From Nuts to...

The Official History of SCUNTHORPE UNITED F.C.

(1899 ~ 2012)

Published by:
Yore Publications
12 The Furrows, Harefield,
Middx. UB9 6AT.

© John Staff 2012

....

All rights reserved.
No part of this publication may be reproduced
or copied in any manner without the prior permission
in writing of the copyright holders.

British Library Cataloguing-in-Publication Data.
A catalogue record for this book
is available from the British Library.

ISBN 978-0-9573862-1-1

Cover photographs:

Front: left to right
Matt Sparrow, Andy Crosby
(holding aloft the Division One Championship trophy
5th May 2007),
Paul Hayes.

Back: from top left
Frank Skull, Jack Brownsword
Ray Clemence, Kevin Keegan
Paul Langden, Steve Cannack,
Alex Calvo-Garcia, Peter Beagrie

Printed by 4 Edge Limited

ACKNOWLEDGEMENTS

GENERAL:

The first acknowledgment is to Mr Steve Wharton, Scunthorpe United's hard working Chairman, the board of directors, and Mr David Beeby, United's Chief Executive, for endorsing this book, without which it would not be possible.

Many thanks must be extended to Dave Twydell of Yore Publications for publishing this second full history. It has been his technical expertise that has put the book together. He has also been responsible for his contacts in producing the statistical section, for which thanks go to Tony Brown of Soccerdata (Every club and every Football League line-up, from 1888, is now available online, see 'www.enfa.co.uk') Dave follows the fortunes of Brentford, and it was pleasing to see that during the 2011-12 that both the Iron and the Bees exercised two diplomatic draws. For the football purist it is worth visiting the Yore Publications web site for more of his work (www.yore.demon.co.uk).

I am very much indebted to the staff at Scunthorpe Central Library for the use of all of their facilities, where I have virtually camped out in the reference section.

It must be noted that the work of James Stott, an early historian and journalist, has to be recognised, as has the part played by the late Len Jacklin. In his senior years, Len passed a lot of notes and photographs on to me belonging to James Stott, and told me to make sound use of them. I sincerely hope that he would consider that everything has been put to good use for the benefit of each and everybody with an interest in Scunthorpe United.

From the point of view of the technical side of the work I wish to acknowledge the assistance of my good friend and neighbour, Mal Hunt, who has set me in the right direction, in the use of wife Christine's computer, in typing the text. In the meantime, Christine lost the use of her computer for more than ten weeks. The final thank you is to the longest finger on my right hand, which has punched out 165,000 words.

PICTORIAL:

Most of the photographs from the last forty five years are my own work, and I thank the Club for giving me permission to record the history of the Iron with my camera.

Some photographs are from Scunthorpe United's own collection and publications, and many thanks are extended to Dave Beeby for allowing me to use them. Phil Cook, Mark Dickinson and Simon Wright are the trio of current photographers, Mark Turtle, Derek Smith and Ian Hewitt, and the Picture Company of Ashby High Street have been responsible in the past. Those photographs used are a superb credit to their work.

A number of the oldest photographs have the names of photographers on the reverse, and these are gentlemen who lived in the first five decades of the twentieth century. The work of Singleton, Wilmore, Lenton, Hainsworth, A.H. Sandars and Gerard are hereby recognised. Some of the photographs of the later photographs were taken by Harold Caine, and thanks go to his family for allowing their use. Len Plumtree is the late artist of the cartoon sketches, and thanks to Dave Johnson for the use of Harry Johnson's pencil drawings.

My appreciation is given to Mrs Doris Haigh and Mrs Queenie Brownsword for photographs of the two Jacks, and to Len Sharpe for the use of his collection.

My personal collection contains numerous photographs from over the years, that have no identification as to the photographer. I have made every effort to trace the rightful owner of the work, in each case, to allow publication. Should anyone not have been acknowledged, may I offer my sincerest apologies. If this is the case, may I hope that compensation will be gleaned in that they have assisted in illustrating part of the history of the Club, that has graced the town over the last one hundred and thirteen years. At no stage has advantage been sought from the efforts of others, but all energy has been focused for the benefit of Scunthorpe United.

DEDICATION

I wish to dedicate this book to my wife Christine, and my two sons John Michael and Robert James.

Christine has been my wife of twenty years, and has suffered my fascination of Scunthorpe United throughout. Without her help, comfort and understanding many of my ambitions would not have been accomplished. My two sons have worked hard through university, and made me proud of the completely different ways each has made a success of life. Both of them have been brought up in the true light of Scunthorpe United.

The Nut

The Iron

INTRODUCTION

It is amazing what messages can be sent via a Christmas card, but the one that I received from Dave Twydell of Yore Publications, in 2011, started the ball rolling on this latest presentation on the history of our beloved Scunthorpe United. Time passes without anyone noticing its rapid advance, and incredibly it had been thirteen years since the Official Centenary History of Scunthorpe United, 1899-1999 was first launched. The question he posed was, has anything much happened in the meantime?

We all known that the response is that the Club have achieved so much.

The most important feature of this book is that it is completely different to what has gone before, even though the journey it takes is a similar one. In the earliest section of this latest volume, a huge amount of extra detail has been discovered in the years from 1880 to 1912. At the other end of the spectrum, the twists and turns of the most recent thirteen years come under the spotlight. Of course, the section in between has been revisited, and more information is included.

Those supporters who know me will be aware of my vast collection of Scunthorpe United photographs, and it is pleasing to have the opportunity to share a completely new set with everyone. The same can be said of the statistics, where a concentration has been made of the period covering the Football League era.

It has been a labour of love, particularly in retirement from almost forty four years on the steelworks, to document the latest list of Scunthorpe United stars. From Steve Torpey to Billy Sharp, and Ian Baraclough to Andy Crosby. Perhaps if you prefer Peter Beagrie and Joe Murphy or Paul Hayes and Gary Hooper, they are all here, as well as many others.

It has been my privilege to be the Club's Historian, a title I do not take lightly. Several days a week I am usually sat in one library or another, searching for more information on Scunthorpe United. The history of the Club cannot be found sat in front of the television, and so this book is an illustration of my latest efforts to bring extra facts to light. Let me also say that I am honoured to know, and talk to so many people through the common bond of our football club

The author, and Club Historian, John Staff holds the Play-Off trophy in 2009. Fifty-four seasons a supporter and still going strong.

CONTENTS

THE STORY

1	The Early Years	6
2	A Midland League Baptism	16
3	The Testing Twenties	21
4	Waiting For Another Title	34
5	Post War Nuts	58
6	The Third Division North	68
7	A Champoinship	86
8	A Pinnacle Of Achievement	92
9	Another Slide	104
10	Basement Blues	112
11	The Long Road Back	121
12	Farewell To The Old Show Ground	143
13	Glanford Park, The First Phase	156
14	An Almighty Fright	184
15	A Change In Fortune	196
16	The Iron Roller Coaster	204

THE STATISTICS

Seasonal Statistics 1949-50 to 2011-12	220
League record Summaries	286

THE TEAM GROUPS

Memorable Seasons	288
The Squads: 1999-2000 to 2000-12	292
Yore Publications	298

THE EARLY YEARS

1880-1912

There can be no denying that the County of Lincolnshire has made a significant contribution to the sport of football. Brigg Town made a mark in season 1879-80, when the club entered the F.A.Cup competition, but lost 7-0 to Turton of Lancashire, in the First Round, away from home. In 1881, the Lincolnshire F.A. launched the Lincolnshire Cup and Spilsby became the first team to hold the ornate silver trophy. During the Summer of 1892 the Football League decided to add a second string to its bow, and when the Second Division was launched, Grimsby Town and Lincoln City became founder members. Within the space of four short years they would be joined by Gainsborough Trinity, when they too were accepted into the fold.

The discovery of iron ore by Rowland Winn on his land in North Lindsey rapidly brought an explosion of the population to this part of Lincolnshire from the 1870s. The town we know today as Scunthorpe was then made up of five separate villages, namely Frodingham, Crosby, Brumby, Ashby, and Scunthorpe. Each village originally had only a few hundred inhabitants, but this soon changed with the growth of the iron and steel industry, which brought thousands of people to the area. Conditions of the heavy work were tough, and the working man saw football as a suitable recreation to enjoy when it was done. A change in the working time table assisted their needs with the introduction of the half-day off on Saturday.

The first known club to lace up its boots in Scunthorpe was Scunthorpe Town, although in the south of the district Ashby could boast of Ashby Town. Scunthorpe Town played on a ground known as the Kempe fields, in Crosby, but they later also used a pitch next to their new headquarters at the Oswald Hotel, on the old Frodingham Road. Frodingham Road then is what is the present Scunthorpe High Street. Indeed, from 1894 the Cup matches were played as a special events at Crosby, while lesser games utilised the pitch adjacent to the Oswald Hotel.

It is believed that the Town club started about 1880. Unfortunately, the sports reporters of the time did not appear to have left the comfort of their desks to relay any news of Scunthorpe football until October 31 1885. It was on that date that Scunthorpe Town were beaten 5-1 on a sojourn to play Brigg Town Reserves, and the score was published in the following week's paper.

Information on football was scant throughout the 1880s, to say the least. Not only would Scunthorpe Town play against Ashby Town and Brigg, but they also enjoyed meeting teams from Crowle, Barton, and Winterton. They took part in the Lincolnshire Shield, as well as the Richardson Cup and Grantham Cup.

The remaining fixtures were made up of friendly matches. Away travel was often by horse drawn cart, but the advent of the Manchester Sheffield and Lincolnshire Railway opened up a whole new world. Soon matches against clubs from Gainsborough, Grimsby, Doncaster, Market Rasen and Nottingham were on the fixture card. The 1890s saw the blossoming of two more local sides. Frodingham Rovers became part of the agenda from 1893, and twelve months later Frodingham and Brumby United, a side to become one of the Edwardian power houses of the local scene, first ran out onto the field of play.

On a good day Scunthorpe Town could outclass the opposition, as they did on December 28th 1895, when Barton Rovers were thrashed 10-0, no doubt suffering from a Christmas hang-over. However, on October 10th 1886 the Town team were similarly found to be out of salts, and went down by an 18-0 cricket score to Gainsborough Trinity. In the 1895-96 campaign the Town men reached the Semi-Final of the Lincolnshire Shield, losing to Spilsby Town. During the 1896-97 season they competed in the first known competition with the title of the 'Lincolnshire League' along with six other teams, which included the reserve teams of Grimsby Town and Gainsborough Trinity. Unfortunately, this was to be the last year of their existence, and they succumbed to a certain amount of apathy, when only the secretary turned up for a pre-season meeting in the Summer of 1897. After that the Scunthorpe Town team failed to run onto the field of play ever again.

When the door closed for one club, so it opened for another, called Brumby Hall. Brumby Hall may have started as a junior club, but this ambitious side was anxious to fill the void. Formed in September 1895, this new club quickly established itself as the new kids on the block, and a force to be reckoned with. They had strong backing, and the drive of Devonian solicitor Mr R.A.C.Symes, who had recently qualified and set up a business in the district. He was known as Reggie to his friends, and became a distinguished gentleman of influence, helping set up a number of football teams in the district. Reggie was to assist the running of several football teams, served on the committees of the cup and league competitions, and he also qualified as a referee.

Brumby Hall at first played at Brumby Hall, then on a ground to the north of the district, once used for the Scunthorpe show. It was not long before the pitch became known as the Old Show Ground. The first reported game took place on September 28th 1895, when they took a 7-1 beating at the hands of the Scunthorpe Town second team. In just five years Brumby Hall were considered to be able to field the strongest eleven men in the area, and proved the point by crushing the Second Battalion, Doncaster, with an emphatic 11-0 result on February 21st 1899. At the end of the 1898-99 season Brumby Hall's record stood at P22 W17 D4 L1 F82 A21.

An Edwardian map (dated 1907) of the expanding spread of Scunthorpe, showing the close proximity of the two grounds of Scunthorpe United and North Lindsey United, just to the West of the populated area. The 'Sports Ground' was referred to as the Crosby Ground, where North Lindsey United played, and the 'Football Ground' was the Old Show Ground, home of Scunthorpe United.

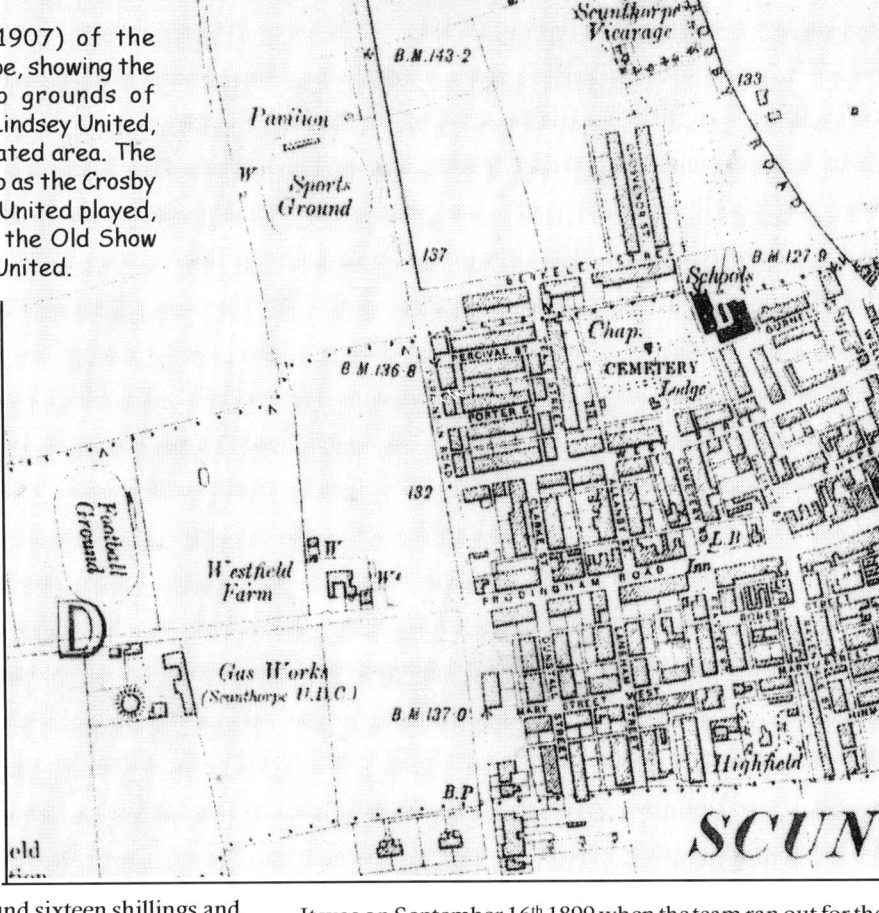

The North Lincolnshire Star newspaper of September 2nd 1899 reported on a dinner of the Brumby Hall Football Club, held the previous Tuesday evening at the Beeston Hall, using the headline "Football Amalgamation". Presided over by Mr R.A.C.Symes, it was resolved to amalgamate with other clubs in Scunthorpe under the title of Scunthorpe United. One of these was thought to be the North Lindsey Iron Works team. More than one hundred players, officials and supporters unanimously upheld the motion, and soon August 29th 1899 the new club was officially formed. Scunthorpe United inherited funds of one pound sixteen shillings and six pence, about £1.82 in today's money. Reverend H. Ashcroft was elected President, Messrs. J.R.Downie, of the former North Lindsey Works side, and W.Sandwith, from the Brumby Hall club, would share the duties of the secretary, Mr Fred Dobbs was to be the team captain, while Mr Symes was part of a large representative committee. It was also agreed to run a junior section to develop young talent to progress to the first team.

When the 1899-00 season began the new Scunthorpe United used the same Old Show Ground as Brumby Hall had played on, although on some occasions in the early days it was reported that they played at Crosby, where another set of facilities existed, where the Town club had used previously. Old maps of the area suggest this was on the right hand side of Frodingham Road travelling North, approximately on the site of the houses of Sheffield Street. Players would change in the Club's headquarters at the Furness Hotel and walk the half mile to the Old Show Ground. One of the reasons for adopting the Old Show Ground was that it was a considerable distance from the nearest public house, to avoid supporters drinking before the match, but it was not frowned upon after the fixture. Later they moved to the Lord Roberts and then the Oswald Hotel. Public houses would be abandoned when the Old Show Ground had its own offices and changing rooms.

It was on September 16th 1899 when the team ran out for the first time. No colours for the kit had been chosen as yet, but information is available to say that United won their first match 4-0 against the villagers of Crowle at the Old Show Ground. At half time the United men were two goals up, and although no goal scorers was noted, J. Charlesworth and J. Dodds received credit for good form. The referee was non other than Reggie Symes. Most games played during the first campaign were of a friendly nature, but the Club did enter the Lincolnshire Shield. It can be confirmed that they met the rivals of Frodingham and Brumby United in the First Round. The original meeting found them squared at 2-2, but Scunthorpe took the honours 3-2 in the replay. There is a report in a Gainsborough newspaper of the Second Round, where Scunthorpe beat Gainsborough Blue Star 5-2 at the Old Show Ground, but after this triumph they lost comprehensively 7-0 at home to a strong Gainsborough Working Men's Club and Institute.

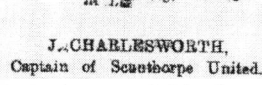
J. CHARLESWORTH, Captain of Scunthorpe United.

Two further cup competitions entered in the first 1899-00 season were the Lincolnshire Cup, and the Hull Times Charity Cup. In the latter cup, teams from the South of the Humber had a series of knockout games to see which club would face the winners of a similar test for teams on the North side. The ultimate winner would earn the 'Hull Times' silver trophy. In the Lincolnshire Cup United lost at the first stage at Morton, 3-1. The Hull Times trophy saw another first time exit, 9-1 away to Grimsby All Saints.

The question was put in the Hull Times newspaper as to which colours the new Scunthorpe United would adopt but after beating Morton Swifts on October 21st 1899, from near Gainsborough 3-0, it was revealed that the team looked smart in their new shirts of green and white stripes. It is known that by 1904-05 season the Club had changed to claret and blue to emulate Aston Villa, a top club of the Edwardian era.

When United's first season had concluded it was reckoned that £80 had been taken at thirty three first team and reserve matches, and the club finished with less than £1 in hand after expenses. The first eleven showed a record of P18, W8, D2, L8, and it was estimated that each of this team's fixture would probably been attended by an average of 300 spectators, and as many a 500 on the better days.

The dawn of the 1900-01 season would bring new opportunities for teams in the North Lindsey district, and Scunthorpe United took advantage to embrace them all. The key element was that of a league, but in addition a second cup competition was entered for. The league was to be known as the North Lindsey League, and would mean greater duties for Reggie Symes to perform. This division originally consisted of five clubs, including Ashby Town, Brigg Town, Frodingham and Brumby United, Winterton, and Scunthorpe United. This was to give a cast iron guarantee of eight matches. The cup competitions entered were the existing Hull Times Charity Cup, and the Lincolnshire Shield, which meant Scunthorpe United could not be so certain as to how many games they could expect.

This required the programme to be supported by some interesting friendly matches. The increased popularity of football brought about greater coverage from the local press especially in the second half of the season. In the Lincolnshire Shield, United reached the Second Round, when they were in action against Gainsborough Rovers, at the Crosby ground. It is understood that this match was drawn 1-1 and the replay lost. The situation in the Hull Times Charity Cup is a little more interesting, because in January Scunthorpe United appeared to have been knocked out of the competition by Frodingham and Brumby United, but a protest must have been up held for them to continue.

ALBERT BOWSKILL,
Captain of North Lindsey United Football Club, Scunthorpe.

Three weeks later the tables were turned and Scunthorpe won 4-2. They were not eliminated until the Lincolnshire section Semi Final, when they lost 3-1 to Grimsby all Saints on neutral soil, at Brumby Hall.

The novelty of a league was a great success, and the North Lindsey League captured the imagination of the football loving public in the district. The inaugural was not to be won by Scunthorpe United. The pleasure of that decision was between Ashby Town and Frodingham, but Scunthorpe's cracking 6-2 victory over the Town club at the Old Show Ground in the March of 1901 virtually handed the silver cup, presented by Sir Berkeley Sheffield, to the Frodingham men. At least Scunthorpe would not be wooden spoon holders. This honour went to the gallant lads of Brigg Town.

Before the season closed in 1901 there was just time to start a new six a side competition at the Old Show Ground, based on points for goals and corner kicks. This was to be a big attraction with both the public and players alike, and would run annually at Easter.

Once the cricketers had put away their bats at the waning of Summer, Scunthorpe United found that the constitution of the North Lindsey League had changed. Despite some initial success, Ashby Town decided to resign. Broughton Rangers, Scunthorpe St John's and Scunthorpe Centrals were happy to join the select gathering, and Frodingham were in a position to defend their title. Scunthorpe United preformed far better in the North Lindsey League of 1901-02. They were confident in all games against the other two Scunthorpe teams, St John's and the Centrals, while contests with Broughton and Brigg brought maximum points. On the first Saturday in November Broughton were crushed by an unequalled 18-0 score. For much of the campaign Scunthorpe United headed the table, but everyone knew it was the battles ahead with Frodingham that would decide which club could have Sir Berkeley's prize. Late in the season the two unbeaten sides met before large crowds of about 800 supporters on each other's ground. On both occasions Frodingham squeezed home by the narrow margin of 1-0. The retained the silver pot, but Scunthorpe gleaned enormous satisfaction from the Runners-up place.

Scunthorpe United had more to be pleased about in the Lincolnshire Shield. In the First Round they defeated Scunthorpe Centrals on the Show Ground 5-1, then had a first class 4-1 victory over Frodingham and Brumby, the new enemy, also at home. Eventually Gainsborough Wednesday saw them off in a thriller at the Old Show Ground. United took a three goal cushion into the halftime break, but had a disastrous second half, losing 3-4.

Scunthorpe United's growing band of followers still had two more cup competitions ahead to wet the appetite in 1901-02. Not only was there the Hull Charity Cup to think about, but a new cup called the Grimsby Charity Cup allowed them to have a chance against the cream of junior soccer from the Grimsby district. This was supplemented by some high profile friendly matches. In the Hull Charity event United did well to reach the third stage, but lost 4-3 to Frodingham following a replay. There was some success in the Grimsby Charity Cup, and they were in favour by reaching the Semi Final, but went out to an experienced Grimsby Tradesmen. They went down 5-1 on the neutral territory of Frodingham's Brumby Hall Ground.

Events of the Summer months of 1902 brought about a profound change to the structure of two of the clubs in North Lindsey. The move was orchestrated by the North Lindsey League and agreed to by all clubs, officials and players. The final summery was reported in the Lindsey and Lincolnshire Star of August 30th 1902. The concluding meeting had been presided over by Mr R.A.C.Symes and involved the dissolution of two clubs, the Scunthorpe Centrals and the Scunthorpe St John's. From the pool of players the best were selected to become part of a new club, to be known as North Lindsey United. Money was set aside to pay for a new kit, which would be of maroon and blue halves, with white shorts.

R.A.C.Symes, a leading light in the progress of Scunthorpe football for thirty years from the turn of the century.

They would have their own committee, and money was made available to rent the ground at Crosby to play all of their home games. The new side would enter all leagues and cup competitions, which the secretary would need to look into with immediate effect.

The remaining players would form a second club, to be titled North Lindsey Bees. All the arrangements made for the United club would be repeated for the Bees. The door was also left open for a long established club, Frodingham Rovers, to join the Lindsey League provided their finances were up to scratch, and this came to fruition.

The above alterations meant that Scunthorpe United had new neighbours, only half a mile away, in the North of what is collectively called Scunthorpe. Those in the know were well aware that North Lindsey would be a significant rival to the Scunthorpe United ambitions, but eventually time would tell that an old enemy would become an ally. In the immediate future virtually everything on offer was entered into by both of these two teams.

The luck of the draw brought Scunthorpe United face to face with North Lindsey United in the Lincolnshire Shield Second Round of 1902-03. This resulted in progress for the North Lindsey men, when they won in a replay at the Old Show Ground. In the North Lindsey League each club won its home fixture, which is just what Frodingham and Brumby United wanted, as they steamed to the third consecutive title.

The 1903-04 season brought a second league to the Lindsey district, and Mr Symes was at the helm making arrangements.

Scunthorpe United outside their headquarters at the Lord Roberts Hotel. The ball dates this as 1902-03 season.

This was to be known as the Gainsborough and District League, played in the Northern division by the teams in North Lindsey, and the Southern division for the clubs around Gainsborough. The winner of each division would meet in a Final to decide the destiny of the Moreing Cup, so called after an official who donated it.

During the first competition Scunthorpe United and North Lindsey were joined by the Frodingham men, Ashby Town and the villagers of Barnetby. This was a time for the North Lindsey United men to flex the muscles and show their worth. They topped the table and then met Gainsborough Working Men's Club and Institute on April 16th 1904 for the Moreing Cup. An unfortunate broken leg to an opposition player was not what anyone bargained for, but North Lindsey United missed three penalties gallantly lost 1-0 in the Cup Final.

The North Lindsey league of 1903-04 brought a return of the 'resurrected' Ashby Town to the division, but once again Frodingham raced to glory at the top, and Scunthorpe United became the Runners-up. The Frodingham club would not to have it all their own way, especially in the newly introduced Frodingham Charity Cup, which was born in their neck of the woods. It was to become another sought after prize, but the surprise package of the tournament turned out to be North Lindsey United, who made the trek to the last tie at the expense of Winterton Rovers, 13-1, and Barton St Chad's a team beaten 3-2, following a protest. On the last day of the season, April 30th 1904 they met the same Gainsborough team that took the Moreing Cup away from, and this time each club had a full compliment of players. Johnson and Bedford gave North Lindsey a first half lead, but the Gainsborough Working Men pulled one back after the break. A tense tussle continued throughout the remainder of the game, but North Lindsey hung on 2-1 to claim the Frodingham Charity Cup. It was the first trophy won by a team specifically from Scunthorpe. The match was played at the Old Show Ground, and their officials and players could only look on in envy. The full North Lindsey record for 1903-04 was P33, W24, D3, L6, F131, A35.

Should Lady Luck have had no inclination to flirt with Scunthorpe United in the past, she certainly changed her mind in the 1904-05 season. Little football appeared in the press for that season, but thankfully the Lincolnshire F.A. has the hand book of clubs in the North Lindsey district, written by Reggie Symes, in its archives.

From this valuable document the fixtures for the 1904-05 season have been preserved. Scunthorpe United's journey for the 1904-05 North Lindsey League would include playing the old rivals of Frodingham and North Lindsey, as well as Broughton Rangers and Barton St Chad's. None of these teams could match the Scunthorpe charge as the Club remained unbeaten., On March 18th 1905 the first North Lindsey League trophy was in the hands of the Scunthorpe captain, after a drawn game against Barton St Chad's left them untouchable. They could not find the same form in the Gainsborough and District League, but made progress on two other cup fronts. The first was the Winterton Charity Cup, the winners of which would be presented with a tall elegant silver cup. In this tournament Broughton Rangers and Ashby Rising Stars gave no obstacle to the Final tie.

A Scunthorpe United photograph dated 1904. Members of this team went on to win the North Lindsey League, the Winterton Cup and the Frodingham Charity during the 1904-05 season. Players include Danson; Holder and Smith; Lockwood, Hollingsworth and Foster; Cox, Barrick, Francis, Free and Brown.

The climax of this charity event was held on the Humberview Ground at Winterton on April 1st 1905. Scunthorpe United had to overcome Frodingham Rovers in order to seize the trophy, and they set about the task in a workman like fashion. Foster scored a pair of goals, Fewster notched a hat-trick, one of which was a penalty, and Barrick rounded it off to make a round half dozen, all without their own goalkeeper being troubled. There could be no doubt that when the Scunthorpe captain went up to receive the trophy his team deserved to win the honour.

The concluding piece of the Scunthorpe United success for 1904-05 was in the Frodingham Charity Cup. Morton Swifts were crushed 5-0 in the Second Round at home, then Frodingham Rovers fell 2-1, over at Frodingham, in the Semi Final. The Final took place on April 29th 1905 against Gainsborough Working Men's Club and Institute, also at Frodingham. Scunthorpe went a goal down, but pulled back level by the interval from an own goal. They took the lead through Free in the second period, when he converted a penalty, and the scoring was completed by a brilliant individual goal from Cox, over on the right wing. United took the trophy as the team won the match 3-1, and after the game the team were met by a band. A procession made its way through the town, and during the week it was reported that the club's supporters wore claret and blue favours in the club colours.

It is at this time of celebration that above all, one man deserved special credit. He was Mr W.T. Lockwood, who had held office faithfully throughout all of the lean times, and would continue give a life time of service. William Lockwood was an architect by profession, and he came from a sporting family. He surely would have been a celebrated player like his brothers had not he suffered an injury as a youth, which made it necessary for him to walk with a crutch.

The success of the Gainsborough and District League was to be in the hands of the North Lindsey United men, and they won nine and drew one of their fixtures, which gave them the Northern Division title.

(Above) The North Lindsey League trophy, won by Scunthorpe United in 1905, and 1906, by North Lindsey United in 1908, and Scunthorpe and Lindsey United in 1911 and 1912. (Below) Mr William Thomas Lockwood, a man who was a founding father of Scunthorpe United. He served the club in all senior capacities, including Chairman, until his death in 1943.

In the Moreing Cup Final they once again crossed swords with Gainsborough Working Men's Club and Institute, playing on the Northolme Ground of Gainsborough Trinity. For the game, Lindsey fielded a weakened side through injuries, but despite this, Fisher dribbled through for the first goal, then Morley shot them 2-0 ahead. Next it was Gainsborough's turn to rally, and they pulled back the score to 2-2 before half-time.

During the run up to the interval North Lindsey lost the services of Bedford with concussion, but they played up supremely well in the second session. The winning goal came not long into the restart, and was shot through by Albert Bowskill off a defender. The final score was a deserved 3-2 victory for the North Lindsey men, and Fred Tune, the winning captain, gratefully accepted the trophy.

The strong constitution of the Scunthorpe United team was maintained for the 1905-06 season. Once again information is difficult to find in the newspapers, but seven months after the year began and the North Lindsey League Championship flag was flying over the Old Show Ground. There was also a Runners-up place in the Gainsborough and District League, which was topped by the neighbours of North Lindsey United up the road. Their supporters also witnessed an incredible record, set on October 14th 1905, when Barnetby were beaten by an unparalleled 23-1 score in the Lincolnshire Shield.

In 1905 the Charlesworth family, who ran the Oswald Hotel on Scunthorpe High Street, decided to introduce a charity cup to raise money for the cottage hospital on Rowland Road. This was to be called the Charlesworth Charity Cup, but would often be referred to as the Scunthorpe Nursing Cup. Scunthorpe United eventually reached the Semi Final of the tournament, where they beat Grimsby St John's on the Show Ground pitch, 2-0, after a replay. A missing micro film prevents knowledge of the Final being available, but information later documented reveals that Scunthorpe United received the winners medals.

The 1906-07 season was a reminder to football enthusiasts that the Frodingham was a sleeping giant, and not one that had been slain. In the Gainsborough League the Frodingham men took the top spot, then added the Frodingham Charity Cup and the Charlesworth Cup to their trophy cabinet. The North Lindsey League was still considered to be the blue ribbon event and a tighter competition unfolded. Scunthorpe looked to have stolen a march on Frodingham, when they beat them 7-2 at the Old Show Ground. Frodingham retaliated by winning 2-1 at Brumby Hall. In the Spring Scunthorpe lost a vital game to North Lindsey United, but Frodingham faltered too. The final table revealed that both teams had finished on the same number of points.

The problem was that the rules of the North Lindsey League stated that the Champions must have more points than any other club. A simple rule change was not quite straight forward, and so the representatives went to the Lincolnshire F.A. for guidance.

Their decision was to tell the League to go back to its committee and have the member clubs agree to change the rules to include a Play-Off in times of a tied division. This came to be passed, and on Christmas Day 1907 the decider was played at the Old Show Ground. Scunthorpe scored in the first half, but two goals following the change round gave the 1906-07 North Lindsey League to Frodingham.

At the time of this decider the 1907-08 campaign was well under way. For some inexplicable reason Frodingham could not fire its gun when it came to the Lindsey League. During the season the Champions slumped, having barely won a game. The main contenders for the summit were North Lindsey United and Scunthorpe United, and it made a refreshing change when the men from Crosby had their name etched on the silver trophy for the first time.

Although the North Lindsey League was snatched from their grasp, success would reach the Scunthorpe club, from a different source. In 1907 the Lincolnshire F.A. withdrew the Lincolnshire Shield, and replaced it with the Lincolnshire Junior Cup. In the First round a cameraman captured the moment of the team leaving its new headquarters at the Oswald Hotel, to play away at the Ashby Rising Stars. When the results were published Scunthorpe United's was not to be found. The had won, but did not send the result to the Lincolnshire F.A., and suffered a fine of two shillings and six pence.

It was fortunate that this faux pas was not repeated in the Second Round, when Gainsborough Amateurs were trounced 10-1. The Third Round brought United a local derby at home to Scunthorpe All Saints, and they were made to work hard for the fruits of a 4-2 score. At this stage, should the Lincolnshire Shield be used as a yard stick, the team was sailing in uncharted waters.

News of the next stage of the Junior Cup brought great excitement to the Club when it was learned that they had a home tie against Lincoln St Catherine's. Little did the officials and players know that fortune would go hand in hand with controversy when events got under way.

The match was played on the Saturday after Christmas, and United celebrated an apparent victory. At the time when they were expecting to hear of their opponents for the Semi Final, a wire was received by the Scunthorpe secretary from the Lincolnshire F.A. saying that the St Catherine's had put in a protest that Scunthorpe had played an illegible player, and it had been upheld. The problem was that a man name Morley in the Scunthorpe team had once had a trial for Lincoln City and was considered to be a professional. The decision of the Lincolnshire F.A, was to have the match replayed in Lincoln, and Scunthorpe be without the services of Morley.

The replayed tie took place on February 8th 1908, and at the interval led by a goal scored by Frederick Smith. The Lincoln club equalised after the players had turned round, and the tie was even on ninety minutes. In extra time Scunthorpe showed the greater stamina, and when they hit two more through Foster and Fisher, the protests were laid to rest.

Scunthorpe United would be followed by more controversy in the Semi Final. Luck gave them home advantage over Spalding on a cold grey Leap Year's Day at the end of the month. The clouds hung heavy and in freezing conditions snow was on the way. It did not help matters when Spalding arrived later than sanctioned, and according to the local newspaper this important match finished as a 2-2 draw. The truth is completely different, and the author of this brief note on the most important match ever to be played at Scunthorpe could not have been anywhere near the venue.

What really happened was that Scunthorpe took a 4-0 lead, when the heavens opened, and dumped an avalanche of snow on all and sundry. The referee suspended play on the hour, but when conditions improved he invited both teams to take to the field. Scunthorpe agreed, but the Spalding captain refused, stating that they had a train to catch back to South Lincolnshire. When all of the facts were put before the Lincolnshire F.A. it only took a few minutes to promote Scunthorpe United to the Final, to be played at Blundell Park on Good Friday, April 17th 1908 against Cleethorpes Town.

On the morning of the match, an estimated crowd of 2,000 were in the ground when the match kicked off. Grimsby newspapers suggested the match was a dour affair, perhaps because their favourites would not receive the cup. Scunthorpe United offered a stiff defence and took the honours when goals by Brown and Barnham gave them a 2-0 lead that was threatened but always repelled.

United's captain was a happy man when he received the cup, and relaxed with his team to watch Grimsby Town lose 1-0 to Wolverhampton Wanderers in the game that followed in the afternoon. When the players finally arrived back in Frodingham and Scunthorpe railway station they all received a hero's welcome.

When the secretary released the fixtures for 1908-09 season, it was discovered that Scunthorpe United would be involved in two leagues and as many as six cups. North Lindsey United would have something similar to chew on. Scunthorpe United had added the Horncastle Cup and the new Ironstone Cup to the list. In addition, the Club was to take part in the Lincolnshire Senior Cup, a reward for the Junior Cup triumph. This enabled them to receive a visit from the full Lincoln City first team, where in September a record crowd saw them lose courageously, 2-0.

During the coming season the team was to reach the Semi Finals of three competitions. In the Frodingham Charity Cup a weakened eleven lost 1-0 at Crosby to Ashby Rising Stars. The Hull Times Charity Cup brought an exit at the hands of North Lindsey United, at the Old Show Ground. A few days later the North Lindsey lads lost, at the same venue, to Cleethorpes Town. Thankfully there was a positive result in the Charlesworth Cup. Scunthorpe had to battle hard to get beyond Grimsby Haycroft Rovers, then beat Cleethorpes in the half final. In the Final they came face to face with Grimsby Rovers, and needed to be at the top of their game. A 4-1 result saw that they did at least hold one trophy up before their patient supporters.

In the North Lindsey League there could be no stopping the resurgent Frodingham and Brumby United. Although Scunthorpe United were becoming the ambitious power base, there was still a vital ingredient missing on the on the field of play. Twice Scunthorpe United had made an application for membership to the Midland League, in 1907 and 1908, and each time they had seen the door closed in their faces, a move the Frodingham men could not contemplate. Over at North Lindsey United, the Crosby team had a determined committee, but had been losing support. Behind the scenes there were beginning to start whispers that the neighbours might be talking to each other about the future, and trying to put a spanner in the Frodingham works, so that trophies went in the other direction.

When the 1909-10 season opened, it would be the last time that Scunthorpe United and North Lindsey United had separate identities. Scunthorpe United still harboured ambitions of a higher grade of football in the Midland League. To attract attention to their ambitions they arranged more friendly matches against top class opponents, and took the massive step forward by becoming the first team in the district to enter the F.A.Cup. On September 18th 1909 they ran out onto the Old Show Ground pitch to face Withernsea with the following line up;

Wogin; Parrott, Barrick; Garrett. Fewster, Foster; Hollin, Clapham, Carr, Cox and Harrison. Although the play was tight in the early stages, United went into the break 2-0 to the good, and finally swamped the opposition 8-0. The record shows that Cox, Hollin and Clapham each bagged a brace, while Harrison and Carr topped up the rest. Two weeks later the Crystal Palace Final dream was over when they lost 4-0 at York City, a club not directly connected with the modern day team of the same name.

Despite the attraction of the F.A.Cup, the 1909-10 season was to be a disappointment for Scunthorpe United, and for the first time since 1904 the team would fail to deliver one trophy. Down the road at Crosby, North Lindsey United was in the same boat. Those whispers began to increase, and dialog took place between the officials of the two fractions. This was to be made public on April 9th 1910, when a meeting took place at the Institute on Winterton Road, to explore the common ground. Mr Symes presided over the gathering and laid out the benefit's the two clubs would gain as one, and how their finance would improve under an amalgamation.

Before the evening was over the merger was agreed, and the identity of the new club be known as Scunthorpe and Lindsey United. It was decided that the Old Show Ground was to be the headquarters and that money used to pay the rent. A committee was elected and included Messrs W.T.Lockwood, G .Mann, G. South, G .Brown, F .Allen, and F. Cox of Scunthorpe United, and W. Clarke, P. Coombe, R.A.C.Symes, F. Tune, F. Morley, A. Fenwick, W. Blenkin and A. Kell of North Lindsey. Mr Lockwood and Mr Coombe would act as honorary secretaries.

On June 1st 1910 a second meeting took place at the Central Hall, but it was poorly attended by no more than fifty persons. Despite this, Mr F. Mason pushed on with the necessary requirements, and votes were taken for various positions. Mr Symes was elected president, Mr Coombe became vice president and secretary, while on the field Frank Hollin was captain, with Fred Holland vice captain. In addition a huge committee of seventeen names was voted in. It was unanimously agreed that the new club enter the F.A.Cup, the North Lindsey League and all the various cup competitions, including the Lincolnshire Junior Cup. Once the Old Show Ground had been secured, the Club would build dressing rooms for the players to change in. Mr Lockwood moved to adopt a report of the sub committee, and offered a vote of thanks to the Chairman, seconded by Mr Holland and duly carried. At the end of the procedures the new club was alive and kicking, and Scunthorpe and Lindsey United prepared for the future with the ultimate objective of Midland League football.

The first match that Scunthorpe and Lindsey played was on September 23rd 1910, when they beat a Hull City junior side 3-2.

The team on that historic day was Bailey; Parrott, Long; Barrick, Holland, Wardell; Leaning, Holland, Fenwick, Cox and Brown. After all the sweat and toil Fred Cox was the hero with a hat-trick of goals.

When the Club got into its competitive gear, the North Lindsey League was still the competition everyone wanted to win. Unfortunately the Gainsborough and District League had folded, but the new United had opposition from Frodingham and Brumby, Ashby Rising Stars and North Lindsey Midgets. On this occasion the North Lindsey League would be closely fought, and not without protest. When the final table was drawn up in 1911 it revealed that Ashby Rising Stars had one more point than Scunthorpe and Lindsey. The problem revolved round a player in the Ashby team called Johnson. The League rules stated that each man must live within six miles of his club's headquarters, so teams could not import the cream of talent from outside the district. Johnson lived at Winterton.

A number of stormy meetings took place to try and sort the problem out, and in the end the matter had to be referred to the Lincolnshire F.A. The crucial part of the argument was specifically over the match between Ashby Rising Stars and the North Lindsey Midgets. If Johnson was unable to play the two points would go to the Midgets, Ashby would lose two, and Scunthorpe would have an extra point on Ashby and be Champions. In a calmer atmosphere those not involved decided that the honourable way would be to ask a local surveyor, Mr Cobban, to measure the distance between the Ashby headquarters at the Brown Cow public house and Johnson's home in Winterton. His decision was that it exceeded six miles and Scunthorpe and Lindsey became the 1910-11 North Lindsey League Champions.

The rest of the 1910-11 season had other moments of note, including a long run in the Lincolnshire Junior Cup. United enjoyed a run beating North Lindsey Midgets, Brigg Britannia, Barton Terriers, Lincoln Liberal Club and the a Semi Final, against Cleethorpes Town, that booked a Final against Grimsby Rovers. The Rovers were the best men to face United all season, and at Blundell Park deserved to beat the team in claret and blue by a 2-1 margin.

In the Charlesworth Cup Final Scunthorpe and Lindsey played an exciting match against Grimsby Rangers. The fixture was the last of the season, and United came back from 2-1 down to force extra time at 3-3. Unfortunately they lost their footing and surrendered the chance of a gold medal when they conceded one more goal, to lose 3-4. However, a polished performance in the Frodingham Charity Cup Final saw them beat the old enemy of Frodingham and Brumby United. It was a keenly fought contest, with an edge to each tackle. All the goals were registered in the second period, and favoured Scunthorpe, as the captain and vice captain, Hollin and Holland scored in the 2-1 triumph.

The 1911-12 season was to be an unparalleled success for Scunthorpe United, and had hundreds of the town people flocking up the Clayfield Road, what is Doncaster Road today, to see the team in action. It so happened that the committee loaned the use of the football field to the cycling club, and so the first soccer was not played until the first Wednesday of September in 1911. It was here that the team announced its intentions, by beating North Lindsey Juniors 8-1 in a warm up friendly.

The initial competitive test arrived a couple of weeks into the calendar, when they played York City in the Preliminary Round of the F.A.Cup. York would turn out to be a stiff test, but a good crowd witnessed a keen game, and home advantage tipped the tie the way of United. Events swiftly moved on to the First Qualifier, where they had to cover foreign soil at Mexborough. It was essential that they put up a quality performance, because the Yorkshire men were of Midland League status, and it would demonstrate the strength of the playing staff. Although they lost the tie 3-2, the team did not disappoint in its ability to compete.

When it came to the North Lindsey League Scunthorpe and Lindsey had no equals in the race to the title, and the only loss of points were from the occasional drawn games. While the rest of the teams knocked lumps off each other United cruised to the top of the pile, and had Sir Berkeley Sheffield's silver cup presented in April.

One trophy that did elude the Scunthorpe men was the Lincolnshire Junior Cup, but they had only themselves to blame. They made steady progress to the Semi Final, where they met Lincoln South End away from home. Most of the side had a surprisingly poor day, losing 5-1, for which the sport correspondent in the Star newspaper gave a critical analysis of each individual responsible. There again, the same journal defended the team when it lost the Bellamy Cup Final at Blundell Park in Grimsby against Cleethorpes Town, 3-0. The report of the game was just as critical of the officials, who appeared to give the Town club all of the vital decisions. This was especially so when the referee was said to have jumped up and down to applaud one of the Cleethorpes goals.

Scunthorpe and Lindsey United's success was to follow as cups came their way in quick succession, and April was a particularly busy month. The first Final of the knock-out trophies arrived on April 6th 1912, when the before mentioned Cleethorpes Town team felt the force of the Scunthorpe men at Brumby Hall. In the Final of the Grimsby Charity Cup the Meggies were thumped 4-0 in a one sided encounter.

The Frodingham Charity Cup was the next challenge, and it was the old Frodingham enemy that remained the only barrier. A much harder effort was required this time, but an early goal by Rusling sealed the victory on April 13th.

It is said that when the vicar of Frodingham, Crypian Rust, presented the trophy he said in his speech that Scunthorpe were a tough nut to crack. From this a new nick-name was said to be born and the team became known as the Nuts. It can be confirmed that these were his exact words, but the team had been referred to as the Nuts a few months before this statement.

A week hence and the United were in line for the Ironstone Cup. The opponents were the highly respected Grimsby Haycroft Rovers, but the smart money was on another Scunthorpe victory. Once the first whistle blew United were quicker thinking and faster of foot. Two goals in each half destroyed the opposition, and another cup was seized. It left just one trophy for United to capture, and that was the Charlesworth Cup. A pair of Rusling goals, one either side of the interval, did the damage, and for the fourth consecutive Saturday the Scunthorpe captain was the presented with a silver reward. In all the players had amassed a total of five trophies, and to mark the occasion the committee paid for a special gold medal to be struck and given to each of the individuals who deserved to be honoured.

There was no disguising the desire of the Club to break out of the local challenges and fight their football in the Midland League, on a National footing. Scunthorpe and Lindsey United made its application, and Reggie Symes attended the Meeting in Nottingham on June 8th 1912 with Paul Coombe. They believed they had the right credentials to become new members.

The situation in the Midland League was that four clubs had resigned their places, but the bottom two, Worksop Town and Denaby United had sought to be re-elected. Applying to join the Midland League were the hopefuls of York City, Goole Town, Halifax Town, Mirfield Town, and Scunthorpe. After careful consideration the Chairman announced that the bottom two clubs had secured their immediate future, and to bring the division back up to strength four out of the five applicants would be given entry.

Each prospective club was given two minutes to state their case, and Reggie Symes used his solicitors fluent tongue to convince the committee that Scunthorpe and Lindsey had all the correct paper work to succeed both on and off the field. When all of the talking was over it was Mirfield who were the unlucky ones, and Scunthorpe had a Midland League Club. Paul Coombe stayed behind in Nottingham to take arrangements for the new set of Midland League fixture, while Reggie returned by train to Scunthorpe. Before he went he just had time to send a wire to William Thomas Lockwood to convey the exciting news. Mr. Lockwood was at Frodingham watching cricket when the message arrived. Famously, it only said one word, and that was " In".

News of Scunthorpe and Lindsey's successful application quickly spread through the entire district. On Monday June 17th 1912 Mr Symes addressed a packed meeting at the Assembly Rooms to discuss how to finance this expensive venture for the Club. Mr Symes was of the opinion that the best way forward was to form a Limited Company and issue shares. It was his proposal that a nominal capital of £500 be an affordable sum in ten shilling shares. There would be no problem with the legal side of the business, which he would personally take on at no cost what so ever. To a great sound of cheering he then asked supporters to put their hands in their pockets, and £50 was raised on the evening, which rose to £66 by the time of the next meeting. The Cub's Annual General Meeting was held at the Blue Bell Hotel on July 3rd and was a jolly affair of ale and cigars to celebrate all the bounty of the 1911-12 season. More money was put in the kitty after a few pints had loosened the wallets, then a final more formal meeting was held, back at the Assembly Rooms on the evening of July 24th.
It was at the gathering that a draft copy of the Articles of Association, required by law, were read out by the secretary Mr Coombe. A short debate ensued before they were accepted, and Scunthorpe and Lindsey United, from the Summer of 1912, had become a Limited Company.

Mr Symes told those present that the local firm of Pallisters had been asked to make further improvements to the changing rooms they had previously constructed, and that the considerable sum of £100 had been invested in erecting a wooden stand on the ground. This would provide accommodation for 340 patrons paying an extra sixpence each to view the matches in greater comfort. All that remained now was to assemble a team ready for the first battle on September 7th 1912, when the first fixture was away to Leeds City Reserves.

> **IN !!!**
> Just that little word! all that appeared on a wire sent to Scunthorpe and Lindsey United's charmain, Mr. W. T. Lockwood, at the Frodingham Cricket match last Saturday. What did it mean? Why the local football team which practically carried all before them last season has been
> **ELECTED TO THE MIDLAND LEAGUE.**
> It is unnecessary to repeat all last season's performances, figures speak for themselves.
> Played 38; won 27; lost 4; drawn 7; for 116 against 38.
> Four Charity Cups and the Lindsey League Cup! What a record!

The wire sent back to the town confirming Midland League entry in 1912.

A MIDLAND LEAGUE BAPTISM

1912-13

The first Saturday of September 1912 heralded the opening of the programme Midland League, and Scunthorpe and Lindsey United arrived at Elland Road ready for their clash against Leeds City Reserves. At kick-off, a crowd of 5,000 spectators included 300 from the iron stone district of North Lincolnshire. Weather conditions were excellent for football, as the Nuts lined up with the following team: Wogin, Parrott, Burkhill, Drury, Henderson, Brown, Hollin, Hill, Waldon, Cox, and Bell. In the event, this team would give good account of themselves. They did not concede a goal until late in the game, and harshly had a goal chalked off for offside. At the end of ninety minutes that goal proved to be the difference, but a great deal of satisfaction was taken from the performance.

It was just one week later when Scunthorpe and Lindsey played their first home fixture against Notts County Reserves, in front of more than 2,000 supporters. The committee had decided to make two changes to the team, and Hall was brought in for Hollin, while Pearce was preferred to Cox. The problem was that Pearce had not been registered in time, but the paperwork could have arrived on the afternoon train. They began the match with just ten men, but after twenty minutes admitted defeat and brought Rusling, a local player, on instead. The Nottinghamshire team scored during the confusion, and a 1-0 loss was repeated.

F.A.Cup headlines in 1912.

United's first Midland League results were most disappointing, and continued with a 7-1 thrashing, at Sincil Bank, against the junior Imps of Lincoln. At least Bell did make some history by becoming the Club's first Midland League goal scorer. Fortunately the Nuts did far better in the F.A.Cup competition, travelling to beat Brodsworth Colliery 3-2, where Pearce managed a brace, one of which was a penalty kick, and another fine effort came from Walden. Three further defeats followed the Cup success, including a 9-1 humiliation in the away match at Notts County. It was only another F.A.Cup victory, over Goole Town at the Old Show Ground, that stopped supporters from demanding changes in the board.

It was soon realised that the cream of local talent needed strengthening with some experienced players. This prompted them to sign a man who had been at the top of the sport, and his name was Harry Burton. Harry had been part of the Sheffield Wednesday team that in 1907 lifted the ornate silver F.A.Cup trophy at the Crystal Palace.

He fitted straight into the Scunthorpe team at full back, and in his first game the improvement was immediate, away to Mexborough. Walden put the Nuts ahead, but they needed an equaliser by former Grimsby Town left winger, Tommy Bell, to go into the break level. In the second half goals continued to flow. The Scunthorpe side went 3-2 up, as Walden dribbled round the stranded keeper, then made history by scoring a hat-trick goal. Mexborough reduced the arrears, but Bell completed a capital display with the last word. He glided past two defenders and put the ball into the bottom corner of the net, making a 5-3 result.

Once Scunthorpe and Lindsey United had their first points on the board, everyone gave a great sigh of relief. It was as if a huge weight had been lifted off the team's shoulders. It could not have come at a better time, because the next fixture was the local derby at the Old Show Ground against Gainsborough Trinity, playing in their first season following relegation from the Second Division of the Football League. An attendance of about 2,500 broke the ground record, paying the considerable sum of £53. Each spectator was to have their four penny worth of entertainment. Goals by Bell and Pearce, the latter for a spot kick, helped the Nuts to a 2-1 lead, but Trinity were on top of their game in the second period, and went home with a point from the 2-2 draw.

The fixtures in November brought a strange twist, when York City were played three times in four fixtures. The pair initially drew 2-2 up the Clayfield Road, now Doncaster Road, in an F.A.Cup clash, where all strikes happened in the first forty five minutes. To make sure the Club was up to speed in the Midland League, the team had next to travel into Yorkshire to meet Rotherham Town on their Clifton Lane Ground. United lost 2-1, and then made arrangements to meet York City, two days later, under the shadow of York Minster. They kept up the pace until into the second half, then faded in a 4-5 thriller. This was despite Rusling, Walden, twice, and wee Shem Hill all making the net bulge. The team barely had time to unlace their boots, when it was necessary to face York City again, but in a League fixture. The boys in claret and blue rose to the challenge and played the best football of the saga. A brilliant win was beautifully setup by a George Walden hat-trick, and another goal from Tommy Bell tipped the scales the way of the Nuts, with a close 4-3 score.

The approach of the Winter still saw Scunthorpe at the basement of the Midland League, but they were gradually climbing out of the re-election places.

The introduction of Harry Burton was certainly a factor as he dictated the play at the rear of the field, and George Walden, a former Rotherham Town forward, was making the front end of the side a lot sharper. Through the dark days of the cold months Scunthorpe steadily improved, but it was when the Spring flowers began to show that United really blossomed. From March 1st 1913 until the end of April only two of the last fourteen matches ended in defeat. These were both played away from home, against the Wednesday Reserves, and Rotherham County, the latter's captain would be the one to take the Midland League trophy. Whereas the Nuts could not buy a win at the commencement of the campaign, April brought an abundance of four in the space of a dozen days. Of these, two are worth singling out.

The arrival of Sheffield United Reserves had seen other teams stutter against the junior Blades, but United put them to the sword, with a handsome 3-1 score. In the next game the Nuts travelled to the town with the leaning church spire. At Chesterfield they played an open style of football, and were rewarded with a 4-2 score, and two more points towards the total.

The 1912-13 Midland League final table revelled that Scunthorpe United had recovered to occupy the fifteenth position. Their record was played 38, won 13, lost 17, drawn 8. The team had scored 55 goals, and conceded 78. Everybody in the town was very happy with the initial outcome, and the predictions of a collapse of the Club proven to be fruitless. The team could look forward to the future in the Midland League with confidence, and special praise went to the local players, who had stepped up a gear from the North Lindsey League.

Players like goalkeeper Johnny Wogin and Shem Hill would go on and serve the Nuts until years later, when senior years eventually caught up with them. Others, such as Frank Hollin, Buck Parrott, Fred Smith from Winterton, Danny Sylvester, and Billy Long, had all acquitted themselves and had to be congratulated. They had been paid far less handsomely than some of the senior stars, like Drury, Bell, Spelvins, Henderson, Wagstaffe, Watkins and Burton. Men of their calibre would expect a wage of £2 per week for their services, and for Scunthorpe and Lindsey to survive, the board needed to dig deep. Even at that price, the wage bill was happily maintained at around £25 per week.

(Top) Billy Henderson, the ex-Grimsby Town player, who captained the Nuts in 1912. (Below) George Walden, leading scorer for the Nuts in 1912-13, and joint top in 1913-14.

1913-14

For a short while the attention of sport turned to the white flannelled players of the Scunthorpe Town cricketers, as they spent time knocking the ball to distant boundaries. While that was happening, the directors took time to sift through the lists of players seeking new clubs for the 1913-14 season. It might have been strange at the time, but they decided on signing four men from Leeds City, in an effort to increase the Nuts stature within the Midland League. These included brothers Arthur and Hugh Roberts, plus Tommy Mulholland and Tommy Morris. The defence would benefit from the addition of Tommy Morris and Arthur Roberts. Morris was to wear the captain's arm band at the centre half position, while Arthur played at full back. Hugh Roberts took up on the right wing, and Mulholland was his inside partner.

Two other new men were also added to the attack. A left winger named Root was considered to be one of the fastest men to tie up his boots in the Midland League, having bade farewell to Derby County. He was joined by Bradbury, a former top marksman of Oldham Athletic. Once Bradbury had fitted into the centre forward position, the Scunthorpe battle wagon was ready for the new campaign.

The interest Scunthorpe and Lindsey had created with the new signings generated an army of six hundred supporters to journey to Lincoln to see them in action against the Imp's second string. It was a day of sweat and toil for all the forwards, as the defences of both teams held firm. A goalless draw divided the spoils. During the next Saturday's game, the four ex-Leeds City men raised the tempo for the visit of their former club. United earned victory number one of the campaign, and Bradbury and Root scored first goals in the claret and blue, as the Nuts won 2-1.

United appeared to have made a pretty good start to the year, but in the next match, away at Rotherham County, the short comings of the team were brutally exposed. A crowd of more than 5,000 Yorkshire folk watched, as the home side tore the Nuts to shreds. At the tea break Johnny Wogin must have suffered from back ache, after picking the ball out of net five times, and little improved in the second part. In the end the team had to lick the wounds of a 7-0 thrashing.

One of the County goal scorers was Herbert Lloyd, who would serve United for many years until retirement in numerous capacities.

Thankfully, the defeat at Rotherham County had no long term lasting effect on Scunthorpe and Lindsey. The restoration of Morris to the defence, after injury, had the desired result in the following fixture, for the visit of Chesterfield. The men from Saltergate were sent packing with a 4-0 resounding win by the Nuts, where three of the goals came in a brilliant second half spree. It was just the boost that the team needed. It set them up for progress in the F.A.Cup, where lowly Mildland Leaguers Mexborough were dispatched from the competition, but only after a replay. Ironically, the two clubs then met for a third consecutive game, and like on the previouis Saturday, the League match ended in a stalemate.

The Second Qualifying Round took United to York City, and 5,000 people paid £133 to see the City men reverse a one goal deficit, to win 2-1. Scunthorpe could now concentrate on the Midland League, where November was a most productive time for the Club. At home the Nuts were invincible, and took maximum points for visits by Rotherham Town, Worksop, Mexborough, and Castleford. On their voyages the wins continued at Leeds City Reserves and in the return fixture at Castleford. The attraction of Sheffield Wednesday Reserves saw the record crowd rise to 3,000 and £80 was taken from gate money. At the turn of the year Scunthorpe and Lindsey were in a healthy position just above the halfway position in the table.

During the Winter months the Scunthorpe team continued to please its supporters by maintaining the comfort zone within the Midland League table. This was assisted by the introduction of two player into the first eleven. Jack Thompson took up at inside left just into the Autumn, but the true potential did not come until Ernest Wood arrived in March. Wood scored on his debut against Rotherham Town, then hit hat-tricks in consecutive games, as the Nuts became the masters of Sheffield United Reserves, 3-2 at Bramall Lane, and York City, 4-1 at the Old Show Ground. The advent of the First War saw many young men sign up to fight for King and Country. Ernest was one such lad, and sadly he lost his life.

Scunthorpe and Lindsey United finished the season in seventh place on a ladder of eighteen rungs. This would have been greatly improved upon, but for trials carried out by giving young players chance to prove themselves in the first team. Results suffered to the degree that all of the last remaining fixture ended with the surrender of points.

A determined looking Bill Bradbury, a man who was the Club's centre forward in 1913-14 season.

The board kept a keen eye on the financial side of the operations, and were all heartened by an increase of the average takings to £61 per match, considering that four fewer matches were played than in the previous season. At least the books roughly balanced, and they could look forward to the future.

1914-15

The advent of the 1914-15 season was completely overshadowed by the ominous threats of hostilities throughout Europe, which finally developed into the First World War. This would alter the whole fabric of society and rip families apart. The question would arise as to the ethics of playing football when men were out in the fields of war, but the sport would continue until the end of season, until peace once more returned. At Scunthorpe preparations had already began, and one of the biggest changes occurred with the resignation of Paul Coombe as secretary. He was to be replaced by Harry Allcock, who would complete his first season in office, and become a familiar face at the Old Show Ground.

The Scunthorpe board of directors had made careful considerations as which players they might bring into the squad of men for Midland League football. They were mindful of producing promising young talent, which saved a considerable amount of money, but also knew that there was no substitute for proven men. One person of experience that they attracted to the Club was Charlie Pinch, a half back, who could play any of the three positions along the centre of the field. It was said that Charlie, who signed from Preston North End, had a wonderful voice, and would entertain his team mates on the way back from their travels, with a variety of different songs.

Charlie was to be joined by Jimmy Monaghan, a winger from Sheffield Wednesday. Jimmy was said to be an artist with his right peg, and could put a ball on the nose of his centre forward each and every time. He went to the First World War to fight and lost his sight at the Battle of the Somme. Mercifully it was restored after surgery. Another player was Fred Smith, who initially came all the way from Southampton to play at left half. He decided to enlist, and was killed without kicking a ball in anger at the Old Show Ground. Two men who did play throughout the coming season were both for the left side of the attack. The Club took Clarke from Sheffield Wednesday and Platts of Lincoln City. It was said that both of them were speed merchants, who gave defenders a run for their money.

The journey of the 1914-15 season began at home to the junior Mariners of Grimsby, but only £35 was taken on the gate at the Thursday evening match. United wore a smart new kit for the occasion, and marginally deserved victory. This came from a better response after the interval. Wood, Clarke and Platts did the damage to the Grimsby Town Reserves, and a 3-2 win was most welcome. Two days later, United were thrashed 5-0 at Leeds City Reserves, a most disappointing score considering that the opposition had propped up the table in the previous campaign. At least confidence was restored when the team returned home, and gained their ever point against Rotherham County. The County men were held 1-1 on the Show Ground pitch by a resolute Scunthorpe side, not wishing to let them have an easy ride towards a third Midland League title. Wee Shem Hill had returned to the starting eleven to score United's point. This was to start the Scunthorpe team on a run of six unbeaten League games and eased the Nuts in the upper half of the table. It was not until October that United came crashing back to reality, with a thumping 2-6 disaster at Castleford.

At this time Scunthorpe and Lindsey had embarked on their annual F.A.Cup voyage. United were drawn away to Hull Old Boys at the Preliminary stage, but for a guarantee in gate money the tie was switched to Scunthorpe. A Clarke hat-trick was a feature of the comfortable afternoon's work, which was reflected in the 5-1 score. This lined the Nuts up against Grimsby Rovers, a familiar name from pre-Midland League days. The Rovers had the handicap of injuries during the game, but managed to restrict the Nuts to a 4-0 advantage. Clarke once again stood out with two goals. In the Second Qualifying Round Scunthorpe and Lindsey were confronted by the might of Doncaster Rovers, a former Football League club. Local rivalry brought more than 2,500 interested parties to the Old Show Ground. They were to bare witness to the keenest of struggles, which was won when Robinson, a capture from Rawmarsh Athletic, scored the only goal. Scunthorpe United bowed out of the competition in the next round, when they lost 5-1 at the Victoria Pleasure Ground, against Goole Town after a replay.

Once United returned their attentions to League football, they proved to be no more than an average side, able to beat the chaff, but lose to the more accomplished clubs. On December 12th 1914 they produced one of the best displays for some time for the visit of the big rivals from Gainsborough Trinity.

Edwin Burkill, alongside trainer Marsden, an accomplished full back in each of the Club's first three Midland League seasons.

The War had had a marked effect on gate money, and even this attractive fixture only produced £24 from the box office. On the command of ' play up the Nuts', the team took advantage of two first half slips, and drives by Robinson and Armitage brought home the bacon with a 2-0 score. Unfortunately, this would herald a particularly lean spell for Scunthorpe followers, and on Christmas Day an uninspiring goalless draw for the visit of Goole Town became a rare treat, as times became hard on the field of play.

The results did little to assist the desire to watch football, as did the pinch being felt in the town as a result of the hostilities. Many of the residence had answered Lord Kitchener's call to serve the King, and the men folk who would have filled the terraces were away at the front. The Club had come in for an amount of criticism but the squeeze on the income meant that there was little they could do. It was with regret that the team was asked to take a pay cut to reduce the demands on the cash flow, and the difference between what was coming in and the bills that needed paying was an ever widening one. Scunthorpe United's Chairman, Mr A.J.Raynor, went as far as writing a letter in the Grimsby Telegraph to explain the situation, and to say that even with a cautious approach the Club needed a minimum of £40 per week, just to make ends meet.

A meeting was called on January 5th 1915, at which Mr W.T.Lockwood opened the books to show that the Club was deep in the red. The figure indicated that a further debt of £400 would require assistance to cover. In the mean time the coffers had only £1 in hand to pay the wages for the coming Saturday's visit to Gainsborough. Despite the black situation the directors dug deep into their own pockets and United struggled on, but the Nuts were thumped 5-0 at the Northolme.

Shortly after this humiliation, Scunthorpe United began to improve, encouraged when Chesterfield were beaten 3-1 at the Show Ground, and the Hull City junior Tigers, 4-1 on the other side of the Humber. Another inspired performance came at Heckmondwike, where the Nut were in cracking form to win 6-0. Wood, Ibbotson and old boy Rusling all scored a brace, four of which came in a motivated second period. The season wound down with three home fixtures on the card, starting with a remarkable 5-5 draw for the visit of Rotherham Town.

Only a small gate saw the thriller, which had the lead change hands in the last five minutes, then each team settled for a tied match. Rotherham even had to borrow a reserve player from Scunthorpe, when they turned up shy of a full compliment of men. Before the week was over, the team finished the season by beating Mexborough 5-0 and Castleford 4-0.

It was a great relief to reach the finishing line at the end of the 1914-15 season, especially in view of the dwindling gates. Figures indicated that on many days the attendance was less than a thousand spectators, and perhaps as low as five or six hundred. If it had not been for the financial support of the directors, the Club would have had to pull the plug on the Midland League. The table declared that United breasted the tape in thirteenth place, a little worse off than twelve months ago. Wood led the goal scoring charts with fifteen successful strikes, followed by Ibbotson on ten and Platts on nine.

Players were all thanked for their fine efforts and released to follow other activities, many of them joining up for the King's shilling. Those who did stay local to the town would be able, for another season at least, to play in a limited number of friendly games, organised against similar strength teams.

The main consideration for the board of directors was what might to happen to the Old Show Ground pitch. Concerns were that it would be dug up for allotments, and they wanted to preserve the surface, ready for when football resumed after the War. They managed to secure grazing rights on the field, so the problem was resolved to some extent. Harry Allcock promised to look after the books for a short while, which would be for the rest of his working life. For the period from September 1917 until April 1919 no official business was conducted, and effectively the Club was closed down.

(Top left) Ernest Wood, with the ball at his feet, was the leading goal scorers in 1914-15, but sadly never returned from the First World War. (Top right) John Wogin, a brilliant utility man, able to perform either side of the First War for Scunthorpe and Lindsey United. (Below) Harry Allcock, the devoted secretary from 1915 until 1955.

THE TESTING TWENTIES

1919-20

The whole of the Country rejoiced when the guns fell silent on the battlefields of the First War. Men came home to their loved ones, and wanted to return to normality as soon as possible. Once their lives had settled down they looked to the Nation's favourite sport of football for recreation. Everyone connected in the game was only too happy to come out of hibernation, and pick up the pieces of where they had left off.

Scunthorpe and Lindsey United began the long road back to the Midland League by announcing that from May 21st 1919 Harry Allcock was to be appointed full time to the salaried post of secretary. He was instructed to use the Athletics News journal, the most universally used football paper of the day, to seek out as many promising young men at the right price, to fit in the Scunthorpe team for the forth coming season. The first signing was not a player, but that of a trainer, Tommy Moran, in May 1919.

Before not too long, the new players began to arrive outside the main entrance of the Old Show Ground on Henderson Avenue. One of the most notable was that of ex-Irish International Jack Hanna, formerly of Nottingham Forest, who stood at five feet ten inches tall. He was an amazing character, who was said to enjoy a tipple, like many a true Irishman. His ability in front of the goal post was sometimes astonishing, as he plucked the most difficult of shots out of the air, and his anticipation was that of an old professional. The directors could also call on the services of Johnny Wogin, who was still a long way from hanging up his boots, and had years of experience on his side. It seemed that John was as enthusiastic as ever, and only too happy to help in the green jumper, whether for the first eleven or the Reserves.

In the defence, United signed a pair of useful full backs in Bullivant and Robinson. Bullivant was one of a number of players that had seen service at Lincoln City, but Robinson was last seen active at Barrow, in the North West. The centre half position would be the berth of Matthew Robson, another man who had worn the red and white stripes of Lincoln. Along side of this able pivot was Shem Hill and ex-Lincoln End player Hobson. Shem was as fit as ever, and just as clever in the middle of the park, but before too long Tommy Wield, yet another man of Lincoln City fame, joined for the left half position

Jack Hanna, Scunthorpe and Lindsey United's ex-Irish International keeper for the two seasons after World War One.

The Scunthorpe and Lindsey United forward line was to include Butler, Spavin, Mahon, Lemon and Booth. Ernest Butler was from Stillington, just North of York, and was said to be a gentleman both on and off the field. He was very fleet of foot, and a great assistance to his inside right, Jack Spavin. Spavin was a well built young forward from Goole Town, who had an eye for goal and a mean shot to match. At the sharp point of the team, United employed John Mahon of Shirebrook. This marksman was a football artist, and was criticised by some for his dainty footwork, which might have been better suited to a higher grade of football. On the left flank Charles Lemon came just into the season, from a Sheffield League club, Sheffield Amateurs. He was for the inside left position, where he linked up with winger Booth of Sheffield United. Booth was a good crosser of the ball, and weighed in with the odd goal. Before the football got under way the technological revolution arrived at the Old Show Ground. Permission was granted for the Grimsby Telegraph to install a telephone line at the ground to speed up reporting of the Club's activities. This was situated in the main stand, and was ready for the opening fixture.

The season began on Saturday August 30th 1919, when a healthy crowd of close to 2,000 spectators were all in place, as the team emerged from the tunnel to play Rotherham County Reserves. Now that the Yorkshire men had been elected to the Football League, future encounters were with that club's second team. It was noticed that prices of admission had increased, and gentlemen had a shilling to find, ladies were six pence, while school children were three pence. One of the reasons for these higher fees was connected with the purchase of the Old Show Ground. A quote of £7,000 had been received, but rejected as being far too much. Consequently money had been forwarded to rent the facilities once more.

The game with the County Reserves was a most entertaining affair, and both sides put up a marvellous showing after such a lengthy period of inactivity. Play was of an even nature for the opening forty five minutes, and honours equal at 1-1. After the breather United stretched their legs to run out 4-1 winners. Spavin added to his first half strike with another goal, then Butler and Hobson were on hand to complete the scoring.

United returned the compliment at Rotherham for their next fixture, then went to play at Halifax. Both matches failed to yield a satisfactory result, but an improved performance brought a point from a goalless draw, at home to Sheffield United Reserves. One of the best results of the campaign was in beating Grimsby Town Reserves at Blundell Park, 2-1, but the visit to Gainsborough eclipsed even that score. At the Northolme the Nuts turned on the style with a 4-1 resounding conclusion..

The F.A.Cup produced a lot of local interest, when Goole Town were chosen to visit United's Lincolnshire camp, at the Preliminary stage. In the past, the team from the Yorkshire port had always caused the Nuts a problem, but not so this time, as the 7-0 slaughter suggested. Brodsworth were next in line, but an away tie was reversed to be played in Scunthorpe, for a guarantee on the gate. The colliery men fought every inch of the way, and United followers were pleased to hear the final blast of the whistle, as the Nuts stood slightly ahead at 2-1. Scunthorpe and Lindsey expected to travel further in the competition, when Cleethorpes Town were faced in the Second Qualifier, but a resolute defence helped the Meggies upset the odds with a 1-0 surprise on the Old Show Ground.

The Christmas fixtures brought two excellent games for Scunthorpe and Lindsey, both being against the junior Imps of Lincoln. On Christmas Day Scunthorpe were hosts and ran up a superb 6-0 result, during which the promising Jack Spavin did no harm to his reputation by scoring four times. The result prompted more than a thousand Scunthonians to make the return trip to Lincoln on Boxing Day, some of them arriving on bicycles. The afternoon was bright, crisp and cold. Many of them sat on a grassed bank at the ground, enjoying a Yule cigar, the aroma of which filled the air. The team played up to expectations and Lemon had them yelling with delight as he opened the scoring, in a far tighter match. The Imps pressed for parity, but it never came. Indeed, it was Cox who made matters safe for the Nuts and register the double with the deciding goal. On returning home, the visiting supporters were met by a snow storm, and many did not arrive home until the early hours.

At this time there were a couple of extremely important activities that effected the Club. On December 6th 1919 a price was agreed to buy the Old Show Ground. It was settled at £2,980, a much smaller price than originally demanded.

J. W. Ackroyd, United's full back from 1920 to 1922, who was encouraged to the cheers of 'good old Acky'.

The Club decided on January 6th 1920 that the share capital should be increased to £6,000 in ten shillings issues, so as to raise some of the funds. A further meeting took place on March 6th to agree all of the changes and proposals.

The other major development surrounded their prolific forward Jack Spavin, who had been attracting scouts from all over the Football League. It was reported that on February 24th 1920 United's board approached him with an offer of £6 per week, back dated to the beginning of the season. However, two days later Nottingham Forest made a firm bid of £340 to transfer him away. This sort of money was an astronomical amount for Scunthorpe and Lindsey, and too much to be turned down . Within the blink of an eye Jack walked out of the Old Show Ground, and would wear the red and white of the Foresters. This departure immediately cut through any hopes the Club harboured of the Midland League title, but the transfer was out of necessity, not lack of ambition.

The loss of Spavin caused the team to experience difficulty in scoring. At first Mahon went to the inside berth and a number of centre forwards were tried, in an effort to get back on the goal trail. If anything, it was Charlie Lemon who took over the mantle of the marksman role, even though for some unexplained reason he could not please one boisterous section of the crowd. At least the final month of the season ended in a flourish, when the remaining five matches on the card all yielded points of some description. This useful bounty of eight points hoisted the team into third place in the table, the best they had ever achieved.

In the April run in, Scunthorpe United had played two fixtures against the newly formed Leeds United. This team came to existence in the November of 1919, when Leeds City disbanded, by order of the Football Association, for irregular financial activities. Leeds United were allowed to perform in the Midland League, playing catch up with two matches each week. Scunthorpe won 3-2 at the Old Show Ground, and drew goalless at Elland Road.

The closed season, during the Summer of 1920, brought a number of meetings up and down the length of the County, as teams jostles for positions over the proposed formation of a Third Division Northern Section. In the South similar moves were taking place in forming a Third Division South. The discussions would continue for another year before anything definite occurred, and Scunthorpe United were definitely an interested party. Perhaps this was a step too far for the Club, at this stage in its development, and they would remain on the edge of the proceedings.

1920-21

Talks of a Third Division were put on the back burner, as the board sought to find the right type of men to patrol the Midland League for them. One of the problems was that players were demanding higher fees, and top earners expected £6, an offer made to keep Spavin at the Old Show Ground. Men with Football League experience even demanded a signing on fee before they would entertain a club. In the light of this background, United only retained the services of Hanna, Wogin, Lemon, and Broadhead, who was a centre forward introduced late in the last year, to added power to the attack.

On May 11th 1920, Scunthorpe United signed a prolific left winger called Fred Tunstall. This player had boots that could do everything. He was master of the dribble, could cross the ball onto a sixpence, and was no slouch when it came to goal scoring. Fred had everything a team would wish for, and it was not long into the fixture card when scouts rolled up to see what he had to offer. Tunstall only played nineteen games for Scunthorpe, when he was signed by Sheffield United for £1,000, the biggest fee in history received by a club outside the Football League. He would go on to play for England, and score the only goal of the F.A.Cup Final in 1925, as the Blades beat Cardiff City at Wembley. Not everybody heard the message of Fred's departure for Bramall Lane, because the day after he signed Peter McWilliam, the Manager of Tottenham Hotspur, arrived in Scunthorpe hoping to see the young winger play. He was disappointed to know that Tunstall was in the Sheffield United team facing Spurs, at White Hart Lane in London.

One of United's other useful signings was that of the old head of Herbert Lloyd, as a left half and a captain. He was able to bark orders round the park, and assisted in Tunstall's promotion. In addition, United offered contracts to the Duffus brother, John and Robert. They would operate in opposite sections of the field. John was a marksman, who could play along side either Lemon, or another youngster named Simpson. Robert tended to be found around the central defensive position. Both men had grown up in Scottish football and it added an extra degree of grit to the way they engaged the opposition. In the full back places, Scunthorpe and Lindsey were guided by Herbert Lloyd to sign Ackroyd from his old club Rotherham County, while Arthur Betts was his left sided accomplice. Ackroyd was to become a favourite with the crowd for his all out effort, and they would frequently shout for 'good old Acky'.

Betts was a man who had previously played at Newcastle United, Derby County, and Hull City, and had a no nonsense approach to the game, at the end of his football career. The final signing was that of Matthew Robson, returning to the club to make a stronger impact. For the other sections of the pitch, there was a leaning towards bringing in local men for a chance.

One of these was school teacher Alex Moore, who would serve both the Club, and Scunthorpe as a whole, for all of his life. He became an excellent winger, but was restricted because of his teaching activities.

The season started poorly, much to the dismay of the 4,000 supporters who walked up to the Old Show Ground to see a disappointing 3-1 loss, to a highly rated Notts County Reserves side. The team did manage to put some points on the board by winning 1-0 at Bramall Lane, on the first Saturday of September, and gradually made an improvement. What was noticeable was that at first the team lacked a dynamic goal scorer, and won its games by low scores. This was thanks pinching an odd goal and a rock solid defence, urged on by Herbert Lloyd. One of the outstanding performances was at the Old Show Ground against the newcomers of the Midland League, Nottingham Forest Reserves. The team did not forget its shooting boot on that occasion, and wrapped up a 4-0 result with scores by Lemon, Tunstall, and a couple more from Simpson. Remarkably, all the main action was done and dusted in the first forty five minutes. The approach to Christmas brought a temporary loss of form, but the holiday period itself produced at hatful of points. Over Christmas, United had a pair of fixture to play against Hull City Reserves, and they won 3-1 at Anlaby Road, in Hull, then beat them 4-1 at the Old Show Ground. This was followed with a brilliant 5-3 result on the banks of the River Trent, against the Forest Reserves. It put them near the top end of the table, which was policed by Notts County and Lincoln.

Scunthorpe and Lindsey United would enjoy a decent run in the F.A.Cup, staying in the competition until the end of November. They would have no inhibitions about scoring in the early rounds, against some of the weaker teams. In the last week of September that they met Hull Brunswick Institute, and brushed them aside 6-0. Then Bentley Colliery became the second visitors, but proved to be no obstacle in the 3-0 result. This was followed by a smooth 4-1 performance at Grimsby, where 2,000 spectators paid £80 to see them beat the Grimsby Charltons by 4-1. It was not until the Third Qualifier that Brodsworth Colliery caused them some bother. The gate at the Old Show Ground was swollen to 5,000, but they were unable to see the Nuts deliver the final blow, and a 1-1 stalemate required a second looking at the job, in Yorkshire during the mid-week. This also failed to find a decider through two hours of goalless soccer. The final solution was a Second Replay, at Bramall Lane in Sheffield. For this tie the United produced its secret weapon, because Alex Moore was available to for selection. More than 8,000 spectators were in position at the first whistle, and Alex played a vital part in the 3-1 success. Not only did he notch a goal himself, but was instrumental in the build up to the others. The rest of the strikes came from Harvey and Simpson, and eased the Nuts into the last qualifier.

At the Fourth Qualifying Round stage of the F.A.Cup, Scunthorpe were gifted with a home tie against Mansfield Town, up the Clayfield Road. The weather was described as damp and foggy, the latter effect spoiling the view of a record 6,000 crowd. Some thought that it was too bad to make a start, but trust was put in the judgement of the official in the black uniform. Play was virtually impossible to follow, but those nearest the front could see that Scunthorpe were monopolising it. The single goal was scored by the visitors in the first half, but only those at the Crosby end had a chance of glimpsing it.

The F.A.Cup may well have produced some of the highlights of the year so far, but the party on New Year's Day must have come at least a close second. Scunthorpe rubbed salt in the Trinity wounds with a 4-1 emphatic result, which made Roebuck the talk of the town for his hat-trick. Simpson added the final visitors goal, before what was said to have been a record crowd on the Northolme. There were more fun and games when the Nuts met Lincoln City, rejected from the Football League for one season. Against the senior team, United had previously lost at Sincil Bank twice, once in the Midland League, and another in the Lincolnshire Cup. At the Old Show Ground, there was to be no stopping United. It was a tight defensive tussle that earned the victory from the back of the field. Scunthorpe scored their only goal before the interval, from the accurate boot of left wing man Jenkins, who made his run from the middle of the park.

The unfortunate part of the goal was that young Jenkins collided with the post and broke his collar bone. It took some time to get him in a comfortable position to leave the field, and in those days there could be no substitutions to fill the hole. It was reported that Ackroyd and Betts played out of their skins from that moment, taking no chances, and punting the ball well clear at every opportunity. Jack Hanna used huge amounts of saw dust so that he could grip the greasy ball, and enjoyed the best game of his Scunthorpe career. In the middle, Robert Duffus had a blinder, organising the troops, where every man was a hero. Eventually, Scunthorpe and Lindsey United held on to the 1-0 lead, and at the final whistle jubilant supporters rushed onto the pitch to hail their brilliant warriors. This was only one of eight defeats suffered by Lincoln City, and they were to be crowned Champions of the Midland League for the 1920-21 season. It was somewhat of a mystery that Jack Hanna was not retained at the end of the year, but allowed to drift off to Workington.

Scunthorpe United finished the season in fourth place in the table, after they beat Halifax Town 5-0 in the closing match of the season. Only the records of Chesterfield, Notts County and Lincoln City were superior to that of the Nuts.

Despite the creative performances of Scunthorpe and Lindsey United's team, the directors decided to give a number of key men their cards. As well as showing the door to Hanna, they did not offer terms to the Duffus brothers, Charles Lemon, Matthew Robson and Ernest Butler. To replace a player, Scunthorpe United could expect to put as much as £10 in a man's pocket, and pay a wage of between £4 and £5 per week, depending upon his quality and experience.

The Club had some outstanding business to tie up the with the respect of the purchase of the Old Show Ground. This came late in the season, on March 8th 1921, when its was announced that the legal work had been concluded, and the ground had been secured. It would bind the Club into a large mortgage to pay off, but the future was in their hands. In an effort to ease the burden of the public, in the tight economical times of the day, it was agreed to let the unemployed in at half price. The last word was at the top of the Club, where the Chairmanship changed hands as Mr W.T.Lockwood was succeeded by Mr Paul Coombe.

1921-22

Scunthorpe and Lindsey United brought into the team a new custodian for the forth coming campaign by the name of Bates, from Crystal Palace. He was selected until November, then Johnny Wogin was brought out of the Reserves to take the green jersey. Something similar was experienced at centre half, where United went back to sign the Brodsworth Colliery centre half, called Brandon, a player that performed with distinction against them in the Cup. When he was found wanting, they opted for John Duke from Grimsby Town to fill the void. Duke was a hard as nails central stopper, who took no prisoners. Additions came in the forward department, with the signatures of Vic Witham, a strong player and Harry Maycock, a speedy winger or inside man, while young Meredith improved match by match, under the watchful eye of Hebert Lloyd. Later in the season United gave the reins to another Herbert in mid-field, when Herbert Crookes was brought into the team. It was said that Crookes was deadlier heading the ball at goal, than his accuracy with a shot from the boot.

Scunthorpe started the 1921-22 season in fine style with a draw and three wins, but then in the League they faltered, starting with a 3-0 disappointment at the Northolme, against rivals Gainsborough, where a win mattered most. This uncertain form continued until the end of October, when a number of significant changes took place. It was during the last week of October that the board announced that they had decided to offer Herbert Lloyd the position of player manager. Herbert was quite happy to oblige. There was to be another change in the Club's training staff, as Tommy Moran was leaving for a similar post at Rotherham County. He was succeeded by Charles White from the racing cycling family, at the princely sum of three pounds and ten shillings per week.

Scunthorpe United line up for the home fixture on September 3rd 1921, when they beat Wath 2-1.

From left: Witham, Broadhead, Meredith, Brandon, Ackroyd, Bates, Gibson, Lloyd, Richards, Betts, and Maycock.

In the F.A.Cup, Scunthorpe United began the tour out on the road at Retford, where they were pushed to gain a safe passage via a close 2-1 result. The same could not be said of the First Qualifying Round for the visit of Hull Holderness, who turned in a hapless performance, and lost by the incredible score of 10-0. The next contest was against old friends from Brodsworth Colliery, but United made sure there would be no marathon this time, and did the job first time round, winning 4-1. News of the Third Qualifier brought a great deal of excitement to the local football circle, when it was learned of a visit to Gainsborough Trinity.

On the day of the game the play was evenly matched, but Trinity went a goal to the good before the tea interval. Scunthorpe came out, all guns blazing, but without penetrating the Trinity goal. Their keeper was Elijah Scott, a former International, and a well known soccer personality. All of a sudden United won a penalty, but Scott protested to an unprecedented degree, just to put Ackroyd off his kick. The gamesmanship did the trick, because when the penalty was taken the Scunthorpe man stumbled, and miss hit his shot. Scott dived to save, but had to wait until the ball arrived, then strutted about in triumph. Trinity scored a second, and Scunthorpe had lost the opportunity.

The Club was still short of fire power at this stage in the season, and from late September until the middle of December the Nuts only had one Midland League winning game.

A search was made to find a marksman of shear quality to change the situation. The response was to sign ex-International and Chelsea player Robert Whittingham. Robert Whittingham was a solidly built man, who could put his foot right through the ball when shooting, and had neck muscles that propelled the leather towards the target. His introduction had an immediate effect, as he scored on his debut against Barnsley Reserves, on Christmas Eve, and the team worked like Trojans to achieve a 4-1 result to make the supporters happy.

The inclusion of Whittingham in the team was remarkable. The side went on to win eight consecutive matches, and steamed towards the top section of the table. Over the Christmas holiday they extracted all four points on the table against Lincoln City Reserves, and Whittingham scored in the home leg. Then Herbert Lloyd got in on the act, with the only score of the game, which killed them off at Sincil Bank. During this period of continuous success there could be no parallel to the 6-0 hammering dished out to the junior Mainers, of Grimsby Town. This run only had a temporary stop, when they narrowly lost 3-4 at Worksop, but then continued with another eight unbeaten ventures, six of which finished with maximum points.

Scunthorpe and Lindsey United ended the campaign in fourth place in the table, behind the Champions of Worksop, followed by Grimsby Town Reserves and Sheffield Wednesday Reserves.

When supporters considered the leaner times of the Autumn, it was a remarkable achievement. The only cause for concern was the financial side of the Club's affairs, which called for a meeting, but thankfully the darker clouds blew away when there was a slight improvement in the gate money received. This would become an increasing theme as time went on.

The 1921-22 season finished with the board looking to do some ground improvements to the stand on the West side of the park, and Mr Pallister was asked to quote for the work. When word was returned, the extension to the facilities was going to be quite taxing on financial resources. To pay the cost, the board went to the bank to request a loan of £4,000. It was decided to offset the cost of this by offering eight mortgage debenture shares at £50, with an excellent rate of interest, but this price was later reduced to £10 to encourage a wider public demand. It had soon been realised that running a football club was not a cheap affair.

1922-23

Scunthorpe United began the year by searching to plug the holes left by the departures of the Summer. At first they were happy with Johnny Wogin to use the goalkeepers gloves in the first few months of the season, but the approach of December brought a change of opinion. The board thought it appropriate to give Norman Reynolds a chance from the Normanby Park Works team, and his confident performances were sufficient to give him the job permanently.

Scunthorpe United would make alterations in the defence to try to reduce the number of goals conceded, and popular employees like Broadhead and Ackroyd were given permission to leave for other clubs. In their places the Nuts took on the services of a tough Oscar Hargreaves, from Rotherham County, at centre half, and big Reg Smith, a right sided full back, to partner Arthur Betts on the left. Herbert Crookes dropped into the half back section of the field, as Herbert Lloyd was seen less on the field in the coming season, but Shem Hill had no problems keeping up the pace. If the team was short there was always the possibility of Alex Moore, who had developed into a cultured player for attack or engine room, when his teaching job allowed it.

Scunthorpe and Lindsey would dearly have loved to retain the services of Robert Whittingham, but this prolific marksman came at a price, just beyond the Club's means. Sadly Robert was not to enjoy a long career, because he passed away aged only thirty six. Much of the forward line was kept at the Old Show Ground, including Maycock, Witham and Meredith. These were supplemented by an inside man called Rushby, but the centre forward berth continued to be a thorn in their sides for sometime. James Retford, once of Barnsley, was given a chance, as was former Gainsborough scorer Talbot.

In the end they found what they were looking for as the season unfolded, and took Gittos from Staveley Town in Derbyshire. With all the crew in place, the Scunthorpe ship hoisted sail and was ready for the year ahead.

The Nuts began the campaign on a lush Old Show Ground pitch, where the grass had recovered after a rest from football. In hot conditions, on the final Saturday in August, the new team managed the most promising of starts, beating Notts County Reserves. Vic Witham and Oscar Hargreaves supplied the ammunition, while the defence held firm all afternoon. The 2-0 success was followed by a dismal performance on the following Saturday, when at the same venue Hull City plundered the points in a 1-2 reverse for United. The loss of concentration was only temporary, because in the two consecutive weekends the double was gained over Rotherham County Reserves. At this time Vic Witham had managed to score in all but one of the games.

It was at this point in the calendar that United found goal scoring a problem, and three matches in the Midland League programme failed to produce a single goal. At least a point was taken at Castleford, when the defence managed to keep the Yorkshire men at bay, but a 6-0 hiding at Denaby was a cause for concern. The solution was team changes, and here the introduction of Gittos was immediate, when he came into the frame just into October.

Scunthorpe and Lindsey did not have to play in the F.A.Cup until the First Qualifying Round, where they met Grimsby Charltons before a moderate crowd. It was at this game that Gittos was given a debut and went on to score the first of many for the Nuts. Rushby notched two more, and the Charltons could offer no resistance. In the end the team were hardly extended, and enjoyed the expected victory without breaking sweat, 3-0.

The Cup threw up the mouth watering prospect of a visit to their enemy down the road at Gainsborough. Fate had given them an away tie, the week after they were scheduled to visit in the Midland League. In the first match the points were shared from the 2-2 result, where Gittos enhanced his growing reputation with a brace of goals. This set the scene for the knockout competition, where the last man standing took the prize. United were on their metal that afternoon at the Northolme. They only conceded one goal at the back, and forged in front with goals by Rushby, and the master of the class, Alex Moore. It set up a nail biting finish, with goal mouth incidents galore. In the end it was the Scunthorpe supporters that left the ground with the broadest smiles on their faces, and the claret and blue team won the spoils 2-1. This effort allowed Scunthorpe another away journey in Lincolnshire, for the third stage of the F.A.Cup, this time to Boston. An equally close game keep all and sundry on tender hooks, until the crowd went for the buses home. All that separated the teams was a well directed strike from inside left Harry Maycock.

The team eventually came unstuck, when they lost 4-2 at Worksop Town, a club that was to finish third in the Midland League.

The team took quite some time to make a significant improvement in its wandering, in the Midland League. Perhaps one of the turning points arrived on the last Saturday before Christmas, 1922. The team were scheduled to meet the same Nottinghamshire team from Worksop Town, full of confidence after the Cup tie. This time they would be less secure, because ground advantage was with United. Once the match was under way, it was obvious that United would not be stung by the same fate as last time. They were able to swing the ball about in the Worksop penalty box, causing plenty of confusion. From one of these crosses Gittos made a connection and was unlucky to see the leather hit a post, then be cleared. It was not long before he made amends and scored with a bullet diving header, then increased the lead with a calculated low drive, well beyond the grasp of the forlorn goalkeeper. The unfolding game brought chances at either end, and Worksop would not be denied. They reduced the lead, and the result was still in the balance. Any doubts were laid to rest, when Gittos beat two defenders and found the space to fire home. Such quick thinking make this young player a valuable asset, and Coventry City came in for him at the close of the fixtures.

The Worksop Town result began a sequence of nine undefeated matches, which rocketed the Nuts in the right direction in the Midland League standings. They may have rubbed shoulders at the top end of the division, but it could not be maintained. There were some encouragements, such as beating Grimsby Town Reserves 4-2, and a rewarding 4-3 visit to Hull City Reserves. The best result of the year came on the final day of March, for the arrival of Rotherham Town. Supporters cheered a Talbot hat-trick, plus two more from Gittos, all with no reply.

On April 13th 1923, Scunthorpe and Lindsey United were hit by a disaster of unparallel magnitude. It was on that dark day that a fire swept through the West Stand completely destroying all in its wake. The Club lost the whole of the shelter, along with the changing rooms and a full playing kit. It could not have come at a worse time, because it had just been announced that the Club was in debt to the enormous tune of £2,158. Immediately an appeal was put into place and a sub-committee headed by Mr Talbot Cliff and Mr Paul Coombe was formed. Harry Allcock drew up a number of letters to send to request money for assistance, but the Club showed its true grit by refusing to cancel the match against Sheffield Wednesday on the day after the catastrophe.

Scunthorpe and Lindsey United did remarkably well to finish this sorry season in sixth position in the table, despite suffering two 3-0 loses in the closing pair of fixtures. At board level there were great concerns over the future of the Club.

This had been not only compounded by the fire, but also by the alarming drop in attendances. A gate of under 2,000 spectators was now the norm, because money around the town was less than plentiful. The directors knew that they had taken on a big task in securing the Old Show Ground, and the payments for the mortgage hard to find. In this desperate situation they were not alone, because most other teams were in the same boat. It was a case of soldiering on and hope for better fortune in future.

1923-24

The 1923-24 season brought the brush sweeping away most of the old guard, to allow a different brigade to have their chance. Johnny Wogin was still at the Old Show Ground, by his duty would be in the second eleven, while Norman Reynolds continue to be preferred. The older man was always on hand, and filled in on one occasion when injury kept Norman out for a week. In the field, three regulars had played their last appearances for United, and sad farewells were exchanged. Arthur Betts left to coach the local Lysaghts Works team, while wee Shem Hill could not continue after a knee injury failed to respond satisfactorily to treatment. In the middle of the park Herbert Lloyd had retired as Player Manager, but was asked to continue to serve the Club as the trainer. On the other hand, the steely eyes of Oscar Hargreaves would continue to frighten attacker in the centre of defence. Meredith remained on the books and was joined by Jimmy Forbes, a left winger from Lincoln City. The pair would not stay at the Old Show Ground for too long, because Blackpool snapped them both up at the end of September for a combined fee of £650. It was cash that the Nuts could ill afford to turn down, and eased the mounting problems at the bank for a short while.

To overcome the departure of these exceptional performers, United brought to the camp an inside right named Broksom, from Rotherham County. They also found another suitable candidate for the attack in a lad called Burkinshaw, who had done very well at a resurgent Denaby United. On the left side of the attack they gave terms to a very fast Rotherham amateur player by the name of Foster. He was so nippy down the wing that supporters nicknamed him 'Mumtaz' after a racehorse winner of the time. Young Foster provided the crosses for his inside left, Walter Raby, a man who had served at Lincoln City. The real signing was that of the old Brigg born war horse, Joe Kitchen, who had played for years at Sheffield United in the First Division, and had won an F.A.Cup medal when the Blades beat Chelsea in 1915, and he scored into the bargain. Joe was not one to brag of his former glories, but put his head down and continued scoring for Scunthorpe and Lindsey.

During the season the half back line took some time to settle down, and a number of combinations were tried. The centre half situation was solved by the inclusion of Richard Ashmore, a strongly built lad from Doncaster.

To Ashmore's right, the Nuts offered a trial to a tall customer called Frank Skull, from Middlesbrough. He was to demonstrate control, distribution and coolness under pressure. His signing was a shrewd move, and Frank soon was in harness for an association of a decade of more than three hundred appearances. On the other side of Ashmore, United utilised a local lad called Millson, who was picked up in local soccer at the Ashby Mill team. All that remained was a partner for Oscar Hargreaves, and he was to be a hard tackling Southerner, named George Bradbury. George was a suitably strong man for a full back role, coming from Clapton Orient, close to the Thames. However, when Hargreaves suffered a broken leg at the mid-point of the fixture card, United were compelled to bring in Franklin from the second string.

Scunthorpe and Lindsey had to travel to Fulford, the old ground of York City, when they resumed in action. Neither side could find a way through some stiff resistance from the defenders, who took the honours in the bland goalless stalemate. It took them until the fourth match to record their first success, and that was at home to new boys Sutton Town. Joe Kitchen showed his worth by popping up for the winner, in a closely contested 2-1 match. At least the run of fixtures gave Scunthorpe people every opportunity to cheer the team. This was because the fall of Midland League fixtures, supplemented by the Cup, meant from the end of September until into December the team was only away from home over one weekend. Once team selections found the correct combination, results started to pick up. They headed in the right direction with some entertaining victories. Boston United were slain 2-0, when they arrived at the Show Ground in October. Grimsby Town Reserves fared less well, losing 3-0. Joe Kitchen continued to shoot the goals, bagging a brace, while White had stepped up from reserve football and made a name for himself with the third.

In the F.A.Cup United began by bursting the balloon of Grimsby Rovers, when they were beaten 5-1. Two weeks later, and the Nuts crushed Cleethorpes Town 5-0, putting an end to their dream of Wembley. Perhaps the visiting centre half should have kept closer to Joe Kitchen, because he hit a hat-trick. Home advantage assisted in beating Gainsborough, in a close encounter which finished 2-0. A crowd of 5,000 watched as first Joe Kitchen, and the Frank Skull produced the goods for United.

Then Boston United succumbed by a similar score. The Fourth Qualifier, against Rotherham Town, gave Scunthorpe every opportunity to make progress. However, a goalless disappointment, which included a missed penalty, handed the initiative to the Rotherham club.

On the Thursday of the next week the whole assembly met at the Clifton Lane ground of Rotherham Town. Both teams knew by then that Rotherham County awaited the outcome, and would be the visitors to the victor's stadium.

Both teams refused to budge an inch of territory, and little could be found between them. It was that cunning old fox, Joe Kitchen, who was the only player to find the net, and the Nuts had reached the First Round Proper for the first time in their history.

There was a period of only eight days before the team went back in Cup action again, on December 1st. A crowd of 4,152 wrapped up against a chilled breeze to watch the contest between the United and County. This would surely be the home side's greatest test, because the Rotherham club had made a solid start to life in the Football League. Scunthorpe soon had a grip of the game, and took advantage of the room allowed for a passing game. Everyone raised their performance, and they held the lead at 1-0 when the interval arrived. This was thanks to a thunderous shot, high into the net by Joe Kitchen. This lead lasted long into the second half, when a strange refereeing decision changed the match round. A Rotherham free kick resulted in pressure on the Scunthorpe goal, and a melee developed near the goal line. Reynolds dropped on the ball, but the referee, some distance away, indicated that all the ball had crossed over into the goal. A draw needed settling at Millmoor, and Rotherham County made sue that United's journey was a fruitless one. They battled hard for ninety minutes, but Rotherham were superior by 2-0.

Back in the bread and butter of the Midland League, Scunthorpe and Lindsey put the strength found in the Cup to good use. They went through December and only suffered one defeat, at Mexborough, and similarly the same Yorkshire team became their only conquerors in January. In that time the Nuts inflicted their own destruction, gaining double wins against Rotherham Town and Lincoln City, the latter cheering up the Christmas spirit.

Scunthorpe and Lindsey United beating Gainsborough 2-1, in 1924.

At Rotherham, Raby was the hero, scoring all three goals, then another hat-trick further improved his rating for the visit of Gainsborough Trinity, as each score favoured Scunthorpe 3-0.

From the middle of March until the third week in April, United's beer went a little bit flat. They could only muster four goals and one paltry win. They got the froth back on the pint in the last two fixtures, which both finished with 4-0 home wins. These were against Worksop Town and Doncaster Rovers Reserves. The consequence of this resulted in the team being seated in sixth position in the table, but the goals total only numbered fifty nine, and was the smallest to be registered since before the First World War.

1924-25

The whole foundation of Scunthorpe and Lindsey United's football was shaken in the Summer of 1924, and threatened the existence of the Midland League itself. Chesterfield had been a prime mover in forming a new Midland Combination League, for Reserves sides of clubs in the Football League. It meant that most Football League clubs took their reserve side out of the Midland League. Only Lincoln City remained loyal to the cause, and a drastically reduced number of fixtures were available for each club to play. The financial implications would be enormous, and only solved by a subsidiary competition, which ran from March. Virtually every club was running on a shoe string and only surviving with the generosity of their directors.

It had been customary to make sweeping changes during the closed season in the past, but this was not necessary in the atmosphere of the present situation. Norman Reynolds was more than an adequate custodian, and in some quarters the opinion was that he could cope in the Football League. In the background, Johnny Wogin was comfortable as coverage in times of absence and showed the enthusiasm of a school boy when playing for the Reserves. In front of the keeper, George Bradbury was still in line for a call to duty, but little was seen of Oscar Hargreaves after his serious injury. His left full back role generally went to George Greaves, but another injury blow to Bradbury meant that Shearsmith of Grimsby would partner him.

The middle of the park only needed one tweak to its machinery. Skull and Millson had passed their tests with flying colours in the engine room, but the would require a new central pivot. For this position the Club signed Burnham, but an early injury took him out of the equation for a short while. When he got the all clear it was found that he was up to scratch and proved a worthy fighter.

The forward line showed many changes as the year progressed but would frequently show a combination of Cammack, Dawson, Shaw Green and Clarkson.

Of these the stars included Clarkson, a small man of considerable speed and accuracy in the pass, who generally could be found on the left wing, but would switch if necessary. In the middle the directors had found a marksman called Shaw, who was of deadly precision, and was guaranteed to pepper the goal throughout the duration of a game. It was unusual for him not to accomplish some sort of damage to the other side's defence.

Before the first wheels could turn on the field of play, the board of directors announced that Mr Paul Coombes had released his position as Chairman, and in these extreme times Mr Talbot Cliff would be at the helm. With this in mind, United started the fixtures with three defeats in the opening four games, not the returns they would wish for. A packed house did enjoy the pleasure of watching the team beat the Trinity, when the men from the Northolme arrived on September 13th 1924. United played up in style to win, as Cammack and Shaw warmed the Scunthorpe hearts with the strikes in the 2-1 result. The early season problem for United was the lack of goals, and enough injuries to keep the trainers busy massaging the bruises for weeks. They did not begin to gel until the easy victory over a poor Sutton Town, on foreign soil, at the end of October. Scunthorpe ran out as 5-0 masters of the opposition.

In the past United had made some extra money from a number of games in the F.A.Cup. This was one of those occasions when all additions were most welcomed. Sadly it would not transpire in 1924. They did overcome the challenge of Barton Town, but a 2-1 passage was hardly an endorsement against a team of local status. In the First Qualifying Round United were drawn to play at home to Lincolnshire rivals Boston United. The Stumpites rolled up for the match with a brick wall defence, and try as the did, the Nuts could not penetrate it. After the goalless draw Scunthorpe travelled to the South of the County and were brushed aside by a 3-0 result.

On November 25th 1924 Scunthorpe and Lindsey's directors called a meeting to explain the dire strait the Club's financial position was in. This was in light of the match at home to Worksop only being attended by 1,272 spectators, who paid a mere £65. Already the board had found the money to pay the wage bill, and for their part, the players accepted a reduction in remuneration of twenty five percent. Already the Club had lost £300 on the season and the overdraft at the bank had reached £987, with a figure of £2,700 committed towards the purchase of the ground. On top of these figures was an amount for £760 owing on the price of two stands. The board appealed to the public for greater support, or their actions might have to be terminal.

It was obvious that a huge amount of money had been loaned on the Club's behalf, and the directors had stood as guarantors. With debt rising all the time, the moment had arrive to put a stop to the situation before it got out of control.

The conclusion was that the club would have to wind up, and Harry Allcock was asked to compose a letter to the Midland League tendering the Club's resignation. At the same meeting a sub-committee was elected to sell off all of the Club's assets, so that its creditors might be paid off. Scunthorpe and Lindsey was on the brink of no longer existing.

The directors had already agreed to the sale of part of the land on the East side of the Old Show Ground, when at the last minute the board had a change of mind. They approached the Barnsley Brewery in respect of taking over the mortgage of the ground. When this was agreed it meant that the directors could guarantee £400 of the debt, on the loan from the bank. This would enable them to take out more loans to keep the Club afloat. Some extra revenue came from the Supporters Club, who did their best to put as much money through fund raising to where it was needed most. Before the next set of fixture could be forth coming, Harry Allcock wrote a second letter to the Midland League headquarters, withdrawing the resignation.

On the field of play this was not to be the great year of glory. The team did not show the same grit and determination demonstrated by the board when the times were hard. The only exception was Shaw who did his best to register in every game, standing out like a beacon in the darkness. From December 6th Shaw scored in all but one of the next fourteen games. This included a hat-trick at Frickley Colliery, when the team showed a slight lift around Christmas. The main fixtures finished when Shaw hit four goals in a 5-4 thriller with Wath, and left United in seventh place in a table of fifteen.

The subsidiary competition went even worse for United, when only two of a dozen games were accomplished with the Nuts ahead of the opponents. Needless to say that the Scunthorpe men were rooted to the bottom of this small section of six teams. When the curtain finally came down on the 1924-25 season everyone at the Club was pleased to hear the first cricket ball smacked to the boundary rope.

1925-26

There was much better news of the Midland League in 1925. Six more clubs from the Midlands and North had successfully applied to join, and now had a far healthier membership of twenty one clubs. This would make a meaningful competition, and no need to be supplemented by a worthless subsidiary league. Such a move gave Scunthorpe's board confidence to take the next steps.

The directors decided to virtually start again with the forwards, and only Clarkson was retained for the left wing. There was a welcome return of Vic Witham to the forward line, following two years away. Even Shaw had been allowed to depart, as this season they would use Crawley, the former Worksop sharp shooter, and Charles Vowles, who previously came from Barrow via Exeter City. On the right wing Dawson was tried, but as time went on Tommy Lawrie was given the nod.

The central belt of the team was to use a player named Wilson at centre half, while to his right Frank Skull could still do no wrong and had no rivals for the number four shirt. On the other flank, Evans won the regular spot, and Glennie of Oldham Athletic paired up with Liversege to occupy the full back places. Goalkeeping was still in the hands of Norman Reynolds, who appeared to improve with each game. John Wogin could still be relied on to fill in the gaps in times of injury and illness. Each year he would pick up the odd appearance, and this term was no different. The way Reynolds moved between the post suggested a League team might snap him up, and then Wogin would be worth his weight in gold.

The team began with a worthy win at home to Alfreton Town, 2-1 but lost the return fixture in mid-week by 4-1. This was to be the only defeat in the opening seven fixtures. Once the team selection discovered a regular combination, the football public of Scunthorpe found that they had a forceful and entertaining side to watch again. The star of the show was Vowles, who proved to be an absolute wizard as a marksman and made Frickley Colliery suffer with a hat-trick in the 5-0 resounding victory. The odd game did see the Nuts fail to register, but these matches were far and few between. Usually the trio of Witham Crawly and Vowles would see that the supporters with the claret and blue favours had something to shout about.

The F.A.Cup was to produce more sustenance this year for United, with greater progress made. A day at the seaside was rewarded with a 4-0 squeeze on Cleethorpes Town. Those who took the train from Frodingham and Scunthorpe station, at the bottom of the High Street, enjoyed a hat-trick from Vowles. Another Grimsby club, the Haycoft Rovers, were next to the chopping block, beaten 5-1, and Crawley was responsible for four of the goals. The next round was the Second Qualifier, for which the old enemy of Gainsborough Trinity came to town. The match attracted a good following, but Scunthorpe needed to concentrate in order to keep their lead. Twice they had it and twice Trinity equalised. Eventually the Nuts had to settle for a replay, and were made to pay the price. Gainsborough scored the single goal through ex-Scunthorpe player, Alex Moore.

When the team arrived at the New Year they had been pleased to spend most of the time in the top half of the table. Should they have been a fraction more consistent, they could have been challenging at the very summit. The two Christmas games, both against Long Eaton, were fine examples. On Christmas Day they lost the away fixture 5-1, but made amends on Boxing Day, by winning 5-3 at the Old Show Ground.

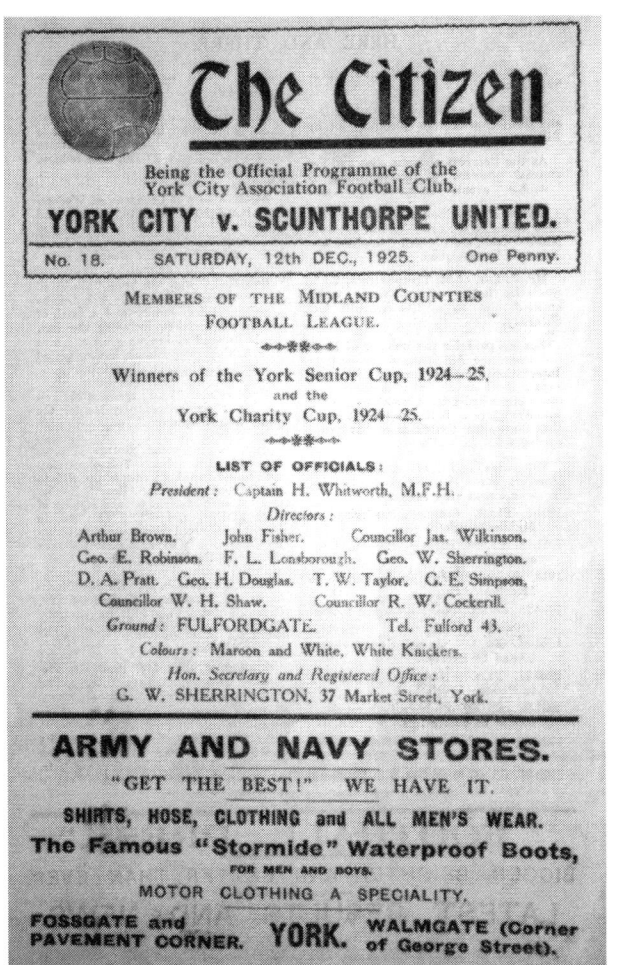

York City versus Scunthorpe United game in 1925 at the old Fullford Ground, which finished in a 1-1 draw.

At the turn of the year bad weather lost a fixture, but in the first week of January Loughborough were beaten 3-0, followed by a 9-2 loss to the Lincoln City second squad. This was an extraordinary score, considering the teams had earlier drawn in Scunthorpe. Then a couple of weeks down the road, and the Nuts went to Loughborough, only to lose 6-1.

After the inconsistency at Loughborough the team returned to winning ways, beating Castleford 5-1 on foreign soil. The Yorkshire club propped up the League all season, so it was not such a surprise, but four goals in the game from Vowles all added to the total. This was not his only high scoring feat of February, because a fortnight later he scored another three into the Shirebrook net, as the team won 4-1. The hat-tricks were still not finished, and he registered his final one against Newark Town in the closing match of the calendar, at the Old Show Ground, when United won 5-0.

The contrast in the team that ended this season could not have been greater than with the side of twelve months before. The school of 1925-26 only failed to scored in just five of the forty games in the Midland League, and three of those were goalless draws which gained a point apiece. The public had turned out in slightly larger numbers and it was a refreshing change to watch a team with a bit of steel. The final table found Scunthorpe and Lindsey in seventh position of twenty one teams, only ten points behind the Champions, Mexborough, and six in arrears of Runners-up Mansfield, who had thoughts on a Football League place. At least the directors had a base to build upon.

The statistics revealled that United had mustered eight six goals during the whole Midland League season, which was eight more than those scored against them. Vowles had created a record for a Scunthorpe United player, by scoring thirty four goals, two more than the noble effort of Shaw. In addition he scored five more in the Cup. Next on the list was Witham with seventeen strikes, followed by Crawley, who could boast of fourteen, with six more in the Cup.

1926-27

The stucture of the Midland League altered slightly for the 1926-27 campaign, because Castleford failed to gain re-election, and Mansfield Town decided to play their football in another League, so they might promote their chances of entry to the Football League. One club was admitted to made the body up to twenty interested parties, and that was a Nottinghamshire team of Heanor Town. With these routes changes the Scunthorpe United bus was ready to roll.

The directors decided on a ruthless approach to the playing staff, and only Frank Skull and Norman Reynolds were considered for further regular positions, although it goes without saying John Wogin was never very far away when required.

During the Summer months a rumour started to spread round the town that the board was seeking the signature of an old England International centre forward, but they remained tight lipped when ever the subject was brought up. It was then announced that this was true, and the directors had successfully approached and signed Ernie Simms, the former Luton, South Shields and Stockport County player. Big Ernie had won a place in the England side in a game against Northern Ireland, whilst on the books at Luton in 1922, and was proud to own his cap. This man was a marksman of top quality, and still had many goals yet score to. He came at a price, but it would be well worth the cost. At his suggestion, United offered terms to his inside partner Joey Johnson at Stockport, who also knew where to put the ball and it was a move that paid dividends. The right flank was completed by winger Thompson, formerly of Sheffield Wednesday and Portsmouth, who would supply a stream of crosses for these two experienced campaigners. The left section of the attack brought in Tommy Allen for the inside position, and Fred Alford at left wing. Tommy came from last season's Champions, Mexborough and had an abundance of skill.

Fred stood only five feet and six inches, but was grease lightening, and tricky with it, having seen service at Lincoln City, Barrow and Everton.

The mid-field trio was to be made up of Frank Skull, Charles Smith and George Hunter. It should be noted that Frank Skull was a tall man, but stood alongside Charles Smith he seemed tiny, because Smith was three inches greater in height, and of a built suited to the rough and tumble of the Midland League. Over on the left side of the midfield George Hunter, from Doncaster, was even taller at more than six foot. Hunter came with a suitcase full of experience, having been at clubs at the corners of the land, including Exeter City, Southend United, and Sunderland. This line was supported by full backs McKenzie and Holland. McKenzie was a man who had played at a number of clubs and was just the sort to bring the best out of young Holland, who had been spotted at Bolsover Colliery playing football. He would always be issuing words of encouragement to his fast developing partner. The final piece of the puzzle was the return of Alex Moore as a utility man from his errant wanderings at Gainsborough.

The season began in earnest at home to Frickley Colliery, and they zipped the ball about with confidence, winning 3-1 at a canter, with goals by Tommy Allen, George Hunter and Charles Smith. They continued in a winning streak at new boys Heanor Town, picking up two more points from the 2-0 score. It was only then that they met some sort of resistance, visiting the home of Champions Mexborough. They were soundly beaten, but made sure they learned lessons from the 4-0 reverse. The problem proved to be a minor hick-up, and two days later they punished the junior Imps of Lincoln City, by 4-1 and a Simms hat-trick announced his arrival. The team was to steam on to a twenty match unbeaten sequence, starting with this result.

On September 18th 1926 Scunthorpe and Lindsey launched their F.A.Cup campaign with a record equalling 10-0 demolition of Hull Holderness, a team used to such results against the Nuts. Simms scored another trio, Johnson and Allen notched a braces, while Alford and Skull made up the total. Only Thompson of the forwards failed to register, probably because he was always out on the wing knocking crosses in for the others.

Frank Skull was the first man who played three hundred games for Scunthorpe and Lindsey, and could be found in any of the three half back positions.

The theme was repeated in the First Qualifying Round for the visit of Grimsby Haycroft Rovers, who were shown no mercy, and spanked 7-2. All those in attendance knew that something of this nature would happen, but it was still a brilliant feeling to cheer, as Johnson Simms and Allen were all able to hit a couple of goals each, while Smith came out of defence to make up the oddment. This latest result was rewarded with a Second Qualifying Round tie in Yorkshire at Selby Olympic.

Scunthorpe and Lindsey were unaware of the strength of the Selby team, but had nothing to fear, except a Cup upset from one of the minnows. On the appointed Saturday in October it was to be the defenders who took the eye, and Simms and company were not allowed to dictate. Neither side could make an impact on the scoreboard, much to Selby's credit, but Tommy Allen hit the only goal in the replay.

Scunthorpe and Lindsey supporters enjoyed the F.A.Cup, and turned out in guaranteed greater numbers to see the drama of the knock-out challenge. It made a pleasant change to the Midland League, as the Club advanced on two fronts. The luck of the draw had the Nuts make the sixteen mile or so trip down the A159 to Gainsborough, and every form of transport took the army of supporters to see the match. It turn out to be a real Waterloo with both sides firing guns that did some damage. Three times the blue shirts of Trinity breached the United goal, but three times they shot back in sharp reply. At 3-3 the episode required settling at the Old Show Ground, and the match attracted 5,000 people to swap shifts at the steelworks. This time it was to be a cagey affair and defenders were not as generous. The tie was won by the trusty boot of Ernie Simms, who rocketed a shot into the net.

The visitors for the final qualifying stage of the competition was Kettering Town, a team from Northamptonshire, but the Poppies must have at least been equals to reach this stage of the competition. It was a miserable Autumn day that greeted both fans and players alike. The visitors brought a small but noisy band of their own supporters, but the weather restricted the gate to 3814 spectators. When battle commenced play was even, but reports in the newspapers suggested some element of luck attached to the first Kettering goal, which gave them an interval lead.

In the second half Scunthorpe were not long in finding an equaliser goal from Joey Johnson, but late in the match Kettering found a way through the mud, and notched the killer blow, winning 2-1.

The exit from the Cup was an avenue for the team to continue to make progress in the Midland League. All thoughts of defeat were cast aside one week later when Ilkeston were beaten 5-3, then a visit to Alfreton, and a call from Long Eaton, both brought the opposition 6-1 thrashings. It cannot be empathised how free scoring Ernie Simms was, and week after week he was hitting the headlines with hat-tricks or more. At Christmas his goals had United top of the pile, and looking strong to maintain the top spot. In the space of two Saturdays in January the team scored fifteen goals. They humiliated Shirebrook 8-1, and then Grantham 7-1. Simms made a contribution of seven goals in the two matches.

The list of conquests was almost endless, but the one that hit the headlines was when Sutton Town were beaten 10-0 in the Midland League, and Ernie Simms scored a double hat-trick, thus creating all sorts of records. Those watching on the terraces at the Old Show Ground could not believe their eyes.

Scunthorpe and Lindsey United were crowned Champions of the Midland League weeks before the end of the season. They strolled in eleven points better off than the Runners-up Boston, with a far superior goal average. The Scunthorpe record stood at P38, W28, D4, L6. During the season a massive total of 121 goals had been scored but a tight defence conceded just 44.

This outstanding team made its own history, and was so consistent that it virtually picked itself, and few players appeared, other than the regular eleven throughout the campaign. Understandably Ernie Simms topped the goal scorers with fifty eight in both competition, followed by Tommy Allen, who was credited with thirty five, then Joey Johnson, who was responsible for thirty one.

Scunthorpe and Lindsey United had experienced years of struggle at all levels since it was conceived from the Brumby Hall club in 1899. It had almost gone out of existence a few short months ago, but this team had made the Club and its supporters proud. Each and every man had played beyond the call of duty, to secure a marvellous victory that focused the whole town in the National spotlight. There can be no question that if this team had operated in the Football League Third Division Northern Section, it would have been a front runner. Above all the board needed congratulating for all the risks and effort they had put in. Now was a time to savour the rewards of the Championship trophy and prepare for the times ahead.

The first Scunthorpe United team to win the Midland League Championship, in 1926-27 season.
Back row: Allcock(Secretary) Smith, Skull, McKenzie, Reynolds, Holland, Hunter and White(Trainer).
Front Row: Thompson, Johnson, Simms, Allen, and Alford.

WAITING FOR ANOTHER TITLE

1927-28

The situation going into the 1927-28 season was a much healthier one, thanks to the wonderful achievement of the Championship team. Interest was much greatly increased in the Nuts, and the board knew that if the gates were to be maintained, then so too had the standards on the field, or it would be back to square one. The Club was still not out of the woods as in respect of the financial burden that for twelve months had been forgotten in favour of the exploits of Ernie Simms and the rest of the team. At least the blackened scar of the fire had now been erased and the work on the West Stand completed to satisfaction.

The thought of breaking up the Championship squad could not bare thinking about, but inevitably it happened by natural progression, as Reynolds, McKenzie, Thompson, Smith Alford and Johnson all decided to move to other vacancies. In this respect the directors hand their hands tied, but at least there was consolation in the fact that Ernie Simms was still on the books, and they could build another team around his goal scoring foundation, but only if the Club could afford it.

Scunthorpe and Lindsey started the repair with a new custodian by the name of Watts, who was recommended whilst playing for Bradford Park Avenue, but the board was not happy with his progress and he was replaced by a local player by the name of Unwin. This young lad was a tall bean pole of a man, who had no difficulty touching his fingers on the cross bar with his outstretched arms. There was still a swan song from the evergreen Johnny Wogin, who made five appearances in the keepers jersey, before hanging up his boots for good, after the Loughborough game March 31st 1928. In the full back places Holland was to have a new partner, when ex-Worksop and Portsmouth player Len Severn put pen to paper. He was not the tallest pencil in the box, but could keep up with the fastest wingers and saw that their crosses were blocked and came to nothing.

The middle of the field still had the benefit of Skull and Hunter, but the centre half post was given to a man called Murphy, who stood more than six foot tall, having played for Norwich City and Southend United.

These changes were nothing compared to the forward line. Ernie Simms would still be the main part of the striking force, but over on the right wing Harry Wainwright was signed from Sheffield United. His inside man was Brooks, a local product from the Normanby, who was put to use. There was another chance given to a Santon based youngster before the end of the year, named Jack Bowers. Both Maw and Bowers would be sold on, and reach the top of the game, winning International honours, but that was still a long way off.

The last on the forwards was for the left wing berth, which went to a former Worksop Town player called Foster, but again the team could fall back on the services of Alex Moore in times of shortage. After all, the coming Midland League season was extended to forty four matches.

When the Midland League committee met in the Summer of 1927 it decided to open its doors to a number of Football League clubs to allow their reserve teams to join the fold. These included the reintroduction of Grimsby Town, Notts County, and Nottingham Forest. In addition Scarborough, a strong North Yorkshire club, had also been granted permission to perform. Scunthorpe and Lindsey opened their account with a comfortable visit to Newark Town, and, as expected, returned with both points when they plundered a 5-2 result. Brooks scored twice on his debut, but in the next match the Nuts faced the new boys from Scarborough and soon realised how tough it was going to be to retain the title. Not only did Scarborough win 3-2 at the Old Show Ground, but the red and white kitted men completed the double back at their own Seamer Road Ground, in Scarborough.

The changing of the seasons brought the leaves on the trees to turn to brown, and also turn Scunthorpe United's fortunes with it. They were able to beat old friends from Nottingham Forest and Gainsborough, then registered seven goals twice. One of those events was at Heanor Town, 7-4, when Simms clattered the opposition with a hat-trick, and the other at home to Staveley, 7-2, when Tommy Allen did an encore.

Scunthorpe football fanatics had high hopes of another enthralling run in the F.A.Cup. The Preliminary Round started a much shorter journey of Cup exploits, at home to Cleethorpes Town. Scunthorpe and Lindsey had no inhibitions in rolling over the Meggies with a 5-2 stroll. Ernie Simms made the best of the extra space afforded him, and helped himself to four of the goals.

The First Qualifying Round gave United a sticky trip to Gainsborough. The Trinity board had taken advantage of signing two former Nuts, and McKenzie and Shaw were players that both sets of supporters in the 4,500 crowd knew all about. Goal scoring was an art that had not left Shaw, and he had scored six times for the Trinity against Boston a few weeks prior to the Cup tie. A wall of noise greeted the players at the beginning of the match, and a 3-0 result meant that it was the Northolme section that was still cheering on ninety minutes. The Midland League was proving not to be as easy in the current year as in the past. Ernie Simms was an expensive acquisition, but well worth the increased demands of his pay packet.

1927-28: In the second half of the season after the transfer of Ernie Simms to York City, when Jack Bowers, (middle of the front row), was the principal marksman. Bowers would play for England when at Derby County.

Where other players were not up to scratch, Simms certainly was. Scunthorpe gradually slipped down the table, and a position hovering just above the half-way mark soon made it apparent that the Midland League title could not be retained. A nail was knocked in that particular coffin at Christmas. To make for a most disappointing holiday period, Scunthorpe first lost the double to Grimsby Town Reserves, then haplessly tossed away two more point, 3-0 at Staveley, in the first game of 1928. The only compensation was the win over Grantham, squeezed in between those games on New Year's Eve.

There had been gossip going around the town that Ernie Simms was attracting attention from other clubs. He kept adding to his total, which rose to thirty goals when three more hit the back of the net against Newark Town, as United inflicted a 7-2 mauling. It might have been the fact that the Championship was now well out of the Club's grasp that played a role in the decision of the board. During the first week in February there was confirmation that Ernie Simms was about to leave the Old Show Ground and sign for York City. On Saturday February 11th, United had a fixture at York, and standing hands on hips on the opposite side of the field was Simms. It was he who did the destruction of his former club, and City won 2-1.

The loss of Simms was not as damaging as at first was to be thought. The mantle of scoring was assumed by the local boys, Jack Bowers and Arthur Maw, who impressed every time they laced their boots. In terms of percentages, the figures of Bowers matched those of Simms, when young Jack needed only nine games to score fourteen goals. The team was to run into some fine form, and only lost once in the final nine fixtures. It was too late to make an impression higher up the table, but gave hope for the future.

In the final analysis Scunthorpe and Lindsey United had the eighth best record of twenty three teams, but were far off the pace set by Gainsborough, who took the title. The team gathered twenty three wins, which was six more than they were beaten in, and a tally of one hundred and eighteen goals were registered, but only eighty five conceded. Some directors questioned their own decisions as to if the Championship men been given greater incentives to stay, but hindsight is a wonderful commodity, and the financial struggle far from over. At least the lessons learned would act as a yardstick for the future, when the balance between affordability and talent had to be weighed up again.

1928-29

When the list of fixtures landed on Harry Allcock's desk for the coming year, it was obvious that United would be involved in a marathon. No less than twenty six teams had lined up to try and claim the Midland League prize, and that meant a fifty match programme, and a lot of travelling. Those clubs with the biggest squads would be favourites to forge ahead.

The big news of the Summer was the transfer of Jack Bowers for a sizable fee to Derby County. This marksman would be a bargain for the Rams, where he became the record goal scorer at the club in the 1930-31 season, with a total of thirty seven strikes. Bowers assisted County to the second place in the First Division of 1929-30 season, and represented England three times. After leaving Derby he joined Leicester City, and his goals helped the Foxes win promotion from Division Two. However, the Club did retain Unwin for goal, Severn in the full back role, Skull for midfield, and forwards Maw and Allen.

The huge number of fixture meant a vast number of men were used in dibs and drabs, but the main partner for Len Severn was Frank Hill for the left back place. In the centre of the park Edward Mooney was a player that was said to have a cheery disposition as central pivot. Skull continued at right half, and a stocky man called Bailey occupied the far side. The centre forward position took quite a long time to resolve and seven men were tried without satisfaction, until Smith became the regular player, into the second phase of the season. A similar situation occurred on the right wing, and was not sorted until October, when Wadsworth became a partner to Maw. The left flank was less problematical, as Tommy Allen, a popular crowd pleaser, linked up with Webb.

The picture was finished with Unwin in between the posts, but after four matches the green jersey was passed to Watson, who used his position in authority until February. It was a this point in time that the directors had been given notice of another goalkeeper, named Walker. For a time Walker had given service at Sheffield Wednesday, and once he signed for the Nuts the job was handed to him until the season finished.

Scunthorpe and Lindsey United started the fixtures at home to Hull City Reserves with a dismal goalless draw. This was the beginning of one of the worse starts to a season, when they won only one out of the first eight League matches, at home to Doncaster Rovers Reserves. It was only slightly better than the poor beginning made during the 1912-13 season, and it was easy to suggest that an unsettled team was the reason for the misery. The nadir of this run came at Shirebrook where shame faced Scunthorpe players left the field after a 7-0 lesson of the basic arts in football.

Supporters of the Club welcomed the changes made to the side, as performances gradually improved and shortly the team began to climb back up the table to a position somewhere nearer the middle belt. Unfortunately these early pantomimes put a severe dint in any ambitions the Club had of rubbing shoulders with the leaders, and making an impact on the title race. At least the F.A.Cup was to put the smile back on everybody's face and the road started at Barton , where the Town club put up a brilliant exhibition on the banks of the Humber, but lost out to the professionals by a 3-2 score.

They next journey was to Spalding, which brought back memories of a snowy day in 1908, when they both met at Scunthorpe in the Lincolnshire Junior Cup. This time, in the South of the County, United triumphed again, winning 3-0. The Second Qualifier was at home to Cleethorpes Town, and provided a goal feast, which the Nuts won 4-3, followed by another away success at Boston, won narrowly 1-0. Only Grantham stood in the way of the Scunthorpe and a prize draw in the First Round Proper.

Ground advantage was with Grantham, and they put it to good use. Arthur Maw scored for the Nuts, and they were considered rather unlucky when another effort was disallowed. In the end a 1-2 result was an unfair reflection of the shift the team produced, and they missed out on playing Rhyl Athletic at the next stage.

The arrival of the New Year saw a different team run out of the tunnel at the Old Show Ground, judging by the results and performances. United went back into the top section of the table, accelerated by a run of only one defeat in thirteen matches. At Christmas the entertainment was provided by the junior Mariners of Grimsby. Scunthorpe and Lindsey gave no presents, and took all four points on offer with two identical 2-1 victories.

It was not all a bed of roses for the team, as they found out in the early part of the New Year against Mansfield Town. The Stags had returned to the Midland League, but were determined to rise to play in the Third Division of the Football League. A lot of investment had been put into the Nottinghamshire team, and they were streets ahead of all other sides at the summit of the division. Scunthorpe and Lindsey would fall to the Stags mastery, like many others. At the Field Mill Scunthorpe made every effort, and were fortunate to only lose 5-0. At the Old Show Ground it was the same story, but this time 3-0.

It was left until the last match of the season to produce the best result. Scunthorpe and Lindsey had never played host to Wath Athletic, but after a gruelling season their legs were fresh as ever. It was a small crowd that turned up, in pleasant but cool conditions, to see the Nuts raise the temperature at 7-2. Both Smith and Calladine scored hat-tricks, and Tommy Allen made up the remainder. Those who walked up to the ground came away very satisfied.

When this result was tucked in to the equation United finished eleventh in the twenty six horse race, a country mile behind Mansfield. Statistics declared the Nuts winners on twenty occasions, and losers just sixteen times. The goal difference was positive, but generally the report suggested that the pupils must try harder. A variety of men had been responsible for scoring United's goals, but Smith was given the most credit for registering nineteen in less than half a season, closely followed by Allen with seventeen.

The 'Scunthorpe Hospital Cup' was an annual event between Scunthorpe United and an invited Football League club, to raise money for the local hospital. United drew 1-1 with Doncaster Rovers on April 29th 1929, and are pictured with the trophy they shared for six months each.

The football season was wrapped up in May with a new innovation, the Grimsby Telegraph War Memorial Hospital Cup. This was to be an annual event to raise money for hospital funds. Scunthorpe and Lindsey would play a top club for ownership of the trophy for a year, and crowds flocked to support the charitable venture. The guests in 1929 were the friends of Doncaster Rovers, who brought their Football League eleven for an entertaining draw. The Cup was shared on this occasion, and a correct call to the toss of a coin had it handed it to the Scunthorpe captain for the first six months.

1929-30

Scunthorpe and Lindsey United received a bid for their talented young forward Arthur Maw during the Summer, and they were only too willing to allow him to make progress at a higher level. Arthur was starting his career in the Football League at Notts County, and the Magpies were happy to send a cheque in the post to the Old Show Ground. Harry Allcock took this to the bank so that the debt could be reduced, but the situation was still critical. The assembly of the team began with the acquisition of Bromage from Frickley Colliery to fill the goalkeeping position, and at least this was not to cause the problems of a year ago.

He was able to remain as a servant for a number of uninterrupted seasons, such was his ability, and injury only precluded him from one match. To support Len Severn in the full back role the board found John Baynham who was born in Somerset, and was recognised as a tough tackling customer. Across the half back line Skull and Bailey were given the green light to continue, and had a new centre half in Cooke, of Royston, to keep them company.

The forward line was initially led by Arthur Smalley, but he so impressed during some epic League and Cup battles that Blackpool asked the priced, and another cheque reach the bank. After that, Baldwin spearheaded the attack, having perfected the art at Oldham Athletic. The inside positions went to the rapidly developing youngster from last term, called Calladine, and former Portsmouth favourite Stringfellow. This left Simmons to take up on the right wing, and Beynon on the left. Beynon had arrive from Halifax Town via Swansea Town, and put in a number of class performances to enhance his reputation. This completed the general picture of the team, which would soon become a balanced outfit, once it got to know each other.

The Midland League season commencing in the Summer of 1929 was to be yet another fifty match slog, with players on overtime for many mid-week callouts.

It all started in the sunshine at the Old Show ground when Hull City's Tiger Cubs rolled up. The players did not need bottles of water, because during the match a thunder storm broke and drenched them, but it was the home side that cut the mustard in a 3-1 win. The month of September was a productive one for the Nuts who only lost once on the sojourn to Lincoln, for the match against the Imps second set. The most outstanding display came when Gainsborough arrived outside the Old Show Ground and were peppered to the tune of 5-0. The list of marksmen included Stringfellow, Smalley, Calladine and Beynon, but Calladine was the toast of the team with two goals. One of his was a low hard shot which bewildered the Trinity keeper as to where the ball would finish. October had just three matches, owing to Cup duties. Only one produced a victory, and that was against Rotherham United Reserves, a club formed out of the amalgamation of the Town and County clubs. The biggest surprise was a loss at Gainsborough by 4-1, where defensive errors left the team to blame for the result. There was no wonder United could not trouble the top positions in the table with returns like these.

Scunthorpe and Lindsey United were ready for embarkation in the F.A.Cup and this was to be a record breaking season that saw them smash barriers that in the past had seemed impossible. All journeys start with the first step, and for the Nuts it was on a small pitch at Selby Town, already starting to lose its grass. Scunthorpe had to work hard for the 3-1 victory, which only came late in the day. The result presented the team with a match against the other team from the same town, Selby Olympic. The Nuts were already acquainted with the Olympic, but hoped that ground advantage would give them confidence. The Yorkshire opponents proved just as robust as on the previous occasion, and Scunthorpe were pleased for a 1-0 win. This came via a goal scored from a corner kick incident, and was a victory not taken for granted until the last whistle. At least supporters appreciated the fight put up by the visitors, and could now look forward to Goole Town at the third stage. This was to be exactly the same sort of struggle. It was watched by 3,329 spectators, who saw the Nuts take a 2-0 first half lead, but concede a last minute penalty goal, and go through.

The Third Qualifying Round landed United a local derby against the villagers of Broughton Rangers, many of whose visiting supporters also followed the fortunes of the Nuts. Despite the local rivalry, only 2,100 made the effort on the afternoon. Rangers had done extremely well to reach this distance in the F.A.Cup, and equally so to hold the Nuts to a two goal lead at the pause of play. After the break was over, Scunthorpe got into gear and won 7-0. The Nuts could afford to play Kennedy from the reserve team, and he scored four of the goals. The public was still not convinced when United played their Fourth Qualifying Round at home to South Kirkby, and only 2,206 were on station for the kick-off.

Scunthorpe and Lindsey had the handicap of injuries during the game, but this was offset by the sending off of a visiting fullback. Scunthorpe scored first, conceded an equaliser, then ran amok in the second half, winning 6-1.

The club at last woke up the Scunthorpe public's interest, when they took on the challenge of Hartlepools United in the First Round of the F.A.Cup. The team to represent them was as follows: Bromage, Severn and Baynham; Skull Cooke, and Bailey; Simmons, Stringfellow, Smalley, Calladine and Beynon. At the beginning of play a record crowd of 5,305 was in position to cheer the players on. Scunthorpe were on top for long periods of the match, and had several chances to go ahead. The surprise was that Bromage was hardly troubled, but United had to wait until the forty third minute to go ahead. The ball was sent down the centre and Stringfellow passed it to Smalley. His quick thinking allowed him to put his foot through the ball and direct it beyond the Pool custodian. Pandemonium broke out on the terraces at this, and it was the encouragement that the team deserved.

Scunthorpe kept up the pressure on Hartlepools in the second half, and the pace of the game was just as frantic. Shortly into the second period the Nuts were hit with a blow, when Bailey went for a ball, and collided with his opposite number. He was out cold and had to be carried from the field, then revived by the doctor. In the final moments the visitors went in vain hope of an equaliser, but it never arrived. At the end of the game pandemonium returned, as happy supporters ran onto the pitch to slap the backs of the players. On the following Monday Scunthorpe folks gathered round the radio to discover that their team would be at home to Rotherham United in Round Two.

The Second Round of the F.A.Cup was played two weeks later on December 14th 1929, at the Old Show Ground, and the record attendance was extended to 8,030. Scunthorpe fielded the same team that got the better of Hartlepool, and pushed Rotherham all the way. Smalley shot them into a fourth minute lead, Calladine increased it in the seventeenth minute, then an unfortunate own goal reduced it to 2-1 at the interval. After the players returned to the field, Scunthorpe again took up the initiative and extended the lead when Simmons slipped the ball through for Calladine to score his second. Rotherham reduced the deficit from a penalty, then were fortunate to equalise with little time remaining.

On the following Thursday the same players rolled up their sleeves to resume the conflict. Rotherham United raced out of the blocks and twice Bromage had to pick the ball from the back of the net. Scunthorpe reduced the arrears when a penalty was awarded, and Beynon made sure with his blasted shot. When the players emerged from the tunnel after the ten minute break it was those supporters from Scunthorpe that shouted next, when Smalley hit a sweet volley beyond the home keeper. Rotherham regained the lead, but Calladine caught a cross just right with his head, and it was level at 3-3. Going into the last ten minutes and it was the fitness of the full time players of Rotherham United that was to ride the storm the best. Scunthorpe tired trying to keep up the pace, and conceded two late goals. It was a valiant effort, and not quite over yet. Beynon made sure that Scunthorpe had the last word, with a goal in the final minute. Everyone was breathless, and a 5-4 result spelt the end of the gallant run, but it had replenished the coffers. Rotherham went out to Nottingham Forest in the next round, losing 5-0.

Once the F.A.Cup run was over the team concentrated on the Midland League which perhaps did not contain the same glamour as the knock-out competition. This last series of games had raised the Club's profile as a team that could play attractive and direct football. Even the loss of Smalley for another cheque did little to halt the team's progress and the balance of the team was not effected to any noticeable degree. They still had enough fire power left in the ranks to find the victories to lift them up the table. United enjoyed the company of Calladine, Beynon and Baldwin, all of which would register twenty goals or more, before time was called on the season.

The 1929-30 season was to have a number of memorable moment yet to be savoured. Scarborough were the runaway Champions of the Midland League, and scored one hundred and forty three goals. On February 1st they played hosts to Scunthorpe, in the depths of the Winter weather, but the Nuts failed to pay homage, and fought hard for a creditable 1-1 draw. They even had the audacity to take the lead in the sixtieth minute when Stringfellow hooked in a Beynon cross. Another close affair saw them beat Lincoln City Reserves 2-1 at the end of March. Witnesses at the Old Show Ground saw City miss a number of chances, but the Nuts were able to score a goal either side of the one of the junior Imps. Theses were probably better contests than when Staveley Town lost 9-0 on their visit, in April. In was not all sweetness and light, because they had two disasters, against Bradford Park Avenue Reserves, which were lost 5-2 at home and 9-0 away. Perhaps the transfer of centre half Cooke to Hull City had some influence on this.

When all the dust had settled, the table showed that Scunthorpe United had reached seventh of the twenty six contenders. It was a satisfactory effort in, view of a certain amount of disruption. The honour of topping the Nuts goal scoring chart went to Calladine, who had to be congratulated for a fine year of thirty two strikes. In total the team had scored the magnificent sum of one hundred and twenty four goals, whilst conceding only ninety eight. The finances had been eased significantly by the windfall from the Cup games, which twice brought the unexpected bonus of a record gate at the Old Show Ground. They would find more money forth coming from Rotherham United, who had taken a shine to Frank Skull, United's right half. Even with that cash in the bank there could not be room for complacency, and the Club was still far from debt free.

1930-31

The decade of the Thirties would see attitudes and society change. Money was to be as tight as ever, and little spare cash was to be found in the working man's pocket. Football was still the principal sport, but Scunthorpe and Lindsey United would have to produce the goods to compete with other interests To make sure they were prepared for the new challenges contracts had been offered to Bromage in goal, Baynham at full back, Bailey in mid-field and Stringfellow and Beynon in the attack.

The chosen replacements for the team looked to be men of pedigree. In front of Bromage, Webster was selected as the right full back partner for Baynham. Webster came with credentials from Sheffield United, Lincoln City and Walsall. The loss of Frank Skull to Rotherham was minimised by the signing of Ernie Pattison from the same club. Pattison showed he had some tricks of his own and gained the affection of the crowd. When the need was felt, Pattison moved forward into the attack as a prolific marksman, and threatened danger anywhere near the posts.

When Pattison was at half back, he stood alongside a six foot giant called Hilton, who signed from Notts County. When his tour of duty was cut short, a Scottish player named Ross took up the mantle, being equally tall and more effective. On the far side Bailey continued to play with aplomb. At the same time as the arrival of Ross, Scunthorpe directors discovered a young forward called Joey Johnson in Grimsby, a different man to the one who played in the Championship side of 1927. Johnson was to develop into a cultured half back of some considerable class, eventually being transferred to Bristol City and on to Stoke. At the Victoria Ground he was summonsed by the Football Association to play for England.

It may have taken some time to settle down, but the directors chose their preferred forward line as Oakton, Stringfellow, Rawlings, Green and Beynon. Oakton had been brought in from Grimsby Town, Rawlings had impressed at Boston, while Green was from the other side of Doncaster at Denaby. A number of fringe players were utilised, of which Wainwright was given the most opportunities, coming off the books of Sheffield United.

From the turn of the first ball, on the grassy pitch at Wombwell, it was obvious that it was going to take some time for the new men to find some sort of understanding, as the 3-1 defeat against a weaker side indicated. They did turn the tables on Wombwell in the next fixture at home, but did not get a proper grip until they crushed Rotherham United's second team 7-2. In October they showed their frailties, when a not so clever experienced saw them stutter to a 6-2 defeat on a visit to Oakwell for a clash against Barnsley Reserves.

The directors chose at this point in the procedures to promote Pattison to the forward line, and with an instant success He netted twice at home to Loughborough, and United won 4-2. Then he added another pair at Scarborough, to yield a similar result a week later. If that was not enough, the next two Saturdays brought hat-tricks, as Notts County and Chesterfield both had their reserve sides sent packing.

The number of games Scunthorpe and Lindsey had to play in the F.A.Cup was reduced in 1930, because they had reach the First Round last term. It was not until the Fourth Qualifier that they were expected to come to the table. They could expect a strong opponent at this stage of the competition, and had to confront Worcester City, at the Old Show Ground. In the past, they had taken Kettering too lightly, and would not be remiss this time. On November 15th the two teams met before a crowd of more than three thousand. They saw the Nuts play at the top of their game, and win by three clear goals. Pattison was on fire this time and weighed in with a pair, while the other was supplied by Beynon, on the left. In the First Round Proper a local derby was the calling, at Gainsborough. Scunthorpe knocked on the door all afternoon, despite the efforts of Pattison, but this time he could not weave his magic. Trinity sneaked just one goal, and went into the hat for Round Two.

Once United returned to the business of the Midland League, Pattison continued to conjure the goals. At Chesterfield, a roller coaster of a game finished honours even at 4-4, and Pat, as he was known, plundered a hat-trick. Then at Frickley Colliery, on the Monday after Christmas Day, he was responsible for four goals in a remarkable 6-0 score.

In the period just after New Year, Scunthorpe United hit a patch of form which was akin to a piece of cork bobbing up and down in a choppy sea. One minute it was up and the other it was down. At the end of January three consecutive games were lost, then a quartet of fights gained the maximum reward. On the down side, Lincoln rubbed the salt in the wounds 5-0 at the Old Show Ground, but on the up side the Mariner's Reserves were mastered 4-3, a team who would be Champions. This fluctuation in form coincided with an injury to Pattison, but then the severity of the Winter eased and was replaced by a wind swept March. It was then that the Nuts had two encounters with Nottingham Forest, a team of men on the fringe of the title race. The men of Sherwood sharpened their goal arrows for the visit of Scunthorpe and Lindsey, and fired them true.

Charlie Cross played from 1929 until 1938, making 274 appearances.

The score was an incredible 9-0 humiliation on that Thursday afternoon, and Maid Marion could had scored if she had been playing. The sides met again two days later, on the Saturday, at the Old Show Ground, and the Nuts implemented three team changes. A much harder battle took place, and, believe it or not, the men in claret and blue rose to the occasion an stole a 1-0 victory through Pattison.

The daffodils were in evidence for the last throws of the dice, as the football calendar was coming to a close. United still had time to produce a couple of performances that went beyond the call of duty. At Mansfield, the introduction of Joey Johnson caused quite a stir. He hit the Nottinghamshire lads with a hat-trick at the Field Mill. The Nuts squeezed one more goal than the Stags, and came home 4-3 to the good. Twelve days later and Scunthorpe and Lindsey sank Bradford City Reserves' chances of the title, by winning 3-1 at the Old Show Ground. The Valley Parade boys finally lost the title on goal average.

If the Club had been able to orchestrate performances like those every week, the team would have been in the same shoes as the Grimsby Town Reserves. Instead, the year fizzled out with two inept home displays against middle of the road teams from Chesterfield and Mansfield. This dropped the Nuts into eleventh place in the final table, a slightly worse position than what had been anticipated. It would give board had plenty of ammunition to consider a number of options.

The Summer break was welcomed by some, and a rest taken from standing on the cold terraces of the Old Show Ground. Others had to work on, and the land was scoured to find the right blend of youth and experience. When the shadows of late Summer fell long across the grass supporters, hoped that the squad of players assembled would do the Club justice.

1931-32

Scunthorpe and Lindsey were very fortunate to have such a reliable goalkeeper in Bromage, who would have no contenders for the green jersey. He had demonstrated how composed he was under pressure at all times, and only serious injury occasionally precluded him from duty. His full backs would be Cross and Baynham. Charlie Cross was a local boys, who made his first tentative steps in the first eleven last season. He was to be one of the success stories of the side, and retained his shirt throughout the year.

The centre half position was selected from either Wilson or Grainger, while Staniland and Stimpson stood either side as the halfbacks. Jack Staniland was a tall young man, who had played for Broughton Rangers at a lower level. The step up to the Midland League would cause him no bother, and he, too, became one of the stars of the show. Stimpson came from Nottinghamshire, and gathered his experience whilst on the books of Mansfield Town and Notts County. Grainger was given the first opportunity as the central pivot, having Hull City stamped on his passport, but he was succeeded by Sheffield junior Wilson. Evidence reveals that when the needs must both were selected at the same time. Through the season injury and inconsistency gave at least five men a chance to claim the number five shirt.

The forward line was to be unrecognisable from that of the previous year. Supporters missed the guile of Pattison, and at fist the directors handed the role of chief marksman to Adams, but had a change of mind when his gun was found to be firing blanks. They needed to find a man who was up to standard, and shortly into the fixture card Methven was brought in to fit the bill, most satisfactorily. Methven was a man who always scored goals, and in the past Derby County and Sheffield United had benefited from his energy. His inside men would finally be Hubbard and Dawson. Hubbard was a September starter from Manton Colliery, and despite his youthful qualities, was adequately up to scratch at inside right. John Dawson was from Louth and secured a place in the team without conceding it to any other competition. On the right wing Daws was the first man to use the shirt. He was a local product, who was later succeeded by Tucker, a player found in local football at Rotherham.

The left wing berth was initially given to Isaacs of Louth Town. Although he performed reasonably well he lost his place to Walter 'Ginner' Reed. Walter was a local player who had feet that could talk, once they were inside a pair of football boots. He could slip round opponents like a ghost in the night, and his left foot sent over a stream of accurate crosses to his forwards. It was not long before there was a queue of scouts knocking on the door to watch his progress. Eventually he was invited to London by Herbert Chapman, the famous manager of First Division Champions Arsenal, for a trial. He impressed sufficiently for them to offer him a contract and in March 1932 he signed.

Scunthorpe and Lindsey United made a bold enough start to the campaign in the Summer of 1931, winning both of the first two fixtures by an odd goal, at home to Mansfield Town Reserves and Boston. They were unable to pick up another win under their belt for a further four matches, from which a solitary point was gleaned. The last in this package was an important defeat by three clear goals at Gainsborough, and the natives returned home restless. It was a this moment that team changes were implemented and Mexborough became the victims of a rejuvenated side, and lost 4-1 to the Nuts at the Old Show Ground.

After this match Methven was installed in the team for the return of Gainsborough, on home territory. Alterations saw as many as six members of the team on the opening day of the season dropped for the visit of Trinity. The men of the blue and white kit were a formidable combination, and completed the double over United, but it was the signal for better results to come.

The month of October had Scunthorpe and Lindsey in the discomfort of a mid-table placing in the League. Their fortune turned for the better through the goals of Methven, who scored in all of the next three games. Each time the club was able to gain victory, and on all occasions four goals were scored. From these matches maximum points came against Rotherham United Reserves, Frickley Colliery, and Barnsley Reserves. During the next month F.A.Cup duties only allowed for two Midland League fixtures, which took the Nuts by bus to Mexborough and Barnsley. Supporters who made the trips witnessed two 6-1 results, but the transport to be on was the one going to Mexborough, because the Barnsley score was a defeat. At least the Mexborough result brought some relief because the double had been secured against the Yorkshire club.

Scunthorpe and Lindsey United were given exemption from the early rounds of the F.A.Cup, and did not join the party until they played Sutton Junction at home, on the second Saturday in November. The tie was a Fourth Qualifying Round match, and Scunthorpe took no chances against the unknown quantity. They sprinted out of the blocks and completed the afternoon with no doubts as the better team, having won 7-1. The hero of the day was inside man Hubbard, who scored three, Methven added a pair, and Grainger and Dawson were on hand for the rest of the total.

There was great jubilation in the town when the draw was completed for the First Round of the Cup. Scunthorpe and Lindsey were lucky enough to be graced with a visit from Rochdale of the Third Division North. The Lancastrians would be a formidable opponent, but by no means invincible. On the appointed day and at the appointed hour 4,800 hardy souls wrapped up warm to see the Nuts take on the Dale. United set their stall out accordingly and matched Rochdale in every department. Their patience was rewarded by a 2-1 win from the keen struggle, and the triumph was gleaned by the sheer hard work. The a courageous team effort produced goals by Methven and Hubbard.

The Second Round of the F.A.Cup brought Scunthorpe and Lindsey United in contact with their first adversaries from London. Queens Park Rangers, of Loftus Road, would have to journey North to the Old Show Ground, for fight to the death. The London and North Eastern Railway company put on an excursion from Kings Cross for the benefit of supporters of the team in the West of the Capital.

This was to swell the expectant crowd to marginally short of the record, at 7,993. When the Rangers ran out onto the pitch it was obvious that the Third Division South side were an athletic group of men, with their shirt of blue and white hoops. Scunthorpe and Lindsey were very well prepared and urged on by the majority of the crowd they rolled up the sleeves ready for battle.

Reports of the Cup tie against Queens Park Rangers suggested that the Londoners had it all sewn up their own way. Scunthorpe and Lindsey were never given the chance to stretch their legs and get a grip of the game. The score of 4-1 to the visitors was a true reflection of the play, and when United's supporters headed for the road home there could be no complaints. The single consolation was a penalty goal, converted by full back Baynham. Rangers followers had a long but happy trek back South and would see their team beat Leeds United in Shepherd's Bush 3-1, but then take another lengthy journey up North, only to lose to the big boys of First Division Huddersfield Town 5-0.

Scunthorpe soon resumed in the Midland League, and picked up the pieces with a close encounter against the Forest Reserves, winning 2-1. This brought them to the Yuletide programme, which during the decade to come would feature a pair of fixtures against the Grimsby Town Reserves. At this time the Mariners first team were on the verge of promotion to the First Division, and boasted one of the strongest second elevens. The Mariner's Reserves squad had claimed a trio of Midland League wins, and would be placed second at the end of this year. Times would be suitably hard for the Nuts, and try was they did, they conceded the double to the fishermen, going down at home 4-2, on Christmas Day, and losing 3-0 at Blundell Park, on Boxing Day. The sad tale of the holiday period was far from over. At Wombwell, United continued their woe, losing 5-3, and twenty four hours later the misery was completed at Bradford Park Avenue, where they capitulated 6-0 to the side that would be proud Champions.

This poor set of result plummeted the team towards the wrong end of the table. The results of the team in a reverse gear had an unsurprising knock-on effect at the turnstile, and numbers tumbled as a result of the waning interest. At least the Club began to rally through the rest of January and the crisis was averted. The journey improved, as the team pulled itself up by the bootlaces and gained victories over Frickley, Grantham, and Chesterfield, then suddenly the chill of the Winter did not feel quite as cold. A glance at the regularly picked team saw that only Bromage, Cross Baynham, Staniland, Stimpson and Dawson had remained in contention continuously.

During the last two months of the season Scunthorpe and Lindsey played the remaining ten games of the season. The returns were best described as mediocre and a meagre harvest of two wins and four draws just about summed up the general trend of the whole forty six match trail.

A last post was bugled at Newark in May, and the team went out with a whimper, losing 2-1. The lack of a goals scorer throughout the calendar made all the difference. When the Midland League table was examined in the sports editions, it showed that United were in ninth place, a marathon away from Bradford Park Avenue Reserves, who needed a Play-Off game with Grimsby Town Reserves to decide the Championship. During the term Scunthorpe had taken forty five points, whereas the top teams made seventy five.

Scunthorpe and Lindsey United had time to reflect on the previous year of work and there were some positives. At least the F.A.Cup had provided extra revenue, and the Club had been lucky enough to reach as far as they had ever ventured. The sale of Walter Reed went a long way to paying for some of the expense, when receipts fell at the gate. Team affairs could have been of a higher standing, but a number of local men had worn the shirt with pride, particularly Staniland and Cross. A further scrutiny of the League table was not quite as damning, because the only other team to finish above them, that was not the Reserve side of a Football League club, was Scarborough.

1932-33

The board of directors knew they would have to search the four corners of the land to put the strongest team in the field for the challenge of the year that was about to start. Midland League football was reaching even higher standards and only the best would survive. Scunthorpe started with Bromage in goal, but his throne was threatened by the agile Gordon Young, who succeeded him after a handful of games. The highly recommended former Sheffield Wednesday custodian was to become king of the castle for the next few years to come.

In the full back positions the board made an almost unheard of decision by retaining both of the previous incumbents, and Cross was to continue to partner Baynham. The same could be said of Staniland, who had ownership of the right half berth for a second spell, playing in virtually every game. There was to be a combination of Millson, Barke and Sharman to swap and change in the other two half back roles, depending on availability, and which was the flavour of the day. This was not the first tour of duty for Millson at the Old Show Ground, who had had sought improvement with Charlton Athletic in 1928, and was a better artist for the experience in the South.

The forward line of 1932 was to be led by Price as the main goal scorer, and he was accompanied on the right side by Hubbard from the old class of twelve months ago, who showed enough skills as an inside hit man to deserve another chance. Chapman was the other inside forward, from local circles, while Tucker and Murfin were in charge of the left flank. Tucker was the final player was deemed good enough to be offered another contact, in lieu of prior satisfactory work.

Perhaps the advantage of this squad of performers was that they would, by and large, be kept together as a unit, apart from inevitable injuries, and not chopped and changed on the whim of the board.

The fixture list was kind to Scunthorpe and Lindsey, and gave them a pair of games against the team that would finish hopelessly adrift of everyone else. Wombwell would only manage two wins during their whole sorry campaign, and conceded four goals short of the double hundred. The Nuts were cast iron certainties to beat them in each encounter, but in view of those statistics, should have done better than results of 3-2 way, and 3-0 at home.

In the next two matches Scunthorpe had to face Scarborough in a double header. This was to be a more meaningful tour of duty and gave the players an idea of the real standard to expect. The men from North Yorkshire rolled up outside the main entrance on Henderson Avenue and meant business. Scunthorpe had no answer to the cut and thrust of their play, and were baffled into a 4-0 loss, in front of their own faithful. It did not orchestrate well for the trip to the seaside, seven days hence. Scunthorpe felt the full blast of the breeze from the North Sea, and also from the wind off the ball, whizzing six times into the back of their net, with the Nuts having no reply.

Pride was restored for the visit of Gainsborough Trinity, a team who's presence was only to attract the attention of 2,600 football minded folks. It turned out to be just the derby thriller that was necessary to lift the spirits. Hubbard came in from the right hand side to score his first of the season, and put the Nuts ahead with a thunderous drive. The lead stayed with them, and was increased following the ten minute interval. Baynham was up in support of the front men, when he made use of an opening, to made the score 2-0. The all round supremacy was completed by Murfin, who stole in from the left to finalise the score at 3-0.

Victory over Gainsborough was a cheerful beginning to a five match unbeaten run. There could be no doubt in the minds of the claret and blue followers that the climax of this was when the giants of Bradford Park Avenue Reserves were smitten by a 3-0 blaze from the Nuts, at the Old Show Ground. Within a fortnight Bradford extracted revenge with a 7-0 mauling, which left local enthusiasts perplexed.

Results of this nature saw Scunthorpe United just about on the correct side of the half way line in the Midland League table, which was little different from in previous years. The team made every attempt to play a tidy brand of football, not always getting the desired rewards for the effort put in. The turnstiles always seemed as if they needed oiling, because they never turned as freely as the directors would have hoped, and finances were putting increased pressure on the Club's resources.

Scunthorpe and Lindsey United were thrust back into the action of the F.A.Cup once the fireworks had been let off one week earlier. They had been drawn at home to Burton Town, from the Midlands, and hoped the Cup campaign would get off to a bang. In the end they had no need to fear, as Murfin had his shooting boots on for a hat-tick, and Hubbard was as reliable as ever for a fourth, in a 4-1 cruise into the First Round Proper.

In no way could Scunthorpe claim to have been given any sort of luck when it came to the draw for the next section of the F.A.Cup. The thanks they received for beating Burton was the long and winding road into Cumberland, to play in the North West corner of England, at Workington. Little was known about the Cumbrian club, but the ride was to be a tiring one for the selected eleven. Few supporters made the journey to support the team in the barren spaces of Borough Park. It was a match where everything went against them, and on the afternoon each error was punished by a goal from the opposition, in the red and white colours. A disappointing ninety minutes finished with a 5-1 defeat, and only Tucker's goal could momentarily lift the spirits.

Once the F.A.Cup had been put to bed until next time, United made amends the following Saturday. In the more familiar surroundings of the Old Show Ground, they enjoyed a confidence boosting 5-0 thrashing of the junior Millers of Rotherham. The joints of this win were soldered by a hat-trick from Chapman. In the next outing, the team went to the Minster City of York, where they picked a scrap with the local Reserves and won 4-2, after the foundations were set before the break with a 2-0 lead. One week later, just as the Christmas decoration were going up, the nightmare returned, and Lincoln took them by the scruff of the neck, and caned them 7-1 at Sincil Bank.

Christmas had its mixed blessings. On Christmas Eve United won at home to Bradford City Reserves, then escaped punishment on Christmas Monday, when the fixture at the Old Show Ground was abandoned because of fog. They trailed 3-0 to Grimsby Town Reserves at the time. The next day they had no such luck at Blundell Park, when an improved display still culminated in a 1-0 defeat. They received a lot of credit for the performance, which put them in good heart for the rest of the holiday programme. Grantham had their noses tweaked 4-1 on New Year's Eve, when the lads next put their boots on, once again playing in the shadow of the Henderson Avenue Stand. The first match of 1933 was scheduled on the first Monday of the year, and required the Nuts to duel with the Colliers of Barnsley Reserves. At Oakwell they mastered the freezing conditions far better than the home camp, returning with both points and a handsome 4-1 win. The run continued unbeaten throughout all of January, and saw five consecutive straight victories.

During the rest of the harshness of Winter Scunthorpe and Lindsey's men won about the same number of games as it lost. Few teams inflicted any lasting damage on the team, but both Denaby and Loughborough launched 1-5 attacks against them on when United visited. At the Old Show Ground the side had a fortress, and it provided the majority of the points.

The month of April was to be a busy time for the tired troops, but they soldiered on and had some excellent displays, starting with a 3-1 reduction in Loughborough's prosperity up, the Doncaster Road once referred to as the Clayfield Road. At Easter, the team dipped its bread when the Cubs of Hull City were played on the far side of the Humber. United had good support in the Anlaby Road crowd on Good Friday, most of which had crossed by ferry boat. Scunthorpe began in workman like fashion, and enjoyed the comfort of strikes by Price, Hubbard and Tucker. Gordon Young, in between the Scunthorpe posts had a quieter afternoon, and only picked up one ball from behind him.

The team returned home for a lifeless goalless draw the next day against Frickley, then prepared to take on the Tiger Cubs, again. This time the City Reserves were frighten out of their wits, as United ran riot, and Hubbard was the Nuts hero with four crisp shots in the 6-0 drubbing. The taste of blood gave Scunthorpe the appetite to continue in the scoring mood, when five days later, at Newark, they hit the same sort of form, winning this skirmish 6-3. The season concluded with three home matches. Those with Grimsby and Chesterfield were lost, but the final one with Newark completed the double, when they waved farewell to supporters, winning 4-2.

The record Scunthorpe finished with, in the Spring of 1933, told a tale of a rise in the table of one place to eighth. The team had played five games less but conjured five more wins. The goals scored column had risen by twenty one goals, to the respectful total of one hundred and four. This compared with exactly one hundred conceded, just one more than twelve months ago. These were some of the best figures since Ernie Simms had led his crew to the top of the table in 1927. In this light the directors were very happy.

Further scrutiny of the figures showed that the gate receipts had remained constant. There had been a loss of some income, compared with other seasons, when the F.A.Cup did not produce the same revenue as when extended runs in the competition had been enjoyed. The supporters had made every assistance and gave a generous donation of £100 to starve off more difficulties. The directors had done their own dipping into their own pockets, and a crisis narrowly avoided. The Barnsley Brewery, who had sorted the mortgage continually smiled on the Club, but they still had to be prudent.

1933-34

Scunthorpe launched its ship in 1933 with every optimism, because of the return of a number of errant players to the forward line, some of which had left the Club for a fee. Both Arthur Smalley and Ernie Pattison had made it safely back and would soon be joined by winger Walter Reed. The directors had also managed to secure the signature of Paddy Mills, who was Barton based, but a Hull City marksman of considerable reputation. It was predicted he would do well in the Midland League. Paddy was also quite able to fill in at half back when it was required. The forwards would be complimented by Allen at inside left and Barry on the left wing. When the team was lacking in numbers a local boy named Bill Sumpter was an adequate replacement. In later life Bill would become editor of the Scunthorpe Star newspaper.

The half back line had a new centre half, which was a position handed out to Nicholson. Jack Staniland was favoured over on the left side, and his old position went to Norman Davidson. Charlie Cross resumed his old right back slot, and had Frank Hill as his left sided accomplice. Bromage left the Club, and was thanked for his services, while Gordon Young was everyone's choice in between the sticks, because of his athleticism and apparent magnetic gloves.

The cold blast of the economic situation was felt through all corners of the Midland League, and others that had not managed to survive the storm as well as Scunthorpe and Lindsey, had gone to the wall. No less than six clubs had resigned their places, and the fixture list only contained thirty two matches. This would have serious consequences, if an alternative could not be found. Fortunately, the clubs in Lincolnshire all got together and formed the Lincolnshire Senior League. This was to provided a number of attractive derby matches to make sure the coffers never ran dry. Scunthorpe and Lindsey United would be joined by the Reserves sides of Lincoln City and Grimsby Town, plus Grantham, Gainsborough and Boston. This League would be a complement until it folded at the beginning of the Second War.

The season opened in fine style for Scunthorpe, as they piled on the agony for Barnsley, beating them 5-0. Pattison was the man who led the way, scoring a hat-trick and leaving the Yorkshire men licking their wounds back to Oakwell. On the Wednesday the bus made its way up the winding coast road to Scarborough, and Pattison bagged a couple in a 2-2 draw, at a ground which in the past had been problematical to the Nuts. In successive matches, United beat off the challenge of Boston and Gainsborough in further away visits, and Pattison continued to score. Scunthorpe supporters were beginning to wonder what trainer Herbert Lloyd had put in their tea. This was especially so when they arrived back at the Old Show Ground to thrash Chesterfield Reserves, who had a strong team, but did not see what hit them, when they lost 6-0. Pattison, who had scored in every game, scored twice, as did Barry, while other came by way of Swain and Allen. It was only a 2-0 defeat at Rotherham that spoiled the Scunthorpe record, who would keep on scoring, despite the loss of Pattison through injury.

For their sins at Workington, a year ago, Scunthorpe had to regroup and fight in the early stages of the F.A.Cup. They began in the First Qualifying Round, at home to Selby Town, on the last day of September. Only a moderate crowd was on hand to see them ease through with a comfortable 4-1 victory, which was started by Bill Sumpter scoring his first Scunthorpe Cup goal. Humber United caused even less trouble in the Second Qualifying Round, beaten more emphatically 5-0. Concerns were not raised when Louth Town were drawn, and the Lincolnshire junior club lost 4-1 at the Old Show Ground, at the third stage. Then it was Heanor Town who were the visitors in the Fourth Qualifying Round of the competition. Those in attendance saw a keen fight, in which the Nuts did not have the game all their own way. Heanor fought viciously and inflicted a couple of deep wounds, but two goals by Pattison, and others from Sumpter, and full back Cross, up in a rare visit to the forward line, gave United the 4-2 ticket they needed.

F.A.Cup fever brought a great deal of excitement to the football community of the town. It was soon spread to every quarter that it was to be a home tie with Accrington Stanley, in the First Round. A gate of 6,500 was to pack the Old Show Ground, as every seat was taken. Scunthorpe And Lindsey were the first men to show, and Reed and Sumpter fired in balls that created chances for Smalley and Allen. In the middle Paddy Mills was causing Accrington's defence all sorts of problems, testing the goalkeeper on a couple of occasions. The deadlock was broken by young Bill Sumpter, who dashed in from the right wing and sent an angled ball well beyond the reach of the visiting custodian.

The cheering echoed round the ground, and United went into the dressing rooms for a cup of hot tea in the happier frame of mind.

Scunthorpe players in happy training mood in 1933, led by Norman Davidson at the front of the queue.

Ten minutes later the twenty two mud splattered players were out working again. United made a number of opportunities, enough to make the game safe, but could not convert any of them. Accrington began to play up, using their football League experience to penetrate the Scunthorpe defence. Scunthorpe and Lindsey would be punished for not taking advantage when they had it. The old Reds of Accrington came back late in the game to find an equaliser, and silence the Scunthorpe cheers.

The 1-1 draw meant more travels for the Nuts in midweek, as their bus made it over the Pennines to Peel Park, where folks have hot pots to keep out the cold. A poor crowd of just 3350 was on hand at kick-off to see the replay. This time the Lancastrians would not be taken lightly. Scunthorpe were pressed back and Pattison's supply of crosses was snuffed out. At half time the team in red and white had forged into a one goal lead, and made sure the pace was maintained in the second period. The gallant Lincolnshire men conceded twice more, and finally bowed out with a 3-0 score, which was a poor reflection of their hard fought efforts.

Meanwhile, Scunthorpe had not forgotten the importance of the Midland League, And the months of October and November found them in fine fettle. During that period they were committed to four games and won the lot, including an 8-1 poke in the eye for Rotherham United Reserves, which allowed Bill Sumpter to keep his first ball for a hat-trick.

Scunthorpe and Lindsey United had reached their zenith, but now came the fall, thanks to an almost complete collapse in December. It all started with a bunch of roses, when Bradford City reserves were cut down to size, by 3-2 at the Old Show Ground. The customary cheers went up for goals, twice from Pattison and another through the work of Paddy Mills, but Scunthorpe had struggled for the win and Frank Hill was knocked out when the ball hit him. In the next game at Doncaster the team struggled even more and the fluidity was missing.

They returned home with tails between their legs, beaten 4-2. Next came the disaster to beat them all. On Christmas Day the team put in an inept display at Blundell Park, against the junior Mariners. The 5-1 result was justice to the better team. On Boxing Day the two teams met up again on the hard Old Show Ground pitch and this time United were blitzed by a humiliating record 9-3 reverse. Local supporters were numbed. Christmas was off the menu as far as Scunthorpe was concerned.

Scunthorpe and Lindsey had time to clear their heads for a while, with three matches in the Lincolnshire League and County Cup. Once the did get back on their Midland League horse again they began to ride as well as before, but the damage had been done to their chances, where early results might have suggested that they could scoop the title. The finger of blame for the nine goal salvo was pointed firmly at the Scunthorpe stand-in goal keeper, called Lamming. He would not be offered the green jersey again. Few other changes were made and the consolation was that the Mariners would win the title for the second season on the trot, and in thirty two games netted one hundred and twenty seven goals. A little bit of pride was restored when virtually the same team beat York City Reserves 6-1 three weeks later.

The rest of Scunthorpe and Lindsey's season was not to be greeted with the same enthusiasm. The lost to Grimsby had left a heavy heart, and destroyed confidence in the team. Gates would not recover and it was down to the hard core of a couple of thousand supporters, who were there through thick or thin, whatever the weather. Some of them voiced interesting opinions of the team and the board of directors, more in frustration than malice. After the beating of York, the team only managed one more win, at home to Notts County, until March. They even were in the doldrums at Mexborough, and lost 6-2, to a team wallowing the mud at the second to bottom place in the division. Injuries to key members of the team did not help the cause, and for a while either Mills or Pattison was out of action on the treatment table. It was as if everything was conspiring against them all at once. The team was to lose six of the last eight matches and it brought them down the table. At least the small band of loyal followers who did keep the faith had a 5-3 victory at home to Bradford City Reserves to savour. Then on the final day of the season, Mexborough were put to the sword 6-0 and Bill Sumpter had them smiling with his second hat-trick.

The new Lincolnshire League was considered to be a great success and brought the necessary revenue that had been anticipated. Grimsby Town Reserves not only became the Midland League Champions, but also the Champions of this League. Over the course of the year they would be a complete nuisance to Scunthorpe and Lindsey, winning all four matches. Gordon Young in the Scunthorpe goal will have every reason to try and remember the Lincolnshire Senior League match at Blundell Park. The brave keeper was knocked out twice during the game, trying to do his duty. If there was a consolation, it was that Scunthorpe were just the same in taking advantage of Gainsborough and won all five of their meetings.

There was one piece of silverware that did sit on the table at the Old Show Ground. The Club entered the Doncaster Invitation Cup, and probably had their best match in the series against Gainsborough, in the Semi Final. Here, the teams met on March 1st and United hung on to a 3-1 half time lead to win 5-4. In the Final, Selby Town were the Old Show Ground visitors, on May 3rd 1934. Scunthorpe stole a march on the Town team, 3-1, where all strikes came in the later part of play.

The Hospital Cup show piece game was played on April 23rd, during the 1933-34 season, and Sheffield Wednesday were gracious enough to bring their First Division side and won 3-1 before a crowd of 5,000 spectators. It was such a success that they would be invited back as the regular guests.
The labours of the Midland League saw Scunthorpe in seventh place in the table. It was not quite what was hoped for after a glorious start. At least they had won one more game than they had lost, and scored three more goals than conceded. Of all the non-League teams in the competition, Scunthorpe had performed the best. They were still in dire straights with their finances, but just keeping afloat. The whole of the Country was in a depressed state and Scunthorpe as a town was struggling, but despite the gloom there was still football to look forward to at the end of the Summer of 1934.

1934-35

The 1934-35 Midland League contained a number of changes to its ranks. York City had pulled the plug on its Reserve team in the competition, but four others were there to swell the division. Frickley Colliery and Grantham were making welcome returns, while Peterborough United and Norwich City Reserves were unknown quantities, entering for the first time.

The construction of the Scunthorpe team confirmed a large number of the old school had been retained. Gordon Young was back in goal, and Charlie Cross took the shirt of the right full back. His partner was usually either Roberts or Harrison at first, but later, when Skull returned from his tour of Rotherham, it allowed Nicholson the drop further back and be the better candidate for the position. Before the arrival of Skull for centre half, the early mid-field combination was usually Mills Nicholson and Barkley, a slightly built lad, but Norman Davidson figured very much in evidence as time progressed, allowing Mills to wander up in the attack. When the team settled, the attack was led by either Pattison or Mills, accompanied by inside men of Noble and Allen. Belting up the wing would be found Barley on the right and Lax on the left.

Once the heat of the sun had waned, the end of August brought back the interest in football. Scunthorpe and Lindsey began their programme at Mexborough, against the club they played on the last day, just months ago. On Yorkshire soil United took an expected 3-1 result, and the cobwebs were blown away, thanks to goals scored by Ernie Pattison, Sid Allen and George Lax. United came back home in fine spirits, ready for the new boys at the Old Show Ground, when Peterborough asked permission to play. The Posh proved to be an extremely stubborn opponent, and had a defence like a castle wall. Scunthorpe battered it all ninety minutes, but to no avail, and had to be content with a scoreless draw. Five days later, on the Saturday, Scunthorpe found their shooting boots against one of the weaker sides in Denaby United, and managed to please the audience with a 4-2 sortie. Everything seemed to be going according to plan, until the arrival of a much changed Gainsborough Trinity. In this home encounter, the Nuts fell to their County rivals, and had poor finishing to blame as the answer. They were all square at the half-way point, but lost a grip late on, losing 3-2.

Scunthorpe and Lindsey United only made moderate progress as the Autumn leaves floated to earth from the trees. Windy days did not bring gusts of high numbers of goals into opponents nets, although the team did make every effort, and were always around the mid-table mark or better. The results were mirrored in the takings from the gate, and the cash bags going to the bank always had room for more coins. It was almost time for the F.A.Cup, and they were put in the right mood with an inspiring 4-2 result, where team work was the order of the day.

United did not enter the Cup competition until the Fourth Qualifying Round, on November 10th, when they meet the force of Kettering Town. The Poppies arrived on the long journey from Northamptonshire, and would be a difficult opponent. Scunthorpe should have won the match, because they were the better of the two teams, and held a 2-1 advantage at the break, through strikes by Allen and Lax. On the day, the Kettering goal keeper was the outstanding player, which accounted a great deal towards the 2-2 result, and more work down South for both sets of players during the mid-week.

On the following Thursday the players were all in place at the Rockingham Road Ground, to see which of them could deliver the knockout punch. Kettering Town had assumed the role of favourites on the heavy ground, sticky with mud. Only once had the Nuts won an away Cup replay, but they were determined that this was about to change. Kettering were first off the blocks, and Gordon Young was called into action several times to dive and push the ball round the posts for corners. He only slipped up once, but Scunthorpe had their own opportunities, and were far more accurate. At half-time it was the visitors who were leading 2-1. The second period was just as frantic, but again it was edged by the Nuts, who eventually succeeded 3-1, thanks to two goals from Lax and another, drilled from the right by young Barley.

When United went into the match at Kettering the players all knew that the prize was a visit to Highfield Road to play Coventry City, a decent competitor in the Third Division South. This was part of the key to the inspiration against the Kettering men, and they did their best to prepare for Coventry with extra training. On November 24th 1934 Scunthorpe played in front of 12,939 spectators, the biggest attendance to ever witness them play. The gross takings were a staggering £722, and a slice of the cake worth £290 was put on the Scunthorpe plate. On the day the Nuts were out of their class, and overwhelmed by the whole occasion. It was 3-0 halfway through and 7-0 by the finish. The generous Coventry crowd gave warm applause to Gordon Young for a courageous performance, which contained a dozen saves of distinction. Should Scunthorpe have remotely looked like beating Coventry, they could have faced Hartlepools United away from home in the following stage.

The gloom of the approach of the dark days of December, and the miserable cloudy skies had parallels in how Scunthorpe and Lindsey United played after the Cup thrashing. Two games, in particular, were remembered for how the Nuts could not cope with the pressure from teams that could only be described as superior. At Norwich, the Scunthorpe men played against the eventual Runners-up on the old Nest Ground, before the Canaries moved to Carrow Road. The report stated that Norwich played at the top of their game. United were better in attack, without probing, but the back quarters buckled under the onslaught. The 5-0 score was fair in every way. The same could be said of the short voyage to Anlaby Road, to play the Hull City second team. After a good start they faded away, and when two of the Tigers scored hat-tricks, it led to the Nuts being overwhelmed again, 7-1 this time.

Defeat at Hull was the precursor to the Christmas Day episode, against Grimsby Town Reserves, three days later. Memories of last years debacle had not gone away, and rankled with supporters in North Lindsey. This year the junior Mariners were not quite so strong, but were still a formidable foe. The Christmas holiday brought a bigger than usual trail of folks swarming into the four corners of the Old Show Ground, and an estimated 3,000 crowd was ready for the action. It was obvious that previous lessons had been learned, as Cross and Nicholson stuck much closer to their wide players, while Frank Skull had a head to every ball into the area. Gradually the confidence was back in the Scunthorpe team, and they played as supporters knew they were capable. It was to be the tightest of games, and the only division was a goal scored by local boy Sid Allen, the inside left. At least that particular ghost had been exorcized.

At Blundell Park, on Boxing Day, Grimsby restored the advantage, when they beat the Nuts 3-0, but it was not the thrashing that had been administered in the past. A much heartened Scunthorpe side met Norwich City Reserves at the Old Show Ground, on the Saturday between Christmas and the New Year.

This time the Nuts were no shrinking violets and match the yellow and green kitted men every inch of the way. Only 1,000 persons braved the cold, and those who did saw a thrilling battle. All the goals were fired in the first forty five minutes. United were said to have been at their best to gather the points and inflict only the second defeat of the season on the high flying Canaries.

The Norwich result was the first of a run of four wins out of five, only spoiled at Doncaster. This flurry of good form brought a lifting of the gloom for a short time. February was much more of a difficult month, because the goals dried up, and there was a lack of points as a direct consequence. It was not until the buds appeared on the daffodils in March that the situation altered for the better, but any frail hopes of bothering the top positions were only a dream for the ardent supporter.

The poor run of form came to an end on April 19th 1935, on Good Friday at Scarborough, at the Seamer Road Ground. The home club was crippled with debt and unable to afford a decent side. United ripped them apart, forgetting the woes of their own, and returned with a handsome 5-3 result. The match saw a Scunthorpe player register the team's first hat-trick of the season, blasted home by Paddy Mills. Other goals came from Sid Allen and George Lax. The next day revenge was taken out on Hull City Reserves, with a 4-2 execution of the Tiger Cubs. Easter was completed in fine style, when Scarborough arrived in Scunthorpe on the Tuesday, and the head masters handed out a 6-2 caning. The name mentioned in dispatches this time was Noble for the completion of his trio of strikes into the back of the net. All that remained now was for two away games to finish off the business for this term of office. At Park Avenue, United went down to Bradford Reserves, then picked themselves up to sort out Frickley Colliery 5-1, against the background of the coal spoils.

The conclusion of the season was that United had not fared as well as in the previous years, and were the eleventh best of the twenty who took part. They only managed sixty seven goals this term, and conceded eighty two. This was the main reason why gates had slipped at an alarming rate. The compensation came from the run in the F.A.Cup, which was at least, a topic of conversation in the public houses. A major factor in what the board could afford to put in place on the field of play was the continuing theme of the shoe string budget. All these troubles could be put to bed for a short duration whilst the Summer took the attention away from the sport.

1935-36

The new opportunities brought fresh hopes to the club, as optimism clenched everyone's thoughts once more. The shifting sands of times made the Scunthorpe and Lindsey board think it was time to keep up with present trends in the game and appoint a player manager.

Herbert Lloyd had not been void of success when he first acted in this respect, and now was the time to repeat the experiment. The person chosen for the venture was Thomas Crilley, a former Derby County full back, who was signed off the books of South London club Crystal Palace. He was able to command operations from the left side of the field, ahead of keeper Gordon Young, and opposite Charlie Cross.

In the middle of the park Frank Skull was not to be the prominent personality of the past, but his skills would be used in the reserve team to help bring through the youngsters. Instead, the solid figure of Yorkshire man Mal Millington was to start on the epic voyage of more than fifteen years of service at the Old Show Ground. Mal came to the Club from Torquay United, and was the type of player that had the face of a rugby player, and could run through steel plate. Millington would have Davies and Barker as his half back partners. Jeff Barker was another player that would make a significant impact. The local youngster was to have two spells at the Club and eventually become coach, working for United until retirement.

The Scunthorpe forward line was to face lots of changes as the season went on, and while Noble and Allen would not be shifted, a combination of Oates, Chapman Pattison and Sumpter would be in and out of the team all the year. There was to be a new leader of the attack, and a man called Snaith fitted the bill. Generally he was assisted by Kilsby, Noble or Lewis on the right of the field, and Roberts or Lewis on the left.

The Scunthorpe squad opened its doors at the end of August to Mexborough, for the opening fixture. The 2-2 result brought encouraging headlines from the newspaper who thought it to be a promising display in a rousing game, which finished square at 2-2. Next, a 3-0 loss at Gainsborough was unlucky and did not mirror the play. Scunthorpe's men carved enough chances in the early stages, but were hit with a sucker punch later on. A series of three victories followed, starting with a 2-0 win against the reserves of Bradford City at the Old Show Ground. They were at home again, when Trinity called in for the second fixture, and this time United could not be denied. The drama of the match was in the last minute when two penalties were awarded. Gainsborough equalised, but in the time added Scunthorpe had their own Davies shot was parried by the keeper, but Davies was able to head the rebound into the net for the winner. This run was concluded by an in credible 8-5 victory away to Lincoln City, which stood at 4-3 in the Nuts' favour at the interval.

The Lincoln City Reserves match certainly created an aggregate record, and later in the season the junior Imps won 4-1 at the Old Show Ground. For the time being, the euphoria was brought to a close when the team lost 6-1 at Burton Town, not far from Birmingham.

The F.A.Cup gave the Nuts the chance to make progress, when their ball came out of the hat just in front of Denaby United. The match was the magnet for 3,000 supporters to trouble themselves to march up to the Old Show Ground, and found the Nuts in the best of form. Denaby could not stop the onslaught from United's rampant forwards. Goals came from Snaith and Lewis, who each banged in a pair. Although the visitors did have the consolation of one goal, the 4-1 result did justice to Scunthorpe and Lindsey's efforts.

The Old Show Ground was used for the ceremony, when the urban district received borough status, in October 1936.

News of the First Round of the F.A.Cup brought a great dismay to Scunthorpe football supporters, because for the second year running the team had a trip to Highfield Road, to play Coventry City. It was fresh in people's minds how the team had lost heavily last year. Player Manager was keen to see that the men had a different preparation, especially in lieu of the fact that Coventry were the lead side in the Third Division South, and on the way to they title.

The match was played on Saturday November 30th 1935. An attendance of 11,590 arrived at the ground in time for the first turn of the ball from the centre spot. Scunthorpe had enjoyed some special training to prepare for the match, and at the start of the game they chose the following eleven: Young; Cross and Crilley; Davies Millington and Barker; Kilsby, Lewis, Snaith, Roberts, and Allen. Coventry City had a big strong powerful side, but Tom Crilley made sure the Scunthorpe lads kept their shape, and were not over run, as was the case twelve months ago. All through the first forty five the Sky Blues probed, and on just one occasion Gordon Young's goal was breached, in the seventeenth minute. Orders were still to hold tight, and Scunthorpe gave as good as they got. The defining moment was on sixty five minutes, when Barker took a free kick. Lewis flicked it cleverly to Snaith, who banged it in from four yards out. This helped the Nuts to a creditable 1-1 draw. The hero was not the goal scorer, but Gordon Young, who saved countless times.

The replay was fogged off in mid-week, and patrons had to wait until the following Monday for the battle to resume opposite the new Baths Hall. At the appointed hour of kick-off 7,084 supporters had found time away from the steelworks to watch the progress. The majority were horrified to see that Coventry City were ready to catch Scunthorpe cold with two goals in the first ten minutes.

The Nuts might have been stunned, but they did not show it. From the moment the first throats roared for a revival, the team responded. Kilsby won a free kick directly in front of goal, which allowed Davies the chance to shoot through the wall, and reduce the arrears. Seconds later the ball was won, knocked forward to the attackers, where Kilsby set up Roberts to slam home the equaliser. Before the half time whistle sounded, Kilsby was in the thick of the action again. This time he was the supply train for Lewis, who fired a canon into the Coventry net to send the crowd delirious with delight, and Scunthorpe led 3-2.

The crowd was still buzzing when the break arrived. It was like the bell ringing, at the end of the round, for a boxer battered on the ropes. After the ten minute break United continued to get into the City faces, not giving them the slightest breather. The tie was still not safe and in the electric atmosphere the Nuts needed another goal to make quite sure. It came from Kilsby, who had made something for everyone else, and was the hero of the hour with the final unstoppable strike. There could be no doubt now as to who was the man of the match, and as to which name would be on every person's lips in each black hole in the steelworks. Scunthorpe and Lindsey were cheered off the park, 4-2 winners at the end of this Titanic epic.

Progress to Round Two meant a journey to the Wirral to play Tranmere Rovers of the Northern Section, who did their homework on Scunthorpe. It was an equally difficult tie as the Coventry game, and the team had used up a lot of energy in the Coventry encounter. Nine days later, and a defeat at Bradford City Reserves under their belts, United were ready at Prenton Park.

This time there would be no upsets, and Rovers showed the class of a League team to win 6-2. On the following Monday morning the broadest smile was that of the bank manager, when secretary Harry Allcock banked the cheque.

Scunthorpe and Lindsey United supporters had the pleasure of the company of Grimsby Town Reserves to look forward to, just before they sat down to Christmas dinner. This time there would be no spoiling of the feast or even a close call. The junior Mariner were stuffed like turkeys, and cooked in the oven in the full heat of a 5-0 roasting. Every forward, except Sid Allen scored, because he was too busy supplying the ammunition, and Snaith took the back slaps with two of the five goals.

Tom Crilley had to declare himself injured for the Boxing Day rerun at Blundell Park but Frank Skull was a useful warrior to deputise. A large and noisy band of steelworkers risked the wrath of their wives to be in attendance. A much tighter game was staged in front of the Pontoon Stand, but the Nuts were always in the ascendancy. It is this game that was the more entertaining spectacle, which Scunthorpe won 3-2.

The second half of the season contained one particular match which would produce a return, which stuck out like a sore thumb, and that was played not too far away at Mexborough. The Yorkshire team did not enjoy the best of years in the Midland League, but did manage an opening day draw in Scunthorpe. On this occasion they were swept aside after an injury to the goalkeeper became a major second half factor. The 1-1 score was quite pedestrian at half time, but by the end of the procedures the home side had been humiliated by an incredible 8-3 score. All of the Nuts forwards scored, and Snaith made the magic trio.

The Midland League table found Scunthorpe in eleventh place, but could have seen an improvement, if they had managed a better goal average. This could have raised them three places. In total seventy three goals were registered in forty games, four less than were conceded. Snaith was the leading goal scorer with twenty three in the League and the Cup. However, there was a beautiful silver cup won, when the team only lost one Lincolnshire Senior League match in ten outings, to become the Champions.

1936-37

Despite the continuing picture of austerity at the Old Show Ground, the directors had been happy with Tom Crilley and allowed him to continue as the Player Manager into the next term. His role on the field was to become a diminishing one and he barked his orders more often than not from the touchline. This meant that Charlie Cross would mainly be partnered by Bill Jones from Blackhall Colliery for his left sided full back, when Crilley was not up to the mark.

There was to be another goalkeeper, to replace Gordon Young, who was lured away. He was a huge lad called Earnshaw, and came from the other side of Doncaster at Denaby United.

The centre of the park was to be dominated by the popular Mal Millington, who was the overwhelming choice for the centre half position. At first he would have Jeff Barker calling all the shots, a local boy in the left half position, but talent of this high degree was attracting attention. When Aston Villa waved the cheque book, a note for £400 floated the way of Harry Allcock to bank. This prompted Sid Allen to drop out of the forward line, where this versatile young man was able to fill in at half back with aplomb. Harry Stocks, a Grimsby junior player, took the remaining place.

The Scunthorpe forward line would suffer numerous changes during the coming months. Only local lad Stan Norris, who had been a junior player at Leeds United, would keep his place. A stream of players included Horton, Moses, Beckett, Smithson, Porter and Gill would be pieced into the jig-saw. The most noteworthy of these were Smithson and Porter, who would score the vast majority of the goals. Smithson came with credentials from Aldershot and lately Scarborough.

All of the changes to the front end of the team had a consequence when the goals came to be added up, and a meagre tally of seventy seven was a reflection of the upheaval going on. It was simple to suggest that more money ought to be thrown at the situation, but it simply was not there to throw. What they had was what they would have to try and improve with.

The team had a mixed bag of nuts for the first couple of months of the season! They got off on the wrong foot, losing 3-1 at Newark on the opening day of the campaign. Faith was restored with a draw at home to the Tiger Cubs, and goals by Beckett and Porter beat the Trinitarians 2-0. Then a total of six defeats in October brought the Nuts down to earth with a bump, and the corner was only turned just into November with a confidence boosting 5-1 result at the Old Show Ground, against Frickley Colliery.

The Frickley result was immediately prior to the beginning of their F.A.Cup expedition, which was to take them to Gainsborough. To set the scene, the local rivals won the return League match on the Northolme, 3-0. Gainsborough started as odds on favourites to win, but the Nuts were determined to do well after recent disappointments. They put the shutters up and played what the press described as one hundred percent defence. Millington had an outstanding game, and other praise was handed to Cross and Jones, the two full backs. Little separated the teams on the afternoon, and a replay was a distinct possibility. However, the all important goal came Scunthorpe's way from the boot of Stan Norris, who was proving to be the find of the season.

The next part of the F.A.Cup was the First Round Proper, when the Football League teams made the competition more interesting, particularly from an increase in the amount of gate money. Fate offered her hand to Scunthorpe in the form of an away tie at Walsall, in Staffordshire, about one hundred miles away. The Saddlers were still in the mood to tell anyone who wanted to listen how they had recently beaten the mighty Arsenal, at their Fellows Park Ground, and they were hardly to be bothered by what Scunthorpe could offer. On the day, Walsall were always in the driving seat and won comfortably, 3-0.

Scunthorpe and Lindsey United turned the ignition back on their Midland League car with one of the best away score of the season, once they had said their goodbyes to the Cup. On a visit to the banks of the River Nene, they proved to be too much of a handful for Peterborough United. The 5-3 returns were as unexpected as they were welcomed. The Posh defenders were turned inside out by Smithson, on the London Road Ground, and had no answer to his mastery. On the day he scored four of the Nuts goals, and Norris was on hand to stab home the other, in what was an entertaining sortie.

The holiday programme had the tasty tit bit of Burton Town, up in Lincolnshire on Christmas Day, and the 2-0 result was as much in doubt as that there would be poultry for dinner. The team then experienced some turbulence in the next two games, being heavily clobbered 7-0 at Grantham and 6-1 at Bradford Park Avenue Reserves. There can be no hiding from the fact that this was not good enough, and some harsh words were said. The team became shuffled a little and gained a victory over the Bradford men, even though it was only 1-0, and Moses was in command of the scoring.

The pick of all the matches played during this year would certainly be the two against the Champions, Barnsley. From the first kick-off, the Reserves of Oakwell were head and shoulder superior to any other Midland League club. They took the title by a mile, and only lost eight games during the whole course of the fixture card. They did not roll into Scunthorpe until the first cold Saturday of February. On a day when gloves were in order, Barnsley were mastered by the Nuts, by a small 2-1 margin, but the home players were always on top. All the damage was done in the first period, and young Stan Norris was the one to fire the Scunthorpe gun in the 2-1 result. Scunthorpe made the journey into Yorkshire for the away leg, and might have gained inspiration from the wonderful smells drifting from the Brewery, the owners of which had helped them with their mortgage. They held their nerve and repeated the 2-1 trick, thanks to strikes by Porter and a penalty goal from Bill Jones.

The return of Porter from injury gave the Nuts a far better finish to the calendar than when they started. Once he was restored to duty the goals began to flow again.

He was able to score in eight consecutive matches, and singled out Denaby United for special punishment. In their visit to the Old Show Ground, they were blitzed 7-2. He was not alone in this final spell, because Smithson repeated the four goal feat, away at Bradford City Reserves, in a 4-1 pounding. A week later he scored three times on the road at Meadow Lane, against Notts County Reserves, when an invigorating performance beat the Magpies 5-2.

There can be no denying that football is a surprising and unpredictable sport. With this in mind, the next match United played was at bottom placed Frickley Colliery, who at the time had won just two of their forty fixtures. Scunthorpe and Lindsey expected to stroll onto the ground and be passed the points, but it was not going to happen. On the Thursday afternoon only the smallest of crowds of a few hundred saw them generally in command, but completely blotted out by the coal miners in front of the target. The final score was a total shock, and Frickley won the honours with a 2-0 score. At least the Nuts won the last two games, both at home, to Notts County Reserves and Rotherham United Reserves.

Scunthorpe and Lindsey United had hardly set the world on fire in the 1936-37 campaign. The Midland League table could no lie on their behalf, and the place of fourteenth rung on the ladder was less than the standard they hoped to achieve when the ship first sailed. Tom Crilley packed his bags, and did not take a second glance to see if a new contract was put on the table. He would be remembered for the F.A.Cup exploits, and not the routine of the Midland League, where consistency probably mattered far more. The idea of having a manager in charge was put on the back burner for the moment, and the system of the directors picking the team restored.

One part of Tom Crilley's defence was the team that he was leaving behind had the nucleus of a strong squad that could take the Club forward. In this respect his work had been far from wasteful. Other teams had seen the benefits, and Manchester City decided that they could make use of a rapidly developing young player called Emptage, and another fee, this time for £250, helped ease the finances.

1937-38

The board of directors examined the team for the coming year and decided that the whole of the first two lines of the team were quite adequate. This would mean a regular selection of Eric Earnshaw in goal, Charlie Cross and Bill Jones for the full backs, and for the band across the middle, there would be Harry Stocks, Mal Millington and Sid Allen, whenever they were free of injuries. When Cross was out towards the late end of operations Clark came in to assist. Then a rethink for the goalkeeping position saw Wilf Poxton replace Earnshaw.

The news for the forward line was that the directors had secured the signature of Harry Johnson, a former Oldham Athletic and Southend United marksman of repute. Harry was a tough customer, who could handle himself where it hurt in the box, with heavy tackles going in and elbows from defender causing no problem. It would not be long before his name would be mentioned in the pubs around the whole district.

Harry Johnson was to be joined by Stan Norris, Jimmy Lewis and Fred Betts from the school of 1936, plus Jack Wilkinson and George Baldry who arrived in the Summer. These men were complimented by Whittaker from October, and Betts was the subject of an unwelcome approach from Sunderland who lured him away in a fashion not considered gentleman like by the board. Sunderland were said to have tried to smooth things over by sending a cheque, but this was returned.

The wonderful point about this present collection of players was that it knew what it needed to do and with Johnson in charge of the forward line the goals were beginning to flow. They got the green light in the first the fixture, at home to Denaby, and cracked in five goals with no reply. Harry Johnson scored two, Betts another two and Wilkinson, on the left wing, got the fifth. Early scores were quite satisfactory, as Johnson led a cavalry charge each week, but the conceding of the double to Gainsborough suggested that the side was not the finished article as yet. Despite the odd rocky moments, the team did contain a number of jewels which would shine as time proceeded.

Some of the more entertaining games did not produce the scores that supporters might have wished for. An example was for the game thirty miles down the road at Lincoln, where seven goals went flying into the net, but it was the Imps who took the lion's share with four of them. Harry Johnson had done his best with a hat-trick, but was short of the winning bonus.

The F.A.Cup brought the Nuts some mixed blessings. The Fourth Qualifier was against a strong Grantham team, from the South of the County. Thankfully the gods had sorted the team a lay in bed, and not the handicap of travel. The two teams knew all about each other, having played a goalless draw in Grantham. The Cup tie was to be anything but void of goals. The attendance of 3,314 spectators were happy to see Jack Wilkinson open the scoring, and the Scunthorpe men found their power had them two points ahead going into the break. In the second part of the match the play was more even, but just as quick. The goals continued to pile in, but Grantham were always in a catch up position. Finally, they had to admit defeat, as Scunthorpe finished 4-2 winners. Wilkinson hit a hat-trick, and Johnson could not have his nose pushed out for the other.

The First Round Proper gave Scunthorpe a Humber derby against Hull City. A continuous stream of Scunthorpe supporters made it across the water in the paddle steamers and at kick-off the attendance was 6,000 at the Anlaby Road Ground. United often had their work cut out against the Tiger Cubs, but the Tiger first eleven had sharp claws, and set about causing some nasty scratches. United had to raise the white flag, and accept defeat in a 4-0 mauling.

Scunthorpe and Lindsey returned to League action by taking out their frustrations out on Mansfield Town Reserves, 4-1, but then ran into a head wind, and lost three matches on the belt. They recovered in time to meet the team who would be Champions, Shrewsbury Town, three days after Christmas. There was a large gathering on the Old Show Ground, and they saw Norris and Allen score the goals that helped the team to a fine 2-1 victory. This close encounter was probably a classier game than the 5-2 thrashing of Newark, on New Year's Day, during their travels, or the thrill a minute ten goal epic at Bradford City Reserves, which ended 6-4 to the Nuts.

The brakes were not put on the Scunthorpe train until it ran into the Shrewsbury station. At the Gay Meadow, Shrewsbury were invincible, and showed all the skills that would make their captain eligible to take the Midland League trophy. They cast the Scunthorpe challenge aside with little effort, and took the points with a 5-1 score.

After the loss at Shrewsbury, United had four home matches to show their own supporters that they had not lost their edge. These would bring three wins plus six points and adequately demonstrated that no harm had been permanently done. The best of the sequence, in terms of results, was the 4-0 thrashing handed out to the Notts County Reserves. For separate reasons, the Bradford park Avenue match will be remembered for Johnson's hat-trick in the 3-1 score, but Lewis was responsible for another trio, when Lincoln were chopped down by a 4-2 result. In the final phase of the season Scunthorpe had an opportunity to gain a small amount of revenge for the Cup defeat. At Easter they went back over the water to Hull, on Good Friday, and without the presence of the big Tiger, cuffed the Cubs about the ears, winning 2-1 through two Jack Wilkinson goals.

The team had no Saturday fixture, but met the Cubs again on the Tuesday. United put in a sterling performance of power and flare, crushing their striped subordinates 7-1. It was as good as they had shown the Old Show Ground faithful all year. Norris Lewis, Clarvis and Wilkinson all grabbed a piece of the action with a goal, but the largest slice of the cake was the hat-trick by Harry Johnson, who fired the biggest gun.

The swan song, as far as home games were concerned, was against Grantham, who had sneaked in by the back door to be the second placed team, behind Shrewsbury.

Neither side showed any tired legs and kept a thrilling episode going up until the last minute. There were chances galore, and many taken. A breathless crowd enjoyed a 4-3 carnival, and it was not until the man in black called time, that Scunthorpe emerged as the winners.

The season finished with a single goal defeat at Nottingham against the Forest Reserves. It mattered not, because at last the Club had produced a team that was capable. They finished in sixth position of twenty two teams. Twenty two games were won, but only fifteen ended in disappointment. It had been a few years since one hundred goals had been scored, but these lads managed nine more, yet only conceded seventy eight. Harry Johnson was the toast of the forwards for his thirty eight goals, and Mal Millington was the hero of defence.

Scunthorpe and Lindsey United harboured a burning ambition to make even greater achievements, and the Football League had now become the goal of the directors. They were not alone, and a long queue of similarly minded clubs had the same intentions. These clubs included Shrewsbury Town, who had superior credentials. Scunthorpe first considered the Third Division North in 1921, but the size of the town and the gates they were getting made it inappropriate at that time. The expanding population and a stronger playing staff meant that an application to join the Football League was a reality. The Summer of 1938 saw the directors attend the Football League A.G.M. and put in its first application, but it received no votes from the existing members. This would become an annual pilgrimage for the foreseeable future, until the tide turned.

The application had shown that Scunthorpe and Lindsey United had turned a corner, and looked to the future with a lot more confidence. The extra size of the town had proportionally increased the gates. Transfer fees and Cup ties swelled the coffers. The Club could not be considered rich by any means, but the huge debt was now manageable, and not the millstone threatening their existence.

In the past the directors had toyed with the idea of a player manager on two occasions. The experienced had left them with mixed feelings, and for the immediate future it had been abandoned. Having said that, they signed Tom Jones, the former Welsh International, who had been captain of Manchester United. Tom was at the twilight of his career, but was still as athletic as ever, and could give the youngsters a run for their money. He was to be the full back who would muster the troops on the field.

he Scunthorpe United eleven that were presented with the Lincolnshire League trophy, following a 7-2 victory over Gainsborough Trinity, on April 25th 1938. Captain Harry Stocks has the silverware.

1938-39

Scunthorpe and Lindsey did not believe it necessary to sign a whole host of players during the closed season, because what they had they could build upon. In goal Wilf Poxton had no rivals for his green jersey. Charlie Cross had said his good byes, to move into local football, and left Tom Jones and Bill Jones to be the full back pair. In times of injury Thorpe was an adequate replacement, and figured in the early stages. The ex-Norwich and Wolves man was a utility player, and once filled in at centre forward in Harry Johnson's absence.

In the middle of the park, Stocks, Millington and Allen were sometimes complimented by Jack Staniland, and whatever the combination, it was a strong one. This left the attack, in which Harry Johnson was the sharpest of arrow heads. He was to have two new inside men, in Sammy Nightingale and Eddie Fleetwood. Sammy was a sure footed youngster with poison in his shot, and his young legs had the speed of an antelope. Eddie was at the opposite end of his career, but brought masses of experience, having been at Blackburn and Barnsley. He was a cunning old fox and used his head rather than his legs, but also had a lethal strike. On the wing, Stan Norris and Jack Wilkinson were asked to continue to serve as before.

The team of 1938 set off hunting like a pack of wolves, and some of the results did not always reflect how much they were in command. Harry Johnson scored nine goals in a practice match before the rocket was launched. It went up at Mansfield, where the Nuts had a gentle warm up, beating the Stags second team 2-0, creating a good impression.

On the next Monday evening, 4,000 supporters were at the perimeter wall to see the 10-3 destruction of Newark Town, which sent a warning shot to the other clubs of their intentions. Harry Johnson scored five times, and the Club went on a ten match unbeaten run, scoring goals at will. They only tasted their first defeat at home to Forest Reserves, who had some first team experienced men in their ranks. Even then, it was they that opened the scoring in the 3-2 loss, and missed a hatful of chances.

The advent of the F.A.Cup had United playing from the First Qualifying Round, and brought them into contact with a section of the senior local clubs. Barton Town were the first men to feel the blast of the Scunthorpe attack. They swapped venues for extra cash and were crushed 9-1 at the Old Show Ground, as Harry Johnson scored five times. Appleby Frodingham works team played a little better, losing only 4-1, as Johnson scored a hat-trick, while Stocks made up the difference. The third local conquest was Lysaghts Sports works team, who lost by a record 11-3 score. It was Harry Johnson who plundered five goals, Sammy Nightingale smashed four, and the others were launched from the boots of Stan Norris and Eddie Fleetwood. Such was the ferocity of the scoring that many in the crowd simply lost count.

The arrival of November saw the team in a rampant mood, and they started at Newark with a 3-0 romp, that completed the double over the Nottinghamshire club. They then continued in the F.A.Cup, with a sojourn at home to Boston United. A healthy crowd of 6,250 saw a proper battle this time, but Scunthorpe took an early command, as Nightingale and Johnson had them 2-0 up at the interval. The Stumpites did pull one back late in the game, but the Nuts kept them at arms length to win 2-1. This set the stall out for the visit of Grimsby Town Reserves. It was a day when the Mariners Reserves were put in their places, as United thrashed them 5-0.

(Top) In 1937 Scunthorpe United signed Harry Johnson, who was the leading goal scorer of 1937/38 and netted 69 goals in all competitions in the 1938-39 Championship season. (Below) A sketch of George Baldry drawn by Harry who was a competent cartoonist, including caricatures of all his colleagues.

At the time Harry Johnson showed his considerable skills in front of the posts, as yet another hat-trick went on record.

The last roll of the dice for the month was at home to Lancaster City, in the F.A.Cup First Round. This might not have been the attractive tie that was dreamed about, against a top Football League club, but Scunthorpe supporters responded by swelling the gate to 7,600 patrons. Lancaster soon demonstrated that they were more than worthy opponents, and every Scunthorpe player knew that they had to be at the top of their game. Lancaster exerted some early pressure but Eddie Fleetwood was the first marksman to put his foot through the ball, and the Nuts were 2-1 ahead in the tea break. They continued to fight just as hard as time went on, and scored two of the three goals that arrived in the second half. A 4-2 victory had the faithful in jubilant mood, streaming back home for their suppers.

The Second Round of the Cup did bring a smile to the faces of the fans, because this time they had been selected to play at the Old Show Ground against Third Division South outfit Watford. On December 10th 1938 a record breaking attendance of 11,800 supporters were in place ready to roar the Nuts on. The Scunthorpe side lined up as follows: Poxton; T. Jones, and Staniland; Stocks, Millington and Allen; Norris, Fleetwood, Johnson, Nightingale and Oxley.

Once the game started the packed house saw Scunthorpe fly out of the blocks and made a series of raids. Harry Johnson almost put the Nuts ahead with a powerful header, and Watford had their own chances through Dunderdale, their burly leader. It was not long into the procedures that a tragic collision between Dunderdale and Poxton changed the whole course of the game. The two men raced for the same ball, and a sickening crack was heard. Poxton lay in a heap clutching a broken leg and had to be gently eased onto a stretcher, then carried off the field.

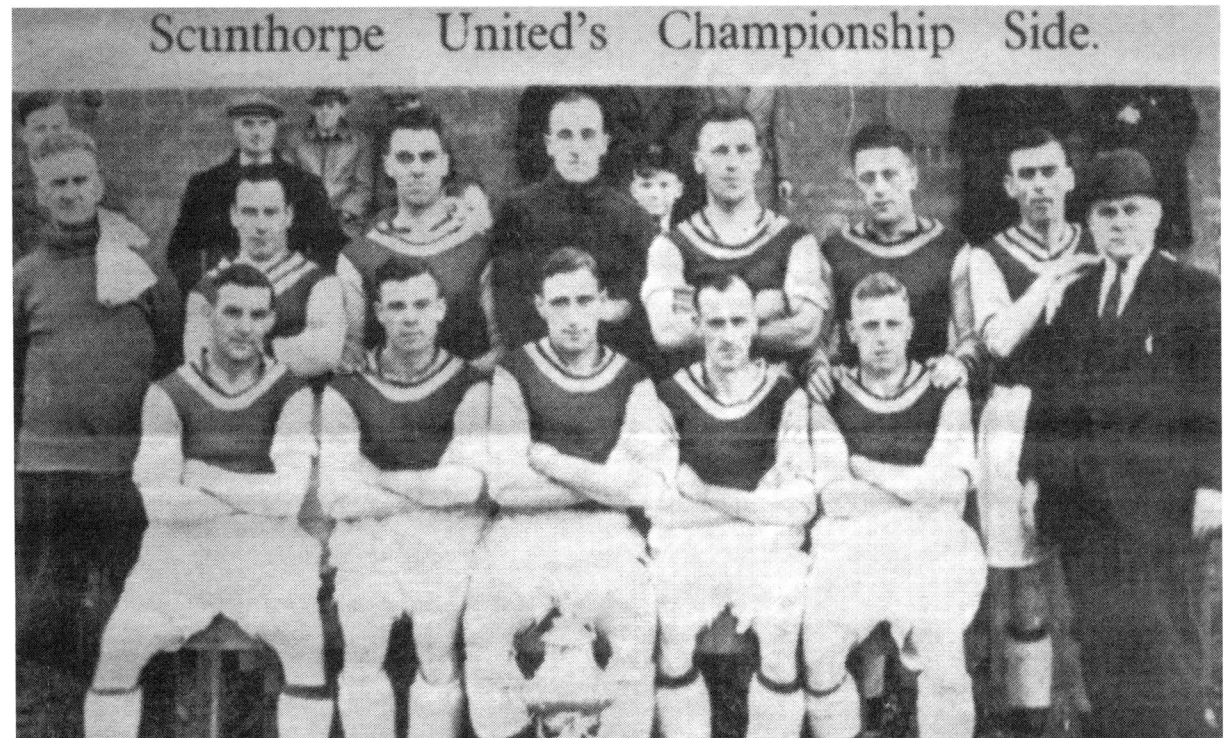

The Scunthorpe United Midland League Champions of 1938-39 with the trophy. This photograph came from a Scunthorpe United programme for a special friendly match with Barnsley to publicise the Club, in preparation for their application to join the Football League.

Staniland offered to take the gloves, and Stocks dropped to full back as cover. For quite some time the accident took thoughts away from football, but gradually Scunthorpe came back into the fight. They may have been considerably handicapped, but the crowd urged them on in patriotic union. The men in claret and blue were given a life line, when Oxley burst into the box, on the left of the penalty area and was tripped. A penalty was awarded, and from the spot Tom Jones led an example by giving them the lead.

The sympathy might have been on the side of the non-League underdogs, but Watford were only interested in self preservation. In the second half they ran hard at the ten men, and Dunderdale was to be the undoing of the gallant Lincolnshire battlers. He scored twice for the Hertfordshire team, the winner coming ten minutes from time. In the next round Watford played away at Tottenham. For Scunthorpe it was what might have been, because the press suggested they had already beaten better sides than Watford. There was satisfaction in knowing that when all the coins were put into the bags for the bank, a sizable amount would reach their account. Some of this would help to find a goalkeeper to replace the brave Poxton. Tom Jones recommended that they sign an old Manchester United colleague of his, called Clunie, and at Christmas a deal went through.

December brought a famous record beaker to Scunthorpe, when they Played Notts County Reserves. Dixie Dean, the sixty goal in a season ex-Everton man, had been transferred to Meadow Lane, and was asked to assist the County second eleven. During the ninety minutes he was policed throughout the game and hardly had a sniff of the ball. Scunthorpe had their own machine in top gear, and ran out 8-0 winners, as every forward was on the marksmen list.

The only real setback of the season was to be felt just before Christmas, when the team found themselves wrong footed by the tune of 5-0, at Bradford City Reserves. This was at a time before Clunie was established in goal, and local players of no experience filled in, and Stocks and Nightingale were retired through injury. Just for once the whole team suffered from a cold. This was quickly forgotten the following week, and they were all back to their cheerful selves in beating Bradford Park Avenue, at the Old Show Ground, by 5-2 on Christmas Eve. Christmas Day fell on a Sunday, but on Christmas Monday United scored a remarkable 9-1 victory over a hapless Denaby United.

Harry Johnson had the honour of equalling Ernie Simms record of scoring six goals in the game. Although United then went on to lose 4-2 at Shrewsbury, they met up with Denaby, at the other side of Doncaster, on January 2nd 1939. Clunie must have been frozen, because all the action was at the other end, and the Nuts recorded an away victory of 10-0. What added to spice the party was that every forward scored twice.

John Campbell, third from the left, watches his effort about to be held by the goalkeeper Middleton, in a practice match in 1939.

Scunthorpe and Lindsey United played like a battleship steaming to sink every enemy target. The thrashing of Denaby was the start of a twelve match unbeaten run, and only three more loses would be recorded for the remainder of the season's commitments. Supporters were always confident of victory, and the only uncertainty was how big it be, and how many goals Johnson would score. They were blessed with a team that fired like a Gatling-gun up front, had the pistons of a Sir Nigel Gresley streamliner in midfield, and could rely on a defence that was as tight as a champagne cork. Harry Johnson stood out in a complete team of stars, and still had time for a hat-trick against Barnsley Reserves and a quartet against the Doncaster Rovers second eleven.

Scunthorpe and Lindsey United finished the Midland League season at Frickley Colliery, in front of a crowd increased in number by celebrating Scunthorpe supporters. The team had won the title weeks ago, and the 2-1 victory just added to the total. If anything, this was a more prestigious title than the one taken in 1926-27, because more games were played against a stronger opposition. The final record showed statistics of P42, W28, D8 L6 F133 A 64. It should be noted that Harry Johnson had scored fifty of this incredible total, as well as fifteen in the F.A.Cup and four in the Lincolnshire Senior League.

The season finished with three exhibition matches, which were attended in large numbers. Barnsley came to play in a friendly match to salute the Champions, then there was the Champions verses the Rest of the League match. United signed off their football activities by playing Sheffield Wednesday in the Grimsby Telegraph Hospital Cup. The Barnsley match, in particular, was used as a platform to promoted United's bid for Football League status, and many guests were invited from the voting clubs.

They would have been impressed by the facilities, which now included a stand that covered the back half of the terrace at the Fox Street end of the ground, and was completed during the past season. The stadium now had a roof on three sides of the rectangle.

Scunthorpe and Lindsey United attended the Football League A.G.M. with a delegation, headed by Mr Talbot Cliff. This time they had put a great deal of thought and preparation into the bid. It included a brochure containing six significant reasons why the door should be opened to allow the Club into the Third Division North. The main points included the fact that the Club had an average 5,200 gate, developed the ground, and had the backing of the businesses of the whole district. They also stressed that team was of a playing strength capable of the Northern Division, and the ground capacity had risen to contain gates of up to 15,000. Finally, they intended to produce a succession to players through a nursery system.

The Scunthorpe delegation had countless meetings lobbying for support. Some gave encouragement, while other were quite blunt. Grimsby Town nailed its colour to the mast and gave outright assurances, as did Sheffield Wednesday, but when the votes were counted only four delegates supported the Scunthorpe cause. It was a disappointment, but not altogether one that was unexpected. The weary party made its way home wiser for having taken part, but ready to sort out business for 1939-40.

1939-40

Scunthorpe and Lindsey United decided to implement some changes to team that won the Championship, and this caused some dismay in many quarters. Poxton had still not recovered and Clunie had been allowed to leave. A replacement keeper was found at Boston, when Jenkinson unpacked his case. The next two divisions of the team were left unaltered, but changes were brought to the forward line. Campbell came via Leicester City and Lincoln City to pep up the attack, while Fleetwood and Arthur Maw, who had returned from his successful travels, would be the inside men. Rickards from Notts County took over the right wing spot, while over on the left, John Millington was a winger, once at Swansea Town. Other favourites remained on the books, but initially Johnson, Norris, Staniland and Nightingale would have to wait patiently for a turn.

Scunthorpe followers were still not convinced. The team started with two victories, at Rotherham, and when Shrewsbury visited, but they showed plenty of short comings in losing to the junior Mariners 1-2, at home in the third game. Campbell had scored in each of his three outings, but still could not hold a candle up to Harry Johnson. While this debate was raging in the pubs around Scunthorpe, the German Army had marched its troops into Poland and the whole of the globe was to be plunged into the Second World War. Within the week, Great Britain would be fighting with Germany.

Emergency meetings were called throughout all levels of football. Everything was cancelled immediately and contract suspended. A whole list of players put their belongings back into the suitcases and headed for homes in all corners of the land. Only the local men remained, sufficient to form a team of reasonable strength for whatever might be forth coming. Harry Allcock was instructed to use the phone and arrange a number of friendly games, until something substantial had been agreed. Invitations were sent to Grimsby Town, Gainsborough Trinity, Lincoln City and Bradford Park Avenue. At least arguments over team selections would cause less bother now.

The pool of players left allowed either Mayberry or Middleton as the goalkeeper choice. Full back selection was taken from Bill Jones, Jack Staniland or former Southampton player Pickering. There was no problems in the half back line, which remained unaltered. Norris resumed his right wing berth, but when he joined the war effort, Greaves was the selection. Fleetwood and Maw were the inside men, while Sammy Nightingale was to roam the entire line. Swain was a player from Grimsby for the left wing, and it would not be too long before Harry Johnson was back where he belonged, as prolific as ever.

The friendly arrangements served their purpose in terms of continuity, but a more meaningful unofficial league system, run in two separate parts, was to operate from the end of October. Scunthorpe found that Peterborough would be the main rivals for the honours, when everything had been completed. In the first part of the new competition only Frickley Colliery beat the Nuts in the first ten games.

Mal Millington, Scunthorpe United's dominating centre half, who played more than three hundred games for the Club, either side of the Second World War. He was also a guest player for Grimsby Town during the hostilities.

Sammy Nightingale took over the mantle of goal scorer, and was on target in eleven of the fourteen matches, notching five against Boston at home, when United won 7-0, and six at Gainsborough, on the Northolme, as Scunthorpe won 8-2. The team then drew at Peterborough, but lost a remarkable game to them at the Old Show Ground 6-3. This did not stop them heading the first table, two points better off than the Posh.

The second part of the competition was to be uncompleted., because of the intensity of the War. Scunthorpe and Peterborough each failed to play one fixtures. Of those played United had scores of note against Boston at home, 8-2, and Grantham away 8-0. Overall they managed to lose only two games and finish one point in arrears of Peterborough, but a point more on aggregate. The committee decided to award the unofficial competition to Scunthorpe and Lindsey United.

Football for Scunthorpe was now concluded. They would not enter anything except friendly games. Harry Allcock was in charge of the books, and the Barnsley Brewery Company had been generous in the terms of the loan. This should have closed the chapter for the duration of the War, but Grimsby Town made an approach to use the Old Show Ground for its War League home fixtures.

Grimsby Town used the facilities at the Old Show Ground until 1943 and could and expect two or three thousand people to turn out to cheer them on. They gave opportunities to Scunthorpe players to join their line up, and Harry Johnson, Harry Stocks, Bill Jones and especially Mal Millington turn out in their colours. Other teams would be filled with the stars of the day, some as guests for lesser teams, and the likes of Len Shackleton and Peter Doherty plied their trade at the top of the Doncaster Road. The highlight of Grimsby Town's stay was when they reach the Semi Final of the Northern Cup in 1942. A record crowd of 11,896 watched them lose 3-2 to Sunderland in the Second Leg, after they had drawn goalless at Roker Park.

At the end of 1943 Grimsby Town thanked Scunthorpe for their hospitality and returned to Blundell Park, leaving the Old Show Ground a ghostly shell. Little football activity took place on the turf, as youths kicked cans for their football amusement. It was not until the Spitfires had chased away the enemy and peace had been declared that any life would be brought back to the ground, and the roar of the crowd would once again breath fire into the bellies of the warriors in the claret and blue colours.

POST WAR NUTS

1945-46

The end of the War could not come too quickly for everyone throughout the whole of the world, and virtually everyone's life had been changed for ever. The German High Command had been beaten into submission, and Hitler was no more. Across all of Britain church bells rang the news of the peace, and soldiers returned to their families to pick up the threads after the disruptions. It would take sometime to return to normal but the first steps had been taken in the right direction.

Football had its own recovery to find, and some players would not return, others would be too injured to play again, while others had lost their opportunity through the passage of six years. Scunthorpe and Lindsey would be touched in exactly the same way, but some of the younger men from 1939 would step proudly forward to wear the claret and blue colours again, in 1945. They would find other enthusiastic youths willing to step up to the mark both at the local level and further a field. The Midland League was to find nineteen teams ready for operation, and the 1945-46 competition was recognised as an official one, a year before the Football League became up and running.

Scunthorpe and Lindsey welcomed back a familiar face to the goalkeeping position when it started back, in the August of 1945. It was of course Wilf Poxton, who was last seen in official action on the floor in the Cup games with Watford. He was back with a smile, to offer his loyal service and safe hands. He was to be utilised in virtually every game.

The full back pair would be two former players of considerable service, as Charles Betts and Jack Staniland returned, having been at the club since the beginning of the thirties. Charles had played for years in the reserves, and was familiar to many supporters, while Jack played a part in the last Championship side. They would be joined by George Lax, another experienced old campaigner, who was at Wolves before the War. He was signed to make use of his coaching skills for the younger players.

The belt in the middle of the park started with the irrepressible Mal Millington back in harness, and ready to go. It was as if there had been no break, although he had enjoyed the extra running with Grimsby Town. He was the pillar at centre half and had Sid Allen, another stalwart, as the partner on the left side. This was later to be occupied by as big mobile local lad, called Alan Leeman, and when he was in place Sid Allen drifted out to the left wing. In the right half spot, United discovered another local boy, named James Burnip, who was skilful enough to claim a place for the whole season.

The star of the forward line was the speedy Jack Marroitt, another local youngster, with deceptive feet, that mesmerised full backs. He was versatile enough to be able to play either wing, and would earn the Club money when transferred. The rest of the forward line consisted of Readhead, who came from the Lysaghts Sports works team, for the other wing, then a combination of Fleetwood, Carver and Leeman, up from mid-field duties. Harry Johnson struggled to get back to form, and was only occasionally called to duty because of injury. He would not waste his talents, because he became another of the coaches. Carver took over as the main goal scorer, having once been at Mexborough, and would be a surprising success. When March arrived, so did a softly spoken Scotsman called George Wallace, an inside forward from Aberdeen. He was an absolute wizard on the ball, and could ghost past bemused defenders with ease. George was to be part of the scenery throughout the next six or seven years.

On August 25th 1945 the first shrill note was heard on the referee's whistle for the visit of Mansfield Town Reserves. Football supporters were so relieved to hear it, and the sport was back on the field, being playing where it should be. Scunthorpe were by far the masters, against a young set of lads, who gave little in the way of opposition. In the late Summer sunshine the Nuts cruised to a 6-1 victory, with goals from Marriott, Leeman a pair and Carver a hat-trick. They deserved their victory, because of the way they were able to find each other with the ball. It was just the tonic that the people of Scunthorpe needed, as some of the spectators were still in uniform.

The first month of the fixture card was to reveal that United had assembled a strong squad under the circumstances. They lost the next match 3-0 to Notts County Reserves, but actually this was against the first team. At Lincoln City they took the game by the scruff of the neck and return home with the points from the 3-0 result. For those who went to Sincil Bank, there was the sight of Eddie Fleetwood showing the younger element how to score the goals, with a brace, plus another came from Readhead. This led to the first local derby against Gainsborough Trinity. Supporters of both camps were hungry to see the action, and at the Old Show Ground, United ran out 4-1 winners, being superior in every department. The goals this time were credited to Carver, but most encouragingly a hat-trick by Alan Leeman.

It was soon realised that the strength of teams playing in the Midland League had increased. There would no easy rides, making up the numbers, and unable to cope against the bigger clubs. From now on supporters could not expect any high scoring games to happen on a regular basis. Each separate match was to be a close battle, and the Nuts had to play with patience and keep the game tight. A raising of the bar was beneficial to everyone concerned, and tactics would play an even greater importance.

During the Autumn, there was the wonderful sight of the brief return of Harry Johnson. The long layoff for the War did nothing to help his cause, and he returned a battle scarred warrior, but was given a marvellous reception from an appreciative crowd. Many of them remembered how, in his prime, he had help wrestle the Midland League Championship with a sparkling display of goal scoring. It was to give the rest of the team a boost as, he played a three match cameo.

The F.A.Cup for the 1945-46 season was to be played on a two legged basis in the competition from the First Round, just for one year. Qualifying Rounds would not be effected, and Scunthorpe became interested from the Third Qualifying Round. The draw gave them a home tie against the Lysaghts Sports club, which contained many former Scunthorpe players, but only 1,200 supporters were attracted to the match. Scunthorpe had the pleasure of Harry Johnson for the game, and thanks to two goals scored by his initiative, the Nuts won 4-1. Sid Allen and Jack Marriott supplied the others.

On the first Saturday of November, the team were ready for the last of the qualifying positions, and faced Yorkshire Amateur, at the Old Show Ground. The crowd did at least more than doubled to 3,500, for this important game. The Amateurs turned out to be a full set of battlers, and did not allow the Nuts to settle on the ball. They took a lead into half time and Scunthorpe did their best to play catch up. In the second half Fleetwood did give the local crowd something to cheer about, but it was the Amateurs who went through 2-1.

Once United made its Cup exit, they did manage to find some flare in the next two games, played at home, when points were won against Barnsley Reserves and Ollerton Colliery. Barnsley were beaten 2-1, while the crowd enjoyed a five goal feast against the Nottinghamshire miners, as the Nuts won 5-1. The Scunthorpe team had the return of Stocks and Swain to help them, and had a three goal cushion by the mid-way point. Carver scored twice, and others came by way of Fleetwood, Marriott and Swain.

The approach of the holiday period brought some excellent entertainment for the supporters of Scunthorpe and Lindsey, but they did not all end in victory. Christmas Day saw the traditional fixture against Grimsby Town Reserves, at the Old Show Ground, and an attendance of 3,500 watched a closely fought match. The Mariners team contained men of First Division experience. Although United took the lead through Carver, they had to settle for a 2-2 draw, Carver also getting the second. The next day, at Blundell Par, 2,046 patrons saw another see-saw epic which swayed one way then the other.

In the end, a free kick Grimsby Town's way led to the deciding goal, and a lot of sweat resulted in a 4-3 defeat. On the Saturday of the Christmas break, United made amends by beating the junior Imps team 4-2 up the Doncaster Road, then threw any advantage away in the mud at Frickley, losing 5-4. Mal Millington could only look in disbelief, with his hands on his hips, wondering where it had all got wrong after running himself into the ground.

The Club implemented an number of team changes in the second half of the season, and the side did not operate quite as well. A direct result of this was a slip towards the middle of the table. Some men did perform reasonably well in the limited opportunities offered to them. This was especially in the forward line where hat-tricks were scored by Priestly Sheen and Burton. None of these men could match the presence of Carver, who managed to score all four of Scunthorpe's goals when beating Denaby United 4-1, and became the leading marksman.

During the March of 1946 Scunthorpe United announced that they would build the future round their experienced defender, George Lax. He was going to be the Club's third Player Manager. It was a move that made all parties happy, until just after a fortnight George received another offer from Hull City, and the board were happy to let him depart.

The year was to end in a whimper at Ollerton, in the shadow of the coal heaps. Towards the final matches, the Club always tried a few team changes, in view of the year ahead. This might explain how they lost 3-2 to Ollerton Colliery, when points had been anticipated before the match. After all of the statistics were gathered Scunthorpe featured in sixth place in the Midland League table, a satisfactory return after years of turmoil.

1946-47

The news of the closed season in the Summer of 1946 was the signing of Ted Catlin, a full back who had won the top honour with Sheffield Wednesday. Unfortunately he was only to play a handful of game for the Nuts, and so it did not prove to be the most productive of moves.

The goalkeeping position was to remain in the hands of Wilf Poxton, and he had Harry Reed from Yeovil, and Stan Cooke from Rotherham as full backs. It was said that there were some strange sounding accents, as folks tried to understand their conversations. Jack Staniland and Mal Millington remained in the half back section, and were joined on the left by the old Barnsley War time International, Bernard Harper. Harper was a man who had been round the block a few times, and would bolster that department with skill and robustness. Further up the park the forward line was to have two local boys as wingers. Jack Marriott was on the right, while Arthur Robertshaw patrolled the left.

During the season Marriott became such a hot property, that Sheffield Wednesday offered the huge sum of £2,000 for his transfer. The departure co-insided with the return from War of Stan Norris, who had been captured by the Japanese in the jungles of the Far East and badly treated as a Prisoner of War. His return to fitness was a relief for all to see, and he quickly recovered his old zest.

The main player in the coming games was Percy Bowers, otherwise known as Timmy, and he would be the new king. His rate of fire was to match that of Ernie Simms and Harry Johnson, and the mystery was that he did not play at a higher level. His discovery was the same as a modern day Billy Sharp and whenever he went on the field, the chances were that goals would be scored. The inside men around Bowers would be James Wynne, a notable marksman, George Wallace, Alan Leeman, and a player called Hydes, signed from Newport County.

The strange co-incidence was that United opened the season with the same home fixture against Mansfield Town Reserves, as twelve months ago. This time the attendance, watching with shirt sleeves rolled up, had a real epic unfold in front of their eyes, as the junior Stags took a lead in the first minute of play. At half time this was reversed 2-1 in the Nuts favour, and the full motion picture was not settled for certain until the end. James Wynne claimed three goals, while Timmy Bowers and George Wallace scored one each, as the result finished at 5-4 to Scunthorpe.

It was not long before this Scunthorpe team was purring along like a Rolls Royce, and able to compete with all comers. I was soon apparent that Timmy Bowers and James Wynne could score at will and the news of hat-tricks would not be uncommon. The situation might have slowed when James Wynne became injured, but Bowers was just as able to cope as a marksman with the support of Marriott and Robertshaw supplying the bullets. The capacity of the double spearhead was aptly demonstrated when each of them were responsible for one when Notts County Reserves came knocking. Then, in a rare goal marathon, Frickley Colliery were unable to give an answer to Bowers scoring four times, and Wynne three, in a 9-0 demolition.

The failure of Scunthorpe and Lindsey, in the previous year to make the First Round, required extra homework in this year's completion.

George Wallace, a player from Aberdeen, who joined the Nuts in 1946. He was an inside forward of dazzling feet, and a deadly shot, able to bridge the gap between Midland and Football League football.

It might have been a distraction, but Norton Woodseats, of Sheffield, had to be met in September, and it was to be remembered for a goal by Eddie Fleetwood in his farewell performance, rather than the 5-2 result. Haworth Colliery received the same treatment at the Old Show Ground with a similar result, then visits to Rawmarsh Welfare and Wombwell Athletic saw them sure footed with positive 3-0 and 5-2 results, to earn a passage to the Fourth Qualifying Round.

The F.A. Cup was to fix Scunthorpe and Lindsey with a visit from Boston United, a team familiar to them. When the referee blew his first whistle, the Nuts started like a tornado, and quickly mastered both the conditions and the opponents. Goals were fired in at regular intervals and the Stumpites could not cope with the onslaught. Timmy Bowers soon had two strikes to his name, then two more came from Robertshaw and the mercurial George Wallace. At half time the enemy had surrendered at 4-1, and United saved its energy in the last forty five, knowing the job was done.

Scunthorpe and Lindsey United were not strangers to the First Round of the F.A.Cup, and they were given the relatively short journey to Bootham Crescent to play York City, of the Third Division North. These were the type of games they would have to face if ever they gained Football League status themselves. On the day of the game a depression had dumped gallons of water on the pitch, and when the referee saw his own reflection in all corners of the playing area he called it off until the following Wednesday.

Conditions were much improved at kick-off, but it was extremely muddy. The afternoon start did not stop a crowd of 7,849 being in place to view the game, with about a thousand arriving from Scunthorpe. It was after only four minutes that these Lincolnshire folk would be jumping for joy. The magical feet of Wallace slipped a neat ball through to Robertshaw, who glanced up, and crossed to Marriott. Young Jack, controlled first time, then drilled the wet ball hard and low beyond the advancing keeper, into the inviting net.

The remaining eighty six minutes were packed with skilful football, brilliant saves, near misses and lots of endeavour. The stars for Scunthorpe would be found in the defence. Every man put his life on the line for the cause. Wilf Poxton stood out for extra praise, as he repelled dozens of shots.

In the last five minutes one in particular was noticeable, when he found himself one on one with a attacker in front of goal. Wilf was straight down at his adversary's feet and whipped the ball away to spontaneous applause from the crowd. Eventually the Nuts held out to record their only away F.A.Cup win on the foreign soil of a Football League club, when they were of non-League status themselves. The only sympathy was for the laundry lady who had to wash the kit after the game.

It was not long before the next episode unfolded in the F.A.Cup, and the journey this time took them to the South of Yorkshire, to play Rotherham United. Millmoor was familiar to the Nuts, but they were not up against the junior team on this occasion. Rotherham United were considered to be one of the strongest teams in the Northern Section, and this was to be proved on the day. The Millers quickly established themselves as the masters, and a two goal lead demonstrated which team was dictating the play. Scunthorpe were to be rewarded for a gallant effort by a fine strike from Timmy Bowers, but returned home empty handed from the 4-1 lesson.

Over the Christmas holiday United had three local derby games to keep the chill of the Winter away. It all started at Lincoln, where the Imps junior eleven were unable to keep pace with the Nuts, and victory came from a 3-0 jog. On Christmas Day the Mariners Reserves hit town, and 5,000 throats roared the gladiators on, in an incident packed match. No side could show an overall mastery, and despite Timmy Bowers being on the mark with a hat-trick, the teams tied at three goals each. This theme continued on Boxing Day, before 7,000 excited folks. James Wynne engineered United the lead, but once again the valiant effort of all the twenty players earned a point apiece from a 1-1 result.

Another draw was recorded at Mansfield, immediately afterwards, then the team slipped in the ice at Denaby United, on New Year's Day, 3-2. This stutter was not to be the general trend, and the following three matches all finished with healthy goal packed victories. These were at Notts County Reserves, and home to Bradford Park Avenue Reserves, plus the second fixture with Denaby. It was at this time when the British weather took a grip, and a cold plunge of Artic air settled over the entire Country for a number of weeks.

In those times a referee would sanction a start in some of the most atrocious conditions, that are not tolerated today. Even the frozen pitches of 1947 could not allow some games to go ahead, and the football season would have to require a long extension.

The story of Scunthorpe and Lindsey United's yarn would be crammed into April and May, and was not terminated until June 14th 1947, next door to the Summer holidays, at Ollerton Colliery. The Nuts continued to play a smooth well oiled game of cultured football, and attracted large attendances to appreciate their work. They did their best to keep pace with Grimsby Town Reserves, who would lift the trophy. United's attempts for glory were thwarted by injuries sustained by Wallace and Cooke, which had a baring on the later results. It took an extra six weeks to sort out the fixture congestion, but a resting place of fourth did not flattered the months of concerted effort. Timmy Bowers had maintained his amazing strike rate, and scored sixty in all competitions, which rated him with the other giants of the past.

Mr Scunthorpe United, Jack Brownsword, who played from 1947 until 1964. A dedicated club man, and scorer of fifty Football League goals, all but one from the penalty spot.

An extended season gave the Club more time to give thought to the application to join the Football League. The position of Scunthorpe United had been enhanced during the resumption of football after the War and the directors received nods of approval at what they brought to the table, but in essence little had changed. The senior figures that ran the sport were single minded and not ready to alter the system. It was as if the directors were running up a blind ally, and be patient. They decided that the only way was to strengthen the Club on the field, and hope that headlines like those after the Cup tie with York would make them noticed throughout the Country.

1947-48

The directors continued to work tirelessly to improve the standing of the Club, and it was announced that Bernard Harper would supplement his left half position with the role of Player Manager. Mal Millington was as fresh as ever, and took the centre half position, while Alan Leeman became the right half, as Jack Staniland played a decreasing first team role, after years of much appreciated service.

In the back quarters, Wilf Poxton was gradually retired with Jack Staniland to the second eleven, and he was to hand over the woolly jumper to George Rymer. The full backs positions both saw change, and Cook and Reed faded into the background in favour of Albert Watford and Jack Brownsword. It was twenty four year old Brownsword who would be the big star of Scunthorpe and set all sorts of appearance records, and become a goal scoring full back. Jack was an unassuming lad who worked hard, ran hard and tackled like a spitting Cobra. He would earn the praise of the top personalities in the game, whilst still keeping loyal to Scunthorpe. Bill Shankley, the great Liverpool manager, once remarked that Jack was the best uncapped full back in the entire Country. This epic marathon was to start on Thursday 28th August 1947 before 6,700 spectators, at home to Scarborough, and it was Jack that scored the only goal from the penalty spot.

The forward line remained virtually unchanged, as Timmy Bowers was at the sharp end, George Wallace continued at inside forward along with Stan Norris. Arthur Robertshaw resumed at left wing, but had another partner, called Rowney, on the right wing, as his opposite number.

Timmy Bowers nets in an F.A.Cup tie against Rawmarsh Welfare in 1947. United won 8-0, and Timmy, real name Percy, scored five times.

During the later part of the Winter, James Johnson made a handful of appearances in the forward line, and trials were handed to others to find a new balance. The final signing of the year was another significant one for United, but came too late in the day to make a lasting effect on this season. Dick Taylor was taken from the books of Grimsby Town, to replace the aging Mal Millington. Dick was a quality player, who was used to life on a regular basis in the First Division with the Mariners. He was to be the new backbone of the defence, earning lots of accolades for his towering performances. It was unbelievable that a player of this calibre could be allowed to be released to play at non-League level.

Scunthorpe and Lindsey United might have needed some time to find the right players to settle into the most effective unit they could put onto the park, but the Nuts were the envy of most other teams, and made a formidable combination.

The attack was razor sharp, but could not be expected to rattle home the one hundred and twenty one goals of last term. This was of no consequence, because the trio of Rymer, Watford and Brownsword gave them a defence that was water tight, and Millington was always in the thick of things to clear the ball skilfully or unceremoniously, it mattered not.

The Scunthorpe express train instantaneously went off to a flying start, beginning at Bradford City Reserves. Bowers hit a pair of goals, while other from Wallace and Norris made up the 4-1 result. During August they squeezed out maximum points from three outings and headed the early table. September was a less certain time, and they lost three games and won once in the six matches they had to perform in. The victory was an emphatic one, at home to Gainsborough Trinity, and was watched by a record Midland League crowd for Scunthorpe of 9,100, who paid £594 for the pleasure. United never let the visitors in blue have a moment of rest, and won 3-1 through the guile of goal scorers Bowers Norris and Rowney. It was Gainsborough's first defeat of their fixture card, and there could be no complaints.

The third week of September brought an additional match in the F.A.Cup, and this tournament would see the scorers find their shooting boots. United drew the oldest club in the World for the Preliminary Round, called the Sheffield Club. The minor team was simply out played, and hardly managed to get too near the Scunthorpe posts. A 5-1 result justified Scunthorpe's superiority. This allowed a visit from Rawmarsh Athletic in the next round, and this bunch of Yorkshire lads were blitzed out of sight, 8-0. They were unable to cope with the wizardry of Timmy Bowers, whose wand conjured five of the goals. It was not until Denaby United came for the Second Qualifying Round, that a team rolled up to make a meaningful contest of the tie. Here a proper struggle took place, and the game was not settled until late in the day, thanks to some stiff resistance from the Denaby back quarters. They only made one slip, at the end of the clock, and missed the shot on the run of Rowney, coming from the right side of the posts.

The Cup trail continued at the Old Show Ground on November 1st, with the arrival of Norton Woodseats, for another pop at the Nuts, and this time they were far stronger in their preparation. Scunthorpe played a young up and coming lad, named Pinchbeck at centre forward, and Timmy Bowers drifted out to the left wing. The experiment was a success, as Pinchbeck scored twice in the 2-1 win, and United marched on.

The Fourth Qualifying Round brought the return of Gainsborough, who had responded to Scunthorpe's triumph at the Old Show Ground with a win of their own at the Northolme. The intrigue meant that Harry Allcock could have sold the seating tickets three times over, and the stadium was full to bursting, yet again. The official figure was 9,905, and they watched a cracker of a match open mouthed. Trinity were the first to open an account, and led at the forty five minute mark. Scunthorpe kept their powder dry until the second half and fired four canons into the Gainsborough rigging, through Pinchbeck, Rowney, Robertshaw and Bowers. They proved to be the Trinity nemesis once again, winning 4-2.

In the First Round of the F.A.Cup, Scunthorpe were sent to the other side of the Country to do battle with Runcorn, not too far from the port of Liverpool. Scunthorpe knew nothing about the opposition, but soon found them a team that would take advantage of any mistakes. United had by far the greater part of the play in the first three quarters of an hour, gaining a 2-1 lead. Mix ups in the middle of the defence would be the down fall of the team, and three disastrous times they were made to pay. A 4-2 loss was the medicine they were made to swallow, and the only ones to blame were themselves. If the team did receive any sort of consolation, it was in the admirable way that Pinchbeck had conducted himself at centre forward. It impressed the watching Everton scouts, and the Goodison Park club paid Scunthorpe £2,000 for his signature.

The loss of Pinchbeck was not noticed in the team, because they resumed battle at home to Ollerton Colliery, and won 7-1. Timmy Bowers was selected at centre forward, and repaid the faith in him with a record equalling double hat-trick, only the third in official competitions, in the history of the Club, that this had ever taken place.

With all of this activity going on it was immanent time for the Christmas bonanza against Grimsby Town Reserves. The theatre of football rivalry brought large crowds celebrating the Yuletide with samples of their favourite tipple, making a happy atmosphere. Neither of the two teams would disappoint, and fought as if they were two boxers slugging it out in the ring. Each side would deliver a 2-1 knock-out blow on their own ground. This was to be eclipsed, on the day after Boxing day, with the third match in three days, when Peterborough United came to the frozen North. They found the Scunthorpe machine running in top gear, and while the Nuts hit seven goals, they were only posh enough for one. The main marksman was Timmy Bowers, who scored three times, while Rowney notched two, and Wallace and Norris completed the others.

The cold Winter month of January was a generous one to United, and they remained unbeaten. It put them at the top end of the table, which saw Shrewsbury Town in the driving seat.

Already the Nuts had visited Shropshire and returned with a point. February started with the return match at London Road Peterborough, but the Posh were far stronger on their own patch, and United lost 2-1. It was a minor blip on the radar, and Scunthorpe returned immediately to winning ways, taking points from the next six games.

The last two months of the calendar found United in top form going into the finishing straight. Four games were won in March, and five in April, this included the important fixture at the Old Show Ground, with Shrewsbury. This match saw the Scunthorpe boys answer all the questions proposed by the Shrews, and they had the points in the bag, when all the goals came in the first half, as Jim Johnson was twice on hand to score. This left United on the second rung on the ladder, but marginally out of the reach of the Shropshire men. Time and opportunities were fast running out on Scunthorpe and Lindsey United, who realised that Shrewsbury would not be caught. This was confirmed when Boston United put a nail into their title hopes, with four matches remaining. The last fixture on the calendar was at the Old Show Ground to Lincoln City Reserves, and it was not until after this finale that they conceded their home record. This remarkable achievement meant the honour of being second in the table for the 1947-48 season in the Midland League, seven point behind Shrewsbury, but one more than Nottingham Forest Reserves.

It was with these credentials that all of the hopeful non-League clubs headed to the next Football League A.G.M. but each of them, including Scunthorpe, received the same blank expressions from the men in charge. They had no alternative but to return to the same familiar circle of the Midland League, where at the worst they would enjoy the company of old friends, and the fruits of there labour were still appreciated. The Summer was to be spent making sure that the Scunthorpe team could keep up appearances in the year ahead.

1948-49

In the Summer of 1948 the newspapers heralded the return of a local man, Jeff Barker, who left as a boy for Aston Villa. He moved on to Huddersfield Town, and was back where he started, as a battle hardened warrior. Jeff was to become the new captain of the side, using his authority with the armband. He would stand alongside Dick Taylor, a master of the central defence. Mal Millington was not to have his nose pushed out of the way just yet, and any injuries to the half back quarters would see Taylor moving to a half back position, and Millington operate from the centre. The right half place was not as simple to decide. At first Lee was given his chance, but then Dai Davies and later Eddie Lindley all had a run in the first team.

The old season had seen the last lines of defence finish as George Rymer in goal, and Watford and Brownsword as the full backs.

Their behaviour was exemplary and no reason could be found to stop them continuing. They picked themselves every time throughout the coming year, and the trio was only disturbed by an injury to Jack in the number three shirt, so he could not make the home visit of Doncaster in April.

The forward line was to see the majority of the changes during the year in front. Timmy Bowers was unable to play until the second half of the season and George Murphy took over as the goal scoring spearhead. Murphy was a larger than life character, who was known as Spud. He had been an old stalwart for West Bromwich Albion and Hull City, and it was not unheard for him to ask for a sub on his wages to have a flutter on the horses. George Wallace remained as the inside left, but on the other side Rowney had to share the duty with John Taylor. The right wing found Little in the number seven shirt, because Stan Norris decided to retire from Midland League duties, while out on the other side it was Whitehead who became the left winger. In March the Club was not happy with the conduct of Murphy, and he was offered his cards. This brought Whitehead in from the wing and Watson to his former berth.

The loss of Murphy could have been damaging, but it opened the door to allow the incredible skills of Jimmy Whitfield, from Grimsby Town. Whitfield was another gift that the Mariners were able to discard, and he had played many games in the Grimsby Town first team squad, particularly at inside forward. The new look forward line was not to alter the general direction of the team, and it was to produce much of the same.

The first match in the circle of events was to take Scunthorpe and Lindsey United to Sincil Bank, to play the junior Imps, and they gained revenge for the embarrassment of losing their home record to them late last term. The Nuts were keen in attack and sound in defence, coming home with a 4-1 victory. Spud Murphy and John Taylor were responsible for two goals apiece. They went on to gain maximum points from the first four matches, the 3-0 pounding of Shrewsbury Town holding the greatest significance, before 8,000 people. It was not until they lost 1-0 at Gainsborough, and 5-2 to Forest Reserves in Nottingham that a reality check was taken.

Dick Taylor signed for Scunthorpe United in the Summer of 1948 from Grimsby Town, and played at the heart of the defence until 1954.

Once the Forest setback was out of the system, the team found an incredible ten match winning Midland League run which shot them to the top of the table. This invigorating form saw them beat York City Reserves 5-0 on their travels, get the better of Gainsborough 4-3, in front of 9,874 supporters, and thrash Frickley Colliery 7-0. Revenge was eked out against Forest Reserves which actually saw them miss three penalties but win, and the attendances boomed like never before.

Scunthorpe and Lindsey United would not be called into action in the F.A.Cup until the Fourth Qualifying Round in 1948, and they had some business to sort out at home to Selby Town. It was always a battle, as a crowd of 6,343 could testify to, but generally they were always ahead of the game. Murphy scored in each half and ninety of hard toil won the tie 2-1.

The First Round of the F.A.Cup brought them to The Shay, to slug it out with Halifax Town, on a foggy day late in November. The players all lined up and the crowd began to roar, but the density of the fog was so bad that the referee had no alternative but to call a halt before a ball was kicked. On the following Saturday they started again, and this time a 15,000 crowd saw a defensive battle take place, Neither side could find a breakthrough, and two days later they tried to sort it out in a second time in Scunthorpe.

The replay created much interest in local circles. Every seat was sold, and Harry Allcock was confident that the Old Show Ground would be stuffed to the seems and every last corner filled with supporters. At the kick-off, on the afternoon of December 6th 1948, a record attendance of 12,736 was in place, smashing the previous ceiling by more than a thousand.

The noise coming from the roar at the Old Show Ground could be heard at Keadby, such was its intensity. Each set of troops was just as keen as ever to impress, and a number of chances were created. George Rymer in the Scunthorpe goal showed a clean pair of gloves, and the defence domination continued. At half time no advantage was found, and it was to take something out of the ordinary to inch one of the teams into the lead. It came when Scunthorpe won a free kick, just outside the Halifax box.

The men in the blue shirts erected a wall to protect their keeper, but found that Spud Murphy had muscled into it. Jeff Barker took three paces back, then raced forward and shot the ball at Murphy. Murphy ducked, allowing the ball through the gap, and sailing into the net. This was to be the only goal, and the match winner.

The delays in the schedule meant that the Nuts knew that they would have another home tie in the Second Round of the F.A.Cup, and Stockport County of the Third Division North, would be their guests. This was to take place five days later on December 11th 1948. At this match the gate rose further still, and was bursting at 13,775. For the first time ever receipts of more than one thousand pounds went over the turnstiles. It was to be another memorable afternoon of silky football skills, and defences were the talk of the terraces. Dick Taylor was magnificent at the heart of the battle, while Jeff Barker was the heart beat of the mid-field. Up in the front lines Wallace jinked his way round the Stockport back quarters. The only score was made by Stockport County, deep in the game and Scunthorpe bowed out 1-0. There was an interesting question, accompanied by a photograph, as to whether a Scunthorpe shot had crossed the line.

The brilliance of the team in the F.A.Cup was to continue right up until the Christmas period. It was only on Christmas Day that, to the dismay of the 8,000 supporters, United's luck deserted them. A keenly fought dispute ended when the Mariners Reserves held on to an early goal to win 1-0. The next day, on Blundell Park, the same intensity of battle could not find a winner. Each team scored once, and had to agree to split the spoils.

Scunthorpe a Lindsey United were one of a group of four clubs at the top end of the Midland League, headed by Gainsborough Trinity. The holiday period had not done the Scunthorpe cause much good, because they tasted another defeat on New Year's Day, at Notts County Reserves. The team did not get back into winning ways until the following Saturday, when Peterborough United called by. United won comprehensively, and the Posh goal was scored from the penalty spot, in the 4-1 triumph. Two more wins during the month kept them in with a shout, and results in February brought a suggestion, that if other scores went for them, they could go one better than last year. Certainly the spirit was good when the team beat Bradford Park Avenue Reserves 5-1 at home.

At that moment it looked possible for the Nuts to do something special, but then they began the let the opportunity slip through their fingers. Three conclusive trips on the road ended in defeat. The team went down at Grantham, Bradford Park Avenue and Peterborough, while Gainsborough were stealing a march. The remainder of the month saw Scunthorpe stage a recovery, and the presence of Timmy Bowers gave lots of hope. At the far end of the month of March, they registered two handsome victories of 4-1 at Newark, against Ransome and Marles, and 5-0 at Frickley Colliery, making good reasons to celebrate.

Then it was all thrown away at the Old Show Ground, when they went down 3-1 to Grantham, on the first Saturday in April. The rest of month reaped some sterling results, especially when three of four points came against the Hull City Cubs at Easter. However, it was a visit to Shrewsbury that put to bed all talk of the Championship coming to Scunthorpe. They had no answer and no excuses for their poor defence that lost them the chapter by a 5-1 score. In the final phase, United finished with three home fixtures. Four points were yielded from the first of these. Scarborough were narrowly defeated 2-1, then a hat-trick from Timmy Bowers helped to break the resolve of Bradford City reserves by 5-0. On the last Saturday of the season they could have retained the second place in the table, but losing to Boston United dropped them to fourth.

The usual pilgrimage to lobby for support to join the Football League was met with the same stalemate. Teams making the application to become members were all told the same story. Member clubs did not think it right to expel another club, just for a bad season finishing in the bottom two. After all, somebody had to go cap in hand every year. This brought a change of tactic from the Scunthorpe delegation, headed by Ernest Plowright, the owner of the Scunthorpe and Frodingham Star newspaper. The opinion was expressed that if there were too many planes in the sky, then there was the need for a bigger airport.

When Scunthorpe's delegation made the suggestion of an increase of the League it was met with indifference, which was not unsurprising. Many of them did not want to dabble with a change in the rules and regulations. Some member clubs had Chairmen that said they agreed with the move in principle and would vote in favour, but did not wish to put it forward themselves. The Scunthorpe delegation knew that a lot more midnight oil would have to be burned if something concrete was to be worked out. Finally, a basic outline was drafted and it was agreed to increase the number of clubs in each of the two Third Divisions by a further two entries. The move was to be proposed by Sheffield Wednesday and seconded by Everton.

The next day, at the Football League A.G.M., the proposal received the necessary backing, and was passed. At least some headway had been made, even though the four fortunate clubs still had to wait twelve months to be voted in. Scunthorpe's band of directors had done the hard work, and now set about building the team for the next Midland League season.

1949-50

There was a suggestion circulating that Scunthorpe and Lindsey United were about to sign another goalkeeper. During the next few weeks it was learned that this was the case and the Club had approached Chesterfield about the services of George Thompson. The two clubs agreed a fee of £250, which United were happy to pay, in lieu of the tidy sum of money that had been received from their run in last year's F.A.Cup. It seemed a huge amount of cash, but when George was seen in action, he was considered well worth the investment.

In front of Thompson, the full back duo was to consist of Jeff Barker and the immovable Jack Brownsword. Watford had left the Club, and Barker was a capable deputy. These would stay intact as a unit until injury to Jeff Barker.

The regular half back line would be Maurice Conroy, Dick Taylor and Joe McCormick. Conroy was formerly employed at Accrington, while McCormick was once of Oldham and Rochdale. Dick Taylor, a tall slender man with a characteristic bald top, was another player never to miss during the year ahead.

The forward line was to benefit from the presence of a big Southerner from Tottenham, called Leslie Heseltine, but he could not hold his place when Timmy Bowers was in line for duty. Jimmy Whitfield showed all the class of a League player, being able to also fill in at centre forward, and George Wallace continued to dance through defences. The wingmen were to be Albert Wilson and Alec Malcolm, the latter an ex-Barnsley player. The great advantage for this squad of men was that it was settled and there was no need to shuffle the pack, except for the inevitable times of injury.

Scunthorpe and Lindsey United began the season with a fluent brand of neat attractive football, which brought an eight match unbeaten run from the start of the season. The first six home matches were rewarded by the maximum twelve points, during which eighteen goals were scored and none conceded. It was the type of form that could only be dreamed about, and just went to show how good a custodian they had in George Thompson.

The solid start made to the campaign had an influence on the numbers of people going up the Doncaster Road, which had risen in the milder weather to around the 8,000 mark for most matches. The visit of Gainsborough Trinity was to create a record for Scunthorpe in the Midland League of 11,573, a remarkable figure indeed. It had not been unheard of for the Reserves to enjoy the support of crowds of just over 3,000. The Scunthorpe following had made Timmy Bowers the centre of their adulation. He was in the twilight of his senior career, but in the early part of the season notched nine goals in three outings. Two of them arrived against Gainsborough, three went into the Grantham net, and finally four took Goole Town by surprise, at the Old Show Ground.

The silk smooth run of the team was halted at York, when the Nuts lost 1-0 to the Minster team's second squad. This was followed on the next Wednesday with a second defeat, on the River Ouse, at Goole Town, who beat them 2-1. It gave the other leading clubs a chance to gain lost ground, and came as a timely reminder to those team members that needed a nudge.

Scunthorpe and Lindsey showed no permanent signs of damage, and went on a run of eight matches, of which seven received the maximum two points reward. York City Reserves proved to be the thorn in their side, and a 3-1 loss handed them a deserved double over the Nuts. At the same time Nottingham Forest Reserves, a leading contender, found themselves 3-2 in arrears when Scunthorpe left the City Ground, on the banks of the River Trent. Then, on Guy Fawkes night, seven goals were picked out of the net by the visiting Doncaster Rovers keeper, when the real fireworks went off.

The team was to be dealt a severe blow during the shortening days of the Autumn. Both Albert Wilson and Joe McCormick would be out for some considerable time with broken collar bones. Next to go on the sick was Jeff Barker, who suffered a broken toe, but this was not to keep him from missing a majority of the action.

It was in November that thoughts turned to the F.A.Cup, when Scunthorpe came to the competition at the Fourth Qualifying Round. The team found that they had an invitation to be hosts to Goole Town. The local derby brought a lot of interest and the Old Sow Ground had little space when the time of kick-off approached. Scunthorpe would not have the best of fortune, because this was the game when they lost McCormick, and also missed a penalty. There was no wonder that the match finished inconclusive as a goalless draw.

A replay was arranged for the next Saturday afternoon at the Victoria Pleasure Grounds, and was to be an eye opener for anyone who could see. Indeed, the day was shrouded in fog, and little could be made out of what was going on in the middle of the park. The cheers and groans indicated that Goole had taken a 2-1 lead at the interval, then increased it to 3-1, with the passage of time. The situation was becoming ridiculous, as virtually none of the play could be followed. Ten minutes before the end, the referee consulted the two captains and abandoned the game to a chorus of boos from the home supporters. When they started again on the next Tuesday, Goole Town repeated the trick, and this time the 3-1 score stood. United could concentrate on the Midland League.

One of the consequences of the long injury list was that it allowed the directors to take a look at some of the younger players in the second team, and promote them to see what they were made of. The pick of the bunch was Len Sharpe, who made his debut three days prior to his seventeenth birthday. United were at home to Forest Reserves, possibly the strongest team in the division, and lost 2-0. Len was utilised as a right winger, and kept his place for four games. He even managed to score in the last of the run, against Rotherham United Reserves, and only relinquished his position when Timmy Bowers returned to fitness. Ten years later and Len Sharpe was still a crowd favourite, established as a quality mid-fielder.

The old stalwarts were made of tough old stuff, and healed sooner than most would have thought. Both McCormick and Wilson were sufficiently mended to run out for the visit of Bradford Park Avenue Reserves on the last Saturday of January. Both of them scored goals, in what was an overwhelming victory, which finished at twenty to four in a 6-1 success. The major difference on the day was in the superior tactics used by Scunthorpe, and the remaining strikes included a hat-trick from Jimmy Whitfield, while Lennon notched the sixth.

Scunthorpe and Lindsey United maintained their challenge throughout the entire season. It must be said that the injuries did have a serious effect, especially over the Christmas holiday, where loses occurred on the road at Grimsby and Grantham. The rest of the campaign was a solid performance, in an effort to keep pace with Forest Reserves, Grimsby Town Reserves and to a lesser extent, Peterborough United. It was only in the dying phase of the fixture list that United realised that Forest Reserves were not going to be caught, especially when Easter arrived. They went over to Boothferry Park to claim a 5-0 win over the City second eleven, on Good Friday, but lost to them 1-0 at the Old Show Ground, on the Monday. The Nuts finished the campaign with four consecutive 2-1 victories, three of them on their travels.

The final Midland League table found Scunthorpe United nestled in the third highest place behind Champions Nottingham Forest Reserves, and the second placed team, Grimsby Town Reserves. Three more wins for the Nuts might have changed history, but a huge amount of satisfaction was taken out of a memorable year.

During the early part of the closed season Scunthorpe and Lindsey United made preparations for one of the most important phases in their fifty one year history. Ernest Plowright, and local M.P. David Quibell were ready to attend the A.G.M. of the Football League, and canvass for support of the bid to claim one of the newly created places in the Third Division North. The delegation made sure they were aware of all the Chairmen of the member clubs that they would need to target. They had all the ammunition they required to promoted the Scunthorpe United case and say why they deserved a place above all the others. A number of meeting were arranged at various hotels and gentlemen's clubs in order to lobby for support, and the bar bill to soften the minds of those in power was enormous. This mattered not, because the competition of other teams trying for the same aims was considerable. When the time finally arrived at the main meeting, the delegates re-elected the bottom two clubs of each of the two Third Division. Then came the voting for the four extra places. The Third Division South was to be boosted by the election of Colchester United and Gillingham. When it came to the Third Division North the Scunthorpe delegation would be in for a heart stopping surprise. The votes for this section revealed that Shrewsbury Town had won the ballot, but Workington and Wigan Athletic were tied equal in second place, and Scunthorpe and Lindsey United were out on a limb in fourth. They simply could not believe it.

Jeff Barker, United's captain in the last season of the Midland League in 1949-50, and the first of the Third Division North a year later.

The Chairman of the Football League meeting announced that Shrewsbury would be given a place in the Third Division North, and all other clubs would go into a second ballot to find a conclusive result for the remaining fixture card. The blood started returning to the Scunthorpe delegates faces, as they realised they had been thrown a life line. It must have been like being at the dentists waiting for the next set of votes to be cast, and another count taken. When it was all over another incredible result brought more gasps, because this time Wigan Athletic topped the pole on the same number of points as Scunthorpe.

Further consultations took place on the top table to find a solution. This time there was to be a straight fight between Scunthorpe and Wigan, with a winner takes all at the end of it. The tension was numbing for the parties involved. Eventually the drama came to a climax, and the results declared. Wigan Athletic had gained eighteen votes, while Scunthorpe and Lindsey United and poled thirty. The Scunthorpe party were cheered and it was hand shakes all round. They had succeeded in their aim to take the Club into the Football League after a journey that started in 1899 in humble surroundings.

The news was splashed across the front page of the Scunthorpe Evening Telegraph, and soon spread round the whole district. It was greeted with great excitement, and supporters could not wait for the new season to arrive. Plans were made to bank the area behind the Doncaster Road end, and to see that it was safely paved. This effectively increased the ground capacity to more then 15,000. A full time manager was made a priority, and money immediately put forward to strengthen the team. The whole of Scunthorpe was buzzing. They even decided to change the Club's nick-name from the Nuts to the Iron to reflect the main trade of the town. From this point the Club would be referred to as just Scunthorpe United. The full name was still retained, but not officially altered until an uncharted date late in the decade.

THE THIRD DIVISION NORTH

1950-51

An expectant queue of Scunthorpe United supporters wait for the gates to open on August 19th 1950 for the first Football League game, against Shrewsbury Town.

rose early on the morning of Saturday 19th August 1950, and Harry Allcock, Scunthborpe United's secretary, was quickly on his way to the Old Show Ground. This was the day that both he and thousands of other people in Scunthorpe had been waiting for. It marked the Club's baptism in the Football League Third Division, and there were dozens of jobs to attend to hours before the crowds started queuing at the gates.

The closed season had been busier than ever before, and one of the most important jobs had been to find a manager to guide them in the first tentative steps in the Football League. The man selected was the former Arsenal and Wales International full back, Leslie Jones, who had won the top honours in the game. Since his retirement from the field, he had taken his coaching badges, and was quietly confident that he could take the Club forward. He was not the kind of man to make rash promises, but would take the time to watch, listen and bring the young players through into the first team squad. Leslie Jones would find a number of Welsh players for the team, and the word was that everyone was learning to speak Welsh so that they could all communicate.

During the build up to the new campaign Leslie Jones had cast his eyes over the defensive part of the team and was happy with most of what he saw. George Thompson was of a class suited to the League, and Jeff Barker and Jack Brownsword were all capable artists for the full back roles. At right half Bill Allen was signed, with a great amount of experience, from York City. He was to partner Dick Taylor and Joe McCormick. This combination was tried for the first few games, then the chance was given to Jack Hubbard, a Summer transfer from Scarborough. The trial proved to be a first class succes, as Hubbard went to right half, and Allen swapped to the left. A decade later and Jack Hubbard and Jack Brownsword would still be the regular choices. From time to time, a strapping young local lad named Dick White was given a stretch of the legs, and he was to become another valuable asset.

The forward line was the area of the park to be most effected. George Wallace dropped for the moment into the Reserves, not wishing to turn full time. It only left Jimmy Whitfield as the remaining former Midland Leaguer.

The new forward line was to be spearheaded by a rugged Welshman, called Ted Gorin, who was happy to get stuck in where it mattered. Last year he had been the leading marksman for Cardiff City in the second team. The insidemen would be chosen from Jimmy Whitfield, Joe Payne who came from Newport County, and Mal Rees, a player signed by way of Barry Town. Out on the right wing United took on board a small, but nimble, Harold Mosby from Rotherham United. He was a good crosser of a ball and became a crowd pleaser for his work rate. The other wing berth went to former England International Wally Boyes, who won an F.A.Cup Runners-up medal with West Bromwich Albion before the War. He was next door to forty in age, but used his experience and head, rather than dashing about. The season was not very old when the Club splashed out £900 for the talented Horace Cumner, another Welshman, from Watford, who was to play the majority of games at left wing. Once everyone got to know each other, Scunthorpe United were ready for action.

The fixture card for the opening day was to bring the two new clubs together at the Old Show Ground, so what was a baptsm for Scunthorpe United was the same for their opponents, Shrewsbury Town. At three o'clock the visitors were well represented in the 11,847 crowd. Leslie Jones selected the following team for this historic occasion: Thompson; Barker and Brownsword; Allen, Taylor and McCormick; Mosby, Payne, Gorin, Rees and Boyes.

The game was a very even affair, and neither side wished to

(Above) An informal moment with the players and a game of cards. Manager Leslie Jones is nearest the ash tray, where most of his team have a cigarette! (Below) On October 7th 1950 Scunthorpe United players enjoy watching a junior match at St James' Park, Newcastle, before tackling Gateshead in the afternoon. The men in a line include Jack Brownsword, Ted Gorin, Dick Taylor, Jeff Barker, Horace Cumner and Harold Mosby, while Jack Hubbard is behind Brownsword.

start the new era with a defeat. Both camps could point to the back line for the stars of the show, and George Thompson and captain Jeff Barker both stood out for the Iron. After ninety minutes of worthy endeavours the two advarsaries retired without a shot beating the goalkeepers, and a 0-0 result left honours even.

During mid-week United were back in action, just down the road at Sincil Bank, to meet Lincoln City. A gate of 16,857 saw them play their first away match, with just one team change. Jimmy Whitfield replaced Joe Payne. The distinction of scoring the first goal went to Ted Gorin, but despite this, the Iron lost 2-1. They counted themselves extremely unfortunate, because a Dick Taylor header was ruled out for an infringement, and travelling supporters let the official know what they thought of his decision.

The inclusion of Jimmy Whitfield, the ex-Grimsby Town man, was a huge success. He not only scored on the Saturday, in the 1-1 draw with Mansfield Town, but added a second during the mid-week return, of the Imps. The crowd record was beaten at this match, and the ceiling raised to 14,840. Here there was little difference between the two teams, and this was reflected when the result was a declared as another 1-1. Three days later the crowd record was under threat once again, on the Saturday. This was for the arrival of the eventual Champions, Rotherham United. In the end, the attendance fell a couple of hundred short, but the team produced a marvellous defensive performance to earn a creditable goalless goal.

Scunthorpe United had made a tidy start to the season, but had yet to satisfy their eager supporters with that much needed first win. The football public had been very patient, but had to

wait until the sixth game of the list before it happened. The visitors to the Old Show Ground were Oldham Athletic, and it took a by Jimmy Whitfield to make the dream come true, his third so far. The 1-0 win was the talking point of all the pubs, and in every corner of the Steelworks. The only disappointment was that the crowd had shrunk to a little less than 8,000. Oldham Athletic would figure in another of the early 'firsts' for the Iron. Eight days later, United played in a see-saw game at Boundary Park, and won 4-3. Ted Gorin scored twice, and Jimmy Whitfield and Harold Mosby fired one apiece. The significance was that it registered both the initial away win, but also the maiden double.

On November 11th 1950, Scunthorpe United met Hereford United away from home in the F.A.Cup Fourth Qualifying Round. Jeff Barker is about to have his penalty kick saved, and United lost 1-0.

At the end of September the fixture card took them to Peel Park, for a match in Lancashire, with Accrington Stanley. Here, the team fired on all cylinders, and recorded a thrilling 3-0 result for the few hundred travelling supporters. Ted Gorin was on hand for all three of the goals, and in so doing, became the first Scunthorpe United player to score a hat-trick of goals

The four new boys in the Football League were not given permission to enter the F.A.Cup competition at the First Round stage, but were expected to fight the Fourth Qualifying Round. Scunthorpe United were unlucky in the draw, because it required the lengthy jouney to Hereford United's Edgar Street Ground. The match was a tight affair, and one that Scunthorpe should have earned at least a draw from. In the end they lost 1-0, and Jeff Barker, who was the inspiration on the field, blotted his copy book with a vital penalty kick miss. It was a wiser set of players that made it back in the Lincolnshire Road Car bus, along the winding lanes from Herefordshire.

Scunthorpe United were coping far better with life in the Third Division North than Shrewsbury Town. The approach of Christmas saw the Shrews struggling in or just on the bottom four point in the table. Scunthorpe were much handier placed in the mid-table, far away from trouble. It was the Yuletide programme which gave them a pair of matches with Wrexham. In the first, it was Wrexham's turn to make it to Lincolnshire on Christmas Day, to play the Iron. Horace Cumner came in from the left of the posts to shoot the opening goal, then the win was sealed by an own goal. On Boxing Day, United arrive at the Racecourse Ground and were beaten this time 3-1, leaving honours even.

A feature during the first few months of the season had been the impressive form of Ted Gorin, the Club's robust goal scoring centre forward. His performances could be guaranteed to be consistent, and several scouts had followed his progress. When January arrived, Leslie Jones had to face the prospect of losing him, because Shrewsbury Town had put an offer for his services, to alter their flagging fortunes.

A move to Salop suited Gorin, because he would be nearer his family in Wales. United shook hands and waved good bye to the man who had netted twelve goal for them. Supporters wondered if the cheque received would be worth the loss of goals, but Dave McCelland was brought out of second team duty to fill the gap admirably. He was a huge lad who could handle himself, and when he retired from football Dave joined the Police force.

In April Scunthorpe United drew a line in the sand by registering their biggest win in the Football League. The visitors were New Brighton, a team now defunct, that came from the Wirral. Scunthorpe United ripped the struggling team apart. They won 6-0 through two pairs of goals by Dave McClelland, and Len Comley, plus another from Joe Payne, and a penalty converted by Horace Cumner. The result completed another double, but the Iron would not play them again, because at the end of the season they lost their place to Workington.

Scunthorpe United terminated the first year of operation in the Football League on a muddy Prenton Park pitch, which was void of grass. They lost the match narrowly by a single goal. After the game the final table had them seated favourably in twelfth position, the best achieved by any of the four new apprentices.

The team had gained three doubles, but conceded none. Their home record declared that they had only lost one match, when York City won at the Old Show Ground, and during the whole of the calendar only nine goals were conceded on their own turf. This could not be matched by any team in all four divisions.

1951-52

During the closed season, Scunthorpe United released three players, and would see no more of Joe Payne, Wally Boyes and Mal Rees. In addition, Jimmy Whitfield decided on a move to Southport, for which a fee was banked. Some of the replacements would come from the second team, and Len Sharpe and Dick White were promoted when the opportunity arose. George Wallace was too valuable to leave in the shadows, and still able to balance a full time job as an electrical maitenance man, with his football commitments. When the right moment came, other chances fell to Peter Platts and young George Gray. The team also had cover from a South African goalkeeper, Norman Malan, who deputised efficiently in times of rare injuries to George Thompson.

Most of the team changes circulated around the forward line, for the second Summer running. Ray Powell had been signed from Swansea Town, as a centre forward to sharpen the attack. At first, Jack Hubbard was utilised as an inside right, but as time progressed he slipped to right half, then finally to right full back, as the permanent replacement for the aging Jeff Barker. When this happened, Arthur Hall, from Goole Town, came to prominence as the right inside man, while George Wallace was to the left of Powell. The wingers would operate as Harold Mosby on the right and Horace Cumner on the left. Team matters were to be complemented by the arrival of the sure footed inside man, Jimmy Rudd from Rotherham United, via Manchester City, for £1,500. Len Sharpe once asked him why he had a stud missing on the toe of each boot, and he responed by saying it assisted him to swivel past his opponent.

In the other parts of the team its was more or less the same status quo. There was only to be minor changes, and an experience Cecil Sterland was signed from New Brighton, for an occasional run at right half. Similarly, John Babes, a former Arsenal trainee, had a handful of appearnces at full back when Jeff Barker sustained an injury, but he did not become a regular feature.

Training in the 1951-52 season. George Thompson races the balding Dick Taylor and John Babes.

It was not long into the season, when the Club made the shock announcement that Leslie Jones was parting company with Scunthorpe United. He had taken exception to some criticisms, and he thought his authority had been undermined. His record was a sound one and stood up to scrutiny, but his resignation was accepted with regret, and a successor was to be sought in the fullness of time. The board was not in a hurry to find the new manger immediately, and left trainer Bill Corkhill, a softly spoken Irishman, who played last at Notts County, in charge. It was a smooth transition, but resignation followed on the board. Alex Moore a former player, and now a headmaster, took over as the Chairman.

A crowd of 10,315 supporters, standing in shirt sleeves and Summer dresses opened up a roar to greet the players at the first match of the second season in the League, for the visit of Bradford City. There were streams of sweat on the twenty two red faces at the end of an entertaining and fruitful afternoon. Only Horace Cumner's strike separated the teams, but this was enough to make a happy start for the Iron. During the next ten matches the only victory was at the railway town of Darlington, where goals by Cumner Platts and Wallace put United on the right tracks. The management upheaval would not help the situation, but at least some points were harvested from drawn fixtures. One of the notable scores was a 4-1 loss at Lincoln City, who would win the Championship. Never the less, it was not a neighbourly experience savoured by the Scunthorpe followers.

The lean spell of winless games came to an end after three consecutive draws, and was again on distant travels, this time at Wrexham. It was a long trek to make, but the faithful few who visited from Lincolnshire were rewarded when Scunthorpe hit form and won 2-1. The toast of the trip was Ray Powell, who sank his Countrymen with both of the goals in the second half, and the last minute Wrexham strike arrived too late to make an impact.

The Iron team that beat Wrexham 2-1 on October 6th 1951. On the back row are Jeff Barker, Len Sharpe, Dick Taylor, George Thompson, Jack Brownsword, and Bill Allen. The front row includes Jack Hubbard, George Gray, Horace Cumner, Ray Powell, George Wallace and Jimmy Rudd.

The annual pilgrimage in the F.A.Cup began at the First Round, with a visit from the lyrically sounding Billingham Synthonia Recreation. They were an amateur team from the North East of the land, not too far from Newcastle. At kick-off a lot of Geordie accents could be heard exchanging pleasantries with the locals in the 9,861 crowd, and the visiting team turned out to be a set of hard grafters. From the point of view of a contest, it was done and dusted by the half time Oxo drink. The Iron led 3-0 through strikes by Jack Hubbard, George Wallace, and Ray Powell, and that is how it remained at through the rest of the match.

The Second Round of the Cup was a little special for Scunthorpe United and all the supporters, because they had drawn Millwall of the Third Division South. This was the first time that Scunthorpe had ever played in London, and many of the population had never set foot in the Capital before. The pundits gave the Iron no chance what so ever, expressing the view that Northern Third Division teams were not as strong as those in the South.

On the afternoon of the game, a crowd of 22,702 was noticeable for a blend of Lincolnshire accent mingling with Cockney ones, which made an interesting mix. This attendance was the biggest that had watched any Scunthorpe United match.

It was a day for defenders to win the argument, and George Thompson had a field day. Through the whole of the ninety minutes each side fought hammer and tongs. Scunthorpe had an anxious time when Harold Mosby had to leave the field after a bang on the head, and the Iron played with backs to the wall. They held on to a goalless draw, but Mosby collapsed after the game and was detained in hospital with concussion.

Despite the injury, Mosby was back in the team, which remained unchanged for the replay, on the following Thursday. The prize for the winners was a tantalizing draw, at home to Tottenham Hotspur. This had the Old Show Ground packed with 13,580 supporters on station, and they were to see United at their best. Both teams took time to settle to the pace, but after the initial blocking of punches, it was Scunthorpe United who dictated the play. It was not until eight minutes from the break that Scunthorpe seized the lead. Millwall were slow to clear a ball from a crowded goal mouth, and it was gathered by Cumner, who lobbed to Jimmy Rudd to hook it into the net. Great efforts were made by the Lions to equalise and they certainly had their moments. The game was taken away from the Londoners ten minutes from time by the £2,000 man, Ray Powell, who flashed home a perfect pass from Mosby on the right wing. The same combination produced a third goal, headed by Powel, two minutes from the end.

The noise bellowing from the Old Show Ground could be heard all over the town, and most of the district had noted all three cheers go up. Ray Powell took all the back slaps for two strikes, but it could not have been possible without the team effort, where Len Sharpe had played like a veteran. Of all the players on the park, Jack Hubbard was said to have covered every blade of grass on the pitch.

Scunthorpe United had a Third Division programme to consider before they could think abut the Third Round against Tottenham, and they began two days after beating Millwall with another confident performance over Hartlepools United, winning 2-0. This was the beginning of the holiday period, which gave them two fixtures against Grimsby Town. Each contest was to end in defeat, but it just went to show how fortunes had changed. In 1947 United played the Mariners Reserves on Christmas Day, while the Grimsby Town first team had a goalless draw in the First Division, with Chelsea. At Scunthorpe, a record League attendance of 15,734 spectators saw an entertaining battle. United continued the journey with loss at Oldham, but a double secured with Darlington.

On January 12th 1952, Scunthorpe United line up in their smart claret and blue colours to meet Tottenham Hotspur, the First Division Champions of 1951. The Old Show Ground was never to see such times, and the record crowd was shot to pieces, as 22,652 spectators made an unbelievable sea of faces. St. John's Ambulance men had a lot of fainting cases to deal with, and young children were passed over heads of adults to the front to secure a better view. The favours of navy and white were much in evidence on coats of the visiting supporters, as Scunthorpe United lied up: Thompson; Barker and Brownsword, Hubbard, Taylor, and Sharpe; Mosby, Hall, Powell, Rudd and Cumner.

The game was to see Scunthorpe United try to play a cultured brand of football, and match the aristocrats, which was possibly their undoing.

Dick Taylor beats the Millwall inside right, Constantine, to the ball in the F.A.Cup Second Round replay at the Old Show Ground, on December 20th 1951.

Tottenham half expected to be pushed off their game by some rough tactics from a lesser side. This was to give Spurs more space, which the London side, packed with Internationals, put to good use. Attacking the Fox Street end, Spurs took a seventh minute lead through Duquemin, and generally held the upper hand for the rest of the half. The second half brought another goal after fifty four minutes for the same player, who slid the ball past Thompson. All this time the Iron were running at full speed, but not getting any reward. The third and final goal arrived fifteen minutes from time, when Bailey shot under George Thompson, who was unsighted. This performance prompted the newspaper to say it was hard luck Scunthorpe, but well played.

The Tottenham game does still survive as a black and white film, lasting less than a minute as a news item. Although United had been eliminated, the bank balance did prosper from the adventure. At the end of it all the board approached Bill Corkhill to offer him the job of Scunthorpe United Manager full time. He took a puff on his pipe and quietly asked where he was required to sign.

It was after the Cup tie that Dick White was used as a centre half during a long absence of Dick Taylor through injury. Another signing took place, following a 5-1 defeat at Southport, orchestrated by Jimmy Whitfield. It may have been that Whitfield was home sick and asked the question in a quite corridor, but a couple of weeks later he was re-signed by Bill Corkhill, and came back to play in claret and blue.

Two weeks later and Corkhill picked up a big bustling centre forward from Mansfield Town, called Sid Ottewell, who a similar sort of contender as Ted Gorin. Ironically, Ottewell scored his first Scunthorpe goal at the Old Show Ground, against his former employers. This was when the Iron beat the Stags 4-1, towards the end of March. The rest of the goals came from Mosby Cumner and Rudd.

The Iron finished the season on an unbeaten run of four draws and a couple of wins. This put the team on the same number of points as last season, but two places worse off, in fourteenth position. At home, the Old Show Ground was still a fortress, and only Grimsby Town and Lincoln City managed to penetrate its defences, to steal the points, and these were the only two teams to plunder doubles. Ray Powell was the leading marksman for the year, with seventeen goals, three more than Horace Cumner. In the short space of time Sid Ottewell had eight, from an impressive fourteen appearances. Although the average League crowd was down, this was more than compensated for by Cup attendances.

1952-53

The business conducted late in the day of last season did not stop some activities taking place during the Summer of 1952. Sammy Cox was offered terms as a right full back to run with Jack Brownsword, but after a few games it was realised that there was no parallel to Jack Hubbard. During the year Jack Brownsword missed three games, which ended a sequence of one hundred and thirteen consecutive appearances, in December. The short absence was filled by a tall player, named Eddie Lockwood.

In the mid-field engine room, Bill Allen left the Club, and was replaced by Andy McGill, a very capable customer at right half, from Bradford City. Andy was to feature in this belt of the park for four solid years of dependable service. At centre half a fully fit Dick Taylor was still king of the castle, but there were still to be found chances for Dick White and Len Sharpe. The problem these two lads had was their National Service, where her majesty came first, and they could not always get leave. When Taylor was fit, Bill Corkhill found another task for young White as a centre forward, and this had its successes.

Bill Corkhill also took another glance at his options in the forward line. He had spotted a tall Yorkshire man, called Jack Haigh, who was playing at inside forward for the Liverpool second team, but had played an odd time in the First Division. Jack had an awkward style, which caused a nightmare for defenders, and he was to prove to be an extremely shrewd signing. Jack was to appear in the Scunthorpe United colours more than three hundred times and score more than seventy goals. Figures like these soon made him a crowd favourite, as he switched from Anfield to the Old Show Ground. Another Summer signing was Alan Daley, who was a winger that was able to fit either side of the field.

This tricky young player had been noticed in a Midland League match whilst at Boston United. The centre forward position was never satisfactorily solved. Les Mynard arrived from Derby County, but was not totally the ideal candidate. Next Les Broadley had a go, but the former Goole Town man had his short comings, and Sid Ottewell had a run. The position was then offered to Jimmy Whitfield, who possessed a terrific shot and performed slightly better. The forwards would be supplemented by continued service of Horace Cumner, and Harold Mosby.

Scunthorpe United did not get off to the best of starts to the fixtures, and could only glean one point from a 2-2 home draw with Stockport County in the first four outings. This was not a suggestion of anything alarming in store, only a slow beginning. Two of the matches were against the highly rated neighbour, down the road at Grimsby. The Mariners won all four points over two games, watched by more than forty thousand spectators, including a record League crowd of 18,974, at the Old Show Ground.

The corner was turned when Rochdale turned up for the seventh fixture, halfway through September. Jubilant Scunthorpe United fans clapped and cheered as the team went nap, and goals came from McGill, Mynard, Whitfield, Mosby and Haigh. United won the day 5-1, but the problem was not entirely solved. To alter the engine room, Bill Corkhill went to his reserve strength and gave a try to a slightly built Yorkshire lad called Alan Bushby. He fitted into the left half position like a hand in a glove, propelling the forwards on. After his inclusion in the team, at the end of September, he gave Corkhill the confidence to include him every week. Scunthorpe United drew on his debut against Gateshead and then went seven further games unbeaten, six of which ended in victories.

It was during this run that Scunthorpe enthusiasts had to wish farewell to their brilliant goalkeeper George Thompson. Each week a gaggle of scouts had noted his skill and improvement. Preston North End came in with a bid for him, and the board did not want to hinder his progress in the First Division. George would cope with all the obstacles to his football life in the fast lane, and the highlight of his career was to play at Wembley for the Lily Whites in the F.A.Cup Final, when they lost to West Bromwich Albion. The effects of losing such a class player was cushioned, because waiting in the wings was a capable deputy in Norman Malan.

It is probable that the most outstanding match during this unbeaten sprint was the visit of Accrington Stanley, early in November. Scunthorpe supporters had plenty to cheer, in an action packed match. The Iron won the thriller reasonably easily, by 5-2, but the prominent feature was that of Dick White, who stood in at centre forward, whilst home on leave during his National Service, and scored twice. Two other goals came from right winger Alan Daley, and another from the penalty spot from Jack Brownsword, who inherited the regular job of penalty taker for the first time this campaign. It was in converting penalty kicks that Jack would set a goal scoring record for a full back.

The time of year soon was upon the team for the usual antics in the F.A.Cup, and the luck of the draw was to see them at home to Carlisle from the far North West frontier.

It was to be the tightest of contests, against a team placed higher than they were in the Northern Division. Success did not happen until the seventy four minute, when Jimmy Whitfield met Alan Daley's cross, with the Carlisle keeper unsighted. The reward for the 1-0 win was a second trip to Hereford, where they lost in 1950. This time the heroics of Norman Malan in goal earned a replay from a goalless stalemate.

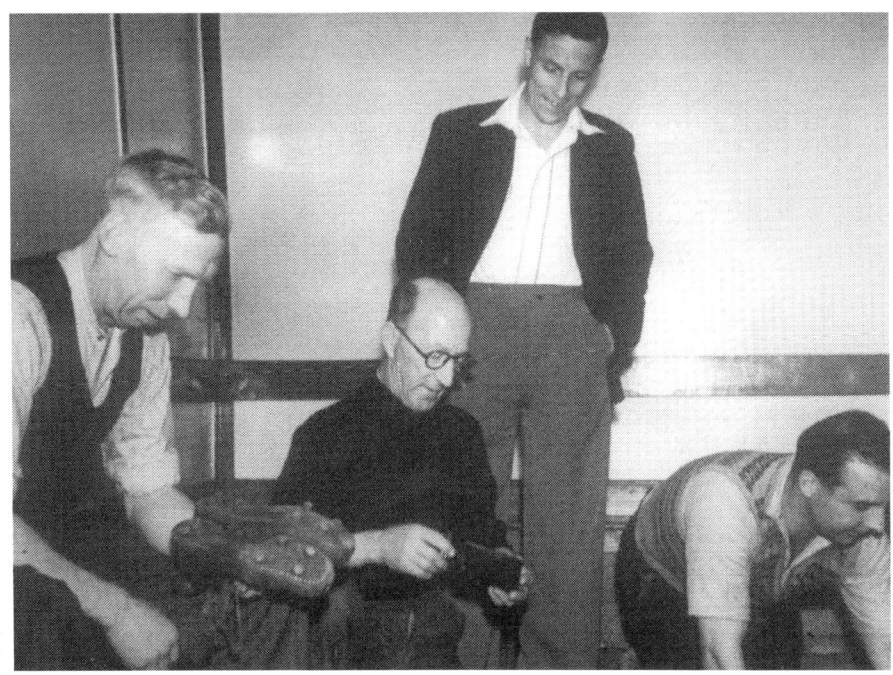

Time for inspections in 1952-53. From the left; Manager Bill Corkhill, Masseur Charlie Johnson, Jack Brownsword, and a member of the ground staff.

The replay was given a Thursday afternoon schedule. A crowd of 10,631 managed to make suitable excuses from work. Scunthorpe realised a break through would give them command, and it came on two minutes. The ball was crossed into the middle, and the Hereford keeper dropped it, whilst challenged by Dick White. As it dropped White was able to put a foot through it and crash it into the net. At half time a rejuvenated Hereford stole an equaliser, but League fitness eventually told over the non-Leaguers. Eight minutes from time, jimmy Whitfield took the ball out to the right of the posts, followed by three defenders. As they approached he shot the ball into the net from an almost impossible angle.

The carrot dangled before the two teams, as an incentive to win, was the money spinning Third Round tie up in the North East, at Roker Park, to play Sunderland, a team that had yet to be relegated from the First Division. For the moment, that would have to wait until after the New Year celebrations.

The month of December started brightly enough for Scunthorpe United, when a visit to Wrexham not only broke Welsh hearts, but broke their home record. A 3-2 away win was completed by Jack Brownsword's penalty goal. From that point onwards it tended to slide down hill. Barrow stealing a win at the Old Show Ground might have been bad enough, but a record 8-0 loss at Carlisle, on Christmas Day, spoiled the party. If that was not the last straw, a 2-1 reverse at the Old Show Ground on Boxing Day to the Cumbrians certainly was. Pride was not restored until New Year's Day at Southport, when the Iron won 3-2.

On January 10th 1953, Scunthorpe United ran out of the tunnel to find the awesome sight of 56,507 faces, all contributing to a deafening roar, at the huge Roker Park arena. This was the biggest attendance that had ever watch the team, and it was a record that would not be broken for more than fifty years. Bill Corkhill made sure that he fielded his strongest available eleven, which consisted of the following men: Malan; Hubbard and Brownsword; McGill Taylor and Bushby; Mosby, Haigh, Ottewell, Whitfield and Mynard.

Scunthorpe United had experienced the silky skills of the First Division when they met Spurs in 1951, and they knew that they would have to raise the tempo. From an early time in the game it was obvious that Shackleton and Ford would be the danger men in the Sunderland team, but Dick Taylor cut out the balls coming into the box, while Hubbard and Brownsword sprinted time after time to stop the wingers making an impact. Malan in goal was very well shielded, but he dealt with every stray ball shot at him. In the attack Jimmy Whitfield and Jack Haigh made sure that Threadgold in the home goal was tested. The tactics continued to work, and half time saw the goalless state continue.

The Scunthorpe men kept the First Division Internationals at bay, and a replay was looking a possibility, until ten minutes from time, when Sunderland made the break though. The ball found its way to Shackleton, with space to himself in the box. The inside left flicked it to Ford, who just got enough power on his shot to beat the grasp of Norman Malan, and it glided gently into the corner of the net.

This might have tolled the bell for a lesser team, but not Scunthorpe. Urged on by the three thousand strong claret and blue army of supporters, they won a corner with four minutes remaining, through Sid Ottewell's persistence. Les Mynard put over the perfect outswinger towards the penalty spot, which Andy McGill met with his head in story book fashion. It was a truly magnificent equaliser. The Scunthorpe section erupted in joyous salute, and the Iron had a courageous replay.

The epic game made sure that Harry Allcock was fully employed, organising the arrangements for the Thursday replay. He was to oversee the printing of tickets for another bumper crowd of 21,624 expectant supporters, packed up tight to the fence so that players called almost feel their breaths. Les Mynard had received a knock up at Sunderland, and was replaced by Horace Cumner, as the only Scunthorpe change.

The pattern of the game continued much as it had finished on Saturday. The two teams could hardly be separated in terms of class. It was as if two thorough bread racehorses were neck and neck in a classic. The Iron thought that they had a lead when Jimmy Whitfield fired the ball in the net, but a linesman's flag was raised for Harold Mosby, way out on the far side of the pitch, nowhere near the play, for offside. This decision was followed by Sunderland taking the lead before the half time whistle, as Wright side footed the ball into the target.

At the beginning of the second spell the home crowd roared their team on, and the players did their level best to respond. The star of the show was birthday boy Alan Bushby, who was twenty one on the day. He ran himself into the ground and was involved with all of the significant moves of note. The Scunthorpe equaliser came from his free-kick, which Alan Daley headed home. A delirious packed house gave thunderous applause, and shouted for the winner. Unfortunately, when it arrived it was not the gallant Third Division men who would get it.

A moment of training in the 1952-53 season. Harold Mosby gets in front of Dick White, with Dick Taylor to the right.

Trevor Ford had received an injury, and spent the time out on the wing as a passenger. Ten minutes from the end the ball broke clear, after some concerted Scunthorpe attacking pressure. It ran loose on the edge of the box to where Ford was waiting. For a moment he forgot his wounds and crashed the leather beyond Norman Malan's dive. It crashed into the net, to seal the match at 2-1. Once again the poor man had the glory but not the prize.

The F.A.Cup had not caused Scunthorpe United to lose any of the edge off the form in the Third Division North. Two days after going out of the Cup, they met Bradford City before an attendance a third as big as against Sunderland. Those loyal supporters who turned out in the cold were rewarded by a competent display, which took both points. Jack Haigh led the charge with a fine goal, then Jimmy Whitfield and Alan Daley made sure that the game was beyond City. To round the result off, Jack scored his second, making the final score 4-0.

In the March of 1953, the board gave Bill Corkhill permission to sign Gordon Brown from Wolverhampton Wanderers. It was another example of the manager's foresight. At first Brown was play as a right winger, and in so doing cracked home four goals. Corkhill reassessed the situation in the months ahead and utilised him as a striker with bewildering results. Gordon Brown was to become one of the goal scoring sensations of the period.

When supporters reached for the Saturday Telegraph football paper on the first Saturday of May, it contained the Third Division North final table. Scunthorpe had achieved the fifteenth rung on the ladder, the worse of the three years in the division, but ironically with two more points than the other two seasons. The F.A.Cup highlight had earned a reasonably thick slice of cash, and some of this could prudently be invested in new players. Above all the board had a good deal of satisfaction at the continuing progress inching the Club forward in the right direction.

1953-54

The closed season of the Summer of 1953 brought speculation as to where the team was going to be strengthened. Bill Corkhill had been back to Anfield for one of his signings, and negotiated for the transfer of a small, but immensely talented versatile winger called Merfyn Jones. Merfyn was lightening fast, and as slippery as an eel. During his time at Liverpool, Merfyn had played four first team games, and was well acquainted with Jack Haigh. They would all be joined by the Cockney tones of inside forward, Jack Gregory, from West Ham United. Jack had two dozen Second Division games under his belt. He was about to set up a goal scoring machine with Jack Haigh and Gordon Brown that would set records, and be the envy of others.

The year would not see the efforts put in by some of the second team players go unrewarded. When Norman Malan was injured, Scunthorpe born Peter Barley deputised with great credit. On the wing or at inside forward there was a run for Harry Roberts. At centre half Lincoln born, but Scunthorpe junior, Brian Heward made his first tentative steps in the senior team, and would develop into a classy performer.

Once the ball started rolling on this latest campaign, it was obvious that the talent on view was superior to all that had gone before. They demonstrated this in the opening gambit, at Blundell Park Grimsby, where previously the team had been pushed about, and lost all points. This time, an attendance of 18,246 watched Scunthorpe match the Mariners in every department, and the home team could not find any advantage. The breaking point was to arrive on seventy seven minutes, when a Jack Haigh centre reached Jack Gregory on the six yard line. It was perfectly placed for him to head well out of the reach of the Grimsby custodian, and sew up the game.

Scunthorpe United continued on the road at Gateshead, on the Monday, and returned with a goalless draw. Five days later, Iron supporters saw the men in claret and blue at home for the first time, and the team did not disappoint. York City came knocking, and probably wished they had not. Scunthorpe dominated the play for long periods but had to wait until the fiftieth minute to open the scoring. Alan Bushby won possession from a melee just outside the box, and fired it past an unsighted keeper.

Two others by Gordon Brown sent the Scunthorpe section of the crowd home happy, with the 3-0 score. The team did not concede its first goal until they played the second game in the series with Gateshead, at home. Gateshead took the initiative, but Jack Brownsword equalised with a penalty kick.

The Iron had played a slick brand of football, and would not taste defeat until the fifth match on the list, at Southport. It was a thrilling, but unrewarding match for the team, who tried their best to recover from a two goal setback, and did not help themselves by losing a goal, at 2-1 down, to a penalty. At one stage they were 4-1 in arrears, but rallied to narrowly lose 4-3. One of the reasons for early successes was the settled nature of the team, but an injury to Jack Gregory brought in Harry Roberts for a month. Then Bill Corkhill was faced with a difficult choice to make, at centre half. His influential central pivot had a rival, and Corkhill had to select the right moment to retire Dick Taylor from first team matters and allow Dick White to take over. The end of September was the time to change the team. Dick would still play in some games, but chiefly went into the reserves and a coaching role, to pass his knowledge on.

The advent of November saw Scunthorpe United involved in a remarkable match at Bradford City. The attendance of 8,039 was not one of the Yorkshire team's biggest of the season, but it was certainly opinionated. They had Scunthorpe heads for the chop, but it took until the fiftieth minute to find a break in Norman Malan's defence. The crowd were announcing the Scunthorpe United team's doom, when in the last thirteen minutes the apple cart was upset. A Sharpe cross was not cleared properly, and found its way to Merfyn Jones, whose ground shot was a goal all the way, for the equaliser.

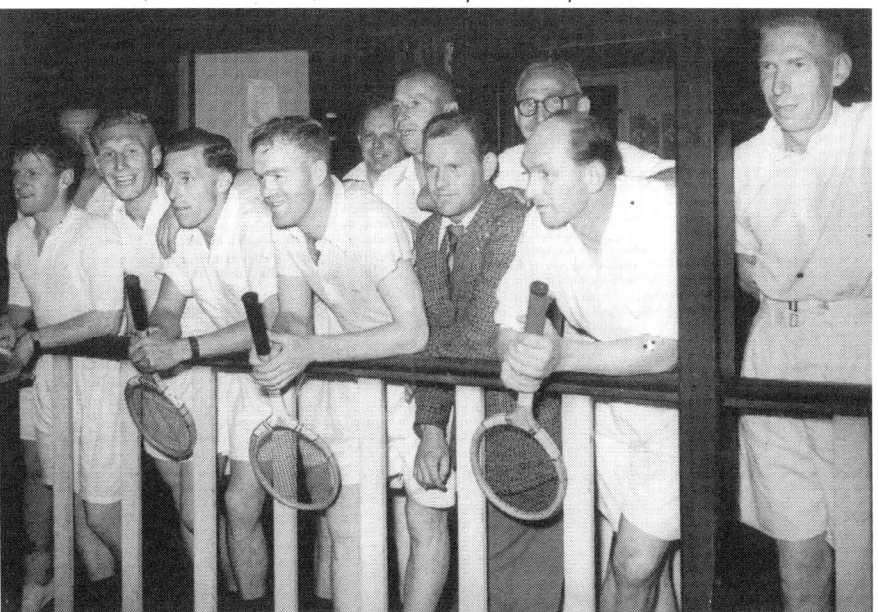

Any one for tennis? A group of players enjoy relaxation away from their chosen sport in 1953, and leaning on the rail include Merfyn Jones, Alan Bushby, Jack Brownsword, Jack Hubbard, Harold Mosby Dick Taylor and Bill Corkhill.

The Scunthorpe United team that beat Halifax Town 3-2 on November 28th 1953. Back row (L-R): Hubbard, Sharpe, Malan, White, Bushby and Brownsword. Front row: Mosby, Haigh, Whitfield, Gregory and Roberts.

Then good work by Jones and Sharpe made an opportunity for Jimmy Whitfield to pinch an unlikely lead. Right upon the final whistle it went messy for City, when Brownsword tucked a penalty away, low and hard, to finish off the score at 3-1. At that moment there were few opinions to be expressed.

November brought the F.A.Cup into everyone's focus, and a visit from Lincolnshire rivals Boston United. Their arrival had older supporters harking back to the days of Midland League football, before the War, when the two clubs met regularly. On this occasion the Iron would not play a neighbourly game, but went all out show how time had widened the gulf between the two clubs. Scunthorpe punished every last mistake, and all but run up a cricket score. At half time they were 4-0 ahead, and stretched it to 9-0 by the final whistle. In the closing stages each forward had his name on the score sheet, except Harold Mosby. The team ethic was put to good use, as the forwards spurned the chance of more goals just to set up Harold. His magic moment brought the biggest cheer in the last minute of the ninety.

Before the Second Round visit of Bournemouth, Scunthorpe United lost 5-1 at Carlisle, which was not good preparation. On the other hand Bournemouth arrived at the Old Show Ground with a clash of colours and had no change of kit. The only solution was for the Iron to borrow the black and white striped shirts of Lysaghts Sports, and when they ran out of the tunnel they could have been mistaken for Grimsby Town. Thankfully, the attendance of 12,005 did not need to rub their eyes to tell the teams apart. They were to be treated to a keen Cup tie, in which Scunthorpe dominated, but were denied by the agility of the visiting goalkeeper, who was credited as man of the match.

The all important division between the two adversaries happened eight minutes before the referee signalled the half-way mark. United supporters were roaring approval as Len Sharpe sent a high ball into the goal mouth to Jimmy Whitfield, who tapped it back for Gordon Brown to hammer home.

This set the team up for an all important League match, on the Saturday before Christmas, with Grimsby Town, but on the morning of the game there was an important distraction. Jack Brownsword had just about enough time for his wedding, at Burton upon Stather church, along with other players and officials. The popular left back had the game of his life, and Scunthorpe beat the Mariners 2-1, in the best clash of the two teams yet. Scunthorpe's goals were both scored in the first half by Whitfield and Gregory. Grimsby then pulled one back, and Jack caught the last bus back to Burton with his bride.

The Third Round of the F.A.Cup took the Iron all the way to the Racecourse Ground, at Wrexham, against a Welsh team that had been beaten in Scunthorpe in the Third Division North. A Cup tie would not take this into account, as both teams set out their battle plans. The match started off in Scunthorpe United's favour and by half time Bushby and Mosby had given United a healthy lead. Wrexham returned to the pitch with the words of the manager ringing in their ears. On seventy minutes the Welshmen had turned the match on its head and led 3-2. Another Alan Bushby goal, with just two minutes on the clock, restored the parity at 3-3, and a replay was ordered.

On the Thursday afternoon the Old Show Ground turnstiles clicked to the tune of 12,862 supporters passing through. Using home soil the task in reaching the Fourth Round for

Scunthorpe took Portsmouth to an F.A.Cup Fourth Round Second Replay in 1953-54, at Highbury in London. Dick White heads the ball off target, while Jack Brownsword guards the line.

the first time was still to be a difficult one. The team was to have a blistering first half. To begin with, Jack Gregory netted a header from an Andy McGill cross, then Jack Brownsword was ice cool from the penalty spot. Right up on half time Jimmy Whitfield scored from an acute angle to make the tie almost safe. The only unfortunate part of the game was an unlucky own goal by Jack Hubbard, but Scunthorpe had made their own F.A.Cup history, by winning 3-1.

The Fourth Round of the F.A.Cup handed Scunthorpe United a marvellous opportunity to make the headlines by pairing them with Portsmouth, who twice had been the First Division Champions in the short time since the War. Snow needed to be cleared from the pitch, at a time of freezing conditions, but at kick-off a record unequalled Scunthorpe home crowd of 23,735 spectators covered every conceivable space within viewing distance of the pitch. Scunthorpe United lined up as follows: Malan; Hubbard and Brownsword; McGill, White and Bushby; Mosby Haigh, Whitfield, Gregory and Jones.

The game was played at tempo in its entirety, and Scunthorpe made sure they matched Portsmouth speed for speed. Portsmouth soon showed that they could take advantage of the smallest opening, and did so in the eleventh minute. The ball ran loose down the Scunthorpe left, hotly chased by Brownsword and Harris. Before Jack could slide it back to Norman Malan, Harris got a foot on it first, to divert it past the Iron keeper and into the net. Portsmouth remained ahead until the fifty sixth minute, when the continuous Scunthorpe pressure told to good effect. Mosby set the ball rolling with a dash on the left, followed by a looping pass into the middle. Merfyn Jones scored the brilliant goal by hitting a cross shot past the Pompey goalkeeper, which set the Iron fans roaring. There was even the question of a second Scunthorpe goal by Jimmy Whitfield, but the referee said the ball did not cross the line before the Pompey keeper clung on to it.

The 1-1 score required a long journey by bus, on the Wednesday, and the snow had reached the South Coast, meaning another clearing operation at Fratton Park. At the kick-off at least two thousand Scunthorpe people were in place in the thirty thousand strong attendance. Scunthorpe began the game facing a strong breeze and made good account of themselves. The opening goal went the way of the home team, minutes before the halfway break. Malan and Brownsword both went to clear the same ball, and it spun away to Henderson, the Portsmouth left wing man. In one movement he was able to guide the ball into the net, for an easy goal. Scunthorpe United would not get back on terms until after they had return from the tunnel. The creator was Andy McGill, who threaded a defence spitting ball through the middle of the park for Merfyn Jones to flash on to, and poke it past the home custodian. It was not altogether a surprise, but it was going to require extra time to sort the tie out.

Portsmouth did not appear to be too thrilled at the prospect of over time, but took the lead again, just into the first half of it. Harris looked to be causing no danger with the ball, until he found the perfect pass to Henderson in space, and the winger shot home has second strike beyond Malan. United appeared to be sunk, but their never say die attitude brought a swell to their chests, as they found another leveller.

Jones was the hero once again, smashing home a shot, that flew into the net off the goalkeeper's arm, from an Alan Bushby pass.

Scunthorpe United's name was blazed across the sports pages of every National newspaper for holding the First Division giants a second time, for the right to take on Bolton Wanderers. The Second Replay was held at the Highbury Ground of the Arsenal, on the Monday, after a 2-2 draw at home to Crewe. This time it was to be a bridge too far, and a tired Scunthorpe United were cut down to size 4-0, in front of twenty four thousand supporters. The dream was over, but the glory was permanent.

When Scunthorpe United returned to the duty of the Northern Section, they were still a force to be reckoned with, although not able to challenge the runaway leaders Port Vale. They did produce and exemplary performance at Vale Park and became one of only seven teams to earn a point at the venue, which remained an unbeaten fortress. The other noteworthy matches came at Easter from a trio of fixtures against Barnsley, who would be the Runners-up in the League, and Halifax Town. Scunthorpe United gave Barnsley a jolly good pasting at the Old Show Ground, with a 6-0 score, on Good Friday. They then took Halifax Town apart 3-0 at the Shay, on the next day, then completed the double at Oakwell, on Easter Monday. It was in this third match that Jack Haigh notched the only goal of the game.

When all the dust had settled on the efforts for the season, it was not too difficult to work out that this team was the best the Club had ever put into the field. They finished third in the Third Division North, and went further in the F.A.Cup than any Scunthorpe team. The Cup attendances made an aggregate of one hundred and thirty thousand, and League attendances were up almost seven hundred per game. Jack Gregory finished the campaign on sixteen goals, and five others all scored eight or more. It just needed a little bit of luck, and Scunthorpe might find themselves at the top of the table next year.

1954-55

The team for the 1954-55 campaign virtually picked itself, and contained little in the way of team changes. Two alterations that were necessary both involved utilising the versatile Jack Hubbard moving out of position, for others to fill in. Alan Bushby was out of commission for two months after the opening game, and Jack played in his left half position. This allowed the tall figure of Harry lamb to take over at right full back. Towards the close of the season Jack played at inside right in place of Jack Haigh, who lost a major slice of the tail end of the campaign. Otherwise it was business as usual.

Although it cannot be confirmed because of lost records, it is believed that during the next twelve months the full title of the Club was officially shortened to just Scunthorpe United.

When Scunthorpe United supporters attended the first match of the season, they were delighted to see that some of the money from the F.A.Cup had been invested at the Doncaster Road end. The whole of the area behind the goal was completely covered and the terrace was suitably sculptured with a new neat concrete blocked floor, a vast improvement in comfort. Another development of United's F.A.Cup run was that the Sunday Pictorial newspaper decided to award a cup to the team that performed the biggest giant killing feat of each season. This was to be known as the Sunday Pictorial Giant Killers Cup.

The new covering provided a complete contrast to the open terrace that had the old gas works as a back drop in the early days of the Midland League. It also acted as a shade in times of sweltering heat, and had brilliant acoustics, as was tested when Jack Haigh scored twice in the 2-2 draw with Halifax Town.

Scunthorpe United supporters were probably more focused on the second match on the calendar, which would see them in devastating form, away at Blundell Park to Grimsby Town. An attendance of 19,736 spectators roared the teams onto the park. Home supporters thought that they would be in for a field day, as the Mariners drew first blood with a goal in twelve minutes. When all of the noise had died down it was Scunthorpe that totally dominated the game, and Andy McGill had them back on level terms with a shot that was assisted with a lunge from a desperate defender. In the second half, goals by Jack Gregory, Gordon Brown and Merfyn Jones destroyed the Town, and the Iron won 4-1.

A visit to York City, on the following Saturday, finished 3-0 to Scunthorpe and Jack Gregory poached a hat-tick. However, it was the return match with the Mariners that was at the front of all supporters minds. The Old Show Ground had little space left for the assembly of 15,547 spectators. Grimsby Town did not contain the skilful men of in previous meetings, and the crowd was incensed by some rough tactics which had Gordon Brown limping. Then a difference of opinion between Jack Gregory and Hughes, his opposite number, resulted in both of them receiving their marching orders from the referee. This did not stop Scunthorpe taking command of a match, that failed to live up to expectations. It was not until the eightieth minute that the best player on view, Merfyn Jones, ran onto the ball and blasted it in the target, for the only goal of the game. Scunthorpe should have had one more, but Jack Brownsword had a spot kick marvellously save by the Grimsby man in green.

At the end of September, Bill Corkhill had only chosen from thirteen players, and it was obvious that this squad of men would be, at the minimum, as good as last year. The team was up with the front runners, which included Accrington, Barnsley and York. At the end of the Autumn Scunthorpe United had recorded a win over each of them.

One of the most productive returns came at the beginning of October, for the visit of the high flying Accrington Stanley, and this attractive fixture added a couple of thousand to the attendance, which at kick-off stood at 11,370. They were soon stamping and cheering on eleven minutes. Andy McGill took a free kick that was not punched clear enough by the keeper, under pressure from Jack Haigh, and the ball whistled into the net by Gordon Brown. Phil Turner scored on his debut, then Jack Haigh made it 3-0 at the break. The final goal did not come until Gordon Brown scored it, a minute from the end, making the result 4-0. Not every game went according to the same plans, and at Hartlepools United the team had misunderstandings in defence which led to a 4-2 defeat.

In November, the F.A.Cup First Round took the Club wandering in the North East to play Horden Colliery. At this time the area was a hot bed of smaller clubs that did particularly well in the various cup competitions, including the defunct Amateur Cup. Horden provided a stiff test for the Scunthorpe professionals, but a goal by Andy McGill on forty nine minutes was sufficient to make sure that there would be no upset, even though the miners kept them on their toes.

The Second Round of the Cup brought back memories of the nineteen thirties, when for the third time the Club received an invitation to play Coventry City, away from home. It was in the mud of Highfield Road that the Scunthorpe challenge became stuck. They lost a goal on the quarters hour, then surrendered three in ten disastrous second half minutes to lose 4-0. They could think more about their aim to win Second Division football, but would still have enjoyed the trip to Huddersfield that went begging. Instead, a hat-trick by Jimmy Whitfield, plus one other from Gordon Brown, cheered up a day in Chester, which finished 4-2.

At the end of March, Scunthorpe experimented with different inside men, from the time they lost Jack Haigh through injury.

The treatment room in 1954. Jack Haigh comes under scrutiny watched by Malan, Taylor, Brownsword, Whitfield, Mosby, Bushby Brown and Jones.

The visit of Hartlepools United brought Jack Hubbard use of the number eight shirt, to see what he might conjure up. Jack was to completely rejuvenate the whole front line and Scunthorpe took the initiative in the twenty third minute. A movement by Gordon Brown and Merfyn Jones allowed a cross to be connected hard and low by Jack Gregory. Then Jack Hubbard took over. He scored Scunthorpe's second before the break, which gave the Iron a platform to work from. In the second phase the Pools reduced this to 2-1, but sheer hard work by Hubbard produced a trio of goals in the last thirteen minutes, thus rounding off a tremendous afternoon at 5-1.

The Hartlepools United game was the beginning of the final rush towards the end of the campaign, during which only a sojourn to high riding Chesterfield, at Saltergate, resulted in the loss of all points. On their travels, the most profitable match brought two points via a second half strike by Gordon Brown, at Gateshead, but the match was a dull one. At home, the 6-1 pummelling of Oldham Athletic was anything but dull, and Brown, Hubbard and Gregory each scored twice.

At the end of all the proceedings, Scunthorpe United's late run raised them to the same place as last year, which was another third position in the table. The points total was one greater, and the average crowd was up fractionally to just short of nine thousand per game. A poor performance in the F.A.Cup was costly, and the revenue massively reduced for this season.

Congratulations had to be offered to Gordon Brown and Jack Gregory, who had a reputation as one of the deadliest strike forces in the Third Division North. Gordon hit twenty three goals, and Jack one less. Both Gordon Brown and Dick White were ever present throughout the whole season, while eight men played forty or more times.

(Left) Bill Corkhill shows Harold Mosby, Andy McGill and Dick Taylor how to fix studs in a football boot in 1954.

(Right) Concentration is etched on the face of Captain Andy McGill, as he is followed by Jack Brownsword (slightly to the right), Harold Mosby and Gordon Brown.

(Below) The Scunthorpe United team that was unchanged in the final three matches of the 1954-55 season: Back Row (from the left), Hubbard, McGill, Malan, White, Bushby, and Brownsword. Front Row: Mosby, Whitfield, Brown, Gregory and Jones.

1955-56

Scunthorpe United only made a handful of signings for the coming season, but the team was to experience far more alteration than Bill Corkhill would have preferred. He started in goal, where Norman Malan was to find pressure from Peter Marshall, a tall brave young man, who made his baptism last term, having signed from Worksop Town. At the end of the year Peter would play almost three times more often than the veteran Norman. A centre half Dick White was the automatic choice, and had grown in stature so much that at the end of October he was signed of a sizable fee of £8,000, by Liverpool, and would eventually captain the Anfield team. The void was to be filled by Brian Heward, not strange to the first team, and having served a thorough apprenticeship in the Midland League second team. The other defensive position would be sorted by Hubbard and Brownsword, but Harry Lamb came back when Hubbard was required in the half back line.

The half backs would remain as McGill and Bushby, but John Barrett and Len Sharpe helped out in times of injury. In the forward line, the main change was on the right wing, which was to be dominated by a fast Portsmouth man, called John Davies. Davies linked up in brilliant fashion with Jack Haigh for the right flank. When he was unavailable, Glasgow born Bobby Callaghan, from Scottish junior football, was a keen performer. The rest of the team was much of the same as twelve months ago.

Scunthorpe United made an uncharacteristic start to the season, by losing the first two matches of the campaign to Bradford Park Avenue and Mansfield Town, both on their travels. Amends were made with maximum returns from the next three matches. The revival began in the first home fixture, against Oldham Athletic, where Bobby Callaghan was praised for a terrific debut for the Iron. He capped it with the opening goal on twenty eight minutes, and Jack Haigh scored the winner, when put through by John Barrett. The final score was 2-1. In the second encounter, with Mansfield, the Stags were not up for the battle at the Old Show Ground, and lost 3-0 in mid-week. A 2-1 victory up in Cumberland over Workington restored all the faith in the team, and the Iron went nine games without being mastered.

The loss of Dick White took the team some adjusting to, at a time of a string of four League matches that ended empty handed. In his final match, United went down at Accrington, followed by more defeats in games at home to Darlington, and others at Gateshead, and Tranmere Rovers.

The pendulum by now had swung round to the time of battles in the F.A.Cup, and duty called for a home visit of yet another team from the North East. This occasion was set for the visit of the miners of Shildon Colliery, a team that had fought hard to get this far. Scunthorpe were surprised by the enterprise of the pitmen, who played with plenty of vim. The teams went into the break goalless, and it took them fifty four minutes before wing man John Davies rifled Scunthorpe into the lead. Once the gun was fired, it went off three times. Other goals were scored by Gordon Brown and Jack Gregory, as fitness began to tell. Scunthorpe had stayed on their feet, stood on the potential banana skin, to win less comfortably than the 3-0 score suggests.

The flavour of meeting teams from the North East continued in Round Two. The Iron had to make their way to meet the famous Cup fighters Bishop Auckland, of the Northern League. Bishop Auckland were no strangers to Wembley having played there on a number of occasions in the Final of the Amateur Cup. The Bishop Auckland ground was effectively three sided, but 13,500 spectators crammed into it to view the match, only five hundred of which travelled from Lincolnshire. It was a typical F.A.Cup tie, played with pace and passion, but the battling Bishops, like the Iron, could not beat the goalkeeper, despite a good number of attempts. The 0-0 score needed more attention at the Old Show Ground five days later, on the Wednesday.

The afternoon of the Cup-tie was ideal for neat football, and for the 9,923 spectators on hand to view it. In the replay, United were strengthened by the return of Gregory for young Parrott, and Davies was preferred to Callaghan. It would make all of the difference, but supporters had to be patient and wait until the last fifteen for the goals. The first came from a header from John Davies, which put a lot of the pressure on the Bishop Auckland side to find an equaliser. It was their undoing, because the visiting keeper quickly rushed out of goal to take a throw in to save time. Unfortunately for him, Jack Hubbard anticipated the ball, and lobbed it into the empty net, and the game was effectively over at 2-0.

Christmas day fell on a Sunday, so United had to make their way to Bradford City on Boxing Day. The Bradford City side were evenly matched with Scunthorpe, comfortably placed, but away from the action at the top of the table, dominated by a resurgent Grimsby Town and Derby County. Each team would make their own contribution to a Christmas cracker. It was a game strewn with action thrills and above all a sack full of goals. Scunthorpe would gain nothing out of the 3-4 loss, except praise from a less opinionated holiday crowd. Scunthorpe had time for revenge twenty four hours later, as Andy McGill had a storming game against his old club. Jack Haigh led the way for the scorers, closely followed by Andy McGill. A 2-0 success was much merited.

The treat of the New Year was the Third Round of the F.A.Cup at Rotherham United, who were a strong Second Division side, capable of beating anyone in their own league.

It was a biting cold day that greeted players and supporters, alike, but it did not stop 16,144 hardy souls passing through the turnstiles, an estimated two thousand of these travelled the thirty odd miles from Scunthorpe. The first half was to be the most frantic, and produced the goals, while after the break both sides settled to play their best football. Scunthorpe shocked the crowd by scoring first, on twenty four minutes. Rotherham gave away a sloppy corner, which Jones dropped at the near post. The Rotherham keeper palmed it, but only to where Gordon Brown was ready to pounce. Brown leapt forward and headed it firmly into the net. Just as folks were contemplating a hot Bovril, Rotherham equalised from another corner, when it fell for Grainger to volley through the busy area, between the posts. Honours were even at 1-1, and had to be tested again on the coming Thursday.

The value of the F.A.Cup trophy brought another huge gate to the Old Show Ground, of 13,362. Snow and ice had to be shovelled from the pitch to make sure of a prompt start, and those at the games would be in for a treat. The players would play on a surface less than perfect for football, but they were roared on by the throats of the excited supporters. Scunthorpe fans were first to cheer a goal, when Merfyn Jones had his shot parried, but Gordon Brown side footed through the rebound. Rotherham United were unshaken but hit back on forty minutes with a driven equaliser, that Peter Marshall was blameless for.

After the players returned from the dressing rooms, United took the game to Rotherham. Ten minutes after the resumption Gordon Brown led the cavalry charge again, lifting a ball out of the mud, high into the target, and out of the way of the hopeful goalkeeper. The crowd went crazy, and shouted for more. Within moments Brown had his hat-trick with another accurate drive, smashed purposefully into the net to make the score 3-1. Rotherham United were anything but dead and buried, and as time ran short, the lead was reduced to 3-2, making sure they were still in with a chance of pulling the game out of the fire. Some anxious times may not have made it easy for the Scunthorpe hearts, but the pain was removed by a very late header into the net from John Davies. Rotherham had now to admit defeat at 4-2, after a noble, but fruitless effort.

Scunthorpe United had a Fourth Round tie to consider, at Second Division Liverpool, but before then they had to concentrate their minds on a visit from highly placed Derby County. They tried to do neighbours Grimsby Town a favour in the title race, but lost the match 2-0.

Before the team travelled to Anfield, Bill Corkhill faced a goalkeeping crisis. His regular keeper Peter Marshall could not move his neck for a boil, and all other choices had broken bones. Prior to travelling he called a summit of his senior staff and had a long hard conversation. He then asked Peter to the treatment room, and told him he wanted him to be brave.

Rotherham born Jack Haigh scored seventy goals for Scunthorpe United from 1952 until 1960, and is ready, on the far right, in case of a slip from the keeper.

A gang of men held Marshall down and a hot needle was taken to the offending area. In the morning Peter Marshall was different again and would play the game of his life.

At Anfield, an assembly of 53,393 was the size of the crowd that gave Liverpool and Scunthorpe the roars of encouragement as they ran onto the field. Liverpool would make sure that the Iron knew they were in for a battle and forced the play. Ironically, it was Scunthorpe who drew the first blood. Jack Gregory picked up a centre from Jack Haigh, and slid the ball delicately under the diving goalkeeper on twenty two minutes, and four thousand visiting supporters went wild.. Billy Liddell shot Liverpool level on the half hour, then Payne, on the right wing, had the team in red 2-1 ahead on fifty four minutes, with a simple tap in, from a headed pass.

Peter Marshall, the Scunthorpe United goalkeeper in 1955-56 season, punches confidently clear.

It was now Scunthorpe United's turn to show their hand. John Davies made and shot the goal, coming in on his own from the right, but hitting it into the net with his left foot, with fifteen minutes to play. Scunthorpe United looked like they might cause a Cup shock, when not more than a minute later, the same player fastened onto a loose ball in the box, and gave it the same punishment. Both sets of supporters were stunned for different reasons, but the Liverpool bacon was saved in the final minute with a second Liddell goal, to make the ninety minute score 3-3.

Tickets were in great demand for the replay, on the coming Thursday, but winter weather caused a postponement until the next Monday. At the time of kick-off 19,612 spectators packed the ground like a filling in a sandwich. Snow had to be cleared from the pitch, and the Old Show Ground was a muddy mess. Liverpool adapted to the conditions far better of the two teams, and were first to find a lead through Liddell. The next major drama was to be a penalty kick to the Iron. Jack Brownsword was the most reliable of spot kick takers, but this time he missed his target, and the groan was heard at his home in Burton.

At half time Bill Corkhill spoke quietly to inspire his troop, telling them to remain tight, and push up when the opportunity presented itself. When they entered the field again they played much smoother football.

It was not long before the patient strategy paid off. Merfyn Jones dashed down the left wing and lifted the sweetest of balls onto the head of John Davies, who planted it where it was well out of reach. At one goal each the game was still open to all comers, but after ninety minutes, extra time was called upon to sort the job out. Liverpool made sure of the prize when Arnell scooped the winning goal in the final phase. For their efforts the tired Scunthorpe lads received a standing ovation from the crowd.

The second half of the year could not compare with that of the first. The team on view was never able to come back to the Third Division North programme and repeat the same progress made by the sides that finished third. They always were an above average eleven, that could match the best. A prime example of this was over the Easter holiday, which had been selected for a pair of fixtures with Grimsby Town, who would shortly be back in the Second Division. Each side won 1-0 in their away game. At the Old Show Ground the attendance was 19,067, which is a figure unparalleled for any Scunthorpe United Football League fixture.

The last foot steps of the season saw the team unable to score any goals, and momentarily sank them just below the half way point in the table. The last two matches, at Halifax Town, 3-0, and Chester, 5-3, brought a rally and raised the team into ninth position in the Third Division North final table.

There would be two very sad farewells to say at the end of the 1955-56 season. Bill Corkhill decided that he could take the Club no further, and he had successfully applied for a similar post at Bradford Park Avenue. Supporters were saddened to hear the news, and the board extended good wishes to him on behalf of everyone at Scunthorpe. Also leaving was dear old Harry Allcock, who had reached retirement age. He would still be round the corner at Theodore Road waiting for match days, and was not really leaving at all.

A CHAMPIONSHIP

1956-57

In the Summer of 1956 the board of directors had the difficult task of finding a successor to the genial Bill Corkhill, a man that would be a considerable act to follow. In the end the directors were all unanimous as to their choice, and he was the former Blackburn and Blackpool full back Ron Suart. Once Suart was in office his job was going to take some time to find the right blend, but although his background was as a defender, his logic was built on attacking football. He was also able to make a recommendation as to a suitable person to fill the post of secretary, and Ray Oates arrived from Blackpool with all the right credentials.

Ron Suart began his team changes by bringing in a big centre forward called Doug Fletcher, the type man that was hard to knock off the ball, from Bury. At first he replaced Jack Gregory, but the partnership of Brown and Gregory was soon to be operating once again. In September George Luke was added to the forward line from Sheffield United, and the changes would necessitate Gordon Brown being used on the wing. Other alterations were made at centre half, where Malcolm Hussey was transferred from Rotherham United, but in the end Suart found that local product Brian Heward was the choice above others.

Scunthorpe United did not fire the Suart era off to the most promising of starts, losing at home to Darlington at the first hurdle. Supporters did not need to be alarmed, because the next three games yielded points, and two of them brought wins at Barrow, and home to Southport. Statistics showed that Gordon Brown had scored in all games, and he continued in September at the first Humberside derby with Hull City. The Tigers had been relegated from Division Two, and 11,004 spectators greeted them out of the Old Show Ground tunnel, in what resulted in a 1-1 draw. This was all part of an eight match unbeaten run, the best result of which was the thrashing of Halifax Town, 6-1. On this occasion, the new men Luke and Fletcher both scored, and the Iron had a purple patch of four goals in a fifteen minute spell.

In November, the gauntlet was thrown down to Rochdale, at the Old Show Ground, in the First Round of the F.A.Cup. It may have had a sleepy first half, but after the first forty five minutes the game woke up. Gordon Brown missed a penalty, which was hotly disputed to have crossed the line. Then the Rochdale right winger was sent off for an incident with Jack Haigh, and finally Gordon Brown fired home the only goal of the game.

The team which lost to Darlington on the opening day of the 1956-57 season. Back row (from the left): Hubbard, McGill, Marshall, Hussey, Bushby and Brownsword. Front row: Whiteside, Haigh, Fletcher, Brown and Jones.

At the Second Round stage the Iron had every chance of dismissing Wrexham at home, despite the absence of Gordon Brown through injury. The Welshmen were all stubborn fighters, and on the day a lack of punch produced a goalless draw. This took the cast of the play to Wrexham for a Tuesday afternoon sort out. Gordon Brown was back to match fitness, and Jack Gregory had the Iron in a commanding position, two goals ahead at half time. Football is an unpredictable game, and not too many punters, at this stage, would have been able to guess the final outcome. First Wrexham drew level, then in extra time they blitzed the Iron with four further goals, and the 6-2 score meant that they would face Reading, and not Scunthorpe United.

Already Scunthorpe United followers knew that this was not going to be a headline season. Back in the Third Division North the results had not been inspiring, and the Iron could be found sailing along in mid-table, against a head wind. They had an attractive pair of Christmas fixtures to look forward to, against Derby County, a club on the way to the Third Division North Championship. At the Baseball Ground, the difference in class was obvious to see, but Ron Suart saw what standard United needed to achieve there own aims. On the day, Scunthorpe could only count the cost of a Christmas Day 4-0 battering. Little changed on Boxing Day, at the Old Show Ground, and another battering was handed out, 4-1. The weather was not in favour of football, but even then a crowd of 4,103 was far lower than was expected for a view of the would be Champions. At least those who did roll up did have an Andy McGill penalty to cheer.

At New Year the new team began to take shape. Terry Charlesworth was given a chance in goal with some success, from local circles. Another local boy was Barry Horstead, who was Brigg born, for the right full back position, when Jack Hubbard became injured toward the end of the season. Barry was to be a huge addition to the back quarters, and was just as happy in the half back line. From the forward line, Jack Gregory said his farewells to move back to the South, nearer his home, to play at Aldershot. His departure paved the way for Scunthorpe to approach Sheffield United for a blond bombshell of a forward, called Ronnie Waldock.

Ken Hardwick, a goalkeeper who already had a Third Division North winners medal when he was signed by Ron Suart from Doncaster Rovers in 1957.

Ronnie had a canon of a shot, possessed an athlete's dash and was no mug with his head. He showed how prolific he was by destroying Chesterfield with his first Scunthorpe hat-trick in February, when Scunthorpe won 5-1.

The inconsistency of results was not to be resolved through the rest of what remained of this campaign. A degree of revenge was eked out over Wrexham, when they rolled up for a League match, and the cagey F.A.Cup game was not repeated. Both teams threw caution to the wind, and a 4-3 thriller blew the cob webs away. This was to be the final victory of a mediocre season, and the last seven matches yielded three loses and four draws. A bright spot was the signing of a vastly experienced goalkeeper, Ken Hardwick from Doncaster Rovers, for the remaining four games before the closed season. Ken had already won two Third Division North Championship medals with the Rovers, and was in a different class. The rest of the year was best to be consigned to history, as Scunthorpe United finished fourteenth in the table.

1957-58

Before Ron Suart could add to his squad, he had the bitter pill of losing one of his aces, Gordon Brown, who was sought by Derby County, now the Rams were of Second Division strength. A little sugar of a £5,000 cheque sweetened the taste, which would be put into further investments. A large percentage of this went for the purchase of local boy Jack Marriott, who departed to Sheffield Wednesday in Midland League days. He had been since transferred to Huddersfield Town, and was the exciting finished article for either wing berth. The rest of the money brought in an experienced mid-field general called Frank Marshall, at right half, from Rotherham United. He would see that the engine room ticked along in fine fashion.

When the team was assembled, Ken Hardwick would have Jack Hubbard and Jack Brownsword as his full backs. In the middle of the park it was to be Frank Marshall, Barry Horstead and Alan Bushby, with support from Len Sharpe and Brian Heward on several occasions. The forward line began as Jack Marriott, Ronnie Waldock, Doug Fletcher, Jack Haigh and Merfyn Jones, with John Davies not too far from the action.

In November, a tall goal scorer called Eric Davis was the last major signing from Plymouth Argyle. Eric might have been a late starter, but he almost caught Ronnie Waldock up as the Club's leading goal ace.

Scunthorpe United started the season in confident style, atSaltergate against Chesterfield. The 1-1 draw saw Jack Marriott score on his return debut, but the gentle beginning did not hint of any of the fireworks that were to come. They stepped up the tempo in mid-week with a second journey, this time to the Prenton Park, on the Wirral peninsular, against Tranmere. They had to put up with the annoyance of the home side taking the lead, but the forwards were able to slip the ball through to allow Ronnie Waldock the opportunity to equalise. The same man raced onto a pass by Merfyn Jones to shoot United ahead, before the first forty five minutes were up. The next goal came after the resumption, when Marriott found Waldock, then Waldock passed to Fletcher, and the big man fired the Iron 3-1 in front. Ten minutes from time the scoring was curtailed as Ronnie Waldock took advantage of a defensive error to finish his hat-trick.

On the following Saturday another emphatic victory took place at the Old Show Ground. Darlington found themselves dismantled by the Scunthorpe attack, and did not help the situation by conceding three goals in a five minute spell. Jack Marriott notched a pair, as did Waldock, while Doug Fletcher completed the rout at 5-0. This team was starting to turn up the heat, and would soon be heading towards the top of the table. Midway through September United touched the summit, when the early leaders, Bury, slipped up. The Iron men were not to taste a first defeat until the final match of that month.

Six Iron men indulge in a game of leap frog in 1957.
From the left, Jack Marriott and Frank Marshall;
Ron Waldock and Eric Davis; and Jack Brownsword and Brian Whitnall.

Len Sharpe keeps his eye on the ball. Len was one of two players that had made Midland League debuts for the Club, and were part of the Third Division North Championship side.

It came when a solid performance by Bradford City took both points, as United lost 2-0 at the Old Show Ground.

In October, Scunthorpe United joined the modern world of football by installing floodlights at the ground, at a cost of £16,000. Each corner of the pitch had a green tower supporting thirty lamps, and they would be a feature of the horizon for thirty years. They were switched on for the match against Rochdale on October 3rd 1957, and Jack Haigh and Albert Stokes became the first goal scorers, as 11,636 spectators turned up for the novelty.

In November, with Scunthorpe United handily placed in the League, it was time to meet Goole Town in the F.A.Cup First Round. The Midland Leaguers would not be an easy nut to crack. Scunthorpe appeared to be on the way to success, when Doug Fletcher forced an opening and shot the ball home.

A number of chances went begging, and after half time Goole Town equalised from the penalty spot. Any thoughts of an embarrassment were abolished when Jack Marriott put the perfect ball into the centre for John Davies to crack into the target, and Goole were sunk 2-1.

The Third Division North was turning out to be a four way fight between Accrington Stanley, Bradford City, Bury and Scunthorpe. The Bury team would be played on consecutive Saturdays at the Show Ground, in the League then the Cup. The Lancastrians were beaten on the first visit, 1-0, by a Waldock goal. Seven days later, the thought of Scunthorpe United and Ronnie Waldock would have sickened them. He scored another goal in the Second Round of the Cup, and the Shakers limped out of the completion, 2-0, thanks to Merfyn Jones being accountable for the other strike.

In the Third Division North, the Scunthorpe machine was purring along nicely. Many of the wins were by an odd goal margin, and slowly but surely the points kept on being added to the total. The Bury League match was the first of a tremendous fifteen match unbeaten run of Third Division fixtures, which was not broken until they took a tumble at Wrexham, in the first match of April, at the Racecourse Ground, 1-0.

The secret of the run was team spirit, work rate, and a determined forward line that could always be guaranteed to cause problems.

The first week of January paired Scunthorpe United in the F.A.Cup with Bradford City, who had already won at the Old Show Ground, so the Yorkshire men arrived full of confidence. At the time, the Winter had its grip, but temperatures hovering just above freezing did not prevent 11,645 spectators braving the cold conditions. The main feature of this important Cup tie was Scunthorpe knocking the ball into the City net on three occasions, but the referee only allowed the one by Jack Haigh to stand. It meant for an uneasy last part of the game, but Barry Horstead, Jack Hubbard and Jack Brownsword had exemplary games, and Ken Hardwick was well protected. The 1-0 result was a reflection of a close encounter, marginally deserving of a Scunthorpe win.

Scunthorpe United were experiencing life in the fast lane, being top of the Third Division table and in the Fourth Round of the F.A.Cup. Accompanying the success were gates of close to ten thousand for each game.

When the F.A.Cup draw was announced it seemed that life would get even faster, because the had been gifted a visit to First Division Newcastle United in the next stage. Every coach was made available, and five trains were fully booked to take an army of 5,000 supporters to St. James' Park. Perhaps the fact that Newcastle United had won the Cup three times in the decade had something to do with it.

At kick-off, conditions could only be described as treacherous, and a postponement avoided by an army of volunteers clearing the pitch of deep snow. To imagine the state of the pitch, think of Ashby Park on a bad day! The match was to be attended by 39,407 hardy souls, stamping their feet to keep the feeling in them. Scunthorpe United selected the following team; Hardwick; Sharpe and Brownsword; Marshall, Horstead and Bushby; Marriott, Waldock, Davis, Haigh, and Jones. Ron Suart had brought in Len Sharpe, when he lost the services of Jack Hubbard, but Len played the game of his life.

Once the first whistle sounded for the start of the game, it was Scunthorpe United's men who were the best to adapt to the terrible conditions. They showed no respect to the International stars of Newcastle United, and the home support was given a scare, when Ronnie Waldock stretched to get the ball in the net but was flagged marginally offside. The fright became a reality.

Left winger Merfyn Jones was a provider of many assists of goals during the 1957-58 season, but this one he he scored himself, thought to be in the F.A.Cup against Bury.

Jack Haigh received a bang on the head and fell limply to the ground, out for a moment. He was concussed and needed several minutes to come round. When the referee invited him to leave the field for a breather he refused. Seconds later United received a corner, and he rose majestically above all others to head United into the lead.

The Scunthorpe travellers went crazy with delight, and it was just the talking point the United crowd wanted. In the privacy of the dressing room Newcastle would not have had the same gentle assessment enjoyed by the Scunthorpe team. They came storming out from the break and set the home supporters alight with an equaliser. At that point in the match most people would have expected them to take command. Instead it was Scunthorpe's turn to shine, and in a similar incident to the first goal, Eric Davis out stripped all challenges to head Scunthorpe in front for the second time. It was difficult to see which team came from which League division, as Newcastle began to play second fiddle. The final nail in the coffin for the Magpies arrived with fifteen minutes left on the clock and was the sole work of Eric Davis. He won the ball close to the half way line, made progress to the middle of the park, tricked past a defender, then composed himself for an unstoppable drive into the net. What a score and what a triumph! Scunthorpe United's gallant battlers were the toast of the F.A.Cup for the 3-1 success.

It was a triumphant army that made its way back home. The Club found out that they would receive Liverpool in the Fifth Round of the competition, who now had Dick White captaining the team. Artic weather disrupted any chances of special training, and all the Iron had to test themselves before the next Cup tie was a visit from Workington, which resulted in an honourable draw, at 2-2. Conditions had improved immeasurably by the time of the kick-off, and a near record crowd officially declared at 23,000 had the stands and terraces creaking. Ron Suart decided in his wisdom to keep an unchanged team.

Eric Davis scores one of his pair of second half goals against Newcastle United in the Fourth Round of the F.A.Cup.

The game was to be like a game of chess, as each side tried to out fox the other. Chances were seen at both ends of the park, but the goals remain intact.

If anything it was Liverpool that ruled the first three quarters of an hour, but after the ten minute break Scunthorpe took control. The game looked as if it might be heading towards an Anfield replay, when the visitors struck in the dying moments. Alan A'Court, out on the left wing, found the perfect cross to Bill Murdock, who let fly low to Ken Hardwick's right, and scored just inside the post. It was too late for Scunthorpe United to come back, and at the end of the game Dick White was the first to lead the congratulations for his old club. For this marvellous Cup run, which knocked out Newcastle, Scunthorpe United received the Sunday pictorial Giant Killers Cup.

Shortly after the Liverpool Cup game Scunthorpe United would be faced with another disaster. On Sunday March 16th 1958 Ron Suart had been working at his desk, when some children rushed in to inform him that the stand on the East side of the Old Show Ground was in flames. The fire brigade was called, but the wooden structure was completely destroyed in minutes. There was no question of any postponements, but problems of where to accommodate season ticket holders caused a headache. Plans were drawn up for the first cantilever stand to be erected at a football ground anywhere the whole of the Country, as a replacement of the ruins. The final parade of matches would have to be viewed from the remaining three sides of the ground.

A packed Old Show Ground for the F.A.Cup Fifth Round tie when Scunthorpe lost 1-0 to Liverpool. Jack Marriott, in the dark shirt, looks for an error from Younger in the visiting goal.

The beginning of April it was noted that had Bury drifted slightly off the challenge of the top spot, but Bradford City and Accrington Stanley were hot on the heels of Scunthorpe United. If the Iron wanted to return to the summit, they must win the games in hand caused by the F.A.Cup sojourn. The busy month started for the Iron with defeat at Wrexham, then consecutive home victories over Hartlepools United, and the return of the Red shirts of Wrexham. What followed immediately afterwards was a journey to North Manchester to play Bury, who still thought they could get back into the frame. On the afternoon little could separate the teams, but Bury showed more accuracy in front of goal, and their two goals out weighed the strike by Jack Haigh.

At this stage of the campaign Scunthorpe United were playing two games each week. Another win arrive at the Old Show Ground to Barrow, but then the alarm bells sounded when two home points were thrown away for the match against York City, and it could have been a fire engine going off when the Iron came a cropper at Stockport County.

This was a time for cool heads, and Ron Suart showed his composure to settle the team. The loss of Ronnie Waldock through injury had contributed to the troubled times, and Suart turned to Albert Minton for the most important game of the season. Scunthorpe United had an away journey to play one of the main rivals, Bradford City. Albert was a big strong man but he had a gentle nature. On the bus trip to Valley Parade, Ron Suart calmed his nerves, and talked him into being the nastiest monster ever to lace up a pair of boots. The ploy worked and dear Albert was the toast of the team, scoring twice, and leading the side to a magnificent 3-2 victory, knocking the main opposition off course. Eric Davis notched the other Scunthorpe goal, and Albert returned to being his genial self.

Only three matches remained and promotion to the Second Division was tantalisingly two points away. Two days later and the team had a date with Chester, at the scarred Old Show Ground.

Champagne is poured by John Davies for Len Sharpe, and Barry Horstead. United had just beaten Carlisle United 3-1 in the final game.

A Third Division North Winners medal of 1957-58.

A crowd of 10,403 roared as the teams filed out of the tunnel, but the script did not go initially according to plan. Chester upset the plot by taking the lead, sinking Scunthorpe hearts. Jack Haigh brought the crowd back to life with the equaliser, but that was not quite enough. It took a goal from Eric Davis five minutes from the final whistle to finish the work off. Playing in all white with claret trim, Eric rushed into the box and stooped low to head home from close range. The Iron had won the match 2-1, and would be crowned Champions of the Third Division North.

Scunthorpe United would be the last team to receive the prize, because from next season the North and South Divisions would be mixed, to become the Third Division and Fourth Division. Now that the weight was off their shoulders, United enjoyed far more freedom in the last two matches. At Hartlepool they took victory through Eric Davis scoring twice, in a 2-1 contest. It was at the last match of the season that Frank Marshall received the Championship trophy, in front of 12,555 appreciative supporters. The game was on May 1st and was a rearranged mid-week finale with Carlisle United. In the Carlisle goal was an old friend, George Thompson. He was first to shake hands with Jack Brownsword, both of these men having played in United's first League fixture.

Scunthorpe United finished with a 3-1 carnival, through strikes by Eric Davis, Jack Haigh, and Jack Brownsword, who placed the ball on the penalty spot, then hit it hard and low, bang in the corner of the goal on the floor. It gave Scunthorpe United a seven point advantage over second placed Accrington Stanley. Twenty nine games had been won, thirteen of which were on the road. Another eight games gave them points from draws, making a total of sixty six points. During the year eighty eight goals had been scored and just fifty conceded. Ronnie Waldock was the leading League scorer with twenty one goals, while Eric Davis managed seventeen. Above anything else, the name of Scunthorpe had been spread through the land by a football team from this Lincolnshire town, who played in claret and blue at the Old Show Ground.

A PINNACLE OF ACHIEVEMENT

1958-59

During the closed season, Scunthorpe United had been rocked with the news that Ron Suart would not be renewing his contract at the Old Show Ground. Instead he was taking up a similar post at Blackpool, the club he had played for. This required the directors to advertise the job, and the man they chose was Tony McShane, who had gained his managerial experience at Chesterfield. The book makers had put odds on Scunthorpe United being in for an automatic relegation, and his job was to make sure it did not happen.

Tony McShane decided that the policy of allowing the promotion sides time to prove themselves would suit most people. He was forced, however, to say his goodbyes to John Davies going to Walsall, and Doug Fletcher off to Darlington. This enabled him to bring in a left winger called Billy Ormond, from Barrow, and injury to Merfyn Jones gave him the first three appearances of the year, but no more. A familiar face for the next twenty years arrived at the Old Show Ground during this Summer, but not for team matters. It was Charlie Strong, who was to act as the Club Physiotherapist.

Scunthorpe United's first Second Division fixture was at home to Ipswich Town, at the Old Show Ground, on August 23rd 1958. Before the game, Commander Wells opened the new 2,500 seated cantilever stand, which also had sheltered standing accommodation for a further 1,000 people, to the applause of 13,317 supporters. They would view a fast open game, with chances for both sides. The first goal was scored by the Suffolk visitors through Tom Garneys, but they would not hold it for too long. Ronnie Waldock knocked a neat ball to Eric Davis, and he drove through the ball, making it sail into the net. The score finished 1-1, and the first point was in the bag.

The next two games were both away from home, at destinations that were previously just places on the road map. It was to be part of a sharp learning curve, and slack defending cost them a hat full of goals. They lost 3-0 at Swansea then 4-0 at Bristol Rovers. It was not until Swansea Town arrive at Scunthorpe that a calmer, and more cultured approach, brought the all important first win. The Swans were packed with Welsh Internationals, but could not cope with the pace of the United attack. They were put on the back foot with strikes from Eric Davis and Ronnie Waldock before half time. Swansea found the net themselves in the second period, but conceded a third goal, when Davis was on target for the second time. A 3-1 win was just deserts for a workman like effort.

The first half of the season was difficult time for the Scunthorpe team to pick up points. It put them in the bottom pocket of the table, but they were not in the relegation two places. Attendances remained higher than before, because of the attractive football on offer and the abundance of stars that the big clubs brought. Even in defeat, the Iron ran off the pitch with their heads held up.

Examples of tough fights in the Autumn that failed to bring in wins included a brilliant 2-2 draw at home to Derby County, which saw the return of Gordon Brown in the County black and white colours. At Stoke the home support was generous in complement, when the Iron lost 4-3, and 17,488 spectators watched Sheffield Wednesday beat United 4-1 at the Old Show Ground, and only had a Jack Brownsword penalty as compensation. A week later the posh Londoners of Fulham had to clap the Scunthorpe efforts for a 1-1 draw, against the team that would finish second to Sheffield Wednesday.

Midway through October, Tony McShane dipped into the transfer market, and signed Peter Neale, a versatile half back or defender, from Old ham Athletic. It was a shrewd piece of business, because Neale was as tough as old boots, but creative with it. He was to make more than two hundred appearances in the Club's colours, and become known for his dyed blond hair. Unfortunately his debut was marred by a 6-1 loss at Middlesbrough, noted for a Brian Clough hat-trick.

Scunthorpe United kept their heads above water with a quartet of 1-0 wins which started at home to Barnsley. It continued at Bristol City and Huddersfield Town, then ended just before Christmas opposite the Baths Hall, for the visit of Cardiff City, after the original fixture was lost to fog. These successes came within the space of seven matches, but was barren of points when Liverpool beat them 2-1, in the same period, at the Old Show Ground.

Christmas threw up the cream of a pair of fixtures against Sunderland, experiencing a first ever season outside the top division. On Boxing Day, United were at home to the men in the red and white stripes, and a bumper holiday crowd of 14,509 spectators wrapped up warm to be present. It was an absolute cracker of a game, and started with Scunthorpe shooting into a two goal lead, through Ashurst slicing the ball into his own net, then Peter 'Noddy' Neale increased it. Sunderland made a fist of it, and in the second half they pulled the score back level. The climax came seven minutes from the end, when the ball came back to Len Sharpe after a free kick had been taken, and he rifled the best goal of his career with his trusty left foot.

Jack Haigh wins a heading duel in the match at Derby County's Baseball Ground in January 1959.

United may have won the day 3-2, but up at Roker Park on the following afternoon, they could not gain the same foot hold. A series of mistakes were all punished severely and only a Peter Neale goal could cheer the few hundred fanatics who made the journey to the North East.

The New Year was started with a point from a less than memorable goalless draw with Bristol Rovers. What was noticeable was the debut of a new Welsh under twenty three goalkeeper, called Ken Jones, signed from Cardiff City. He was soon to succeed Ken Hardwick, who was thirty five years of age. Ken Jones was acrobatic and quite a character, and would be the main stay of the gloves for five years.

All thoughts by this time were fixed on the F.A.Cup Third Round tie, set for January 10th 1959. Scunthorpe United had drawn the Cup holders, Bolton Wanderers, at the Old Show Ground. The gate was more than double the average for the visit of England International centre forward Nat Lofthouse, to 23,706, the second biggest gathering for a football match ever in the town.

The ground was covered by a thin layer of snow, and new lines had to be drawn to mark the pitch. A sea of bright faces followed each movement of the ball, and a haze of cigarette smoke rose from those who had lit up. Scunthorpe put up a brave fight, but were always the second class citizens. Nat Lofthouse showed why he was the England centre forward with two immaculate drives, despite Barry Horstead trying to keep pace with him through ninety minutes of chasing. A 2-0 result handed a tie with Wolves to Bolton, and Scunthorpe could think about staying in the Second Division.

The small amount of cash from the Bolton game allowed Scunthorpe United to do some trading in the transfer market, and they started by bringing in Peter Harburn from Everton. He was a tall awkward player, who had a lot of power in both headers and his shot. This allowed Eric Davis to move away to Chester, and leave room for one more forward to arrive, close to the end of the season. This was a well built inside man or centre forward called Peter Donnelly, from not far down the road at Doncaster. Like Harburn, Donnelly knew where the goal posts were.

Scunthorpe felt no immediate benefits from these alterations and actually lost six consecutive matches, before a change in fortune. The tide began to turn in Yorkshire, by the coal heaps of Barnsley, at Oakwell. It was here that United narrowly stole the points, 1-0, through a Harburn winner.

This was to put a stake through the Barnsley heart, because defeat was to keep them anchored at the bottom of the pile.

The Easter holidays were now upon the team, and they added another point on Good Friday at Lincoln City, who were not out of the mire themselves. A crowd of 14,679 packed the terraces around Sincil Bank, and in the milder conditions a 3-3 battle gave everyone cause to celebrate. Although United lost 3-1 at Sheffield United on the following afternoon, they welcomed the Imps to the Old Show Ground for a game under lights, on Easter Monday. Scunthorpe United had hinted at changing their kit, and played in an unusual blue strip. The initial drama was an injury to Ken Jones, and as he laid on the floor senseless, Jack Brownsword palmed a shot away from a certain goal on target. It took Jones some time to come round, and had no chance with the spot kick. In the second half Scunthorpe United got into full stride, and pummelled City with three goals. Peter Donnelly scored twice and Peter Harburn one, in the 3-1 triumph.

On the following Saturday Scunthorpe United secured their first ever win in London, when they beat Charlton Athletic 3-2, in the massive sixty thousand capacity bowl of the Valley. The Iron were almost safe from relegation, as Grimsby Town looked to have taken the sticky end of the spoon, with Barnsley also virtually doomed. At home to Bristol City, Scunthorpe United took a further point from a 3-3 draw. The talking point of the game was a three times taken penalty kick by Scunthorpe, at the Fox Street end of the ground. Jack Brownsword missed twice, but each time the keeper moved, so the rules at the time meant a retake. Eventually Jack was retired and Peter Donnelly scored.

Scunthorpe made sure of sufficient points with victory at Ninian Park Cardiff, when a top dollar performance beat the Bluebirds on their own patch, 2-0. In mid-week Scunthorpe United lost 3-0 at Anfield, to Liverpool. This was to be the last match for the Club with Tony McShane in charge. He had given notice to leave the Old Show Ground and take up a post outside the game. The board of directors received a number of applications, and selected Bill Lambton, the Grimsby Town trainer to succeed.

Scunthorpe United played the final game at home to Huddersfield Town, on a very wet day on April 25th 1959. Bill Shankley was in charge at Leeds Road, and had with him his Scottish scoring sensation, Denis Law, who was only eighteen. Denis scored two cheeky goals, and Town won 3-0.

A rare photograph of Scunthorpe United during the tour in France in 1959.

It was Bill Lambton's only game in charge, because after three days he resigned and went back to Grimsby.

During the Summer, the board went through the whole process again, and this time they selected the former Stoke City and England War time International half back Frank Soo. Frank had a Chinese father and a English mother, and was to be a wiser choice for the post. The end of Summer would give him the opportunity to prove himself worthy of football management.

1959-60

Scunthorpe supporters had two new innovations for the coming year, the first of which was a change of colours. It was said that the claret and blue kit did not stand out as well under floodlights, and was replaced with white shirts, blue shorts and old gold facings. On the ground the second improvement was at the Fox Street end, where the half cover at the back of the terrace was removed, and the whole area covered.

The closed season brought a gradual break up of the promotion squad, which started in goal, with Ken Jones being preferred to Ken Hardwick. At right full back Jack Hubbard decided it was time to retire and spend time coaching the junior team. Frank Marshall was transferred to finish his career down the A18 at Doncaster, while Merfyn Jones still had sufficient petrol in the tank for a finale at Crewe.

The right full back partner to Jack Brownsword was to be Dennis John, a dark haired stocky lad with lots of speed, from Swansea Town. He had a golden voice to go with his football, and became a recording artist in South Africa when he retired. Martin Bakes joined him as was a slightly built young fellow from Bradford City, who was a good crosser of the ball for the left wing, and would adapt well to the Second Division. Martin was to remain in the area and become a respected school master.

Scunthorpe United would start the campaign in 1959, mirroring what they did the year before. An opening day draw with Bristol City was earned by a Brownsword penalty. Two nasty defeats came on the road at Plymouth and Huddersfield, before Plymouth were sunk by a blaze of guns by Len Sharpe and Jack Haigh, 2-0, in mid-week. Jack scored another goal at Rotherham to win another point, but defeats lost any reward from a trip to Liverpool and the visit of Cardiff City, who turned out to be the promotion dark horses.

The calendar next opened up on an attractive home match with the not so mighty Liverpool. A crowd of 11,822 greeted the teams onto the pitch, and watched a highly entertaining 1-1 draw. Peter Donnelly scored for the Iron and every citizen of the town present cheered the goal. When Jimmy Melia scored for Liverpool every voice of the roar had a Liverpudlian accent. At the end of the game all of the Liverpool supports left the ground to head back to the North West. It had been a number of years since Second Division Liverpool had won a trophy!

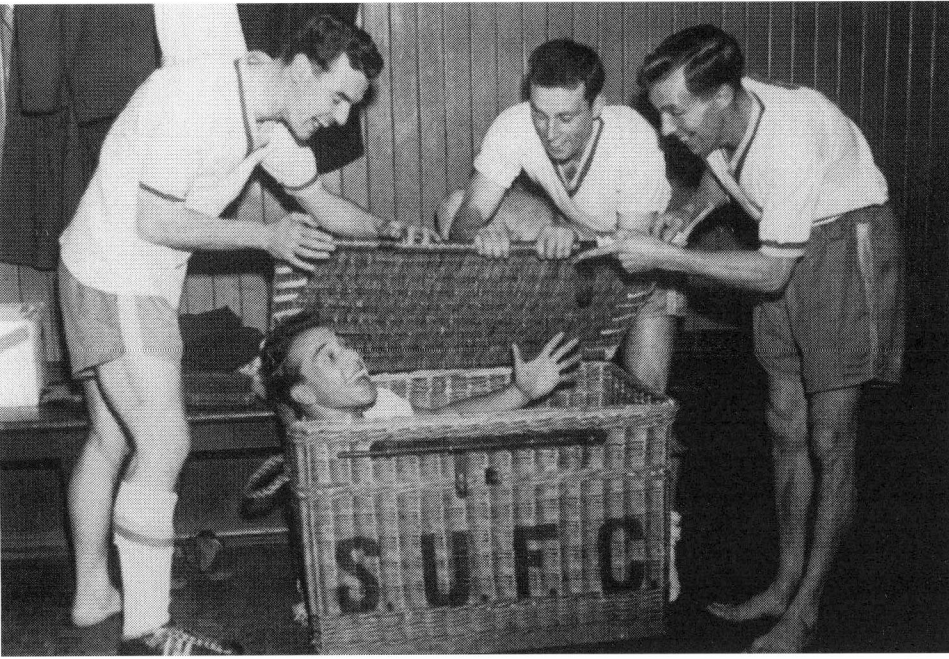

Barry Thomas is caught in the kit basket by Peter Donnelly, Dennis John and Jack Brownsword in the Villa Park dressing on November 28th 1959.

In September and October another round of changes took place. Ronnie Waldock packed his bags and left for a short stay at Plymouth, then went on to Middlesbrough. Then Peter Harburn decided on a transfer to Workington.

Coming into the Club as a forward replacement, Frank Soo had discovered a man who would change the furniture significantly. He was Barry Thomas, a former Leicester City player, taken from Mansfield Town for a fee. Barry was a stocky player with fast muscular legs, and a barrel chest. In the next two and a half years the name of Barry Thomas would be on everybody's lips for his sensational goal scoring. He arrived about the same time as a tall centre forward named Harry Middleton, who had been playing at Wolverhampton Wanderers, and would link up with Thomas. Another welcomed face was that of the old captain, Jeff Barker, who was taking up a post as the first team trainer.

Barry Thomas made his debut in an absorbing 1-1 draw, at home to Sheffield United, attended by 15,384 spectators. They saw the Iron earn a point, when Jack Marriott equalised a Blades lead, all within the first thirty minutes. A fortnight later the Middleton-Thomas combination first got together for a visit from Ipswich Town. Harry Middleton made a dream debut by scoring a minute into his debut, fed by a ball from Peter Donnelly. Scunthorpe held the lead up until half time, but were hampered by an injury to Barry Thomas, who remained up front for all but five minutes, as a passenger, giving nuisance value only.

Ipswich took advantage against ten effective men, and turn the deficit into a 2-1 lead. In the very last minute Barry Thomas over came his pain to score and equalise at 2-2.

Barry Thomas was out for five matches, but the team won twice and drew a couple without him. His comeback was at the Old Show Ground, for the tour by Sunderland. Thomas scored a late goal on his return to activity, but a brace of goals from Peter Donnelly gave the former Doncaster man the deserved headlines, in the 3-1 victory. Ever since the Ipswich match, Frank Soo had given Ivor Williams a run from of the second team, and he had shown no sign of nerves. In the next match, the Iron had to pay their first call at the massive sixty thousand capacity Villa Park. The Aston Villa versus Scunthorpe game was to feature on the 'Match of the Day' football programme, later that evening. What it did not convey was a hand injury to young Williams, who was hampered throughout long periods of the contest. This was a major contribution to the 5-0 loss and Ivor returned to the second team after his recovery. In retirement from the game, Ivor Williams has stood for years on the terraces as a loyal supporter.

The irony of the setback at Villa Park was it gave the team a lot of resolve, and the players bounced back one week later, to inflict a crushing 5-0 defeat on Lincoln City, in the local derby. Bakes scored on two minutes, Thomas on five, and Middleton had them in the driving seat on thirty three minutes at 3-0. The punishment continued with a Brownsword penalty seven minutes from the restart, and Middleton completed the rout with six minutes on the clock. Ken Jones was in green and kept a clean pair of gloves.

On the second Saturday of the New Year Scunthorpe United's men faced a challenge from Fourth Division Crystal Palace, in the Third Round of the F.A.Cup. Palace put up a great fight with a workman like performance, but Heward was excellent in the Iron defence, and Haigh was creative in attack. Harry Middleton flicked the ball into the net, from a near post position, when put through by Peter Donnelly, and Scunthorpe had it sealed at 1-0. The Fourth Round of the competition was to be kind, from the travelling point of view, and Third Division Port Vale came up from the Midlands. The team in amber and black stripes raced up the field in the second minute for their first attack, and slid the ball past Ken Jones, in the Scunthorpe goal. During the next eighty eight minutes the Iron went all out on attack, but could not break the Vale door down, and United lost 1-0.

Scunthorpe United earned a creditable 1-1 draw at Leyton Orient on December 12th 1959. In the white shirts, from the left, are Brian Heward, Jack Haigh, Dennis John, partly hidden and Len Sharpe.

The calendar was now turned over to show the picture for February, and the view of the Old Show Ground was much more secure than a year ago, although work still had to be done to avoid relegation. The attack of Haigh, Donnelly, Thomas and Middleton made the difference, and goals were never too far away. The month was to open at home to Hull City, who had one foot in the bottom two positions, following promotion in 1959. At kick-off the crowd of 10,885 spectators had less visitors than would have been expected from the mighty Tigers. Those that did travel would have to marvel at the efficiency of the Scunthorpe team, who gave nothing away, but fired three live shells into the Hull net. Goals by Harry Middleton and Peter Donnelly had the Scunthorpe dressing room warm at the interval, and Barry Thomas sunk City out of trace, in the second forty five. Further embarrassment was caused by a penalty kick being saved by Ken Jones, as United won 3-0.

A feature of the back end of the season was the introduction to first team football of some up and coming youngsters, and Frank Soo was not afraid to give them the reins. At the end of March, Bob Pashley came into the team and scored on his debut, at the Victoria Ground, against Stoke City.

It constituted one of the best performances on record that year, and other goals by the two wing men, Jack Marriott and Martin Bakes, rounded off an impressive 3-1 win. Tom Passmoor and Tony Needham were also given a chance in the defence. There was time for just one last appearance, in an emergency, for Jack Hubbard. He played in the right half berth, at Lincoln City during the penultimate game.

Scunthorpe United finished the 1959-60 season on fifteenth position in the Second Division League table, with three more points than last year on thirty six. It might have been more, with a little more application in the last three matches, which yielded no points. Mr Jack Wharton, the Chairman of the board, was highly satisfied with Frank Soo, but was forced to accept his resignation as manager, when he left to take up a position coaching abroad. Mr Wharton was happy to shake Frank's hand and wish him all the best of fortune from everybody at the Old Show Ground.

During the Summer Scunthorpe United received plenty of mail for the post of a new manager. When the short list had been drawn up, and interviews took place, the directors knew the name of the successful applicant. He was the former York City and Darlington boss, Dick Duckworth. He came from a sporting family, and was a pre-War player with a string of clubs, and cut a striking figure with his balding head, and large waist. When the season began he would put his thoughts into practice.

1960-61

Dick Duckworth soon got his brush to work, and transferred two of United's forward players. It was with deep regret that Jack Haigh was allowed to leave the club, and go to Doncaster Rovers, at the town where his family lived. Jack's proud record spoke for itself, with seventy one goals in three hundred and sixty appearances, he had served with distinction. Peter Donnelly had played his last Scunthorpe game, and was to be part of an exchange deal that would take him to Cardiff City, and ship Joe Bonson, another goal scoring forward, to the Old Show Ground. Joe took some settling next to Barry Thomas, but his value was in passing the ammunition, rather than firing it.

The forward line was further fortified by the inclusion of Welshman Brian Godfrey from Everton. This inside forward possessed a Welsh under twenty three cap, and would be a prized asset at inside forward. A another signing was that of Joe Turner, a goalkeeper from Darlington, as cover for Ken Jones. When United lost 4-0 at Rotherham in February Joe was included in the first eleven until the end of the season. The last signature was that of one of the classiest wing halves to ever pull on a Scunthorpe shirt. He was Scotsman Archie Gibson, from Leeds United, who must have possessed considerable talent at the club to let such an artist go. Archie could dribble past opponents in the most dangerous of situations, with not the slightest chance of losing the ball. He made the ideal captain on the field of play.

Scunthorpe United started the season in fine form, suggestion that a comfortable season lay ahead. A draw at Charlton, secured by a Thomas goal, was followed by a crushing 4-0 victory over Ipswich Town, the team that would the Champions.

Another home game yielded a point with Leyton Orient, but a devastating 5-2 thrashing of Derby County, at the Baseball Ground, brought about of the silence of the Rams. Joe Bonson scored his first two Scunthorpe goals, and others followed from Brownsword, Thomas and Godfrey.

In the October of 1960, Scunthorpe embarked upon a new competition, which was born during the season, and was to become a regular first team fixture on the calendar from then on. It was the League Cup, which took them to Rochdale of the Fourth Division. At first the League Cup was met with indifference.

This might account for Scunthorpe United's draw at Rochdale being followed by a 1-0 loss at the Old Show Ground, in the replay.

Scunthorpe United brushed away the League Cup dismissal, and returned to the League as though it was a minor irritation. This team could dish out a punch on the nose against the best of teams, as Portsmouth found out in November. The Portsmouth team led by a goal after four minutes and seemed to be in charge. Then Scunthorpe fired a five goal salvo, to sink their victory, 5-1. Thomas and Godfrey scored two apiece, and Len Sharpe notched the fifth. In the next home game, two weeks later, a similar team spirit gleaned a point from a lost cause, against Sunderland. A generous amount of defending allowed the North Eastern men into a 3-1 lead, but they were denied, with two goals in the final eight minutes, as Scunthorpe rallied. Bonson reduced the deficit, then cool Mr Brownsword scored an eighty ninth minute penalty.

Jack Brownsword was to be the Club's saviour at Christmas, when they trailed at home to Brighton 2-0. This time he went one better, and scored two penalty goals to earn a draw. Another point came on the long haul down to the South Coast when the two sides shared a 1-1 result.

The F.A.Cup was to bring a peach of a Third Round tie, that was to feature Stanley Matthews and a whole host of International, stars in a match at home to Blackpool. It was a game that is a legend with older supporters, who were privileged to watch the contest, in the crowd of 19,303. Scunthorpe United had to contend with the absence of Jack Marriott with a stomach problem, but Harry Middleton filled the gap. On the afternoon of the Cup tie the pitch was in reasonable condition, and the temperature not as cold as it could be. United ran out of the tunnel as following: Jones; John and Brownsword; Gibson, Horstead and Sharpe; Middleton, Godfrey, Thomas, Bonson and Bakes.

This was to be the type of game, written in the pages of a boys comic book for sensation. One of the noticeable features of the match was how Brownsword never gave Matthews an inch, following him over every blade of grass he touched. Joe Bonson put the Iron in front on the fourteenth minute, but by the break Mudie and Charnley had reversed the lead. In the second half, Scunthorpe United were dynamic. Bonson equalised moments after the resumption, and he completed his hat-trick in the sixty ninth minute, and United led by 3-2. Duckworth ordered a change of tactics that brought Barry Thomas into the middle from a wide berth, and a minute later Barry increased the lead. Then he fired two more goals in the remaining ten minutes, to make an unlikely score of 6-2. No wonder it has become a fable.

The Fourth Round produced a second thrilling game, and Norwich City, led by captain Ron Ashman, arrived at the Old Show Ground. Norwich scored first, but Martin Bakes had United level on thirty one minutes, sixty seconds after the opener. Norwich took the lead with a fantastic Punton goal, from the tightest possible angle. In the second half, gift defending allowed the lead to be stretched to 4-1, and United were out of the competition. At least the double over the Canaries in League matches was compensation.

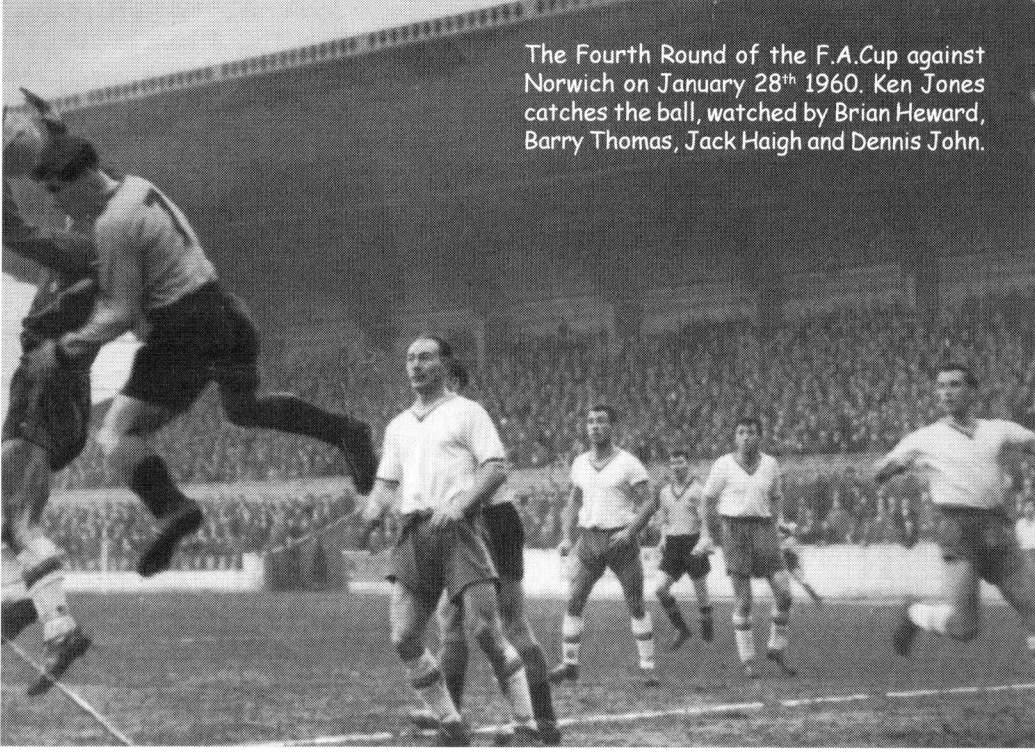

The Fourth Round of the F.A.Cup against Norwich on January 28th 1960. Ken Jones catches the ball, watched by Brian Heward, Barry Thomas, Jack Haigh and Dennis John.

When Scunthorpe United returned to the Second Division fixtures they continued to keep the pace, very comfortably in mid-table, thanks to the leadership of Barry Thomas at the front of the attack. He was one of the fastest men in the division and could out sprint all comers over a short distance. This campaign saw him take the Scunthorpe record for the most goals in a season, with twenty six to his credit. In one game, at home to Sheffield United, the Blades goalkeeper took a quick goal kick. Thomas anticipated the move, pinched the ball and put it into the net. The referee disallowed the goal, unable to believe it had left the area and gone into play. There were 10,873 pairs of eyes that disagreed.

Towards the end of the season Dick Duckworth gave promotion to a number of players to the first team, some of them had appeared odd times before. These included Derek Hemstead and Tony Needham into the defence, Arthur Thorpe for the wing, and a very useful lad called John Kaye at inside forward, from Goole Town. They all had their merits, but young Kaye made the most impression as a goal scorer. The introduction of these younger men did not slow the team down, as perhaps it may have done, twelve months ago. The final five games of the year yielded four draws and a win, which was when Plymouth made the three hundred and forty miles North. The visit to Elland Road was worthy of note, because only 6,975 supporters bothered to turn out, a figure beaten by some of their Midland League crowds, around the time of the Great War.

After Scunthorpe United drew 0-0, in the last fixture of the year, at Luton Town, it left them in the unbelievable position of ninth in the table. Whatever was happening at the Old Show Ground, it had the Club going in the right direction.

1961-62

Transfer activities during the Summer of 1961 saw Harry Middleton depart for Walsall for a small fee. The money was ploughed straight back into team affairs, and. the forward line would not suffer from his loss. On the right wing United took on board Andy Wilson from Sheffield United. Andy had a good turn of speed and the accuracy of passing as a useful weapon in his armoury. More money was invested in the mid-field belt, where Ron Howells came into the engine room, from Portsmouth, to improve its efficiency. This was just as well, because Len Sharpe was to suffer through injury, and little would be seen of the old stalwart. The coming year was also to see the emergence of a small versatile local lad, called Barry Lindsey, who would motivate defence, mid-field and forwards alike, through his hard running.

The puzzling part of this period of time was United's gates. Last year an improved team performance saw a significant down turn through the turnstiles, and the opening game this term only attracted 7,965 spectators for the visit of Brighton. Those who were on the terraces saw a wonderful exhibition of Second Division football, terminated at 3-3. Jack Marriott converted a penalty, in Jack Brownsword's one absence of the season, and others came via Brian Godfrey and Barry Thomas.

In the next four days another point was taken at Norwich, but two Barry Thomas goals should have won the match. Unfortunately, the defence allowed the Canaries back into the match from 0-2 down, and United again showed frailties in defence, losing the next game to Bury 4-1. This was not repeated, at the Old Show Ground, for the second encounter against the Carrow Road men. Norwich City conceded two more goals to Thomas, but this time the defence was water tight, and the victory there to be savoured.

Scunthorpe United began an experiment with Friday evening football at this time, and the fixture against Charlton Athletic was the one that set the ball rolling. The Londoners were beaten 6-1, and never knew what hit them. All of the goals arrived in the first forty five minutes, as Scunthorpe relaxed in the second period. Thomas, Marriott, Thorpe, Brownsword, a trade mark penalty, and a pair of strikes by Brian Godfrey made for continuous thunderous applause from a crowd of 9,639 supporters in the blue white and old gold coloured scarves.

Exactly two weeks later, the floodlight frenzy brought a host of goals in the Rotherham United game. More than eleven thousand supporters watched a seven goal bonanza, which the Iron won 5-2. The pick of the bunch was a thirty yard screamer from Barry Thomas. A free kick was taken by Archie Gibson, directly in front of the goal, and he passed the ball no more than three inches to Thomas. The shot was just a blur.

The arrival of October saw statisticians making a quick tally of goals that Barry Thomas had scored, and it was revealed that the number was eleven. No wonder that the scouts were beginning to notice him. In the last match of September he started a seven game consecutive run, which had him scoring in every encounter, and effectively doubled this total to twenty two. He scored twice in the match against Southampton, noted for the sending off of England International Terry Paine and Ron Howells of Scunthorpe. Barry did the same against Newcastle, and then netted four times, in a 5-1 trouncing of Plymouth Argyle. All of these successes were treats at the Old Show Ground.

It was undeniable that the most memorable match of the year was for the visit of the highly rated Newcastle United, who had slipped from First Division grace. A crowd of 13,988 clapped and cheered the players onto the park, a figure that would not be exceeded all year. This was a night when all the stars shone bright in the sky and at pitch level as well. Newcastle men were swiftly out of their blocks, and had the large contingent of Geordie supporters alight with two good strikes by half time, through Allchuch and Suddick. This was to fire up Scunthorpe for something special in the last forty five.

The Scunthorpe United supporters were the next ones to be on their feet, only minutes after the tea break. Jack Brownsword did his usual with a penalty kick, into the bottom corner of the target. Archie Gibson was having an inspired game as captain, and his pass set John Kaye off at pace, running onto the Newcastle defence. Kaye looked up, passed to Barry Thomas, and in the blink of an eye United had a seventieth minute equaliser. The noise was so great that conversation as impossible, and the volume was to be cranked another notch. Five minutes later Ron Howells had the ball on the left, and sent over a high inviting cross, that Thomas raced off in chase, with the speed of a cheetah. He stretched his neck out at the final second, managing to get enough on the ball to deflect it past Hollins in the Newcastle goal. Scunthorpe were high and dry at 3-2, and Hollins hit out at the goal post in sheer anger.

Scunthorpe United started to rub shoulders with the teams at the summit of the Second Division table. Results put them not too far from teams like Liverpool, Leyton Orient and Sunderland, who would sort out the promotion places at the end of the campaign. At this time the rules allowed just two teams to go up. Scunthorpe United became popular enough to be the feature of the second half live commentary match on B.B.C. radio, when they travelled to the South Coast to play Brighton and Hove Albion. The broadcast started with Scunthorpe United 3-0 ahead, but there was to be no extra scoring, and that would be the concluding result.

Scunthorpe United entered the Christmas holiday in line for a pair of matches against Leeds United. On Boxing Day, Archie Gibson was in his element for the tussle at Elland Road, against his former club. His great game was over shadowed by the performance of Barry Thomas, who gave Jack Charlton, a World Cup Final player to be, the run around. On the day Barry was untouchable, and scored four times during a 4-1 triumph. It was only a pity a frozen pitch postponed the match at the Old Show Ground.

Barry Thomas was on the brink of stardom, and had even been invited to train with the England squad. Speculation was that a big money transfer was not too far away. For the moment, his focus was on the pair of matches United had to face, in the F.A.Cup and the League, at Charlton, immediately into the New Year. The Cup match was to end 1-0 to the home side. One week later a brilliant match produced a high scoring 3-3 draw. In it, Barry Thomas was to score his last Second Division goal for the Iron. During the following week Scunthorpe United hearts were broken with the news that Barry Thomas had been transferred for £40,000 to Newcastle United. To sweeten the pill, Newcastle offered Ken Hodgson at cut price as part of the deal, and John McGuigan might follow, after a week end of thought. This turned into fruition, and although they lost one terrific marksman, they gained two others, plus some considerable amount of cash in exchange.

The legacy of Barry Thomas was indelible, for thirty one goals in twenty four matches, and he would never be forgotten.

The loss of Barry Thomas to Newcastle did not toll the bell on Scunthorpe United's activities with the top clubs in the division. A visit from Liverpool demonstrated that they would continue to perform satisfactorily without him. A goal by Ron Howells aided a 1-1 draw, and once John McGuigan got into his stride, he was to average one in every other game. John Kaye was a player that would take his new opportunity as a goal scorer, and registered in consecutive weeks after the Liverpool draw. This included the only goal at Millmoor, against Rotherham United, and the second Scunthorpe strike in the 3-1 beating of Sunderland on home soil. In the same February month, the Iron beat Don Revie's Leeds United boys 2-0, when the frost hit game could be played.

Scunthorpe United continued to entertain the crowds, even though numbers at home they were still down. At Southampton they took part in a March goal marathon, which saw them on the wrong side of a record aggregate 6-4 score. Another entertaining loss was at Newcastle United, where they suffered 2-1, and Barry Thomas and John McGuigan each hit goals against their old clubs.

At the beginning of April Liverpool had the top spot in the table stitched up, but Scunthorpe had a thin slither of a chance of the second place. They started the final six matches in confident style, by beating Derby County 2-0, then they moved on to Leyton Orient and won with a goal by John Kaye in nine seconds, 1-0. More points were gathered at home to Preston, and away at Huddersfield. If it was not for two defeats in the remaining pair of fixtures, they might have had an improvement, but still would not have caught Leyton Orient. Injuries to key players did not help in the last gasp effort.

The table for 1961-62 declared that Scunthorpe United possessed the fourth best record in the Second Division, and therefore would be classed as the twenty sixth best in the entire Football League. This was the zenith of the Club's sixty three years of existence, and revealed a remarkable transformation from the days of the North Lindsey League. Barry Thomas had produced the perfect platform, but others were now continuing the tradition of this small Lincolnshire club, which had been watched by an average attendance of 9,957 spectators per home League match. It was hoped to see that this tremendous work was repeated in the years ahead.

Barry Thomas, who had a predatory instinct, scored ninety six goals for the Iron, including thirty one in the 1961-62 season.

1962-63

The closed season of 1962 was to be notable for two significant departures. It was sadly learned that the Club had to say farewell to Len Sharpe, after service that stretched back to the last remaining link with the Midland League. He went with everyone's best wishes to fill a similar role in the Hull City mid-field. Later, when his first class career was at an end, Len would be just down the road, managing Ashby Institute, in the Midland League. Leaving with Len, was full back Dennis John, going to London at Millwall.

The right full back position was first filled by Mike Gannon, signed from Everton, having been part of their second eleven. He was succeeded for a while by Derek Hemstead, but then Barry Horstead made the shirt his own property. Later in the season Gannon found use for his services at left half. Most other places in the team remained unchanged from the previous year.

Scunthorpe United got off to a positive start, with a 2-1 victory in the sunshine at a warm Old Show Ground. Ken Hodgson shot the opening goal of the campaign, and a sliced clearance by Tony Knapp, ended in his own net, to assist in a 2-1 victory. The team suffered 3-0 loses in the next two meetings, at Chelsea and Grimsby Town. The temporary stay of Chelsea in Division Two for a year, brought a match which saw Scunthorpe run off their feet, but this was not so at Blundell Park. It was that the Mariners made United pay dearly for defensive errors.

Every dog has his day, and this was certainly the case against the mighty Chelsea, who would be promoted as the second placed team in the division.

On the last Tuesday of August, 10,976 spectators rolled up at the gate to see a memorable match. Scunthorpe United included two youthful faces in the team, Derek Hemstead and Barry Lindsey. Throughout the match not one of the United team could be said to be overawed by the occasion, and it only took nine minutes before Ken Hodgson fed John Kaye, and the former Goole man fired the first salvo into the Chelsea net.

The game was to now take a nasty twist, because Derek Hemstead fell awkwardly on the ground, and when Charlie Strong attended to him it was discovered his collar bone was broken, and precluded him from any further action. Despite the heavy handicap, United continued to match the Londoners stride for stride. Moments before half time John Kaye found more space to launch another missile, and Scunthorpe were 2-0 in front. This lead was to be severely tested after the break, but some resolute defending preserved it. Archie Gibson was the experience in the middle, while Barry Lindsey never stopped running. The day was finally secured in the last ten minutes, when, unbelievably, John Kaye scooped another ball into the net to complete his hat-trick, and United were 3-0 winners.

Scunthorpe United would make a small piece of history at this time. The Chelsea match was the first of five consecutive victories, which also included Bury away, then home games against Newcastle United, Rotherham United and Swansea Town. The Swansea visit was on a Friday evening before the rest of the division played, but for a brief period of eighteen hours, Scunthorpe United sat at the pinnacle of the Second Division.

In the League Cup United had been drawn away to Southampton, but ninety minutes could not separate the teams, and the 1-1 result required a replay. The second match went into extra time, and at 2-2 it still was not resolved. A second replay, at London Road, the home of Peterborough United, was needed before United took a 3-0 advantage. In Round Three, a trip to Sunderland was terminated at 2-0 against them.

The team returned to the duty of Second Division football, and from November went on a nine match unbeaten tour, which included four victories. They enjoyed a draw at Newcastle, which won the first ever point at St James' Park, and another at home to Grimsby Town, thanks to a rare gem from Archie Gibson.

The Grimsby match was at the start of one of the coldest Winters on record, and no further football would be played on the Old Show Ground until March 7th 1963. During the freeze up, United did manage to win at Plymouth, and draw 1-1 at Portsmouth in the F.A.Cup, with a John McGuigan goal. These were two extremes of the Country which could just keep warm enough to play football. The first match the Old Show Ground was fit for purpose was the return Third Round F.A.Cup tie with the Pilgrims, which United had command of, but threw away, losing to a late winner, 2-1. The irony of the fixture card was that Portsmouth were back in North Lindsey for a League match at the weekend, and two days after the Cup tie they had the same score inflicted on them, as Hodgson and Wilson scored goals for Scunthorpe.

The Football League was busy rearranging football fixture for every team and the back log required an extension to the season, which even delayed the F.A.Cup Final. One new date brought Preston North End, freshly relegated from the First Division, to Scunthorpe under the floodlight. Only 7,002 spectators were on hand to see one of the deadliest displays of the year. United had no regard for former status, and ripped the Lily Whites apart with a devastating 4-1 display. John McGuigan was the main architect with two accurate strikes, and others followed by Andy Wilson and Ken Hodgson.

At this time, Derby County found themselves at the wrong end of the table, and had one foot in the relegation grave. It came something of a surprise that a half decent squad like Scunthorpe United should lose 6-2 to such a weakened outfit. Two of the goals were own goals and two scored from penalties. This game was highlighted as part of a Nation wide soccer bribes scandal. Ron Howells was found guilty of fixing the match, and was sent to jail for the shame he brought on his self, Scunthorpe United, and the sport of football.

The season was starting to dwindle away, and Dick Duckworth tried to ring the changes, as United headed towards mid-table safety. Andy Crawford was brought in as a replacement for Jack Marriott, who was at the senior end of his career. Crawford came from West Ham and was able to play at inside forward should he be required. Tom Passmoor found an up grade when Peter Neale was not available. Then in goal, Brian Reeves, a Blackburn Rovers product, was utilised when Ken Jones was injured.

The team changes did not have any adverse effects on the results, and the points came trickling at an acceptable pace. A concern was raised over the size of the gate, which had dropped in one case below six thousand. This was not a figure that would sustain the current level of football. During this elongated part of the fixtures, Scunthorpe produced a top draw performance to beat Stoke City at the Victoria Ground. Stanley Matthews had returned to his old club, and was assisting them to the Second Division Championship.

The television cameras were there to record the events for the Nation, in glorious black and white. Stoke were expected to be hailed the Champions that afternoon, but Scunthorpe spoiled the party. They inflicted only the third home defeat of the season at Stoke, as strikes by McGuigan, Kaye and Hodgson gave a 3-2 victory to the visiting Iron.

The events of the football year were all concluded after Scunthorpe United lost at Rotherham, on May 17th 1963. A final table reflected that United had finished in ninth place in the list of Second Division teams, and had fifty seven goals in the bank. John Kaye emerged as the leading marksman, having netted thirteen times, one more than Ken Hodgson. The average crowd was 8,851, but over the second part of the fixtures was far less. Many stay away supporters pointed to the sale of Barry Thomas as the reason for their absence.

1963-64

Scunthorpe United supporters would discover that during the Summer months, to their dismay, a number of key men had been transferred. The most important of these was the latest leading goalscorer, John Kaye. West Bromwich Albion had been keeping tabs on him, and came in with a bid of £40,000, which the board found difficult to refuse. Two other forwards had played their last games at the Old Show Ground were Brian Godfrey, who was to depart for Preston, and John McGuigan, heading to the South Coast at Southampton. Although further cheques were placed in the bank, it was not the team changes the bulk of the army of Scunthorpe followers wished to see.

Quite a number of new faces would be tried in the various positions, some of which proved to be ineffective. One of the successful Duckworth signings was that of Irish International Ian Lawther, an inside forward from Sunderland, who did add some pep to the front quarter. At the turn of the Christmas holiday, United signed another proven forward from Rotherham United, named Alan Kirkman. He made every effort to induce some ideas to the front end, at a time of pressure. In January Scunthorpe would add David Sloan, from Irish club Bangor, to the ranks. He was to gain Irish under twenty three honours in the coming years, then become a full International at a later date. David was just the type of young, exciting blood the team needed.

During the months ahead, Duckworth tried a number of different forwards in an effort to find any sort of blend. Some men would only play small roles, and each worked hard, but only supplied degrees of partial satisfaction. The list included Keith Ellis, Cliff Mason, Jim Conde, and Andy Smillie. The fact that there was so much rotation spoke volumes as to how successful this section of the team really was. Certainly, the number of stop gap players cost a lot of money, and raised questions as to the wisdom of the original sales.

The start of the 1963-64 season was nothing short of an unmitigated disaster, and the team crashed to five consecutive defeats on the bounce, and nose dived to the depths of the League. The next two games resulted in draws, both at the Old Show Ground, to Sunderland and Swansea Town. The latter game was the first that they actually managed to score two goals in one ninety minute period.

Barry Horstead was a local produced player. Seen here in the match at Stoke City's Victoria Ground. United caused an upset by beating the Champions-to-be 3-2.

Half way through October the team had just four points, having lost every away game and possessed a big zero in the wins column. Mercifully, the thirteenth match, at home to Middlesbrough, brought a release from the pain, as a slightly more composed performance yielded the first win. It mattered not that the result was a narrow 1-0 difference, as Andy Wilson scored the all important goal. Although the team lost at Preston seven days later, Scunthorpe United entered November and things began picked up a little, thanks to three consecutive matches being won 1-0. One of these was on the road at Charlton. Just prior to Christmas there was even a suggestion of a complete recovery, as the meagre 4,986 attendance began to wonder, at the game with newly promoted Swindon Town. The Iron produced a workman like performance to win 3-0, but it was a rare oasis.

At Christmas Scunthorpe United had the daunting task of playing a fallen giant, who just happened to reside at Maine Road. Manchester City and Scunthorpe United were scheduled to play each other in the pantomime season. The first act was over in the big City, and at half time the teams were level at 1-1. At the end of ninety minutes Scunthorpe had received the equivalent of the custard pie, losing 8-1. Two days later the teams resumed at the Old Show Ground. This time there was more of a semblance of a game. City had the whip hand, and won 4-2, but at least Scunthorpe United did have some shape, plus goals by Brownsword, a penalty, and Kirkman, on his home debut.

At the start of the New Year Scunthorpe United were in a relegation fight, along with Grimsby Town, Swansea Town and Plymouth Argyle, while Bury wished they had a touch more meat on the bone. The Iron had lost at the first stage of the League Cup to First Division Stoke City after a third game, and were about to enter into the F.A.Cup. Scunthorpe United supporters hoped that a change of competition might bright a change in fortune.

The Third Round of the F.A.Cup gave the Iron every opportunity of progress, when they drew Barnsley from the division below, at home. On January 4th 1964 a constant stream of folks made their way up the Doncaster Road to swell the crowd to 11,160. Almost half of these had travelled from Yorkshire, as many Scunthonians were voting with their feet. Those in attendance saw a rip roaring typical Cup tie, in which a 2-2 draw was a reflection of an even game. United should have claimed victory, when Wilson and Lawther gave them a 2-0 lead in the second half, but Barnsley scored twice in the last five minutes, to complete a remarkable come back. At Barnsley, the home team were slightly the better set of players. Jack Brownsword twice converted penalty kicks to send the match into extra time, but it was then that the home club claimed the winning goal, taking the tie 3-2.

January was to continue to be a bleak month for Scunthorpe United, and from the four other fixtures played, only two draws accounted for any sort of salvation. These were at home to Norwich and away at Derby, as both scores finished 2-2. On the down side, the visit to Swansea Town ended in a miserable 4-1 defeat, and at Southampton the 7-2 result was a product of everything the Saints touched turned to gold. A small consolation was the goal scored on his debut by David Sloan.

The inclusion of David Sloan did put some vim into the forward line, as this young up and coming star did his best to inject some life into the attack. February brought two noteworthy matches. Scunthorpe won only their second game of their travels, on the first day of February. At reserve fixtures, it was traditional to broadcast over the loud speakers the score every fifteen minutes. Usually five hundred hardy souls turn up for the North Regional League fixtures. The gloom was evident, as United plummeted to a 3-0 deficit at Portsmouth. Then announcements followed, one after another, of a fight back, and eventually the Iron won 4-3. Ken Hodgson hit a trio and Andy Smillie a fourth. The winning strike did not happen until the eightieth minute, when it was buried into the net by Hodgson.

A week later and David Sloan was the hero. A two goal Rotherham United lead was neutralised by strikes from Barry Lindsey and Andy Wilson. Rotherham still had enough petrol in the tank to take a 3-2 lead into the break. Scunthorpe may have had a sizable helping of luck when the Millers lost their goal keeper, and Madden scored an own goal, but the Iron worked hard for victory, and David Sloan scored the winner, one minute from time. For the second week United were 4-3 winners.

On February 22nd Scunthorpe United prepared, to receive Southampton, at the Old Show Ground. John McGuigan did his old club no favours, when he had the ball beating Ken Jones after just thirty seconds. Up to now Jack Brownsword had scored forty eight goals for Scunthorpe United, since they entered the League, all from the penalty spot. Now his luck was to change. In the fifth minute he received the ball on the left, and noted that Godfrey, in the Saints goal, was off his line. Jack looped the ball from fully thirty yards over the keeper into the net and he was rewarded with a huge cheer from the 5591 spectators. Unfortunately Martin Chivers scored another for the visitors, eight minutes later, and the Iron lost 2-1.

On March 30th 1964 Derby County arrived at the Old Show Ground. There was still a slim hope of avoiding relegation, but it was fading fast. On that occasion Scunthorpe United re-established their determination to stay up, with a 3-2 win. The greater significance of this Friday night victory was the winning goal, scored from the penalty spot by Jack Brownsword. It marked the fiftieth goal of his career, and set the courageous veteran a British record for goals by a full back.

Scunthorpe United went into the last two games of the season knowing that only two wins would save their bacon. The first of these was at home to Newcastle United, a team of men that were positioned in no mans land. At half time nothing had stirred the former giant, which gave the Iron hope of a bite of the points in the last three quarters of an hour. They ran out with words of encouragement from Dick Duckworth ringing in their ears, and played a tight sensible patient game. Ian Lawther put Scunthorpe United in the box seat, when he seized a chance on the right of the park, and rifled an accurate shot beyond the grasp of the Magpie in the visiting goal. Some anxious moments followed, but fears were eased, when Keith Ellis settled the game at 2-0, with a side foot from close range. It was a shame that only 6,434 supporters turned out for such an important fixture.

Scunthorpe United played the last match of the season at Leeds Road, against Huddersfield Town. Before kick-off the situation still needed something to go wrong for either Grimsby Town or Plymouth Argyle before Scunthorpe could survive. On the day there was no doubt that Scunthorpe gave it their best shot. The Town fought to establish a two goal lead at the interval, but the Iron engineered their way back, with two goals from a motivated Keith Ellis. Unfortunately Huddersfield scored deep into the game and the dream of Second Division football was shattered.

For a moment everyone felt dazed, and the severity of the situation would not sink in for some time to come. Scunthorpe United had finished bottom of the table, and dragged neighbours Grimsby Town with them. It too late for anything else to be said or done, but time to pick up the pieces and move on.

ANOTHER SLIDE

1964-65

The sombre mood at the Old Show Ground was obvious to see, and the new set of fixtures did not receive with the same enthusiasm as in the past. The loss of status was to be matched by a loss of the class of players that had seen the Club through its days of glory. Archie Gibson went to Barnsley, at the tail end of last term. Tom Passmoor was on his way to Cumberland, to help Third Division Carlisle United. Ken Jones chose the path to Charlton Athletic and remained in Division Two. Jack Marriott decided that it was time to hang up his boots, after close to twenty years, and concentrate on a career outside football.

Another senior player was in a similar position, and the Peter Pan of the team, Jack Brownsword, was not far behind him in retirement. During the coming year Jack was to only play three games, bringing the curtain down on a career of three appearances short of the six hundred mark in the Football League, one hundred and twenty in the Midland League, ten in the League Cup, and he must have set some sort of record by appearing in every single F.A.Cup game United played from 1947 until 1964. Jack was not quite finished, because he was to be a familiar sight, running on to the field with an ice cold sponge, ready to revive wounded soldiers.

The Shrewsbury goalkeeper is challenged for a cross by David Sloan at the Fox Street End of the ground during the 3-2 victory in September 1964.

The new breed of men signed as replacements included Barry Betts from Manchester City for the defence, and Jack Bannister of West Bromwich Albion, for the middle of the field. Jack Hutton came via Hamilton for the right wing and Barry Ratcliffe arrived from Blackburn Rovers, for the left wing. In October, United allowed Andy Smillie to depart for Southend United, but brought in Dick Scott for the engine room from Cardiff City, and his cultured feet made a difference. Scunthorpe United began life in the Third Division with a home gate of 5,562 against Bristol City, and the crowd, in Summer gear, enjoyed a value for money thriller. Bristol City were the first men to make the all important breakthrough with a goal past Brian Reeves on sixteen minutes, but just after the half hour Ian Lawther found the equilibrium.

Alan Kirkman put United ahead five minutes after the restart, then a quick fire burst of goals saw David Sloan score two goals either side of a strike by Ian Lawther, all within a lightening four minutes. Bristol City recovered their composure, and pulled one back, but the result was 5-2.

Any thoughts of the Iron making a quick return to the golden age of Second Division football were soon dismissed, as August finished with a point at Gillingham and defeat to Queens Park Rangers. September contained a couple of bright spots, including a home win against Shrewsbury Town, 3-2, in which Brian Reeves saved a penalty five minutes from the end, after Peter Neale handled. There was good news from a trip across the Humber to play Hull City. Over five hundred travelling supporters saw 'man of the match' Ian Lawther in fine form, and out smart the Tigers with two strikes, in a 2-1 victory. Late in the month, United beat Southend United 2-1 at the Old Show Ground. When Barry Betts missed a penalty, it was the team's third waste of the year, showing how much Jack Brownsword was being missed.

On September 29th 1964 Jack Brownsword was called into the team for the very last time. The visitors were the men of Workington, and 4,993 spectators bid dear Jack farewell. United drew the game 1-1.

On October 9th 1964 Scunthorpe United decided that their less than popular manager, Dick Duckworth, should be relieved of his duties. The team found themselves floundering in mid-table, were out of the League Cup and needed a change of direction. In his place United selected Fred Goodwin to take over. Fred was a former Busby Babe from Manchester United and lately of Leeds United. He had retired for the game, but was willing to put his boots back on to assist in team affairs, when full fitness returned. Scunthorpe supporters soon warmed to his genuine approach, and he became a popular choice.

Fred Goodwin did have his hands tied to a greater degree, but he persuaded the board to spent £20,000 on bringing back Barry Thomas from Newcastle United. Barry had been injured and was never exactly the same player that left the Club. Never the less, it was welcomed by everyone, and represented a big slice of hope. United drew goalless on his return debut with Colchester, but the gate increased by two and a half thousand from that which saw United lose to Darlington, in the F.A.Cup. Fred then promoted two younger players, pledging a future based on youth development. Stuart Bramley, a slightly built blond local player, came in at inside forward. He was to be joined by Ian Harper, a young man with similar credentials, for the left side of the mid-field. All three men enjoyed each other's company at Bristol City for the first time. The team finished the game with nine fit men, and received applause for managing a 2-2 result, assisted by two Barry Thomas strikes.

Christmas was approaching, and the Iron had a visit from Queens Park Rangers. Scunthorpe United showed their fighting spirit, by knocking the stuffing out of the Londoners with two goals within ten minutes of the start of the second half, to win 2-1. The revival was made doubly difficult by yet another penalty miss.

Six days later, against Grimsby, a Boxing Day crowd brought 10,867 spectators into the fresh air, up the Doncaster Road. Mariners' supporters thought that their team would make Christmas turkeys of the Iron, but it was not to be.

Jack Hutton (outside right) signed for Scunthorpe from Hamilton in the 1964-65 season.

The pitch had an inch layer of snow all over it, and although Grimsby may have played the smarter football, United's direct approach earned the 2-1 win. Barry Ratcliffe scored the first, when he nipped in to intercept a poor back pass on twenty two minutes. Town equalised seven minutes later, but Alan Kirkman, the best Scunthorpe player, sealed the result ten minutes after the break with a close range shot, when others had been blocked.

In the New Year, United struggled to keep pace, particularly at home, where victories were far and few between. On the road, some distant journeys were made much more pleasant with results of 3-1 in Devon against Exeter City, and 1-0 in Essex against Southend United. The solution was to find new blood, but money was tight, because gates had plum- meted, and the cash from transfers virtually all gone. Fred Goodwin did manage to buy two fresh faces. In goal, Geoff Sidebottom had played at West Bromwich Albion and Aston Villa. He was in the Villa goal for one of the legs of the League Cup Final of 1961, and he was of a class better than the Third Division. Another brilliant capture was that of ginger haired Bobby Smith, a Manchester United second team player of considerable experience. When he stepped out of the shadows of Old Trafford he would make a significant difference to the right side of mid-field. This, and the promotion of young goal scorer Frank Barton, set the scene for the future.

At the end of the fixture card Scunthorpe United slumped to five consecutive defeats, which was the reason why only 2,587 spectators turned up for the last home game on the list, against Luton.. This was the smallest attendance at any Football League match ever staged at the Old Show Ground. When the Hatters arrived for the match, they had only the remotest chance of avoiding relegation to the Fourth Division, a far cry from when they played in the F.A.Cup Final only six years ago. The match was to be one to live in the memory of all those that attended.

Match action: The Scunthorpe United versus Peterborough United game in October 1964. United lost 3-2 - a thrilling first Football League meeting of the two sides.

Andy Wilson scored on two minutes, Barry Mahy, from the Channel Isles, scored on three minutes, and Stuart Bramley increased the lead at the seven minute mark. Luton composed themselves to reduce the deficit on the half hour. In the second half Barry Thomas zipped the ball into the net from all angles, and scored a record five times. Three of these were in a bewildering four minute spell. The 8-1 triumph remains a record Scunthorpe United victory.

The last match of a disappointing year was at Griffin Park, Brentford, and a less than inspiring performance surrendered the last two point in a 2-0 loss. Scunthorpe could be found in eighteenth position in the table, which is not what supporters had wished for in August. Nobody blamed Fred Goodwin, who was starting to find the right blend of men for the job, but he needed to get rid of the players that did not fit into his plans. One player that had said his farewell was Ian Lawther, who signed for Brentford in the House of Commons, because the Brentford Chairman was a Member of Parliament.

1965-66

During the closed season Fred Goodwin managed to unload six more players off the wage bill. Waving good bye were Brian Reeves, Alan Kirkman, Barry Betts, Jack Bannister, Andy Wilson and Tony Needham.

The departures left the door open for the introduction of a tall mid-field general, called Keith Burkinshaw, an experienced tough Yorkshire man, who was at Workington. He would make up the mid-field, along with Bobby Smith Barry Horstead, Dick Scott and occasionally Peter Neale. Dick Scott was to disappear from the team just into the New Year, and eventually move to Lincoln City.

In the forward line, Scotsman John Colquhoun joined from Oldham Athletic, and was a marvel at left wing. Mick Ash made the short journey from Sheffield United to play in either inside position. At the beginning of September United successfully secured the signature of Queens Park Rangers leading marksman Brian Bedford, and soon it was he who would fire the bullets for the Iron. Then local youngsters Monty Brown, Frank Barton and Keith Lindsey had more work to do, having developed through the reserves. Keith Lindsey was the younger brother of Barry, who was now a versatile jack of all trades around the team, which spoke volumes of how successful the Scunthorpe training system was.

Scunthorpe United started the season with a marvellous performance away to Hull City, which yielded no points. The Tigers went ahead in five minute from the penalty spot, but Monty Brown equalised with a goal which rated as a contender for the best of the season. He beat just about every defender on an amazing run, which ended with a cannon into the net. Although Scottish winger Jack Hutton scored on fifty eight minutes, two Ken Wagstaff strikes gave City a 3-2 win.

Scunthorpe United began the 1965-66 season with a 3-2 loss at Boothferry Park, against Hull City. Derek Hemstead, on the left, and Dick Scott are the Scunthorpe players in all white.

A second defeat followed at home to Mansfield, but the Scunthorpe locomotive was in full steam to beat Reading 2-0, in the last fixture of August, at the Old Show Ground. It was during this game that Scunthorpe United made a small piece of history by making a substitution for the very first time. Barry Lindsey was unfortunate enough to become injured, and Barry Mahy ran onto the pitch to replace him. This was to be the only victory in the first eight matches of the season, and saw United tumble to the bottom place in the table. Eventually, the gears began to turn, starting with a welcomed 3-1 win at Oldham athletic, in which John Colquhoun scored against his old club.

Scunthorpe United's rise up the table ran parallel with a brilliant run of away form and five consecutive matches ended in victory, including those at Brentford, Swansea,. Workington, York and Shrewsbury. At Swansea, the 4-3 result was an absorbing goal feast. The York match was a rearranged game, played on a Saturday evening, and had the voice of support from a band of Hull City supporters returning from a postponed match in the North. A first class performance was won 3-1, with goals by Sloan Bedford and Ash. At Shrewsbury, the Christmas game was won 4-1, thanks to a hat-tick by Brian Bedford, an a fourth Jack Hutton. The next day the tables were turned on United, when Shrewsbury won by the same score, in an excellent encounter at the Old Show Ground.

In the meantime United, visited Crewe for the First Round of the F.A.Cup. Scunthorpe were always on the back foot, and a moment of madness saw Keith Lindsey making an early walk to the dressing rooms. The Railway men won 3-0, and deserved to make progress to the next stage.

Once the New Year arrived, it was time for high flying Hull City, boosted with a large windfall of cash from the Needler family. The imminent rise of City to the Second Division swelled the gate to 15,570. From the first kick of the ball there was never any doubt as to the Tigers claiming the points, but Scunthorpe United made them fight every inch of the way. In the end, everybody received value for money, and Scunthorpe won praise from the 4-2 defeat.

Brian Bedford wins his header in a match in the 1965-66 season, during which the former Q.P.R. man was United's leading marksman with twenty two goals.

Hull City would be Champions of the division, with Millwall next in line. Already United had been to London, and drawn 2-2 at the Den. The Iron led 2-0 but lost victory in the last five minutes. There was a similar pattern of play unfolded at the Old Show Ground, in March. A rip roaring game saw United 4-2 in advance, but pegged back to 4-4 in the last five minutes. The Lions' goalkeeper was a young Alex Stepney, who would later be a European Cup winner, in the colours of Manchester United.

The one game of the season that Scunthorpe United's supporters will remember most, was during Easter, at Blundell Park. On Good Friday, the Iron had the difficult task of facing Grimsby Town on a pitch that was a soft mess of oozing mud. The Mariners made the most of the conditions, and took a one goal lead into the dressing rooms. Fred Goodwin rallied his troops, and David Sloan led the charge, which brought him the personal satisfaction of a hat-trick. If it had not been for the courage of Harry Wainman, in the Grimsby goal, the score could have been more than the 3-1 victory to Scunthorpe United. Four days later and these two teams served up an entertaining 2-2 draw in Scunthorpe. Scunthorpe United had not finished scoring hat-tricks in this season. On the following Saturday Workington came South, to the Old Show Ground, and lost 4-1. This time it was Barry Thomas that netted three times, and David Sloan notched the other.

Late in the year, Scunthorpe United gave a debut to a young goalkeeper from out of second team football. He was Ray Clemence, who appeared four times, starting with the home match with Swansea Town. Clemence would become a regular performer from next season, and go on to be noted as one of the all time greats with England, Liverpool and Tottenham.

Scunthorpe United finished the campaign with a run of form which brought three wins and three draws from the last six outings. This hoisted the team into a satisfactory fourth place in the table, aided tremendously by the creditable total of twelve away victories. Brian Bedford was the leading goal scorer on twenty two, while David Sloan had fourteen, and Barry Thomas ten. On the down side, the average crowd had dropped five hundred per game to 5,184.

1966-67

The situation at the bank only allowed the Club to bring in one player to the squad. He was a tall dark haired Scottish man from Raith Rovers, called Frank Burrows, and what a good acquisition he turned out to be. He instantly fitted in at centre half to plug the defence. In order to save money Fred Goodwin brought into play a lot more of the local lads, developed within the Club. This was to include extended runs for Ray Clemence, John Barker, the son of trainer Jeff, Don Welbourne, Stuart Taylor and Frank Barton.

During the first half of the year, United allowed some experienced men to leave the Old Show Ground. Brian Bedford went back to London, and joined up with Brentford. Stuart Bramley would play most of the time in the reserves, before heading to Plymouth. Perhaps the saddest farewell was said to Barry Thomas after ninety six Scunthorpe goals, off in November to Barnsley.

Scunthorpe United got off to a poor start to the campaign of 1966-67, and had not been inspired by the World Cup performance of England three weeks before. They lost all of the first three matches and Fred Goodwin wanted to teach his senior professionals that if they were not up to the job, then it was time to try the youngsters. In the match at Grimsby Town the Scunthorpe team was flooded by younger players, against a rampant Mariners team, packed with experience. It was like the first day of the Battle of the Somme, and United were cut to shreds. There was blood on the pitch when the gallant lads fell 7-1, and even relied upon Brian Bedford to score the last defiant goal of the slaughter. Fred Goodwin made a public apology and restored some of the old guard. For those of the younger element that did survive, the experience stiffened their resolve

After the Battle of Blundell Park, United's play began to pick up, starting with an unexpected win in the following match, on the long road to Swansea. United won 1-0 via a fourth minute goal from Barry Lindsey. This was followed, on the next Saturday, by an enterprising 3-2 victory on the occasion of the visit of Middlesbrough, which attracted 3,948 spectators through the turnstiles. United may have scored first through Stuart Bramley, but needed two late strikes to overcome the North Eastern men's advantage. These Scunthorpe goals were scored by Barry Lindsey and Frank Barton. The game marked the last appearance for Peter Neale, when he replaced Barry Horstead as a substitute.

Within the next ten days United met Grimsby Town, this time at the Old Show Ground. The crowd was swelled by supporters from the other end of the A18 to 11,105, expecting another bloody mess, but this time the troops held their line, and earned a courageous goalless draw. Eventually United crept up the table and occupied a position of safety, just below half way.

The F.A.Cup found Scunthorpe United making the thirty mile journey down the A15 to Sincil Bank, to play Fourth Division Lincoln City. Scunthorpe United supporters making the trip by the Lincolnshire Road Car football special became stuck in traffic and missed Frank Burrows, used as a temporary centre forward, opening the scoring. Lincoln equalised in the twenty second minute but a moments before the break Burrows scored again. In the second half the teams traded blows until Scunthorpe won the game 4-3 with seven minutes on the clock. Frank Barton had made it 3-1, but ex-Iron Joe Bonson and Jim Grummett equalised. Then came the late winner from Barry Mahy.

Shortly after the Lincoln City match, the Club announced that they had accepted the resignation of Fred Goodwin, who was going to America to be part of the new American football scene with the New York Generals. He was to take Geoff Sidebottom, Mick Ash and Barry Mahy with him, as part of the playing staff, and Scunthorpe United received £10,000 for their transfer fees. Until a new man was found, Keith Burkinshaw was to take temporary charge of the managerial side of the affairs.

The Second Round of the Cup brought the Iron to the Field Mill, the home of Mansfield Town, and the tie took place in January, a month later than usual. Over Christmas the two teams had met in the League, and each had gained a home victory. On the day of the game Scunthorpe dominated the play, but Mansfield scored twice to take command where it mattered. United gained a late goal by Neil Foxon, but it was too little too late.

When Scunthorpe got back into the groove of League football they uncovered a rough diamond that was going to shine in the centre forward position. He was local steelworks electrician Graham Rusling. He had been playing in the Lincolnshire League, and knew the physical side of the game well. His debut was at Swansea, and Graham made the dream start, by scoring the second goal in the rewarding 4-3 result. It was top fare from both sides, and showed that the team had not suffered from the loss of Bobby Smithy to Grimsby Town during the week.

The first team was to be eclipsed, at this time, by the activities of the Scunthorpe United Juniors in their F.A. Youth Cup competition. Round by round they made progress until a victory at Port Vale gave them a Semi Final clash with Sunderland. The format of the F.A. Youth Cup was for a two legged contest at this stage and although they narrowly lost both ties, it was a monumental achievement to reach this position. The Sunderland team contained a number of names that would win the senior F.A. Cup for Sunderland in a few years time. Many of the Scunthorpe team would take up duty in the lower divisions with the Iron. Scunthorpe continued to trundle along just below the half way point in the table, very much as before.

(Left) Barry Mahy, was a utility player from the Channel Isles, who went with manager Fred Goodwin into American soccer at the end of the season. (Right) Three young Scunthorpe United players training, which include Ray Clemence in the centre of the picture. Ray was United's regular keeper during the 1966-67 season, and left for a career of stardom at Liverpool, Tottenham and England.

The end of the fixtures was now within touching distance, and a less than average finish saw United win two and lose five of the last seven matches. This included loses in the last three fixtures, and the final game of the year brought an attendance of only 3,544, at home to Swindon Town. The Saturday Telegraph football paper that night revealed that the team had finished the campaign in eighteenth place on the ladder.

1967-68

Scunthorpe United began the new campaign still without a manager, and having to face life searching for a new custodian. The Club had received an offer from Liverpool to take Ray Clemence, their star goalkeeper, for a fee of £18,000. He was to start an apprenticeship in the Central League team that would take a number of years before he was ready for first team soccer at Anfield.

United selected Brian Arblaster from Chesterfield as his replacement, but Steve Drake from Goole and Jim Lavery, a locally produced lad, also had a chance. In front of them, the team was very much as before but there were some signings. These included Dave Harney, a Jarrow born lad, at centre forward from Grimsby Town, and Peter Foley, a Glasgow native for the wing, from Workington. Peter had been recommended by Keith Burkinshaw, having played together at Workington. He may have had a Scottish accent, but Peter had the honour of being the first of many black players to proudly put on the Scunthorpe United shirt.

The team started the season in a modest way with two draws, one at Peterborough and the other at home to Mansfield. The next two matches finished in defeat, 4-0 at Watford, and 1-0 on the long trek to Bournemouth. There was enough evidence on view to suggest that this was to be a long hard season ahead. At the end of September they did manage to have two wins under their belts. The first was when they squeezed narrowly past Southport, and David Sloan notched the only goal of a less than inspiring home match. They functioned far better on a visit to Oldham, where a see-saw match ended 4-3 in their favour. Frank Barton, scored one, David Sloan managed a pair, and a delighted Barry Horstead scored one of only four goals of his ten year career.

In the League Cup, the early season knock-out competition took Scunthorpe United to Doncaster Rovers, and they returned home unscathed, with a 2-1 result. This was to earn them the prize tie of a home match against Nottingham Forest of First Division fame. The attractive visitors drew a crowd of 13,523 to the Old Show Ground, to see the Forest stars. One of them was Scunthorpe born Ian Storey-Moore, who led the visitors attack. United's defenders made sure he was tracked all evening, but with less than ten minutes left, he slipped the lead, and scored the only goal of the game.

When the team returned back on parade in the Third Division they were unable to secure a win in any of the four games following their success over Oldham. The strain was beginning to tell on Keith Burkinshaw, who was doing his best to juggle life as a player and that of a manager.

The last straw was when the Iron lost 5-2 at home to Walsall, and frankly looked out of salts. It was then, that the board decided they must take on a full time manager.

The man that was chosen for the job was Ron Ashman, the former Norwich City full back, who had made a record number of appearances with the Canaries, and for a short time was their manager. Ron made no rash promises, knowing he was taking charge of a weak team in a lowly position, without a bundle of cash to spend. Generally speaking he was found to be a softly spoken man, but would bite when the occasion called for it. His appointment was to build a strong bond between the man, the Club and the supporters, which was to last in one form or another for more than thirty years.

A work out round the Old Show Ground pitch for Jim Currie, Graham Rusling and Don Welbourne.

Ron Ashman was to become known for bring up to Lincolnshire a conveyer belt full of talent from East Anglia. A long term injury to David Harney necessitated the signing of Steven Deere, from Norwich City, to fill the sharp end of the attack. Before long Steve was cultivated into one of the best central defenders in the lower leagues. He also brought in a mobile mid-fielder, called Mel Blyth, from Yarmouth, who was to go up in the football world as time went on. It was at the Christmas period that Jim Lavery was the preferred choice of keeper. When every one was in place, they did manage to scrape three out of four points from Oxford United, a team that was to top the table. The climax was at the Manor Ground, where United had a coupon busting 3-2 victory. Steve Deere scored two of the goals, and David Sloan netted the other.

This match was to signal the last game for Frank Barton in the Scunthorpe shirt. The motivation for the departure was purely money, which was put on offer by Carlisle United, and had to be taken. The Club had suffered an early F.A.Cup exit to Halifax Town, and gates were at an all time low. A few weeks later and the highly rated David Sloan was sold for the same reason, to Walsall.

Bad weather caused the next couple of games to be postponed, and when they returned to action a 3-0 loss at home to Grimsby Town showed how many problems the team really had. With the situation as it was, some of the money received went on three shrewd signings. The first of the cash went on the balding Bill Punton, from Sheffield United, who had been a long time colleague of Ron Ashman, at Norwich. This man was a winger who had the trickiest feet imaginable, and was similar in style to a modern day Peter Beagrie. Next he chose George Kerr, a Scottish inside forward with plenty of flare at this level, from Barnsley. His third master piece was former Leicester City inside forward or mid-fielder Terry Heath, from Hull City. Terry was another crowd pleaser of tremendous ability, who could win a match on his own. Added to these inspired signatures was promotion to the first team of reserve player Graham Foxton, a full back of huge promise. Graham was Harrogate born, and would represent the Club for the next five years. Years later, Graham was pleased to support the Iron from the seats.

During this extremely difficult time, United would see the last of Barry Horstead. At the end of February he appeared in his last game for the Club at Colchester, during a 1-0 loss. Barry had been a loyal servant of just over three hundred and fifty appearances over the last eleven years.

Scunthorpe United in the Costa Blanca in 1968. The four players carrying the flag are, from the left, Graham Foxton, Terry Heath, Barry Lindsey, and Jim Lavery.

He was now heading the way of many of the Third Division North Championship side, into retirement and a game of dominos at his favourite Brigg pub.

The irony of football is that even in the darkest hour a team can produce the most unexpected scores, and the return match at the Old Show Ground against Colchester was one such example. The team produced its best result of the whole year, and won 5-1. John Colquhoun netted twice, while other came from Bill Punton, Terry Heath, making his Scunthorpe debut, and Steven Deere. The team contained just five survivors from the side that ran out on the first day of the season.

During the last twelve matches of the campaign, United would only win two games, even though they managed to score in all but one of those fixtures. Swindon Town, and Torquay United were the oasis in the desert, with scores of 3-1 and 2-0 respectively.

This was not good form for a team that started March starring relegation in the face. The last straw was a 2-1 defeat at Holker Street, Barrow, on May 11th 1968, when Scunthorpe United played their last Third Division match for some time.

The final table of the 1967-68 season showed that Scunthorpe United had the worst record in the Third Division of any other club. The defence had surrendered eighty nine goals, and on the road two wins and two draws told its own tale. In total a meagre fifty six goals had been scored, and David Sloan was the long departed leading scorer with ten. Ron Ashman had seen many prized assets sold on, but had done his best to replace them. Perhaps if he had been in charge since the beginning of the campaign the outcome might have been different.

THE BASEMENT BLUES

1968-69

Scunthorpe United's fall from grace had happened in the space of four short years, and life would not be the same. They may have been forced to sell some of their better players to the top clubs, but it had a snowballing effect, and money could not replace the skills honed from years of practice. Supporters had to live off the small crumbs from matches against the poorer relations of the Football League, of which they were one.

Many Scunthorpe people were unhappy with events at the Old Show Ground, and a large number would not ever return, feeling the Club had let them down. For decades the sales of Barry Thomas and John Kaye were quoted examples of why they continues to stay away. Those faithful bunch of supporters who believed in tomorrow could look round and see that their numbers were less than half of what was expected for a Third Division North Fixture.

The board knew only too well of the situation on the terraces, but events had taken place, and it was time to move on. They would make every effort to see that the Club was put back into better shape, but unfortunately they were forced to sanction the departures of two more men. Before the season was opened Frank Burrows was sold to Third Division Swindon Town, and then Mel Blyth departed for Crystal Palace, in the Capital. Each of them was to taste promotion with their next club, and for Mel Blyth a transfer to Southampton was eventually rewarded with an F.A.Cup winners medal at Wembley.

Ron Ashman wasted no time in finding new players and replacements. He had never been happy with his goalkeeping position, and decided that he had just the man in mind, down at Norwich. His choice was Geoff Barnard, who was in the Carrow Road second team, although on six occasions he was called into the first team for action. Scunthorpe United moved from a year of chopping and changing, to using one keeper for every game.

In the centre of defence, Ashman used the services of a big man called Ray Holt, from Halifax Town. His height was used to fill the void left by Frank Burrows. Either side of Ray, Ron Ashman used two younger players that would make three hundred appearance for United. Angus Davidson was a man on the small side, but had the bite of a terrier and the stamina of a marathon runner. He was a utility man from Grimsby Town, used mainly at right half. On the left side of mid-field, Don Welbourne had blossomed into a really culture performer, able to match any opponent in speed and distribution. When either was not available, Barry Lindsey was always on call.

Few changes took place in the attack, until into the first part of the fixtures, when another winger was signed from Rotherham, who was a different Andy Wilson.

Scunthorpe United began football in the Fourth Division, deep in Lancashire, at Rochdale, and soon discovered that life was not to be a picnic. Only Geoff Barnard prevented the Dale scoring a hatful of goals, and the home side raced into a 3-0 lead. Thankfully, this was made more respectful, by goals from George Kerr and Steven Deere that made the loss 3-2.

The first steps in Fourth Division football suggested that Scunthorpe might not shake the division up, but they would be comfortable. The first point went on the board after a drawn game against Brentford, and a Friday night squabble with the neighbours at Belle Vue, in Doncaster, brought plenty of entertainment, but no luck from the 3-4 rough and tumble. On the following Monday, a polished performance at Colchester yielded a four goal bonanza without reply. George Kerr scored twice, and Terry Heath and Steven Deere netted the others, to record the first win of the season.

League Cup had not been a competition of any tradition for Scunthorpe United, and it had been the custom for them to sign out early. In 1968 the team did manage to make some headway, starting in the First Round, at home to the Millers of Rotherham United. A modest crowd of 4,643 watched a keen struggle, in which two goals by Steve Deere edged the Iron to a 2-1 victory. The Old Show Ground gate more than doubled to 11,098, when Lincoln City drove up the A15, for the local derby, in the Second Round. This time the same score had Scunthorpe United reach the dizzy heights of the Third Round, thanks to two strikes by George Kerr, which sent the toilet rolls onto the pitch in celebration, as was the vogue of those times.

The third stage of the League Cup brought a bumper crowd to the Old Show Ground, when for the only time the Iron faced the mighty Arsenal in a competitive match. The game was played in a constant down pour of rain, making a soft pitch ideal for slide tackles. The weather did not prevent 17,230 spectators drip their way into the ground. From the point of view of a contest, this game certainly had nothing, as the 6-1 advantage to the Gunners suggests. Even the single Scunthorpe goal was an own goal, but they stuck to their tasks manfully, and it was still an enjoyable occasion.

During the closed season, it had been put to Jack Brownsword that there was a useful lad called Kevin Keegan, who might just make it. After an assessment Jack help bring Keegan to the Old Show Ground to begin his apprenticeship, just the same as anyone else.

Keegan worked hard, and on September 16th 1968 he was promoted to the first team, into a right wing berth, for the visit to Peterborough. The Iron lost the match 3-2, but the significance of the evening was that it launched the career of the Kevin , who to become a household name. His first taste of the big time was in the match against the Arsenal.

During the Autumn, Scunthorpe United played their F.A.Cup First Round tie at Borough Park Workington, and made no impact, losing 2-0. At this point in the calendar, United were nothing more than a middle of the table team, and gates had dropped to below three thousand. Ron Ashman knew that the inclusion of a striker who was able could score goals, would make all the difference. He went back to Norwich, late in December, and signed Nigel Cassidy, a dark haired man with a Mexican style moustache. Nigel knew exactly where the target was. Alongside George Kerr and Terry Heath he was to make a difference to the attack. It also gave Steven Deere the opportunity to drop back into the defence and blossom in a defensive role. Ron gave another chance to local product Nigel Jackson and the youngster played a handful of games in the left full back position, eventually becoming a regular over the next few years.

The value of Nigel Cassidy in the team was appreciated during a match in January, against Grimsby Town, a team that would have to seek re-election to the League. It was to be a revenge meeting, because the Mariners had won 2-1 earlier in the campaign at the Old Show Ground. At Blundell Park there would be no such repeat, and for once Scunthorpe United looked to be in control. The only goal of the game was a picture book header by Nigel Cassidy, who out jumped everyone, to plant the ball into the net, at the railway end of Blundell Park.

The Winter of this season was a severe one, and some matches had to be rearranged. It gave the Club the strange finale of five consecutive home games. The effect was to reduce attendances to the two thousand mark, which was a drain on financial sources. At least the team was to use their own back yard as an advantage, and three of the matches ended in favourable victories.

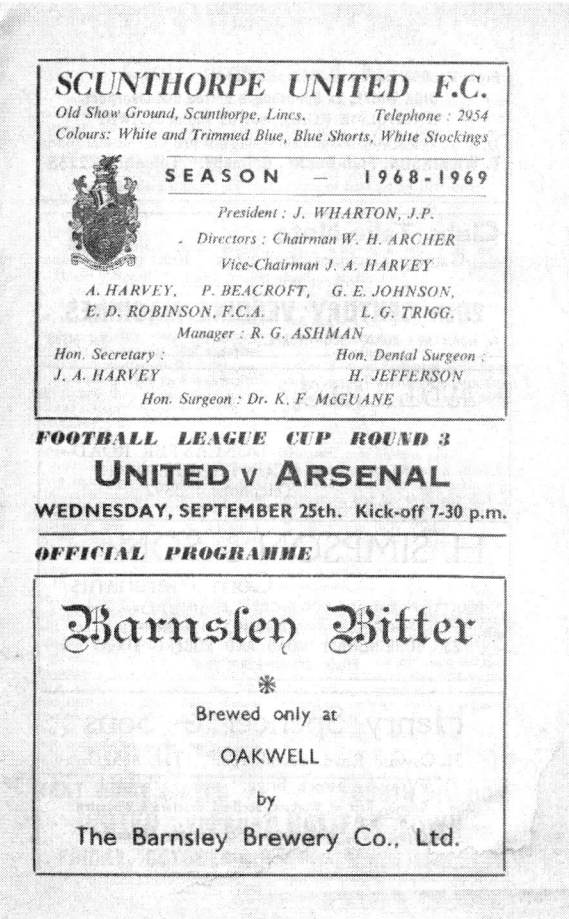

Kevin Keegan

George Kerr was United's joint leading goal scorer with fifteen goals in all competitions in the 1968-69 season.

The last game on the fixture card was against Southend United. Nigel Cassidy and Graham Rusling both score twice, and United were 4-1 to the good, when the floodlights failed. Normally the match would have been abandoned, but because the result would have no baring on other events, the Shrimpers agreed to finish the game in half light.

The conclusion of the fixtures saw that Scunthorpe United had eased into sixteenth position in the table, a much lower place than United's band of supporter would have hoped for. There had been no challenge for promotion, and the average attendance was 3,650 per match. In all competitions, the leading marksman place was shared by George Kerr and Terry Heath, who each scored fifteen goals, but Nigel Cassidy was coming up fast on the rails, with eight goals since the New Year

1969-70

During the Summer of 1969 Scunthorpe United received an offer for their locally produced defender Derek Hemstead, who was an experience campaigner of more than two hundred and fifty battles. His fee was banked to help the finances. Ron Ashman unloaded other players to ease the burden on the wage bill, and Bill Punton went to Yarmouth Town, while Andy Wilson left for Corby Town. The rest of the team was very much the same as finished the previous year, with no new faces for the time being.

Scunthorpe United decided to change the Club's colours at this junction, and the blue white and old gold altered to blue and white, then became white with blue facings. Now, a completely different approach was made, and for the pre-season friendly with Leicester City the Iron ran out in an all red strip. Over the years this would be come red and white.

Scunthorpe United began the year with two defeats in the Fourth Division, and another, at home to Hartlepool in the League Cup. They then rallied, and took the maximum point from the next three games, the best result was the 3-1 win on the road at Boundary Park, Oldham. Steven Deere, Angus Davdison and Nigel Cassidy put the smiles on the handful of supporters who made the journey. The general trend of results gave United a better standing than twelve months ago, but they would not challenge the top places in the table.

In October, United started to play far better, and went on a run of six consecutive wins, something almost forgotten. This success was preceded by the signing of Mick Atkin, a local footballer, who was a school teacher by trade. Mick was a ginger haired central defender that was to play a vital role in keeping a water tight defence, and saw Steven Deere move out to the left half position. The run included a victory at Lincoln City, which had the unusual sight of television cameras capturing Nigel Cassidy scoring twice, in the 2-1 away triumph.

The real story of the year had yet to be revealed, and started in the First Round of the F.A.Cup, at the Moss Rose Ground of non-League Macclesfield Town. United had control of the game, and pinched the lead through a Terry Heath shot, after Graham Rusling's effort was blocked. They should have increased this superiority, but chances went begging, and Macclesfield earned an equaliser, which led to a second game.

The replay brought the interest of 5,131 spectators up the Doncaster Road on the following Tuesday evening, and Scunthorpe made sure of no upsets. The game was high scoring at 4-2, which kept the crowd in good spirits. Kevin Keegan was the star of the show, with two goals, and others followed from Graham Rusling and Nigel Cassidy. The killer blow was two Scunthorpe strikes in the space of three minutes, to make certain the tie was always out of the Silkmen's reach.

In the Second Round Scunthorpe had to travel to the same County of Cheshire, this time to meet Stockport County, from the Third Division. Stockport were strugglers in the League, which was quite apparent from their approach to the Cup tie, and Scunthorpe returned with a goalless draw. It meant another floodlight drama, watched by 5,646 supporters. United ripped the County team apart in the re-match, and were full value for a 4-0 demolition. This time the scores came from Cassidy, Kerr a brace and Keegan. The candidate for the best effort was definitely George Kerr's second goal, which started with a thirty yard run, and finished with a razor sharp shot, that had the net bulging. Such a high number of accurate strikes empty the toilets, of all the toilet rolls, which cascaded over the cross bar in celebration each time.

The Third Round of the F.A.Cup landed United with a home match against the Lions from Millwall, and brought back memories of 1951. On a fresh January Saturday 7,675 folks wrapped up warm to attend the game. Ron Ashman told his troops to keep it tight, because a team like Millwall, in the Second Division, would take no prisoners. A solid defence was the platform to built an attack from, but patient players would win the day. With this in mind, United gave the visitors no room to stretch their legs. They next had to deal with the handicap of losing Barry Lindsey through injury, after twenty minutes, but Mick Atkin filled the gap beautifully. Within ten minutes of the substitution, it was the Scunthorpe supporters that roared for the first goal. Steven Deere was able to move up to a forward position, on the edge of the box, and when the ball came to him he kept his body over it, to sent it back along the ground and into the net.

The second opportunity was also to fall to the Iron. George Kerr caught Keith Weller in possession, passed to Terry Heath, and Terry hit the squared ball first time into the net. At 2-0 Scunthorpe's men were in a strong position, but the threat never went away.

Millwall did score, through Bolland, but the last minute strike was too late to make the impact the visitors wished for, and 2-1 result was enough for Scunthorpe to make the next stage.

Scunthorpe United had at last aroused the interest of local football fans. The Fourth Round tie was just the money spinner the Club needed, away to Sheffield Wednesday of the First Division. It prompted an army of seven thousand supporters to mobilize, and at the kick-off they made a strong voice for the team in the 38,047 crowd. The match was the first to be played in the new decade, on January 3rd 1970. Ron Ashman chose the following team: Barnard; Foxton and Barker; Deere Atkin and Welbourne; Keegan Cassidy, Kerr, Heath and Davidson; substitute Rusling.

The conditions for the time of the year were reasonably good for football, and it was not long before Sheffield Wednesday used them to get into their stride. After only four minutes, the home team brought thunderous applause from their followers with the first goal. A Sam Ellis header was on its way into the net, but Graham Foxton managed to get his own head on the ball, in an attempt to knock it over the bar. He was desperately unlucky to see the ball come back into play, and gift Jack Witham the easiest of chances, virtually on the goal line.

The next fifteen minutes would be crucial to Scunthorpe United's survival, and in defence Steven Deere led by example. Gradually they managed to stem the flow of Wednesday attacks without further damage. It was noticeable that Terry Heath was coming into his own, and on one of his searching runs he was upended, in the twenty first minute. George Kerr took the free kick, and squared the ball to Steven Deere. John Barker had made a dash up the field to support the attack. Deere clipped him the ball, and he dive low to head it beyond Springett, the Wednesday keeper, into the net. In the drama of scoring Baker had been kicked unconscious by a Sheffield Wednesday boot, quite accidentally. While supporters celebrated the goal, he lay on the ground motionless, and would not wake up until he reached the Sheffield Infirmary. Graham Rusling was called into the fray and Ashman had to shuffle the pack.

Scunthorpe United were naturally boosted by the goal, and played the game with a refreshing freedom. In the second half Terry Heath dominated the play with a man of the match display. Time and time again he ran at the Wednesday defence. In the seventieth minute it was his pass, intended for Kevin Keegan, that won a corner. George Kerr sent over a long ball to the far post, where Nigel Cassidy had been waiting. Nigel timed his run to perfection, and sent a looping header back over the defence, and the ball landed on the other side of the goal, just inside the post. United's massive band of support went wild and urged the team to score more. They did have their further chances, but settled for the 2-1 victory.

The Fifth Round of the F.A.Cup was the greatest distance the Club had ever reached, but there was little to compare the strengths of the two different Scunthorpe teams that achieved it. On this occasion, Scunthorpe United had to play Swindon Town at the County Ground. Swindon Town were men of Second Division quality, and were the League Cup holders. British Railways put on two trains, and the match was attend ended by 24,612 spectators.

On the day of the game the pitch was so heavy it was like a treacle pudding, and frankly the match should never have started. The travelling supporters would meet up with a former Iron, because Frank Burrows was at the heart of the Swindon defence.

When the game did begin, it was Scunthorpe United that scored first, on ten minutes. Steven Deere cleared the ball out of the back quarters, and found George Kerr. George looked up and threaded the perfect pass for Nigel Cassidy to run onto. Nigel dashed at top speed, and beat off a challenge from Burrows, to fire the ball past the Swindon goalkeeper. As of that moment the rest of the match belonged to Swindon, and they made more of the muddy condition, running up three goals, and eliminating the gallant Lincolnshire lads from the competition. A 3-1 score was no disgrace, and the players had all enjoyed the glory that went with the F.A.Cup.

Now that the Club found themselves out of the Cup, Ron Ashman had to get his squad focused back on the Fourth Division. The knock-out competition could hardly have been called a distraction, but while it was on the team had won just once in a dozen matches. At least they managed to gain back to back wins at the end of February, from at trip to Hartlepool, and a derby visit from Lincoln City, both of which saw the team work hard for 2-1 results.

The season had just two months to run, and was to finish in April, because of the World Cup in the Summer of 1970. At this stage of the campaign, United were in a middle of the road position, averaging a point per game. During March they had one of the best games on the fixture list, which brought the most favourable result. Newport County made the long journey from the South West, and ran into a Scunthorpe team in storming form. Nigel Cassidy was the outstanding forward with a brace of goals, and George Kerr and Angus Davidson were the two other marksmen, in the 4-0 romp.

April only had three scheduled matches, and in the first of these Scunthorpe United travelled to play an away match at Bradford Park Avenue. George Kerr gave United a lead for the half time break. In the second half he scored another, along with others from Terry Heath, Nigel Cassidy and Angus Davidson. The 5-0 score was a record away win for the Club in the Football League. This was Bradford's last home match of the season, and they would not be re-elected back into the League during the Summer. Within a few short years the Bradford Park Avenue club sadly went to the wall.

Another club has risen from the ashes, and plays in non-League football, guided in 2012 by John Helm, the well known television commentator.

A rare shot from the last ever League game of Bradford Park Avenue in 1970, where the home side lost 5-0 to Scunthorpe United' in the dark shirts.

Scunthorpe United finished the year with a draw at Workington, and a loss at home to Wrexham, who needed the points to win promotion. The end result, as far as the table was concerned, was a moderate improvement to twelfth position on the ladder. Gates had increased very slightly to a figure of 4,424 for each game. The honour of being the leading scorer fell to Nigel Cassidy, who netted twenty five goals in all competitions. Another attacker coming in for some praise was Kevin Keegan, who was starting to bring the scouts to the Old Show Ground.

1970-71

During the Summer, when most football minded people were watching the Brazilian magic in the World Cup, Ron Ashman was tending to team affairs, ready for August. He decided to release Steve Drake, the goalkeeper, and Ray Holt at the centre of defence. All his out of contract players re-signed for the Club, avoiding that particular headache. With his meagre resources he brought in the slight figure of Colin McDonald, from Norwich, for the forward line. He also took on a local right winger, named Terry Muldoon. Terry only played once for the team, and sadly passed away before the fixtures were concluded.

The 1970-71 season started for Scunthorpe in glorious Devon, with a trip to play Exeter City. United had to be content with a one each draw, when Kevin Keegan opened the scoring for his side in the second half. There was a suggestion that a corner might have been turned, when the home part of the fixtures began, and Southend United were beaten 3-0. George Kerr initiated the onslaught, and this was followed by rare goal by Graham Foxton, before the first forty five minutes were up. Terry Heath bagged the third after the tea break, and Geoff Barnard in goal was not troubled during the whole test.

Scunthorpe continued the early part of the fixture list with what is best described as inconsistency. The situation was not helped by a serious injury to Barry Lindsey, which finished his ten year career.

His place was initially taken by Chris Kisby, a young player who had progressed through the ranks at the Old Show Ground. Eventually, Terry Heath took over the right half place, and freed up room in the attack.

The fourth Division was to see Scunthorpe United as a poor home side initially, but much more adaptable on their travels. Example of this could be found from hard fought battles at Aldershot Bournemouth and Newport County. At home disappointments occurred in games against Oldham Athletic York City and arch rivals Grimsby Town. The tour of the South Coast to Bournemouth saw them peak in form. Not many clubs would go to Dean Court and win, but Steven Deere had a blinder. He policed the Cherry's highly rated striker, Ted MacDougall out of the game. Before supporters had time to warm themselves with a Bovril, Steven had put the Iron in front and Angus Davidson supplied a second, for an unassailable lead.

Scunthorpe supporters were not completely starved of points at home, and two wins at the Old Show Ground followed on immediately after the visit to Newport. They won by three goal margins against Exeter City and Peterborough United. The Exeter match was by way of goals from Kevin Keegan, and Nigel Cassidy, who hit a pair. The Peterborough match was in mid-week, under lights. The Iron took a 2-1 lead into the break, and moved the score in the last forty five to 5-2. Keegan and Cassidy did their reputations no harm by scoring additional strikes, and the others came via John Barker and Terry Heath, who notched two.

The Autumn was to see events on and off the park make a profound change to team affairs. Unfortunately, the highly rated George Kerr was to break his leg in a Lincolnshire Cup tie at Gainsborough, which ruled him out for the remainder of the football year.

The next event was when Oxford United came and offered £20,000 for Nigel Cassidy, and money of that nature was not to be sniffed at. The cash helped to pay the bills, and left Ron Ashman with a little surplus to invest in the team.

Within a few weeks, United signed London born Tony Woolmer, from Bradford Park Avenue, to replace Nigel Cassidy. Tony had his hair on the long side, with noticeable side burns, but would not be as prolific a marksman as Cassidy. Next on Ron's shopping list was a tough character, called Harry Kirk, who was a useful wing man at Hartlepool. He soon fitted into the team, and made an impact with his foot work, and accurate crosses. Harry's no nonsense approach made him popular with Scunthorpe supporters of all ages.

(Top) A ticket from the F.A. Cup-tie (Above) Steve Deere scores against in the 1970-71 season against Southport at the Old Show Ground.

November brought Scunthorpe United checking the post to see what the F.A.Cup had to offer, and they were summonsed to play at Prenton Park, against Tranmere Rovers of Division Three. The game was a closely fought one, marked by Tony Woolmer's first goal for his new club. A 1-1 result was followed by a goalless draw in a long yawn, which produced very little excitement in one hundred and twenty minutes of football. At the end of the evening the two clubs tossed a coin to see who would choose the venue for the Second Replay. When Tranmere won the decision, Goodison Park was arranged to take the match.

The Second Replay was to be just as tight for the 7,235 spectators that echoed shouts of encouragement round the huge cathedral, at the home of Everton Football Club. Those in attendance wondered who might be the person to find the target, and going into extra time neither goalkeeper had picked the ball out of his net. The vital breakthrough was made by Graham Rusling, in the additional thirty minutes.

He was put in a position by a pass from Kevin Keegan, where he could not miss, but still needed two stabs, before he scored.

Mansfield Town must have almost fallen asleep, waiting to find out where they would travel to for the next part of the contest. The Stags were also in the Third Division, but it cut no ice with Scunthorpe United, who were not so goal shy this time. The Old Show Ground was comfortably filled with 7,656 spectators, many travelling with the away team. At half time the score sheet was still blank, but a minute into the second half Graham Foxton put a purposeful ball into the box. Tony Woolmer challenged the keeper, who let it drop, and Graham Rusling gratefully scooped in the first goal.

This strike brought the crowd to life, and they were to cheer once again, when the ball was punched out, but only as far as Harry Kirk. Harry quickly controlled the ball, and had enough time to send a shot whistling past the ears of the keeper for his first goal in Scunthorpe United's red colours. The same player became very popular with home fanatics, when he sent in another a ball from the left, right into the path of Graham Rusling, and the big man with the cheeky smile made it 3-0, and the game was out of sight.

Supporters could not understand why the Iron found F.A.Cup games a challenge, but the regular League pattern never hit the same heights. After beating Peterborough United, the team did not win another Fourth Division fixture for another ten games, and only three of these were drawn matches. The worst part of this sequence was a 5-1 loss at Haigh Avenue, against Southport, and United had only the crumbs of comfort of a Kevin Keegan goal. It was not until Scunthorpe United played Peterborough again that the spell was broken, with a 2-1 victory at London Road.

The luck of the F.A.Cup took Scunthorpe United to play West Bromwich Albion, at the Hawthorns. The Albion were of top quality First Division class, and full of International stars. One of these was England International Jeff Astle, who led the England attack in the World Cup Finals in Mexico. They also had John Kaye, the former Scunthorpe player, in mid-field. Steven Deere was given the difficult task of marking Astle, all through the ninety minutes, and the Iron man had an outstanding game. United matched the Baggies in every department, and even had a crowd of 21,960 spectators wondering if Tony Woolmer had given the visitors a shock last minute goal. The referee saved the blushes when he blew for a foul. At the end of the match no side had scored.

The replay was postponed, and not played until the Monday of just a little more than a week later. A healthy crowd of 15,926 was in position at kick-off to roar the teams onto the Old Show Ground. Scunthorpe United continued to refuse to be bossed about. It seemed that all of the real chances had been created by Scunthorpe, and in the thirty third minute they took the initiative. Harry Kirk crossed a highly tempting ball, which was just out of Jim Coombe's reach in the West Bromwich goal. Steven Deere went up to meet it in the crowded area, and did enough to deflect it into the net.

The shock spurred the Baggies into action, and it was a different side that left the dressing rooms for the second half. Scottish International Tony Brown scored twice, and Jeff Astle hit another to make the final score 3-1. At least the Cup had overflowed for the Iron in their time of need.

Scunthorpe United continued to do just sufficient in their League programme to be far enough away from trouble in the bottom four places, because that would mean seeking re-election, to ask permission for another set of fixtures. During March the team managed two straight wins, to ease the situation, in the home meetings of Colchester United and Lincoln City. These were made possible, thanks to the inclusion of Paul O'Riley, Scunthorpe United's first dabble in the loan market, from Hull City.

Colchester United had just caused a sensation by knocking Leeds United out of the F.A.Cup, and it was big news, because this Leeds team had been winning all the honours. Colchester could not build up the same head of steam against Scunthorpe, and Tony Woolmer and Paul O'Riley scored the two vital goals in the 2-0 success. Paul went one better in the Lincoln City encounter, scoring twice, and another shot by Colin McDonald guaranteed two points from the 3-1 triumph. In the end it was the Imps that finished in the bottom four.

Scunthorpe United went on to finish the season with three wins and seven losses from the last seven fixtures. They said their farewells with an enterprising performance which beat Workington 4-0.

This left the Iron in seventeenth table place in a bunch of teams on the same number of points. One more win could have raised them several position further up the ladder. Terry Heath was the leading scorer on ten goals, while Kevin Keegan scored nine, and the F.A.Cup saw to it that the Club kept its head above water.

The last piece of business was conducted right on the point of everyone at the Club thinking about Summer holidays. For long enough there had been speculation about their young starlet Kevin Keegan. In May, Bill Shankley, the great Liverpool manager, rang the Old Show Ground and made an offer of £35,000. It was a staggering amount of money, and a fee readily accepted by the Scunthorpe United board. Ron Ashman accompanied Kevin to Liverpool, who was photographed outside Anfield, smartly dress in a suit, sat on a dust bin, waiting to see the new boss. Kevin was a man of the people, as he still remains, and he worked hard at Scunthorpe to earn his chance. This was to be the beginning of a career that hit the World stage. Scunthorpe United supporters are still proud to mention the name Kevin Keegan.

1971-72

When the new season was about to dawn, Ron Ashman had already invested a small amount of money in forward line of the team. He had been to Lincoln City and signed Rod Fletcher as an all out marksman. Rod was a serious man, who was another qualified school teacher, and was content to run at the front end of the team. He also looked to hone Dave Hutchinson as a goal scorer. Dave had been prolific in the lower leagues at Brigg Town, but although he was a willing horse, he was not able to bridge the gap and make it at the senior level. The forward line was to benefit from the return to match fitness of George Kerr but that was not until October. On his way out of the Old Show Ground was Graham Rusling, who would join Goole Town.

The 1971-72 season started badly for Scunthorpe United, with two derby game losses. On a sunny day at Blundell Park, United had their colours lowered by the old enemy, Grimsby Town. The 4-1 result mirrored everything needed to be known about the game. The only bright spot was a debut goal by Rod Fletcher. In mid-week a crowd of 5,864 supporters saw United lose 1-0 at home to Lincoln City, in the First Round of the League Cup, and go out at the first stage for the third consecutive year.

The Fourth Division fixtures brought Lincoln City back to the Old Show Ground on the Saturday, and the loyal few dropped to 4,468 supporters. The Iron decided to leave Woolmer out and instate Chris Kisby. It was to prove to be a winning move, against a much improved opponent, but Scunthorpe played a brand of inspired soccer not seen for some time. Terry Heath scored the first goal to get the crowd it its feet, and Nigel Jackson stroked away a penalty in Brownsword fashion, now that the old master had been coaching him. The final result of 2-1 fully justified the points going to the Scunthorpe team. This was the beginning of a nine match unbeaten run which contained six wins, five clean sheets, and Geoff Barnard conceded the minimal number of five goals.

In October United's run came to a shuddering halt, when less than three thousand spectators witnessed a useful Bury side win 3-1 on their own ground at Gigg Lane. The question being asked of the local supporters was not about the Scunthorpe game, but did they want to change their name to Manchester North End? In the next encounter, an extremely efficient Grimsby Town side completed the double over Scunthorpe at the Old Show Ground, and their could be no complaints from the Scunthorpe camp, as 11,510 pairs of eyes would testify.

During November, the Iron clad ship set sail for the choppy waters of non-League South Shields, in the F.A.Cup. United's defence that had been so water tight, started leaking goals, but in the highly charged atmosphere of the occasion produced a 3-3 sensation. Steven Deere scored United's first, but most welcomed was the first two goals from George Kerr, since his return. In the replay South Shields played above their status, and caused a real Cup shock by beating United 3-2 on the Old Show Ground. It was the first time, as a League club, United had lost to a non-League side in the competition.

There can be no denying that the exit from the Cup was a wasted opportunity, which might have brought another cash bonanza. It prove not to be as costly as at first it appeared. The absence of extra fixtures allowed the Club to go on an extended unbeaten Fourth Division League run, which started the week before they embarked upon the chaotic F.A.Cup voyage. The first match was a 2-0 home win, against Workington. Five days after the Cup game the team found their way back to winning form on the long journey to Gillingham, where a solo run by Rod Fletcher sent the ball into the net for the one and only time. In the following match, at home to Chester, Scunthorpe triumphed 2-0, and Colin McDonald added his name to that of Fletcher in the goal scoring column. The unfortunate part of this game was an serious injury to Don Welbourne, which was to end his season forth with, on the slope of the Old Show Ground pitch.

Christmas was almost upon the team, and seven days in advance of the Santa making his annual tour, United were down the Road at Doncaster Rovers. Most of the game was controlled by the Iron, and Geoff Barnard needed some exercises to keep warm. The first goal was to come as a result of Rod Fletcher heading into the net from a corner. He was to receive a bang in the face from the fists an apologetic Rovers keeper for his troubles. The second goal wrapped the game up, and was scored by George Kerr, when he shot through a crowded scene into the net.

Scunthorpe United's Christmas fixture was on Monday December 27th 1970, and a bumper crowd of 6,940 spectators were on hand to see Hartlepool put up a cracking performance and thoroughly deserve a point from a tremendous 2-2 draw. Colin McDonald and George Kerr hit the Scunthorpe goals into the back of the net, but the one scored by George was down to the generosity of the visiting defence, or it might not have been a happy Christmas. Another aspect of the game was the groin injury to Terry Heath, which was to preclude him for the rest of the fixture card.

The industry of Scunthorpe United hoisted them up with the leading pack in the New Year, as the confident run continued. On February 19th 1972 the Iron had an intriguing battle on their hands in West London, against Brentford, a team in the promotion mix. The Iron men were blessed by a great sway of support in the 11,910 attendance, and they offered a huge voice of continuous encouragement throughout the ninety minutes. When the match kicked off, the pattern of the play found Brentford as the aggressors, but making no headway against a solid Scunthorpe defence. At the sharp end, Rod Fletcher was a lone wolf relying on breakaways, but it was from one of these that United scored. A shot from Fletcher was only punched clear as far as Colin McDonald, who catapulted it back into the target.

Brentford immediately retaliated, going in search of equilibrium. Graham Foxton and John Barker had to gallop like never before, and Geoff Barnard got his gloves behind a number of broadsides. In the fifty sixth minute the Bees were stung again. A grass cutting ball up the field found Rod Fletcher, and after steadying himself, he shot hard and accurately into the net, before the keeper could narrow the angle. Two minutes from time Brentford allowed Fletcher to use his back door key again, as they bombarded the Scunthorpe defence at the front. A similar breaking move allowed the forward runner to notch his second goal, and round off a remarkable 3-0 result.

In the next match the Iron continued with another 3-0 score, at home to Exeter City, but on the first Saturday in March the unparalleled run of fifteen unbeaten matches, ten of which were wins, came to a halt. This wonderful achievement started in November at home to Workington, and finished at Borough Park, Workington, when the men from Cumberland squeezed the extra juice, to scrape a 2-1 win.

The approach of Easter saw Scunthorpe as one of five teams contesting four promotion places. It was going to be a tense time for everyone connected with Scunthorpe United, and Charlie Strong was the busiest man at the Club, patching up the wounded. Ron Ashman was so restricted by injuries that if a player did not need a crutch, he was selected. On Good Friday, the team played the first of two away games in the North East.

At Darlington a clean sheet and a Rod Fletcher goal made for a fruitful first leg. United stopped over night in a hotel, and twenty four hours later, the Iron lost by the same score at Hartlepool. Their nemesis was former team mate Bobby Smith, who inflicted the fatal blow in the dying ten minutes.

The holiday period games finished with a tussle against mid-table Aldershot, at the Old Show Ground, by this time looking bare without a blade of grass. Harry Kirk's goal helped to take the last Easter egg, as United won 1-0. The deepening injury crisis had forced Ron Ashman to blood yet another youngster in the game, just to make up the numbers, but Peter Markham enjoyed a debut to be proud of. The performance of the team, as a whole was best described as jittery.

On the Saturday of the following weekend, United kicked off in the evening, so as to avoid clashing with the Aintree Grand National. Their opponents were lowly men of Stockport County, who were in the bottom four, and had won only once on their voyages all season. The Iron produced a performance that had the power of a wet lettuce, and played with the confidence of a rabbit caught in the headlights. Stockport County were blameless in taking full advantage to win 2-0. The only consolation for the Iron was that other promotion minded competitors were having similar uncharacteristic results.

Scunthorpe United continued to inch nervously towards the finishing line, and on the following Tuesday 5,916 supporters were on station for the next nail biting episode, at home to Cambridge United. The visitors were too far adrift of the promotion places, and played with a freedom of a prisoner released from his chains, so much so that it was they who took the lead. Scunthorpe regained their composure, and won the tense struggle 2-1. Rod Fletcher twice proved how lethal he was in front of goal, with a couple of headers into the target, each time the cross was from the boot of Harry Kirk.

At this late in the calendar, the fourth place in the promotion push appeared to be between Lincoln City and Scunthorpe United. The Iron were to travel to play Reading, a team that had Steve Death to guard their posts. Scunthorpe lost the day 2-0, but sunken spirits rose when news came through of a surprise home defeat of Lincoln by Darlington, the only loss the Imps would suffer at Sincil Bank all season.

The match that would eventually clinch promotion was played at the Old Show Ground on Tuesday April 25th 1972, when a slick Southend United team arrived needing one point for their own promotion. This was Scunthorpe's final home match of the fixtures and became a magnet for 8,540 supporters. The main ingredients of the game included a fourth minute Harry Kirk goal, curled wickedly into the net, directly from a corner kick. This was followed by a soft gift from the Scunthorpe defence to allow Southend in for an equaliser on the stroke of half time. A further forty five minutes of superb endeavour from both sides provided a nervous time for the viewers, but no further goals. At the end of the game the visitors celebrated their untouchable position, while home supporters still had to wait and see.

A group of Scunthorpe United players were enjoying a quiet beer at the Wortley Hotel one evening later, when it was learned that Lincoln City had drawn goalless at home to Crewe and the mathematics meant that Scunthorpe United had won promotion. It was hugs and handshakes with colleagues and supporters alike, as the fourth place was firmly secured. It was just as well, because visits to Cambridge and Newport yielded no rewards.

Ron Ashman was an unassuming sort of a man, who took promotion with an inward smile, and soon started the work of building for the future, rather than getting involved with a lot of fuss. He had to be congratulated for being the architect of an unbelievable year. His tactics were based on the stingiest defence, which conceded a mere thirty seven goals, and an attack that worked on a shoestring, aided by nineteen Rod Fletcher goals.

The Club had wonderful team spirit and a first class work ethic. It was a team that contained a high number of players that had been developed at the Old Show Ground, while the rest cost peanuts. Every step of the way, the journey was hampered by serious injuries to key players, and despite all the setbacks United held off the challenge of Lincoln City, to win promotion by a solitary point. Heaven only knows what would have been achieved with a fully fit squad.

The goal that effectively sealed promotion in 1972, scored directly from the corner kick by Harry Kirk, against Southend United. The 1-1 result guaranteed both clubs would

THE LONG ROAD BACK

1972-73

The 1972-73 season was a watershed for Scunthorpe United, which began with the euphoria of promotion, but was to signal the toughest ten years in the Club's Football League history. It would rate with the darker days of the Midland League, when the team almost went out of existence, and lived hand to mouth. Scunthorpe would continue to be a selling club, just to make ends meet, because it was the only way to survive.

There was no fat on the bone to consolidate their hard won Third Division status. This did not phase Ron Ashman, who signed three men that could be guaranteed to do their utmost for the team. Graham Collier was a utility mid-field player of slender build, who wore longish dark hair, and was signed from Nottingham Forest. At the City Ground he had a sprinkling of first team games to his name, and would add drive to the middle of the park. In attack Ashman had returned to his old school of Norwich, where he successfully acquired the signature of Gary Sargent. Gary was the type of player never to admit defeat in chasing lost causes. Finally Mike Williams was taken from Hull City as an understudy to Geoff Barnard, but Geoff was unmovable from between the posts.

Scunthorpe United began the season with a workman like performance, which was to hide the frailties, that would become apparent as time went on. They beat a Swansea Town team at the Old Show Ground, who suffered from a void of attacking ideas, and would have problems of their own. United took a lot of credit from the 1-0 victory, made possible by Steven Deere's header from Harry Kirk's corner, deep in the contest.

The rest of the opening month was quite encouraging, with just one solitary loss recorded, at Tranmere. This was out weighed by three points gleaned from two home fixtures. Steven Deere earned a point against Wrexham when he scored, but Walsall were undone by a dual salvo from Rod Fletcher and Harry Kirk. The League Cup story was to reveal the reverse side of the coin in the conflict with Chesterfield. At first, United held the Derbyshire men in a stale goalless draw opposite the Royal Hotel, but at Saltergate Ashman's lads were flattened 5-0.

September was to begin in a modest sort of a way, with a point from the long haul to Bournemouth. When Rod Fletcher thumped the ball into the net to level at 1-1, supporters could not have envisaged that the team was to embark on a disastrous slide. The Iron suffered six straight frustrating defeats, and they must have felt like the officers leading the charge of the Light Brigade. This unmitigated catastrophe dumped Scunthorpe United at the wrong end of the table, down with the dead men in the relegation places.

There was to be a far better approach in October, and the blood was staunched against Brentford, when at last the defeats were halted. Brentford had won promotion in the position immediately above United last term, and were struggling in the same manner. All that separated the teams was Don Welbourne's only goal of the game. Scunthorpe used this as a platform to gain a draw at Burden Park, against Bolton Wanderers. The Trotters would be Champions of the division, but they were thwarted by a Scunthorpe rear guard action. United salvaged a point, and needed to do a lot of chasing to get it in the goalless result.

When the dark evenings of November, arrived Ron Ashman emptied the cash machine of the few pounds left in it to spend on Neil Warnock, who was a journeyman midfielder at Hartlepool. Neil was to become a noted manager, but his Scunthorpe debut was at Rochdale. The match was memorable for the first away win of the season, 2-0, and a brick thrown through the window of the coach carrying supporters from Lincolnshire. The absence of a huge pane of glass made for a freezing two hour return trip home.

The problems of the Third Division would be put to one side for a moment, when the F.A.Cup became the priority. Scunthorpe United travelled to Hartlepool, where Neil Warnock was quickly reacquainted with his former colleagues. Ninety minutes of honest toil brought no goals, nor did two hours at Scunthorpe in the replay. Both teams played with steel doors on their defences, and supporters were desperate for a glimpse of a goal.

A Second Replay was staged at Roker Park, Sunderland, at the suggestion of the Hartlepool party, after the spinning coin fell in their favour.

United's only visit to Ewood Park - a Third Division match that was lost 3-0.

At last, in this match supporters could open their lungs to cheer a goal, and Hartlepool took their chance early in the game. It appeared that the Fourth Division men would win the day, until four minutes from the end of normal time. The drama was an unfortunate own goal by defender Malcolm Dawes, when worried under pressure by Terry Heath. Roker Park then became the theatre for another thirty minutes longer. Three minutes from the conclusion of extra time, Harry Kirk took a short corner. From the return pass he put a pin point centre onto the head of Steven Deere, who gratefully accepted the gift, and United were through 2-1.

United never had a moment of rest from football before taking on Halifax Town in the F.A.Cup, because two League matches had to be played. Less than three thousand supporters were present to see them beat Shrewsbury 1-0, but away at Bristol Rovers they had their knuckles rattled with a 5-1 defeat.

In the F.A.Cup, United had a score to settle with Halifax, because the Shaymen had already won at the Old Show Ground, in concerns of the League. This time Scunthorpe United gained revenge, but via the hard route. Terry Heath and Rod Fletcher fired the shots that should have sealed the tie, after less than half an hour. Halifax made great advantage of some errors at the back and by the hour mark had clawed back the deficit. Thankfully, ten minutes from the end, a punch by the keeper fell on the head of defender John Barker, who sent the ball looping over the crowds in the box, and into the back of the net.

United returned to League action, and a 2-0 loss at Port Vale was about par for the course. They were expected on paper to lose in the following game, at home to Notts County, but the Iron put up a courageous performance, which confounded the Magpies. Angus Davidson scored the only goal in the first half of the match, in which the tough Scottish character was brilliant. The rest of the afternoon contained backs to the wall football, but Scunthorpe held out. Notts County would win promotion at the end of the year, four points behind Bolton.

The next match on the list was at Grimsby, on Boxing Day, where the Mariners had adapted far more comfortably than the Iron to the Third Division. Scunthorpe fought with much vigour, but could not match the mobile Town team.

Utility man Stuart Pilling sogned in 1973 from Hull City, and he went on to play almost three hundred games and score thirty one goals, in nine years.

A crowd of 16,580 waited for the inevitable, and United finally collapsed to a Lew Chatterley goal, which stole the match for Grimsby Town, 1-0. The holiday games finished at home to Tranmere Rovers, and the visitors completed the double when the Iron gave a tired performance, in which they were sunk 5-1.

The New Year began with an uplifting 2-1 victory away from home at Wrexham, one of only three defeats in Wales for the Welsh Robins. This set the Iron in good heart for the F.A.Cup Third Round at home to Cardiff City, of Division Two. The Bluebirds attracted a gate of 6,379 spectators, and it did not take them long to see where the class lay.

However, the Scunthorpe boys raised their game, and deserved credit for their contribution to the fight given in the tie. Twice they went behind, and twice they achieved equality, the third Cardiff City goal was a bridge too far. Don Welbourne scored United's first, with a nicely placed header, and Harry Kirk volleyed the second from twenty five yards.

It was in January that Scunthorpe United's season turned sour. They went on a twelve match run without a win, which included seven consecutive loses. This pitched Scunthorpe United firmly at the foot of the table, adrift from the nearest team. It was not terminated until midway through March, when the team scrambled a 2-1 win over Rotherham. Supporters abandoned the cause in droves, and against Watford only 1,687 loyalists were there to echo shouts of reassurance from the stands. When the wind blew the huge medal gate at the Doncaster Road terrace could be heard banging a melancholy beat as it vibrated to a stop, until the next gust repeated the sequence.

United finished the season drawing their last two games with 1-1 scores. The first was at home to Blackburn Rovers, on the Lancastrians only ever visit to Scunthorpe, and the last at Walsall, marked by the debut of utility man Nolan Keeley, from Great Yarmouth. Nolan would play in every out field position for the Iron, in a career of marginally short of three hundred games, and forty four goals. The end of the game was a great relief for the core group of two thousand Scunthorpe United supporters, who were emotionally drained, and in need of a compete rest from football.

1973-74

During the closed season football followers were given a further knock, when it was learned that their respected manager was leaving the Old Show Ground to take up a similar post with arch rivals Grimsby Town. Ron Ashman was going to replace Lawrie McMenamy, who had been lured away to Southampton. The board of directors received thirty four serious applications for his post, and selected Ron Bradley as the successor. He was new to management, but had been a coach for a good number of years.

The playing staff would go through the usual changes, and the first was the retirement from the game of Nigel Jackson, who did not respond to treatment on a knee injury. United received an offer from Hull City for the considerable services of Steven Deere, who was now a proven defender of quality.

The Tigers made two players available as part of the deal. The first was Ken Houghton, an experienced stalwart of the Humberside club's rise up to the Second Division. He was to be used on the right side of the pitch in an advanced mid-field or wing position. The second was an exciting prospect called Stuart Pilling, who would have a career of similar statistics to Nolan Keeley. Young Stuart was to develop into a versatile performer, who wore his Scunthorpe United heart on his sleeve. He never had a bad game, and could have played many more games if he had not been hampered by a shoulder injury.

Other men that unpacked their suitcases included Barry Lynch, a full back from Grimsby Town, and Bruce Collard, a West Bromwich Albion second team player for the middle of the field, and a youthful Richard Money, for the back quarters from Lowestoft Town. Richard was to have three spells at the Old Show Ground, two as a player, and another as the manager.

The 1973-74 season brought the Iron back in line with a level of opposition that they could deal with, but they left their blocks slowly, losing to Lincoln City 1-0 at Sincil Bank in the opener. Supporters were treated to a 3-0 victory over Barnsley in the Old Show Ground curtain raiser, but by the end of the fifth game, the Club found themselves in twentieth position in the League, after they were sank out of trace, down at Gillingham, losing haplessly 7-2. In the League Cup United had to meet Peterborough United in a two legged tie. Fortunately, the Iron won 4-3 on the aggregated scores.

At the end of September Ron Bradley made a modest offer to Blackpool for Chris Simpkins, a mid-field man, who was once of Hull City, and had a reputation of being as tough as old boot. The engine room received the necessary boost, and United put up a convincing performance in the League Cup against Bristol City of Division Two.

The goalless draw was to earn a replay which was subsequently lost 2-1, in Bristol. One productive move that came out of the League Cup was the borrowing of Eddie Woods, on loan from the Ashton Gate club. The most significant contribution the Bristol man made was at home to Brentford, where he scored twice. The result was 4-1 to the Iron, and three of their goals were scored in the first ten minutes. It seemed disappointing to have to wait until the seventeenth minute for the fourth, and the Bees sorted the final goal before the end of the first session. Simpkin and Keeley scored the other two Scunthorpe goals.

The F.A.Cup brought a struggling Darlington to the Old Show Ground for the First Round of this ancient club competition. The Quakers arrived as the team that propped up everyone else in the Fourth Division table. Both sides did their level best to produce an entertaining game, but a strong wind spoiled matters. A meagre crowd of 3,191 came to its feet, when Ken Houghton scored the only goal past Morritt, the star man in the visitor's goal.

Scunthorpe United received a schedule to play Mansfield Town in the Second Round of the F.A.Cup, at the Field Mill, and they had good preparation at the Old Show Ground, by defeating them 5-3 in the League, only a week before. Although this had no baring in the Cup match, it raised the confidence levels, and United came away to fight another day with a 1-1 draw. In mid-week the floodlights were turned on for the replay, that had little to choose between the two sets of the players. It was never going to be a repeat of the eight goal thriller of the League, but it was settle in the fifty second minute, when indecision opened a path for Neil Warnock to shoot the only goal of the game.

United were at the junction of the Christmas holidays, and on the Saturday before the festival, the team ran out at Hartlepool to be greeted by the smallest crowd ever to watch them in the Football League. Only 832 persons put their hands together to welcome them onto the field. The apathy was transferred to the Scunthorpe team's performance, who lost most disappointingly 3-0.

In the next two matches, both played at the Old Show Ground, they gave a hint at what they could really do. On Boxing Day, Doncaster Rovers found the cutting edge of the Scunthorpe sword too much. Stuart Pilling and John Barker shot the goals in an exhilarating 2-1 display. Three days later an even better performance was enjoyed against the would be Champions, Peterborough United. The score was repeated, but Graham Collier and Nolan Keeley were the men who had the supporters jumping with joy. Anyone think of getting carried away with present events was given a reality check, as Scunthorpe crashed 5-0 at Barnsley, on New Year's Day 1974, where the Oakwell Brewery was within two years of closure.

It was on the January 5th that United went to London for the Third Round of the F.A.Cup to meet Millwall, a team they could not keep away from.

Ron Bradley made sure they were properly coached to face the Second Division men. The plan was to put extra men at the back and look to hit the Londoners on the break. It was to be a long ninety minutes, but it worked, The Lions were restricted to one goal, and late in the preceding United nicked an equaliser through Graham Collier. It was a happy set of players that came back on the bus from the Capital.

Scunthorpe United played the return match on the afternoon of Tuesday January 8th, because of a power strike, for which the Government put a ban on the use of floodlight for sporting activities, and the Country suffered electricity cuts. The match was remarkable because of the only goal, scored by Scunthorpe, after just twelve seconds.

No doubt the routine had been practiced many times before, but at kick-off United lined up with five men on the halfway line between the centre spot and the wing. This was a most unheard of and a confusing situation. Ken Houghton passed the first ball to Graham Collier, who eased it back behind him to Chris Simpkin. Simpkin ran forward towards the left of centre, and gave short pass to Stuart Pilling. Pilling looked up and lobbed the ball over the keeper for 1-0, and the rest is history.

Scunthorpe United needed to wait to see if they would play Newcastle United or Hendon in the Fourth Round of the Cup, and no disrespect to Hendon, but supporters were pleased that it did turn out to be up in the North East. On January 26th 1974 Scunthorpe ran out at St James' Park to the thunderous appreciation of 37,870 throats. Ron Bradley selected the following eleven for the game: Barnard; Collard and Lynch; Simpkins, Welbourne and Money; Houghton, Pilling, Warnock, Keeley and Davidson.

Scunthorpe United played an excellent game of cultured football, promoted by short neat and precise passes. Newcastle were big and skilful through the entire team, but Scunthorpe United had the travelling supporters on their feet first.

Scunthorpe reached the F.A.Cup fourth round, where they lost in a replay to Newcastle United 3-0, at the Old Show Ground. Desparate defending is required from the Iron, in dark shirts.

A collision between Jim Smith of Newcastle and the referee led to a bounce up close to the centre spot. The Magpies won the ball, but when Alan Kennedy attempted a back pass, Nolan Keeley intercepted, and flicked the ball into the target. Richard Money then hit a post, and Ken Houghton put wide when McFaul in Newcastle United's goal was beaten.

In the second forty five minutes Newcastle left the tunnel a different team, and put a lot of pressure on the Scunthorpe back lines. Fifteen minutes into the restart and Terry McDermott set a twenty five yard screamer into the net, out of the stretch of Geoff Barnard's reach. The rest of the game was a case of all hands to the pumps for survival, but they just managed to hang on to the 1-1 draw.

On the following Tuesday, a crowd of 19,028 spectators braved the cold conditions to welcome the twenty two players to the Old Show Ground. This time the International stars of Newcastle United made sure there was to be no further embarrassment. One man in particular was to stand out, and that was a Magpie with a London accent. Malcolm MacDonald was the England centre forward, and he stamped his authority on the match from the off, taking no notice of some interesting suggestions from the home support. He scored two brilliant goals, and Barrowclough added a third, to emphasise the difference in class between the teams. United may have lost 3-0, but were by no means disgraced.

Once United had been eliminated from the Cup, they hit a bad patch of Fourth Division form which brought the meagre rations of two draws and no wins in a seven match spell, starting at New Year. When the goals dried up, Ron Bradley went into the transfer market and signed Dudley Roberts from Mansfield Town, while Les Andrews was used on loan from Wolves for two months. They both linked up in the 2-2 draw at Mansfield Town to score United's goals, but form at the end of the year was patchy, to say the least. In the last ten games three were won, two finished as goalless draws, and the remainder were all lost, including the final three fixtures of the card.

It was hardly inspiring football, but left the Iron safe in fifteenth table position. Not one bit of surprise was expressed, when the average gate fell to an all time low of 3,029. The board could only thank goodness for the F.A.Cup.

1974-75

Scunthorpe United released a number of players during the closed season, and no more was to be seen of Mike Williams, Ken Houghton and Bruce Collard. One of the main replacements was Alan Sproates, who had notched up more than three hundred appearances at Darlington. During the previous season, the Quakers had loaned him to neighbours Hartlepool, and Alan took the opportunity to find new pastures. Ron Bradley was to use him, at first in a forward role, but then he dropped back into the spaces of mid-field.

Scunthorpe United retained their tradition of bringing players through the junior ranks, and at left fullback John Peacock came in for half of the games to partner Peter Markham. John was a Leeds born young man, who would settle in during the next couple of years. To add cover to the goalkeeping slot, Ron Bradley brought back Jim Lavery, from non-League football, for a short spell but Geoff Barnard was always the supporters number one choice. Other newcomers included Steve Earl, Derek Charnley and Eddy Taylor, all for minor roles. Derek Charnley was to use every different shirt number in the next two years, expect that of the goalkeeper.

On the opening day of the football year, the Workington versus Scunthorpe match, at Borough Park, certainly was not the Wembley Cup Final clash. It was, however, disappointing to learn that it only attracted 1,656 supporters, less than one hundred of which arrived from Lincolnshire. Perhaps it was to be explained in the fact that these two clubs would be at the very base of the division for most of the season. At least Angus Davison did make the return journey a little more pleasant, when he hit a second half equaliser, to register a 1-1 result.

At this early time of the football calendar the League Cup was a priority for the Iron, and Sheffield Wednesday, from the Second Division, called by the Old Show Ground for the first match on home turf. United played extremely well, and had the luck of winning a penalty kick. This was promptly dispatched by Angus Davidson into the corner of the net and Scunthorpe upset the bookmakers' odds to win 1-0. The draw for the Second Round took them to the massive hall of Maine Road, Manchester, to play against the Internationals of Manchester City. Only 14,790 spectators saw United chase their own shadows and lose 6-0, five of the goals coming as they tired in the second half.

In the first two months of the season, Scunthorpe United found the basic art of putting the ball in the net an almost impossible task.

They only scored six goals in the opening ten games, and did not win until the eleventh of the season, at home to Barnsley. A crowd of 2,157 spectators were lifted by Neil Warnock's goal, and then it was a case of holding on for the remainder of the match, and see that every ball was kept as far away from Jim Lavery's goal as possible.

The shocking form continued unceasingly throughout the Autumn.. United had won only two games when November arrived, and the were like a canoeist without a paddle, heading straight for the rocks. On November 7th 1974 Ron Bradley put his hands up and admitted defeat. He was a complete gentleman, and offered his resignation, which the board accepted with immediate effect. The reins were passed to Jeff Barker on a temporary basis, until a suitable choice could be found. It was not too long before Dickie Rooks, the former Sunderland, Middlesbrough and Bristol City player was appointed as the new manager. His task was to hoist the Club back to respectability.

In an effort to put some money in the direction of the board of directors, the Council made an offer of £70,000 for the Old Show Ground. It was very tempting, but in hindsight it was best that it was politely rejected.

Dickie Rookes had barley had time to try his seat out in his new office, when it was time for a visit from the non-League team of Altrincham, who were a decent club, with aspirations to join the Football League. In the First Round tie, in Scunthorpe, they looked the better of the two sides, and United were pleased to hang on for a replay. Over at Altrincham United were humbled 3-1, and appeared to be a sorry side for most of the ninety minutes.

When the New Year began, the situation at the Club was still a total mess. The team had managed to gather a pathetic four points on their travels, all of which came from drawn matches. At home they had still only two victories to their name, and it was a scramble to see if they could move away from the bottom of the table. If that was not bad enough, the B.B.C. made a programme at the Old Show Ground under the banner of 'Life at the Bottom'. Ironically, on the day the cameras called to film them in action, they beat Newport County 4-1, and Dudley Roberts hit the first Scunthorpe hat-tick since Barry Thomas in 1966. This still did not raise the Iron from the bottom place.

It was hard for supporters to see a way through the nightmare, and Dickie Rooks had no war chest to spend, in a bid to change his personnel. He was bold enough to throw Bob Oates in at the deep end for a debut, as a central defender, and the big youngster played competently to warrant a regular inclusion. Bob came from Leeds Ashley Road junior club, and would play more than three hundred games for the Iron during the coming eight years. Mike Norris also had a trial between the posts, but Geoff Barnard was never too far away.

Following the Newport match, spasmodic wins came, and remarkably the team raised its game on one occasion to beat second placed Shrewsbury Town, 1-0. Consecutive wins were achieved for the first time on the visit of a poor Workington side in the next fixture, but United had a struggle to overcome the Cumbrian men by a 2-1 score.

On March 18th 1975, the Workington result was to be the last time in the season that the team gathered the grateful harvest of two points. United's sorry tale of woe finished by recording three draws and seven disastrous losses. They suffered a crushing 7-0 defeat at Mansfield, on the night when the Stags celebrated being Champions of the Fourth Division. At no moment did any of the lads stop trying, but as a collective unit they were not good enough in this company of football.

Stern faced Dudley Roberts had reason to smile as he became the leading goalscorer at the end of the tough 1974-75 season.

The conclusion was that for the one and only time Scunthorpe United had finished as the bottom club in the entire Football League. They had gained the meagre bounty of twenty nine point, won just seven matches and drawn fifteen. Not one of their matches on their travels had been won. Only forty one goals were scored, but seventy eight went in the Scunthorpe United net. The average attendance slumped to 2,239.

It was with these statistics that the Scunthorpe board had to go cap in hand to the Football League A.G.M. and seek re-election. All of a sudden the boot was on the other foot, and they hoped that their position was not taken by a non-League club. Fortunately, the Club received another chance, and was voted back in quite comfortably, but the shock posted a warning to everybody. There was a huge sigh of relief when the season was finally put to bed, and they prepared for the next step forward.

1975-76

The board of directors knew that a complete make over was impossible, and the piggy bank was empty, but they would soldier on and hope to unearth some talent from somewhere. Optimism and patience remained the key factors.

Dickie Rooks was to lose a number of faces through natural evolution, and this was to offer new possibilities. On the way out were two of the Scunthorpe United keepers. Jim Lavery was not retained, and the popular Geoff Barnard decided to take a job outside the game, after close to three hundred games.

Alan Sproates was emigrating with his family to Australia, and Chris Simpkin moved to Huddersfield, to replenish the coffers with a modest fee. Mick Atkin had the chance to continue as a school teacher, and also left the professional game. Dudley Roberts was shortly to suffer a long term injury, and would play one single game more.

To ease the goalkeeping situation Rooks brought in a young trainee called Alan O'Meara, who was on the small side for a custodian, but during the season he was given an opportunity to succeed Mike Norris. For the middle of the park, Archie Irvine was a former Sheffield Wednesday man, brought in from Doncaster Rovers. Archie was a Scotsman who could play either side of the mid-field, and had blond hair which neatly covered up his ears. To control the central defensive role, United took on board a tall man of experience, from Grimsby Town. He was Clive Wiggington, who was just type to tough competitor that was missing last year.

Dickie Rooks improved his forward line with the injection of two men. The first was Doug O'Connor, who was a wing man from Barnsley. Next John Woodward came as a goal scoring forward from Port Vale, but he had seen service at Walsall, Aston Villa and Stoke. These men would be supplemented by the retained players, which included Peter Markham, John Peacock, Richard Money, Derek Charnley, Nolan Keeley, Stuart Pilling, Bob Oates, Angus Davidson, and Graham Collier.

Scunthorpe United supporters thought it was a case of déjà vu when no goals came from the first six matches. This saw the Iron knocked out of the League Cup, 6-0 on aggregate by Mansfield Town, gain a single point from a goalless encounter at Newport, and resume the bottom place in the division after the defeat at home to Huddersfield Town.

United needed to solve the problem rapidly, and they did so by taking striker Jeff Hemmerman on loan from Hull City. The improvement was immediate, if not permanent, and the team responded with a pair of victories in consecutive matches. The first was a priceless 2-1 win at Hartlepool, and Hemmerman scored the first goal of the season. Graham Collier was on hand for the winner. It was the first away victory since April 1974. At home to Torquay United, United eased to a 3-1 result.

Rooks would have loved to have signed the Hull City forward on a full contract, but he was wanted back at Boothferry Park.

The other alternative was to turn to big Rick Green, who had been scoring goals for fun with the Appleby Frodingham works team. Rick was only too pleased to roll up his sleeves in the team he had supported as boy, and quickly adapted to the rigours of the Fourth Division. His physique was a great asset in muscling into the opposition defences, and supporters warmed to his efforts. The first Rick Green goal was at home to Rochdale, but United lost, and were anchored at the wrong end of the League once again. The team was to show no control of the deteriorating situation, which brought six consecutive defeats. When Workington paid a call the team did manage to sort their problems out and the 1,503 spectators dotted around the Old Show Ground did have a handsome, if not rare, 3-0 victory to salute. At half time no team had beaten the respective goalkeepers, and those present wondered who might break the deadlock. In the next half, Nolan Keeley notched the first goal, while Rick Green was a hero for shooting the other two.

Scunthorpe United were offered no relief in the F.A.Cup. Their task was a difficult one, away to Preston North End, from the Third Division. The team played far better than in recent weeks, but still lost 2-1. Rick Green actually put them in front, on thirty three minutes, with a beautifully placed lob shot, after Richard Money's original effort was punched out. In the fifty third minute, United gave away a penalty for a mistimed tackle, and minutes from the end they were undone by a headed goal.

Dickie Rooks was not happy with the goalkeeping position at the Old Show Ground, and it was obvious that the two young men covering the green jersey needed to regain some confidence. Neither were on the top of their games, as results confirmed. He returned to his old club, Bristol City, and persuaded Len Bond to spend two months, over Christmas, lending Scunthorpe a hand. During his spell at the Old Show Ground Len played eight matches in the Scunthorpe United team, and after two defeats he was able to assist the Club to a pair of points from goalless draws. The best of these was on Boxing Day, at Valley Parade, against Bradford City.

The most notable performance of Len Bond's tour of Lincolnshire was after the Bradford game. United had another Yorkshire opponent, and they were neighbours Doncaster Rovers. A crowd of 5,801 was the biggest attendance to pass by the turnstiles for a League match that season, and United rose to the occasion. All of a sudden, the team that was shot shy was blasting the ball at the goal from all angles. In the fourth minute the policy paid off, and Rick Green slipped a ball in front of Angus Davidson, and the nimble Scotsman danced into a position to fire a superb shot into the inviting net. Peter Kitchen found an equaliser, but after the tea interval John Woodward settled the dispute, when he found some room in the box, and sent a sizzling shot past Graham Brown in the goal. Many more shots were saved or just off target.

Scunthorpe United entered the New Year unable to keep a consistent run of form together. Wins were far and few to be found, and the team had occupied the bottom two positions for the majority of the campaign. Supporters were in despair as to when the team might to sort itself out, and deliver anything like a reasonable performance on a regular footing. Everyone was starting to give up hope, especially when there were rumblings in the National press that clubs that could not cope should be weeded out and replaced by those from the non-League circles that could.

In January, the Scunthorpe United Chairman, Mr Jack Empson, announced the dismissal Dickie Rooks, and within three days Ron Ashman was invited back to be the new manager. His task was simply to see that the Iron survived the current turmoil, and avoid seeking re-election.

Ron Ashman had been working outside the sport, but was keeping in touch with what was happening at his old club. He knew immediately where the solution lay. Confidence would only come with results. Players needed to become fitter, play in their favourite positions, and be encouraged to do the simple things in the game, such as not being generous to the opposition by passing the ball to them.

A tighter game was required at the back, and if in trouble, aim for the top row of the East Stand. The middle of the park had to forget about fancy football and bang the ball to feet every time. The front men had to get wise to firing the ball as many times at the target as they could. If ten shots hit the back wall of the Doncaster Road Stand, but the next one went in, then it was better than dilly dallying about, not shooting at all. If it was necessary, the mid-field could be missed out and the ball knocked up from the back to put Rick Green directly on goal, then so be it

Ron Ashman's first game back was away at Cambridge, and United returned with the prize of a point from a 2-2 draw, thanks to goals by Nolan Keeley and Angus Davidson. The next match was at home to high flying Watford, and although the side lost 1-0, the defence was tighter, and the play was a lot more organised. Interest in the return of Ron Ashman put another five hundred on the gate. They then received the boost of a second away win, at Workington, on the following Tuesday. In this match they squeezed three goals for only the second time in the year. Rick Green notched two of them and Angus Davison the third, in what was a productive 3-2 result.

All of a sudden the penny had dropped, and the team started to get their act together. Rick Green was given the right sort of ammunition, and was finding the target. The win at Workington was the first in a spell of eight matches that contained just one defeat, on the road at Northampton, and contained four wins. Rick Green scored in four consecutive matches, including a 5-1 demolition of Hartlepool, in which he recorded a pair.

Graham Collier arrived from Nottingham Forest in 1972 and gave United five valuable years as a midfielder, playing almost two hundred games

Geoff Barnard, was outstanding, from 1968 until 1977, playing in exactly three hundred matches - a record number for a United goalkeeper.

On March 20th 1976 United entertained Graham Taylor's Lincoln City at the Old Show Ground, which was heaving with a gate of 10,329, to see the Imps on their way to a record number of Fourth Division points. This Lincoln City team really did deserve all the accolades, because they were smooth in every department. Scunthorpe United may have been the poor relations, but give them credit for covering every blade of grass in the chase that led to a 2-0 defeat.

Scunthorpe United had moved off the bottom of the table, but still needed every point to escape the four re-election places. Easter would be a make or break time for Ron Ashman's boys, and they went into it on the back of a five match unbeaten run, that contained a win and four draws. The first of three matches was at home to Bradford City, where 3,254 supporters saw Alan O'Meara keep a clean sheet, and United earned maximum points, through goals from Green and O'Connor. Scunthorpe's revival was starting to sound the alarm bells in camps at Darlington Stockport and Newport, as the Iron forced a way through.

The job was not done yet, but on Easter Monday a legion of supporters went down the Road to cheer the team on at Doncaster. They gave the Iron great vocal encouragement from the cage behind the airstrip end, and United scored only their third away victory, with a 1-0 score, supplied via another Rick Green scorcher.

Twenty four hours later and United put themselves in a strong position for the great escape, at home to Barnsley. A crowd of 4,770 shouted their allegiance to the cause, and United responded in due fashion. The team stuck admirably to the task in hand, and when Doug O'Connor took advantage of a loose ball in the penalty area, his shot on target was greeted with thunderous applause of relief. The two points earned was technically not quite enough to say the job was done, but it would take an unusual set of circumstances for Scunthorpe not to survive seeking re-election.

The last match of the season was the on the distant road to Exeter. Scunthorpe United played a brilliant game and enjoyed a freedom that had not been apparent since they won promotion. The side scored four goals, but lost the thriller 5-4, earning the respect of the Devon crowd, who gave both teams a standing ovation. The result meant that Scunthorpe United had survived, but only on goal average. Three teams all had thirty eight points, and Scunthorpe would occupy nineteenth position, with the best goals ratio of the trio. Darlington also avoided the bottom four, but Stockport could not count themselves so lucky. Before everyone said their good byes, it was handshakes all round. Supporters of the time knew that the whole survival of the Club, in every sense of the word, was down to one man, Ron Ashman. If ever a person deserved a medal it was Ron.

1976-77

Ron Ashman made many changes to the team during the Summer of 1976, the most regrettable one being to decline another contract to the mercurial half back Don Welbourne. Don had suffered an injury, which kept him out of action for long periods of the previous year. He was to be fondly remembered by supporters for three hundred matches of dedication, and was part of the mid-field in the 1972 promotion eleven. Other players that had worn the shirt for the last time included John Woodward, Dudley Roberts, Ray Charnley, Archie Irvine and Mike Norris.

The large number of departures allowed for a small amount of cash to be spent bringing in replacements. Clive Wiggington was joined by a former Grimsby Town colleague, Mike Czuczman, a strong running full back, that tested supporters as to the correct pronunciation of the name, and 'churchman' would be on the mark. He was to be accompanied by a fast winger from Gainsborough Trinity, called Mike Wadsworth, that Ron offered a one year contract to. Mike did not make his name in the game until years later, when he became a respected manager of a number of Football League clubs.

Ron Ashman was still not happy with his goalkeeping position, and to settle the question, he took Glen Letheran on loan from Leeds United, until the beginning of March. Glen was a solidly built man, who had won Welsh under twenty three honours whilst waiting in the wings at Elland Road. Alan O'Meara had to be content to be in reserve. The rest of the team contained established men that had been through the wars, and junior players had now developed into harden campaigners whilst the battle for survival raged on. Youngsters such as Peter Markham, Stuart Pilling, Bob Oates, Richard Money and John Peacock all fitted the bill, while Angus Davidson was a veteran.

Scunthorpe United started the 1976-77 season with two loses, but did a lot better in the League Cup. For the second year they had a two legged tie against Mansfield Town, but wins of 2-0 for each team on home turf, required a replay. Scunthorpe won the toss of a coin for the choice of venue, and at the Old Show Ground a smart performance was rewarded with a safe passage. United triumphed 2-1, thanks to strikes by Doug O'Connor and Mike Wadsworth. The League Cup run was to grind to a halt on the last day of August, when 6,208 spectators turned out on the warm late Summer evening to see them play Notts County. The Nottinghamshire Magpies were of Second Division strength, and the Iron went on to lose respectably, 2-0.

When September arrived, Scunthorpe United were not long in turning out some favourable results from their Fourth Division programme. A visit of Crewe Alexandra produced a 4-0 bonus, and Clive Wiggington got under the Railwaymen's skin, by scoring twice, one of which was from the penalty spot.

When Keeley and O'Connor added others, the Iron supporters in the 3,286 crowd could hardly believe it. During the next two months a further four home victories went on record, and they even pinched the two points on offer at Halifax Town. This lifted the team into eighth position in the table for one brief stage.

The approach of the Autumn, and the golden leaves falling from the trees, was the beginning of more austere times for the Iron. They started a slide in November by losing 5-1 at Barnsley, where the Oakwell was not the happiest of hunting grounds for the team. This was followed by two consecutive home defeats, one in the League to Aldershot, and another in the F.A.Cup to Chesterfield. It was not that all of a sudden the team had become a bad one, and they proved it by winning in Devon, at Plainmoor, the home of Torquay United. News in Scunthorpe of a 3-1 win was greeted with delight by Scunthorpe followers. The main toast was to winger Doug O'Connor, who was in the correct place to put the ball in the net on each of the three occasions.

At Christmas, no further wins had been recorded, although they had two very close matches against Doncaster Rovers at home, followed by a visit to Leeds Road to play Huddersfield Town. United fought hard to gain a point from a draw, aided by a Rick Green strike in contest with the Rovers. The Scunthorpe luck was out on their travels, and they ran their legs off for no reward from the 1-0 defeat against the Terriers. In the New Year the Iron had a greater fortune, and their efforts brought the full fruits of victory in two home matches against Bradford City and Brentford. It was to put the team just under the halfway point in the table.

In the second week of February United received a bid of £20,000 from Chesterfield for big Rick Green, who had made tremendous progress since his non-League days. Rick had been on a goal every three matches, and gave the Chesterfield defence a battering in the F.A.Cup match. Every one wished the pleasant giant good luck for his future career.

The papers for Rick Green's transfer had barely been received at the Football League headquarters, when Ron Ashman was knocking at the door of Brigg Town, to sign ex-Grimsby Town man Jim Lumby, to fill the gap left in the forward line. The two competitors could not have been further apart in terms of stature and style. Jim was slightly built, and was like a ferret, hunting for the ball, rather than as a target man who used his weight. It was not to be long before Jim was on the goal trail, and the transition was a smooth one.

This was not the only alteration to the front end of the attack. Ron Ashman was never afraid to blood the young element, and at the same as Jim Lumby arriving at the Club, a debut was given to Kevin Kilmore, a Scunthorpe born trainee. The two players linked up quite satisfactorily together, and between them notched eleven goals.

The beginning of March found life hard for Scunthorpe United, and they were having to scratch for each win, especially on the road. It put the Club back on the edge of the bottom four positions. At least the six matches of the month brought three wins and three loses to balance the books. The finest result was the 4-1 beating of Exeter City, the team that would celebrate promotion in second place in the table. Jim Lumby scored two goals for the Iron and Czuczman added another. The fourth goal was down to the generosity of a visiting defender, but victory looked assured by half time, when the team held a 3-1 advantage.

Before the season was finally wound up, there was a cameo from Geoff Barnard, who answered Ron Ashman's emergency call for cover. Geoff was applauded at every touch of the ball, and in his first match back he kept a clean pair of hands, to assist the team beat Newport County 1-0. It was to be the last win of the campaign, but United would limp home safely. Eventually, Geoff Barnard made six appearances, which took his Scunthorpe United figures to exactly three hundred games in all competitions.

At the end of the season Scunthorpe United had not had the same scare as twelve months ago, but the rations of three draws and two defeats in the last five games gave them a points total of thirty seven, which was one less than last year, and they fell one place to twentieth in the table. One more position lower would have required them to seek re-election, but they had survived, and that was all that was important.

1977-78

The news of the Summer was that Workington had been disenfranchised from the Football League and Wimbledon voted in their place. It served as a warning to other perennial offenders, regularly finishing in the bottom places, that other teams would step forward, and they would lose their status. A repercussion of Workington's dismissal was that Ron Ashman offered terms to one of their players, Eamon Kavanagh, a mid-fielder who had scored against the Iron in the 1974-75 season, at Borough Park. The middle belt was to benefit from the services of Bernard Bridges, a Doncaster born lad, who had made progress through the junior ranks.

The attack was to enjoy the company of a new winger, called Brian Heron, who was a Scotsman, signed from Oxford United. Brian had not been able to get back into the Oxford Second Division team after recovering from a broken leg, and the change of scenery was to do all parties good. The final quest was for a tried and tested goalkeeper, and Ron Ashman found just the ticket at York City. Graeme Crawford was an excellent choice, and was considered to be one of the safest pairs of hands in the lower divisions. Like Brian Heron, Graeme was also born North of the border.

Making way for these changes, United had to say farewell to five of last years squad. The longest serving player that was to leave was that of Angus Davidson, who had played more than three hundred and sixty games for United, and scored forty six goals in the process. He was accompanied by Graham Collier, who went to Barnsley, Clive Wiggington, departing for a fee to Lincoln City, while Doug O'Connor Mike Wadsworth and Peter Markham next played football outside of the Football League.

Scunthorpe United made a positive beginning to the new set of fixtures, gleaning four points from a win and two draws, in the first three games. The victory was at home to Crewe, who had suffered at the hands of the Iron last year. This time the 3-0 damage was not quite so severe. There was even a short run in the League Cup, which brought Darlington to their knees. At the Feethams, no team found the target, and in the second leg United had a comfortable 3-1 result. The aggregate score was what mattered, and Scunthorpe met Peterborough at London Road in Round Two. This match ended 1-1, and Stuart Pilling fired the Scunthorpe goal. In the replay the team fluffed their lines, and lost 1-0.

At the start of September the team's quest in the League ran up three disappointing consecutive loses, and the light was only turned on for the advent of Wimbledon making their debut at the Old Show Ground. Life had not been a bed of roses for the South London boys, and they continued to suffer in Lincolnshire. The only puzzling point to consider for the 2,618 supporters was how could Scunthorpe play so ordinary and win 3-0? Bob Oates would not worry about that, because he scored twice on the afternoon, and only made fifteen goals in a career of more than three hundred appearances. Jim Lumby added the rest to the Scunthorpe mixture.

Before the season advanced too far, John Kaye was brought to the Club to become the Assistant Manager to Ron Ashman. It was to ease the burden off Ron's shoulders, who was not getting any younger. John was to use his vast experience of more than ten years at West Bromwich Albion and Hull City, particularly in a coaching role.

In October United's form continued to bewilder supporters, and reached its nadir, in the game at Torquay United. The team slumped to a 4-2 loss, and the Iron had the generosity of a Torquay defender to thank for one of their goals. Jim Lumby held the torch for the forward line with the other goal, converted from the penalty spot, and Richard Money was responsible for some sterling work in defence. The dismal result saw Scunthorpe reach as low as the third from bottom place. This match was to mark the debut of Ron Wigg, a player that had as many clubs to his name as a golfer. He had already scored twice against Scunthorpe playing for Barnsley, his last team. Ron was the type of player that floated through games, then would strike like a viper.

Once he was in harness the side was to have a change in fortune. The resurgence may not had been too dramatic, but in the next eight matches, half of them were won, starting with the ensuing tussle against Halifax Town. Jim Lumby managed to get the Scunthorpe circus rolling, when he neatly tucked away a penalty, that Jack Brownsword would have been proud of. Indeed, the penalty taking was much more accurate, and yielded seven rewards through the year. Once Nolan Keeley had the second ball shot firmly into the target, United knew the 2-0 result would give them the points.

At the end of November, Scunthorpe United has a trip into Cheshire for the F.A.Cup. The game was at Edgely Park in contest with Stockport County of the same division. The interest for Scunthorpe fanatics was the non appearance of their reliable central defender Richard Money, who was the gold nugget in the team. It was soon learned that he was in London at Fulham, negotiating personal terms, after a £50,000 deal had been thrashed out. The gaping hole left at the back probably explained the 3-0 exit the team suffered from the senior competition.

The loss of Money from the team required some surgery, and initially Ron Ashman brought Mike Czuczman into the middle, allowing West Ham junior player Steve Davy, who had been groomed locally, to fill in at full back. During the month Jon O'Donnell arrived from Hartlepool, and Terry Cooper came from Lincoln City on loan. Local boy Bob Lee was promoted for three matches from the reserves, and all these changes allowed the team to sail towards the Christmas period.

December was not too unkind to the team, and they went into the holiday matches on the back of a 3-0 result at home to Darlington, which saw the visitors given a sound chasing. United did not have any problems putting opponents down at the Show Ground, but on their voyages they had yet to win. On Boxing Day, they were along the A18 at Doncaster but the all impor-tant first away victory still did not mature. However, when Ron Wigg breezed in out of nowhere, a goal did settle a 1-1 result with the equaliser, to add an important point to the total. The team played better, the following day, for the home clash with York City. Jim Lumby gave his reputation another boost with two goals, as the scouts pencilled down notes after the Iron won 2-1.

The Winter months brought whispers of the possibility of a couple of signings, but the Club kept tight lipped about any deals. All of a sudden, during the first week of February, there was an announcement. Scunthorpe United had negotiated with Hull City to buy their Scunthorpe born midfielder Vinny Grimes, a players of considerable credence, for the engine room department. When John Kaye was manager at Hull he had brought Vinny through from junior level, all the way into the first eleven, and what an asset he was to be.

The month was three quarters through when another major signing was completed. Ron Ashman had been keeping tabs on the Iron's former central defender Steven Deere, who by this time had left Hull City, and was in non-League football on the Yorkshire coast, at Scarborough. During his stay at Seamer Road Steven won an F.A. Challenge Trophy medal at Wembley. When asked the question by Ron Ashman, Steven was packing his bags to head towards the Old Show Ground.

On the occasion of the first time these two quality players ran out of the tunnel together, Scunthorpe United had an away fixture at the County Ground, in Northampton. It was a three sided arena, which staged both Football League and County Cricket fixtures. Scunthorpe United threw off all their old inhibitions and rose to the challenge. They had a band of no more than one hundred travelling supporters dancing on the terraces with two goals. Jim Lumby shot the first and Steven Deere bundled in the second, which allowed the team to end the afternoon as 2-1 winners.

Jim Lumby became United's leading scorer in the 1977-78 campaign, with twenty one League and Cup goals. Seen here scoring one, before his end of season move to Carlisle.

In was just the boost the team required, as they looked forward to the derby clash with Grimsby Town, at the Old Show Ground, in the first week of March. United knew the Mariners were not invincible, because the two team shared a goalless draw, at Blundell Park. This time an invigorated Scunthorpe forgot the hoodoo the Town team usually had over the them, and made sure the visitors knew who the bosses were. United took a commanding two goal lead through the deadly boots of Jim Lumby, one of which was from the twelve yard spot. In the second half Grimsby rallied, but the 2-1 score was soon to be the result. Certainly everyone in the home section of the 7,612 attendance thought the points were going to the rightful home.

During the first week of April, Scunthorpe United received a £30,000 offer from Carlisle United for the Club's highly rated goal scorer, Jim Lumby. It was a welcome return for a lad who cost a small pittance from Brigg Town, after rejection by Grimsby. The last time he ran out in the all red colours of Scunthorpe United was on April 4th 1978, when the Iron won 2-0. Both of the goals were scored by the new kid on the block, Kevin Kilmore. This was also to give a chance to Geoff Crouch from Crowle United, of local football as in inside forward.

The remaining seven games of the season, including that against Newport, produced two wins, two defeats and three draws. Since the dismal performances earlier in the campaign, the team had slowly but surely inched towards the middle of the table. At the end of the fixture card, Scunthorpe United had risen to a respectable fourteenth on the ladder. Understandably, Jim Lumby was the leading marksman on twenty one goals, but Bob Oates and Kevin Kilmore each had eight. It should also be noted that Graeme Crawford, Bob Oates and Nolan Keeley had been ever present through the whole year.

The school report confirmed an improvement, but said the pupil could do better.

1978-79

During the closed season Ron Ashman did not sign too many new players, because of the activities late in the day of the last campaign. He did go back to Hull City to sign a utility man called Dave Gibson, who generally operated in an advanced position. The forward line was also supplemented by Steve Bloomer, from Brigg Town.

The opening of the 1978-79 season began with two legs in the League Cup against Notts County, a team that had just finished the previous year as a Second Division club. Ron Ashman's boys had the toughest of struggles to keep pace with the Magpies, but losing 1-0 at home and 3-0 away perhaps did not reflect the amount of perseverance that the Iron put into the two games.

The task of goal scoring was passed to local boy, Kevin Kilmore for the 1978-79 year, and seventeen strikes displayed his potential.

The Fourth Division fixtures began on the open spaces of Vale Park, in the Potteries, against a useful Port Vale team. Scunthorpe earned a 2-2, but it took a goal right up on the wire to pinch the point. It was scored by that old trooper Stuart Pilling, a player so reliable that by now he had been asked by Ron Ashman to cover every out field position. Little wonder he was a crowd favourite, and deservedly so. This result was followed by home victories against Bournemouth, 1-0, and Huddersfield, 3-1. Remarkably, Pilling scored in each match, making him the leading scorer on three strikes. A further point was yielded from a goalless draw at Doncaster, but unfortunately Nolan Keeley limped out of the battle, and was side-lined for two months.

At the end of September, the team had lost only three matches, all 1-0, but had four wins under the belt plus three draws. They were in a comfortable middle table placing without too many worries. The start of Autumn was not to be quite as rewarding for the Iron, and began with a give away, at home to Newport County. United had every opportunity to win the game, but the useful Welshmen took advantage of United's frailty in the back quarters on the afternoon, and recorded a 3-2 away win. Scunthorpe still had no victories on their travels, and this continued with a defeat at Wimbledon, but a useful point from Hartlepool.

The only victory of the October was a game in conflict with Bradford City, which was liberally sprinkled with goals.

United won 3-2, and the game saw Geoff Couch score his first for Scunthorpe, while Kevin Kilmore notched the other two. One of these kept up the tradition of securing goals from the penalty spot. November finished with a 3-2 loss at Huddersfield, made regrettable for the throwing away of a two goal lead at the interval.

At the end of November, United lined up to face Sheffield Wednesday in the F.A.Cup. The Owls were not the First Division aristocrats of the 1970 battle, but a Third Division team striving to regain former glories. This time the tie attracted 8,697 paying customers. They had to wait until the sixtieth minute for the opening goal on the muddy Old Show Ground pitch. Stuart Pilling picked up a ball, and ran on a speed to the Wednesday defence. When he was not closed down he let fly and scored. While United fans were on their feet celebrating, Ian Nimmo silenced the cheers with the equaliser, and set the visiting fans off in similar fashion. On the following Tuesday night, the same player scored a very late goal, on a particularly cold night, to put Wednesday through.

In the first week of December Ron Ashman used his considerable ability to unearth local talent, and offered a contract to Steve Earl, who was leading the attack of the Appleby Frodingham works team. He was thrown it at the deep end and began almost ever present until the end of the season, as the spearhead of the attack. Steve was not afraid to put himself about, and weighed in with a number of goals to his credit.

Scunthorpe United seemed to wake up with the inclusion of Steve Earl in the team, and on his debut won by a penalty goal, tucked away by Kevin Kilmore, at Torquay. Back to back wins came, when Hereford United found the going too tough at the Old Show Ground, and the 4-2 result was an echo of the ups and downs experienced by both set of supporters. Kevin Kilmore scored twice, Stuart Pilling added another, and Steve Earl notched his first for the men in red. After a point at Darlington, the team rubbed salt in the wounds of Grimsby Town, by beating the Mariners 2-1 in front of 8,008 enthusiastic fans at the Old Show Ground, on Boxing Day.

The last game of 1978 was at home to Rochdale, a team that had no wins on its travels, and were languishing at the foot of the table. During the Saturday morning heavy snow fell throughout the Country and many matches were postponed. Everyone was amazed that the match with Rochdale still went ahead, despite the Old Show Ground being covered with three or four inches of the white gold, and heavy flakes continued to fall. Every turn of the ball seemed to make it increase in size, but the referee was happy for the match to continue in front of the 2,620 spectators. In the end Rochdale won the snow ball fight 4-0. The weather made sure that this was the last football in the town until March.

January was a complete write-off, and in February a loss in Aldershot was balanced by victory at Stockport County, both being 2-0 scores. This was all there was to offer in the midst of the bleakest of Winters. The Old Show Ground did not open for business until March 10th 1979, when York City came to a thawing Lincolnshire. It was then that United missed the opportunity of salvaging a point, when Kevin Kilmore shot three penalties at the York custodian, Joe Neenan. He hit the target twice, but Joe smothered the third, and the Iron lost 3-2.

It took Scunthorpe United some time before the rusty old wheels of the team began to get moving again. They came under the cosh in most matches, as the Winter continued to stretch into the month, unwilling to recede back to the North Pole. However, in one match United did manage to steal two very naughty points against Reading, at Elm Park. An army of volunteers moved a mountain of snow from the pitch, so that the Friday evening fixture could go ahead. Nolan Keeley scored in the first few minutes, and for the rest of the time the defence took an almighty battering. Miraculously the team held out, and when Reading were crowned Champions, the only dent in their home record was against Scunthorpe.

The rest of a packed March programme was to continue with an inconsistent run of form, and only brought a further win from the visit of Port Vale. An exasperated Ron Ashman thought it was time to see what another of his young army of reserve players could do. He promoted David Hall, a Scunthorpe apprentice, into the left side of mid-field, and the Doncaster born lad did sufficiently well to warrant his inclusion until the end of the season.

April was an equally swollen month, as far as fixtures and rearranged games were concerned. United held their own, and of nine games played three wins, three draws and three defeats was about par for the course. Of all those matches, the main theatre was at Blundell Park, against the mighty Grimsby Town, heading to a second place in the table. The fans in the black and white scarves were convinced the Iron would be put to slaughter, but the sense of occasion brought United through safely. They were content to register a point from a 1-1 draw, and Eamon Kavanagh did the damage.

The horrific Winter weather meant that matches continued to be played into the middle of May. Scunthorpe United finished their card with a little flourish of three consecutive wins, including one at Halifax, in the final burst of the football year. Goals by Couch, Grimes and Gibson produced a 3-2 victory, which made the surprising total of five on the road. In the end, Captain Grimes had led his troops into twelfth position in the table, and the honour of being the top marksman went to Kevin Kilmore, for his tally of seventeen. The players could now fly off to the sun and leave the problems of football behind, until it was time for the pre-season training slog.

1979-80

It was not long before everyone was back in training, trying to knock off the odd extra pounds, but one player that was absent was Mike Czuczman, who had been transferred to Stockport County.

The ranks of the team were to be increased by a tall utility man called Malcolm Partridge, who could be just as happy in attack as at the back. The former Grimsby Town man would be a welcomed addition. Ron also spotted an excellent right winger, Paul O'Berg, at non-League Bridlington. Paul was on the small side, but possessed an accurate cross, and was capable of beating his man. It was apparent on his Football League debut that he would fit in so brilliantly well. Within a short space of time Ron Ashman promoted Chris Cowling to the forward line. Chris was a tall local player who would make the best of his opportunity, and settled with the senior squad on the right side of the field.

In the League Cup the Scunthorpe United ball was followed out of the hat by that of Grimsby Town. The Mariners had a strong team, that was heading places, and they won the first of the two legs at Blundell Park 2-0. In the return match United put up a brave performance, but Town repelled everything that came towards their goal, and neither side scored. The situation in the Fourth Division began in a similar vein, and the first three matches all had the Iron trailing on the final whistle. At Portsmouth the team received a severe 6-1 mauling, with just a Stuart Pilling strike as a minor consolation. Although it was early in the season, the result dumped the Iron to the bottom of the table, and a long term injury to Vinny Grimes was not to assist the situation.

Ron Ashman was given permission to spend £25,000 and bring Rick Green back to the Old Show Ground from Notts County. He went straight into the side and 1,471 souls saw him score in his return game against Bournemouth, as United won 2-1. Within a fortnight Grimsby Town came in with an acceptable £60,000 cheque for Kevin Kilmore. Almost before the ink was dry on the forms, Ron went out and brought in one of the most brilliant marksman for this level of football that the Club could have hoped for. He was Steve Cammack, who cost £15,000 from Chesterfield. Steve was a fair haired lad, who could score from all angles with both feet and his head. He was a first class player, and a superb person to have around.

Once everyone was in place, United showed what they could do in two home matches. Huddersfield would be the Champions, but they were held to a 1-1 draw at Scunthorpe, and Rick Green proved his worth again. The floodlights illuminated the pitch in mid-week for the York City encounter, and Scunthorpe delighted the 2,365 patrons with an exhilarating 6-1 performance.

The chief architect was Malcolm Partridge, whose hat-trick included a penalty. Rick Green scored twice, and Steve Cammack fired the first of many in his Scunthorpe United career. The York City goal was the last of the evening, and Peter Lorimer, the former Leeds United and Scotland man put it away.

Bob Oates played almost three hundred and fifty games for Scunthorpe United from 1974 until 1983.

Scunthorpe United continued to struggle to find consistent form, which led well into the Autumn. This saw them lose the away League match at York City, and slip at the first fence in the F.A.Cup to Rochdale, in Lancashire. Ron Ashman tried a new goal keeper by bringing in Jimmy Gordon from Reading, and he paid Grantham a small fee for a tall Scottish central defender, David Dall. John Kaye knew of an ex-Tiger at Chelsea in the second eleven, and it led to midfielder David Stewart being taken from Stamford Bridge. Dave had the quality to have won a full cap for Northern Ireland, and he would fire up the boiler room, where Vinny Grimes was still struggling with injury.

Throughout the early part of the Winter, and into the New Year, the Club hovered around the bottom four positions. It was not until another new face appeared that they finally began to rise up the table. He was Graham Pugh, from Barnsley. Graham was to wear the number seven shirt, and operated in an advanced position on the right of the field. He came with a pedigree, having gained a losers medal in the F.A.Cup Final for Sheffield Wednesday against Everton. On his debut, the Iron faced up to Portsmouth with a completely different attitude, and put one over Pompey, when Malcolm Partridge scored the only goal of the ninety minutes.

The weather spoiled part of the football programme, but in February the team had a mixed bag. They began by picking up a point at the Old Show Ground, drawing 3-3 against Bradford City. United should have made more of the match from the comfort of a 3-1 lead. The next game was a complete 5-0 disaster against Doncaster Rovers, at Belle Vue.

Thankfully, the team made amends at home, when Lincoln City were beaten 1-0, before a derby gate of 3,672. Most of them happily cheered when Stuart Pilling was up for the single goal.

The numbers through the turnstiles were never large at this time of day, but to boost the figures Ron Ashman was to bring in a big hitter. He was the England Cricket Captain Ian Botham, who had been a follower of United's fortunes, and trained with them during his cricket closed season. Ron Ashman signed him on a non-contract basis, and he was used as an old fashion centre forward. He was first employed as a substitute at Bournemouth, one Friday evening, on the South Coast. United recovered from 3-0 down to gain a draw, and had two goals from Stuart Pilling plus another from Dave Stewart to thank for the rescue act.

The opening fixture of the 1980-81 brought United in conflict with Aldershot; captain Vinny Grimes in flight during the eventual 2-2 draw.

The last leg of the football year, during April, brought United into a better frame of mind, and they only lost one match. The team managed three 1-0 victories, and another of 3-0, in the last home fixture against Northampton Town. There was even the joy of a third away win, at Rochdale. This was a rare occasion, because the team continued to suffer road sickness on their travels. It was at this late stage of the football year that the Club entered into negotiations with York City, with the view of exchanging goalkeepers. Graeme Crawford returned to Bootham Crescent, while Joe Neenan was to become the regular custodian for Scunthorpe United.

The last match on the list was an away visit to Hereford United, and about thirty hardy Scunthorpe supporters made the voyage. They were rewarded by a point from a 1-1 draw, and clapped and cheered heartily when Stuart Pilling popped up with the Scunthorpe goal. Sadly this was the last glimpse United supporters would see of Steven Deere, who had been a superb servant to the Club, and had played in more than three hundred and eighty appearances for the Iron. He was to take a career outside the game.

The extra point elevated Scunthorpe United to the dizzy height of fourteenth in the table. It was quite astonishing, because they never surfaced higher than nineteenth before the end of March. Away form was still the main cause for concern, and the average crowd of 2,266 was the second smallest on record. Credit for the top marksman went to Malcolm Partridge for his total of fifteen in all competitions.

1980-81

The cash flow at the Old Show Ground was always a problem, and to ease the situation Ron Ashman was forced to prune the wage bill. A number of players had to be told they would no longer be required at the Club, and these included Jon O'Donnell, David Hall, Geoff Couch, Steve Earl and Dave Gibson. In addition, the team was depleted by the loss of Nolan Keeley, who was transferred at a small fee to Lincoln City.

The new season was to see a welcome return of a much fitter Vinny Grimes, although Chris Cowling suffered injury, and Rick Green was unavailable until October.

Ron Ashman was to bring in four men to join the party, the first was Nicky Jarvis from Grantham, for a full back role. At the centre of the defence, United went to local club Barton Town, for a towering London born man, called Alan Boxall. Despite the lack of senior football, Alan was able to step up to the mark, particularly in the second half of the campaign. The next man was Anton Lambert of Long Eaton, a young leader for the attack, which produced mixed fortunes, and less was seen of him in the New Year. Finally, United brought in the vastly experienced Phil Ashworth, a mid-fielder from Portsmouth. Phil actually had his roost in Burnley, and played as a trainee with Blackburn when he first started.

It was not long into the fixtures when Scunthorpe United realised they would not be at Wembley winning the League Cup, because they bravely lost to Barnsley, 3-1 on aggregate.

In the League, the opening gambit was at home to Aldershot, but the warm Summer afternoon only brought 1,325 motivated football supporters up the Doncaster Road. A point was salvaged from an entertaining 2-2 draw, which satisfied all and sundry. Vinny Grimes announced his comeback with the first goal of the new calendar, and Steve Cammack made certain of a point with the other.

Scunthorpe United then went on a familiar pattern of results, drawing two and losing three of the following five matches. Scunthorpe did not gain the initial victory of the Fourth Division campaign, until the seventh game, when they travelled to Darlington. Joe Neenan kept a clean sheet, and Steve Cammack supplied the winner, but it was two ordinary teams on view.

Before the chilly nights set in, Ian Botham tried to brighten up the mood with a cricket match as a fund raiser, at the Old Show Ground. The presence of the England Cricket International prompted five hundred spectators to pay to watch an interesting experiment. This was one of a handful of ideas to raise awareness in the Club, when just fourteen shareholders attended the A.G.M. with the board.

The win over Darlington was the first exercise in a run of six unbeaten matches, which rocketed the team into tenth place on the ladder. When Stockport County arrived, the Iron shot a hole through their unbeaten record, by beating them 2-0. On twenty minutes Steve Cammack controlled a spinning ball, left a defender floundering on his backside, and drove the perfect drive into the net for one of the best goals of the season. The second goal was just as firmly struck by Paul O'Berg, and the anxiety was over before the break.

It was to the credit of Steve Cammack that he was able to continue to score, and two of his strikes helped gain the double over Darlington. The 3-0 result was played opposite Henderson Avenue, and a Malcolm Partridge penalty made sure of no resurgence from the demoralised Quakers.

The F.A.Cup had been unkind to Scunthorpe United in recent years, and it was not since 1974 when they last won a tie. At long last this was to briefly change, and United raised the stakes for the visit of Hartlepool United, beating them 3-1, on a muddy Old Show Ground pitch. A crowd of 5,165 was twice the average, and most expected United to struggle, against the side that had taken three League points off them.

In the first half Rick Green made space for Vinny Grimes to put his boot through the ball and launch it goal bound. Hartlepool responded with an equaliser, cleverly chipped over Joe Neenan. In the second period, Rick Green chose his moment, on the hour mark, to head the Iron in front. Then Malcolm Partridge stroked home a penalty, to make it game set and match to the home team.

The Second Round of the competition found Altrincham at the Old Show Ground, for the second occasion. On the day of the game no goals was scored, but it was a very physical match, and Joe Neenan was to suffer more than any other player. In the replay a similar pattern of football continued. The whole turning point of the tie involved Joe. When he caught the ball, on one occasion, he raised his knee out in front of himself. An Altrincham player ran into it and was hurt. In the opinion of the referee Neenan was guilty of dangerous play and was sent off. It was a contentious point to say the least, and was a contributing factor to the penalty award which led to Scunthorpe losing 1-0.

After the controversy, United supporters were pleased to play a Fourth Division match, and expect a games of football in the purest sense. Tranmere Rovers were a good excuse to avoid the High Street crowds and Christmas shopping, but only 1,664 people took the opportunity. Tranmere had much more of the game, but it was Anton Lambert who headed the Iron into the lead. Both teams battled on to find supremacy, giving the public something to get excited about. They had to wait until Dave Stewart was brought on as a substitute, before he was able to shoot the decisive goal and give a 2-0 advantage. The rest of Christmas went a little sour, and they lost 1-0 at Mansfield, then took a point from the 2-2 home draw against Bury.

The New Year started for the Iron on January 10th 1981, when the visitors were the Posh of Peterborough United, seeking a possible promotion. In the early stages of play the Peterborough team appeared by far the better team, and had the lead on five minutes. If it had not been for some keen goalkeeping by Joe Neenan, the Posh might have been out of sight. The moment their guard went down, Steve Cammack found Rick Green, who side stepped his defender, and cracked a sweet shot into the corner of the net, and at 1-1 the points were shared.

Scunthorpe United produced a mini revival, but it did nothing to swell the brilliant band of two thousand supporters. This was not enough to sustain the Club, and in February they had to part company with John Kaye, their Assistant Manager, purely for financial reasons. At the same time they received a call from Lincoln City, up in the dizzy height of second place in the table, destined for promotion. In the team was former favourite, Nolan Keeley, in the changed green strip of the Imps. A crowd of 4,848 added a little extra to the coffers, and witnessed a tremendous struggle.

Lincoln were blessed by the goal scoring talents of Gordon Hobson, who shot his team into an eleventh minute lead. The Imps took charge of the events, but Alan Boxall kept the defence together. In the sixtieth minute Paul O'Berg chipped in a neatly taken equaliser, which set up a brilliant finale. Lincoln looked to have stolen all of the points, when Hobson scored the Imps second goal, with two minutes left.

The Wigan goalkeeper gathers the ball in the 4-4 draw that finished the 1980-81 season, at the Old Show Ground.

The noise hadn't died down, when Stuart Pilling made himself the hero of the hour. He burst through at full throttle, waited until he could see the whites of the opposition's eyes, then drove the ball with the speed of a bullet, into the net. What a climax! Everyone stood on their feet to applaud one of the favourite men of the time for his commitment.

Stuart Pilling was just the type of player to be in the right place at the right time, when an important goal was required. He did this against Southend United, the team keeping Lincoln City off the top spot. The match was noteworthy, because it was one of the first Sunday kick-offs, and brought a crowd of 3,605 up the Doncaster Road. Stuart scored a similar goal on this afternoon, when the ball was back heeled to him by Steve Cammack, and he knocked it home with his trusty left foot. Rick Green shot the second, six minutes later, after neat foot work by Paul O'Berg. The two goal cushion was reduced to a final score of 2-1 in the last few moments.

Scunthorpe United announced that they had decided to make some changes to the managerial side of the running of the Club. Ready for next season, Ron Ashman was to become the General Manager, and they would search for a younger man, possibly a player manager, to sort out the team affairs. At the end of March, with the season running short, Ron took his men to promotion minded Doncaster Rovers, for a Friday evening fixture. The Scunthorpe team dominated the game, but in the true spirit of a side going places, Rovers stole both of the points, like a thief in the night, with an only goal of the event. The season was in its final phase, when York City called in at the beginning of April, and helped to make a contribution to a frenzied match.

It was a game that had the keepers reaching to pick the ball out of the net five times, before the referee had blown for the half way point. Rick Green made himself popular by scoring twice, and Dave Stewart notched the other. The tempo eased after the resumption, and 3-2 remained the score. This was to be followed by two loses, at Hereford, and at Bury. The match at Gigg Lane was a damaging 6-1 thrashing, where the team turned in a sorry performance.

Scunthorpe United sprinted over the finishing line in the dash of the last three matches, making it appear as though they were seeking a last gasp promotion place. Mansfield Town lost 2-0 at the Old Show Ground, and at Tranmere the boys brought back only the third away win of the football year, with a 2-1 victory. The curtain was brought down on a 4-4 roller coaster game, at home to Wigan Athletic. Paul O'Berg and Steve Cammack scored two each, and all twenty two players left the field to the applause of the 1,704 supporters in the ground.

It was a tremendous finale to Ron Ashman's remarkable career in charge of team affairs. He had guided the Iron into sixteenth position, and Steve Cammack was the leading scorer on sixteen goals in all competitions. Ron Ashman had kept the Club alive on the scraps of whatever players he could find. Whenever he produced a player, and Ron unearthed scores, they had to be sold to pay the debts. He could never hoped to produce a sustained team for a promotion push, because the best men had to disappear into a wealthier clubs, who inevitably benefited from his hard work. The board knew what a first class manager he was, and he was never heard to complain once.

1981-82

The news that local supporters had been waiting for, was the signing of John Duncan to take the post of Scunthorpe United Manager. John Duncan was a Scotsman, who made the grade at Dundee, then went South to the bright lights at Tottenham Hotspur. His next move was to Derby County, and it was from here that he took the job as a player manager, but like those player bosses before him, supporters would have to be patient to see him play.

One of John's first signings was Andy Keeley, a former Tottenham apprentice, who was a half back at Sheffield United. He was joined by Dave Hughes of Lincoln City, a man to be employed in a defending role, and in September Paul Moss was a useful addition to the forward line. Paul came from just across the Humber at Hull City. The Club took on two new apprentices, in Neil Pointon and Vince Duffy. At first it was Vince who was called into action, but Neil Pointon developed into an accomplished defender, who would play at the top level in the game.

The inclusion of these recruits made of the exit of others. Top of the list was the leading marksman, Steve Cammack, who was to be transferred for a fee to Lincoln City, and play in Division Three. The list was to continue with Jimmy Gordon to Boston, Phil Ashworth to Cambridge, and Nick Jarvis returned to Grantham. Finally, Graham Pugh left with his Cup Final medal to go to Matlock Town to become a Gladiator in non-League football

The Club, at this time, had a debt of £140,000, and could go under at any time. The crisis was as great as those terrible days of the Midland League, when the shutters were almost put up. To ease the Club's financial pressures, Scunthorpe United played a friendly against the full Liverpool side at the Old Show Ground. They also increased the cost of admittance by twenty pence for adults, to one pound fifty pence, and pensioners and juniors would need to raise eight pence for each game. To help with the running of the Club, Mr David Wraith became the Vice Chairman, with a view of moving Scunthorpe United forward. He had his own business, and the acumen to sort the finances out, but the debt was a massive figure to deal with.

One major change that supporters had to take on board was a change in the Football League rules, that would reward three points for a win, in a bid to cut out negative play. On the field, Scunthorpe United began with a pair of games against Mansfield Town, and that was as far as the League Cup venture was going to go. A goalless draw at the Old Show Ground and 2-0 defeat away meant that they exited on aggregate. In the Fourth Division an ordinary start was made, thanks to draws at Northampton, and at home to the once famous Blackpool. The long haul to Torquay finished in a disappointing single goal loss. It took the fourth League match, at home to Tranmere Rovers, to bring the joy of a maiden victory and the first three points. Wins would be like buses, because another followed immediately behind. This time it was against the visiting Hartlepool team. Both of these results were registered as 2-1, and Paul Moss was a goal schemer on each occasion.

Unfortunately, the road went down hill from here on, and the team found it impossible to sculpture another positive result from the next eleven matches. Only a 4-4 match, against the fallen Tigers of Hull City, was anything of note, and attracted 3,575 spectators. United were behind three times, and trailed 4-2 at one stage. The City supporters cursed the waste of two penalty awards, which Malcolm Partridge tucked away and helped to save the Iron's bacon. Needless to say, Scunthorpe sank like a stone in the ratings.

Scunthorpe United's next win was caught on camera, when the 'Match of the Day' team did a feature on the lower divisions. They were away at the Shay, playing Halifax Town, a team in a similar predicament. It was the Town that opened the scoring, but a Chris Cowling header brought parity. The winner did not arrive until the seventy fifth minute, when Paul O'Berg set Paul Moss free, and his shot cannoned off the under side of the bar. United returned the happier for a 2-1 result.

In the F.A.Cup, Scunthorpe United had to play host to Bradford City, who had already beaten them in the League. John Duncan urged supporters to turn out and support the Club, the effect of which was that 3,339 enthusiasts filed through the gate. They were to see a tough game, which brought a number of injuries. Paul O'Berg had to leave the field after one, in the second minute, following a high tackle. United put on a brave face, and were rewarded for their patience in the seventeenth minute, when Dave Stewart found Chris Cowling in space, and he angled a shot past the goalkeeper. It was a case of all hands to the pump for the remainder of the play. The rough play was not finished yet, and an interesting tackle left David Dall a limping passenger, when he was challenged in the second half. On ninety minutes, the one goal was all that separated the teams.

At the end of November, John Duncan brought two men to the Club. The first was a tall solid defender from Leeds United, named Tony Arins, who was willing to drop down the divisions just to guarantee playing. He was a utility man, used mainly in mid-field or the defence. He was to arrive at the same time as George Telfer, a quick, goal scoring forward, who had tried his luck in America, with San Diego Sockers. George was once playing for Everton in his younger days, and had that little bit extra.

These two new lads first played as a unit in the goalless draw, at home Port Vale, but then football went into hibernation with a spell of Artic weather, which hit the game for a month. It was not until January 2nd 1982 that United could run onto the park and continue with the F.A.Cup.

Fate took them to Gresty Road, to play Crewe Alexandra. In the League, Crewe took full command and won 3-0, and so a 3-1 Cup victory was a pleasant surprise, and put an unexpected extra few bob in the kitty. Chris Cowling, George Telfer and David Dall supplied the goods, and for George it was his maiden strike for the Iron.

Hope was that Scunthorpe United's coffers might be boosted by a trip from a First Division club when the Third Round of the F.A.Cup was made. No disrespect was intended, but a home tie with Hereford United from the same division, did not set the imagination racing. There was still a thin layer of snow on the pitch for the kick-off, and Hereford were no doubt the superior team. United only earned a draw from a Dave Stewart equaliser, after the visitors held sway at the forty five minute point. In the replay at Edgar Street, United bowed out with a 4-1 defeat, and only had a moment to cheer, when Vinny Grimes diverted the ball into the net. At least some money was forth coming.

Back on League duty, United lost to Blackpool in between the two Hereford ties, but then were rejuvenated with three consecutive victories. Initially, Northampton Town were felled at the Old Show Ground, 2-1. Then the Iron won only the second match on their travels, at Tranmere 1-0, and it was Rick Green who was on station to do the trick. A similar result won the points at home to Mansfield Town, and David Dall supplied the ammunition.

On February 11th 1982 Scunthorpe United called an emergency press conference. They had to announce a number of unpleasant measures which had to be implemented, if the Club was going to survive. The first was that Mr David Wraith was to become the new Chairman, and Mr Jack Empson would exchange his position to be the Vice- Chairman. Regretfully, three members of the senior staff would be asked to leave the Old Show Ground. These included the General Manager, Ron Ashman, the physiotherapist, Charlie Strong, and the Secretary, Mrs Sheila Louth. A fighting fund was set into motion to raise £50,000 as soon as possible.

Within days the supporters became mobilized. Fans offered to donate money from wages, a sponsored walk to the away match at Peterborough raised more than seven hundred pounds, and a disco made another one hundred pounds. The supporters club chipped in £3,000, and that was just the start of it.

Within a short period of time, Scunthorpe United introduced Don Rowing to the Club as the new Secretary, and fund raiser. On the occasion of his first match there was a lighting failure, and all the cash bags had to be counted by candle light. This he would soon get over, and Don was to be in office for more than twenty years. Another of his early duties was to confront a stranger who turned out to be a bailiff, but he was soon on his way when David Wraith supplied the necessary cheque.

At this manic time of rapid change, the Iron had to get on with trying to keep out of the bottom four, and results of late found them within the re-election zone. In February they came up against Sheffield United, from the other steel making centre. The Blades were spending their one and only year in Division Four, and would celebrate their escape as Champions, in May. At the Old Show Ground, 8,105 noisy neighbours clapped and cheered, as the two parties trotted out onto the brown Old Show Ground pitch. The vast majority of the crowd were from Yorkshire, expecting a pint, a pie and a pile of goals.

The Sheffield crew may have had the first two, but it was Scunthorpe that caused the first shock, as early as the fifth minute. Vinny Grimes curled over a tempting free-kick, and Paul Moss stretched his neck to meet it and plant the ball in the net. Throughout the whole match, every player played out of his skin. After sixty six minutes George Telfer played another trump card, hitting a ball on the run, high into the Sheffield net. It was not until the dying minutes that a penalty pulled one back for the Blades, playing in a yellow and Brown striped shirt. Scunthorpe held on for a coupon busting win, only the fourth defeat the Sheffield United team had to choke on all year.

This was to be the last win that the team managed for a further nine matches. One match in this run was a loss when Ian Botham received his full debut. It was at home, one Friday evening, to Wigan Athletic. The Iron crashed out 7-2, in what was an unparalleled record defeat on their own soil. This form was exasperated when a number of senior players were given their cards in an effort to save more money. The likes of Stuart Pilling, Rick Green and Malcolm Partridge fell victim to the current position, and it was with deep regret that supporters had to say farewell to old servants in this manner.

John Duncan had to sign a number of players to fill the void on short term contracts, or loans. These included Ronnie Goodlass, Stuart Hamill, Alan Thompson and Gordon Boyd, but none would stay beyond the end of the season. Ronnie Goodlass was the most noted of these, for having played for Everton in a League Cup Final. The manager did make one signing in April, with an eye on next year in mind. The board allowed him a small margin to re-sign Steve Cammack, who never settled at Lincoln. Steve knew where he was really wanted, and he was exchanged for Dave Hughes, who was more suited to Sincil Bank.

The events of the year made seeking re-election, for only the second time in their history, almost inevitable. Between the beginning of April and the end of the fixture card, in May, only one result ended with a Scunthorpe victory, that being against Rochdale. The 2-2 score against Bury, in the third last match of the campaign confirmed United's plight. At the final count the Iron had finished second from the bottom of the table. Fortunately, Scunthorpe United had no trouble in securing the necessary votes to retain the Club in the Football League.

The lesson was noted by everyone at the Old Show Ground, and steps were taken to see that it never happened again. During the season the financial position was eased by the generosity of Nottingham Forest, who sent a full first team to play Scunthorpe United in fund raiser. This was followed by a second special match, between a Jack Brownsword eleven and a John Duncan eleven. It was to bring World Cup winner, Jack Charlton out of retirement, and see the return of Kevin Keegan for one game. The crisis was not over, but at least the darkest clouds had passed over, and a certain amount of normality returned to the Old Show Ground.

The Jack Brownsword friendly was see Scunthorpe United run out in the all red colours for the final time. A movement was afoot, during this time of upheaval, to return to the favourite old claret and blue kit, which the Club had originally played in. The board were happy to go along with popular demand, and at first the new shirts would be blue with claret facings, but in future became more like the traditional colours that were everyone's favourite. It was written that a gipsy's curse said that the team would never win a trophy until the Club returned to the claret and blue, but it was purely a myth.

1982-83

During the closed season of the Summer of 1982, John Duncan found that he was to be hampered by the loss of Paul Moss and Tony Arins, who were seeking employment outside the game. He also decided not to offer contracts to David Dall and Steve Davy.

John Duncan had been shrewd in his choice of replacements, starting with a six foot two inches tall, left sided mid-field man, called Les Hunter. Les was a highly motivated man, signed from Chesterfield, who could fill in the centre half position if required. For that central position, United originally utilised Alan Boxall, but the signing of Steve Baines of Walsall took Boxall into the right half position, and Baines became the automatic choice as the central pivot. Another man that was to operate from the right side of the middle row was Martin Fowler, a well built lad off the books of Stockport County.

The forwards would benefit from a well balanced young man, called Noel Parkinson, who was a slightly built player from the second team at Ipswich Town. He could also be used in the half back line, when required. Another player that was not on the tall side was the talented Dennis Leman, from Sheffield Wednesday. He was at his best on the left side of the advanced troops. John Duncan introduced Mike Angus on loan from Middlesbrough, but the loan deal stretched to three months. Mike was a forward player, but another loaned man, Peter Cartright from Newcastle United, fitted into the middle belt. Perhaps John Duncan's two best promotions during the campaign were those of Chris Cowling and Neil Pointon, who had worked tremendously hard to be recognised as fully fledged members of the first team.

The pre-season friendly games received a boost, when Tottenham Hotspur brought the F.A.Cup with them to play Scunthorpe United, before more than five thousand supporters. The mighty Spurs had just won the trophy at Wembley, beating Queens Park Rangers, and were managed by Keith Burkinshaw, the former Scunthorpe player. It was a carnival atmosphere, and Tottenham, led by Glen Hoddle, won 5-0.

The year started in earnest, up in the North East at Hartlepool with a goalless draw, but folks without a ticket would still have squeezed in, because the attendance was 1,009. On the following Tuesday, United played Grimsby Town in the League Cup, now to be referred to as the Milk Cup. At home, in the first leg, United gave a good account of themselves against the Mariners, who were in Division Two. The Iron thought they had snatched a late equaliser, but as the team celebrated, the Town went straight back down the park to grab a 2-1 winner. One week later, United went to Blundell Park for the return leg, by which time they had drawn their first home League match 1-1 against Aldershot. The goalless draw in the Grimsby backyard showed that this team of John Duncan's was on the march, even though they would make no more progress in the League Cup.

Scunthorpe United continued to be a reformed character, and the team thumped a bewildered Stockport County 3-0. George Telfer and Chris Cowling had the job sewn up by the tea time, and another beautiful strike from Telfer put the finishing touch to a brilliant three point exhibition. Only 1,335 spectators watched the match, but after an unbeaten run of nine matches, the crowd rose to 7,483 for the visit of Hull City, who were rubbing shoulders with the Iron at the top of the table. The contest was tight, like a chess match, and a goal in the last five minutes made it check mate to the Tigers.

Scunthorpe United did not flounder after this minor set back, and took maximum points out of the next two games. First they mesmerised Mansfield Town at the Field Mill, 2-0, then made better use of chances to beat Tranmere Rovers, at the Old Show Ground 2-1. The beauty of the Scunthorpe team was that although they had a marvellous marksman in Steve Cammack, the goals were also being spread amongst the other members of the squad.

At the end of October, Scunthorpe United made a new innovation for the match at Torquay. Instead of the arduous six hour coach drive down to Devon, the team flew from Holgate airport, close to Gainsborough. It was worth it, because they were far less exhausted, and were worthy of a 1-1 draw, made possible by the boot of Steve Cammack.

Immediately after returning from Torquay, United had back to back victories at home to Port Vale and Northampton Town. It was Steve Cammack that scored the only goal in the first of these against the Vale, in an even contest.

The story was different with the Cobblers. Paul O'Berg grabbed a brace, while Steve Cammack, playing his best game so far, weighed in with at hat-trick. The 5-1 victory spoke for itself, and raised the name of Scunthorpe United to the top of the table for a brief moment.

United were in fine fettle to tackle the next job in hand, which was at Darlington in the First Round of the F.A.Cup. The team had all bases covered, and looked as if they just needed to be patient for the winner. It came after fifty two minutes, when Steve Cammack rose majestically to head the ball into the net at the cricket field end of the ground.

There was a pause for two League tours of duty before the next round, and their colours were lowered by Bury at the Old Show Ground, but Hereford United surrendered to them at Edgar Street. In the Second Round of the Cup, United were at home to the green and white colours of Northwich Victoria, a team who were original members of Division Two in 1892. Scunthorpe needed to see that there would not be a shock result. Chris Cowling put them ahead, but the Victoria men equalised on the stroke of half time. A stiff talking to at the break made sure the team had the right mind set, and they went through when Paul O'Berg made the final score 2-1.

Scunthorpe United went into the New Year in touch with the leaders, but hovering around fifth position. The reason for the slip was two defeats of 3-1, in away journeys at Blackpool and Halifax Town, during December.

At the start of 1983, the F.A.Cup brought them in contact with Grimsby Town once again. The had been gifted home advantage, and 11,010 spectators enjoyed a fast entertaining match, which might have been made more memorable if a couple of goals had been scored. On the following Tuesday, fans travelling from Scunthorpe took advantage of a fish and chip supper along Cleethorpes front. At Blundell Park, the Iron slipped up against a stronger side, and lost 2-0.

The result at Grimsby Town was the start of suggestions that all was not well between John Duncan and Chairman David Wraith. The apparent situation simmered on for a few more weeks. Then it was announced that John Duncan was to part company with Scunthorpe United, which left many, not close to the situation, totally bewildered. On February 2nd 1983 a further statement declared that the former Leeds United and England International Allan Clarke was to be the new manager. Clarke was always known as 'Sniffer', and that is the name that David Wraith was said to have called his pet dog.

Allan Clarke had his first game in charge at home to Bristol City, and the team struggled to eek out a 1-1 draw, which came courtesy of a Noel Parkinson strike. This was the second of five consecutive drawn matches, which pushed them to the edge of the promotion fringe.

The most notable of these was at Hull City, where 14,252 supporters saw Dennis Leman hit the Scunthorpe goal in the 1-1 score. After inspecting the troops, Allan Clarke expressed the opinion that there was still work to be done if they were to go up. His words of wisdom put them back on the road to winning ways, when they thrashed Tranmere Rovers at Prenton Park, 4-0. The remarkable victory was via strikes from Dennis Leman, Noel Parkinson, and Steve Cammack scoring twice.

Scunthorpe United were to be rocked with the news that an injury to Noel Parkinson in training, was in fact a serious broken leg, which was to keep him out of the game for a year. Allan Clarke responded by taking on a experienced forward, called Mike Lester from Bradford City, who was the type of player that could turn a game with one subtle pass, or one wicked shot. He also gave a chance to Tommy Graham, a Scottish born player looking for a club, having last been at Doncaster Rovers. Allan Clarke threw down the gauntlet and told him to earn himself a contract. He was given immediate access to the first team on the right side of the attack.

It was at the beginning of April, when the team knew that they would not be able to make an impression on the top spot in the Fourth Division table, but promotion was still a possibility. It came at a time when wins at home to Halifax Town and away to Rochdale were followed by defeats at home to bottom of the table Hereford, and most disastrously, 5-1 at Colchester.

For a few days United were nothing short of stunned, but once over the initial shock, they got back to winning ways with a glorious battle against Blackpool, in the safer territory of the Old Show Ground. It was not for those of a nervous disposition. Blackpool twice led during the game, and twice they were pegged back. Chris Cowling put the Iron ahead, then Greenall made it even. Steve Cammack was to have the last word for Scunthorpe, when a Neil Pointon free kick was headed out of defence to him, and he volleyed it back into the net for a 4-3 result.

The clock was now ticking down on the final matches of the season. The Iron picked up another three points, when Peterborough lost at Scunthorpe, but at the very end of April they lost one of the most important matches of the year. It was at Gigg Lane, where Bury won the upper hand 1-0. The result allowed the Shakers to leap above them in the table, dumping them down to sixth place. Two home matches followed for the shattered Scunthorpe forces, and Allan Clarke stressed that maximum points had to be secured or promotion was out of the window. All went well in the first trial against Swindon Town, who were slain 2-0. Next up were the men of the North East from Darlington. All seemed to be going according to plan, when Steve Cammack gave the Iron a two goal lead, but crazy defending allowed the Quakers to equalise, and the 2-2 result threw two precious points away.

The scenario was that Scunthorpe United had two matches left, at Port Vale and Chester. If they won both of them, and Bury lost their final match at home to Wimbledon, Scunthorpe would just sneak home. It might not be over until the fat lady sang, but she was somewhere down the corridor clearing her throat.

The first hurdle was at Port Vale, before a packed crowd celebrating the home side's guarantee of promotion to the third tier. It might have been the euphoria of the occasion that put Vale off guard, but Scunthorpe United produced a tremendous workman like performance. Each man played to the limits of his ability, and the team savoured a 1-0 victory, when Chris Cowling rose above the defence to power the ball into the net with his accurate header.

On the last Saturday of the season a long row of buses lined up outside the Old Show Ground to take several hundred hopeful fans to Sealand Road, Chester. At the start of the game there must have been almost one thousand Scunthorpe supporters in the 2,560 attendance. The Iron would be without Paul O'Berg, who was injured at Port Vale, and Ian Webster came in for his one and only appearance of the year.

Over at Gigg Lane Bury, their management had stolen a march on Scunthorpe by setting their kick-off fifteen minutes after the start of the Chester game, so they knew exactly what they might need to do. The Bury task was not to be easy, because Wimbledon were top of the League. Once the match had began at Sealand Road, there was a crowd invasion on the pitch. It was totally good natured, and involved over one hundred of them in fancy dress. It was akin to time wasting, lasting exactly fifteen minutes. They then dissolved back into the terraces to behave for the rest of the afternoon. Every now and again they would jump up and down excitedly in salute of a goal scored by Wimbledon, as the news came through on radios, to let the players know the score.

(Top) Steve Cammack scored twenty five League goals, earning him the Fourth Division 'Golden Boot' award. (Below) Mike Lester beats his Swindon opponent. United won 2-0 with Lester scoring the second goal.

In the meantime, the Scunthorpe job against Chester was not to be straight forward. On fifteen minutes Tommy Graham was first to react to a loose ball from a half cleared Steve Cammack shot, and he scooped it into the net for the first goal. The lead only lasted eight minutes, when Chester came back with a scrambled goal of their own. There were some anxious moments right into the second half. The only consolation was that Bury were behind to Wimbledon, and would eventually lose 3-1.

If promotion was to be achieved, the Iron needed to score, and the winner did not arrive until the eighty second minute. Ian Webster put over an inviting cross, and Les Hunter met the ball with a beefy header. Grenville Millington, the Chester Welsh International keeper, could only parry it away. It dropped nicely for Tommy Graham, who fired it back sweetly on target into the net. At that moment the roar was like a champagne cork being popped, and the terraces exploded into colours and movement.

There were still nail biting seconds to knock off the clock, but eventually that glorious pin point in time arrived and the fourth promotion place was secured. It was the moment that every Scunthorpe supporter present would remember for the rest of their lives. Against all the odds, and against Allan Clarke's first impressions, Scunthorpe would play next season in the Third Division. Tommy Graham was the hero with the two goals, and would earn his contract. Steve Cammack scored twenty five League goals and took the Golden Boot award for the division.

An impromptu celebration was staged in the Chester directors box, and Scunthorpe supporters partied long into the night. Every face wore a smile for the trip back home.

FAREWELL TO THE OLD SHOW GROUND

1983-84

David Wraith was to show what sort of a canny business man he was, when it was revealed that he saw to it that the Club took out an insurance policy on winning promotion. He knew that the elevation to the next division was to mean higher wages and bigger transfer fees. The policy was to yield £50,000, a tidy sum indeed. The premium might have been high, but the risk brought a massive bonus.

Allan Clarke was able to bring in some new players and his first was a full back for the back four positions. Paul Longden was signed from Barnsley, having had a sprinkling of appearances with the Oakwell club. At Scunthorpe he went straight into the first team, and was equally happy on the right side or the left. This was to begin a career of close to ten years in the claret and blue colours. United also brought in a big strong central defender named John Green, from Rotherham United. He justified his fee by being ever present during the year ahead.

The mid-field was boosted by the presence of a bearded Mike Brolly, who was a former Mariner, signed from Derby County. His skill level was apparent from the beginning, and just what was required for the Third Division. For further up the field, Clarke took two youngsters from Sheffield United. These were the promising Julian Broddle and Geoff Day. From his own junior ranks, the year was to hold glimpses of Dave Hill, Simon Snow, Robbie Holden and Ian Webster.

On the other hand, the revolving door at the Old Show Ground was to be an exit route for five regular first team players. The most notable of these was Bob Oates, who was to have the last fling of his career at Rochdale, and the old stalwart left with the best wishes of all supporters. He was joined on the way out by Steve Baines, George Telfer, Martin Fowler and Andy Keeley. It was not to be long into the activities of 1983-84, when Alan Boxall, Dennis Leman and Les Hunter went in the same direction.

For many years the Football League had stoutly refused to allow advertising on any part of the playing kit, but gradually pressure from the clubs forced the rule to be altered. Scunthorpe United first used shirt sponsors during this season, and the official sponsor was the borough council. The logo 'Scunthorpe E Z' was smartly printed across the middle of the claret and blue shirt. The letters standing for 'Enterprise Zone', and would be seen for the next twelve months.

Scunthorpe United began the long trek of the season by drawing in the League Cup, at home to Doncaster Rovers, 1-1. During the match, Steve Cammack scored his first goal of the new football calendar. The second leg was not played at Belle Vue until the second week in September, when the Iron lost in torrential rain 3-0.

In the Third Division programme, Scunthorpe United made a tidy start, earning a goalless draw at Port Vale. Then they won 3-1 at home to Exeter City, who had ex-England International Gerry Francis in their ranks. When another goalless draw went into the book, for the match at home to Oxford United, everything in the garden seemed to be rosy.

In the first home League game Tommy Graham and the Exeter City goalkeeper Len Bond both wait for a descending ball; between them is the visitors player manager, ex-England man, Gerry Francis.

One month later, at the end of September, the Iron had been put in their place, and were on the fringe of the bottom four relegation positions. They did have the reward of a 1-0 win over Bolton Wanderers, but had lost consecutive results, 4-0 at Plymouth, and catastrophically 6-1 at home to Southend. Allan Clarke had done something similar to Fred Goodwin years ago, and blooded too many young players in one team. The only cheer all evening was a penalty conversion by young Robbie Holden.

The month of October was to see the inclusion of a talented half back, on loan from Nottingham Forest. He was Danny Wilson, who had the legs, skill and brain to be going places. His appearance at the Old Show Ground certainly brightened up the place, and he made his presence felt. The best two matches of his five game spell started with a remarkable 5-1 beating of Wimbledon, opposite the Baths Hall. His contribution was two goals, one of which came from a penalty, and the senior professionals were happy to see him convert it. In the following game, immediately before his departure, United played a major part in a 5-3 extravaganza against Sheffield United, at Bramall Lane.

The woes of the League could be shelved for a moment, when November arrived, and they put up a strong resistance at home to Preston North End in the F.A.Cup First Round, watched by 3,484 loyal followers. Steve Cammack made the most of a penalty award, and tucked in the only shot to beat either of the keepers. This allowed them to extend a warm welcome to Bury in Round Two. The Iron were always a cut above the Shakers, and gained the initiative, thanks to an own goal sliced into the net, and a second goal fired home by in form Steve Cammack. The 2-0 result put them in the hat with the big fellows.

Before Allan Clarke and his men had time to think about the knock-out competition, they had more work to do in the bread and butter of the Third Division. On an extremely wet Saturday in December, the team put in a tremendous effort to over come the class of Gillingham. Steve Cammack angled a penalty kick into a corner of the target, and Chris Cowling scored a second. At the rear of the field John Green shielded Joe Neenan and a 2-0 result was thoroughly warranted.

The Iron would not win another League game again until the middle of March. In these days of three points for a win, of the twelve matches played, eight finished in draws, which caused problems.

In an attempt to shake up the pack, Allan Clarke brought in a couple of new faces. He signed Mick Matthews from Wolves for the mid-field, at Christmas, and during the holiday period made use of Ian Botham's rest from cricket duty. In January Alan Whitehead was taken on loan from Brentford to sit in the middle of the back four. Bad weather restricted his stay to one appearance, but Clarke had seen enough to wish to sign him. When the asking price dropped to £34,000, the move became permanent in March. Derek Bell was added to the list of players in February, when he was brought in from Chesterfield, to try to add some goals to those being scored by Steve Cammack.

The tale of the F.A.Cup was to bring great excitement to the faithful band of Scunthorpe United supporters, when it was discovered they would have a day out at Elland Road, where the Iron had to confront Leeds United. The once proud Peacocks were a strong Second Division team at this point in their history. A crowd of 17,130 stood up to cheer the two sets of warriors onto the pitch. Allan Clarke must have had mixed emotions because this was the ground where he had won his top honours as a player. The rest of United's squad got stuck in, and contributed to an entertaining hour and a half. Tommy Wright put the team in all white into a first half lead, but it was not going to be their day entirely. Steve Cammack came up with a late equaliser, stabbing the ball into the net from close range whilst under pressure from a Leeds defender and the keeper. Brave and effective, if not skilful. The 1-1 result brought the whole circus back to the Old Show Ground and a huge 13,129 attendance saw the same score repeated.

Julian Day receives praise for his goal in the first of the two replays, versus Leeds United in the F.A.Cup.

The night was to be a long one. Ninety minutes of football yielded no scoring, then thirteen minutes into the extra period Tommy Wright fired Leeds into the lead. Two minutes later, it was the turn of teenager Geoff Day to find the leveller. Before everyone departed for the night, the clubs tossed a coin to see which one would stage the second replay. Fortune favoured Scunthorpe, and six day later the battle was to recommence, back at the same venue.

When the 13,312 crowd turned up for the second replay, they looked round and noticed that something was missing. The roof had been blown off the East Stand in a violent gale on the Thursday evening, that following Leeds United match. Thankfully, the evening was dry, if not a breezy one, and the rest of the structure was sound.

The trilogy was to be fought at pace, and the Scunthorpe lads were unconcerned by the opposition. Mike Brolly had a slice of luck on twelve minutes, when his intended cross was caught by the wind and dropped behind Scottish International goalkeeper David Harvey, into the net. Tommy Wright scored his hat-trick goal for Leeds, but it had taken this third match to achieve. There was a possibility of Leeds United gaining the upper hand at this stage, but it was snatched from them by Steve Cammack, as the interval approached, and he drilled United into the lead for the second time.

The frenzy continued unabated after the break. Immediately after the restart, Mike Lester took hold of the ball on the left of the edge of the box, and rifled United 3-1 to the good. The last Scunthorpe goal came from the feet of Tommy Graham, who made the tie safe in the seventieth minute with another unstoppable drive into the roof of the net. In the final ten minutes, Leeds reduced their embarrassment to a final score of 4-2, but little Scunthorpe had won the right to go to West Bromwich Albion for the Fourth Round.

The saga of the F.A.Cup continued when four thousand tickets were sold to Scunthorpe United supporters, but the match was postponed because of inclement weather, and played on the next Tuesday evening at the Hawthorns. A total of 18,235 spectators shouted their allegiance when teams entered the field. Scunthorpe played with great credit against the First Division aristocrats, and might have gone into the lead, had not Jim Barron been in such wicked form. In the end, this was where the Scunthorpe train hit the buffers. The vital moment of the tie was on the fifty seventh minute, and came from a corner kick, which was clearly a goal kick. The ball was swung over, and in the melee Noel Luke forced the ball home. It was hard on Scunthorpe United, but the Cup had made its mark on the season for the Club.

In matters of the League, United decided to invest in the team with some more new faces through the loan scheme. Richard Pratley was brought in for two months, from Derby County, for the left side of the mid-field.

Late in the football year Simon Steele came from Brighton, to ease the burden on Joe Neenan in goal for the last five matches. There was welcome news of Noel Parkinson, who reappeared in March, now that his broken leg was completely healed.

On March 17th 1984 Scunthorpe finally won another Third Division match. Bradford City happened to be the visitors, and local fanatics in the 3,274 crowd were understandably relieved to see the Iron win 2-1, at last. The Scunthorpe men who made the score possible were Steve Cammack and Mick Matthews.

Scunthorpe United had only one victory in the next six games, which did little to hoist them out of their relegation positions. When they did find the right form, they produced a performance worthy of praise. Plymouth were the visitors to the Old Show Ground, and the Iron beat them 3-0. One week later and the Argyle men played Watford in the Semi Final of the F.A.Cup. At Easter another polished performance saw them miraculously raise their game and puncture Hull City's promotion ambitions. Most of the 8,286 crowd had come to support the Tigers, but the visitors had rubber teeth, and lost 2-0. These two scores stood out, only because they were unusual victories. On the Club's travels, the team had yet to win, and it was not until next term when it would happen.

Scunthorpe United said farewell to their own supporters on a high note, beating Burnley 4-0 at home. It gave a small flicker of hope. The flame was virtually extinguished at Gillingham when the team earned a creditable draw, which was not enough. The maths meant that they had to beat Rotherham by a hatful of goals in the final away game, in order to overhaul fifth from bottom placed Brentford on goal difference. In the end, United suffered a 3-0 loss, which was accelerated by an unlucky John Green own goal at the beginning of the match. They had put in a tremendous effort, but finished three points short of safety.

1984-85

During the closed season there were rumblings of discontent over the management of Allan Clarke. Paul O'Berg left the Club for Wimbledon, and John Green and Steve Cammack put in transfer requests. At board level David Wraith resigned as Chairman, owing to business commitments, but said he would remain a director. It was proposed to put the Club up for sale to attract some new money into the coffers. If that was not enough, a dry Summer caused cracks to appear in the Old Show Ground pitch, and completely disrupted pre-season training.

On Friday 24th August, Mr Tom Belton was proposed by Mr Cooper as the new Chairman, and seconded by Mr Alston. Mr Belton agreed that he would become the new Chairman, but only if Mr Wraith left the board, and Allan Clarke be dismissed as the manager.

This was passed unanimously. The sale of the Club was immediately withdrawn, and the Assistant Manager Frank Barlow was put in charge of the team's first match, away at Chester, from which they earned a 1-1 draw. On the eve of Scunthorpe United's Milk Cup game, at home to Mansfield Town, Frank Barlow was officially given the job to manage the Club. At a later date Allan Clarke received an undisclosed sum for wrongful dismissal.

Frank Barlow was to be a popular choice as manager. He started by watching his side beaten at home by Mansfield Town 1-0, but in the second leg United won 2-1 at the Field Mill. Those two away goals, by Mike Brolly and Chris Cowling, earned a pair of lucrative fixtures against Aston Villa in the next round.

The Iron enjoyed much of the play at the Old Show Ground, and the display brought them a deficit of only 3-2 against the strong First Division men. At Villa Park a 1-3 score was also quite in order, considering the differences between the teams, and the Iron finally lost 6-3 on aggregate.

United would suffer from a number of injuries, and the upheaval behind the scenes showed that they should have signed more players. Frank Barlow did what he could, but the first illusive win did not mature until the seventh game, at home to Halifax Town. The 4-0 result was quite timely, because the team had sunk to the second from bottom place on the ladder.

October was to be far more productive, and although it started with defeat at Peterborough, the side managed three pointers on three occasions. The initial one of these was at Northampton, and constituted the first win away from home since the promotion clincher at Chester. A handful of loyal supporters, travelled to see Mick Matthews and Steve Cammack shoot United into the 2-0 unassailable position. At the end of the month, consecutive wins against Torquay United, 2-0 at home, and 1-0 away at Bury, put a completely different complexion to the team affairs.

It was at this junction in time that Frank Barlow made his first sorties in the transfer market. He successfully secured the services of a much travelled full back, named Terry Lees, from Blackpool, although the player had been round quite a few of the clubs in the Midlands. There was a need to sign a goalkeeper, because of a facial injury to the flame haired Joe Neenan. Frank went to Doncaster where he brought in Paul Gregory, a young player who was not on the tall side for a custodian.

An early season game versus Chesterfield. The Saltergate men in the white shorts won the day 4-2, and went on to become the Champions.

This was of no impediment and Paul was used for the majority of the remainder of the season, displaying great enthusiasm for the game.

In the F.A.Cup, United were invited to play away at Nuneaton Borough in the First Round. This club had a real Cup pedigree, and boasted of being one of the top non-League teams at that time. Frank Barlow warned against complacency, and at kick-off United came prepared, playing in an away strip of green and yellow. An assembly of 4,287 spectators crammed into the spaces of the neat little ground, and immediately the Iron knew they had a tough fight on their hands. They took a first half lead in a complete scramble, and Chris Cowling was the last player to touch the ball before it was bundled in. The Borough found a way back and pegged the score at 1-1, with a goal on the break. Although each defence came under fire, that was how the match was to finish.

In the re-match, at the Old Show Ground, United received a shock within the first five minutes, and Nuneaton held a one goal advantage. Try as the did, the Iron could not engineer an equaliser for quite some time, and the visitors caused a number of scares.

It came with a great sigh of relief that on sixty nine minutes Mike Lester scored the equaliser. He received the ball on the left hand side of the edge of the penalty area, and without hesitation, smacked the ball low into the corner of the target, near the post. This was to herald a need for extra time. Steve Cammack sank the Borough side with a close range header four minutes into the period, and their tired limbs could not find a way back.

Scunthorpe United resumed League duty for the duration of a pair of matches, and spectators were being guaranteed a number of goals. Five came along at Hartlepool United in the North East, but United only managed two, both of them coming from Chris Cowling, who was performing tremendously well. One week hence and Wrexham found themselves caught in a gale, when United won 5-2 up the Doncaster Road, and Steve Cammack notched a brilliant hat-trick, while Mick Matthews and Alan Whitehead were responsible for the others.

When Scunthorpe United returned to matters of the F.A.Cup, they found that Port Vale had been drawn at Vale Park. The date was put back a day, so that it was played on the Friday evening, and the home side took the Iron to the cleaners. Port Vale waltzed through, winning 4-1, and even the only Scunthorpe goal was kindly provided by an own goal. It was a great pity, because in the next stage they could have been at Upton Park playing West Ham. In the very next match Scunthorpe returned to play the same side in the League at the very same venue, and managed a 1-1 result.

Much of December was wiped by cold weather, but the Old Show Ground did play host to Ian Botham's Testimonial game. It was Scunthorpe United supporters first chance to see Manchester United perform in the town, and around five thousand people turned out to see the entertainment. The final score was a 5-5 draw, and reflected of how serious the game was taken.

The 1984-85 season League Cup brought two matches in the First Round against Mansfield Town. In the first of these games, at Scunthorpe, United's Mick Matthews challenges for the ball.

At this time little football was to survive the weather, but one match that did was on Boxing Day at home to Stockport County. Only one ball hit the back of the net, and that was struck by the faithful boot of everybody's favourite, Steve Cammack. In January not one match took place on the Old Show Ground, and Scunthorpe played just twice, going down at Tranmere and Chesterfield.

Scunthorpe United began playing in earnest from the February, when the icy weather retreated. They would not hinder the promotion places, but were to occupy a position in advance of the halfway mark up the League ladder. They were playing a smart brand of entertaining football, and usually the public saw a fist full of goals. There were a couple of very exciting young apprentices that had forced their way into the reckoning, and these included Dave Hill in the half back line, and Mark Atkins for the defence, who would each have a career at the summit of the game. These were valid reasons to make the effort to attend matches, but the average gate had slumped to 2,065 per match, over the course of the season.

For the hardy souls that did have the Club's interest at heart, there would be some brilliant entertainment of an unparallel nature to savour. On March 19th 1985 United beat Exeter City 7-1, on a mud splattered Old Show Ground pitch, but the significant marker was the second goal scored by Steve Cammack.

It brought his Scunthorpe United career total to ninety seven, one more than the record held by Barry Thomas. He modestly raised his hand in salute to the crowd, as he was mobbed in celebration, at the conclusion of the game.

This was not an isolated incident. Swindon Town were rattled 6-2, and eight different players of the twenty two put their names to the scoreboard. On April 9th it was time for the visit of Tranmere Rovers, and they were beaten 5-2. Steve Cammack reached another milestone when he notched a brace, and became the first hero of one hundred Scunthorpe United goals. He continued to be the ace up the sleeve, and scored seven more goals in the final five matches. Needless to say, he was the leading scorer with twenty five, in all senior competitions.

The football calendar ended with two 3-3 thrillers, at Rochdale and at home to Port Vale. An attendance of just 1,867 saw the last game of the year, against the Potteries side, and it was hard to wonder what people wished for from the game. Scunthorpe United perhaps did not have the tightest defence to mount a promotion push, but when the Iron finished the campaign in ninth rung on the ladder, Frank Barlow was sleeping much better that some other football managers.

1985-86

Frank Barlow knew that he needed to plug the holes in defence, and found time to select two outstanding defenders from Doncaster Rovers. The first was Steve Lister for a central defending role. Steve was a tall player, who had more than two hundred games of experience under his belt with the Rovers. It did not take long for the Scunthorpe fans to realise that this was a superb signing of quality. At the same time, Billy Russell was to fill in at right full back. Billy had a pedigree which began at Glasgow Celtic, where he was an apprentice.

This meant that the back quarters would include the two newcomers, along with Alan Whitehead, Neil Pointon and Paul Longdon, in front of Paul Gregory.

There was to be a strengthening of the forward line, with the introduction of big John Hawley, a former Arsenal campaigner, from Bradford City. This man was very useful as a target man for Steve Cammack to feed off.

The team was to suffer casualties to accommodate the changes, and Frank Barlow shook hands, and said good bye to Derek Bell, Terry Lees, and Joe Neenan. Neenan had played more than two hundred games in the green jersey, and it was pleasing to hear that he had been fixed up at Burnley. Another player who stepped down was Chris Cowling, who had suffered injury, at a time when he had been playing some of his brightest football.

Frank Barlow chose just one more new face for his team, but he was not to play. It was the former West Ham and Carlisle defender, Bill Green, to be his Assistant Manager. Bill was a tall, quietly spoken man, who instilled confidence in players. He would be a first class choice for the role. Now that everyone was in line, the Barlow army was ready for battle.

Scunthorpe United flattered to deceive when the began the football year. Although they beat Torquay United 4-0 on the opening day, with two goals in each half, they would have to wait eight more games to win another. In addition, the team lost 3-2 on aggregate to Darlington in the League Cup. This pushed the Iron to the wrong end of the table, and it was not until October 1st that another victory was registered. The victims were Crewe Alexandra, who were beaten 3-1. Only 1,443 spectators saw Tommy Graham score in the first period, then Dave Hill and an own goal secured the points later in the game.

The first home match of the season, when Torquay United were thrashed 4-0.

In an effort to achieve greater stability, United paid Portsmouth a small fee for the return of their former starlet, Richard Money, who had since played for Liverpool in the Semi Final of the European Cup. Richard went into the left side of mid-field, and the next five matches were rewarded with points of some denomination. One of these was on Bonfire Night, watched by Preston North End's lowest crowd of 2,007. A goal by Steve Cammack won the spoils 1-0, but after the match Everton came in with a cheque of £75,000 to take Neil Pointon away to a career at the top level.

Scunthorpe would lose the services of two key first team players as, the Winter approached. Mike Brolly and Steve Cammack both suffered injuries, and had to endure a spell in the treatment room. It prompted Frank Barlow to dip into the loan market and bring a talented West Ham youngster named Bobby Barnes, into the forward line. Thankfully the goals of John Hawley and Julian Broddle filled in for Steve's three month absence.

In the F.A.Cup, Scunthorpe had to be content with an away tie at The Shay, in Yorkshire against Halifax Town. This was not to be a barrier to them. Only 1,501 supporters were attracted to the match, but visiting support did not have the best vantage point to see the game on the huge ground. Dave Hill's strike kept the Iron in the picture at 1-1 at the interval. Within five minutes of the restart Julian Broddle seized on a ball, and fired his team in front. Generally speaking, the match was in Scunthorpe's pocket, but it was not secured until Steve Lister went up in the attack and his fine goal made everything water tight at 3-1.

The Second Round of the F.A.Cup gave United a chance to make the next stage, with a home tie, in conflict with Rochdale. The uncertainty of football is one of the sport's attractions, and anyone brave enough to bet on Scunthorpe making progress was to lose cash. Rochdale produced a sterling performance and held the Iron to a 2-2 draw. The onus had shifted by now, and the winners would be treated to a money spinning tie against Manchester United. The Dale made home territory count, and won 2-1 on the evening. All that Scunthorpe had for company was the joy of one Julian Broddle shot hitting the target.

On the Saturday immediately prior to Christmas, Scunthorpe United had a call from Halifax Town. At half time the Iron had slumped to 3-0 down and were only a shadow of the team that won in the Cup. Frank Barlow was normally a quiet man, but it would have been interesting to be a fly on the wall of the dressing room, listening to what he had to say. Whatever was said, it certainly did the trick, and his troops came out with fixed bayonets. The architect of the recovery was John Hawley, who fired in the last senior hat-trick of his career, and the score finished at 3-3.

On Boxing Day, United started a mini revival in which only one of the next five matches finished with no points. The Hartlepool game started the run off and was a treat for the claret and blue supporters in the attendance of 2,495. Mick Matthews was the only goal scorer, and United stole the points with the 1-0 result. The general trend continued through the darkest days of the Winter, as the team selected a high degree of competency at home, but continued to disappoint on their travels. The dreadful away returns were not something new, but there could be no hope of a journey up the table until it was rectified. When the Spring arrived, the Club found themselves out of trouble, but a little to the South of the midway point on the ladder.

The later part of the season was to be pepped up by the inclusion of a number of new men. The first of these was Kevin Dixon, a mid-fielder, who stayed two months on loan from Hartlepool, and when his time was up Frank Barlow put a tick next to his name. In the attack there was a brief appearance of a local apprentice player, called Andy Stevenson, who was to develop in the next few years into a regular first team player. In the middle of March, United took another man off the books of Doncaster Rovers. He was a fleet of foot forward, named Dave Travis, who was a front runner with an eye for goal.

John Hawley dives low to head the only goal of the match at home to Aldershot in March 1986.

Before March was out, Frank Barlow promoted a Scunthorpe born apprentice to the goalkeeping position. This was Paul Johnson, who impressed enough to keep his place until the end of the football year. On the same day that Paul Johnson made his debut, Scunthorpe United welcomed the return of Les Hunter from Chesterfield. He slotted back into his old left side of mid-field position as though he had never been away. He was able to play along side Steve Cammack, who had returned from his injury problems. The final introduction to the team was that of a marksman of immense ability, called Keith Houchen, who signed from York City. Keith had a little bit extra. He was only to play nine matches for the Iron, when he was snapped up in the Summer by First Division Coventry City. Within twelve months Keith was to hold a gold F.A.Cup winning medal in his hands.

April was to see the new brigade make a difference, and in the remaining nine fixtures the team won five of these and drew two. Keith Houchen scored his first Scunthorpe United goal in the 3-1 win against Rochdale, and over in Burnley, United took all three points from the visit to Turf Moor. Houchen was credited with another goal, and his third of the season was denied, when it was recorded as an own goal. It made a brilliant journey home for the four hundred or so travelling army. The season was concluded when promoted Chester City brought a band of supporters with them, but their team would have a thin time that afternoon. The Iron won 2-0, thanks to the goals of Mike Brolly and Steve Cammack. This result put Scunthorpe United in fourteenth place in the final table.

1986-87

During the inactivity of the Summer, Frank Barlow decided it was time for an experienced goalkeeper to fill the position in between the posts. He chose Ron Green, the former Walsall and Shrewsbury player, who was at Bristol Rovers. It meant that Paul Gregory was only to be used as cover. He also opened the door to Alan Birch for an advanced position on the right of the field, from Rotherham United, and Dave McLean came as an experienced right sided mid-field man from Darlington. In the attack he selected a strong running forward player called Steve Johnson, who left Bristol City to take his place as spearhead of the Scunthorpe attack.

The 1986-87 season would throw open opportunities for local apprentices, and supporters could cheer the efforts of Mark Atkins, Paul Nichol and Andy Stevenson. It was hoped that they might tread in the foot steps of the likes of Paul Longden and Dave Hill, who had benefited from coaching at the Club, to make an established career.

Making their way to pastures new would be Mike Brolly, John Hawley and Tommy Graham, the hero of the final promotion push in 1983. Scunthorpe United would also keep a weather eye out for the progress of Keith Houchen at Coventry City.

Supporters of all teams had to get used to a new structure throughout the Leagues. The authorities had introduced the play-off system. The rules would vary as to which teams would be involved, but it was to reduce four teams down to just one to see which club was to win promotion. In Division Four, a trapdoor was to open to swallow the bottom team into non-League football, and promote a team from the Conference in its place, providing the new club had a ground that met football League standards.

Scunthorpe United began the season at home to Northampton Town, the team destined to be the Champions at the end of the football year. The 2-2 result was significant because the first Scunthorpe goal was scored by Steve Cammack, and it was to be his final one for the Iron.

Steve Cammack was now struggling with injury, and he tried loan spells at Stockport and Port Vale to resurrect his career, but in the end he had to leave the first class game. He scored an unparalleled one hundred and twenty one goals for Scunthorpe United in all competitions. This man will always remain in the hearts of the sporting public who were lucky enough to see him play. Steve Cammack wrote his name indelibly in the Club's history and will live with the likes of Jack Brownsword and Barry Thomas as Scunthorpe United great players.

In the League Cup, United came up against the same Darlington that knocked them out of the competition twelve months ago. This time the story was to be different, because the Iron put up two worthy performances to win both of the legs. The aggregate score was 4-1, and defender Steve Lister notched three of the goals, including both of them in the 2-0 victory at the Old Show Ground. The voyage was to hand them a two legged tie against Ipswich Town, of the Second Division. This time the team was to lose 4-1 on aggregate, but supporters and players found themselves richer for the experience.

Scunthorpe United continued to produce results that saw them tripping along fractionally below the halfway line in the League ratings. During the early fixtures there were two that stood out, and both involved home matches against original members of the Football League of 1888. The first was a tussle with Preston North End, a team that was to finish the campaign in the second promotion position. They were hardly up to the task at Scunthorpe, and lost 4-0, the greatest margin they would suffer all year. At the beginning of October the team locked horns with the not so mighty Wolverhampton Wanderers, for the first ever competitive meeting. The Wolves tore into the Iron, and won 2-0. Their fate was via the Play-offs, and they would lose in the Final to Aldershot.

Before too long, Frank Barlow made a number of team changes. The first saw Alan Whitehead transferred to York City.

On the other hand, the manager brought in a right sided forward, named Ian Richardson, who was from Chester City. He was of slender build, and was noted when the Chester side played in Scunthorpe late last term. At the end of November, a marvellous pocket battle ship came for the right side of the mid-field, in the form of David Harle, from Bristol City. His dynamo never stopped running, and his inclusion was a immediate success.

The F.A.Cup provided the Club with another potential banana skin, and a home draw against the former League club of Southport. The players listened to the words of wisdom offered by their manager, and successfully negotiated the obstacle via a 2-0 score. Dave Hill was the marksman of the first half, and Julian Broddle made sure later in the contest. This led them to another bout against a non-League team, and Runcorn were the second Cup visitors. Older supporters recalled the 1947 battle on the Wirral, where Runcorn won, but this time there was to be no upset. The prize went to Scunthorpe, but the 3,006 spectators had to wait patiently until into the second forty five minutes before Broddle notched another Cup goal, and United were through. It was to prove to be a golden goal, because Scunthorpe became paired with Spurs at White Hart Lane in the Third Round.

Over the Christmas holidays, Frank Barlow made two loan signings, and the last appearance of one would overlap with the first of the other. Scunthorpe United borrowed David Reeves, a forward from Sheffield Wednesday. He was a tall slender lad with blond hair, and he made a favourable impact by scoring twice in his debut game at the Old Show Ground, against Exeter City. United went on to win the match 3-1. If the money had been available, it is doubtless he would have been offered a contract. When he left, United took Ken De Mange, an Irish forward on loan from Liverpool. He had already played for Eire at full International level, and was to scored three times in four appearances.

On January 10th 1987, Scunthorpe United took dozens of coaches full of supporters to London, on one of the coldest days of the year, to see them play Tottenham Hotspur. At kick-off, White Hart Lane was sparsely populated with 19,339 spectators, three thousand having travelled from Lincolnshire. Most of the noise was issued from the visitors end, and Frank Barlow chose the following team:

Green, Money, Longden, De Mange, Lister, Atkins, Russell, McLean, Johnson, Broddle and Hill.

Scunthorpe United produced a display which was of the top order. They chased and harried the First Division men over every inch of the park. Gary Mabbutt, the Tottenham captain, put his team ahead, but Steve Johnson fashioned a great equaliser for the break. Once the game went into the second phase, Nico Claesen and Glen Hoddle looked to have secured the Spurs victory with two goals. A comment must be said about the Hoddle strike, because it was a vicious swerving stinger that was worth the entrance fee just to see. Scunthorpe still refused to die, and came back with what proved to be the last goal of the bone freezing day. It was scored by Ken De Mange, and put a respectable seal on a cracking Scunthorpe afternoon all round.

Scunthorpe United went back to the Fourth Division programme, and continued to pursue the loan market. In the middle of January they brought in Mark North, a goal scoring forward from Luton Town, for a month. During his stay he was part of the party that beat Tranmere Rover 6-0, and in his next match Mark scored both goals that beat Aldershot 2-0. Unfortunately, these two victories would be the last for eight lean matches.

The responsibility of the poor showing of the team had to stop at the managers door. Supporters had been patient, but the board could see that the situation was not satisfactory. Everyone respected Frank Barlow, but now was the time for a change. Frank was relieved of his duties, and Richard Money and Bill Green sorted the first team affairs, until a new man could be interviewed for the vacant post. It was during this period of uncertainty that the men in temporary charge, signed one of the cheekiest goal poachers ever to put on the claret and blue shirt. He was Andy Flounders, and he would pinch goals at every angle around the box, taking him to near the top of the tree of all time Scunthorpe goal scorers. He soon got to work, and whistled in six goals in the remaining fifteen matches.

Steve Johnson, the leading goal scorer of 1986-87, receives the prestigious Ernie Storey Player of the Season award from Keith Storey.

The season was quickly ebbing away, and just prior to the new manager walking through the door the team hit the headlines by beating Southend 3-0. What made it special was Julian Broddle's opening strike after only ten seconds.

On April 15th 1987 it was announced that Mick Buxton, the former Huddersfield manager, had been offered, and accepted the job as the Scunthorpe United Manager. It was to be seen that Mick Buxton was a no nonsense type of a manager, who expected a high work rate from his men. In the seven matches he had left of the season, Scunthorpe United won six of them, and drew the other one. The transformation was like a Guy Fawkes night rocket, and it shot them up the table into eighth place, something unthinkable a few weeks ago.

1987-88

The new era had now commenced, and during the Summer months Buxton was to add to his squad. One of his first signatures was that of Tony Brown, another tall central defender from Doncaster Rovers. When it was necessary, Tony could be moved into the left of the mid-field four. He also put out feelers on Kevin Dixon up in Hartlepool, no doubt after some advice from Bill Green. This time the move became permanent, and Kevin was now part of the furniture. The forward line had the injection of a will o' the wisp character called Tony Daws, from Sheffield United. It might have taken this youngster a year to settle down, but once he linked up with Andy Flounders, these two men would be the machine gun raiders of the attack. Neither of them were big men, but they would fire so many accurate cannon shells into the opposition net, that size was the last worry on anyone's mind.

On the other side of the coin, United said their fond farewells to Paul Gregory, Dave Travis and Les Hunter. Unbelievably, Les was returning for his third tour of duty at Chesterfield, and his career must have been unique for four moves to the two clubs.

In the Summer there was some sensational news. It started with a number of alterations on the board. There was an amicable change of Chairman, where Mr Belton stepped down in favour of Mr Graham Pearson, but he agreed to remain as the Vice Chairman. When that was all sorted, there was the announcement that the board had unanimously voted to leave their home at the Old Show Ground, and build a new stadium somewhere in the vicinity of the town. The problem was that the present ground needed too much money spending on it to meet its certification requirements, and the mounting Club debts would not allow the team to be able to function for too much longer. It was a case of move or go under.

The Old Show Ground belonged to the Club, and was a valuable piece of real estate. If they could sell it for development, there would be sufficient funds to pay off all the money owed, build as new stadium from scratch and still have a small surplus to invest in the team. It was a brave plan, and would see the first upheaval of this kind in modern times. Supporters might have been reluctant at first, but once they saw how vital it was, they all endorsed the project. A number of meetings took place and consultations made as to the best location for the new stadium. Happily, this quickly brought everyone into line, and any objections dwindled to nothing.

A spot of defending to do in, early in the last season at the Old Show Ground against Colchester United. The two teams shared four goals.

The firm of Birse and Company became the main contractors, and the sale of the Old Show Ground was agreed with the chain of Safeway supermarkets. Planning permission was successfully obtained to build the new stadium in Glanford, marginally outside the town. It was to be constructed South of the Berkeley circle, on land between the road and the railway. It was difficult to picture where it would be at first, but once the first pegs were hammered into the ground from which the general out line could be constructed, the concept was soon appreciated.

The football calendar opened at home to Tranmere Rovers, and three second half goals by Billy Russell and Andy Flounders with a brace, put the Iron on the route to a 3-0 success. Attention was next switched to the League Cup, now referred to as the Littlewoods Cup. Scunthorpe beat off the challenge of Hartlepool United, 3-1 at home and 1-0 away, to earn the right to face Leicester City, of Second Division fame. The class difference was apparent, but the Foxes had to work hard for the 4-2 aggregate win, as each of the two legs finished 2-1.

At the termination of the League Cup run, Mick Buxton went into the transfer market and brought a Yorkshire man from Crystal Palace. He was Kevin 'Ticker' Taylor, a half back of a superior class for the fourth tier of the game. This was evident by the thought he put into some of his passing, and the accuracy of his feet. Mick Buxton also used the loan card to good effect, going back to borrow David Reeves for a second spell. When that loan period was about to finish, Dave Cowling arrived from Huddersfield, where the manager and player once worked together. Dave Cowling played only one game, and that was on the left side of the forward line. Reeves enjoyed six appearances, and scored four goals, three of these won the match at Hereford, 3-2.

At the end of October, the Iron had only lost three times in the League, all of them being on their travels, and included the visit to Molineux to play Wolves. During that time they had a notable victory at Darlington, where a second half of three Scunthorpe United strikes extended a 1-1 score after the first forty five minutes, to 4-1 at the conclusion. Another victory was watched by 2,872 spectators on the event of Cardiff City dropping into the Old Show Ground, which was looking in a tired state of repair. United had the gift of an own goal to get them on their way, and Kevin Taylor added a second before the halfway mark. In the second section of the game Cardiff pulled one back, but the spoils fell to United, and they won 2-1.

Scunthorpe United sat happily at the top end of the League, but every now and again they were found to be caught napping. One such occasion was when the new boys of the Fourth Division, Scarborough, made their visit to the Old Show Ground. The day was marred by a broken leg suffered by Kevin Blackwell in the Scarborough goal, but the visitors recovered and won 1-0 in the second half.

This reverse had no ill effect one week later, when the First Round of the F.A.Cup was played on the same pitch. The team faced Bury, who enjoyed the comforts of a division higher than the Iron. This counted for naught, and the Shakers were shaken by the only recorded hat-trick, scored by a Scunthorpe full back. Billy Russell notched all three goals in the 3-1 triumph.

In the Second Round, United had a plum tie at home to Sunderland, now residing in the Third Division, but soon to return to former glory. A crowd of 7,178 supporters made the noise of a Concorde jet taking off, as the teams came onto the park. The patrons would receive full value for the entrance fee, being able to witness a battle that makes the F.A.Cup the main attraction. Eric Gates put Sunderland ahead, but in the second half United hit back. Kevin Taylor struck the first for the Iron, then in a grandstand finish David Harle caused the greatest excitement for the home fanatics, as he shot the winner. At 2-1 United were untouchable.

In December, United borrowed Martin Taylor, on loan from Derby County for two months, for the goalkeeping spot, at a time of inconsistency. The League programme was to only contain one victory for Scunthorpe United during the month, and that was at home to Darlington, on Boxing Day. The 1-0 result arrived courtesy of a first half shot aimed by Andy Flounders, and raised the team up into eighth position in the table. Two days later, the Iron took a point at Leyton Orient. Then came two games in consecutive days, beginning on New Year's Day at Colchester, where a slick example of taking chances brought a smart 3-0 result. Tony Daws helped to construct the win with two goals, and Steve Lister provided the other. Back at the Show Ground, United made it maximum points, beating Cambridge 3-2.

It was on Saturday January 9th that United sharpened the axes to do battle in the F.A.Cup, at home to Blackpool in the Third Round. A crowd of 6,217 spectators had a large number of pockets of the tangerine colours of the visiting supporters. It brought back memories of a similar tie in 1961, but there would not be the goal bonanza of yesteryear, and it was the same score at the last whistle as it was at the first. This was the last ever F.A.Cup match ever to be conducted from the platform of the Old Show Ground, and ended a tradition stretching back to 1909. In the replay, Blackpool scraped through with a single second half goal.

When the team returned to League business, they left their foot off the throttle, and managed one point out of the next nine. This was taken from a draw at Newport, and was followed by agony at home to Wolves, and despair at Rochdale. The result was that United tumble to eleventh in the table, the lowest they would occupy all year.

Scunthorpe United in attacking mood at Tranmere in March 1988 season, a game which was won 3-1.

It was in February that Mick Buxton secured a prolific Scottish marksman, named Dave Shearer, from Bournemouth. He had seen service in the colours of Middlesbrough and Gillingham, and was quickly to make his mark at Scunthorpe. One of the most remarkable matches ever staged at the Old Show Ground just happened to be Dave Shearer's debut, when Leyton Orient were the opposing team.

Scunthorpe United played reasonably satisfactory throughout, but hats off to the Orient boys for taking a two goal lead into the final ten minutes. Then came an amazing last three minutes which saw David Harle score twice, and Dave Shearer add the third to pull off an incredible 3-2 victory.

The Leyton Orient game was the first of a seventeen match run to the end of the season, in which the only loss was at the Racecourse Ground in Wrexham. At home to Peterborough, Andy Flounders scored a hat-trick, when United won by five clear goals. Hereford and Hartlepool both crashed to 3-0 defeats, but one of the keenest results was at Ninian Park, Cardiff. The Welshmen would be the second place team in the division, and gained automatic promotion. When Scunthorpe came calling, the Bluebirds lost only their second home match, and conceded their only double. Dave Shearer scored the 1-0 winner in the second forty five minutes.

Scunthorpe United rose up the table and flirted with the automatic promotion places themselves, but lost ground with a run of consecutive draws. In the final League match ever to be played at the Old Show Ground, the Iron had to meet Exeter City.

A crowd of 6,736 spectators turned out to see a parade of old veteran favourites that had graced the place in their younger days, led by the old master, Jack Brownsword. Although it was a day of nostalgia, there was the important matter of the tussle against the Grecians. Dave Shearer scored United's goal, but the result was a 1-1 draw. This left the last day of the season finely balanced. If United could win at Torquay, and Bolton lost at Wrexham, then it would be Scunthorpe that went up.

The game at Torquay had a problem for those supporters wishing to see it, because at Plainmoor the Devon club had a total ban on away fans. This was imposed ever since the visit of Wolverhampton Wanderers when some people, supposedly following the famous old team, wrecked the town. This was no consolation to other well behaved football enthusiast who wished to see a match. The Iron would not be entirely without support, and Exeter City followers had distributed a number of Torquay membership cards when they came up to play their match. Getting in to see the game was equivalent to the Great Escape in reverse. The kick-off arrived just at the moment of a cloud burst, but a refreshed United took a lead through Andy Flounders, then a decisive strike by Ian Richardson won Scunthorpe a 2-1 victory. Before there could be any celebrations, the Bolton result had to be put into the equation, and unfortunately they had won. This meant that the Iron were in the Play-Offs, and by chance their opponents would be Torquay United.

The consequences of that Saturday afternoon, on May 7th, threw up quite a number of interesting scenarios, the first of which was that the bulldozers had to be delayed from starting to demolish the Old Show Ground, until the Pay-

Offs had been completed. Another was that Scunthorpe United successfully appealed, to allow their supporters to attend the match in Devon. Torquay had no choice but to open the terraces, but set a twelve noon kick-off, to minimise the numbers that might travel. It did not stop two buses setting off at four in the morning to be in Torquay on time. In the end, almost five hundred Irons made the voyage.

Another factor was that one of the Torquay men had received a lengthy ban for disciplinary reasons. The Devon club protested against the ban, and he was allowed to play during the Play-Off games, but went on to serve the suspension at a less demanding time.

The first of the two legs was held on the five thousand capacity Plainmoor Ground, which was packed to the gunnels. It cannot be said that the game could ever be remembered as a football classic, or closely fought epic. Instead it was to be noted as a spiteful ninety minutes of gamesmanship. Scunthorpe United's party were aggrieved to have Paul Nichol dismissed for an innocuous tackle that left a Torquay player hurt one moment, and ready for the free kick once the red card had been delivered. In another incident the manager of the home side was sent to the stand for protesting too vehemently. During the match, several Scunthorpe players received knocks that left the team a blooded army.

The bare bones of the match were summed up by the fact that 4,602 spectators saw Caldwell and Dobson give Torquay a 2-0 lead, and Andy Flounders reduced this in the period after the first forty five with an opportunist goal, when the ball was lost by the tall Gulls goalkeeper.

On Wednesday May 18th 1988, the curtain came down on a period of almost ninety years of football history. It was to be an emotional evening because this really was the last time the Old Show Ground was to function as it had done for generations of Scunthorpe football supporters. The attendance of 6,482 included several hundred Devonian supporters, who were all made most welcome. Scunthorpe United had no choice but to select the only fit men available to play. Mick Buxton's team included the following: Green, Stevenson, Longden, Taylor, Lister, McLean, Richardson, Shearer, Daws, Flounders and Hill, substitutes Atkins and Dixon.

The second leg was more in common with the type of football to be expected of an important match, and there was a greater concentration on the game. Both sets of players behaved themselves, and no goals came in the first portion of the play. In the second half, United pressed forward, and left space at the rear, which Mark Loram of Torquay exposed. At 3-1 the tie was lost, but there was still one moment of drama for the Old Show Ground to stage. Only eight minutes remained, when the Iron were awarded a penalty, and Steve Lister was given the responsibility to take the kick into the Doncaster Road goal. He duly dispatched the ball swiftly into the target.

It was too late to find the right formula for an unlikely recovery, and Scunthorpe United went out on aggregate 3-2. Torquay United were wished good luck, but in the two legged Play-Off Final Swansea City beat them, and claimed the place in the Third Division for the following term.

At the sounding of the final whistle, thousands of supporters ran onto the field to claim pieces of the pitch as a souvenir. Others took the favourite seat they had sat in as season ticket holders. Ronnie Barnes, the Scunthorpe United grounds man, dismantled posts so they could be used at the new stadium. It was hoped that the first cantilever stand on the East side of the Old Show Ground might be saved and bought by Doncaster Rugby League Club, but it never matured. The evening was one of sadness, and a time of the last good bye. Twelve hours later and the Old Show Ground was brought to its knees, cut down like in a medieval execution, and pushed into the oblivion of history. It took less that two weeks to clear the site ready for a new construction.

Down at the bottom of the Doncaster Road hill the new stadium was almost completed, and was a neat ten thousand capacity ground, made to order, and fit for the modern age. It stood out as a beacon that many other clubs would wish to copy in the years ahead. This was the way forward, away from the tired grounds that were part of an age of yesterday. Scunthorpe United had held the torch for the sport of football, and Glanford Park was the way to new future.

The last regular League match at the ground, but not the last game!

GLANFORD PARK, THE FIRST PHASE.

1988-89

There could be no denying that the new stadium, to be named Glanford Park, was a model piece of football engineering and put the Club on the map. Everyone was proud of the beautifully sculptured ground, which originally had terracing behind each goal, and featured a unique roof that covered the whole ground in an oval shape. It was worth every penny of the £2.5M investment.

On Sunday August 14th the stadium was opened by Her Royal Highness, the Princess Alexandra, accompanied by her husband Mr Angus Ogilvy, and dozens of specially invited guests, including Mr Graham Kelly, the Secretary of the Football League. A Scunthorpe United eleven played a Football League selected team, managed for the day by Graham Taylor, a man soon to be the England team boss. The Scunthorpe United side even featured Kevin Keegan, who completed the extra special occasion. The star studded team won 5-1, and Dave Shearer had the four thousand supporters cheering, when he scored the Scunthorpe goal. It was a carnival day, for everyone to capture on camera.

Mick Buxton included a Dutchman in the opening of the Glanford Park game. He was Rob de Lang, and Mick tried to sign him, but was thwarted when he was unable to receive the proper clearance by the authorities to play. Instead he brought in Paul Rumble to cover the full back position, on loan for two months from Watford, and Julian Winter from Huddersfield for the attack, just for one month.

One player that would have an influence at Glanford Park was a young goalkeeper from Portsmouth, named Paul Musselwhite. Mick Buxton launched him in at the deep end, and he responded so well that he kept his position throughout most of the football year. Paul was to be joined by Andy Hodkinson for the right of the attack, from Stockport. He was a slender figure with speed, who was to improve with the advance of time. Another attacking minded player brought in by Buxton was that of the reliable Dave Cowling, who had, of course, already played at Scunthorpe on loan from Huddersfield. During the Summer of 1988, hands were shaken on a permanent deal. The final part of the reshaping was to bring in Paul Smalley, a quick tackling full back from Notts County. He was to arrive in October, and was the right sided partner to Paul Longden.

A number of the old guard would not fit into the new era at Glanford Park. Steve Johnson, Alan Birch, Kevin Dixon, Dave McLean, Billy Russell and Ron Green all departed for other destinations. In addition, Dave Hill was transferred to Ipswich Town for a substantial fee, and Mark Atkins went off to play for Blackburn Rovers. A tribunal set the transfer at £45,000. Mark was to expand his game at Ewood Park, and eventually won a Premiership medal with the Lancastrian club in 1995.

On August 27th 1988, Glanford Park began the business it was designed for, and the first Football League match was staged there, before 3,663 spectators, for the visit of Hereford United. The Scunthorpe United team for that historic event was as follows;

The opening game at Glanford Park versus a Football League Eleven on August 14th 1988. Rob De Lang watches, Kevin Taylor shoots.

Musselwhite, Longden, Rumble, Taylor, Lister, Brown, Hodkinson, Winter, Shearer, Flounders and Cowling. During the match Tony Daws came on for Dave Shearer after thirty one minutes of play, and Andy Stevenson was an unused substitute.

The match was to be a close affair at first, but opened up on forty seven minutes, when Dave Cowling wrote his name indelibly into history with the first goal, scored from close range. The second strike was the first by a substitute. Tony Daws took the ball four minutes later, and ran from the halfway line. He was unimpeded by any defenders, and took the advantage with a shot low past the keeper's left post. Hereford then pulled one goal back, but the Iron, playing in claret and blue stripes, were not finished yet. The final word was by 'Ticker' Taylor, who returned a volley into the net from a partially cleared corner.

Three days later and the floodlights were turned on for a match in the League Cup. A gate of 3,820, was incredibly smaller, compared with the one that witnessed the turning on of the lights at the Old Show Ground, but in each case they would warm to a brilliant display. On this occasion, the visitors were the Terriers of Huddersfield Town, who counted ex-England International Peter Withe in their ranks.

The first leg began with the Town team taking a four minute lead, which they held for almost an hour. Andy Flounders equalised, only for Huddersfield to regain the initiative at 2-1. It set the match up for a grandstand finish, and two goals by Steve Lister and Andy Hodkinson gave Scunthorpe a 3-2 lead to take to the huge Leeds Road arena.

The return leg contained just as many twists and turns. Andy Flounders seemed to have put Scunthorpe in an unassailable position with another strike, but then Huddersfield scored two more through Maskell and Trevitt. This squared the tie and the adventure had to go into extra time. It was during this period that another Andy Flounders shot scorched into the net to seal the match at 2-2, and the aggregate score stood at 5-4 in favour of the Iron.

The League Cup saga continued with another two legged thriller against the not so mighty Chelsea, who were a team of Second Division stock for one brief season. They had a reputation of bringing some boisterous supporters from the Capital, but those in the 5,061 attendance behaved impeccably. They cannot have enjoyed the evening, certainly not in the later stages. The interval score was 1-1, and Scunthorpe had provided both of the goals, from Tony Daws and Steve Lister through his own net. Events would change in the second period, as the Iron ran riot with three more goals. These were supplied by Tony Daws again, plus others from young Andy Stevenson, and a fourth from 'Ticker' Taylor. A 4-1 lead was handy to take down to Stamford Bridge.

The second part of the competition was to provide a problem for Scunthorpe supporters wishing to view the match. The football authorities had banned all away fans from visiting Stamford Bridge, because of trouble between the Chelsea followers and Middlesbrough supporters at a Play-Off game in May. It was a strange decision to receive a ban when an event happened months ago, more than one hundred and sixty miles away. At kick-off about fifty supporters from Scunthorpe had found their way into the ground. The attendance of 5,814 was one of the lowest to be present at any Chelsea game throughout the London club's history.

The match saw each side score one goal in the first half of play, then the same trick was repeated in the second period. David Hale scored United's first from the spot, and the other was pushed in by Andy Flounders. After one hundred and eighty minutes, it was little Scunthorpe that immerged triumphant with an unlikely 6-3 aggregate score. Scunthorpe United had a distinguished visitor in September, when the Prime Minister, Mrs Thatcher, called in to have a look round the new enterprise. This was in the week before Grimsby Town met the Iron in a 1-1 draw. The match took place before 6,037 spectators, and Steve Lister made sure of the Scunthorpe point, when each goal arrived in time for the tea break. United drew the next match at Glanford Park to Carlisle by the same score, then let their guard down during the fourth home match, and surrendered their fortress for the first time to Scarborough.

The arrival of November produced the novelty of seeing Scunthorpe United still in the two major cup competitions for the first time ever. The Club had been drawn away to Bradford City, of Division Two, in the next round of the League Cup, sponsored by Littlewoods. Ties were of one game from the Third Round, and United set about the task in a workman like fashion. They were well represented in the 8,011 crowd, and earned a replay from a 1-1 result. Tony Daws took the honours for a second half come back, when he equalised a first half Bradford goal, but the efforts of the likes of Richard Money and Steve Lister, further back down the line, contributed just as much.

Before the Iron returned to battle in this competition, they had sufficient time to play Blackpool in the First Round F.A.Cup, over at Bloomfield Road. It was never a happy park for Scunthorpe to play on, and so it proved again. For all the dashing about, they still suffered a 1-0 loss.

In the League Cup, the replay did not take place until November 22nd, supposedly because of a break for International duty. It made local supporters smile when they heard of the reason, but 5,793 were in force when the battle resumed. This time, that fraction of extra class in the City side edged them through, but make no mistake, Scunthorpe pushed them every inch of the way in the 1-0 defeat.

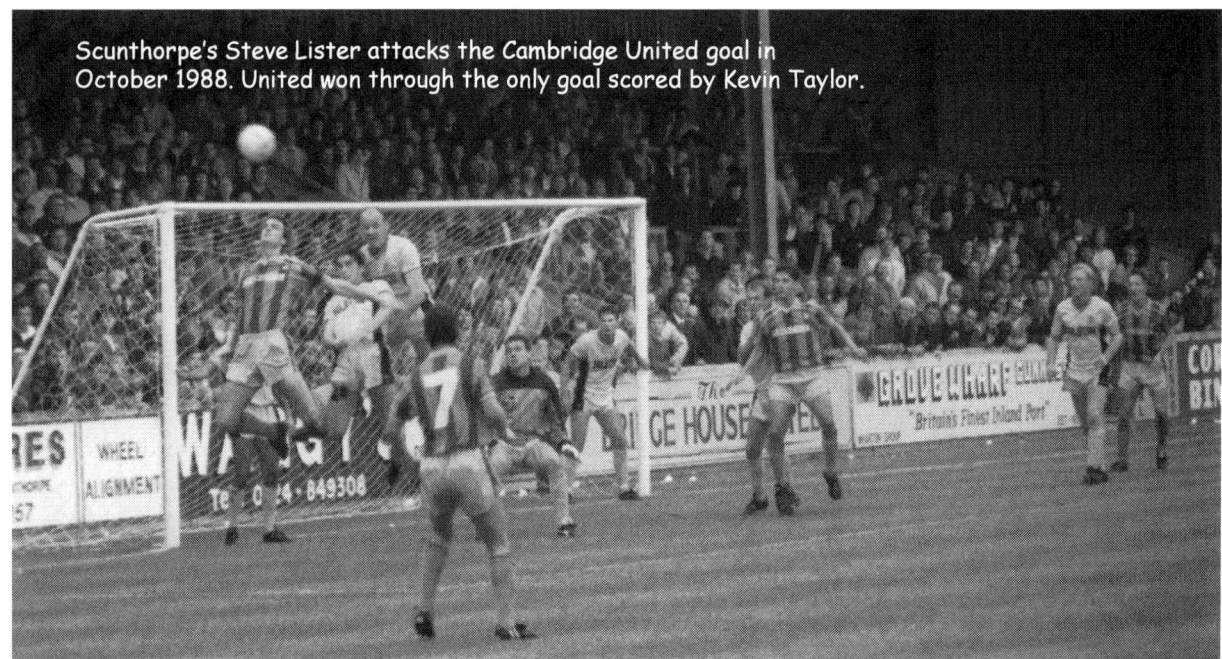
Scunthorpe's Steve Lister attacks the Cambridge United goal in October 1988. United won through the only goal scored by Kevin Taylor.

In December, United would draw three matches and lose one of their Fourth Division fixtures. One of these was on Boxing Day, at home to Hartlepool United. It was to mark the debut of a superb young mid-fielder called Ian Hamilton, from Cambridge United, who was introduced gently from the bench. Ian had a pair of educated feet, that would assist in the engine room, and he was to become an influential player. In this game, the Iron looked to be slipping towards a 1-0 defeat, when a ball was fisted away from the target. The problem was that the hand belonged to an outfield player and not the custodian. David Harle put away the fortuitous penalty award, and saved the day.

On New Year's Eve, United lost 1-0 to Tranmere, and the goal that won the match was a spectacular twenty five yard looping header. This next problem was it was an own goal by Steve Lister, over the head of his own keeper Paul Musselwhite. Never the less, it did become a talking point for a week or two, as did the 5-1 defeat at Halifax Town, which angered Buxton in to making changes.

Scunthorpe United took David Brown on loan from Preston, in an effort to give young Paul a rest from the pressures of his first season, not that he was shouldering all the blame. Mick Buxton next looked what was in the cupboard of the second team, and decided that it was time to upgrade Paul Nichol into the frenzy of the first team. Paul was a tall central defender, who adapted in a positive manner to the rigours of the sport. During February there was the sight of David Cork in a Scunthorpe United shirt, arriving for the mid-field positions on either side of the pitch, from Huddersfield Town. He was not a big man, but showed skill and resilience.

It was fortunate that Scunthorpe United soon overcame their Christmas holiday time hick-up, and went on a spree of six unbeaten matches, five of which yielded the maximum points. The team managed three consecutive away victories, and given a choice, perhaps the 3-0 win up in Cumbria took the biscuit. During this purple patch, the combination of Daws and Flounders as a scoring partnership was proving priceless. It might have been at a lower level, but it was as exciting as Gregory and Brown, or Thomas and Godfrey.

In the final third of the season, Scunthorpe United played like an express train at full speed. Highlights of the stations they passed through included Rochdale at home, beaten convincingly 4-0. Then at Burnley the home side could not prevent a Steve Lister strike in between the post stealing the points. Peterborough lost to a Flounders hat-trick, 3-0. Only a wobble in April, when the team lost at Tranmere and Scarborough, stopped them going top.

The team entered the last leg with three matches in May. The first of these was to produce at record Glanford Park crowd of 8,775, against the eventual Champions, Rotherham United. The men in the yellow shirts appeared to be one of the classiest teams that the Iron had played against all season, and although the game lacked goals, it was a tense entertaining chapter, that kept the custodians on their toes. In the next match, United met a very sorry Darlington, who were sent to the grave of non-League football in the Conference after the result. The Iron totally destroyed them 5-1, and this time Tony Daws took the ball home for his hat-trick. Kevin Taylor and Andy Flounders hit the other two.

After the match, United went into the final episode at Leyton Orient, in London, perched in second place in the table. All they needed to do was to avoid defeat and they would be automatically be promoted. At the Orient, the whole of the massive bank behind the goal was an army camp of the claret and blue. Unfortunately, the team was to play a Leyton side also desperate for the three points for their own Play-Off ambitions. On the day, Scunthorpe United produced an horrific display and slumped 4-1, dropping them back into fourth place. They would be given another game of chance in the lottery of the dreaded Play-Offs.

The cards dealt to the Iron required them to play Wrexham twice, beginning at the Racecourse Ground. Once again the team continued to suffer a headache from the previous match. They put up a lack lustre display, which terminated in a 3-1 loss. It was not the platform that the Buxton boys wanted. In the return, at Glanford Park, the tie was over by the interval, by which time Russell had bagged both of Wrexham's winning goals. It was a disappointing finale to a year, that looked so promising at one stage, but the hard fact was that promotion had disappeared out of the window, and the same journey would have to be traced again next season.

Andy Hodkinson congratulates Tony Daws after scoring against Darlington in the final home game of 1988-89 season. The 5-2 result relegated the visitors to the Conference.

1989-90

During the sunshine months, Mick Buxton strengthened his goalkeepers by bring in Peter Litchfield, from Bradford City, as competition for Paul Musselwhite. Peter started the season in charge, but Paul forced his way back, and by the end of the football year, he had more appearances to his name.

In the out field position, Buxton went back to his old club at Huddersfield Town, and brought in a left sided mid-fielder called Gordon Tucker, who had made his League debut for the Terriers. He then went to Sheffield Wednesday, and signed a huge central defender of the name of Ian Knight on loan. Sadly the big man broke his leg in only his second game, and never wore the shirt again, a huge disappointment for all parties.

One player that United had a look at was Martin Butler for the forward line, but he was not what Mick Buxton was searching for. However, Perry Cotton, a tall young forward on the brink of the New Zealand International squad, was handed a contract. His chance was chiefly in the second half of the fixtures. The main talking point was the £50,000 signing of Gary Marshall for the left wing, from Carlisle United. It was hoped that his presence would promote further goals from the partnership of Daws and Flounders.

The calendar had only just rolled over into September when Mick Buxton brought another of his old players to the Club. It might have cost a bob or two, but the investment in Mark Lillis, a proven marksman, at Aston Villa was a shrewd move. Mark was a bustling front man, who was just as good a supplier of goals as finisher.

To make way for the influx of newcomers, United waved cheerio to Ian Richardson, off to Staines Town in the non-League, while Dave Shearer and David Cork both went to Darlington. Tony Brown decided to depart for Rochdale, and David Harle took the road to Peterborough.

The start that Scunthorpe United made to the campaign was hardly headline news. They lost at Lincoln 1-0, and repeated the trick for the visit of Rochdale. There was similar misery in two matches in the League Cup against Scarborough. A 2-0 loss at Scarborough could not be redeemed at Glanford Park, and a draw put the team from the seaside through, 3-1 on aggregate

The fixture list continued to yield stuttering results for the Iron, but the debut of Mark Lillis came just at the moment of the arrival of Exeter City, a team destined to breast the summit of the division in May. If it was entertainment that was wanted, this match had it all. At half time United had a tough team talk from Mick Buxton, as they trailed 2-1. In the second half they found a gear that had not been used all year, and ran out 5-4 winners. Mark Lillis scored twice, as did Ian Hamilton, and 'Ticker' Taylor made the fifth strike.

In the month of October, United enjoyed varying fortunes in two high scoring consecutive matches. The visit of Colchester United found the guns being fired by Andy Stevenson, Tony Daws, Ian Hamilton, and 'Ticker' Taylor. It was a one sided 4-0 match that sent the Scunthorpe element home happy in the 3,254 attendance. This result prompted about five hundred supporters to travel to Cambridge for the match on the following Saturday, and on a day of gales, United fell victim to a 5-3 reverse. One of the Cambridge goals was worthy of note, because the ball was picked up by a gust of wind high into the air, travelled forty yards and dropped behind Peter Litchfield in the Scunthorpe goal.

The match at Cambridge marked the debut of another Scunthorpe United player. He was a tough mid-field man, called Mark Ward, who was to operated from the right side of the park. Mark came at a price from Leyton Orient, but was a North Eastern lad, who began as a Chelsea apprentice.

In November, the team began the month with two fine victories in the League. At Doncaster Rovers it was brilliant to see the Daws and Flounders combination put a spell on the neighbours, and United won 2-1. This was followed by a mid-day kick-off against Burnley, which brought 4,745 bodies to see what was appertaining. It was a match where all was perfect for the Iron. When the mid-point whistle sounded, Marshall, Ward and Hamilton had hit the shots that hoisted the Iron to a position that was out of reach. One of the strikes, that of Mark Ward's, was from the gift of a penalty. In the second forty five minutes, United made sure of a Peter Litchfield clean sheet, and a 3-0 triumph was richly deserved.

It was now time in the calendar to see what was expected of them in the F.A.Cup. Fate gave them a home tie against the minnows of Matlock Town, and the Gladiators brought several hundred supporters to fit in the 4,307 crowd. They even had the joy of a goal in the later moments of an absorbing game. Scunthorpe had the lion's share of the play, and a hat-trick by the veteran Mark Lillis spoke volumes as to which player controlled the park. Andy Hodkinson was the other goal schemer, and a 4-1 result was a good day out for all concerned.

The Second Round of the F.A.Cup had Scunthorpe United nose to nose with Burnley. This time the other Clarets would show no generosity, and the Iron needed a goal in each half from mid-fielder Kevin Taylor to make sure of a draw. The final 2-2 score required a replay, and took the teams to Turf Moor. This time United owed it to Tony Daws to find an equaliser during the inconclusive 1-1 draw. Eventually, the toss of the coin took the second replay to Burnley. The home side had to be congratulated for their 5-0 success, which was a little unkind on the Iron and the valiant effort they put up.

During December, United would gain solace from just one win, in which Mark Lillis and Paul Nichol cemented the bricks of a 2-1 reward at Hereford. On Boxing Day it should have been more. The match was the local derby against Grimsby Town, and injuries forced Mick Buxton to blood an exciting young central defender named Richard Hall, who would make his way up the divisions. There was little space available at Glanford Park, as 8,384 packed into the place, creating a wonderful atmosphere. At the centre point of the game United held a healthy two goal lead. Tony Daws and Gary Marshall had the distinction of netting the two strikes. In the second portion of the match Grimsby hit back, and the teams finally shared a 2-2 draw.

On Boxing Day 1989 United gave a debut to the highly rated Richard Hall, who is seen clearing the ball in the 1-1 draw with Grimsby Town.

The injury crisis saw Steve Lister sidelined for much of the year, and in January Mick Buxton put his hand in his pocket to buy John Bramhall, a tall, central defender from Halifax Town, who was thin on top. John picked up the nickname of 'Whoosh', because of the huge kick he put behind the ball, to clear it up field.

1990-91

In the Summertime, the board of directors agreed to install a complete area of seating behind the goal in the railway end, for a cost of £40,000. It was intended to pay for the costs from the extra revenue charged for the greater comfort. This would lower the capacity of Glanford Park to 9,183, a figure that as yet had not been reached.

Meanwhile, at a time of pre-season training for members of the team, Mick Buxton was hard at work, making two signings. The first was a grafting central defender called Stuart Hicks. He had the muscle and the guile to compete at the heart of the defence where it mattered most. Stuart signed from Colchester, and it spoke volumes that he and his co-defender, Paul Longden, were to play in every League game. His arrival was at the same moment as that of an experienced right sided wing man, named Ian Miller. Ian was taken from the playing staff of Port Vale, and was a Scotsman who figured in the first half of the football year. Another part of the equation was the inclusion of Richard Hall from the very start of the proceedings. Neil Cox came in from the beginning of October, for the right side of the mid-field. Each of these two lads had been nurtured at the Club, and their rapid rate of maturity brought a posse of scouts knocking at the door.

On the way down the motorway and going out of the ground, United had not offered contracts to Andy Hodkinson, who went to Hyde United, and Gordon Tucker departing for Goole Town.

Scunthorpe United failed to win for ten matches after they beat Hereford. This run included eight draws, five of which were goalless, and four of those were in consecutive matches. It was after these that United exploded back to form, with a 5-0 destruction of Stockport County, and it appeared to be strange to see such a flood of goals after the drought. This was followed by a 1-0 win at Halifax.

At this time Paul Musselwhite was in goal, keeping the clean sheets. He had played in all of the goalless games, plus the two victories, meaning a record of six games without conceding. Two more wins were still imminent, but the record had to stopped when Aldershot notched two goals at Glanford Park. United managed to beat them 3-2. At that match a new giant electronic scoreboard displayed information to the crowd for the first time.

United still had time to win 3-0 at Torquay, where Daws, Flounders and Lillis, all put the ball in the net in the last three quarters of an hour of play. The Torquay result confirmed the second double over the Gulls since the Play-Offs, two years ago. At this junction in time United seemed on course for the Play-Offs, reaching ninth in the charts. However, six games with out a win put pay to these plans. They did have a little flurry of four unbeaten matches at the end of the football calendar, but all hopes of promotion were fading as fast as the sun was going down, at the end of the day over Glanford Park. One of these was at Burnley, where Perry Cotton scored his only goal of the year, and in so doing, gave the Iron a 1-0 victory. This confirmed the double over Burnley, and made compensation for the F.A.Cup exit.

When United greeted Doncaster Rovers for the last match of the season, the 4-1 victory only allowed them to climb as far as eleventh in the table, meaning they could all pack suitcases and go on holiday. Andy Flounders was the top scorer on twenty goals in all competitions, while Mark Lillis had sixteen, and Tony Daws twelve. The supporters also honoured Paul Longden, an unsung hero of the team, with the prestigious 'Ernie Storey' player of the season award.

Richard Hall, Scunthorpe United's number six, is about to sweep Stuart Hick's headed pass into the Lincoln City net for the winning goal. The Iron won 2-1 in September 1990.

Richard Money left to take up a coaching role at Aston Villa in their youth team department. It was not to be long before they would be joined by Peter Litchfield and Paul Smalley looking for fresh pastures.

The fixtures for the 1990-91 card gave United the favour of an opening day fixture against the highly rated Lancastrians of Blackpool, and it was to be a stern test to commence the season. Andy Flounders got them off to a perfect start with a beautiful lob on seventeen minutes, which just evaded the hand of the visiting custodian. This slender advantage was not extended until the referee was about to check his watch, and then the ball fell in the path of Ian Hamilton, who cracked it methodically into the net to make sure, at 2-0.

Before August was out, the Club had the interlude of a pair of League Cup fixture against Carlisle United. The competition was now named the Rumbelows Cup, but a 1-0 loss up in the border lands could not be overturned at Glanford Park. The team was only able to muster a draw, thanks to the shooting boots of Mark Lillis. The 2-1 aggregate score made sure that this footpath to Wembley was now closed.

Once the Buxton boys were back focusing on the League, results started to deteriorate, and only one point was gleaned from the next four results. One of these was a 6-1 thrashing by newcomers, Maidstone United, and constituted the Stones biggest League victory. Scunthorpe United fans were not happy, and aimed the sharpness of their tongues at the Chairman, Mr Graham Pearson. Within the margin of the next board meeting Mr Pearson resigned, and Mr Tom Belton took the reins for a second term of office.

Scunthorpe United still could not find any permanent stability. They managed to squeeze past Lincoln City, 2-1 at Glanford Park, but then went down at home to Cardiff City, and away at Walsall, with scores of 0-2 and 0-3 respectively. It was not until Paul Musselwhite and Neil Cox were selected for team duty, that they conjured up back to back home victories. Against Gillingham, Paul's safe hands kept a clean sheet at one end of the park, and Richard Hall came up into the attack to register the goal, at the other. The 1-0 result was most encouraging. Seven days hence, the team went one better to see off Scarborough 3-0. In this game the name on the lips was that of Tony Daws for two shots into the target, and Taylor glided the third home.

In November, the Iron flexed their muscles in the F.A.Cup. Lady Luck took them over the M62 to play Rochdale, in Greater Manchester. Rochdale were men of middle of the road Fourth Division status, very much like the Iron. It was therefore nothing of a surprise that the two sides managed a goal apiece and had to go to a mid-week replay at Glanford Park. This was to be an elongated affair needing extra time to settle.

The Dale took a one goal advantage back to the dressing rooms, but Andy Flounders shot an equaliser. His Strike was from close range, near the base of the post, shortly after the resumption. The tie was finally wrapped up by Mark Lillis in the additional thirty minutes, shooting into the goal behind which the visiting supporters were sat.

The Second Round of the F.A.Cup kept them at Glanford Park, and on paper they had a sticky tie to deal on their hands. Tranmere Rovers, sailing their ship high at the top of the Third Division, would prove the stiffest of tests. Scunthorpe had the backing of most of the 3,576 paying customers in the ground. Throughout the ninety minutes spectators witnessed a game played at pace, punctuated by incidents of all kinds. At the break, Paul Ward and Mark Lillis had United marginally ahead at 2-1. Each side traded punches in the time after the break, and Andy Flounders made sure that the Iron would breast the tape 3-2 in front. It was a brilliant result, made all the better without the services of Tony Daws and Ian Hamilton, both out injured for more than a month.

There had been a few grumbles of discontent over the way that Scunthorpe United were performing under the leadership of Mick Buxton, but he had no concerns. The team went through December with two draws and a defeat, until they reached the Saturday between Christmas and New Year. A 2-0 result over Carlisle at the other side of the Berkeley circle, lifted spirits. A penalty award in the second section of the match was the key to victory. Andy Flounders put it away and Mark Lillis added another, so that the team had a firm grip on the three points.

The first Saturday of January was traditionally reserved for Third Round of the F.A.Cup, and Scunthorpe United had the long slog down to the South Coast to play Brighton and Hove Albion, on the Goldstone Ground. At the beginning of play a total of 7,785 people were at the old stadium, and saw Scunthorpe under pressure from the first moment. They took a 2-1 deficit into the interval, but kept pace with Brighton's scoring in the second forty five minutes. The 3-2 loss reflected a lot of calories expended, but the reward of goals by Andy Flounders, from the penalty spot, and another brave effort by John Bramall, coming up in support of the attacking men.

Later in the month of January, there would be a number of events to put the Iron in the spotlight. The first was the best result of the year, which saw Andy Flounders score a first class hat-trick, when Aldershot were crushed 6-2. A reflection of how richly the men of Iron were performing prior to this game was in the size of crowd, which contained 2,727 loyalists on parade to see it. The next match was at Blackpool and Scunthorpe could not match the form of seven days ago, losing 3-1, pushing them into thirteenth place in the League ladder. At this point in time Mr Buxton was called before the Chairman, thanked for his hard worked, and relieved of his duties.

The board of directors received dozens of applications for the post of manager, but eventually promoted from within. Bill Green, the tall gentle quietly spoken former assistant, took the helm for a smooth transfer of power. In the first week of his reign he had to sell the two most promising starlets on the Club's books. Scunthorpe United had received a bid of a record £350,000 from Aston Villa for Neil Cox. Neil had played twenty eight first team games in all competitions, but it was enough to convince Villa that this young man would go all the way to the top. Once the ink was dry on the forms Richard Hall took his turn to embark on a £250,000 move to Southampton, in the Premiership. Each of the two lads would develop within the top bracket of the game, but Richard was to suffer with injuries, and his career was not to be as rewarding as the one Neil would experience, for that reason.

One of the next priorities for Bill Green was to go on a shopping spree, in order to fill some of the holes that had been created, and to change a system that had not proven to be a huge success. His first signing was an experienced defender from Barnsley. Joey Joyce might have been thirty, but he had the legs of a Spring lamb, and gave a much needed stability on the right of the defence. The next in line was that of £55,000 right sided mid-fielder, Glen Humphries, from Bristol City. Glen was as strong as an ox, and would run over hot coals if requested. His inclusion was a positive move. Within a month, Bill was down at Ipswich, signing Dave Hill up again, after a broken leg had him out of contention for months. Once the injury was healed, Dave was roaring to go, and stood more of a chance of football at Glanford Park.

The last of Bill Green's signings was the slightly built Mark Hine, a player of more than two hundred games under his belt, from Peterborough United. Mark was to be utilised on the right side in the middle of the park. There was also to be the excellent news of Steve Lister leaving the treatment room, and Bill Green started the ball rolling for another young starlet. On April 27th 1991 he gave a League debut to Graham Alexander, on the right side of mid-field, as a substitute against Chesterfield. Although this was his senior League debut, young Alexander had been used before as a substitute in a Sherpa Van Trophy match in 1988. Graham would eventually play more than one thousand games in various first team competition, and pick up forty Scottish International caps.

When Bill picked up the pieces in the Fourth Division programme, United had sunk to sixteenth position in the table, which was to be the lowest point for them. This was after they surrendered 2-1 at Rochdale, on a dank afternoon. Once the team changes came into effect, they changed their tune, and rose up the ladder. They glided to five straight wins, the best of which was a satisfying 3-2 advance over neighbours Doncaster Rovers, on the wide open spaces of the Belle Vue Ground.

The highest the team climbed to was seventh place, achieved by that extra point gathered out of a 4-4 explosion against Halifax Town, where life was never easy for the 3,134 faithful in attendance. An ace that Bill Green had up his sleeve was that the Football League top brass were shuffling the divisions around. In Division Four, just for one season, there would be four promoted clubs, and Play-Offs for teams occupying places five to eight in the table.

Scunthorpe United maintained their position, mainly thanks to three consecutive home wins against Chesterfield, Darlington, and Wrexham. The fixture list concluded at Edgely Park, against Stockport County. It was a contest best forgotten, because the team received a whipping, losing 5-0. Mercifully, the collateral damage was not sufficient to oust them from the last Pay-Off position.

The football year was extended into May, and initially holidays were on hold until a decision was made over two legs against Blackpool. At Glanford Park, a crowd of 6,536 were at hand to cheer the Iron on. Their chances were dealt a blow when Steve Lister was sent off, for remarks apparently said to a linesman. The team had a struggle on their plate, especially from the time when Blackpool took the lead. A great sigh of relief came from home supporters at the moment that Mark Lillis etched an equaliser into the score sheet, and the team had to take a 1-1 result to Bloomfield Road.

Over in Blackpool, the Iron continued to falter on a ground that was virtually always a burial site for them The second leg was another close affair, and although Dave Hill gave them hope with a lead to take to the rest period, Blackpool came back with two goals later in the match to steal United's thunder.

1991-92

Scunthorpe United began the 1991-92 season with a goalkeeping problem. Paul Musselwhite was unable to play in the opening gambit at Gillingham. It was suggested by Bill Green's second in command, Dave Moore, that for just one match the Club might wish to bring his old team mate, Nigel Batch out of retirement. Nigel was once the long serving Grimsby Town keeper, and he made one appearance for his one time rivals at the Priestfield Stadium.

In the middle of the park, Bill Green was happy to bring Graham Alexander further into the picture of first team football. He added Dean Martin to the frame, also on the right of that section, having departed a similar position at Halifax. It was at the sharp end of the field that Bill was to invest £80,000 in a big front man, named Ian Helliwell, from York City. Not only would Ian score goals, but he was the ideal man to nod down the ball for Tony Daws.

The forward line had two other main players to add to the ranks. The first of these was left sided wide man, called John Buckley. John was of average size, and had his origins at Partick Thistle, in his native Scotland. He had played at a couple of Yorkshire clubs, and was delivered to Glanford Park from Rotherham United. Another forward was a brilliant young black prospect, called Jason White, and he had started as a trainee at Derby County. Bill Green was to continue with his development, and young Jason was to warm the hearts of the public with his huge strides, dashing after the ball. A final word was on Gary Hyde, who was a fringe player from Darlington, who generally came on as a substitute.

Ian Helliwell outjumps the Hereford United defence, in October 1991.

Those leaving Glanford Park would include that old warhorse, Mark Lillis, having a last fling at Stockport County. The list also contained, John Bramhall, going to Hyde United, Paul Ward, fixed up at Lincoln, and Kevin Taylor, who was allowed to drift off to Frickley. The biggest shock was the loss of Andy Flounders, who had scored ninety nine goals for the Iron, but went to Rochdale when he could not agree terms.

Scunthorpe United set off on the voyage to Gillingham on the first day of the fixture card full of optimism, but a series of defensive mishaps led to a blooded nose. They lost 4-0, and quickly had to put that one to bed, ready for the League Cup. The first leg of the First Round was away to Wrexham, and Paul Musselwhite was back in goal. Another loss was inflicted, but at 1-0 this was not terminal. By the time Wrexham arrived at Glanford Park, United had won their first League match, at home to Doncaster Rovers 3-2. They tackled Wrexham just as effectively, and surprised everybody with a superb 3-0 result, which upturned the previous score. What had been encouraging was the distribution of the goals round the team from Glen Humphries, Graham Alexander and Ian Helliwell.

On September 10th 1991, the public of Scunthorpe were treated to a special match by Graham Taylor, the England Manager, who supported Scunthorpe United as a boy, and his father was the Scunthorpe United correspondent for the local newspaper.

He gave approval for the England under twenty one International against Germany to be held at Glanford Park, and 6,984 supporters attended the match, which finished 2-1 to the home Nation.

During September Scunthorpe United started a slow climb in the right direction of the League table. From a run of six games, three were rewarded by victories, and only two finished barren. At Saltergate, the Iron had the most notable of their results, taking all three points in the second half, when Glen Humphries was in the right place to score the only goal of a tight contest.

Attention next was seized by the intrigue of the Rumbelows League Cup. It pitched the Iron in the deep end, with a pair of games against Premiership Leeds United. The first tussle was staged at Glanford Park, and 8,392 roaring spectators applauded a valiant Scunthorpe fight, which brought a goalless draw. It was not so much memorable for the action, but the refreshing spirit purveyed by the Fourth Division minnows. Over at Elland Road the same raw grit produced a gripping retaliation, but the Premiership skills saw Leeds United turn up the heat in sufficient bursts for a comfortable 3-0 win.

Scunthorpe United continued to fire on only three of the four cylinders, but briefly hit full throttle, on November 5th for the visit of Rochdale. If it was real fireworks folks wanted, then Glanford Park was the place to be. Only 2,331 paying spectators took up the offer, but those who did saw their team fired up by rocket fuel. At half time United were 3-0 to the good, and at the conclusion it was difficult to remember that it really was 6-2 to the Iron. Ian Hamilton, Steve Lister, Ian Helliwell, Graham Alexander and Dave Hill from Scunthorpe all scored. Making up the sixth of the total was an own goal, scored by old boy, John Bramhall.

November was to be notable for what proved to be a trio of matches against Rotherham United, which gave the sternest of tests. The initial tussle was at Glanford Park, in a Fourth Division fixture. United always could expect to find the Millers to be a stubborn opposition.

This time the game remained goalless until halfway through the second forty five minutes, when Tony Daws struck. He picked up the ball on the right of the centre spot, and advanced at a terrific speed. Defenders fell in his wake, and from twenty yards out he struck a ball that flew into the back of the target. It was a contender for the best goal of the season.

Seven days down the line and the same scenario took place in the F.A.Cup. This time there was just as cagy a performance from both sides, and Scunthorpe needed to be at their best to survive. Rotherham went back to the changing rooms a goal up, but Ian Helliwell restored local pride with the equaliser.

At Millmoor, the replay was what the F.A.Cup has become famous for, and a full blooded contest had every one up and down in their seats. Twice the Millers led and twice Helliwell and Daws saved the situation. At 2-2 the game entered extra time. Jason White looked to have sealed the victory for Scunthorpe, but then Rotherham bounced back to find a leveller. This was the moment when these two teams made F.A.Cup history. To avoid the congestion of further replays, the authorities introduced the penalty shoot out. Rotherham United and Scunthorpe United would be the first pair of teams to decide the fate of the tie by this method. After all the drama, Rotherham won 7-6.

The F.A.Cup may have knocked United off their horse, but Bill Green decided that to get back on again was the best remedy. He also decided that Paul Musselwhite needed a rest from his duties in goal. To allow this to happened, he brought in Phil Whitehead, an old head, from Barnsley for a couple of months. In his Scunthorpe debut, he kept a clean sheet, and York City were beaten 1-0, through an Ian Hamilton second half strike.

Phil Whitehead was to remain in goal for eight matches. From his baptism, United won four of the next five, to take them up to the end of December. Even that odd game yielded a worthy point at Burnley, and the team were obliged with an own goal in the 1-1 result. One of the most demanding tussles in this run was on the Saturday of the holiday period, against Blackpool. Jason White weighed in with both goals, one in each half, to beat the Seasiders 2-1. This had Scunthorpe United on the fifth perch in the table.

The New Year brought the team down to earth with a bump, when they crashed 4-1 at the McCain Stadium to Scarborough. There was then a week with no fixture, but the boys returned to winning ways at the Shay, in an argument with Halifax Town. Jason White, firmly a fans favourite for his raw courage, scored a hat-trick in the 4-1 success, while Ian Hamilton completed the quartet.

During the Winter months, United maintained their position on the fringe of the Play-Off places. They did experience another stumble in mid-March, with two consecutive defeats.

One of these was quite damaging to moral, as well as to the goal difference. It was a 5-0 defeat at Rotherham United. In the next match they surrendered to Lincoln City, at Glanford Park, which meant the loss of the double over the two fixtures.

The end of the football year was almost in sight, and Bill Green made sure of keeping his powder dry, by cementing two late signings. The first was that of Mark Samways, who was the regular Doncaster goalkeeper, and this pushed Paul Musselwhite out onto the boundary. Another addition to the defence was Matt Elliott, a huge mobile central defender, who was not totally settled at his old club, Torquay United. One viewing of Elliott said that he was playing in the wrong League, and he could make it further up in the divisions. Initially, these two deals were temporary, but then became permanent.

At the first opportunity, these two men were installed into the starting eleven. Scunthorpe United began an eight match unbeaten run to take them to the end of the season. At the front of the firing line were the men of Chesterfield, and they were shot down 2-0. From that point onward the team went into battle with all guns blazing. Game by game, each win inched them a place further up the table. They saved the best until last, and in the final schedule they shot a 4-0 salvo at Carlisle United, at Glanford Park. This terrific effort pushed them up to fifth place in the table, and even had big Matt Elliott on the score sheet for the first goal.

When all the results were analysed, it was found that Scunthorpe United would have a Play-Off Semi-Final against Crewe Alexandra. The first match was to take place at Gresty Road, on the Sunday of the forth coming weekend. Both sides went a little gung ho in the early stages, and warmed the 6,083 spectators, as they traded punches. Hignet put Crewe into a fourth minute lead, but Helliwell equalised on seventeen. Helliwell registered again in the thirty fifth minute, but Naylor squared the match six minutes prior to the break. The excitement was intense and the nerves were jangling. Perhaps a quieter second half, where no more goals were in evidence, brought down pulses to nearer normal speed.

The 2-2 score left both clubs thinking they could still win the prize of the Wembley Final. Glanford Park was packed tight with 7,938 expectant enthusiasts, hoping in the majority that Scunthorpe could find that little bit extra. The one noticeable factor was that neither set of men were giving anything away, and defences took the honours. At the mid-point no goals had been scored, and the same said of the next thirty minutes.

Managers and fans were checking watches, as the possibility of extra time loomed. Then the theatre came to life with an eighty third minute goal. John Buckley put across a teasing ball for Tony Daws to cannon at the Crewe goal.

Dave Hill smashes the ball into the net in the 4-0 success during the last regular fixture, against Carlisle.

It was cleared by Gardiner, helping the defence, but only to the edge of the box, and Dean Martin steamed in to hit the ball, clean as a whistle, into the target.

What a celebration, and what a cauldron of noise. Crewe were stunned, and when the tired legs tried to hit back they were stung again, with only a minute on the clock. John Buckley was the architect, with another curling cross, deep into the penalty box. It dropped sweetly for Ian Hamilton, who rocketed the ball into the net from close range. Conversation was pointless because the cheering was deafening. Scunthorpe United would be the first Lincolnshire club ever to walk onto the hallowed Wembley turf.

Scunthorpe soon found that it was Blackpool that stood in the way of them and promotion. The Play-Off Final was to be played on Saturday May 23rd 1992. A fleet of over fifty buses of all sizes made the way down to the Capital to convey 9,000 supporters to Wembley. It mattered not that they were out numbered in the 22,741 attendance. Every Scunthorpe person wore the Club's claret and blue colours, and the day was a spectacle to behold. Not only was this an important football match, but it was putting the town of Scunthorpe into the focus of the Nation.

Bill Green led the Scunthorpe United team out of the Wembley tunnel and onto the turf, bathed in brilliant sunlight. He held his young daughter's hand, who was the team mascot. The men he chose included: Samways, Joyce, Longden, Hill, Elliott, Humphries, Martin, Hamilton, Sheldon, Daws and Buckley. Jason White and Graham Alexander would be used as substitutes. At kick-off, both defences formed a protective shield round their goalkeepers, and guilt edge chances were at a premium. Samways was only called into action to deal with the routine sort of balls.

At the sharp end, Helliwell and Daws did their utmost to find a way through. The first goal was scored by Blackpool, four minutes from the rest period. It was not spectacular, but it was effective. Bamber, the leading Blackpool marksman, managed to get his head to a loose ball, close to the goal line and headed it to the right of the goal, just inside the post.

It was too late to mount an instant reply, but in the seventh minute of the second half, United levelled with as good as any goal that has ever been scored on the famous ground. The move started just inside the Blackpool half when Dean Martin pushed a neat pass to John Buckley. Buckley found Tony Daws with a ball at just the right height, and Tony followed through with a left foot screamer from distance. What corker! The whole claret and blue section came to their feet in triumph.

Both sides went in search of the winner but it never materialised and a further period of extra time was ordered. By this time, United had the services of substitutes Graham Alexander and Jason White at their disposal. Eventually the whistle sounded for the advantage of neither side, and it was down to penalties.

The penalty shoot out was the most cruel way to decide the fate of a season, but this was the cut throat climax of the match. The Seasiders won the drama 4-3, as the shots of Graham Alexander and Jason White failed to reach the target. No blame was ever attached to these two brave warriors, nor the rest of a brilliant team that had gone so far. For the Scunthorpe supporters it was agony, and hands on head time, while for Blackpool followers it was jubilation, and hands in the air. The journey home was a long quiet one, thinking of what might have been.

The climax of the 1991-92 season was the visit to Wembley for the Play-Off Final against Blackpool. In the second half, United press for an advantage.

The first ball of the campaign was actually kicked at Darlington, in front of 1,489 ardent followers, in the Coca Cola League Cup, on a pleasant Tuesday evening in August. United drew 1-1, with the help of an Ian Helliwell goal. However, in the League, Scunthorpe United began the following Saturday, before the gaze of 1,793 spectators on the vast plains of the Shay Ground, at Halifax. Anyone reaching the terraces late need not have hurried, because no goals was scored. In the mid-week, Scunthorpe saw off Darlington by a 2-0 result so that progress had actually been made on one front.

1992-93

Once the loose ends were tied up over the contracts of Mark Samways and Matt Elliott, Bill Green was able to field very much the same team that did such marvellous work at Wembley. He was to use some of his reserves to fill in the odd gaps, and supporters had glimpses of Paul McCullough, Steve Greaves, and Sammy Goodacre. Bill also loaned Phil Whitehead for a second spell in the goal, and he borrowed former favourite Julian Broddle, from Partick Thistle. There was a suggestion of re-signing Julian, but the asking price was way beyond the budget. It was noticeable that the squad was a little thin in places, and might be stretched.

Those men leaving Glanford Park, sadly, included Steve Lister, who had suffered from injury, and never fully recovered. Another player who was a favourite was keeper Paul Musselwhite, who was to recover his confidence at Port Vale. Mike Hine went off to Gateshead, and Stuart Hicks took up at Doncaster. The biggest burden was the transfer of Ian Hamilton, for £175,000, to West Bromwich Albion. It was to be quite some fellow that would put in the same level of performance as Ian.

The football authorities decided upon a make over for football, and created the premiership out of the First Division. Each division was renamed in step with this, and the fourth tier of the game became known as the Third Division.

The team continued to be unbeaten, and Graham Alexander scored the first goal of the game at home to Shrewsbury, in a 1-1 draw. This was immediately before victory over Walsall, who lost 2-0, to a goal in each half by Elliott and Helliwell. It was not until voyages to Lincoln City and Northampton that defeats were tasted, and in both examples the result was a narrow 1-0. The team then took points from three consecutive matches. A draw at home to Crewe came immediately before wins on the road at Carlisle 2-0, where Ian Helliwell did the trick twice, and at Chesterfield, won 2-1. It was the strikes by Goodacre and White that sent the Scunthorpe army home happy this time. After the Chesterfield result the table had the Iron placed twelfth.

In the League Cup Scunthorpe United had another opportunity of disposing of Leeds United, but once again the Iron were just that little bit too small. In the first leg Leeds had a comfortable 4-1 win, which was about par for the course, and 10,113 spectators paid homage. At Glanford Park the attendance was a healthy 7,419, and on home territory the Iron gave as good as they got. The half time score favoured Scunthorpe 2-1, but in the end the Premiership men fought back to level at 2-2. All the three Scunthorpe goals from both matches came via big Ian Helliwell.

Progress in the Third Division became painfully slow, and in a bid to spice up the team Bill took Steve Charles on loan from Mansfield for a month.

It was discovered that the improvement was still hardly startling, not that Charles was at fault. A number of less than complimentary comments suggested that there was some unrest in the camp. In November, the Club still languished in twelfth League position, while the team prepared for the F.A.Cup.

Scunthorpe United had drawn Huddersfield Town of the renamed Division Two, at Glanford Park, in the Cup. The Terriers were a tough band of men, and United had to play at strength in every department, just to tread water. A goalless draw may not have worn down the pencils of the sports reporters, but it did keep United's slim hopes alive. The whole circus moved on to Leeds Road for the replay.

The replay was the last time that Scunthorpe United would play at Leeds Road, because it was to be replaced in a couple of years by a brand new stadium. On the evening, the Scunthorpe boys deserved a lot of praise for the way they conducted themselves. The Iron came back in the second half from a goal down, to equalise through John Buckley. This engineered a further thirty minutes of football, and sadly they were torpedoed by another Huddersfield goal scoring attack in this part of the game.

Scunthorpe United knew now that the only avenue to success lay in what they could manage in their Third Division programme. The month of December did not bare much fruit for them, and the single joy was at the beginning of the month, against lowly Hereford, when the team played satisfactory enough to warrant a 3-1 win.

On the last Saturday of the year, United played at home to second bottom placed Gillingham. Not only did the Iron go behind, but the side was to suffer a major disaster. Paul Longden was unfortunate to suffer a broken leg. The injury was so severe that it put pay to his career of more than four hundred appearances. A sickened team managed to scrape a 2-2 draw, but only with the help of a late Tony Daws penalty kick.

After the result against Gillingham, United were still in twelfth position, but the board decided that the Club needed a change of direction.

Paul Longden, who had to retire from the game following a broken leg in the last match of 1992, versus Gillingham; Paul wore the Scunthorpe shirt on 455 occasions.

In the first week of the New Year, Bill Green left his post in charge of team affairs. He will always be thought of a complete gentleman and had taken the Club further, in those times, than any other manager. His resources were always threadbare, and many supporters were sad to see him go.

Life at Glanford Park had to continue, and within a week Scunthorpe United called a press conference. The new manager was to be their old player Richard Money, who had graduated at Aston Villa as the youth team coach. It was hoped that Richard was the way forward, and that he could find the formula to a brighter future. Unfortunately, the first two months of his reign produced only a 4-1 win, at home to bottom club Halifax Town. Richard Money brought in a number of new players. These included David Farrell on loan from Aston Villa, Darrell Duffy of Moor Green, Shaun Constable from Leeds University football, Richard Crisp, also loaned from Aston Villa, David Foy from Birmingham, Richard Wilmot of Stevenage and Jason Maxwell from Appleby Frodingham. None of those players made a significant impact at the Club.

Richard Money did sign two players that made the grade, and the first was Nicky Platnauer of Leicester City, a left full back to fill in for Paul Longden. He also acquired Ian Thompstone, a well built left sided man for the advanced positions, from lowly Halifax Town.

During this time United parted with two men that had been part of the success of the past. Richard allowed John Buckley to depart for Rotherham United, for £20,000, in February, and then in March, Tony Daws took the move East to play at Grimsby Town, for a fee of £50,000. Tony had scored seventy one goals in just over two hundred and twenty appearances. Both men went with the best wishes of the supporters.

It took some time before any rewards came from the work put in by Richard Money, but in March four wins were most rewarding, including a sound thrashing of Northampton, 5-0 at Glanford Park. The team achieved another five goals in April, when Rochdale were taken apart 5-1.

The rest of the month contained just one more victory, when promoted Barnet had their colours lowered, 2-0 at Glanford Park, thanks to decisive shots by Sammy Goodacre and Ian Helliwell.

The season finished on a low note, with no promotion or coach tours. The only celebrations were by Cardiff City, who beat Scunthorpe United 3-0 on the final day of the football year, to claim the title. There was a 7,407 attendance at Glanford Park to see the match, but five thousand were estimated to have come from Wales. The controversial point was that the board allowed the away supporters to use both stands behind the goals, and home fans had to leave their favourite position, to use the seats along the length of the pitch. It was clearly a move to make money from the extra thousands who came from Cardiff, but many Scunthorpe supporters never forgave the Club, and stayed away.

1993-94

The closed season was not a time of rest for Richard Money. He took advantage of the playing inactivity to sign almost a new team, starting with a permanent replacement for Paul Longden, who would not come back from his long term injury, called Paul Mudd. The new Paul came from Scarborough, and was to be used for the left full back role. In the central defensive positions Richard Money chose two tall young lads. Russell Bradley was taken from Halifax Town, and would usually operate from the left of the field. Chris Hope came from Nottingham Forest, and had been a regular artist in their second eleven. Chris was to develop into the model professional, and never had a bad game for the Club in the heart of the back four.

The middle of the park already had Ian Thompstone, but he was to have another partner, when Steve Thornber balanced the department, from Blackpool. Steve was once at Swansea, where he won a Welsh F.A.Cup winners medal, which is an interesting thought for a Yorkshire lad. There would also be the presence of Mark Smith, who was an attacking left sided mid-fielder, from Grimsby Town. Mark had actually played for the Iron in 1985, as a second half substitute for twenty minutes at Aldershot, when he was much younger.

In the attack, Money brought in Andy Toman from Darlington. He was of slight build, and played reasonably well before leaving in December for Scarborough. Three men that had more of a presence were Ian Carmichael, Ian Juryeff and Neil Trebble. Carmichael had been discarded by Lincoln City, and he would add to the fire power lost when Tony Daws went to Grimsby. Ian had the muscle to work in close with the defence, to eek out chances that could be turned into goals. Ian Juryeff was a proven goal scorer, and had been round the circuit. United picked him up from Darlington, and he would never be far from the action. Neil Trebble was another big player, and had been in the army, but came late of Stevenage.

He was to be used on the left side of the field, but was considered as a fringe player for the first team.

On their way out of the picture would be Dave Hill, who was going to Lincoln as part of the deal that brought Ian Carmichael to Glanford Park. Ian Helliwell was transferred for a fee to Rotherham, so that some of his money could be recouped. Glen Humphries dropped into non-League soccer at Frickley, and Andy Stevenson went down the road to the Hawthorns, at Brigg Town.

Scunthorpe United began by getting the show on the road at Springfield Park, against Wigan Athletic, and the team managed to win their first ever match on the ground. The opening goal of the season was scored by Paul Mudd in the second half. Mark Smith added a second, and when Mark Samways kept his gloves clean it made a first class start. United drew the next match, 1-1 at home to Bury, then Andy Toman scored the only goal at Mansfield. The League part of the equation was completed in August by a goalless draw at Walsall. The only disappointment was the loss on aggregate of two Coca Cola League Cup matches to Shrewsbury, 2-1.

Scunthorpe United continued to be a force away from home. In September, the Iron won at the new Deva Stadium, against Chester, 2-0. When they beat Carlisle United at Glanford Park on the following Saturday, the team touched fourth in the table. In was not until the final weekend of the month that the second defeat was recorded, and that was 0-2 at Gillingham.

When October was flipped over on the calendar, the team had a mixture of fortune, winning twice, losing twice, and taking a point at Torquay, in deepest Devon. The result that stood head and shoulders above the others was the visit of Northampton Town. United unceremoniously took them to the cleaners. At the break a 4-0 score put them in an untouchable position, and at the end, the 7-0 result was a record for Glanford Park. The team had a hero in each and every position, but the main applause went to Matt Carmichael for his hat-trick. Other names on the marksmen sheet included Ian Thompstone, Mark Smith, Matt Elliott and Andy Toman. Two matches later United further improved the goal difference, with a three clear goals win over Darlington.

At the beginning of November, Scunthorpe United received a bid from Oxford United for their big central defender, Matt Elliott, who was always the centre of attention for some quality performances. On November 5th 1993, Matt signed for a fee of £150,000, plus add on clauses. He would eventually be transferred to Leicester City, play for Scotland, and win the League Cup with the Foxes, which would put a little more into the kitty. Within days of his departure, Richard Money went to Bury and signed the tall ginger haired defender Alan Knill, who had a Welsh International cap to his name from his time at Swansea.

All of the changes were completed in time for the wonderful journey that was the cut and thrust of the F.A.Cup. Scunthorpe United had been drawn to play away at a new non-League club called Accrington Stanley. This was a team treading in the same footprints as an old club of the same calling, that went out of the Football League in 1962, and found themselves wound up by the courts. To accommodate the First Round of the F.A.Cup, Accrington Stanley played the Cup match at Turf Moor, Burnley, on the Sunday. This attracted a gate of 5,816 passing through the turnstiles.

The crowd contained a number of Burnley supporters, and the vast majority of the attendance cheered behind the minnows of Accrington. Andy Toman gave United the lead, but the Stanley had ideas of their own, and kept pace with the scoring into the second half. In the dying minutes, each side had two goals, but Sammy Goodacre would change the game. He was on as a sub, and already had one goal. Sammy upset the Accrington apple cart by scoring the late decisive strike of the match, to win the prize for the Iron, 3-2. The Second Round of the Cup threw up another away trip for the Scunthorpe travelling band. This time they were off to the new Bescot Stadium, which was a clone of Glanford Park, but with red and white paint work. On the day of the fixture, United made sure the team from the same division never got a strong hold on the game. Both sides registered in the first period, and at the end of the match there was some suggestions that Scunthorpe had used spoiling tactics to earn the replay at 1-1.

Richard Money was not phased, and prepared to meet Walsall at Glanford Park. This was to be an almost endless evening, which contained one hundred and twenty minutes of goalless football. Even the penalties went on to sudden death, but it was the Scunthorpe supporters who danced a jig at the 7-6 shoot out result.

At the beginning of December, United were in ninth League position, having gone down to a single goal defeat at Bury. In order to sharpen the attack, Richard Money took on board Damian Henderson, from Scarborough, in a move that transferred Jason White and Andy Toman to the Yorkshire seaside club.

Chris Hope was a gentleman both on and off the field, and played in more than 300 games for the Iron between the 1993-94 and 1999-00 seasons.

Room was made available to promote Christian Sansam from the reserves, and another quality attacking mid-fielder arrived before the year was out. He was the clever Wayne Bullimore, who was not shy to have a pop at goal, and was signed from Stockport County.

The last week of December saw the start of a Club record being set by Matt Carmichael. The Chesterfield game was the first match in a run of eight consecutive games in which he would score every time. Not since the days of Barry Thomas had such similar feats been witnessed.

Scunthorpe United entered the Christmas period on the back of a neat 1-0 home win over Wigan, which completed the double. On the Monday after Boxing Day, the team travelled to Lincoln, where they delivered an out of salts performance, that yielded nothing from the 2-0 loss. Twenty four hours later they improved sufficiently to take a point from a more interesting 2-2 draw at home to a Chesterfield side, not too far behind them in the table. The result meant that the Iron went into 1994 in eighth place on the ladder.

Dame Fortune had given Scunthorpe United a match in London for the Third Round of the F.A.Cup, against the nomads of the Premiership, Wimbledon. The tie was to be played at Selhurst Park, the home of Crystal Palace. Wimbledon never boasted of large crowds, and a disappointing attendance of 4,944 was on hand to watch the proceedings. Dean Holdsworth was the star of the show for the Dons. In the first half he scored twice, and in the remainder of the time he completed his hat-trick. The 3-0 score was only what was expected, and apart from the visit to the Capital, the match was largely a forgettable one for the Scunthorpe supporters.

On New Year's Day, United travelled to Preston, where they claimed a point from a 2-2 draw. Alan Knill and Matt Carmichael scored for the Iron, but there was controversy over the Preston equaliser, which was scored from a throw in taken by Preston, which belonged to Scunthorpe. Two days later Walsall returned to Glanford Park for the scheduled match in the Third Division. This time the emphatic 5-0 thrashing dished out by the Scunthorpe men was in complete contrasts to the stalemates that had been played before in the Cup.

Scunthorpe United would now enter a period of stagnation, and no more victories came their way until the middle of March, when eight winless matches had been completed. At the beginning of that month the Club Chairman, Mr Keith Wagstaff, a successor to Mr Tom Belton, informed Richard Money that the board of directors wished him to take a rest from his duties. This he found unacceptable, and so he tendered his resignation. It was not long before Dave Moore, the team physiotherapist was put in temporary charge and soon restored the faith in the players. Dave had done just about every job at Glanford Park, and was a former Grimsby Town and Blackpool stalwart. Within a couple of weeks the board would decide if he was to take the job on a regular basis.

Dave Moore exorcised the old gremlins and had the side back to winning ways over Crewe Alexandra, at Glanford Park 2-1. Graham Alexander and Steve Thornber took responsibility for the goals, in a tussle that was wrapped up by the middle of the game. This was the beginning of an eleven match run to the end of the fixtures, during which just two matches terminated in defeat. At the end of March, the Iron picked up six points from the visits to Hereford and Scarborough. Mark Smith brought the cheers at Edgar Street, when he scored the single strike of the match. The visit to the seaside ended 2-1, and Matt Carmichael and Ian Juryeff were the Scunthorpe marksmen.

At the beginning of April the Iron made it three consecutive wins, when Lincoln City were beaten 2-0. Graham Alexander scored in the first period of play, and Sammy Goodacre extended it in the second. The team were making a concerted effort to reach the Play-Offs, but had a little too much on their plates to succeed. A lost of 3-1 at Glanford Park to Doncaster was followed by a point at Wycombe Wanderers, where United played for the first time at the new Adams Park Stadium. A second home defeat, 4-1 to the Champions Shrewsbury Town, put promotion completely out of the question.

The disappointment of missing out on a Play-Off place did not stop the team putting up a grandstand finish, beating Rochdale at Spotland on the final day of the season. The last six visits had not yielded a single point, but a bright finale changed all of this. Goals by Thornber and Juryeff made it 2-2 at the halfway stage, but United won by a late own goal from Rochdale attacker Dave Lancaster, who may have forgotten which end of the pitch he was at. The 3-2 win left the Club in eleventh place in the table.

1994-95

Dave Moore, at last, had the freedom to take the Club forward, now that he was officially in charge. At first he was happy with the squad, and only made two changes.

The first was to sign a former team mate of his, Tony Ford, a veteran of many hundred games, who would eventually set a British record for the most number of appearances for an outfield player. Tony was utilised as a full back, but effectively he was able to be used anywhere on the park. On the other hand, it was time to wave farewell to Neil Trebble, who was off up to Preston.

Scunthorpe United kicked their first ball of the season on the sloping ground of the Underhill Stadium, against Barnet, on the Northern fringe of London. The team opened their account in brilliant fashion, and led by goals from Damian Henderson and Ian Juryeff at the forty five minute mark. Barnet pulled one back, but the 2-1 result was fully justified. This was followed by four consecutive home League matches, which started with a loss to Fulham. Another, against Northampton Town was drawn 1-1, followed by a 3-0 credit over Gillingham. In the first week of September, this saga was concluded with a defeat by Carlisle United. This was made remarkable by a late come back from the Cumbrians, who were 2-0 down, and even had their coach Mike Wadsworth on as a substitute. They turned the score on its head to win 3-2.

In the first two mid-week Tuesdays of the football year, United had a pair of Coca Cola League Cup matches to play against Huddersfield Town. The first was at Glanford Park, and they shocked the First Division men with a 2-1 victory to take into the second leg. It was played on the new Alfred McAlpine Stadium, and the Iron came unstuck, by losing 3-0 in very wet conditions. It was a match in which Mark Samways in goal was left exposed on too many occasions.

The remainder of September was punctuated by three consecutive victories, the first came in the North East to Darlington, and others on home soil in conflict with Barnet and Wigan Athletic. United continued their programme through October, and could only muster a single victory. This was on the road at Preston, and was fashioned by a second half strike from Graham Alexander. The 1-0 result was made all the more pleasant when the team found themselves reacquainted with Neil Trebble, who was used by the home side as a substitute.

Scunthorpe United occupied a position of ninth in the table, in the second week of November. This was when the team went to Bradford City, of Division Two, to play at Valley Parade in the F.A.Cup. City fully expected to win, but the Iron raised the stakes, after a shocking start. Bradford City took twenty six seconds to take the initiative. They were allowed the freedom of the park, and strolled the ball through into the goal. The Scunthorpe team took only took three minutes to respond with an equaliser. A cross ball was fumbled by the Bradford custodian, and presented the easiest of chances for Chris Hope to tap in from only a few yards out. Ironically, after all that drama there would be no further goals.

At Glanford Park, 4,514 customers clapped the sides onto the ground. This was to be a high octane charged match, and started with an incident that was the talking point of the game. After only six minutes, Christian Sansam was put through on the Bradford keeper, who made an horrific challenge. Sansam needed considerable treatment, and the custodian received a straight red card.

In the second half, the game sprang into life, and Scunthorpe opened the scoring. Ian Juryeff fired in a shot which came back off the underside of the bar to Matt Carmichael, for a simple side foot into the gaping target. Graham Alexander further increased the lead with a sizzling pile driver from thirty yards.
This prompted the Bantams into a fight back. They pulled away from the abyss with a goal by Lee Power, then equalised, in the time added on, through Dean Richards. This brought another thirty minutes. The legs of the ten men were beginning to tire. The coup de grace arrived on ninety six minutes. Paul Mudd sent a high ball towards the Bradford box, and Scunthorpe substitute Ian Thompstone got his head to it before the reserve keeper could take preventative measures.

The task in hand was now in the Second Round at the magnificent St Andrews Stadium against Birmingham City, on their way back to the higher Leagues.
The match was brought forward to the Friday evening, so that the television cameras could treat the Nation. A crowd of 13,832 left plenty of room for any late comers without a ticket. After ninety minutes of full blooded football no side managed a goal. Usually goalless draws are dull affairs, but this one was the opposite, and each side had a hatful of chances that could have won the advantage.

The tie had been so absorbing that the cameras were at Glanford Park for the replay. This time City took command. It may have taken an hour, but eventually Birmingham forged a two goal lead. Scunthorpe knew that it was to be a difficult road back, but they plugged away and had the reward of a goal from Wayne Bullimore. Wayne was given permission to take a quick free kick. He noticed the Blues were in some disarray, and shot the ball into the wide open space of the unguarded target. City protests all fell on deaf ears, but they went on to face Liverpool after the sound of the final whistle.

The loss at Glanford Park to Birmingham ended a run of twenty six unbeaten home F.A.Cup matches, which marginally fell short of a British record. Although they were out of the competition, a decent size cheque had dropped on the mat from Sky Television.

While all this F.A.Cup drama was unfolding, the Club brought in Max Nicholson for the attacking positions from Torquay United. Immediately before Christmas, Dave Moore loaned a brilliant Hull born young striker called John Eyre, from Oldham Athletic. In two months, John saw the ball fly in the net eight times in nine games. The Club marked his card for future reference, and given time he would have a chapter of his own at Scunthorpe United. In December Dave Moore went over to Scarborough to make the permanent signature of Stuart Young, another youngster of forward potential.

After the Cup epics, United returned to League action, two days after the replay, on a Friday evening, at the smart new Sixfields Stadium against Northampton Town.
It was the day that John Eyre made his debut, and was noted for a close range goal from Alan Knill in a crowded box. It was enough to win the game 1-0, from his first half effort.

This result set the team up for a very happy Christmas indeed, and was the first of five unbeaten fixtures. On Boxing Day, 4,785 spectators braved the cold to view a 2-0 sinking of the Lincoln City galleon. Ian Juryeff scored the first, and then John Eyre whistled in the second, his first in the claret and blue shirt, both arriving after the break. Twenty four hours later, a grand assembly at Belle Vue of 3,852 witnessed a 1-1 draw between the Rovers of Doncaster and the Iron of Scunthorpe. The last act of the old year was carried out at Glanford Park, on the final day of 1994. Rochdale were put to the sword with an encouraging 4-1 result. It was only a pity that 2,653 folks were scattered around the ground to watch the team in such rampant form.

Scunthorpe United entered the New Year and began with a demolition of Exeter City, and the 3-0 score had them in eighth position. This deteriorated to eleventh within the space of seven days, when United suffered a 3-1 loss at Chesterfield, just across the way from the church with the crooked spire.

It was at this time that two results stood out. At the very end of February, the Iron marched North to Hartlepool United, and had one of the best scores of the season. There was no hesitation in the 4-1 beating of the Pool, and began with Alan Knill setting the ball rolling before the interval. In the second forty five, Stuart Young, Steve Thornber, and finally John Eyre, rounded off a super voyage. Seven days later a similar pattern arose against Colchester, as United strolled into a 3-0 lead. In the remainder of the game the brave visitors gradually hauled themselves back, and not only equalised, but defiantly took all the spoils 3-4.

During the later half of the season, Dave Moore shuffled his cards with some new men, as well as allowing Matt Carmichael to move to Preston for a fee. Roger Eli came on loan from Burnley, but could not make an impact in his two substitutions. Next he brought in Lee Turnbull and Neil Gregory for debuts, on the same day, at the beginning of March. Neil came on loan from Ipswich Town and demonstrated his worth as a forward when he scored seven goals in ten appearances. Ipswich would want more money for him than Scunthorpe could afford.

(Right) Graham Alexander strides through the Wigan Athletic mid-field in the early season 3-1 home victory. To the left of Graham is Damian Henderson and Steve Thornber is on the right.

(Below) United defend goalkeeper Mark Samways during the 2-1 win over Darlington, on April Fools Day in 1995. On loan Neil Gregory, in the middle of the picture, nearest the camera scored the two goals.

Lee Turnbull was a right sided mid-fielder, who in truth could play anywhere, and was signed from Wycombe Wanderers. He had a superb North Eastern lilt to his voice, coming from hard working origins in Stockton. Lee was to become team captain, and served in many roles at Glanford Park after he hung his boot up. Noted as a gentleman, he was head of the Football in the Community, a chief scout, and was in a management role when the Club was in between managers.

The door had barely time to close when it was opened to allow Andy Kiwomya to come from Huddersfield, for the forward line, until the remainder of the fixture list.

Andy was a brilliant black lad, that both the Club and the supporters would dearly have loved to have signed for the long term. Dave Moore never neglected the chance to give the young reserves the chance of progress, and two trainees on the horizon were Steve Housham and Michael Walsh. They were both allowed a final burst during April and May in the full back positions.

The season was running down quickly, and the recent signings did have some varying degrees of an effect on the team direction. At the start of April, Neil Gregory scored both goals that beat Darlington 2-1, at Glanford Park.

The team took a point at Wigan, then won on the road at Rochdale, 2-1, as Lee Turnbull and Andy Kiwomya fired the ammunition. Just when a Play-Off position looked a possibility, Scunthorpe lost at home to Doncaster Rovers in a 5-0 shambles.

The football calendar finished on May 6th 1995, when United beat promotion minded Preston 2-1. The visitors knew that the Play-Offs would be their only hope of elevation to the next division. United finished the season in seventh place, but because of reorganisations of the Leagues, the top two went straight up and the places three to six went into the lottery of the Play-Offs. It was the end of another long road, and time to drag weary limbs off on a much deserved holiday.

1995-96

The news from Glanford Park during the Summer was that Graham Alexander had moved on to Luton Town for a £100,000 fee. The money would be most welcomed, but everyone would miss his drive and enthusiasm. He departed with everyone's best wishes. The transfer included a sell on clause, and a similar contract agreement was to pay a dividend. Mark Atkins had just been transferred from Blackburn Rovers to Wolverhampton Wanderers, and United reaped a handsome reward.

Dave Moore was to sanction the departure of more players, and these included Paul Mudd to Lincoln City, Damian Henderson went to the North East at Hartlepool, Mark Smith decided on Boston United, while scorer Ian Juryeff took up with Farnborough Town.

The small amount of cash available allowed Dave Moore to go back to Oldham and secure the signature of John Eyre on a permanent basis, a move that was heralded as a superb piece of business. Up front he was to be partnered by a tall black lad with a long fast stride. He was Andy McFarlane, a Wolverhampton born youngster signed from Swansea City. Further back in the defensive ranks Dave Moore chose another full back called Paul Wilson, born in Bradford, and signed from York City. For the time, these would constitute the new products, along with the familiar faces of last term.

Scunthorpe United began the football year at home Cambridge United, and all appeared to be bright and cheerful. John Eyre had the game off to a wonderful start when he converted the first goal on thirty six minutes, but Cambridge found an equaliser in the second section. Then came an absolute sickener. In the dying moments, the visitors pinched the winner.

The picture in the Coca Cola League Cup was a similar tale. Scunthorpe United had two ties to play against Rotherham United. In the first leg, at Glanford Park, the team produced a slick brand of football and looked to have done more than enough, winning 4-1.

On the following Saturday, United went to Wigan, but they returned a beaten side, 2-1. At Millmoor the Iron gave a display more in character with the Rocky Horror Show. They went 3-0 down in normal time, then baled out 5-0 during the extra thirty minutes of added time. It extinguished all hopes of making some advancement in the competition.

It was not until the third League match that the Iron picked up a first illusive victory. Barnet came up from London, with a handful of supporters, all with strange accents, and were dispatched 2-0. Scunthorpe were obliged by an own goal in the second three quarters of an hour, then Andy McFarlane launched the other. The labours of August finished at Sincil Bank, with a needy point from a 2-2 draw against County neighbours, Lincoln City.

The team still could not find a consistent run in September. They only had a single win over Colchester to show from all of their toil. That was scraped out of a 1-0 victory, when John Eyre was on target in the early portion of the tussle. Dave Moore aimed to strengthen the team by bringing in Imre Varadi, who was an experienced free agent, but this did not work to satisfaction. In October, Jamie Paterson was taken from North of the border, at Falkirk, as a goal scorer for the left side of the attack. He was only a small man, but he packed a powerful punch for the team.

The month of October brought three welcomed victories. The first one was at home to Leyton Orient and yielded a compact 2-0 victory, won by all members of the team pulling their weight. From Mark Samways in goal to Jamie Paterson in the outfield it was a heartening display. A crowd of 2,315 shuffled into Glanford Park to see a goal in each half, by Jamie Paterson, scoring his first for the Iron, and Chris Hope. This set them up for the following Saturday and a three hundred and ten mile hike to Torquay.

The game at Torquay was astonishing to say the least, and even hit the National headlines. Scunthorpe United could do no wrong, and went into the interval 4-1 ahead. If it was possible to do better than this after the break, then the team certainly did. At full time they had a record away win of 8-1, a score that mirrored their best home victory in 1965, against Luton Town. Andy McFarlane led the scorers with four, followed by John Eyre with two, and Alan Knill and Tony Ford with one each. Sadly the Torquay United manager was dismissed after the home team's personal tragedy.

The mini revival continued at Ninian Park, where the once proud International Stadium held 2,024 for the visit of Scunthorpe United. Most of them would have gone home grumbling, because Andy McFarlane netted the only goal of the game. The match was to mark the debut of Phil Clarkson, initially on loan from Crewe, but made permanent from February.

He was probably best described as an attacking mid-fielder, and the fact that the deal was rekindled, spoke volumes for the credibility of the man.

In November, Scunthorpe United played Northwich Victoria away in the F.A.Cup. The game was staged at one of the oldest grounds in the Country, known as the Drill Field. Since then it has been assigned into history. It was a dank afternoon, and the floodlights were needed throughout. All the meaningful action was in the second forty five. Scunthorpe gradually won the upper hand, by taking control of the mid-field.

Tony Ford and Andy McFarlane put United in a commanding position, with two neatly taken shots. Northwich then hit back, firing in one of their own. Before any further drama threatened to knock Scunthorpe's superiority, Andy McFarlane seized upon a misdirected clearance, and had a simple task in side footing the ball home, for a final 3-1 lead.

The Second Round of the Cup kept the Iron at their own warm stable, but they were not able to take advantage from it, against Shrewsbury Town. Each side scored a second half goal, and the responsibility for the Scunthorpe effort was taken by John Eyre. The replay was another tight contest, but it was lost in the first forty five minutes. After giving away an early goal, they conceded a penalty and went into the tea break 2-0 down. The Iron continued to fight in the second half, but Jamie Paterson's strike was only enough to put a brave face on the defeat.

At the moment the F.A.Cup run was terminated, Dave Moore brought a slightly sculptured mid-field dynamo into the team. He was David D'Auria, a Welshman with lightening in his feet, from Scarborough. By the end of the month Dave Moore added a second man to his party, and he was Ryan Jones, on loan from Sheffield Wednesday for two months, as an attacking option on the right side of the park.

The Christmas period was disrupted by the weather, but the three match that were played produced poor results for the team. They entered the New Year on the back of a draw and two defeats. Early in 1996, Scunthorpe United sank to seventeenth in the table, and it had been worse. Once the mixture of new talent was working in the team, the performances picked up, and during the first four matches of January, they claimed maximum points .A win at home to Wigan was followed by three on the Club's travels at Cambridge, Plymouth and Fulham.

The Rest of the Winter was not to be bountiful at all for Scunthorpe United. The team found a reluctance to score, and went on a winless trail of nine matches, and only two points were added to the total. On March 16th 1996 the Club had nose dived to third from bottom of the League. At this moment the board of directors took drastic action to see that the rot did not go any further.

Dave Moore was asked to clear his desk, and another man was sought to improve the Club's ranking. It was not long after the departure of Dave Moore that the shock announcement was made that Mick Buxton was to take a second term of office at Glanford Park. He set to work straightaway, and to his credit, he motivated the players back on the road to recovery.

Two late additions were quickly made to the team. The first was a new goalkeeper, called Gary Germaine, who came on loan from West Bromwich Albion, with Scottish junior honours. The other was Kevin O'Holloran, also on loan, from Middlesbrough, for the back quarters.

Whatever the magic ingredient was, Mick Buxton seemed to be able to find it once he arrived, and the trend was reversed immediately. Scunthorpe United could have slipped on to the trap door at the bottom of the League, but instead they took maximum points from the next five matches. This began at home to Fulham, and the 3-1 result completed the double over the Londoners. The next victory was 4-0 at Glanford Park against Exeter City, and was the biggest home margin all year. Perhaps the most difficult task was at Northampton, 2-1, which was the third in the sequence. The other two were both locally fought battles, against Hartlepool United and Torquay United.

This confidence booster took Scunthorpe United away into the safety of the middle of the table. On the last Saturday of April, there was just time for one more handsome success, and that was away at Scarborough, where United took a 3-1 lead to the break, and finished off the travelling programme 4-1 ahead. Seven days later the lights went out on another football year, with an entertaining 3-3 draw at Glanford Park against Darlington. The attendance of 4,847 was the highest all season, and John Eyre scored twice, while Andy McFarlane hit the other. This result left United finishing twelfth in the table. Andy McFarlane was the leading scorer on nineteen in all competitions, while John Eyre had thirteen to his name. Thankfully, it all turned out to be satisfactory at the end.

1996-97

During the Summer of 1996, Scunthorpe United added two important members to the staff. One was Nigel Adkins a former goalkeeper, late of Wigan Athletic, as the Club's Physiotherapist. The other was another Paul Wilson, but this was Paul D. Wilson, who had played non-League football for Yeovil, but was brought to Glanford Park as the Youth Development Officer.

For the playing point of view, Mick Buxton went to Bury, from which club he brought a right sided mid-field man, who was just as happy working in the defence. He was Mark Sertori, a strong determined player, who arrived with plenty of experience, having seen service at Wrexham, Lincoln and Stockport.

He was to drop anchor at the same time as David Moss came for the forward line. David arrived from Chesterfield with a proven record for scoring goals, but at the end of August he left the Club, and took a full time job outside the game.

The supporters were to see a number of other players that all played a small part, but would not sustain regular first team status. These included Mark Gavin, Kirk Jackson, John Francis, John Borland and Iain Dunn. The Club decided not to offer contracts to Max Nicholson, and Tony Ford, who continued at Barrow and then went on to Mansfield. Also on the way out were Stuart Young, Steve Thornber and Wayne Bullimore, the latter having attracted the attention of Bradford City.

Scunthorpe United began the football calendar in East London, at Leyton Orient, and twenty minutes from the final whistle Phil Clarkson scored the only goal for the Iron. On the next Tuesday evening, United entertained Blackpool from Division Two, in the League Cup. It was to be an all action affair, which saw all the goals scored in the first eighteen minutes. The Seasiders took the lead, but a quick fire retaliation brought a reversal of the score, when David Moss and Phil Clarkson shot Scunthorpe a 2-1 advantage.

On the next Saturday, Torquay United made their way up the M42 to call in for a League fixture, at Glanford Park. Again there was not a lot in it, but Phil Clarkson increased his popularity with a seventieth minute strike. The 1-0 result was sufficient to claim all three points. On the forth coming Tuesday, United took on the challenge of Scarborough, at Glanford Park, but the Yorkshire men over stayed their welcome, and inflicted a damaging 2-0 defeat. August finished down on the South Coast at Brighton. When John Eyre rattled a shot into the back of the net on sixty six minutes it looked good for a win, but five minutes later Brighton levelled at 1-1. Another match in mid-week was to sort out the League Cup, but a 2-0 defeat at Bloomfield Road finished United's aspirations in the competition.

Through the month of September, United continued to have a lukewarm set of results, and could only muster a solitary win, 3-2 at home to Cambridge. At the end of the month Mick Buxton had his eye out for two players. One was a goal scorer of notable reputation in the lower divisions, called Paul Baker. Whereever he went, Paul scored goals, and his arrival at Scunthorpe would continue the trend.

A smart looking Alan Knill led the team on the field as a dominating central defender from 1994 until 1997. He returned as manager from the end of March 2011.

The other young man was a Spanish mid-field player, called Alex Calvo-Garcia. Alex left his native Spain with the hope of fulfilling his football dream of playing in England. He hardly spoke a word of the language, and it was a big gamble. Mick Buxton saw something that was worth pursuing, and Scunthorpe United supporters would take him to their hearts.

On October 5th 1996, Scunthorpe United were away in the Humberside derby to Hull City, at Boothferry Park. Paul Baker went straight into the team and Alex came on as a substitute. The game appeared to be heading for a goalless draw, but woke up in the last two minutes. United supporters went crazy when two goals were cannoned into the net by Phil Clarkson and Paul Baker in quick succession. For Alex Calvo-Garcia it was the beginning of an eight year romance with the Club that he was to call his own.

The month of October brought another fresh face to Glanford Park, but it was one that had been seen before. Mark Lillis was added to the coaching staff for the senior squad, and now the backroom positions had a full compliment. Mark was installed in sufficient time to see the Iron beat Lincoln City 2-0 in the next home match. An attendance of 5,414 was present to salute a goal in each half, from defender Steve Housham, and mid-fielder David D'Auria.

Thing went a little quiet for the next month, and Mick Buxton was hoping for an improvement from the F.A.Cup performance. United had the Yorkshire enemy of Rotherham United to deal with at first, but home territory was to play a key role. On paper the tie was a difficult one, but one grass it was not quite so bad. Paul Baker had the Iron in front on ten minutes, but Rotherham levelled on the quarter hour. David D'Auria restored the advantage by the half hour, and Phil Clarkson made life comfortable twenty minutes from time with a two goal cushion. Right on the blast of the final whistle, Paul Baker put the icing on the cake with the last strike of the game, and United were through 4-1.

The progress was to see Scunthorpe United awarded a Second Round tie at Wrexham, never an easy place to win a Cup game. On the afternoon the men of Iron set about the job in a methodical way, and twice Paul Baker had them in front. The defence had to withstand a continual bombardment in the closing stages, as Wrexham forged forward to try to retrieve the situation from 2-1 down. Scunthorpe United held out until one minute from time, and Wrexham equalised at 2-2.

Whichever team won this replay would receive West Ham United at the third stage of the competition. Paul Baker put Scunthorpe United ahead as early as the seventh minute. This lead lasted until deep in the second period, when Wrexham equalised. Two minutes after the visitors celebrated their goal, Phil Clarkson fired the Iron back into the driving seat. All was looking fine, until a howler by Mark Samways gifted Wrexham a simple tap-in from a misdirected pass. The tie went into extra time, and a demoralised Scunthorpe United lost 3-2.

A fall out from the Wrexham collapse was that Mick Buxton took David Lucas on loan from Preston for two months, to take Samways out of the limelight. This was to be the beginning of the end for Mark, and he was given a loan spell at York City.

During the Christmas period, United played only one game, because of the cold weather disrupting the sport. It was at home to Wigan Athletic, who would be Champions. Glanford Park was only just playable, but there was a five goal bonanza served up. Unfortunately, Scunthorpe managed only two of them. January was much the same. The two matches played were both at home, and a 5-1 bean feast saw them give Hereford United a chasing, but the Iron lost 4-1 to promotion minded Fulham. The Londoners had just had a massive cash inject, and the television cameras caught up with their progress, on the way to the second place in the table.

In February, United would have their own windfall. Matt Elliott had been transferred from Oxford United to Leicester City for £1.6M, and Scunthorpe United would receive £80,000. At the same time, Mick Buxton recruited Brian Laws, who had been manager at Grimsby Town, but was involved in a controversy that led to his leaving the Mariners. He was an experienced campaigner, and able to operate in any position around the park. Unfortunately, Mick Buxton was to lose the services of Phil Clarkson, who chose to move on to Blackpool. It was quite a blow to surrender the skills of such a highly rated schemer.

The loss at home to Fulham was the start of a five match run which saw no wins and only a solitary point registered. At the end of it, United suffered three consecutive 2-0 defeats, the last of which was viewed by 1,524 spectators, who were the only ones not to vote with their feet. The visitors were Chester City, and the board decided that they could not let events continue as they were. Mick Buxton was relieved of his duties for the second time and Mark Lillis became the temporary boss. During his first match in the role, Scunthorpe United recovered their composure to beat Colchester United 2-1.

This left the board a difficult decision, but they resolved it by promoting within Glanford Park. They chose to select Brian Laws as the new Scunthorpe United Manager, and Mark Lillis was to be the Assistant Manager.

Brian Laws

It was the ideal situation, and one that was to bring its rewards for those who were patient.

The new regime brought in half a team to see the Club through the final two months of the season. A major priority was a goalkeeper, and Tim Clarke from York City was the experienced option behind the new pair of gloves. He made his debut on the same day that Gary Jones came on loan from Notts County, to shoot the goals in attack.

Another attacking forward was the slight frame of Jamie Forrester, a Lincolnshire lad from Grimsby Town. He was to link up with John Eyre, and the two would produce another legendary goal scoring spearhead, that would be talked about in decades to come. In the middle of the park, Justin Walker was taken straight out of the Nottingham Forest second eleven, into the Iron's front line. He was to be an instant success. The defence was joined by Sean McAuley, a Sheffield born left sided full back, from Hartlepool United.

There was one other new face that went into the team, and that was Paul Wilson, the youth coach. He came on as a second half substitute at Cardiff, and became the oldest player, at thirty six years of age, to make his first class debut in the twentieth century.

It was not until April when all the players knew where everyone else was on the park. The last few matches on the fixture list would steady the ship, with two wins, two defeats and three draws. In ten matches Jamie Forrester not only demonstrated his speed, but made the contribution of six goals in ten appearances. His double strike, at home to Hull City, was probably the most memorable event, and earned a 2-2 draw.

Scunthorpe United said a fond farewell to their fans by beating Swansea 1-0, with another Forrester goal, but ended the year losing by the same result, at Northampton. The Club managed to round the corner, and finished the fixtures in thirteenth place in the table. Work still had to be done, but the Iron appeared to be in safer hands.

1997-98

Brian Laws may have altered some of the team members, but he was not finished tinkering yet. His main priority was a big strong central defender called Russ Wilcox. Russ was a Yorkshire lad, playing at Preston North End. He had everything in his armoury that a back four player would need, and he would remain at the middle hub for a number of years. He also brought in Jimmy Neil for the left full back role, having seen him develop at Grimsby Town, but the lad did not command a regular place at Glanford Park.

Another ex-Mariner was Craig Shakespeare for the middle section on the field. Craig was once at Sheffield Wednesday and West Bromwich Albion. He was another fringe activist. The forwards would see Dave Regis given a chance up front, but at first he did not do enough to convince Brian Laws. Later in the campaign, Brian had another look, and offered him a second chance. Unfortunately this was short lived, when he received a serious injury in the match against Lincoln City.

Another forward that arrived in September was the exceptionally tall Ian Ormondroyd, a six foot five inch player from Oldham Athletic. He obviously had class but suffered too much from injury.

Ironically, Brian Laws was to have more success with his junior players, when they were handed a first team chance. Paul Harsley was a Scunthorpe born full back, who was rejected by Grimsby Town. Lee Marshall came as a midfielder, who was a Nottingham Forest trainee. Darryn Stamp arrived as a tall wandering forward born in Beverley. All these young men took advantage of the opportunity to improve themselves. The same could be said for Alex Calvo-Garcia, Michael Walsh and Steve Housham.

The end of the line had now come for Alan Knill, who was transferred to Rotherham United, and Paul Wilson went to Cambridge United. Hartlepool United had already taken on Russell Bradley, and now he was to meet up with Mark Gavin. Lee Turnbull left Glanford Park to return nearer home, for a last waltz at Darlington, and John Borland left to play at non-League Accrington Stanley. Andy McFarlane impressed Torquay United sufficiently in the 8-1 roasting, that they came back to buy him. Once Jamie Paterson was fixed up at Halifax Town everyone was accounted for.

Scunthorpe United began the long trek through the forty six game marathon, by picking up all three points at London Road Peterborough. The spice added to the mixture was provided by Jamie Forrester's sixty second minute shot, that left the keeper groping the thin air. On the following Tuesday, the Iron went to the seaside, and beat Scarborough, 2-0, in the Coca Cola League Cup, thanks to a pair of inspired goals from Alex Calvo-Garcia .

The winning theme continued at home to Leyton Orient, and it was doubly lucky for the person who had the golden goal ticket with nineteen minutes on it. This was the moment when Jamie Forrester cracked the only shot to hit the net. Another Tuesday evening, and another night under the lights at Glanford Park, brought Scarborough back for the second leg of the League Cup. Alex was getting the hang of scoring in the League Cup, and his second duo of goals eased the Iron through, 2-1 on the night and 4-1 on aggregate. The first month of the season was wrapped up with a 2-0 loss at Swansea, and another 1-0 home win against Mansfield, and Alex Calvo-Garcia was the goal scoring hero yet again.

September was to continue the trend of the winning streak, and Chester at home, Barnet away, and Hull City at Glanford Park, all felt the force of Scunthorpe United. Immediately prior to the Barnet match, the Iron played their Second Round League Cup tie, first leg at Glanford Park. The match was one of two against Premiership Everton, and the Sky cameras were on hand to see United lose pluckily, 1-0.

Victories in those League matches hoisted the Iron up to the third position in the table. The Humberside derby match drew a crowd of 4,905 to the game, and it was one of drama. Jamie Forrester silenced the noise from the away end, when he had the Iron ahead after only four minutes. On the hour Alex Calvo-Garcia made it 2-0. Unfortunately, United would lose the services of keeper Tim Clarke, who was knocked on the head and left the field on a stretcher dead to the world, totally concussed. Chris Hope became the out field man who donned the green jersey, and received a huge cheer every time he touched the ball. This was to play a part in Scunthorpe United's arrangements for the League Cup match, at Everton.

Tim Clarke was ruled out, but Brian Laws was happy to give reserve goalkeeper Tommy Evans his debut. Scunthorpe United lost 5-0, and the Merseyside giant barely broke sweat, but Tommy made a string of saves, and was the Scunthorpe man of the match.

During the rest of the Autumn, Scunthorpe United kept touch with the top positions in the table, and produced some interesting football. They became the first team to get the better of Exeter City down in Devon, with an exhilarating 3-2 victory. This was not settled until David D'Auria shot the winning goal eight minutes from the final whistle. In another match at Colchester, Scunthorpe United went 3-0 down in the first half, but a goal by Chris Hope and two more by David D'Auria had the Iron fight for a point in the second half, drawing 3-3.

The F.A.Cup paired Scunthorpe United with Scarborough, a team of Yorkshire men that were most familiar to them. Victory was to be a close 2-1 battle, but the visiting bench was angered when at least two shots hit the back of the net and were invalid through infringements. The Scunthorpe goals were scored by Russ Wilcox and Alex Calvo-Garcia either side of the Scarborough effort.

A return to League duty had the Iron in fine fettle for two away wins. These were at Rotherham United, 3-1, and on distant plains at Torquay United, 4-2. At Rotherham it was the deadly duo of John Eyre and Jamie Forrester that shot the goals, the former hitting two. On the Devon road, the vital shots were fired from all parts of the Iron ship. Alex Calvo-Garcia scored the first and last, while David D'Auria and Russ Wilcox turned up the heat with the others, in emphatic defiance. The visit of struggling Brighton was next on the list, at Glanford Park. The surprise was that the Iron were smothered by the Southerners, and went down 2-0.

In the Second Round of the F.A.Cup, the Scunthorpe reward was to entertain Ilkeston Town from non-League circles. The Derbyshire team took the lead on fifty two minutes, and for a time there were some anxious moments. Jamie Forrester settled the nerves with an equaliser fifteen minutes from time, but at 1-1 it was a replay in Ilkeston. This was held on the following Wednesday. United went in front through a goal by Jamie Forrester, when he shot the ball home on the snow covered grass, after just ten minutes. On the half hour, Russ Wilcox increased the difference to 2-0. All went well until Ilkeston pulled one back, twenty minutes from time, which looked suspiciously offside. The clock finally ran out on them, and Scunthorpe United went through 2-1.

Once the team went back on League duty, form began to stutter. The Brighton match was the first in a run of eight straight defeats, in which only three goals were scored, and one of those was an opposition own goal. It made for a sorry holiday period in which the supporters wearing Father Christmas hats saw the team defeated on Boxing day, at home to Notts County by a 1-2 score, then travel to Chester and concede a single goal without reply. The last loss in this sequence was at Macclesfield, 2-0. The match had already suffered postponements, and was played on a bone hard pitch, which had the players tip-toeing like ballerinas.

Towards the final phase of this poor League episode, Scunthorpe United played a Third Round F.A.Cup match at Selhurst Park, against Crystal Palace. A gate of 11,624 supporters saw a Cup fight of the top order, played on a heavy pitch. Both teams went hammer and tongs at each other. It was difficult to guess which of them resided in the Premiership, and which one in the basement. Crystal Palace took the lead on the stroke of half time. Scunthorpe United came out in the second period and threw every thing at the Palace. Brian Laws even brought himself on as a substitute. During the game Steve Housham hit the post, while Jamie Forrester had a goal ruled out for no apparent reason. Wave after wave of Scunthorpe attacks were repelled, but three minutes from the end Crystal Palace sealed victory, to kill the Iron's ambition at 2-0.

Jamie Forrester in action at Crystal Palace. He was the leading goalscorer in the following, promotion, season.

Scunthorpe United managed to get back to winning ways, when they took on Swansea City, at Glanford Park. Tommy Evans was brought into the goal, and Lee Marshall led the attack. The only goal went into the Swans net in the twenty first minute, and the shot was supplied by David D'Auria. This time there was no panic in defence and the 1-0 victory steadied the nerves. Six days later, the team travelled up the A18 to Doncaster Rovers, a team that was sadly in a mess at the foot of the table.

Doncaster had a poor set of players that did try their best, and Scunthorpe were only fractionally better on the evening. Credit went to the Rovers for scoring after seventeen minutes, but six minutes later D'Auria found an equaliser. The winning goal did not mature until eight minutes from the end and was prodded home by Steve Housham in a complete goalmouth scramble.

The back end of the season saw a number of new faces on the park. Thanks to a lot of hard work from Paul Wilson, a conveyor belt of locally produced talent was ready to be tried in the first team. This allowed appearances for Nathan Stanton, James Featherstone, Gareth Sheldon, Steve Nottingham and Wayne Graves. Brian Laws also brought in on loan Matt Murphy from Oxford United, Martin Phillips from Manchester City, Neil Woods from Grimsby Town, and Martin Pemberton of Doncaster Rovers.

The list of fixtures was gradually dwindling away, and the late part of the calendar had Scunthorpe United slowly making positive steps in the right direction up the table. Once they were over the worst part of that difficult period of winless games, the team would only suffer three defeats from the end of January until the last whistle in May. The month of March found the Iron at their brightest, and of the five matches played, three were won and two finished as draws. The 2-0 test against Torquay United completed the double.

In April, the first tussle was against Brighton, a team that would finish second to bottom of the division. They only won six times all season, but completed the double over Scunthorpe, winning their home game 2-1. Thankfully, the Iron would only lose once more all season, and that was in London, at Leyton Orient, 1-0. They finished the football year on a high note by beating Exeter City 2-1 at the back of Doncaster Road, then travelled West to Shrewsbury Town to beat the Shrews 2-0. Lee Marshall and Jamie Forrester sealed the victory with the last strikes of the campaign.

Scunthorpe United missed out on a Play-Off place by just one point to Barnet, although the North London club did have a slightly better goal difference. It left everyone ruing the matches of the Winter period, and the less than perfect showings with Brighton and Hove Albion.

1998-99

The Sunshine of the Summer was just the time for Brian Laws to do his shopping for new team members. In defence his main signing was Richard Logan, a tall determined Yorkshire man who was at Plymouth. This central defender was the experienced crusader that United needed at the heart of the back four. Arriving at the same time was Ashley Fickling, a young man from Grimsby Town, who came originally on trial for some reserve team matches. He was fleet of foot and a hard worker, and Brian Laws thought that he was worthy of a contract.

The attack was to benefit from the inclusion of two new men. One was a huge black lad named John Gayle, who had the type of presence to make defenders tremble. When he arrived from Northampton, it was said that when he introduced himself he added the rider that he had 'come to win the team promotion'. He was to be a brilliant ball winner, and took the weight off Jamie Forrester and John Eyre. Another forward came from York City. He was Staffordshire born Gary Bull who was a regular performer, but nearly always from the bench.

The players that were shown the door to accommodate the newcomers included Michael Walsh, United's promising full back, who went for a fee to Port Vale, where he was to meet up with a former colleague, Paul Musselwhite. Meanwhile, Craig Shakespeare dropped into non-League soccer at Telford, and Ian Ormondroyd retired through injury. The last of the old guard was Mark Sertori, who won a contract at Halifax Town, a club that had returned to the Football League.

Scunthorpe United started the season away at Shrewsbury, on the Gay Meadow, where they won the final match of last year. This time they went down 2-1, but August was to be a productive and busy month. They won the following games at home to Carlisle United, and away at Hartlepool United. Scunthorpe then took on a very strong Plymouth side that were not weary after the three hundred and forty mile trip, and the Pilgrims won 2-0. Better news was heard from United's own long sojourn across to Swansea, where the Iron registered possibly the best of their results. They beat the Swans 2-1 at the Vetch Field, but set the ball rolling very late in the day. The home team took a sixty third minute advantage, but a careless tackle won the Iron a penalty. John Eyre tucked it away, with nine minutes remaining. Scunthorpe won the argument five minutes later, when Jamie Forrester stormed in and flicked a delightful shot into the net.

August had two other conflicts in the equation, when Blackpool were met in the League Cup, now known as the Worthington Cup. At Bloomfield Road, a trickle of 1,813 spectators passed through into the ground. They saw the home team score the only goal of the ninety minutes. At Glanford Park the figure rose to 2,211.

During this game the referee disallowed what appeared to be a perfect goal, turned down a penalty award that most thought was concrete, then booked a Blackpool man for an offence that called for a red card in the opinion of many. United drew on the evening 1-1, and went out on aggregate 2-1. The referee held his hand up afterwards, and apologised.

The players would find that September was not quite as demanding, and only five matches were played. Of these, they only dropped two points, when they took a draw at Rochdale 2-2, but it was an action packed drama. Jamie Forrester gave them the lead in four minutes, but it took a last gasp equaliser from Darryn Stamp to salvage a point. The month finished down at the bottom of the country, just before the land ran out, at Brighton. This time there would be no slip-ups, and the 3-1 result shouted volumes of Scunthorpe United's superiority, at the Withdean Stadium.

The Iron were caught off their guards when they welcomed Halifax Town, back into the Football League from the wilderness of the Vauxhall Conference. United knew not to expect a soft touch, but they were bamboozled into a 4-0 home defeat with a performance which beggared belief. This saw them through into October, when they only had the victory over Rotherham United to show for all their efforts. Even this match had its horrific moments. Scunthorpe cantered into a 4-0 lead, with goals from Russ Wilcox, John Eyre, a penalty, Alan Knill an own goal present to his former club, and Richard Logan. It was now one hour into the games, and from then on it was a real cliff hanger. Rotherham pulled back three goals in brilliant defiance, and were unlucky not to snatch a point for their courage, but it went 4-3 to the Iron.

The three points gleaned from the Rotherham United thriller allowed them to sit on the summit of the League for seven days, until they lost at Leyton Orient. The darker nights of the Autumn gave them poor returns in the League programme, and they sank to fifth in the charts. During this time, there was the highly satisfying defeat of the Humberside neighbours from the North bank. Hull City came to town, and 5,633 supporters witnessed a good standard of football, and a wonderful advertisement for the lower divisions.

The opening goal arrived when John Gayle forced his way through, and fired the ball in the net on ten minutes. City fanatics cheered a thirty eight minute equaliser, but before five minutes had passed, Jamie Forrester rocketed a second Scunthorpe goal into the quivering net.

Goalscorer Alex Calvo-Garcia is congratulated by John Gayle.

Spectators scarcely had time to settle back in their seats after the break, when Hull City equalised. Scunthorpe raced round the park probing for a weaknesses, and on seventy seven minutes Lee Marshall found the gap he needed to shoot the ball in, from inside the box. United took the honours 3-2.

In the F.A.Cup Scunthorpe United were presented with the task of a long haul to play non-League Woking. It was to be a keen contest, and the only goal that separated the teams came ten minutes from the rest break, and was a beauty, scored by Jamie Forrester. He received the ball on his left of the field, ran some twenty yards, then let fly with a perfect shot.

In Round Two, the Iron once again had non-League opponents, but this time Bedlington Terriers were drawn at home. The problem for local supporters was knowing where Bedlington actually was. Brian Laws was quite aware, because they were not far from his roots in the North East, near Newcastle. The visitors were handsomely represented in the 4,719 crowd, and the television cameras called to take extra notice. Everyone had to be patient for the goals, and the first was not until the fifty fourth minute. United were awarded a penalty, and John Eyre promptly obliged with a side foot into the net. The fireworks were not over yet, and ten minutes from the end Jamie Forrester rifled the second goal, that put the match in the bag.

Scunthorpe United stuttered with two League defeats going into the last month of the old year, but over the Christmas period they recovered to take six points from two outings. The match played on Boxing Day at home to Hartlepool was not a brilliant spectacle, but the Iron did work hard for their rewards. All that differentiated the teams was a shot into the net from Jamie Forrester, and the advance of a 1-0 score. Two days further in time, and the team ran out at the McCain Stadium in Scarborough. This time the manner of victory was clear cut. They established a platform on the back of two goals from Chris Hope and Alex Calvo-Garcia. Jamie Forrester smashed two more after the break, and a late retaliation from the home side was far too late. The 4-1 victory had the Iron fifth in the table at the start of 1999.

The F.A.Cup took Scunthorpe United to the Racecourse Ground to play Wrexham. It was to be a seven goal thriller and not without incident. Scunthorpe United gave a good account of themselves, and deserved at least a replay. Only 4,429 supporters bothered to turn up, but they saw Wrexham fire a two goal salvo into the Scunthorpe rigging.

Steve Housham pulled a goal back, but once again the Welsh men went two goals ahead. The climax of the show came when the Iron drew back to level terms. John Eyre scored with twenty minutes remaining, then Paul Harsley made it 3-3 in the eighty fifth minute. Right on time Alex Calvo-Garcia was blatantly tripped in the box. The referee waved away claims of a spot kick, and Wrexham ran down field from the same incident and scored the winner.

The New Year brought with it some team changes. The first was at left full back, where Brian Laws put Nottingham Forest reserve youngster, Andy Dawson, straight in the first team. He then decided that he would make Tommy Evans his first choice goalkeeper. During the later stages of the football year, Brian gave another vote to youth, and Gareth Sheldon came into the attack. Finally, Tony Witter was a black London born player brought during February, from Welling. He was a sturdy player that added strength to the right full back position on the field.

Once the F.A. Cup was put to one side, United continued to be a considerable force in the Third Division. They returned with three quick fire victories over Shrewsbury at home 3-0, and at Carlisle 1-0. Then came the completion of the double against Scarborough, 5-1 at Glanford Park. This was followed by four matches, during which they only took a solitary point. The calendar was now at the end of February, and the Iron were perched in sixth place in the table.

Scunthorpe United began March with three wins on the belt, and the last against Leyton Orient was to have a special significance, although it was not apparent at the time. The team delivered a firm message, with two goals in the second half from Alex Calvo-Garcia and Jamie Forrester. The United did not receive any sort of real setback, until they went on their furthest journey to Plymouth. United came back home with a thick ear from a 5-0 defeat.

The end of the fixtures was now in sight. During April and into May the Iron had nine fixtures, and four wins and three draws gave them a strong representation. Throughout March, and on to the end of the season, the team maintained fourth place in the table.

Tommy Evans became United's first choice keeper from 1998 until released in 2006.

Two of the victories were on the road, 1-0 at Southend United, and 3-2 against Hull City, which mirrored the score of the home fixture. The side could still win an automatic promotion place, but a 1-0 loss at Halifax, and a goalless draw at their main rivals, Cardiff City, put this out of the question, now that only one match remained.

The football year concluded on May 8th 1999, at home to Darlington, and 4,238 saw them just a little too relaxed, and the team suffered a surprise 1-0 defeat. This confirmed the Club in fourth table position. It was time to see what the rest of the division had done, and find out who was up for the Play-Offs with them in seventh place. It was resolved that they would have two matches against Swansea City.

The first match was played on May 15th at the Vetch Field, and was watched by 7,822 supporters. Scunthorpe United had a huge following in the away section, behind one of the goals. It was never going to be an open match full of goals, and for the one game Brian Laws brought back Tim Clarke for his experience. His goal was only breached once, one minute before the break. On the coach journey home Brian Laws convinced his troops that a Wembley Final was there for the taking.

Glanford Park was packed tight for the replay, three days later. Before the match the 7,089 spectators saw Assistant Manager Mark Lillis hold a flag of St George tight in his hand and run round the four corners of the ground to show his patriotic allegiance, while rule Britannia was played over the speaker system. This set the Scunthorpe fans in great voice. After two minutes the crowd was cheering even more. John Gayle found that Andy Dawson was up in support of the attack on the left, and when big John flicked the ball his way, Andy put his foot through it, and it sailed into the net.

After all that excitement, there was no more scoring in normal time. Just before the final ninety minutes were up Brian Laws played his trump card. He swapped Jamie Forrester, who had run his feet into the ground, for the fresh legs of Gareth Sheldon.

Two minutes into the restart, Gareth Sheldon was in the right position to receive the ball from John Gayle, and a simple side foot put the Iron 2-1 ahead on aggregate. Six minutes later it was heads in hands time. Swansea equalised, and set the visiting supporters alight, because at 2-2 they had a vital away goal, and would go through.

The drama was not over yet, and Gareth Sheldon took the centre stage again. Three minutes before the extra time change of ends, Andy Dawson steamed down the left and sent the ball over to where Gareth was lurking. He controlled the ball, and knocked in a cross shot into the other side of the target, and the home supporters went crazy. The volume was never lowered through the remaining fifteen minutes on the watch, but the two exhausted teams had no more energy to drum up another goal. Full credit to Swansea, but the Iron were going to Wembley on the back of a 3-1 score on the night, and 3-2 on aggregate.

The Final of the Division Three Play-offs was played at Wembley Stadium on Saturday May 29th 1999, between Scunthorpe United and Leyton Orient. It was exactly three months to the day before the Centenary celebration of the Lincolnshire Club. The ticket office was busy continuously throughout the build up to the game, and it was estimated that 10,000 Scunthorpe United supporters would be in the crowd of 36,985, being far out numbered by the following of the London club. At the same time, the souvenir shop dispatched thousands of items of merchandise in the form of flags, tee-shirts and hats. When the teams came out of the tunnel and into the sunlight, Brian Laws and his side were met with a wall of claret and blue.

There did seem to be a difference between this Wembley Final, and the one in 1992. The attitude of the earlier visit was to enjoy the day, be proud to be at Wembley, and know that the team would do well. This time there was a steely determination that it was nothing to do with Wembley and a day out. It was to focus every ounce of effort driving back the opposition and gaining a victory by shear hard work. The team picked to do this included: Tommy Evans; Paul Harsley, Andy Dawson, Richard Logan, Russ Wilcox, Chris Hope, Justin Walker, Jamie Forrester, Gareth Sheldon, John Gayle, and Alex Calvo-Garcia. The substitutes were Steve Housham, Darryn Stamp and Gary Bull. Scunthorpe would play in the change strip of yellow and navy.

The only absente was John Eyre, who was very unfortunate to have to sit out a suspension.

The teams soon got into their stride, but it was the Scunthorpe men that were first to press forward. All of a sudden United started to find it easy, and as early as the sixth minute they had the old stadium shaking. The move was started down the left hand side of the pitch. Gareth Sheldon was the architect, when he took the ball to the Leyton goal line, jinxed round a defender, and flipped a simple ball to Alex Calvo-Garcia. Alex neatly glanced the ball into the net, as the goalkeeper dive towards his own left hand post. A great roar of noise erupted from the jubilant Scunthorpe section, as supporters danced a jig. Instead of retaliating, Leyton Orient were forced back into their own half for long periods, and it was a mystery that Scunthorpe did not hold a greater lead at half time.

The second forty five minutes was to be more of a contest, and Orient fought much harder after some reorganising. Russ Wilcox, Chris Hope and Richard Logan made sure that Tommy Evans had minimal work to do, and he was fully alert when extended. In the front ranks, Scunthorpe could have scored more, particularly on two separate occasions, when Paul Harsley and Darryn Stamp had golden chances.

In the end, the referee blew the whistle on the longest hour and a half of football that anyone could ever remember. Everyone of the fourteen men selected played a part, and each was a hero. Alex won praise for his goal, and the media could not make up its mind if Jamie Forrester or Andy Dawson was the outstanding player. One guarantee that was for sure was Scunthorpe United had won promotion for the first time since 1983. The tension was over and only at this moment could the Wembley party begin. It was to be a memory that nobody from Scunthorpe would ever forget. Close your eyes if you were there, and you will see it all again.

Defending during the Wembley Play Off Final. Chris Hope heads clear, assisted by Russ Wilcox.

AN ALMIGHTY FRIGHT

1999-00

When the 1999-00 season was about to begin, Scunthorpe United found that the euphoria of that wonderful day out at Wembley, beating Leyton Orient, had dimmed slightly. The Club had taken a great stride forward on the back of a lot of hard work by Brian Laws and his team, and the goals of John Eyre and Jamie Forrester. Now it was learned that both men had refused to sign new contracts at Glanford Park, and sought their fortune elsewhere. John Eyre took up an offer at his home city of Hull, at Boothferry Park, while Jamie Forrester would try his skills at Utrecht, across the North Sea in Holland.

During the Summer of 1999, Brian Laws did not have the opportunity to sign the replacements he wanted for the forward line, but he did pick up the signature of an amazing West Ham United youngster, called Lee Hodges. Lee was not a particularly tall player, but he was able to fizz round the mid-field with great energy, and what may have been lacking in inches was more than compensated for in skill.

Scunthorpe United were handed an opening day fixture away to Wigan Athletic in their brand new J.J.B. Stadium. The Latics were backed by Chairman Dave Whelan of the J.J.B. Sports Company, and were tipped to go places with his support. On a hot Summer afternoon, United worked hard, but without a recognised attack it was men against boys, and they took the medicine of a 3-0 loss. Although they went down in the next match at home to Wycombe Wanderers, at least Brian Laws had found Richie Humphreys for the attack, on a month long loan from Sheffield Wednesday. Before August was over, Guy Ipoua, a black African from Cameroon, was welcomed to the fold as a permanent signing from Bristol Rovers, to boost the forward power.

Both Ipoua and Humphreys made significant contributions by scoring in the 3-1 win against Bournemouth, and thus securing the first three points of the campaign. Then Ipoua added another goal on the Bank Holiday weekend at Cardiff, where the team showed a lot of resilience to earn a 1-1 draw. One more face would appear in the first team at this time, when local product Matthew Sparrow made his debut at Huddersfield, in the League Cup. This youngster was embarking on a career of more than 300 Scunthorpe United appearances, littered with some outstanding goals, as an attacking mid-fielder.

One of the best signings made by United in the late nineties was that of the tricky mid-fielder Lee Hodges.

It was not long before Scunthorpe United supporters knew how difficult a task the team had on its plate. In first couple of months the Iron were rarely out of the bottom four in the table. Victories were far and few between, but a journey to Layer Road, Colchester, brought cheers from a 1-0 result. The game was decided when Lee Hodges let fly from distance with the sweetest of strikes. Indeed, the month of October was to be one of the most productive periods of the 1999-00 season, aided by two further loaned players. Frenchman Lionel Perez from Newcastle United was a goalkeeper in a class of his own. His reactions were of lightening speed, and he had a character than made him an instant favourite of the crowd. Next, Brian Laws found Clint Marcelle for the front positions, at Barnsley. Marcelle was only five feet and five inches in height, but the West Indian added a punch where it was needed, at the sharp end of the field.

The best performance of the first half of the year came on October 5th 1999, when the Iron played a Sunday match before the television cameras, at Turf Moor, Burnley. It was a day when both Perez and Marcelle made their Scunthorpe debuts, and Scunthorpe fired on all cylinders, against a team that would gain promotion. Ipoua put United ahead 25 minutes into the game with an accurate drive, while at the back Perez delighted supporters with a number of acrobatic saves. A minute before the hour mark he was unable to stop an Andy Payton equalizer, and it looked as though the Lancastrians would take the initiative. While majority of the crowd waited for the Iron to collapse like a house of cards, it was they who took charge, after some hairy moments. Guy Ipoua confounded everyone, when he shot through a sea of legs during a rare attack, and stole an unlikely winner, with just five minutes on the clock.

The month of October ended on an embarrassing note, when United lost in the F.A.Cup, one Friday evening, to non-League Rushden and Diamonds. This First Round tie was played one day ahead of the main event, and the 2-0 loss meant that they were the first League club to be knocked out of the main part of the competition.

November began in fine style with a 3-1 result at fellow strugglers Cambridge United, but there followed a seven match run without a win.

The Burnley goal is preserved by the Claret's goalkeeper from Steve Torpey, on the last day of the 1999-00 campaign, notable for United's relegation and Burnley's promotion.

Brian Laws had little room to manoeuvre in the transfer market for an improvement to the squad, but he used what small amount of cash he did have, to attract loaned men. These included John Cornforth, Morten Hyldgaard, and West Ham youngster Emanuel Omoyimni, who had been caught up in the football laws. Omoyimni played in a West Ham League Cup tie, when he had already been used in the competition when out on loan. For this error, the Hammers were forced to replay a match with Aston Villa and lost the second time round. Omoyimni received threats, and a loan move to Scunthorpe took him out of the firing line. When he scored the winner during Christmas, at home to Blackpool, the lad was certainly a hero in this corner of Lincolnshire.

Scunthorpe United opened new millennium with a 4-1 defeat at Luton, a result hastened by three quick goals immediately before half time. January would only yield one result to savour, and that was when Notts County were beaten by a solitary goal at Glanford Park.

From the overall view, it was obvious that the team would not survive the drop without an injection of new blood. The Chairman, Mr Keith Wagstaff, allowed Brian Laws to bring in three signings. The first of these was a giant six foot three inch tall ball winning forward, named Steve Torpey. He joined United from Bristol City for a record £200,000 fee, but it was to be money very well spent. Steve became a loyal long serving forward man, who scored goals and made many more. Also putting pen to paper was Brian Quailey, a West Bromwich Albion youngster to play alongside Torpey. Brian had played a limited number of Albion games, but was released to further his chances. Both Quailey and Torpey made debuts against Cardiff City.

The trio of signings was completed in March, when Brian Laws persuaded the tall Mark Jackson to leave Leeds United. He had progressed through the ranks as a youngster, and played a handful of senior games in the heart of the defence.

Mark soon demonstrated to his Scunthorpe audience that he was a player of immense ability and courage, and Brian Laws had once again captured another exciting prospect.

At the time when February turned into March, Scunthorpe United were treading water in or around the relegation line in the Division Two table. They looked to have given themselves a real chance on March 7th when they visited the new Millwall stadium on Zampa Road. Although the picture appeared bleak at the interval, the Iron recovered from a goal in arrears and won 2-1. The recovery was started by a Richard Logan equaliser, and became completed twenty minutes from time. Brian Quailey scored the easiest of winners in front of the yawning goal after a Millwall defensive howler.

This windfall was an oasis in the desert, because the team would only manage to create one more victory. It came on the road to Blackpool, where all other journeys had resulted in defeat. This occasion brought the relief of three points, and completed the double over a side who would be opposing them next year. Scunthorpe United were soon confirmed as relegated just as April was finishing. It had been a long tough season for Brian Laws and his tired troops, but everyone was wiser for the experience.

2000-01

During the Summer of 2000 there was no time for sorrow, as Laws and his staff sorted out the contracts for life in the bottom tier of the Football League once again. A number of the Wembley winners of 1999 had already departed, and more were set to leave right now. The arrival of Mark Jackson now allowed the exit of the popular Chris Hope, a gentleman on and off the field. Chris went with the best wishes of all concerned at Glanford Park, and Gillingham paid the handsome price of £250,000 for his services. Other men packing their cases, included Richard Logan, Justin Walker, Lee Marshall, Gary Bull, Sean McAuley, and local boy Steve Housham, who never gave less than one hundred percent.

Brian Laws was not expected to splash the cash during the closed season, because of his late dealings, but he did manage to bring in three more men for a minimum of out lay.

From Oldham Athletic, Stuart Thom was a Dewsbury born man of exceptional height, for the heart of the back quarters. He was brought in on a free transfer, as was midfielder Peter Morrison. Peter was a slightly built young lad, who liked to play a wide game. The last piece of the puzzle was completed by the vastly experienced Nigel Pepper, a signing Brian Laws considered to be outstanding. In Nigel Pepper, Brian had his field-marshal.

Scunthorpe United started the 2000-01 season in a smart new kit, which was essentially all white, with claret and blue facings. The supporters gave them a lot of noisy encouragement on the opening match of the season. United were away at Macclesfield Town, and several hundred camped on the steps of the uncovered terrace in brilliant sunshine. During the contest the Iron played a neat passing game, punctuated with plenty of skilful touches. The all important moment came on 56 minutes, when Lee Hodges picked up a loose ball and dispatched it beyond the home goalkeeper, into the net behind which the Scunthorpe ranks were massed. United's team included: Evans, Stanton, Dawson, Pepper, Jackson, Thom, Calvo-Garcia, Hodges, Sheldon, Torpey, Morrison, and substitutes Quailey and Harsley. Also on standby, but not available were Wilcox, Sparrow, Graves, Fickling, Stamp and Ipoua.

Scunthorpe United looked to build on the first success in the next fixture, at home to Kidderminster Harriers. Unfortunately, during the encounter disaster struck. Nigel Pepper went for a ball and came into collision with a Harriers player. A crack was heard and instantly it was recognised that Nigel's leg was broken. The stricken man lashed out at his opponent in frustration, and as he was gently placed on the stretcher the referee showed him a red card. His suspension was to prove to be meaningless, because apart from a brief substitution during the following year, Nigel's career was effectively ruined. The rest of the team displayed a great deal of character and went on to win the match 2-0.

The rest of August found Scunthorpe United unable to continue as they had started, and the injury to Pepper was probably the root cause. Not only did they fail in the League, but they lost two League Cup legs to Wigan Athletic. Once into September, Brian Laws named Bjarni Larusson as the mid-field replacement for Nigel Pepper. Larusson was from Iceland, and looked to be a skilled and well balanced player, that quickly adapted to the pace of the Scunthorpe play. At the end of the month there was a boost to the forward line, when Guy Ipoua emerged from a spell of injury. By this time the Iron had slumped to fourteenth in the table, thankfully a position that would not get any worse. Fortunes changed on the last day of September, and in the fading heat of the Summer, United showed plenty of character in beating Torquay United 3-0, in front of 2,922 of their own supporters. Two goals by Ipoua brought back a little something that had been missing in his absence.

When the days began to shorten, United strung together three wins on the bounce. A victory at Carlisle was sandwiched between results at Glanford against Shrewsbury, and Hartlepool. The North Eastern men came back a second time, for a visit in the First Round of the F.A.Cup, and brought a good number of supporters for the trip down. It was not to be a day they would wish to remember, because the Iron ran out with a 3-1 advantage, but passage to the next round was not guaranteed until the referee blew the last blast.

In the Second Round of the F.A.Cup, Scunthorpe United's task was a tough one, against Brighton and Hove Albion. The visitors were a team sailing along in the second place in the same division, and it was a title race that they would eventually win. United had already matched the Albion at the Withdean Stadium in a goalless draw, and given home advantage, there was no reason to have any fear. When the play began, United opened the better side, keeping the ball on the ground, whilst using a neat passing game. Steve Torpey slotted the Iron into a sixth minute lead, but Brighton's promising starlet, Bobby Zamora, had the visitors back level on the quarter hour. Each team could have stolen a march on the other, and Tommy Evans certainly cut the mustard for the Iron on several occasions, producing a number of super saves. The coup de grace was delivered by Gareth Sheldon twenty minutes from the end, when he shot through a crowd of players, thus earning the right of passage into the next stage.

Christmas was virtually spoiled, because not one victory was registered from the beginning of December until the completion of January. The month of January also brought frustration, with bad weather causing disruption. During this time Brian Laws brought in Andy Woodward, on loan from Sheffield United, for the defence, and Trevor Berry of Rotherham for the middle section of the team. Brian was unafraid to give chances to his trainee players, and supporters were enthused by the efforts of Scott Brough and Terry Barwick, who gave it their all in every appearance. Sadly there was one loss, which was not bargained for. Peter Morrison broke his leg in a Reserve match against Grimsby Town, and would not be able to resume his career.

The Winter gloom was to be lifted by the bright floodlights of Turf Moor, when the Iron drew Burnley in the Third Round of the F.A.Cup. The Lancashire club could boast of a position of tenth in the Championship ladder, and William Hill was giving generous odds on an unexpected Scunthorpe victory of any sort. The two teams clashed on the first Saturday of 2001, and United soon showed that they would not be the squashed hedgehogs on the road. They sprinted out of the blocks, and within two minutes their passing game saw them weave the ball through the Burnley back line, allowing Lee Hodges to shoot beyond Michopoulos in goal.

This early shock rattled Burnley, and it took them to the stroke of half-time to respond with an equaliser, through Ian Moore. At the break, Brian Laws gave his troops some encouraging words, and two minutes after the interval they were in front once more, as Guy Ipoua smashed a loose ball in between the Burnley posts. From then on Scunthorpe United played with an authority beyond their lowly station, but they were to be disappointed, when a last minute scramble enabled big Lenny Johnrose of Burnley to equalise.

Scunthorpe United may not had gained the result they might have deserved, but they were certainly not dispirited. In the replay, Burnley played a brand of football in keeping with a team with designs on the Premiership. A crowd of 4,709 spectators saw Burnley enter a 1-0 lead in the 73rd minute, through the dazzling feet of Andy Payton. It seemed that United had let their chance slip through the fingers, until five minutes from the end, when they won a direct free kick just outside the penalty box. Up stepped the fair haired Andy Dawson, who sized his kick up like Johnny Wilkinson, in the 2003 World Rugby Union Cup Final. He took a short run and placed the sweetest of curling shots round the wall, and into the waiting net. This act brought on the advent of extra-time, and onto penalty kicks. Scunthorpe comfortably slotted home four out of four, but Burnley made one blunder. It was now down to Scunthorpe United's experienced skipper, Russ Wilcox to bring home the glory. He nonchalantly tossed the ball up, placed it on the spot, and while the crowd held its breath, Russ rammed it home. Players came flying on top of him from all directions in jubilation, as he flexed his biceps to the crowd in celebration.

The Fourth Round of the competition brought Scunthorpe another away tie, against a second Championship club. This time they would have to play at the futuristic Reebok Stadium, the home of Bolton Wanderers, on a crisp Sunday afternoon. This time there was no celebrations of triumph, and a couple of defensive errors were punished severely. Dean Holdsworth showed the class of a top forward in form, and registered a hat-trick, while former England Youth player, Kevin Nolan, scored a brace. This was not the first time that Holdsworth had done this trick against the Iron. The only joy for Scunthorpe followers, watching in considerable masses, was the scoring strike by Alex Calvo-Garcia, on the half hour.

Once United return the League action, they ran into some useful form, particularly in March, when they enjoyed an identical 2-1 result over fancied Brighton.

The visit of Plymouth Argyle in March 2001 produced a 4-1 victory. Brian Quailey has just hit the back of the net, and Torpey is ready to congratulate.

The Iron were looking to sneak a Play-Off place, and a 3-0 victory over Carlisle enhanced their chances, mid-way through April. Then they went and spoiled it by failing to score a goal, nor a point, in the last trio of games. It left the Iron tenth in the table and everyone at Glanford Park was a little disappointed.

Towards the end of the season, Brian Laws did try to stir his squad up by the introduction of a quartet of men. From the junior ranks Lee Ridley and James Cotterill were given the reins, while Kevin Rapley spent time on loan from Notts County. However, the most notable capture was the nimble footed Martin Carruthers, who arrived on a full signing from Southend, to pep up the attack. Brian Laws would have marked the card of this proven goal scorer, from the moment Martin fired the only goal of the match, against the Iron at Roots Hall, earlier in the campaign. Once it the claret and blue colours, Martin continued in the industry he knew best.

2001-02

During the Summer recess, Brian Laws reviewed his troops to see which of his army would be marching on, and which would join the cavalry and ride out. Brian had already given his blessing to allow Guy Ipoua to leave for Gillingham in March, and a small cheque was put in the bank as a result. Going out of the door would also be Ashley Fickling, Darryn Stamp, Bjarni Larusson and regrettably locally born Paul Harsley, who sought pasture new along the M62 at Halifax.

The talking point of the Summer was the capture of the vastly experienced play-maker, Peter Beagrie, a colleague of the manager from years ago. Beagrie had magic in his boots, and could turn players inside out, then back again. He had pin point accuracy with his crosses, just like Phil Taylor on the dart board.

Peter possessed a football brain that was of degree level, and could shoot the ball from all angles. Laws said that Peter Beagrie would put bums on seats, and those who turned up watched in awe.

Beagrie was not the only new man at Glanford Park. The Club also welcomed Carl Bradshaw, who knew Peter at Wigan, their last port of call. Carl had just enjoyed four seasons at Wigan and was a useful addition to the defence. Another new arrival was forward Kim Grant, but he was a wandering minstrel soon to depart. Shortly into the season, Brian Laws decided to sanction the departure of Gareth Sheldon, but he embraced Richard Kell, a former Middlesbrough trainee for the midquarters, from Torquay United. August also saw Sam Croudson arrive on loan for the goalkeeper's jersey, to complete the transfer market activities for the time being. It did not stop the use of the locally produced youngsters making the first eleven. Given an opportunity were Nathan Stanton, Wayne Graves, Jamie Cotterill, Jamie McCoombe and Matt Sparrow.

Whereas the Iron started the previous season with two victories, this term two defeats had them in the doldrums. The tide turned at the third attempt, when Exeter City were beaten 4-0 on the road, down in Devon. Goals came from Maritn Carruthers, Carl Bradshaw, and a brace via the boot of Kim Grant. During the first couple of months, the Iron frequently managed to equal their opponents, but could not find the killer instinct to steal the necessary extra goal. The situation saw too many drawn games and a paltry two matches were won in the opening ten fixtures, dropping the Iron into a mid-table position. The League Cup brought no more cheer, either, because Rotherham United over came them 2-0 at Glanford Park.

Throughout the Autumn a gradual improvement took place. The best performance was a workman like effort that beat Leyton Orient 4-1, on one of the more convincing days. This was followed by a Friday evening kick-off at York City, which yielded three points from a 2-0 excursion. The goals did not materialise until the second half, and were supplied by Martin Carruthers and Alex Calvo-Garcia, who was back from injury. It put the Iron in a more healthy placing of sixth in the table.

Brian Quailey causes trouble for the Shrewsbury Town defence in September 2001. He was a marksman in the 3-1 success.

Attentions next turned to the F.A.Cup, where the Iron had an interesting First Round tie at the Belle Vue ground of Doncaster Rovers. Sadly, Doncaster had made a backward step into the wilderness of the Conference, but thankfully the neighbours would recover. In the 2001 Cup clash, the Rovers put up a tremendous fight in the wide open spaces of this big old ground. It was the home side that took the lead on twenty minutes, but Scunthorpe seized the initiative with goals by Hodges and Carruthers, within the space of three minutes, just before the break. The strike by Lee Hodges stood out as the best of the ninety minutes. He picked up the ball on the left side of the field, just inside his own half, and set off on an electrifying run, which finished with an accurate thunder-bolt from distance.

The second period was just as fast and furious. It was to be the Rovers that were to be celebrating next, when they drew blood on fifty minutes. This tie was eventually settled, when Alex Calvo-Garcia hit the decisive match winner in the sixtieth minute, which gave a 3-2 final score.

In December, Scunthorpe United had a very difficult hurdle to jump if the Club wished to reach the third stage of the Cup. They were due to face the West Londoners of Brentford, a more than useful team. The Bees would reach the Play-Offs of the division above the Iron, but the team in the claret and blue shirts did have home advantage on their side.

The day of the match was one to be well wrapped up from the chill of the air, but a fast flowing game warmed the heart. United took a two goal lead through Carruthers and Calvo-Garcia, but the Bees pulled one back through the work of defender Michael Dobson. Shortly after the Vimto break, Brentford were back on terms, thanks to Ben Burgess getting the better of the United defence. It appeared that Scunthorpe might be over run at this moment in time, but a concerted effort allowed them to hold firm. It was not until a quarter of an hour before the end that Martin Carruthers nipped into the box, and sent the ball crashing into the bulging net. They could not claim to be safe until the last note on the referee's whistle, and then had another 3-2 victory to savour.

A crowd of 4,068 see a Martin Carruthers goal at the end of the 2000-01 season against Carlisle United. Torpey and Rapley survey the scene, as the Iron won 3-0.

Meanwhile, back in the League there were a number of ups and downs for Brian Laws and the army of supporters. Not many people that attended the Darlington fixture of 2001-02 are likely to forget it. The Quakers had two men sent off, and were visibly unhappy with the officials. United kept cool and strolled to a 7-1 victory. Give Darlington some credit, because their only goal came when they were reduced in number to nine players. On another occasion it was equally refreshing to see off the challenge at Glanford Park of the Tigers from Hull. A 2-1 victory made sure it had all gone quiet over there! However, a loss at Sincil Bank, to Lincoln, plus a home defeat to Exeter City, saw United placed just outside the Play-Off places in the table. Perhaps this was the wake up call they needed for the forth coming F.A.Cup game.

Scunthorpe United missed out on a plum tie, and had to be content with an away fixture at Millwall. There was sufficient interest to bring supporters from the North in a fleet of half a dozen buses, and around a thousand throats roared them on from the terraces. This game was always going to be a tough one, because the Lions were highly placed in the division that fed the Premiership. Scunthorpe United stuck manfully to the task ahead, putting up a respectable performance, as Peter Beagrie and Steve Torpey tried to use their experience to guide the youngsters. Millwall had their own ideas, and took the lead on the quarter hour. It only took United five minutes to equalise, when a cross from the left was met by the head of Jamie McCoombe.

For the rest of the half the Scunthorpe defence took a battering, as they did in the second part of the proceedings. The team did not crack until the sixty third minute, when Richard Sadlier scored his second goal of the match, and set the seal on the Millwall progress.

Once the Iron returned to the bread and butter of the Football League, their fortunes were slightly better than before. They singled out Halifax for a thump on the nose, 4-0 at Glanford Park, then had their best way day, beating Luton 3-2 at Kenilworth Road, thanks to a black pearl from Captain Matt Sparrow right on the last whistle.

Three more satisfying points also came in the last minute when the team made the short hop to Boothferry Park, Hull. The Tigers and the Iron were locked at 0-0 into the last few seconds, when a disputed free kick came the way of the Iron. Mark Jackson left his defending duties, and his pin point curling shot flashed the ball high into the net. Every single player joined in the celebration making a pyramid, and while Scunthorpe terraces danced, the Hull ones emptied.

Results like these had United briefly touching as far up as fourth in the table, but this sort of form deserted them. From a point in time half way through March until the end of April, Scunthorpe United lost the ability to assert their authority, and a 1-2 result at Darlington, in the penultimate match of the season, left them with the prospect of playing in the same division next term. At least they did send supporters home happy from the last game on the card, which brought York City to the other side of the Berkeley circle.

Once more, all the meaningful action arrived right on ninety minutes. Martin Carruthers was standing on the goal line, when he nudged the ball into the net

2002-03

Although the disappointment was tangible, Scunthorpe people soon moved their thoughts to the seats on planes, going to the far away destinations in the brochures. While they lay back in the sun, Brian was in his office hard at work deciding who would pass through the revolving door. Anyone thinking that the Club would sign a new team of players would be sadly mistaken, and the only person to join the ranks was Paul Wheatcroft, a former trainee at Bolton Wanderers, but Brian Laws was to change his opinion on the player.

It was not until September that ex-Scottish International Stephen Wright was signed on a short term contract. Although Stephen had not commanded a regular place at any club for some time, he oozed class, and lost little in the way of fitness from his defensive position.. The next new faces were those of Stuart Balmer, signed on a one month loan period from Oldham Athletic during October for a defensive role, and Lee Featherstone, a permanent signature for the mid-field area of the park. Brian Laws decided that this was now the time to give Andy Parton a chance to step up from the Reserves.

Peter Beagrie brought extra class to the team with some dazzling footwork.

He wanted to see if the lad could hit the back of the net, and was at first used as a substitute.

The advent of November saw three more men come to Glanford Park. These were Ian Kilford, Paul Hayes and Cliff Byrne. Kilford was an ex-Wigan player, signed for the middle of the park from Bury. Paul Hayes did not have the same experience, but possessed bags of potential, and was an attacking artist, who was taken from Norwich City.

The final face for the first half of 2002-03 was a solidly built young Irish defender, Cliff Byrne, who made a favourable impression, on loan from Sunderland. His no nonsense approach gave the back four a far tighter grip, and his loan period was extended from November until the end of February.

United started the season with consecutive draws, at home to Wrexham and away to Torquay United. Although August had a crowded programme, the team could only muster a win at home to York City, during that month. Brian Laws told supporters not to panic, because results would soon be forth coming. In the League Cup, the team showed what they could do against a side from a higher division, at Preston.

Action from the Scunthorpe United versus Bristol Rovers match on August 31st 2002, Steve Torpey and Martin Carruthers are seen pressing the visiting defence. The game finished square at 2-2.

Matthew Sparrow drills the ball across the pitch during the 5-1 demolition of Torquay United in October 2002.

They may have lost by two goals to one, but it was an excellent performance, which brought praise from the opposition camp. Stephen Wright gave a quality display at the back, and Steve Torpey had the Iron in front on ten minutes. Preston needed a penalty converted by ex-Iron, Graham Alexander, thirteen minutes later. There was no more scoring, and the match went into extra time. Scunthorpe United lasted until two minutes from the end, then lost 2-1. How courageously they played.

This respectable level of performance appeared to be the trigger for a change of fortune for the Club. Scunthorpe United rose from the second bottom position on the ladder, up to a place near the middle, assisted by back to back wins, at home to Carlisle United, and away at Macclesfield. At the end of October, just as the clocks went back, Iron fans had a Steve Torpey hat-trick to savour. The visitors were the Gulls of Torquay, and they suffered a 5-1 setback. Other goals came by way of Martin Carruthers, and the fast improving Jamie McCoombe, putting the advantage of his elongated frame to first class use. All of a sudden United had reached seventh in the League.

Steve Torpey hat-tricks were like buses, and after a long wait two came along together. Another just happened in his next match, up against Northwich Victoria in the F.A.Cup First Round, played at Whitton Albion's ground. In fresh Autumnal weather, and on a heavy pitch, Steve used his physique to muscle in three times. One arrived prior to the tea break, and two more followed in the final half. His last was a penalty, after a clumsy tackle in the box by a Victoria defender.

The success over Northwich gave United every opportunity of more advancement in the competition, when struggling Carlisle were asked to line up at Glanford Park. Scunthorpe experienced little trouble against the Cumbrians in the League, but dried up in front of the goal in this Cup encounter, which then needed a replay following the goalless draw.

By the time that everyone was in position, at the start of the second match, each camp knew that the prize for the victors was a visit from Premiership Leeds United. This time the effort from Scunthorpe United was top dollar, and they won with a twenty fifth minute goal from Martin Carruthers. He was in a lot of space, when he shot past the advancing keeper.

In the real world of the Third Division, December would find little of cheer for the loyal crew who religiously followed the Iron. It all started with a 1-0 loss on home soil to Bury and continued with draws either side of Christmas day at Hartlepool, and away at Rushden and Diamonds. Relief came on the road at Southend, during the final game of 2002, when the Iron scored two late goals through Carruthers and Torpey to make the lengthy journey a happy New Year at 2-1.

The F.A.Cup Third Round was a complete sell out and brought lots of interest from the media, including television coverage for the small screen. Leeds United were a huge attraction, packed with top International stars, but it was Mark Jackson that was singled out for special attention, having played for both camps. Despite his affinity for Leeds, it was Scunthorpe United that he would drive to victory.

On the day of the game, every part of Glanford Park was filled to the gunnels with 8,329 fans in the ground. It was the first Saturday of the New Year and Leeds ran out with quality throughout the team, from Robinson in goal to Jason Wilcox in attack. Scunthorpe United tried to match them in each department, and played the neat passing game instructed by Brian Laws. The turning point of the tie was to arrive on the half hour, and Leeds took full professional advantage. Matt Sparrow gave the merest of touches to an opponent in the penalty box. The man instantly hit the floor, and Australian Mark Vaduka confidently stroked away the spot kick.

Scunthorpe United tried to get back on terms, but with Peter Beagrie side lined through injury, they lacked a general on the park. The final blow came in the sixty eighth minute, when Norwegian Erik Bakke added a second goal, steering the ball beyond the reach of Tommy Evans, and the mountain the Iron had to climb suddenly got bigger.

When the whistle blew to signal time for a hot bath for everyone, Terry Venables, the Leeds United manager, was first to congratulate the Iron's valiant effort, but now it was back to Division Three.

Thankfully, Scunthorpe United suffered no F.A.Cup hang over, and beat Leyton Orient 2-1 in the following match, completing a trio of League wins on the bounce. The next victory would not arrive until the end of the month, when a decisive 4-1 result, in conflict with Southend United, brought about a well merited double. One of the brightest parts of the brilliant ninety minutes play was the first goal registered by their young starlet, Paul Hayes. When the Saturday Telegraph football journal went on sale later that evening it printed a table displaying the Iron happily up to third place.

Throughout February and March, Scunthorpe United played Jeckle and Hyde. A series of poor returns dropped them as low as the ninth position in the League. Afterwards, a run of three games yielded seven points, to hoist them back up to the fourth rung on the ladder, as Spring officially arrived. One of the disappointing displays, during the less prosperous times, was their first visit to Boston for a Football League fixture. On this occasion just about everything that could go wrong did go wrong.

A summery of the worst parts included a harsh sending off for the Iron, and a last minute winner for Boston by Richard Logan, to seal a 0-1 result. There again and looking on the bright side, a tour of Cumbria saw them on their metal beating Carlisle United 2-1. The goals came from the boots of Andy Dawson and Peter Beagrie, and it was worth the cash just to enjoy the Beagrie somersault in celebration.

At the final stage of the campaign Brian Laws was given permission to bring in three new faces, to give the Club every opportunity to achieve promotion. First he brought in former Brentford attacker Bob Taylor on a short term contract, and then take it for there if it went according to plan. Next in line was Paul Dalglish, the son of Kenny Dalglish, of Liverpool and Celtic fame. Paul was a chip off the old block, and joined for the push up front, on loan from Blackpool. He made an immediate favourable impression and showed the way to the back of the net. Last in the trilogy was Gregg Strong, borrowed from the Humberside neighbours at Hull. He was yet another proven player, plucked by United's clever manager to do the job in the back quarters.

Once the team had settled back down, the Iron were ready for the final push. Scunthorpe United did not begin April in the fashion they would have wished, losing 2-0 at home to Bournemouth, but from that nadir the team started a brilliant rally of five unbeaten matches, of which three would be counted as victories.

(Left): Scunthorpe captain Mark Jackson, a central defender signed from Leeds United.

(Right): A young Paul Hayes in his first spell at Glanford Park concentrates on the ball during the 2002-03 season.

The last home game of the 2002-03 against Oxford United was won 2-0, and Peter Beagrie is about to swing another ball over into the middle.

This included the last two fixtures on the schedule, at home to Oxford, and on tour at Shrewsbury. Sadly, Shrewsbury knew that they had been relegated from the Football League and suffered at the hands of Paul Dalglish, who scored twice in the 2-1 result. At five o'clock, after all the matches for the season had been completed, the final table showed Scunthorpe United to have the fifth most prosperous record and they had secured a qualification in the Play-Offs.

It so happened that in another part of Lincolnshire, Lincoln City found themselves equally excited about the prospects of promotion through the same avenue, and as fate would have it, the two neighbours were to face each other in the two legged Semi Final. On May 10th 2003 the gladiators emerged from the tunnel at Sincil Bank, ready to do battle before a crowd of 8,903 expectant devotees. If anyone thought this was to be a cagey contest in which the meanest defences gave nothing away, they would be wrong. This was a Trafalgar all over again.

The first blows were struck by the Imps. Simon Weaver scored the initial goal on the quarter hour, and then Scunthorpe were further stunned with another, only three minutes later, by Paul Mayo. United had to return the fire quickly to avoid permanent damage, and did so on twenty six minutes through Alex Calvo-Garcia. In full flow Alex picked up a ball repelled by the City defence and drove home a true shot through the crowded penalty area.

The fireworks continued into the second half. Lincoln increased the lead ten minutes after the break, and appeared to have the game wrapped up.

Next it was United's turn to celebrate. Twenty minutes from the end, Alex Calvo-Garcia repeated his scoring trick to reduce the lead to 3-2, and before the cheering had died down, Nathan Stanton came up to support the attack, and equalised with his only career goal so far. The crowd went crazy, and Scunthorpe United went for the jugular. It was a big mistake, because whilst everyone was knocking on the City door at the front, the home side sneaked round the back, and stole two break away goals to make the final score 5-3.

A two goal deficit was always going to be a tall ask in the Second Leg of the Semi Final, at Glanford Park. Brian Laws put a brave face on the events, promising his team would not give in until it finally was too late. On the evening City did the sensible thing by putting up a brick wall defence. United attacked constantly during the whole of the ninety minutes, but with no success. Then, as legs tired and heads fell, Simon Yeo nipped in for a winner to make the aggregate score to 6-3 in favour of the Imps. They deserved to progress to the Final, but the score did no justice to the blood sweat and tears of those in the Scunthorpe camp.

2003-04

When the start of the 2003-04 season arrived, Brian Laws knew he would have to replace two of his most influential players. Full back Andy Dawson had blossomed into a class performer and taken the eye of Hull City, who were prepared to wave the cheque book to secure his services. Another hole developed when Martin Carruthers bade farewell, taking the road to Macclesfield, making it necessary for surgery in the attack.

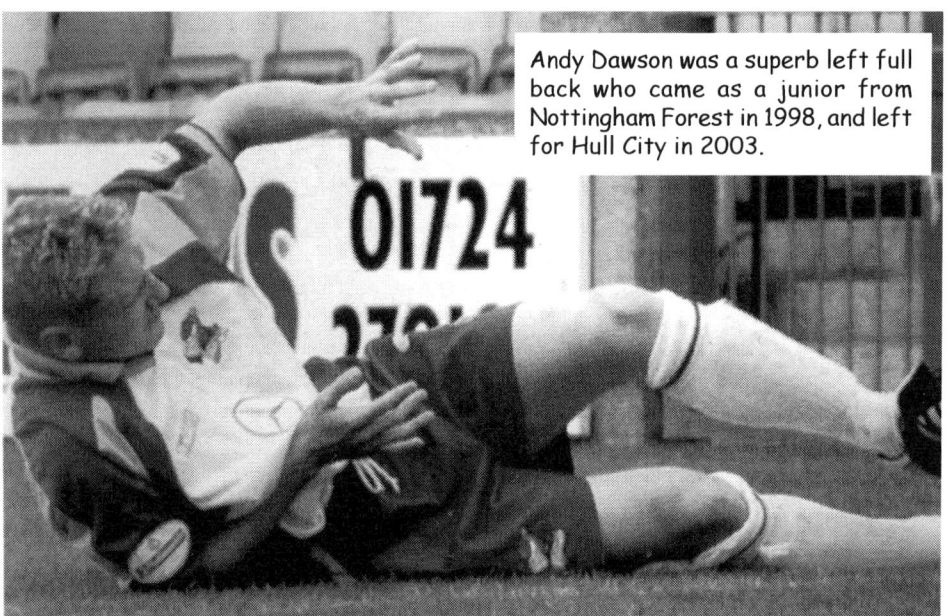

Andy Dawson was a superb left full back who came as a junior from Nottingham Forest in 1998, and left for Hull City in 2003.

In an effort to bolster the team, Brian Laws brought in two permanent signings, plus another which started as a loan until the end of December, but was eventually extended to all year. Cliff Byrne had shown so much commitment during his loan that United returned to Sunderland to take him from their books. This was to sort out the problem of Dawson's loss, and Cliff would become the type of loyal stalwart that would be the cement in the walls for a number of years of honest service. He was joined by another defender, Kevin Sharp, who came from Huddersfield via Leeds United.. The loan ranger, as he would be affectionately known, was Steve McLean, a young goal scorer at Glasgow Rangers. He had been notching many goals in the Ibrox Reserve eleven, and became known to Scunthorpe through a Scottish business acquaintance of Mr. Steve Wharton, on the Glanford Park board.

The season started for Scunthorpe United on a red hot Saturday, at home to Bristol Rovers. Although the team played reasonably well, they lost 2-1, and were annoyed that former Iron, Lee Hodges scored the vital goal. Amends were made in the next outing, when Bury were beaten 3-2. Only a 5-0 thrashing at Mansfield brought any real woe from the first two months of the season, and the team sat in mid-table.

United took a stride in the League Cup by repelling the challenge of Oldham, from the division above, but then fell to the power of the men from Turf Moor, when Burnley robbed them 2-3 at the second stage. Those who witnessed the match had value for money from the entertainment served up by both sides.

The talk of the Autumn months was that of Steve McLean, the young Scottish player, who could not stop scoring. He was to devastate the likes of Cheltenham Town, Huddersfield Town, and Cambridge United with hat-tricks, which yielded maximum points in each case.

The only sour note, at this point in time, was the serious injury picked up by Alex Calvo-Garcia, which would keep him out until the very end of the season.

Scunthorpe United had another degree of success in the Associate Members competition, which bore the sponsors label of the L.D.V.Vans Trophy. Previously, United had never ventured further than the first couple of rounds, but this time they would go much further. Progress started by over coming Shrewsbury, 2-1 at home, and was extended when United became the first team to beat Hull City, in a competitive fixture, at the new K.C. Stadium. They won 3-1 on the evening, then took the battle over to Gigg Lane, against Bury. In poor weather conditions, they required extra-time before over coming the Shakers, 1-0. This saw them reach the Northern Semi Final, when they were outclassed, 4-0 by Sheffield Wednesday.

The F.A.Cup brought more success for the Iron in 2003-04 season. Once again Lady Luck brought Shrewsbury Town to the other side of Doncaster road, and another 2-1 victory put smiles on the Scunthorpe United faces. The Club had the reward of a stiff home tie against Sheffield Wednesday, the fallen giant in the division above. Steve Torpey scored a goal in each half, giving them a fighting chance, but the Owls equalised with two goals in the last ten minutes, bringing the teams back to Hillsborough for a second bite of the cherry. On the evening it was a night for goalkeepers, who both stood firm, aided by strong defenders. The tie went through the allotted time, and beyond extra time into penalty kicks. It was at this moment when Tommy Evans became United's hero of the hour by saving three spot kicks, and the Iron went into the next round, 3-1 on penalties.

The Third Round of the F.A.Cup brought Scunthorpe United another difficult task, when they followed Barnsley out of the hat. At Oakwell, Scunthorpe United played an excellent brand of soccer, which pleased the visiting crowd. A policy of making sure they were tight at the back paid dividends, and United held out for another draw without scoring. The replay was just as close, but a Steve Torpey scoring chance edged Scunthorpe in front in the fourteenth minute. No further scoring took place until the second period. It was in the seventieth minute that Brian laws made a master stroke, by bring the tall Jamie McCoombe into the fray.

Within four minutes, he fastened onto a ball and lashed it beyond the Barnsley keeper, then returned to the centre of the defence, but at 2-0 the tie was in safe hands.

The Fourth Round of the competition brought another memorable day out for Iron fans, all the way down to the bottom of the Country at Portsmouth, on the South Coast. Portsmouth were of Premiership quality, led by everyone's favourite manager, Harry Redknapp. More than 2,000 supporters camped in the seats at what was an open end, but a clear sky meant they would not be troubled by the weather. Portsmouth found themselves with plenty on their plates as the Iron gave good account of their intentions. Eventually, Premiership class made sure of no sort of unpleasant upset for the Pompey Chimes. The Southerners gained a two goal lead, but it was left to Scunthorpe to have the last word. Andy Parton was brought on as a replacement for Paul Hayes, to give him a leg stretch. In the final few seconds the ball came to him just at the right height, and Andy kept his eye on it, and hit a sound volley clean into the net. There can be no doubt that this was the best goal Andy Parton ever scored for Scunthorpe United.

At this point in the season there was no sign of a crisis in the Scunthorpe United camp, but all of those extra games would take its toll, what with injuries, tired limbs and the inevitable number of cards shown to players by referees, which led to suspensions. Brian Laws brought in a number of new faces, including a brilliant young black player named Cleveland Taylor, as an attacking wide man, who won the hearts of the crowd through his non-stop efforts, and broad smile. Another significant signing was that of the vastly experienced Paul Groves, an ex-Grimsby Town artist who had also managed the Mariners. There was also a call to the ranks for trainee Marcus Williams, who was to be baptised into the first eleven.

Scunthorpe United began to tumble down the table as the Spring approached, and ran into a disastrous run of form. Thankfully, they were able to pick up a rare 3-1 win at struggling York City. It was a rearranged evening fixture, and two goals scored by Paul Groves, plus a penalty tucked away by Steve McClean would prove vital to the future of Scunthorpe United.

In the board room a number of changes had taken place, and Mr. Keith Wagstaff was replaced by Mr Christopher Holland as Chairman. On the field of play it was obvious that the performance of Scunthorpe United had turned pear shaped, and the question of Brian Laws future was under review. On March 25th 2004 it was announced that Brian Laws was parting company with the Club, and rumour was that an ex- Scottish International was in line as a replacement. At this point an emergency meeting of directors was called and majority share holder, Mr. Steve Wharton emerged as the new Chairman. He immediately alerted Brian Laws to put away his spade and return from gardening leave.

Brian was reinstated for the fourth from last game of the season, where a plucky Scunthorpe lost 3-2 at promotion chasing Huddersfield Town. The team was in twenty first position in the table, and were grateful seven days later, when a Steve Torpey header grabbed all three points in the 1-0 scrape against Macclesfield, at Glanford Park. The crisis eased a little bit, but was not over yet.

The situation was now that York had sunk into oblivion, and could not pull Scunthorpe into relegation to the Conference. Carlisle had to win both of their matches to pull clear of the Iron. At Cambridge United, Scunthorpe fought bravely, aided by the return of Calvo-Garcia, but lost 3-2. Hearts were in mouths, but the mood lifted, as people waited to rejoin buses for the return home. It was learned that Carlisle had only draw with Cheltenham, and Scunthorpe United had narrowly missed the chopping block. The margin of escape was made clearer after a loss in the final match, at home to Darlington. They actually had just two points more than the Cumbrians. The feeling of relief was parallel to that of a promotion, but in a bizarre sort of a way.

The final act of the season was a good news, bad news story. Alex Calvo-Garcia had sadly announced his retirement from the sport, and the genial Spanish player, who had made many friends at Scunthorpe, would be greatly missed as he returned with his family back to Spain. The board of directors granted Alex a testimonial after the season finished, and supporters turned out in numbers to bid farewell to a firm favourite. In the carnival atmosphere those present may have reflected upon a season which had given them an almighty fright.

A CHANGE IN FORTUNE

2004-05

Finishing third form bottom of the whole Football League in 2004 sent a shudder through the entire fabric of Scunthorpe United. The feeling of going so close to losing the Club's Football League identity was a sickening one, and the board of directors, headed by shipping entrepreneur, Mr. Steve Wharton, would see that it never happened again. It is true that the club had to cut its cloth accordingly, but Brian Laws needed to be able to buy the appropriate tools for the job.

Brian Laws was a clever Manager, and it did not take him long to sit down with his assistant, Russ Wilcox, and return to the Chairman to inform him of his requirements. In essence, the team needed strengthening down the backbone, and then tweaking at the forward end. To do this a goalkeeper of experience and quality was the first priority. For quite some time there had been talk of a return of Paul Musselwhite, who never left his house in the district throughout his career. Paul had spent the last couple of years at Hull City, but was only too happy to put pen to paper.

The second of Brian's needs was a stone wall in the heart of the defence, but one with a football brain who could lead from the back. He had such a player in mind, and that was Andy Cosby, a Yorkshire born man at Oxford United. Andy was pleased to join the Iron and be closer to his roots at Rotherham. Next on the agenda was a mid-field marshal, a ball winner that could distribute passes up the field to the forwards, where the damage could be done. Ian Baraclough, at Notts County, had the educated feet that Brian Laws wanted, and made up the main trio of men on his list. They would be supplemented by a young starlet for the forward line, brought in for two month on loan from Leeds United. He was Andy Keogh, an Irishman of considerable prospects. Within a short time Brian Laws made up his mind that he wished to buy the lad. The problem was that he had gone on loan at Bury. At the eleventh hour Laws put a bid in of £50,000 and made the move a permanent on in the February of 2005.

The first half of the season saw other loans and reserves given a chance. These would include Matt Bailey from Stockport County, Tom Brighton, from Glasgow Rangers and Doncaster born forward Michael Rankine who was given a contract, but utilised mainly as a substitute.

Scunthorpe United began the 2004-05 season at home to Rochdale, and lined up as follows; Musselwhite, Stanton, Ridley, Crosby, Butler, Baraclough, Taylor, Kell, Hayes, Bailey, and Beagrie, while Sparrow and Keogh had runs off the bench.

The team came back from a goal down and scored three times, through Taylor, Hayes, and Sparrow. It was the beginning of an unbeaten opening month, which saw United breast the summit of the division. Only in the League Cup was a loss suffered, and that was away to Nottingham Forest of the Championship, 0-2.

The well oiled machine continued to roll on and received a boost with the return of Steve Torpey and Cliff Byrne from injury. Even a disappointing loss at Lincolnshire rivals, Boston United could not dampen the spirits, as the Iron dropped to fourth in the table, the lowest they would be before Christmas. Scunthorpe United were soon back into gear, and produced one of their best performances so far, against Yeovil Town, a club that had designs on the top spot in the League. On October 23rd 2004, the Glovers came to Glanford Park to lock horns with the claret and blues. Both sides went hammer and tongs at each other, with Phil Jeavons unable to find a way past the huge hands of Paul Musselwhite. The deadlock was not broken until deep into the game, when Andy Butler pierced the Yeovil goal in front of the home supporters end, at Doncaster Road. The Iron won 1-0.

Scunthorpe United were playing with the belief and confidence of a team going places. Between October and the end of December the side embarked on an unbeaten run of ten matches, of which seven contained victories, and the Club maintained a top position looking down on the rest of the division. It was at this time that the Iron entered the fun and games of the F.A.Cup, and Chesterfield from the league above caused them no barrier, as the Spirites were dispatched 2-0 at Glanford Park. Lady Luck gave the club another home tie in Round Two of the Cup, and it was played on a Friday evening before the television cameras. The Welshmen of Wrexham made up the opposition, and they had just announced that they were experiencing financial difficulties, and the prize money would no doubt help their cause. Scunthorpe united could not be found to be in a charitable mood, and a rare goal from the enterprise of full back Lee Ridley, plus another from Matt Sparrow set up a deserved 2-0 passage into the Third Round, when the big boys entered the draw.

On the following Sunday Brian Laws was ready at five in the evening to watch the draw for the next stage. One by one the balls came out of the velvet bag, but no Scunthorpe yet. Manchester United had gone, and at least they would not have to go to Plymouth. Next out was Chelsea, top of the Premiership, and the Scunthorpe ball came immediately afterwards. It was an amazing tie, and it gave the Iron a plum draw against the great Jose Mourinho's men in London.

The climax of the F.A.Cup run was a trip to play Premiership leaders Chelsea.

The game was played at Stamford Bridge, on Saturday January 8th 2005. Both clubs reported a complete sell out of all tickets, guaranteeing a bumper 40,000 crowd. A fleet of forty buses, hundreds of cars and army of supporters on trains left the town for the banks of the Thames where the Chelsea ground was situated in the Capital. Over 8,000 Lincolnshire fans cheered the Iron onto the park, as the two teams left the tunnel to walk onto the neatly cut turf. The pitch had to first be cleared of a sea of claret and blur balloons, but soon the referee signalled the start of the game.

Scunthorpe played in their change strip of all yellow, and were without the services of striker Steve Torpey, but played Michael Rankine in his place. Within eight minutes the match exploded into action, and it was Paul Hayes who became the darling of the travelling hordes. He picked up a ball on his own right, and instinctively hit a low and hard shot past the groping hands of Cudicini in the Chelsea goal. Chelsea showed the irritation of an unwanted fly, and levelled before the tea interval through Kezman.

During the second period, Chelsea were always in command, but Scunthorpe never stopped running and probing. It was the Lincolnshire supporters that made the most noise, even when Chelsea took a 3-1 advantage. On the final whistle there were handshakes on the pitch, and these continued after the game with the opposing supporters. Perhaps the crowning glory was the praise heaped on Scunthorpe United by the generous Chelsea manager, Jose Mourinho.

Within the blink of an eye the Cup, was forgotten and the focus switched back to trying to achieve promotion. January would see the team stutter a little and they lost their top perch. A victory at home to Kidderminster put them back on course, as three points were gleaned from the 2-1 result, and they rose back up to second. Yeovil had by now assumed the summit of the table and were assisted by an incredible number of penalty conversions, which totalled a dozen at the end of the season. United had a chance to steal a march over the Somerset men, but lost an exciting game in the West by 3-4.

Scunthorpe United entered the finishing straight, and at the beginning of March took two precious victories over Rushden and Diamonds, 1-0, and. 4-1 against Cheltenham, which was far more convincing performance. They lost a little ground when three of the next four results yielded three points, all from draws. United could ill afford to slip up at this late stage after all the hard shifts the team had put in. The situation on the evening of the first Saturday of April was that Scunthorpe lay in fourth position in the league ladder, and out of the automatic promotion places, looking up at Yeovil, Southend, and Swansea.

At this moment, thankfully, the Iron cruised back into form, starting with a narrow 2-1 success at the Sixfield Stadium against Northampton, where all the real action arrived in the first period of the encounter. Scunthorpe supporters were back in force to see the next home fixture against Cambridge United, and they were delighted that a 4-0 score helped to promote back to back wins.

United had a sticky wicket to bat on, as they travelled to Grimsby for the last but one away trip, but having already beaten the Mariner, they went without fear. The match finished goalless, but Scunthorpe had enough chances to have sneaked a winner. In the penultimate, played at Glanford Park, United were faced with the task of confronting Bristol Rovers. With all guns blazing, United sunk the Pirates ship in an impressive performance. Steve Torpey was the fans favourite, as his pair of goals took his bounty to a dozen for the year, but leading scorer Paul Hayes and Cleveland Taylor also put their names on the marksmen list. The 4-0 score was exceedingly helpful towards the goal difference.

Andy Crosby receives congratulations for scoring the second goal versus Cambridge United. The final result 4-0.

The whole year of work was to be decided on Saturday May 7th 2005, at the Gay Meadow, where Scunthorpe United had a date with Shrewsbury Town. Their task was to avoid defeat, or they would be wrapped up in the lottery of the Play-Offs. Yeovil could not be caught, but a favourable result could earn the respectable prize as the second placed team. Shrewsbury. made the match an all ticket affair, allowing 2,000 travelling supporters a section of seating and the run of the terrace behind one goal. The Iron, once again, chose to wear the all yellow kit when they walked onto the field, to the welcoming roar of the crowd.

The afternoon was to be an uncomfortable one for all concerned with Scunthorpe United. The team was continually stifled by Shrewsbury, and never allowed to get into its stride. At the back Ridley and Byrne got through some sterling work, while Crosby and Butler shielded. Musslewhite in goal.

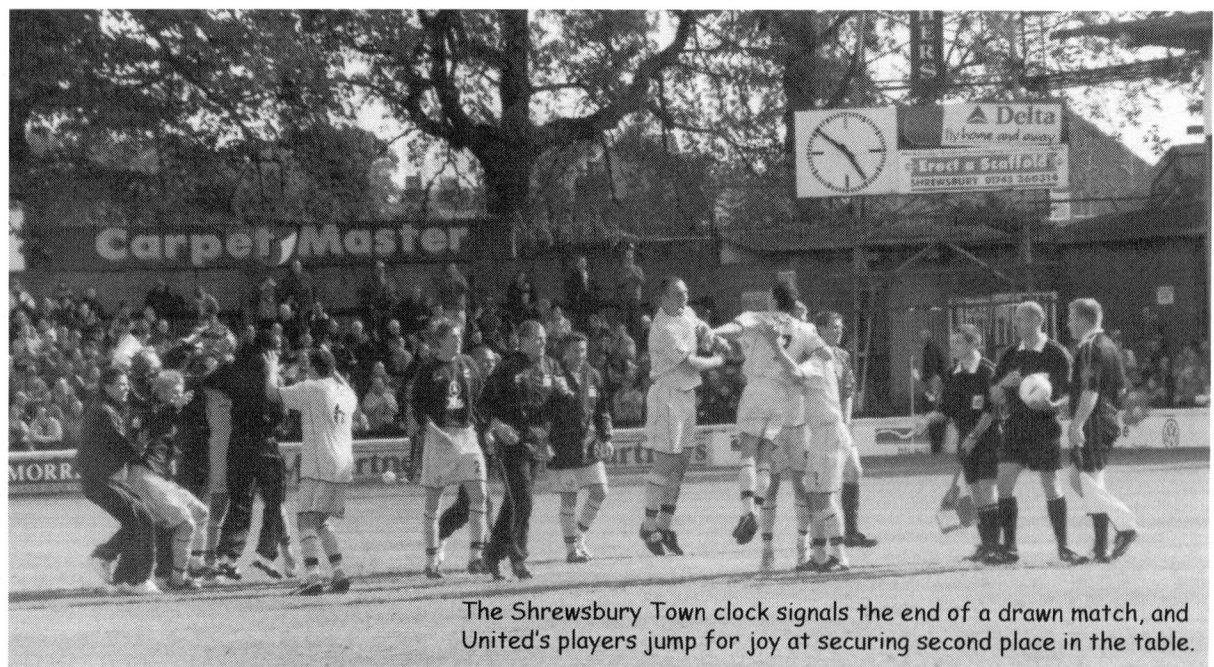

The Shrewsbury Town clock signals the end of a drawn match, and United's players jump for joy at securing second place in the table.

News constantly filtered through of the ups and downs of rival teams, and a first minute goal scored by Swansea at Bury did not help the cause. All this was happening as the clock ticked away the seconds. It was becoming increasingly clear that a goalless draw was looking the most likely result for the Iron, especially when the fourth official put up the board to indicate a minimum of four extra minutes. Once the agony of extra time was over, United had yet another precious point in the bag.

There was a few further tense moments before all the rest of the games had finished, then it finally sunk in that the Iron had taken the second position on goal difference, marginally ahead of Swansea City.

As the reality dawned on everyone, the terraces began to bounce, players and staff hugged each other, and there was an extra special cheer for popular Chairman Steve Wharton. He was on hand to open a bottle of champagne on the pitch, and Amanda Thompson of B.B.C. Radio Humberside grabbed Brian Laws for an interview. It was one of those unforgettable moments that stay for the rest of the lives of those who enjoyed it.

The achievement was reward by the Borough Council, and a civic dinner took place at Normanby Hall. Players officials and staff. made their way in two open topped buses, dressed in best bib and tucker, surrounded by the media. Along a predetermined route thousands of supporters lined the way, waving flags, and holding banners, and cheering as the procession drove slowly past. It was a fitting tribute to the mountain of work that had made the achievement possible.

2005-06

Once the holidays were over, Scunthorpe United were well aware that the immediate task was to consolidate their position in League Division One. Brian Laws knew that to do this he would have to bring in some new faces, and late in the promotion campaign his work began. Already Wayne Corden was signed from Mansfield Town as a wide man, and Richard Hinds, was borrowed from Hull City as a defensive rock. Laws liked what he saw and signed Richard on as a permanent contract. Unfortunately, there was some disappointing news, and it was learned that leading scorer Paul Hayes had decided to join Barnsley.

Scunthorpe United opened the 2005-06 year in West London at Brentford. Although they lost the contest 2-0, there was enough quality to suggest they would stay the course. The team did not have to wait too long before the first points were on the board. These arrived the following Tuesday evening, when Barnsley paid a visit. Paul Hayes did not make himself very popular, when he put his new Yorkshire friends in the lead. Parity was restored before the interval, when ice cool Andy Crosby stepped up to convert a penalty, following a trip in the box.

After the break either side could have won the spoils, but it was left to Cleveland Taylor to score the decider. He made an Olympic dash with the ball and fired in a tremendous drive, that was a goal the second it left his boot. In celebration, Cleveland ran to the manager's dugout and grabbed the nearest object, which happened to be a support belt. This he held aloft like a boxing champion with a World Title Belt.

During August, Brian Laws secured the signature of one of the most influential players of the decade and he brought to Glanford. Park a young man that would make an indelible impact on the immediate future of the Club. Billy Sharp had been spotted playing for Sheffield United Reserves, scoring goals for fun. The minute he put his boots on he just could not stop scoring. Billy was the type of player that young fans will tell their grandchildren about. He made his Scunthorpe debut at the City Ground, against Nottingham Forest, on August 20th 2005. United had been stretched to keep the men of Sherwood at bay, but in the seventy first minute Billy Sharp announced his arrival with a peach of a goal. Facing fully away from the target, he swung round and shot the ball into the net, through a sea of legs belonging to both friend and foe. It was sufficient to pinch all three points.

Scunthorpe United made an unbelievable start to the season and actually touched the dizzy height of second place, when four of the first eight fixtures gave them victories. This could not realistically be expected to be maintained, but it made for a special feeling. Billy Sharp was linking up extraordinarily well with Andy Keogh, and he scored a pair of goals in a 3-3 result at Hartlepool. Keogh returned the compliment by notching another couple at the Galpharm Stadium against Huddersfield, when the Iron gained an unexpected 4-1 advantage.

The early season saw some progress made in the League Cup. United had the blessing of a home tie in Round One, and seized the opportunity to dispatch Tranmere Rovers, who were of the same division. Their reward was a visit from Premiership Birmingham City, which all added to the theatre of the sporting calendar. The Blue Noses arrive in town and took the spoils with a 2-0 score.

During September, the results dried up, but October brought Scunthorpe United far better rewards, especially when Brian Laws introduced some more new talent. Debuts were given to Richie Ryan, Tommy Johnson, and Peter Till. At the end of November, Neil MacKenzie signed for the mid-field from Macclesfield. Another start was given to the tough Irishman Jim Goodwin, who began life in football as a Celtic trainee, but signed for Scunthorpe in the closed season from Stockport. Injury had delayed his Scunthorpe career, but soon he was straight in the mix, along-side Ian Baraclough. Another change was in the goalkeeping position, where Tommy Evans found himself back in favour for a while with the gloves.

It was in November that United found themselves back on F.A.Cup duty and had a wet experience at Gigg Lane against Bury,. in the First Round. Although the Iron took a two goal lead, Bury pulled it back even, aided by some decisions that left the Scunthorpe bench open mouthed. A replay required an evening away from the fire side, and Bury proved to be excellent fighters. The Shakers held firm for the ninety minutes, making sure the contest went into extra time. It was at this moment Tommy Johnson was brought on as fresh legs for Matt Sparrow, and the former Celtic man used all his old expertise to guide the only real chance into the net.

The Second Round provided Scunthorpe United with an even longer journey, as their numbered ball followed that of the newly formed Aldershot Town out of the bag. On the afternoon of the tie, everything was decided by a Scunthorpe move on fourteen minutes. The ball was pushed out wide to Billy Sharp on the right wing. He whipped in a pin point accurate cross to Andy Keogh, running in close to goal. Keogh only needed the slightest touch to beat the helpless goalkeeper, to seal a 1-0 victory, and send the travelling band of enthusiasts ecstatic with delight.

Scunthorpe United began the Winter in the middle of the table. The highlight of December came just before Christmas, when the double was completed over Nottingham Forest, at Glanford Park. Lee Ridley scored the only goal of the first half to get the score board turning, but Forest restored the equilibrium on the hour mark with a penalty conversion. Over 8,000 spectators were kept in suspense as to what the final outcome would be, but Cleveland Taylor blasted the Iron ahead in the seventy second minute, and Mr. Reliable, Cliff Byrne put matters safe right at the death. This result was followed by five draws and maintained the Iron in a respectable position.

Meanwhile, the F.A.Cup had thrown up a delicious tie which was bound to bring a brilliant day out. Scunthorpe United had been drawn away at the City of Manchester Stadium to Manchester City. A crowd of 27,779 was on hand to witness the arrival of the players from out of the tunnel.

Once again it was to be Scunthorpe United that struck the first blow against Premiership opposition. They shook the hosts, when fair haired Andy Keogh, playing in the all black with blue trim away kit, caused the damage. Despite the close attention of a defender and the goalkeeper, Keogh slid in low to stab the ball into the net, from less than a dozen metres out.

The lead lasted into the second half, and then it became the Robbie Fowler show. He danced and dazzled his way to a hat-trick, displaying all the skills of the Premiership star that he was. Whilst he collected the applause and match ball, a decent pay cheque was sufficient to please the Iron. Shortly after the Cup exit, Scunthorpe United supporters had two more names to remember. Brian Laws brought in Michael Rose, a full back from Yeovil Town, for a three month loan spell. Then Steve Foster made the relatively short trip from down the road at Doncaster Rovers, filling a central defensive role. He was soon to demonstrate how brilliant a performer he could be, and Rovers must have had their own reasons for letting him go.

Throughout the first months of the New Year the amazing strike rate of Billy Sharp, plus supplements from Keogh, Hinds Sparrow and evergreen Peter Beagrie, kept the Iron in the picture. Beagrie was always on hand if a penalty was awarded, and could still celebrate with a somersault to thrill the crowd. The gloom of February was lifted by a bright display when United beat M.K.Dons at home, and there was little surprise to note that it was Billy Sharp who stole both of the goals, while at the other end Tommy Evans kept a clean pair of gloves. On the road, United enjoyed a couple of neat wins, 3-1 at Gillingham and the 2-1 in the wide open spaces of Vale Park, against Port Vale. The team certainly did not have it all their own way, and they had reality checks, losing 3-0 at Southend, and 2-1 at home to Swindon Town, a team to suffer relegation in a few weeks time.

Scunthorpe made their own situation safe during the last home schedule. Blackpool brought a large band of noisy supporters, but a pin could be heard to drop when Billy Sharp scored down at their end of the ground, with five minutes left on the clock. Billy notched one more goal, the following week at Oldham. It made his total twenty four in all competitions. At Boundary Park the 1-1 score eased the Iron into twelfth position in the table, a most satisfactory position.

A queue at the Railway End as the Bournemouth goal is attacked in April 2006. The teams eventually shared four goals.

2006-07

Scunthorpe United had achieved their main objective to remain in the division, but as is always the case, changes had been made by the time the players were back in preseason training. The most significant difference was in goal. Both Tommy Evans and Paul Musselwhite would not be given new contracts, and United signed Irishman Joe Murphy from Sunderland, a marvellous character and brilliant keeper, in their place. His understudy would be Josh Lillis, a local product, and son of the former Assistant Manager, Mark Lillis.

Another newcomer was Bootle born Dave Mulligan, a defender from Doncaster Rovers. Through his roots, Dave was a New Zealand International, and when he continued his International career he became Scunthorpe United's first full International in all their one hundred and seven years of history.

It was not too long before Ian Morris, a tall Dubliner, was added to the defence. Ian joined from Leeds United at the beginning of September, as did Danny McBreen, born in the Newcastle in Australia. McBreen was a fraction over six feet tall, and came out of Scottish football at Falkirk, to add an extra punch to the attack. Another young player in line for increased duty was the fast improving full back Marcus Williams, who prospered through work rate and commitment. However, one sad departure was that of Peter Beagrie, who left with everyone's best wishes for a final fling at Grimsby. He then went into a life working in the media. Peter left supporters with so many happy memories, and had helped lay the foundation of the present rise of the Club.

Scunthorpe United began the 2006-07 calendar by losing to an only goal at Bristol City, and they selected the following selection; Murphy, Hinds, Ridley, Crosby, Foster, Baraclough, Mulligan, Goodwin, Keogh, Sharp, Sparrow, while MacKenzie, Taylor, and Torpey stood in the wings for their turns as substitutes.

The Iron continued to make heavy weather of the early part of the campaign. They did not taste their first victory until the sixth match on the card, when the team went to Gillingham and won 2-0. Richard Hinds and Matt Sparrow scored the two goals which helped bring home the bacon. At that time, United experienced a thrilling Carling Cup win, at home to Lincoln City. Scunthorpe required extra time before the battle was won, and for the extra work they only had themselves to blame. Torpey and Mulligan had already edged the Iron in front, but defensive slips cost the team dearly. City took a 3-2 advantage in the time added on, but a rally brought two Scunthorpe goals to snatch the 4-3 win. They needed to thank on loan Villa youngster, Shane Paul, and Ian Baraclough for the goals that eased the nerves.

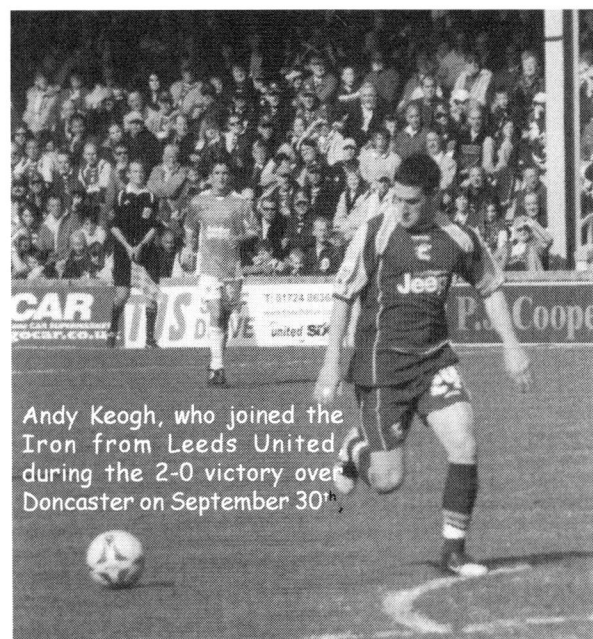

Andy Keogh, who joined the Iron from Leeds United during the 2-0 victory over Doncaster on September 30th.

In the Second Round, Aston Villa dropped in for a change from their Premiership routine. This tie gave the Scunthorpe men the opportunity to pitch their skills against some of the best in the country. A crowd of 6,502 spectators enjoyed an entertaining ninety minutes of good football. Even though Villa did not have the lion's share of the play, it was the older claret and blues who scored a goal in each half. Scunthorpe did have their minute of fame, when Billy Sharp reduced the lead to 1-2, but it was the Villans who went further.

When Scunthorpe United returned to League duty, they found that they were able to notch up the gears, and improve productivity. The turning point was early in September, when Port Vale found themselves on the end of a 3-0 lesson at Glanford Park, which was punctuated by two goals from Billy Sharp and a third via Ian Morris. This was to start the ball rolling on run of six unbeaten matches, which included only one draw. The drawn game was on the distant voyage to the South Coast to play Bournemouth. Scunthorpe gained a 1-1 score, assisted by the sweetest of long range drives by Neil MacKenzie, which went into the net in front the unpopulated end of the ground.

At this moment in the schedule, United enjoyed possibly the best result and performance of the year. The Iron had a mid-day kick-off at the City Ground against Forest. Nottingham Forest were not a side in the habit of losing home League matches, but first half strikes by Cleveland Taylor and Andy Keogh did not make the picture look rosy for the once famous old club. When Ian Morris and Billy Sharp multiplied the score in the second period, there could be no argument as to which was the better eleven. The 4-0 score looked just as compelling on the television later in the evening.

Scunthorpe United continued to climb the table, and found that they were rubbing shoulders with the top teams. Even a loss at home to Brighton and Hove Albion only reduced their standing. to a healthy fourth place. Within a week of this setback the Iron returned to winning ways, beating Bradford City at Valley Parade. Billy Sharp scored the only goal, and the brilliant young goal scorer could do no wrong, notching goal after goal, virtually every week.

Once the Scunthorpe rocket had been launched, nothing looked like stopping it, until events beyond the control of the Club appeared to put a spanner in the works. Over at Hillsborough, Sheffield Wednesday had parted company with manager Paul Sturrock, and they had a fist full of dollars to tempt another successful manager to look after their affairs. It soon became obvious that Brian Laws was the target, and following a period of tight lips and no comment, Brian Laws left Glanford Park, along with his assistant Russ Wilcox, to take up his new post.

On the day after the dust had settled, all of the remaining senior football personalities were summoned by the board of directors to a meeting at Glanford Park. These included physiotherapist Nigel Adkins, chief scout Lee Turnbull, and youth development officer Tony Daws. They were asked to form an interim government, led by Nigel Adkins, who had previously been a successfully managed at Bangor. Nigel Adkins was able to work with people, and had a unique enthusiasm to get the best out of folks. He was full of positives and the players warmed to his working methods. Steve Wharton saw how well the transition of power was, and results continued to maintain the Club in an elevated position up the top of the table. He asked Nigel to take on the position as the new Scunthorpe United Manager, and to this he agreed. Before the time supporters were pulling Christmas crackers, Nigel Adkins introduced his Assistant Manager as Andy Crosby, and Ian Baraclough would become the new Head Coach, while they both continued to play for the team.

During the time of upheaval, the team had the question of the F.A.Cup to deal with. Fortunately, the problems off the pitch did not affect playing matters. It need a lot of concentration to earn a reply from a goalless game against Cheltenham. There was something of a relief when the Iron won the second part of the tie 2-0. This result enabled them to invite Wrexham to play the next stage at Glanford Park, but a stifled performance gave them a 0-2 smack on the nose, and that was it for another twelve months.

The Christmas period started extremely brightly for Scunthorpe United. On the Friday before Santa came down the chimney, the team ran out in London to meet the Lions of Millwall. United had lost the services of Joe Murphy, and Josh Lillis came in for his senior debut. Josh performed admirably on a night when, during an evening when everyone had steam on the breath. He kept a clean sheet, and when Steve Torpey entered the field as a substitute, a slender 1-0 win was secured.

A bit of quick thinking by the old warrior, in front of the Millwall goal, enabled him to prod the ball home. This result was the precursor to a trio of three pointers for the Iron over the festive holiday. When the statistics had been added to the table from results at home to both Chesterfield and Bournemouth, it was Scunthorpe United that sat proudly at the top of the pile. The cold chill of the Winter was replaced by a warm glow for the army of Scunthorpe followers, because from Joe Murphy at one end of the team to Billy Sharp at the other, the players were all motoring at full throttle.

The Club continued to consolidate the top position of the League table, but were continuously being chased by Bristol City, Blackpool, and Nottingham Forest, all expecting the Scunthorpe challenge to fail at any moment. A series of four consecutive draws threatened to hamper the custody of an automatic promotion place, and for a short while the Iron did drop to the second spot. Perhaps the biggest challenge came when Wolves knocked on the door, and lured Andy Keogh away for a fee of £850,000. Nigel Adkins reacted immediately to the anticipated loss of Keogh, by bringing in on loan Jermaine Beckford from Leeds United. On the day Andy rammed his last Scunthorpe goal into the back of the Doncaster Rovers, net at the Keepmoat Stadium, Beckford made his Iron debut. Jermaine was to fit into the Scunthorpe team and continue in the same role, scoring eight goals in eighteen appearances. It was as though he had been playing alongside Billy Sharp all year. The squad was joined by another young signing, with the introduction of Kevan Hurst, an. attacking mid-field man. Kevan originally arrived on loan from Sheffield United, in February, but became a full Iron in the closed season.

It was discovered that towards the end of the season, the more that the chasing pack thought they were going to close the gap on Scunthorpe the better the Iron played. Incredibly, the success at Millwall began a sequence of nineteen unbeaten games, and during the campaign, clean sheets were kept in half the matches played. Joe Murphy was to be acknowledged for his part by being awarded the Golden Glove award.

Meanwhile, the winning post was now insight. A visit to Tranmere Rovers made sure that promotion was guaranteed, and the team won 2-0 on the Wirral. A scrappy first half brought nothing tangible, but Andy Butler was to change the game, returned now from his loan at Grimsby. He raced up to support his forwards, and scored when the Rovers missed his dash on the ball. Jermaine Beckford was responsible for setting up the next goal. He had a run on the left, then a crossed a ball that Billy Sharp connected with, just on the goal line, next to the right hand post.

It was Ironic that the First Division Championship was clinched by the Iron, in Blackpool, at the end of a match that finished with a 3-1 defeat.

Other teams in the race had also lost, handing the prize to Scunthorpe United. During the game, Billy Sharp hit his thirty second goal of the year, thus breaking the Barry Thomas record of 1961-62 for most goals in a season by a Scunthorpe United player. Thirty goals came in the League, and for this feat Sharp was given the Golden Boot trophy for the First Division.

There only remained one final match on the fixture card, and that was at home to Carlisle United. The day was blessed by brilliant sunshine, and both sets of supporters in the 8,720 crowd were in holiday mood. Scunthorpe United played like true Champions and glided to a 3-0 victory. Fans applauded strikes by Cleveland Taylor, still with that cheeky grin, plus local product Matt Sparrow and Jermaine Beckford. Before the game it had been announced that Steve Torpey was not to be offered a new contract, but to honour his loyalty Nigel Adkins put him straight into the team, and when he was substituted at the end, the whole ground stood up to salute the big man. What a marvellous Club servant Steve had been.

At the end of the game a podium was quickly erected and a group of Football League officials assembled. Each member of staff received a golden medal, as did the players following on. Nigel Adkins was the hero of the hour, but the greatest moment arrived when Andy Crosby lifted the championship silver trophy, decked in claret and blue ribbons, high above his head for the crowd to see. At that moment, ticker tape showered the air, changing the entire scene into shades of claret and blue, and then champagne corks were cracked. Steve Wharton was there on hand to take his own salute from an audience who appreciated his own valuable contribution. The whole of the crowd stood and applauded the stroll round the park of the excited players with the handsome cup. It was an unforgettable piece of the jig saw of time. Scunthorpe United would be playing in the Championship League next year and tackling some big city clubs for the first time since 1964. All of that could wait while the team enjoyed the attention of the crowd and milked the moment of adulation.

(Left) Scunthorpe United were confirmed as Champions at Blackpool. Here, Billy Sharp who broke the record for most United goals in a season, scored his thirty second goal. (Below) 6th May: Men, management, mascot and medals after the final match at home to Carlisle, when the Division One trophy was presented.

THE IRON ROLLER-COASTER

2007-08

The release of the Championship fixture card was met with great excitement by the football public of Scunthorpe. They found that the computer had given them an opening day fixture in the Capital for a match against Charlton Athletic, a club freshly relegated from the Premiership.

In the build up to the game the entrance to Glanford Park became like a revolving door, as players arrived and departed. The big absentee was Billy Sharp, who returned to his first club of Sheffield United for a fee of £2M. He left a large hole to try to fill, and broke the hearts of many supporters, especially the ladies. Joining Billy on the way out were Steve Foster going to Darlington, Richard Hinds to Sheffield Wednesday, and Neil MacKenzie to Notts County. Steve Torpey was already known to be leaving, and he became fixed up with Lincoln City, and soon into the season Dave Mulligan headed in the direction of Port Vale.

Although Nigel Adkins had attempted to sign Jermaine Beckford, the move did not materialise, but Beckford was thanked for his on loan service. Instead, Adkins caused a surprise by bringing back Paul Hayes from Barnsley. It was to prove to be a productive transaction, because the best days of his career would always be at Glanford Park. This was part of the reconstruction of the Iron's attack, which brought Martin Paterson to the Club as the main goal scorer. Martin left Stoke City, and although not the tallest of men, this skilful youngster had dynamite in his boots.

Two other players were also brought in for the front end of the field. Jonathon Forte was a black young man, with the body of an athlete and the speed of a gazelle. Scunthorpe picked up his signature from Sheffield United. Ben May was a Southerner, who departed Millwall for an Iron shirt. This new man was big in stature and made a good target man, similar to Steve Torpey.

At the back of the field, Nigel Adkins decided to strengthen the team with another black player. He was Ezomo Iriekpen, otherwise known as Izzy, from Swansea. Izzy was quite a character, who added some steel in the heart of the defence. Iriekpen was to be joined by Kelly Youga, a full back on a half season loan from Charlton Athletic, and would not be available for the opener against his parent club.

The season was barely a fortnight old, when Nigel Adkins plucked Jack Cork, an exciting slightly built player for the mid-field, from the Chelsea junior ranks. What started as a loan eventually lasted all season long. Jack Cork made such an impression, that this brilliant worker had Scunthorpe supporters voting him as their player of the year.

Scunthorpe United kicked off the season in exceptional heat, at a packed Valley Stadium, against Charlton, in wall to wall sunshine. The home side were soon into their stride, and pushed up on the Scunthorpe defence. United held firm and Joe Murphy showed a clean pair of gloves, up until the sixty second minute. It was at that point when Marcus Bent fastened onto the ball and rifled home the opening goal of the campaign. Instead of crumbling, the United players counter attacked, and when they won a corner within the next ten minutes, Izzy Iriekpen was first to it and headed firmly home. The 1-1 score registered the first point of the season.

The mid-week was spoiled by a 1-2 home loss in the League Cup to Hartlepool, but all was forgiven on the following Saturday, when close to 7,000 fans watched at Glanford Park, as goals by Martin Paterson and Jim Goodwin earned the plaudits, with a rewarding 2-0 score.

During the first half of the season, Scunthorpe United managed to keep their heads above water. On September 1st 2007 a particularly entertaining match at Glanford Park against Sheffield United had 8,801 spectators on the edge of their seats until the final minute. Andy Crosby put the Iron ahead, and victory appeared sealed with another from Martin Paterson on the hour. Sheffield United refused to lay down, and came storming back when Danny Webber rifled two goals in the space of four minutes. The Blades supporters went wild with delight, but the game had a sting in the tail. In the time added on for the extras Scunthorpe swung a dangerous ball diagonally across the box. From a position just beyond the far right hand post, Matt Sparrow scooped the ball into the net past a sea of bodies, and the Iron had an incredible 3-2 victory.

Life for the majority of time was not a bed of roses and points were difficult to obtain. A rare victory at Colchester, on the old Layer Road ground, might have been an exception, but the team failed at home to West Bromwich Albion, Watford, Stoke City and neighbours Hull City. When Father Christmas delivered the presents, Scunthorpe United were already fighting a relegation battle. It was at this time that Scunthorpe United had two visits within a fortnight to Deepdale, at Preston. Not only was a Championship match to be played, but the two clubs had been drawn together in the F.A.Cup. Both teams would take a 1-0 win, but for Scunthorpe it was crucially in the League.

Nigel Adkins did not have much of a war chest to dip into, but with what cash he did have to spend he tried to play the loan market to good effect. United gave opportunities to Shaleum Logan, Tomi Ameobi, Seck Mamodou and Shelton Martis.

Andy Butler helps out the attack watched by Martin Paterson in the visit to Crystal Palace.

Perhaps the most outstanding loanee was Liverpool's Jack Hobbs, a towering defender, who was made welcome for two months. Nigel did not forget his own trainees, and Peter Winn was given a call from the bench.

Before January was out, Scunthorpe United made an amazing capture, when they boosted the mid-field belt with the signing of Northern Irish International Grant McCann, from Barnsley. This fair haired artist had all the brush strokes a manager could wish for and it is a wonder why he was allowed to leave Oakwell. Whilst at Glanford Park, Grant would score in an International, and become the Club's first scoring International player. At the same time, Adkins brought in the experienced forward player Geoff Horsfield, on loan from Sheffield United.

The chill of the Winter brought a freeze when it came to United's points total, and they found it extremely difficult to make it ticking over. Certainly victories were thin on the ground. They were unable to pick another three pointer, until a single Martin Paterson goal beat Charlton at home, in February. The next win did not arrive until Coventry City were beaten 2-1 in March, again on home turf. The winning goal was a spectacular volley from for out on the ring wing, hit by Jack Cork. He immediately dedicated it to his father, Alan, who was once dismissed by the Sky Blues.

The season was fast running out for the Iron, and supporters knew that their prayers were not being answered. The only other three points in March came when Ian Morris scored in a 1-0 nail biter that saw the Iron squeeze past Plymouth.

The season just had time for the loan signing of Curtis Weston, who played for Millwall in the F.A.Cup Final against Manchester United, and Andy Wright, an unattached defensive player, who had been studying at a university in America.

Midfielder Jack Cork signed on a season long loan from Chelsea and created such an impression that he was voted 'Player of the Season'.

They did not have time to make an impact, before the Iron suffered confirmation of relegation, on April 12th 2008, with a 2-0 loss at Crystal Palace. After those tears, the team expressed themselves with a greater freedom, and remained unbeaten in the remaining three fixture. They took advantage of Cardiff City at home, in a 3-2 thriller, and were applauded by generous Watford fans for a 1-0 result at Vicarage Road, where Paul Hayes notched to vital strike when only twenty minutes were left on the watch. They signed off in style at Glanford Park, playing fellow relegation candidates, Colchester United, in a 3-3 goal feast.

Relegated clubs Scunthorpe and Colchester drew 3-3 in the final match of the 2007-08 campaign; Paul Hayes scores, after rounding the keeper.

2008-09

During the Summer the talking point was over Martin Paterson, the leading goal scorer, It was alleged that Martin did not wish to continue at Scunthorpe, now that they no longer were of Championship status. Whatever the truth of the matter was, Martin left the Club on a transfer to Burnley, for a decent fee with strings attached.

There would inevitably be changes to the squad, and late in the previous season permission had been given for the popular Cleveland Taylor to leave for Carlisle United. He was to be sorely missed, because of his big heart, and constant running. The same could be said for Ian Baraclough, but Bara would be a little nearer home in a full time coaching role. Andy Crosby was not quite ready to hang up his boots, despite the ever increasing demands of management, alongside Nigel. There was still a last chance to loosen his leg muscles running round Glanford Park. However, the Club did wave farewell during the Summer to Jim Goodwin and Andy Butler, who both decided to accept better offers from Huddersfield Town. Supporters would especially be dismayed with the loss of Andy Butler, a player that they had watch develop from a youngster.

Nigel Adkins was fortunate that the majority of his squad were still in contract, and he had already chosen two men as replacements. One was David Mirfin, a young solidly built, experienced central back four player, ironically at Huddersfield. His defence was like a wall made of engineering bricks. It was planned that he would play next to Kenny Milne, a mountain of a man, at the heart of the defence.

Kenny had been noted in Scotland, playing in the S.P.L. for Falkirk. His shear physique must have made opponents shudder, but he was nimble into the bargain. To make sure the defence had adequate cover, Nigel Adkins also asked the question at Birmingham City about the possibility of borrowing Kristian Pearce. What started as a few months away from home, ended as a full season loan for the tall competent young black lad.

Once the defence was sorted out, Nigel went back to Barnsley to take another middle of the park player from the Yorkshire club. Sam Togwell was soon to settle down with his old team colleague, Grant McCann, and quickly became a strong cog in the gearing.

The forward line was the ultimate section to be fiddled with, and Nigel took three men for this section of the field using his expert judge of talent. From Morecambe he brought in an attacking wide man, Gary Thompson, who had a keen eye for a direct shot into the net. He would connect with Martin Woolford, a non-League player at York City, who looked to have the qualities of a player going places. Call him an attacker or an advanced midfielder, it matters not. Martin would be another string to the bow. The last of the trio was a young dark haired lad called Gary Hooper, discovered at Southend United. He was shy of all publicity and was only interested in playing football, but above all, scoring goal after goal. Gary Hooper would be the equivalent of a lottery win for Nigel Adkins and Scunthorpe United.

Once everybody was in place, Scunthorpe United prepared for the first test of 2008-09, which was a clash with the fallen giants of Leeds United, and Glanford Park was packed to the rafters. Scunthorpe were without Joe Murphy for the first couple of matches of the campaign, and Josh Lillis competently took the gloves. What followed was a tingling game containing a thrill each minute. Gary Hooper scored his debut Scunthorpe goal, but Leeds United equalised, and a face well known to Iron fans, Jermaine Beckford, scored the winner for the visitors.

In mid-week, United had to travel up the A1 in the direction of Hartlepool, for a League Cup tie, and the event turned out to be a complete disaster. Not only did they play badly and lose 3-0, but Kenny Milne suffered a knee injury which would keep him out for the rest of the season. Matters did not improve at the end of the week, in Walsall. David Mirfin was deemed to have fouled as the last man, and received an early red card. United struggled with just ten men and recorded a second defeat.

It was not until Joe Murphy resumed duty that the tide began to turn, not that it was the fault of Josh Lillis in any way. The initial victory came next to the M181, when Peterborough United dropped in. Any folks going for an early half time pie might have missed seeing Paul Hayes stroke home the penalty winner, but like the pies, it was pukka!

This victory was the prelude to the Scunthorpe United wagon starting to roll, and once it was at speed the points began to flow. The team went on a run of nine unbeaten games, only two of which were drawn. The goals came from all round the field, but in particular, from the boot of Gary Hooper, who was an instantaneous hit. Perhaps the highlight of the run was a 4-1 victory at the Withdean Stadium against Brighton. Martin Woolford set the ball rolling, but afterwards Gary Hooper danced his way to a hat-trick.

Another of the results during this time was the beating of Millwall, which silenced the excitable visiting supporters, but not until the final note on the referee's whistle. McCann and Togwell put in a lot of spade work in the middle of the pitch, and this assisted a 3-0 lead after an hour of toil. Goals from Gary Hooper, Paul Hayes, a penalty, and the flight of Matt Sparrow produced the magic moments for the home fanatics. Scunthorpe did not have time for a breather, because the hungry Lions pulled back two goals in quick succession. The last ten minutes were understandably tense, but the 3-2 result briefly lifted the Iron to the pinnacle of the table.

At the beginning of the season, Nigel Adkins named two priorities for the team to achieve. One was the return to the Championship, and the other was to win the Johnstone's Paint Trophy. The journey on the Trophy front was kindly aided by a series of home draws from the numbered balls leaving the bag. Scunthorpe United made positive progress by beating Notts County, Grimsby Town, Rochdale and Tranmere Rovers. More than once they looked to be in for a tumble, but picked themselves up with last minute goals.

Their conquests led them to the Northern Final over two legs, after the New Year, against Rotherham United. In the First Leg, the Iron were untouchable, but only had a 2-0 advantage, because of some outstanding goalkeeping by the visiting custodian. Supporters cheered second half strikes by Martin Woolford and Kristian Pearce. This put a lot of pressure on Rotherham at the Don Valley Stadium. The only chance they had was to conjure up an early goal, but when it did not mature, the odds were on a Scunthorpe Wembley Final. Time was ticking away when on the far side of the field, miles away from the nearest supporters, Gary Hooper efficiently fired the ball from the left and past the keepers outstretched arm.

Running parallel with this competition, United had the usual travels in the F.A.Cup competition. In the First Round they returned to the scene of an earlier disaster at Walsall, but this time their would be no blunder at the Bescot. Although former England player Michael Ricketts blasted Walsall in front, Gary Hooper was just as accurate with his chance to restore parity, before the tea break. Hooper then increased his ranking with a second stinging shot, which put the Iron comfortably in the lead at 2-1. The clinching goal did not mature until the last minute. Nigel Adkins swapped Martin Woolford for the fresh legs of Kevan Hurst. One of his first acts was to send a stunning drive from, twenty five yards out, into the top of the net without the Saddlers keeper able to blink an eye. United won 3-1 to retrieve some pride for previous errors.

The luck of the draw favoured the Iron with a home tie in conflict with the brave non-Leaguers of Alfreton Town. It gave them the opportunity to wish all the best to their former keeper Tommy Evans, who wore the jersey for the Derbyshire minnows. Tommy was warmly applauded by the appreciative crowd, before the match was given the green light. Conditions at Glanford Park were not ideal, as fog masked a clear outline of the players. Scunthorpe put in a workman like performance, and eased into the lead with Ben May's baptism goal. When others were registered by Gary Hooper on two occasions and a fourth by Sam Togwell, United supporters left the ground in a happy mood. Tommy would have left with mixed emotions.

Gary Hooper makes his way through the fog and is about to score in the F.A.Cup versus Alfreton.

The benefit of beating Alfreton was to take a further tour, this time to Watford, for the third hurdle. It may not have been the most entertaining spectacle, but the Iron played an enterprising game, without testing the Championship goalkeeper. In the end they were out of luck and lost by a goal from on loan Polish player, Grzegorz Rasiak.

At New Year, Scunthorpe United lay in sixth place in the table, thanks to dropping points in two drawn fixtures, and the 2-0 loss at the Galpharm Stadium against Huddersfield Town. This position was maintained throughout the colder months, and boosted when the double was completed over Millwall, in the Lion's Den. Despite the intimidating atmosphere, the Iron retrieved the situation from a goal in arrears, with two very late efforts by Gary Hooper.

Nigel Adkins decided to use his loan card in these Winter months, and he introduced three talented players into team affairs. Henri Lansbury was a little dynamo to add power to the mid-field. He was a great success during a spell borrowed from Arsenal, and had the ability to spice a game up with an odd goal. From Southampton Scunthorpe had the assistance of defender Joseph Mills, a slightly built young man with a hot turn of speed.

To added extra meat in the sandwich, Kayode Odejayi was introduced for a short period from Barnsley. This black player was to be a forward with a good physical presence, and also registered a goal in his Glanford Park stay. The final loaned player was a tall useful mid-field man, called Liam Trotter. Liam was an Ipswich player, who impressed sufficiently that Nigel looked to take him on full time, but it did not happen.

The concluding two months of the season was to be busier than ever, and some of the extra bodies certainly helped to share the burden of the work load. Scunthorpe United entered April on the edge of the Play-Off positions, but became focused on the Wembley Final in the Johnstone's Paint Trophy with Southern winners Luton Town. The game was scheduled to be played on Sunday April 5th 2009. A fleet of around fifty buses ferried a large part of an estimated 12,000 Scunthorpe supporters to London, where they were out numbered by Luton supporters in the total crowd of 55,378. It was the greatest attendance at any Scunthorpe United match in over one hundred years of their history.

Scunthorpe United lined up for this historic occasion as follows; Murphy, Byrne, Williams, McCann, Mirfin, Pearce, Landsbury, Sparrow, Hayes, Hooper and Hurst. During the match Wright, Woolford and Togwell were introduced as substitutes for Pearce, Sparrow and Hurst. The Final was played at a fast tempo and contained a lot of good football and goals. Gary Hooper opened the scoring for Scunthorpe, when he fastened on to a ball, fractionally to the right side of the centre of the park and lashed home a shot in the fourteenth minute. Luton Town equalised on the half hour, but just before the interval Cliff Byrne was seen laying on the floor clutching his face. The officials saw nothing, but the pundits on the television voiced some interesting thoughts of their own.

In the second section of the game the play swayed back and forth, and either side could have put away a chance. It was finally left to Tom Craddock to put Luton Town in the driving seat, but just as the Hatters were looking at their watches to see how long was left, Scunthorpe United dug out an leveller. In the eighty eighth minute the ball broke clear to Grant McCann from a melee, and he return it from the edge of the penalty box, flying into the top of the net.

Extra time involved the managers giving words of encouragement, and the demands on players to find more energy from somewhere. In the final analysis, the goal that decided the destination of the trophy came from a mix up in the Scunthorpe defence, five minutes after the restart. In the incident, an effort to try to clear the ball saw it cannoned into the unguarded net, making the result 3-2, and Claude Gnapka was credited with scoring.

When Scunthorpe United returned to the bread and butter of the Division One, their fixtures were rapidly coming to an end. Two draws and a win set up an interesting scenario for the visit of Tranmere, the last of the forty six match schedule. Should Scunthorpe avoid defeat they would qualify for the Play-Offs, but a loss handed Tranmere the same opportunity.

The intrigue of the situation packed 8,029 people into the ground, and supporters appreciated that the men from the Wirral were the best team of the first half. Five minutes before the half time whistle it was the Rovers that went ahead. Scunthorpe United knocked on their door throughout the second period, and had to be patient for their chance of a leveller. It came with two minutes of the season remaining, and the consequence of a needless free kick. The ball came from left to right across the box, and there was the skipper, the inspirational Cliff Byrne, in support of the front runners, to head home. The single point saw the Iron shuffle into the final Play-Off place, and learned that they would play M.K.Dons.

On the evening of the First Leg of the Division One Play-Offs, Scunthorpe United had the home advantage. In defence they had pulled out a secret weapon. It was the towering figure of that old war horse, Andy Crosby. He was given a run in the last half a dozen games, and found the legs still worked, and he could not wait for the challenge. The whole team gave one hundred percent during a warm ninety minutes, but had to be content with a 1-1 draw, handing advantage to the Dons at Stadium M.K.

On the Friday evening of the Second Leg, Scunthorpe United gave a performance as hard as the steel at the Tata Works. Andy Crosby was at the heart of operations, ably assisted by Cliff Byrne. Each of the attacks by the M.K.Dons were systematically repelled and United had odd chances of their own. Time went agonisingly slowly, but half time led to full time and a further thirty minutes of extra time concluded that section of the contest. United had held out, with no goal being scored by either fraction. Now the sweat drenched troops had the pleasures of a penalty shoot out.

The drama of the evening was far from over, and hearts would be in mouths for quite some time yet. Scunthorpe started the ball rolling with the first penalty. McCann scored, Leven scored, Hayes scored, Wilbraham scored Crosby scored, Navarro scored, but at 3-3 Cliff Byrne missed, but fortunately Joe Murphy saved from Puncheon. Trotter scored next for the Iron, and Llera for the Dons, making it 4-4 going into sudden death. The temperature rose as Sparrow missed, then with Wembley beckoning, so did Stirling. Forte, Lewington, Togwell and goalkeeper Gueret all converted consecutive kicks to bring the score up to 6-6. Ian Morris took a deep breath and hammered another into the net to put Scunthorpe United ahead once more. Next to the spotlight was the tallest man on the park, Norwegian International Andre Flo. He placed the ball on the mark, took a nervous step back, then blazed the ball high into the seats at the back of the stadium. Scunthorpe United were through, and everyone went deliriously wild with understandable excitement.

Scunthorpe United would face Millwall at Wembley on Sunday May 24th 2009, to decide which club would be handed a set of Championship fixtures for the coming season. The Club sold close to 10,000 tickets for the second journey in the matter of six weeks to Wembley, and their supporters were out numbered by almost five to one in the 59,661 attendance, another extension to the biggest Scunthorpe United crowd ever to watch them play. Millwall supporters could have a lay in bed on the morning of the game, and their opinion was that they only needed to turn up to claim promotion. United followers began the journey to Wembley starting at 4am, and knew it was strength in the team, not numbers on the terraces that would win the day. Scunthorpe United walked out onto the neat Wembley turf in boiling hot conditions, using the following men; Murphy, Byrne, Morris, Mirfin, Crosby, Sparrow, Togwell, Hayes, Hooper and Woolford. During the game Togwell was relieved by Trotter and Forte came on to replace Hooper.

It was said that the Scunthorpe and Millwall Play-Off Final was one of the best on record. From start to finish it was exciting, played at a high tempo was refreshingly open and contained numerous goal incidents. Scunthorpe managed to get off to a tremendous start by scoring after six minutes of play. Matt Sparrow was the first to react, when Martin Woolford's shot had been blocked, and the Wembley born Iron took his chance close to the goal.

Although Scunthorpe controlled much of the early play, they went into the tunnel 2-1 down at the break. Gary Alexander was the hero for the Londoners, scoring twice immediately before half time, one of which was a thunder bolt of sheer quality, which hit the net before Joe Murphy could move.

Scunthorpe United support could not believe the Iron were in arrears, because they had played so well. Nigel Adkins must have told everyone not to panic and if they all did their jobs, the situation would return to their favour. Any doubts would soon be settled, but it took until the seventieth minute before Scunthorpe found an equaliser. It was Martin Woolford who helped unlocked the Millwall defence, when he burst in from down the left and squared the ball to Matt Sparrow on the other side of the box. Sparrow juggled the ball from right foot to left, which put keeper Forde off his balance and Matt lashed the ball home. The noise greeting the goal was deafening.

Millwall in all honesty should have gone ahead, but Alexander missed a guilt edge chance with a header. History dictates that the coup de grace arrived with five minutes showing on the clock. Scunthorpe United won a free kick, which allowed a chance to fall to Paul Hayes. His shot was only partially cleared, and when the ball rebounded to Martin Woolford, he smacked it low and hard into the Lion's net. The Wembley score board announced a Scunthorpe 3-2 lead, and time soon ran out for Millwall. A roar went up from the Lincolnshire section of the ground to hail the team.

After the final whistle Cliff Byrne smiled all the way up the Wembley steps, leading the rest of his proud team, to receive the honour of a trophy and the deserved medals of victory. The Scunthorpe United achievement was remarkable, and when the champagne corks popped the feeling was amazing. Everyone took time to drink in the victory, knowing how rare these sort of moments are for a club of the stature of Scunthorpe United. The weary band of supporters made their way back to Lincolnshire with pride in their hearts, and the road appeared to be just a little bit shorter.

It was congratulations all round, especially to Nigel Adkins and his staff, the players led by dear old Cliff, and the Chairman Mr. Wharton, on behalf of the board of directors. If anyone should be singled out for special praise then Gary Hooper would take that honour, on account of his twenty four goals. The team received another invitation to a dinner at Normanby Hall, and supporters were out in force for another open top bus tour.

Martin Woolford fires the ball into the net for the Iron's winner in the Play-Off Final.

Cliff Byrne raises the Play-Off trophy to the delight of the team, in May 2009.

2009-10

The 2009-10 season saw the absence of four key players that won promotion. Izzy Iriekpen had left the Club in the New Year, and Kristian Pearce returned to his parent club at Birmingham. Kevan Hurst was released to become a Carlisle United team player, and dear old Andy Cosby hung up his boots to assist Nigel full time.
On his way into Glanford Park was six feet seven inches tall Rob Jones, a central defender from Hibernians, in Scotland. He had captained the Edinburgh club and won a Scottish League Cup medal with them, hence a record £700,000 was attached to his transfer. Then for the middle of the park, Josh Wright departed Charlton for Scunthorpe. Although slightly built, Josh showed all the skills needed for engineering in the Championship. He who link up with another well balanced Irish import, when Michael O'Connor left Crewe for £250,000. Michael was acquainted with Grant McCann through his International caps.

During the first half of the new campaign, United brought in a West Ham junior player to cover the defence. He was Jordan Spence and the loan deal was extended to a couple of months. At the heart of the defence, Niall Canavan was introduced for first team duty as a central pivot from the second eleven. It was obvious that this tall lad was a going places and was a tribute to the efforts of Scunthorpe United's backroom staff. Although his chances were limited, Niall would get regular employment, given time.

Scunthorpe United could not have been handed a more formidable opening fixture to the campaign. Cardiff City welcomed them to the brand new Cardiff City Stadium, and a huge crowd wanted the Iron served up on a plate. The Bluebirds did not disappoint, and United were crushed 4-0. One week later and the thumping was forgotten, because in mid-week progress was made in the League Cup over Chesterfield. Then on the Saturday, a healthy crowd witnessed Scunthorpe United obtain three points at the expense of Nigel Clough's Derby County. It was a particularly encouraging and entertaining performance. Gary Hooper fired them into a 2-1 lead at the break. In the second half the Rams found equaliser, but Martin Woolford nipped in to send the ball low into the net, completing a 3-2 victory.

The rest of August yielded no more points, but September started with an incredible 4-0 win on the road, at Crystal Palace. The goals came from all round the park, as Jonathon Forte, Paul Hayes, Sam Togwell and Michael O'Connor all pencilled their names on the marksmen sheet. The Palace embarrassment was compounded when Murphy kept a penalty out. The week continued on a positive note, and three more points were added to the total, as Preston North End came unstuck under the lights at Glanford Park, four days later. Grant McCann opened the scoring, but a brace of goals from Gary Hooper put the seal on their 3-1 authority.

Meanwhile, the League Cup required a lengthy journey to South Wales, to meet Swansea City.

Defending in numbers at Ashton Gate against Bristol City. United earned a point from a last minute Grant McCann equaliser.

Less than one hundred Scunthonians made the mid-week trek, and those who did saw a memorable match. Niall Canavan headed the Iron into an early thirteenth minute lead, but Swansea equalised with ten minutes to play, and extra time was necessary. Late in the match the Swansea team let their discipline deteriorate and remarkably had three men shown red cards. One of the incidents resulted in a penalty, which Gary Hooper gratefully accepted, and Scunthorpe United kept their own heads to win 2-1.

The Third Round of the League Cup, sponsored by Carling, was a much more pedestrian affair in comparison, and brought Port Vale to the other side of Doncaster Road. No goals was scored in the first ninety minutes, but five minutes into the extra period Paul Hayes scored the goal that put the Iron further into the competition than they had ever ventured. It gave hope of a Fourth Round tie with one of the bid boys, and when the draw was made, the Scunthorpe United ball came out of the bag immediately after that of Manchester City.

The Fourth Round tie at the City of Manchester Stadium encouraged 36,358 supporters to leave the comfort of the fireside to watch the game. Those folk who hoped for an upset would be disappointed, and City raced into a three minutes lead. Jonathan Forte had the joy of an equaliser, when the ball was squared to him for a simple side foot into the open net. From that point on it was the light blue shirts of Manchester City team that displayed the skills of their world class players, and relaxed when the score totted up to 5-1 for the evening.

When Scunthorpe returned to Championship action, they went through a threadbare patch during the Autumn, and did not recover until December. To try to add some spice to the bowl, Nigel brought in a number of loaned men. These included George Friend, a tall defender from Wolves, Bonz N'Gala, another defender of West Ham and Brendon Moloney, a well built mid-fielder from Forest. There were brief chances in goal for Josh Lillis and Sam Slocombe when Joe Murphy could not play in goal.

The Winter of 2009 cum 2010 was a particularly severe one, and Graham Colby and his crew were continuously covering the pitch with ground sheets to keep out the frosts to avoid postponements. In the first week of the New Year, they worked particularly hard to see that the F.A.Cup tie at home to Barnsley went ahead. Home advantage was put to good use, and Paul Hayes rifled United into the next round, with the only shot to reach the back of the net. Another highlight of the match was the return of Kenny Milne as a substitute, after a year and a half fighting the knee injury sustained at Hartlepool. Unfortunately, the his return was a brief one, but Iron fans did get a short glimpse of what might have been from a quality player.

The story of the Iron effort to gather more Championship points continued with arguably the beat performance of the season, on a date immediately after the Barnsley F.A.Cup tie. On January 9th the team rolled up a freezing Pride Park to play Derby County, on a day when three quarters of football was knocked out by the weather. Only under soil heating save the match, but it saw United use the wide open spaces to great effect.

Scunthorpe became one of four side to beat Champions Newcastle United (2-1). Martin Woolford slides in to score the second goal in the 2-1 victory.

Gary Hooper hit a crisp shot to gain them a lead on the quarter hour, and right up on the break Gary Thompson seized on an opportunity to fire in for a handsome 2-0 lead.

The second half brought Derby County back into action, no doubt Nigel Clough would have put a sting their ears during his interval chat. Scunthorpe fought hard to protect Josh Lillis in goal, but conceded an own goal on the hour, credited against Marcus Williams, but it was hardly his fault. At this point the Iron could have crumbled, and the County certainly missed one guilt edge chance that they would have put away on another day. Instead, it was the Scunthorpe fans that were to be applauding next, when a sweet ball was pushed through on the carpet for Gary Thompson to drill low into the net with only ten minutes left on the clock. Not content with matters as they were, Jonathan Forte had the last word, and emptied the home terraces with a shot that zipped in the back of the net, making the all important score 4-1.

In the Fourth Round of the F.A.Cup, the gods blessed Scunthorpe United with another meeting against the mighty Manchester City, but this time City would have to travel. The tie brought attention from the media, and the television cameras were in evidence around the ground ready for the showdown on January 24th 2010. The pattern of play followed a similar path, as in the last confrontation. The Citizens took an early lead, but Paul Hayes fashioned an equaliser. Manchester City eventually began to exert their authority, and in the second half took a 3-1 advantage. Scunthorpe needed full credit for a never say die attitude, and a crossed ball on sixty nine minutes found the back of the net. Boyata was said to have had the last touch, but Cliff Byrne was extremely close to the action. It took a piece of Brazilian magic from £32M Robinho to seal a highly entertaining afternoon at 4-2 to Manchester City.

Scunthorpe United continued to cling to the edge of safety and enhanced their survival chances in March with a trio of consecutive wins over Plymouth and Peterborough at home, while Sheffield United were played away at Bramall Lane.

April was a tough month for them, and they found points difficult to squeeze out. At the bottom Peterborough and Plymouth found their positions terminal. When the final two weeks of matches approached, the last relegation place would be bought by either Scunthorpe United, Sheffield Wednesday or Crystal Palace. The Iron did have one clear advantage, because Palace and Wednesday had to meet at Hillsborough in the final round of fixtures.

Scunthorpe United still had one game in hand over Sheffield Wednesday, and that was at home to a much improved Reading under new management. The maths stated that a draw was enough for Scunthorpe to continue their Championship dream. Reading, playing in green, were not to be found in a charitable mood, and stole a 2-0 lead as the second half progressed. It looked as if it might still end in tears, until Gary Hooper drove home a wonderful shot to give some hope. Then Matt Sparrow turned the ball into the net for an unlikely equaliser right up in the closing minute.

Nigel Adkins and his team went wild with delight, as did the 5,000 supporters with Scunthorpe at heart. They could now enjoy the couple matches of the season, the first of with was an uninhibited 4-3 loss at the Keepmoat Stadium, against Doncaster Rovers. The calendar finished with the traditional Sunday fixture in the Championship, against Nottingham Forest, while others worried about their own safety. In the end, Wednesday could not use home soil to beat a resolute Palace, and a draw sent them tumbling down to Division One.

Scunthorpe United, as usual, earned a 2-2 draw with the Forest the hard way, coming back on the rails from a two goal deficit, thanks to scores by Niall Canavan and Gary Thompson, who had a strong season as a front runner.

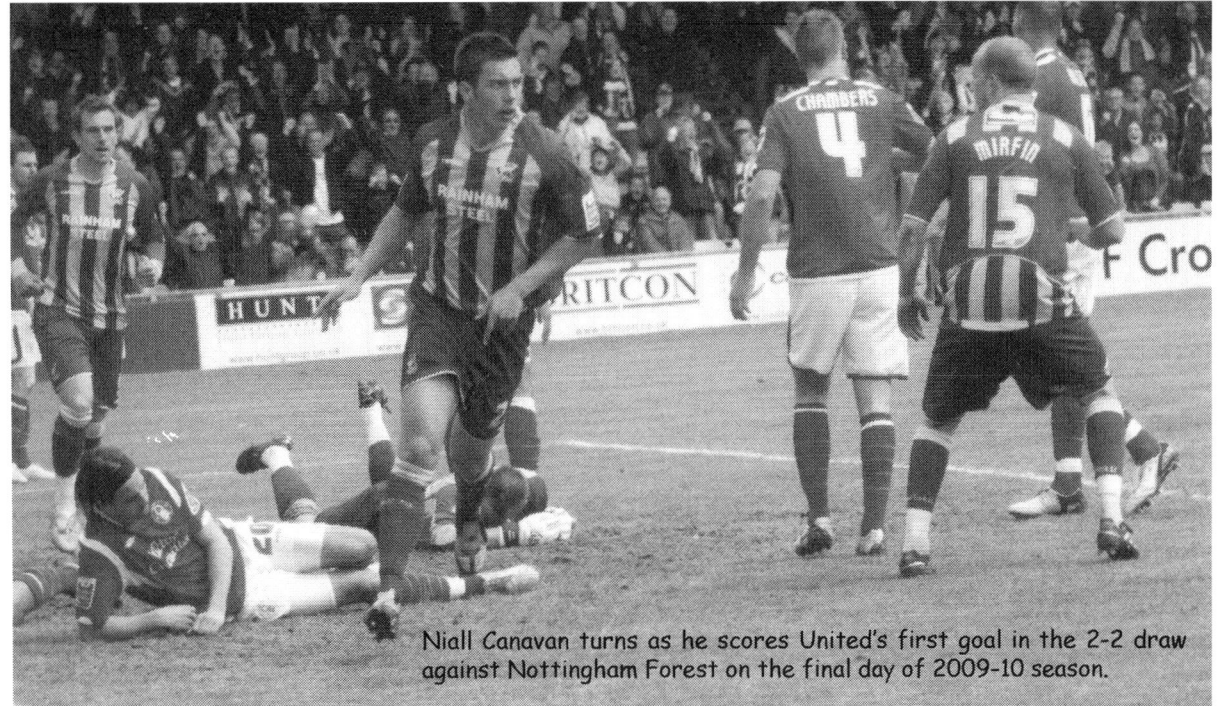

Niall Canavan turns as he scores United's first goal in the 2-2 draw against Nottingham Forest on the final day of 2009-10 season.

2010-11

During the closed season the news from Glanford Park was devastating for Scunthorpe United supporters, as a long list of senior players joined a queue to leave the Club for better contracts elsewhere. Grant McCann, the mechanic in the engine room, departed for Peterborough United. Matt Sparrow, man and boy at the Iron, checked out for Brighton and Hove Albion. Paul Hayes, the scoring wizard of two spells with the Club was going to Preston North End. Marcus Williams, part of the trainee scheme, off to Reading. Gary Hooper, the goal scoring genius of the last two campaigns, had a saga all of his own, but at least when it was resolved for him to go North to Glasgow Celtic, there was a £2M cheque to float the way of Scunthorpe United. The team had a massive hole blown in it and the implications would be far reaching.

In an attempt to repair some of the damage, Nigel Adkins went shopping. For the forward line he chose Chris Dagnall from Rochdale and Bobby Grant of Accrington Stanley. Each of them were of slight build, but had shown that they could find the net in the lower divisions. Now was the time to step up a gear, and score in a higher sphere. They were accompanied by Michael Collins for the middle of the team, who had shown himself to be a capable player more than two hundred times for Huddersfield Town.

The defence was to be boosted by an Irish lad, with a good turn of speed, when Eddie Nolan put pen to paper. At first it was as a loan deal from Preston North End, but the Iron saw his potential, and made it a permanent move. Late in the previous season United took a look at Jim McNulty, on loan from Brighton. This loan was repeated at the start of the season, but the Club never reaped the best of this full back, because of injury, and nothing more would come of it.

Despite the severest of setbacks, Scunthorpe United rolled up at Reading on the opening day of the fixture card and confounded critics by winning 2-1. This was followed by consecutive defeats, at home to Norwich and in London at Q.P.R. Returning to the sunnier side of Lincolnshire, the Iron entertained Crystal Palace, who paraded Edgar Davids, an old Dutch master, in their ranks. He wore his customary black goggles, but was never allowed to show any of his old tricks. This was Scunthorpe's day to shine, and they waltzed to a 3-0 tune, as Jonathan Forte scored twice, and Michael O'Connor slid home a spot kick.

Meanwhile, in the Carling League Cup, Scunthorpe United were handed a invitation to host Oldham Athletic in the First Round. A small crowd of 2,602 turned out on a pleasantly warm evening to see the Iron overcome a goal deficit, to win 2-1. The Second Round of the competition enabled supporters to have another walk up the Doncaster Road as they entertained Sheffield Wednesday. The Owls demonstrated that they were a well drilled side, but could not match the fluidity of the Iron. Scunthorpe United cruised to a 4-2 result, and looked forward to the news of the next round draw. When it came supporters could not believe their good fortune. For the first time in the history of the Club, they would play a competitive game against the mighty Manchester United.

Before the big day Scunthorpe United and its followers were to be rocked to its very foundations.

Rumour had it that a big City club had its eye on Nigel Adkins and wished to lure him away and gain the same sort of success that the Iron had experienced. It appeared that Southampton were courting Nigel's favour, and after a week of speculation he left Glanford Park on September 12th 2010, taking Andy Crosby with him.

Michael O'Connor smartly dispatches a penalty in the 3-0 beating of Crystal Palace in August 2010.

Once again the future of the Club was in turmoil, but Chairman Steve Wharton acted swiftly. Within a short time he approached Ian Baraclough and asked him to take over and become the new Scunthorpe United Manager. Ian was a quiet and honest man who pledged to do his best. He made Kevin Pressman the Assistant Manager, while Steve Parkin slipped into his own former role, to organise the coaching of the team. The new management team was in place on Wednesday September 22nd 2010 for the arrival of Manchester United.

At kick-off a record crowd for Glanford Park of 9,077 made sure that no inch of space was unoccupied in the ground.

Sir Alex Ferguson had his own reasons for not attending, but Mick Phelan was in place instead, and the match was televised, so he would not miss any of the action. There was even a special souvenir programme for folks to digest. After the first turn of the ball, Scunthorpe United had the vast gathering warm to their approach on the game. They showed excellent control, and neat passing. The Iron even produced the surprise of the evening, by starting the score board rolling in the nineteenth minute. Josh Wright had not stamped his authority as a goal scorer at the Club, but now was his moment. He took a ball to the left of centre, about twenty five yards from the goal, then let fly a shot that went like a dart, passing through the triangle made by the post and cross bar.

For the time being that was as good as it would get, because the Manchester United stars took over. Their passing was as smooth as silk, and each football brain was that of an Einstein. Gibson had the Reds level, Michael Owen registered a hat-trick, and Park scored another to make the journey worth it for the travelling fans, some of which did not travel too far. At the very end, Martin Woolford gave Iron fans another cheer, as he rounded off the score at 5-2. There could be no arguments on the evening, but the occasion would stay longer in the minds of Scunthorpe fanatics, than in the memories of the visitors.

It was not too long into his reign that Ian Baraclough dipped into the loan market and borrowed an attacking mid-field player namely Freddie Sears, from West Ham.

Martin Woolford and Eddie Nolan steal possession against Manchester United's Ji-Sung Park, in the League Cup tie.

He also needed an emergency goalkeeper, Tony Warner, once of Hull City, when Joe Murphy became injured. Within a month, Kevin McDonald, a Scotsman who had been with Burnley, was utilised for five substitute appearances in the middle of the park. All of these players were desperately needed, because home wins had totally dried up, and it was not until February that the situation would alter.

On the road, the Iron did pick up some comfort, but it was insufficient to stop them being anchored firmly in the relegation places. They did pick up back to back away wins at Preston and Watford. It was then that a 4-1 loss at Glanford Park, to the White Roses of Leeds United, began the slide in home form. Another three points did come their way at the K.C. Stadium, when Michael O'Connor stole in from nowhere to hit an only goal from close range, right up on the whistle.

The run up to Christmas brought no presents at all for Scunthorpe United, and five consecutive defeats made supporters feel desperate. There was a brief respite at Burnley, in the last fixture of 2010, at a cold Turf Moor. United raised the tempo of their game and beat the other team of claret and blue 2-0. Unfortunately, this result brought the wrath of the Burnley faithful and it resulted in the dismissal of their manager, the former Iron favourite, Brian Laws.

January saw the Iron have a week off from Championship activities, for an outing in the F.A.Cup. They would meet Premiership opposition for the second time in the season, when Everton were drawn at home. A gate of 7028 filed into Glanford Park, on one of the coldest days of the worst Winters for many years. Once again, the team did their best, but were outclassed by the ability of the Merseyside giants. A 5-1 loss was a reflection in the difference of skills between the clubs, but did not tell the tale of United's hard toil.

The January transfer window brought Scunthorpe United as the focus of a considerable amount of activity, and supporters needed to take notes to keep abreast of the dealings. Rob Jones was taken on loan to Sheffield Wednesday, with a view to a permanent transfer, which finally was approved. Martin Woolford, the scorer of the Wembley decider, went to the South West, at Bristol City, and with his move a cheque of £200,000 was said to have been banked. Finally, Nigel Adkins returned to do business with his former club, and paid an undisclosed amount for Jonathan Forte.

In an attempt to alter a rapidly deteriorating position, Ian Baraclough put a lot of eggs in his claret and blue basket. For the central defence he brought in Paul Reid from Colchester, and Michael Nelson of Norwich. Nelson had played for the Canaries, when they plundered the points from Glanford Park, earlier in the year. Both were big powerful men. They were joined by Ben Gordon, a speedy full back from Chelsea, noticed on loan at Kilmarnock. Ian then boosted the middle of the park with Andy Hughes of Leeds United, a player equally at home as a defender, and Mark Duffy from Morecambe, who enjoyed the wide attacking role whenever he could. In attack, Baraclough introduced a little and large combination, with the acquisition of petit Joe Garner on loan from Nottingham Forest, and the big Scotsman Lee Miller, late of Middlesbrough.

The new men had no time to adjust before they were pitched into battle, but results were no better than before. A 3-2 victory over Sheffield United, another club in trouble, was a rare oasis in a desert of disasters. Ian Baraclough looked to be a lonely man on the touchline, as his efforts to improve the team came to nothing. The final straw came one Tuesday evening in a must win game, at home to Preston North end. Instead of coming out all guns blazing, the team capitulated to a humiliating 3-0 loss. Two days later, on March 17th 2011 and the sad news broke that Ian Baraclough had been dismissed from office, but it was not unexpected. The board thanked him for all the work he had achieved, and supporters remembered him for all the valuable contribution he had made to the unbelievable success that had come the way of the Club since he arrival in 2004.

Once again, the Club was in the hands of the backroom staff, guided by Tony Daws and Lee Turnbull. During this state of transition, arrangements were made to bring in Ramon Nunez, a small man on the books of Leeds United from Honduras. He was an instant hit as an attacking midfield player, and was no stranger to hitting the target. At the same time United knocked on the door at Reading to borrow Marcus Williams for the final month of the campaign.

When the last signing had been put into place, United announced on March 31st 2011 that former Scunthorpe player, Alan Knill, would leave his post in charge at Bury to succeed Ian Baraclough. He only had a brief chance to meet the players before the match at Norwich on the following Saturday. Norwich were hell bent on promotion to the Premiership, and Alan Knill was horrified to see his new charges walloped 6-0. The cause was not aided by a sending off early in the match, which not only reduced numbers, but conceded a penalty from which a goal was scored.

The result at Norwich plummeted the Iron to the base of the table, but they regrouped seven days later, to host the League leaders, Queens Park Rangers. Rangers took the initiative with a goal by Hulse on seven minutes, but the Iron rallied and at the end of the ninety minutes held a freak 4-1 lead. They may have just deserved to win, but the goals by Joe Garner, a brace, Michael O'Connor and Mark Duffy flattered the Iron to a degree.

Paddy Kenny is stranded in the Q.P.R. goal as Joe Garner dispatches the ball in the 4-1 win.

The arrival of Alan Knill could not disguise that fact that the willing bunch of players were struggling to keep up with the demands of Championship football. Hopes rose again when United put up a gutsy performance, which beat Crystal Palace 2-1 in London, but faded over Easter when they drew at Coventry and missed the boat, with a poor result at home to Millwall. The 1-2 score guaranteed that Scunthorpe United would be relegated back to Division One.

In the penultimate game, the team took another thrashing, 5-1 at Nottingham Forest. However, the lads went out on a slightly better note, drawing 1-1 with Portsmouth at home, as the curtain came down on the season. There had been optimism that Scunthorpe United would not receive the wooden spoon, especially after the Portsmouth fixture. Results elsewhere meant that the Iron finished with the same number of points as Sheffield United and Preston, but with the worse goal difference.

2011-12

Confirmation of United's relegation soon hit home. The most damaging effect was the loss of almost £4M in television fees. This would mean that they would have to unload the high earners which had taken them to the Championship. With this in mind Joe Murphy, David Mirfin and Josh Wright were allowed to speak to other clubs and not offered new contracts. They would find employment at Coventry, Watford and Millwall respectively. Alan Knill then looked to offload as many of the Ian Baraclough signings as he could, to make room for some of his own imports.

Despite being restricted by the purse strings, Alan Knill initially added two Irishmen to the squad. He brought in Jimmy Ryan, a mid-field man with a quick turn of speed, from Accrington Stanley. This was a permanent signature, but Shane Duffy, a tall central defender, was a half season loan from Everton.

He would play alongside Niall Canavan, a young man who would gain confidence as the other central defender, while the season unfolded.

Adding to the Club's different Nationalities, Knill took on board a useful black French lad, who would patrol the middle section of the park with Jimmy Ryan. This was Damien Mozika, who showed himself to be a neat artist, when signed from Bury, but injury cost the Iron his services for a lengthy spell in the first part of the season. While he was out of the picture Oliver Norwood was loaned for a couple of months from Manchester United. He was of similar style, fitting into the team to the satisfaction of everyone.

Alan Knill also added to the forward end of the team when he offered terms to Andy Barcham, who had been player of the season at Gillingham, and Jordan Robertson, a big man who could hold the ball up, once of Sheffield United. Both of these became full signatures for Scunthorpe United. The only other addition came shortly into the campaign, when the goalkeeping position needed cover after Josh Lillis received an injury which kept him out for a number of months. Through his Manchester United contacts, Alan was able to give Sam Johnstone a two month loan period, but Sam Slocombe pressed him hard for the gloves, and eventually took over in the New Year.

The season opened on the road at Wycombe Wanderers, a club that had won promotion in the previous campaign. Iron followers had to be content with a 1-1 draw, but felt they should have won it after Michael Nelson scored the first of the campaign. They even had a last minute winner chalked off by a linesman's flag. Their travels continued in mid-week, when they visited the small Fraser Eagle Stadium of Accrington Stanley, in the League Cup. On this occasion, Accrington had much of the early play, but the Iron just needed to be patient and won with a late show from a Chris Dagnall penalty and a superb low drive from Andy Barcham.

The reward for beating Accrington was a plum tie, at home to Newcastle United. It brought extra cash from the attention of the television cameras, and Scunthorpe United played well above their station. They took the lead through Chris Dagnall, when he struck the ball home, after a corner incident allowed Michael Nelson to head the ball down to him. It was not until the eightieth minutes that Taylor scored Newcastle's equaliser, then Ameobi hit the winner for the Magpies in extra time.

In the League, Scunthorpe United could not find the killer instinct to gain a win. Injuries were not helping the situation, and Cliff Byrne had still to kick a ball. United did enjoy some entertaining draws, particularly with Sheffield United at home, and away at Charlton Athletic. Scunthorpe were 2-0 down, when Bobby Grant netted twice late on at the Valley. The first win did not arrive until the tenth match, at home to Yeovil at the end of September. Ironically, the next victory was in the following game, on a particularly hot October day at Stevenage. The 2-1 result came with numerous scares right up until the final whistle, and was far from convincing, but most welcomed. The general trend was not towards the comfort of mid-table, but in a downward spiral, as results continued to disappoint. Only three matches had yielded three points before November arrived.

Toi sharpen the defence, one of the shrewdest loan signing made by Alan Knill in 2012 was the return of David Mirfin from Watford, pictured here against M.K. Dons.

In November the team had a break when they went to the South side of London to play Wimbledon, in the First Round of the F.A.Cup. On the afternoon, they played a better game than their opponents, but failed to find the net. It was something they would be punished for in the replayed match, at Glanford Park. Scunthorpe put in another reasonable performance, but failed where it mattered most. Wimbledon scored with one of their few chances and deserved to go through. When the Iron returned to League action they continued to be the draw specialists, and it was thanks to these odds and ends that the points total kept ticking over. The lack of victories sent them to the wrong end of the table, and on Boxing Day a 3-1 loss at home to Bury saw them in the bottom four. The last match of 2011 was also at home, when they engaged fellow strugglers Chesterfield, and they managed to eek out a draw to raise themselves to twentieth place going into the New Year.

Scunthorpe United opened the second half of the programme at Hartlepool United, on the first Monday of the New Year. The team had already lost 2-1 to Hartlepool, at Glanford Park. On their travels, the Iron played in a far more convincing manner. Goals by Sam Togwell and Gary Thompson, either side of the break, put United in a commanding position. It was only when Hartlepool pulled one back, late in the proceedings, that the Iron had a last anxious few moments. The final score of 2-1 was much deserved for the effort of every player.

Up to this point in the season, it could hardly be said that the Iron had set the First Division alight. There had been some grumblings about Alan Knill as a manager, but most fair minded folk knew his hands were tied. Alan had to deal with long term injuries to Cliff Byrne, Jimmy Ryan, Michael Collins and Damien Mozika. The January window allowed him to unload Michael Nelson to Kilmarnock, and Chris Dagnall at Barnsley.

Alan Knill would be able to strengthen the team position by bringing in three players. The first of these was the talented mid-fielder, Josh Walker, from Watford. The move was officially an emergency loan, because of F.I.F.A. restrictions, but it was with the view of eventually being a permanent situation. Next was Christian Ribeiro, a young Bristol City full back, taken on loan for a couple of months. Christian was a full Welsh cap, and proved to be a strong defender. The third signing was Connor Jennings, a twenty one year old forward for the future, from Stalybridge Celtic.

All three men had a taste of the next game at Colchester. Josh Walker put the Iron ahead within seven minutes of his debut, when he flicked the ball into the net. Colchester equalised with a penalty past Sam Slocombe, and that was how the score stayed. The bright side of the game was the improved performance. This was continued at home to Stevenage Borough, and the team ought to have been rewarded far better than the 1-1. In the final match of the month, United were over ran in the visit of high flying Sheffield Wednesday. The Iron lost 3-1, and only had a Jordan Robertson goal to cheer, which was the first Scunthorpe goal for the big striker, and the final one of the match.

In February, Alan Knill brought three quality players to the Club, all on loans. John Parkin was a massive figure at six feet and four inches tall. He was affectionately nick named 'The Beast', but along with an exceptional physique were the skills of a true artist. He was good in the air, strong in the shot, and possessed brilliance at knocking the difficult ball down to a colleague. Big John was joined in defence by a quick moving full back called Jamie Reckord, from Wolverhampton Wanderers, a nineteen year old with England junior honours.

The last piece in the puzzle was the one that all Scunthorpe United supporters were so delighted to see go through, after rumours had circulated. It was the temporary return of David Mirfin, who had only played four League games for Watford since his transfer. At least he was going back to Glanford Park, where, not only was he appreciated, but also wanted.

It would seem that only just now the team Alan Knill wished to see, was starting to line up, and all three new men were in place for a visit of Rochdale. Scunthorpe United secured their first home victory since October, thanks to a 1-0 result. The vital moment did not arrive until the sixty fourth minute, when Garry Thompson took the ball on the half way line. He sprinted up the right, and beat the keeper with an explosive shot.

At the end of the week United added three more points to the tally at Leyton Orient. They had a quite first period, and went into the break a goal in arrears. After the interval, Josh Walker, Andy Barcham and John Parkin all registered goals. The 3-1 result was loudly greeted by five hundred noisy followers, who never stopped the vocals throughout the ninety minutes. Only one further point was gleaned in the month, although the Iron were extremely unlucky to lose 2-1 at Sheffield United. This dropped the Club into the fourth from bottom place.

Scunthorpe United began March in a positive mood by beating Wycombe Wanderers 4-1 at Glanford Park. It was pleasing to see Paul Hayes on loan in the opposition ranks. Those in the 3,811 attendance noted another ex-Iron unsettled. The fixtures next gave United a run of three away trips to make. They started with a bright win at Oldham, who proved to be a handful. David Mirfin and Garry Thompson both scored late headed goals, either side of a Latics equaliser. At Preston a goalless draw was a poor match, but useful point. Next came the long haul down to Yeovil, and after the two hundred and eighty mile trip, the game only just went ahead, when fog impeded visibility. Two equalisers by John Parkin earned a point. The 2-2 draw felt a win, because the last goal arrived three minutes into time added on. An Andy Barcham shot beat the stranded keeper, but was cleared off the line. Big John rammed home the rebound, and the one hundred visitors danced in delight.

The useful unbeaten run, picking up vital points, continued throughout the rest of March, and in each case the opposition provided a stiff test. Charlton Athletic arrived at Glanford Park in the next fixture, and United felt that they had the lion's share of the ninety minutes from a 1-1 draw. Charlton had to be congratulated for finishing as Champions, but had only won two points from the Scunthorpe matches. A visit to Bury produced a goalless famine, but United were happy because their ranks were reduced by a red card. Another draw came from a similar score at home to Notts County, who were a handful at Glanford Park. This match was notable for the debut of substitute Conor McAlney, a young forward on loan from Everton.

Gradually Scunthorpe United had inched themselves out of trouble at the wrong end of the table, and they completed the month with an excellent away win at Chesterfield's impressive new B2net Stadium. It was not a game that started well, because the home side took the lead on twenty minutes. It was just the lesson the team needed to get back into gear. Conor McAlney crossed for Jordan Robertson to equalise ten minutes later.

In the second half Scunthorpe destroyed the opposition with some clinical finishing. Just after the hour mark, midfielder Josh Walker flashed home a Robertson pass, then Robertson hit a cracker into the top right as he viewed the target. The scoring was completed by Andy Barcham ten minutes from time. His dashed into space on the left of the park and hit a low cross shot, to send 957 visiting supporters wild with delight. A 4-1 score was a handsome victory, and the best of the season.

Scunthorpe United continued to pick up more precious points. Exeter came up to Lincolnshire on Good Friday, and the lowly placed Devonians proved stubborn in defence. It was not until hero John Parkin came on as a substitute that the three points were made safe. In the seventy seventh minute Josh Walker found the nimble Jamie Reckord, who threaded the ball to big John. An accurate swing of his right foot saw the ball hit the back of the net, off the arms of the desperate keeper. Easter was completed with another hard working 0-0 at Play-Off hopefuls Carlisle, on Easter Monday, and saw the Iron stretch to ten matches unbeaten. This gave Scunthorpe United a total of fifty points, a figure that in most years guaranteed safety.

The fixture card had only four games left to play, and United returned to action at Glanford Park against M.K.Dons. There may have been a number of injuries, but the 3-0 loss was not only uncharacteristic, but described by Alan Knill as hugely disappointing. The bright feature of the loss was the two substitutions, which brought Connor Jennings back from injury, and gave a debut to young Irishman Robbie Gibbons, who had been signed as a free agent, having played in Cyprus.

Scunthorpe United past another milestone in the next game, at Huddersfield's magnificent Galpharm Stadium. The team played a beautiful passing game, but lost to a goal in the last two minutes of normal time, when a draw should have been the just reward. Around 250 visiting supporters stood and applauded the players toil, but the best part of the afternoon was from other results. Charlton had beaten Wycombe Wanderers and the result meant that the Iron were mathematically safe from the trapdoor of relegation.

All that remained were the two fixtures, at home to Bournemouth, and away on the final day of the campaign at the neat Prenton Park Stadium, home of Tranmere Rovers, on the Wirral. Both matches would contain parallels. Twice the Iron fell behind in the first half, and twice Alan Knill relied upon bringing Gary Thompson off the bench to find an equaliser. Both times the vital pass came from the popular old warhorse, Cliff Byrne, and the two 1-1 draws made a total of twenty two drawn games over the length of the year.

Most fair minded Scunthonians recognised the dramatic turn round in the final months of the campaign. Alan Knill began the year with his hands tied, in many respects, but gradually the team was moulded to what he wanted. His side had lately played a superb passing game, and his use of the loan market had proved to be most valuable, particularly in bringing back David Mirfin plus the introduction of John Parkin to the forward line.

(Above) Sam Slocombe forced his way into the first team and was voted 'Player of the season (Below) The last goal of the season at Glanford Park was netted by Gary Thompson, versus Bournemouth.

In the end the Iron had mustered fifty two points and finished eighteenth in the table. At the final whistle of the Tranmere game, the crowd of several hundred travelling Irons stood applauding the efforts of all the players.

Sam Slocombe had to be congratulated for his tremendous form in goal, which won the former Bottesford Town lad the 'Player of the Season' award. The remaining members of the team had also put in some honest performances.

The last word was with Alan Knill, after the players had waved farewell to the supporters. He walked over to the masses, put his hand on his heart, and gave the crowd a salute. Alan and his backroom staff could look forward to a busy Summer, but after the closed season the army of claret and blue supporters would be back in force, roaring Scunthorpe United on in the 2012-13 campaign. It will be the one hundred and thirteenth year of operation. Be sure not to miss it, and keep believing.

Up the Iron.

1949/50   3rd in Midland League

#	Date	Opponent	Score	Scorers	Thompson G	Barker	Brownsword	Conroy	Taylor	McCormick	Deniff	Whitfield	Heseltine	Wallace	Malcolm	Wilson A	Bowers T	Pigdon	Stanham	Lindley	Poole	Dixon	Barkas	Kirk	Sharpe	Lodge	Thompson E	Wright	Watson	Lemmon	Camm	Ward	Nagy	Millington
1	Aug 20	LINCOLN CITY RES	3-0	Barker 2, Heseltine	1	2	3	4	5	6	7	8	9	10	11																			
2	27	Shrewsbury Town	1-1	Whitfield	1	2	3	4	5	6		8	9	10	11	7																		
3	Sep 1	GAINSBOROUGH TRINITY	3-0	Bowers 2, Conroy	1	2	3	4	5	6		8		10	11	7	9																		
4	3	GRANTHAM	5-0	Bowers 3, Wallace, Barker	1	2	3	4	5			8		10	11	7	9	6																	
5	8	GOOLE TOWN	5-0	Wilson, Bowers 4	1	2	3	4	5			8		10	11	7	9	6																	
6	10	Denaby United	1-1	Whitfield	1	2	3	4	5			8		10	11	7	9	6																	
7	14	Gainsborough Trinity	1-0	Whitfield	1	2	3	4	5			10				7	9	6	11	8															
8	17	NOTTS COUNTY RES	1-0	Whitfield	1	2	3	4	5			10			11		9	6		8	7														
9	24	York City Res.	0-1		1	2	3	4	5	6		8		10	8	9					7														
10	28	Goole Town	1-2	Wallace	1	2	3	4	5			8		10	11	7	9																		
11	Oct 1	BRADFORD CITY RES	1-0	Malcolm	1	2	3	4	5	6				10	11	7	9		8																
12	8	Lincoln City Res.	2-0	Lindley, Wilson	1		3	4	5	6				10	11	7	9		8		2														
13	13	Notts County Res.	2-1	Wallace, Whitfield	1		3	4	5	6		9		10	11	7			8		2														
14	15	YORK CITY RES.	1-3	Wilson	1	2	3	4	5	6		9		10	11	8							7												
15	22	Bradford P. A. Res	2-1	Whitfield 2	1	2	3	4	5	6		9		10	11	7								8											
16	27	Nottm Forest Res.	3-2	Wallace, Barkas, Wilson	1	2	3	4	5	6		9		10	11	7		6						8											
17	29	MANSFIELD TOWN RES	5-1	Barkas 2, Whitfield 2, Wilson	1	2	3	4	5	6		9		10	8									8	7										
18	Nov 5	DONCASTER R. RES	7-0	Barkas 2, Whitfield 3, Wilson, Conroy	1	2	3	4	5	6		9		10	11	7								8											
19	26	NOTTM FOREST RES	0-2		1	2	3	4	5					10	11									8	7	4									
20	Dec 3	Frickley Colliery	1-2	Whitfield	1	2	3	4	5			9		8	11										7	6						10			
21	10	HALIFAX TOWN RES	2-0	Whitfield, Lodge	1	2	3	4	5			9		10										8	7	6	11								
22	17	Rotherham United Res	1-1	Sharpe	1	2	3	4	5			9		10	11										7	6	8								
23	26	GRIMSBY TOWN RES	2-1	Bowers, Whitfield	1	2	3	4	5	6		9		10			7									8				11					
24	27	Grimsby Town Res.	0-1		1	2	3	4	5	6		9		10			7									8				11					
25	31	Grantham	2-4	Whitfield, Lodge	1	2	3	4	5			9		10												8	7	11							
26	Jan 7	PETERBOROUGH UNITED	0-0	Conroy	1	2	3	4	5			9		10	11	7										8									
27	14	DENABY UNITED	1-1	Whitfield	1	2	3	4	5	6		9			11	7									8					10					
28	21	Bradford City Res.	0-3		1	2	3	4	5			9		10	11	7									8	6									
29	28	BRADFORD P. A. RES	6-1	McCormick, Wilson, Whitfield 3, Lennon	1	2	3	4	5	6		9			11	7										6				8					
30	Feb 4	RANSOME & MARLES	3-0	Whitfield 2, McCormick	1		3	4	5	6		9			11							2				6				8	7				
31	11	SCARBOROUGH	1-0	Whitfield	1	2	3	4	5	6		9			11											6				8	7				
32	18	Peterborough United	1-3	Lennon	1	2	3	4	5			9		10	11											6				8	7				
33	28	BOSTON UNITED	3-0	Lennon, Whitfield 2	1	2	3	4	5	6		9			11											6				8	7				
34	Mar 4	Mansfield Town Res.	0-1		1	2	3	4	5	6		9			11											6				8	7				
35	16	Halifax Town Res.	3-3	Wallace, Barker, Heseltine	1	2	3	4	5			8	9	10	11	7										6									
36	18	Worksop Town	3-0	Wallace, Heseltine 2	1	2	3		5	6		8	9	10	11	7										6									
37	25	ROTHERHAM UTD RES	2-1	Whitfield, Wallace	1	2	3		5	6		8	9	10	11	7										6									
38	Apr 1	Ransome & Marles	5-0	Heseltine, Wilson 2	1	2	3		5	6		8	9	10	11	7										6									
39	10	HULL CITY RES.	5-0	Heseltine, Wilson 3, Lodge	1	2	3		5	6		8	9	10	11	7										6									
40	14	Hull City Res.	0-1		1	2	3		5	6		8	9	10	11	7										6									
41	15	SHREWSBURY TOWN	4-1	Wallace2,Heseltine,Brownsword (pen)	1	2	3	4	5	6		8	9	10	11	7										6									
42	20	FRICKLEY COLLIERY	1-1	Heseltine	1	2	3		5	6		8	9	10	11	7										6									
43	22	Doncaster Rovers Res	2-1	Whitfield 2	1	2	3		5	6		8	9		11	7										6							10		
44	26	Scarborough	2-1	Wilson, Malcolm	1	2	3		5	6		9		10	11	7										6									4
45	29	Boston United	2-1	Heseltine, Whitfield	1	2	3		5	6		8	9	10	11	7									8	6									4
46	Ma 3	WORKSOP TOWN	2-1	Malcolm, McCormick	1	2	3		5	6		8	9	10	11	7										6									4
		Apps			42	39	42	33	42	30	1	39	13	33	37	26	12	6	1	5	2	3	6	2	7	21	1	2	4	6	5	2	1	2
		Goals			0	4	1	3	0	3	0	29	11	9	3	13	10	0	0	1	0	0	5	0	1	3	0	0	0	3	0	0	0	0

F.A.Cup

	Date	Opponent	Score	Scorers																													
Q4	Nov 12	GOOLE TOWN	0-0		1	2	3	4	5			9		10	11	7		6						8												
rep	22	Goole Town	1-3	Barker	1	6	3	4	5			9		10	11		9					2	8													

1949/50

	P.	W.	D.	L.	F.	A.	Pts
Nottingham Forest Res.	46	31	8	7	105	44	78
Grimsby Town Res.	46	29	7	10	98	58	65
SCUNTHORPE UNITED	46	29	6	11	99	44	64
Peterborough United	46	23	10	13	91	71	56
Hull City Res.	46	22	11	13	91	64	55
York City Res.	46	25	5	16	103	81	55
Rotherham United Res..	46	20	12	14	79	59	52
Gainsborough Trinity	46	21	10	15	88	74	52
Goole Town	46	22	6	18	76	86	.50
Shrewsbury Town	46	19	11	16	96	86	49
Bradford Park Avenue Res.	46	19	10	17	99	84	48
Denaby United	46	18	12	16	90	72	48
Bradford City Res.	46	18	12	16	91	84	48
Scarborough	46	18	8	20	106	96	44
Grantham	46	17	9	20	95	118	43
Notts County Res.	46	15	10	21	84	82	40
Mansfield Town Res.	46	16	6	23	66	93	40
Frickley Colliery	46	15	9	22	87	94	39
Lincoln City Res.	46	14	11	21	69	82	39
Worksop Town	46	14	5	27	56	80	33
Halifax Town Res.	46	10	11	25	66	99	31
Boston United	46	8	14	24	71	113	30
Ransome & Marles (Newark)	46	13	2	31	58	135	28
Doncaster Rovers Res.	46	9	7	30	63	128	25

1950/51 12th in Division 3(N)

#	Date		Opponent	Result	Scorers	Att	Thompson GH	Barker, Jeff	Brownsword NJ	Allen W	Taylor RE	McCormick JM	Mosby H	Payne EH	Gorin ER	Rees MJF	Boyes WE	Whitfield J	Clelland D	Hubbard J	Bowen D	White R	Babes J	Cumner RH	Mulholland JR	Malan NF	Comley LG	Jones RJ	Conroy RM
1	Aug	19	SHREWSBURY TOWN	0-0		11847	1	2	3	4	5	6	7	8	9	10	11												
2		23	Lincoln City	1-2	Gorin	16908	1	2	3	4	5	6	7		9	10		8	11										
3		26	Mansfield Town	1-1	Whitfield	11637	1	2	3	6	5				9	10	11	8		4	7								
4		30	LINCOLN CITY	1-1	Whitfield	14840	1	2	3	6	5				9	10	11	8		4	7								
5	Sep	2	ROTHERHAM UNITED	0-0		14687	1	2	3	6	5			11	9	10		8		4	7								
6		6	OLDHAM ATHLETIC	1-0	Whitfield	7994	1	2	3		5			11	9	10		8		4	7	6							
7		9	Barrow	0-1		10004	1	2	3		5			11	9	10		8		4	7	6							
8		12	Oldham Athletic	4-3	Gorin 2, Whitfield, Mosby	11980	1	2	3		5	6	11	7	9	10		8		4									
9		16	YORK CITY	0-1		12101	1	2	3		5	6	11	7	9	10		8		4									
10		23	Carlisle United	1-3	Gorin	11167	1	4	3	6	5		11	10	9			8		7			2						
11		30	ACCRINGTON STANLEY	3-0	Gorin 3	7861	1	2	3	6	5		7	10	9			8		4				11					
12	Oct	7	Gateshead	0-1		11167	1	2	3	6	5		7	10	9	8				4				11					
13		14	CREWE ALEXANDRA	1-1	Gorin	11307	1	2	3	6	5		7	10	9			8		4				11					
14		21	Halifax Town	3-3	Mulholland, Cumner, Rees	9512	1	2	3	6	5			10	9	8				4				11	7				
15		28	HARTLEPOOLS UNITED	0-0		10657	1	2	3	6	5			10	9	8				4				11	7				
16	Nov	4	Darlington	2-3	Gorin, Barker (p)	5253	1	2	3	6	5		11	10	9	8				4					7				
17		18	New Brighton	2-1	Gorin 2	3250		2	3	4		6	7	10	9	8			5					11		1			
18	Dec	2	Rochdale	0-2		5336		2	3	4		6	7	10	9	8			5					11					
19		9	CHESTER	2-0	Mosby, Boyes	7089	1	2	3	6	5		7	10	9		8			4				11					
20		16	Shrewsbury Town	1-3	Gorin	7368	1	2	3	6	5		7	10	9		8			4				11					
21		23	MANSFIELD TOWN	0-0		7459	1	2	3	6	5		7	10	9		8			4				11					
22		25	WREXHAM	2-0	Cumner, Own goal (Turney)	8933	1	2	3	6	5		7	10	9		8			4				11					
23		26	Wrexham	1-3	Mosby	9652	1	2	3	6	5		7	10	9		8			4				11					
24		30	Rotherham United	1-4	Cumner	10169	1		3	6	5		7	10	9		8			4	2			11					
25	Jan	6	BRADFORD PARK AVE.	1-1	James (og)	6760	1		2	6	5			8	9		10			4	3			11	7				
26		13	BARROW	1-0	Boyes	7850	1	2	3	6	5		7	8	9		10			4				11					
27		20	York City	0-0		7159	1	2	3	6	5		7	8			10	9		4				11					
28		27	Bradford Park Avenue	2-2	Clelland 2	10246	1	2	3		5		7	8			10		9	6		4		11					
29	Feb	3	CARLISLE UNITED	1-1	Clelland	9247	1	2	3		5		7	8		10			9	6		4		11					
30		10	TRANMERE ROVERS	1-1	Payne	10495	1	2	3	6	5		7	10					9	8		4		11					
31		17	Accrington Stanley	0-0		3433	1	2	3	6	5		7	8			10		9	4				11					
32		24	GATESHEAD	2-1	Cumner, Whitfield	9688	1	2	3	6	5		7	8			10	9		4				11					
33	Mar	3	Crewe Alexandra	0-2		6390	1	2	3	6	5		7	8			10	9		4				11					
34		10	HALIFAX TOWN	2-2	Mosby, Cumner	8447	1	2	3	6	5		11	9		8				4				10	7				
35		17	Hartlepools United	2-4	Comley, Whitfield	5365	1	2	3		5	6	7	8				9		4				11			10		
36		23	Southport	2-2	Comley, Clelland	8206	1	2	3	6	5		7	8					9	4				11			10		
37		24	DARLINGTON	2-0	Clelland, Mosby	8888	1	2	3	6	5		7	8					9	4				11			10		
38		26	SOUTHPORT	0-0		5083	1	2	3	6	5		7	8				9		4				11			10		
39		31	Stockport County	2-1	Cumner, Clelland	6401	1	2	3	6	5		7	8					9	4				11			10		
40	Apr	7	NEW BRIGHTON	6-0	Clelland 2,Comley 2,Payne,Cumner(p)	8588		2	3	6	5		7	8					9	4				11		1	10		
41		14	Bradford City	0-2		13001		2	3	6	5		7	8					9	4				10		1	11		
42		18	BRADFORD CITY	0-0		10287	1		3	6	5		7	8						4				2	11		10	9	
43		21	ROCHDALE	3-0	Cumner 2, Comley	9209	1		3	6	5		7	8						4				2	11		10	9	
44		28	Chester	1-4	Cumner	3778	1	2	3	6	5		7			8				4				11			10	9	
45		30	STOCKPORT COUNTY	3-0	Mosby, Hubbard, White	9175		2	3	6	5		7					9	8	4				11	7	1	10		
46	May	5	Tranmere Rovers	0-1		6990		2	3	6	5							9		4				11	7	1	10		8

| Apps | | | | | | | 41 | 42 | 46 | 39 | 44 | 7 | 37 | 40 | 26 | 18 | 13 | 16 | 16 | 42 | 5 | 9 | 3 | 35 | 6 | 5 | 12 | 3 | 1 |
| Goals | | | | | | | | 1 | | | | | 6 | 2 | 12 | 1 | 2 | 6 | 8 | 1 | | 1 | | 10 | 1 | | 5 | | |

Two own goals

F.A. Cup

Q4	Nov	11	Hereford United	0-1		10527		2	3	4	5	6	11	10	9	8									7	1			

		P	W	D	L	F	A	W	D	L	F	A	Pts
1	Rotherham United	46	16	3	4	55	16	15	6	2	48	25	71
2	Mansfield Town	46	17	6	0	54	19	9	6	8	24	29	64
3	Carlisle United	46	18	4	1	44	17	7	8	8	35	33	62
4	Tranmere Rovers	46	15	5	3	51	26	9	6	8	32	36	59
5	Lincoln City	46	18	1	4	62	23	7	7	9	27	35	58
6	Bradford Park Ave.	46	15	3	5	46	23	8	5	10	44	49	54
7	Bradford City	46	13	4	6	55	30	8	6	9	35	33	52
8	Gateshead	46	17	1	5	60	21	4	7	12	24	41	50
9	Crewe Alexandra	46	11	5	7	38	26	8	5	10	23	34	48
10	Stockport County	46	15	3	5	45	26	5	5	13	18	37	48
11	Rochdale	46	11	6	6	38	18	6	5	12	31	44	45
12	SCUNTHORPE UNITED	46	10	12	1	32	9	3	6	14	26	48	44
13	Chester	46	11	6	6	42	30	6	3	14	20	34	43
14	Wrexham	46	12	6	5	37	28	3	6	14	18	43	42
15	Oldham Athletic	46	10	5	8	47	36	6	3	14	26	37	40
16	Hartlepools United	46	14	5	4	55	26	2	2	19	9	40	39
17	York City	46	7	12	4	37	24	5	3	15	29	53	39
18	Darlington	46	10	8	5	35	29	3	5	15	24	48	39
19	Barrow	46	12	3	8	38	24	4	3	16	13	49	38
20	Shrewsbury Town	46	11	3	9	28	30	4	4	15	15	44	37
21	Southport	46	9	4	10	29	25	4	6	13	27	47	36
22	Halifax Town	46	11	6	6	36	24	0	6	17	14	45	34
23	Accrington Stanley	46	10	4	9	28	29	1	6	16	14	72	32
24	New Brighton	46	7	6	10	22	32	4	2	17	18	58	30

1951/52 14th in Division 3(N)

#		Date	Opponent	Score	Scorers	Att	Thompson GH	Barker, Jeff	Brownsword NJ	Stirland CJ	Taylor RE	Allen W	Mosby H	Hubbard J	Powell R	Hall A	Cumner RH	McLaren R	Gray G	Wallace G	Babes J	Platts P	Malan NF	Lockwood E	Sharpe LT	Rudd JJ	White R	Whitfield J	Ottewell S
1	Aug	18	BRADFORD CITY	1-0	Cumner	10315	1	2	3	4	5	6	7	8	9	10	11												
2		22	Chester	1-3	Hall	7045	1	2	3	4	5	6		8	9	10	11	7											
3		25	Hartlepools United	1-3	Powell	9028	1	2	3		5	6		4	9	8	11		7	10									
4		30	CHESTER	2-2	Cumner 2	6042	1	2	3	4	5	6	7	8	9		11			10									
5	Sep	1	OLDHAM ATHLETIC	2-2	Cumner, Wallace	10389	1		3	4	5	6	7	8	9		11			10	2								
6		6	LINCOLN CITY	1-3	Allen	12967	1		3	4	5	6	7	8	9		11			10	2								
7		8	Darlington	3-2	Cumner, Platts, Wallace	6169	1		3		5	6	7	4	8		11			10	2	9							
8		12	Lincoln City	1-4	Platts	14220	1		3		5	6	7	4		8	11			10	2	9							
9		15	GATESHEAD	1-1	Hall	8539			3		5		7	4		8	11		9	10	2		1	6					
10		22	Crewe Alexandra	2-2	Hall, Gray	5650	1	2	3		5			4	9	8	11		7	10					6				
11		29	SOUTHPORT	1-1	Gray	9297	1	2	3		5	6	11		9	8			7	10					4				
12	Oct	6	Wrexham	2-1	Powell 2	8172	1	2	3		5	6			9		8		7	10					4	11			
13		13	CHESTERFIELD	1-1	Powell	9833	1	2	3		5	6			9	7	8			10					4	11			
14		20	Bradford Park Avenue	2-2	Wallace 2	11203	1	2	3		5	6		7	9		8			10					4	11			
15		27	HALIFAX TOWN	2-1	Wallace, Powell	8729	1	2	3		5	6	7		9		8			10					4	11			
16	Nov	3	Mansfield Town	1-4	Mosby	10300	1	2	3		5	6	7		9		10			8					4	11			
17		10	ROCHDALE	3-1	Powell, Cumner, Taylor (p)	8374	1	2	3		5	6	7		9		8								4	10			
18		17	Accrington Stanley	2-2	Martin(og), Powell	6381	1	2	3		5	6	7	4	9		11			8						10			
19	Dec	1	Stockport County	1-1	Wallace	10398	1	2	3		5		7	4	9		11			8					6				
20		8	WORKINGTON	3-1	Mosby, Rudd, Powell	7113	1	2	3		5		7	4	9		11			8					6	10			
21		22	HARTLEPOOLS UNITED	2-0	Powell, Cumner	7320	1	2	3		5		7	4	9		11			8					6	10			
22		25	Grimsby Town	2-3	Powell 2	19351	1	2	3		5		7	4	9		11			8					6	10			
23		26	GRIMSBY TOWN	1-3	Powell	15734	1	2	3		5	8	7	4	9		11								6	10			
24		29	Oldham Athletic	0-2		16332	1	2	3		5		7	4	9	8	11								6	10			
25	Jan	5	DARLINGTON	5-2	Hall 2, Powell, Mosby, Rudd	7223	1	2	3		5		7	4	9	8	11								6	10			
26		17	YORK CITY	1-1	Rudd	4046	1	2	3			10	7	4	9	8									6	11	5		
27		19	Gateshead	1-2	Cumner	5586	1	2	3				7	4	9	8	11								6	10	5		
28		26	CREWE ALEXANDRA	2-0	Cumner, Powell	6404	1	2	3		5			4	9	8	11	7							6	10			
29	Feb	9	Southport	1-5	Gray	4592	1	2	3		5			4	9	8	11	7							6	10			
30		16	WREXHAM	0-0		6924	1	2	3					4	9	8	11	10	7						6		5		
31		23	Barrow	1-2	Hubbard	7062		2	3					4			11	10	7			1			6	8	5	9	
32	Mar	1	Chesterfield	0-3		10307			3		6		7	4			11	10				2		1		8	5	9	
33		8	BRADFORD PARK AVE.	0-0		8445	1	2	3					4	9		11								6	7	5	8	10
34		15	Halifax Town	1-2	Whitfield	8418	1	2	3				7	4			11								6	8	5	9	10
35		22	MANSFIELD TOWN	4-1	Mosby, Cumner, Ottewell, Rudd	7352	1	2	3	4		6	7				10									11	5	9	8
36		26	Bradford City	0-1		3825	1	2	3	4		6					10		7							11	5	9	8
37		29	Rochdale	2-1	Ottewell, Wallace	1226	1	2	3	4		6					10		7							11	5	9	8
38	Apr	5	ACCRINGTON STANLEY	3-1	Cumner, Whitfield, Ottewell	4801	1		3	4		6	7	2			10									11	5	9	8
39		11	Tranmere Rovers	1-3	Ottewell	9075	1		3	4		6	7	2			10									11	5	9	8
40		12	Carlisle United	0-3		6981	1		3	4		6		2			10		7				1			11	5	9	8
41		14	TRANMERE ROVERS	2-0	Ottewell, Wallace	8066	1		3	4		6		2			10	11	7				1				5	9	8
42		19	STOCKPORT COUNTY	1-1	Ottewell	8305	1		3	4				2			10	11	7				1		6		5	9	8
43		24	CARLISLE UNITED	1-1	Ottewell	7453	1		3	4				2			10		7				1		6	11	5	9	8
44		26	Workington	0-0		5133	1		3	4				2			10		7				1		6	11	5	9	8
45		28	York City	1-0	Ottewell	7827	1		3	4				2	9		10		7				1		6	11	5		8
46	May	1	BARROW	0-0		7103	1		3	4				2	9		10		7						6	11	5		8
			Apps				36	31	46	17	28	25	27	36	31	15	44	6	9	29	6	2	10	1	28	32	19	14	14
			Goals									1	1	4	1	14	5	11		3	8		2			4		2	8

One own goal

F.A. Cup

		Date	Opponent	Score	Scorers	Att																							
R1	Nov	24	BILLINGHAM SYNTH.	5-0	Wallace 2, Powell 2, Hubbard	9861	1	2	3		5	6	7	4	9		11			8						10			
R2	Dec	15	Millwall	0-0		22702	1	2	3		5		7	4	9		11			8					6	10			
rep		20	MILLWALL	3-0	Powell 2, Rudd	13580	1	2	3		5		7	4	9		11			8					6	10			
R3	Jan	12	TOTTENHAM HOTSPUR	0-3		22652	1	2	3		5		7	4	9	8	11								6	10			

		P	W	D	L	F	A	W	D	L	F	A	Pts
1	Lincoln City	46	19	2	2	80	23	11	7	5	41	29	69
2	Grimsby Town	46	19	2	2	59	14	10	6	7	37	31	66
3	Stockport County	46	12	9	2	47	17	11	4	8	27	23	59
4	Oldham Athletic	46	19	2	2	65	22	5	7	11	25	39	57
5	Gateshead	46	14	7	2	41	17	4	4	12	25	32	53
6	Mansfield Town	46	17	3	3	50	23	5	5	13	23	37	52
7	Carlisle United	46	10	7	6	31	24	9	6	8	31	33	51
8	Bradford Park Ave.	46	13	6	4	51	28	6	6	11	23	36	50
9	Hartlepools United	46	17	3	3	47	19	4	5	14	24	46	50
10	York City	46	16	4	3	53	19	2	9	12	20	33	49
11	Tranmere Rovers	46	17	2	4	59	29	4	4	15	17	42	48
12	Barrow	46	13	5	5	33	19	4	7	12	24	42	46
13	Chesterfield	46	15	7	1	47	16	2	4	17	18	50	45
14	SCUNTHORPE UNITED	46	10	11	2	39	23	4	5	14	26	51	44
15	Bradford City	46	12	5	6	40	32	4	5	14	21	36	42
16	Crewe Alexandra	46	12	6	5	42	28	5	2	16	21	54	42
17	Southport	46	12	6	5	36	22	5	5	15	17	49	41
18	Wrexham	46	14	5	4	41	22	1	4	18	22	51	39
19	Chester	46	13	4	6	46	30	2	5	16	26	55	39
20	Halifax Town	46	11	4	8	31	23	3	3	17	30	74	35
21	Rochdale	46	10	5	8	32	34	1	8	14	15	45	35
22	Accrington Stanley	46	6	8	9	30	34	4	4	15	31	58	32
23	Darlington	46	10	5	8	39	34	1	4	18	25	69	31
24	Workington	46	8	4	11	33	34	3	3	17	17	57	29

~ 222 ~

1952/53 15th in Division 3(N)

#	Date		Opponent	Score	Scorers	Att	Thompson GH	Cox S	Brownsword NJ	McGill A	White R	Sharpe LT	Mosby H	Haigh J	Mynard LD	Cumner RH	Daley AJ	Hubbard J	Broadley L	Ottewell S	Taylor RE	Whitfield J	Wallace G	Bushby A	Malan NF	Taylor R	Brown GA	Lockwood E	Charlesworth T
1	Aug	23	Barrow	1-2	Mynard	6254	1	2	3	4	5	6	7	8	9	10	11												
2		28	GRIMSBY TOWN	0-1		18974	1		3	4			8	7	10	11	2	9											
3		30	STOCKPORT COUNTY	2-2	Broadley, Ottewell	8871	1		3	4	5	6		8	7		11		2	9	10								
4	Sep	3	Grimsby Town	0-1		22213	1		3	4			8	7			11		2	9	10	5	6						
5		6	Bradford City	0-0		11525	1		3	4			8				11		2	9	10	5	6	7					
6		11	CHESTER	1-1	Broadley	6695	1		3	4			7	8			11		2	9	10	5	6						
7		13	ROCHDALE	5-1	McGill,Mynard,Whitfield,Mosby,Ha	7381	1		3	4		6	7	8	9		11		2			5	10						
8		17	Chester	1-1	Haigh	5004	1		3	4		6	7	8	9		11		2			5	10						
9		20	Darlington	0-1		5850	1		3	4		6	7	8	9	10	11		2			5							
10		25	MANSFIELD TOWN	0-1		7252	1		3	4		6	7	8	9	11			2			5	10						
11		27	GATESHEAD	0-0		6940	1		3	4			7	8	9	11			2			5	10	6					
12	Oct	2	SOUTHPORT	3-0	Daley, Haigh, Whitfield	5105	1		3	4				8	11	10	7		2			5	9	6					
13		4	Hartlepools United	1-1	Daley	9060	1		3	4				8	11	10	7		2			5	9	6					
14		11	YORK CITY	2-0	Daley, Brownsword (p)	7849	1		3	4				8	11		7		2		10	5	9	6					
15		18	Tranmere Rovers	1-0	Mynard	9156	1		3	4				8	11		7		2		10	5	9	6					
16		25	CHESTERFIELD	1-0	Daley	8319			3	4				8	11		7		2		10	5	9	6	1				
17	Nov	1	Workington	3-0	Whitfield, Haigh, McGill	7348			3	4	9			8			7		2			5	10	6	1				
18		8	ACCRINGTON STANLEY	5-2	White 2, Daley 2, Brownsword (p)	7334			3	4	9			8			7		2			5	10	6	1				
19		15	Halifax Town	1-2	White	7247			3	4	9			8			7		2			5	10	6	1				
20		29	Oldham Athletic	1-0	Daley	14344			3	4	9		11	8			7		2			5	10	6	1				
21	Dec	13	Wrexham	3-2	Hubbard, Haigh, Brownsword (p)	9266			3	4	9		11	8			7	2	2			5	10	6	1				
22		20	BARROW	1-2	White	5434		3		4	9		11	8			7	2	2			5	10	6	1				
23		25	Carlisle United	0-8		9489		2	3	4	9		11	8			7					5	10	6	1				
24		27	CARLISLE UNITED	1-2	White	7325			3	4	9		7	8	11				2			5	10	6	1				
25	Jan	1	Southport	3-2	Haigh, Mosby, Ottewell	4727			3	4			11	8			7		2	9		5	10	6	1				
26		3	Stockport County	1-1	Whitfield	7999			3	4			11	8			7		2	9		5	10	6	1				
27		17	BRADFORD CITY	4-0	Haigh 2, Whitfield, Daley	7356			3	4			7	8			11		2	9		5	10	6	1				
28		24	Rochdale	2-2	Ottewell, Brownsword (p)	5050			3	4			7	8			11		2	9		5	10	6	1				
29		31	PORT VALE	1-2	Mosby	9684			3	4			7	8			11		2	9		5	10	6	1				
30	Feb	7	DARLINGTON	2-0	Haigh, Whitfield	5938			3	4			7	8		11			2	9		5	10	6	1				
31		18	Gateshead	1-1	Ottewell	3980			3	4			7	8		11			2	9		5	10	6	1				
32		21	HARTLEPOOLS UNITED	0-0		7076			3	4			7	8		11			2	9		5	10	6	1				
33		28	York City	2-0	Haigh, Brownsword (p)	7532			3	4			7	8			10	11	2			5	9	6	1				
34	Mar	7	TRANMERE ROVERS	2-0	Haigh, Daley	6796			3	4			7	8			10	11	2			5	9	6	1				
35		14	Chesterfield	1-1	Whitfield	8340			3	4			7	8			10	11	2			5	9	6	1				
36		16	Port Vale	0-4		11371			3	4			7	8				11	2		9	5	10	6	1				
37		21	WORKINGTON	2-1	Bushby 2	6529			3	4				8		10	11		2			5	9	6		1	7		
38		26	BRADFORD PARK AVE.	1-2	Haigh	6117			3	4				8	11	10			2			5	9	6		1	7		
39		28	Accrington Stanley	1-2	Brown	2903				4				8	11	10			2			5	9	6		1	7	3	
40	Apr	3	Crewe Alexandra	0-2		9379				4				8	11	10			2			5	9	6		1	7	3	
41		4	HALIFAX TOWN	1-1	Whitfield	6451				4				8			11		2			5	9	10	6	1		7	3	
42		6	CREWE ALEXANDRA	2-0	Haigh, Brown	5989				4				8			11		2			5	9	10	6	1		7	3	
43		11	Mansfield Town	0-1		7314			11	4				8					2			5	9	10	6	1		7	3	1
44		18	OLDHAM ATHLETIC	1-1	Bushby	10399				4			6	8			11		2			5	9		10	1		7	3	
45		25	Bradford Park Avenue	1-1	Brown	8571				4			6	8		11	9		2			5			10	1		7	3	
46		27	WREXHAM	1-2	Brown	4250				4			6	8		11	9		2			5			10			7	3	1
					Apps		15	3	38	46	11	6	10	24	46	18	23	35	44	5	16	43	40	4	36	27	2	10	8	2
					Goals				5	2	5		3	#	3		9	1		2	4		8	3					4	

F.A. Cup

#	Date		Opponent	Score	Scorers	Att	Thompson GH	Cox S	Brownsword NJ	McGill A	White R	Sharpe LT	Mosby H	Haigh J	Mynard LD	Cumner RH	Daley AJ	Hubbard J	Broadley L	Ottewell S	Taylor RE	Whitfield J	Wallace G	Bushby A	Malan NF
R1	Nov	22	CARLISLE UNITED	1-0	Whitfield	9028			3	4	9			8			7		2			5	10	6	1
R2	Dec	6	Hereford United	0-0		8765			3	4	9			8			7		2			5	10	6	1
rep		11	HEREFORD UNITED	2-1	White, Whitfield	10631			3	4	9			8			7		2			5	10	6	1
R3	Jan	10	Sunderland	1-1	McGill	56507			3	4				7	8	11			2		9	5	10	6	1
rep		15	SUNDERLAND	1-2	Daley	21624			3	4				7	8		11		2		9	5	10	6	1

		P	W	D	L	F	A	W	D	L	F	A	Pts
1	Oldham Athletic	46	15	4	4	48	21	7	11	5	29	24	59
2	Port Vale	46	13	9	1	41	10	7	9	7	26	25	58
3	Wrexham	46	18	3	2	59	24	6	5	12	27	42	56
4	York City	46	14	5	4	35	16	6	8	9	25	29	53
5	Grimsby Town	46	15	5	3	47	19	6	5	12	28	40	52
6	Southport	46	16	4	3	42	18	4	7	12	21	42	51
7	Bradford Park Ave.	46	10	8	5	37	23	9	4	10	38	38	50
8	Gateshead	46	13	6	4	51	24	4	9	10	25	36	49
9	Carlisle United	46	13	7	3	57	24	5	6	12	25	44	49
10	Crewe Alexandra	46	13	5	5	46	28	7	3	13	24	40	48
11	Stockport County	46	13	8	2	61	26	4	5	14	21	43	47
12	Tranmere Rovers	46	16	4	3	45	16	5	1	17	20	47	47
13	Chesterfield	46	13	6	4	40	23	5	5	13	25	40	47
14	Halifax Town	46	13	5	5	47	31	3	10	10	21	37	47
15	SCUNTHORPE UNITED	46	10	6	7	38	21	6	8	9	24	35	46
16	Bradford City	46	14	7	2	54	29	0	11	12	21	51	46
17	Hartlepools United	46	14	6	3	39	16	2	8	13	18	45	46
18	Mansfield Town	46	11	9	3	34	25	5	5	13	21	37	46
19	Barrow	46	15	6	2	48	20	1	6	16	18	51	44
20	Chester	46	10	7	6	39	27	1	8	14	25	58	37
21	Darlington	46	13	4	6	33	27	1	2	20	25	69	34
22	Rochdale	46	12	5	6	41	27	2	0	21	21	56	33
23	Workington	46	9	5	9	40	33	2	5	16	15	58	32
24	Accrington Stanley	46	7	9	7	25	29	1	2	20	14	60	27

1953/54 3rd in Division 3(N)

#	Date		Opponent	Score	Scorers	Att	Malan NF	Hubbard J	Brownsword NJ	McGill A	Taylor RE	Bushby A	Brown GA	Haigh J	Whitfield J	Gregory JE	Jones JM	Roberts H	Barley PJ	Sharpe LT	White R	Mosby H	Underwood GR	Heward B
1	Aug	22	Grimsby Town	1-0	Gregory	18246	1	2	3	4	5	6	7	8	9	10	11							
2		24	Gateshead	0-0		7864	1	2	3	4	5	6	7	8	9	10	11							
3		29	YORK CITY	3-0	Brown 2, Bushby	7494	1	2	3	4	5	6	7	8	9	10	11							
4	Sep	3	GATESHEAD	1-1	Brownsword (p)	11288	1	2	3	4	5	6	7	8	9	10	11							
5		5	Southport	3-4	Brown, Haigh, Whitfield	5640	1	2	3	4	5	6	7	8	9	10	11							
6		7	Workington	3-1	Whitfield 2, Haigh	7367	1	2	3	4	5	6	7	8	9		11	10						
7		12	CHESTER	1-0	Whitfield	10210	1	2	3	4	5	6	7	8	9		11	10						
8		17	WORKINGTON	4-1	Brown, Taylor, Roberts, Jones	10013	1	2	3	4	5	6	7	8	9		11	10						
9		19	Crewe Alexandra	1-1	Haigh	8486	1	2	3	4	5	6	7	8	9		11	10						
10		21	Hartlepools United	2-3	McGill, Jones	5924	1	2	3	4	5	6	7	8	9		11	10						
11		26	PORT VALE	0-2		12630	1	2	3	4	5	6	7	8	9		11	10						
12	Oct	1	HARTLEPOOLS UNITED	0-0		9102		2	3			6	7	8	9		11	10	1	4	5			
13		3	Bradford Park Avenue	2-2	Jones, Gregory	13686		2	3			6		8	9	10	11		1	4	5	7		
14		10	Rochdale	1-1	Mosby	7873		2	3			6		8	9	10	11		1	4	5	7		
15		17	WREXHAM	3-1	Whitfield 2, Gregory	8402		2	3			6		8	9	10	11		1	4	5	7		
16		24	Mansfield Town	1-2	Brownsword (p)	8539		2	3			6		8	9	10	11		1	4	5	7		
17		31	BARROW	3-2	Jones 2, Sharpe	6982	1	2	3			6	8		9	10	11			4	5	7		
18	Nov	7	Bradford City	3-1	Jones, Whitfield, Brownsword (p)	8039	1	2	3			6	8		9	10	11			4	5	7		
19		14	CHESTERFIELD	2-1	Whitfield, Brownsword (p)	8247	1	2	3			6		8	9	10	11			4	5	7		
20		28	HALIFAX TOWN	3-2	Haigh, Brownsword (p), Bushby	8151	1	2	3			6		8	9	10		11		4	5	7		
21	Dec	5	Carlisle United	1-5	Gregory	6550	1	2	3			6		8	9	10	11			4	5	7		
22		19	GRIMSBY TOWN	2-1	Whitfield, Gregory	9985	1	2	3			6		8	9	10	11			4	5	7		
23		25	DARLINGTON	1-1	Brownsword (p)	8035	1	2	3			6		8	9	10	11			4	5	7		
24		26	Darlington	0-3		4518	1	2	3			6	7	8	9	10	11			4	5			
25	Jan	1	Accrington Stanley	1-0	Gregory	8729	1		3	4	5	6	7	8	9	10	11						2	
26		2	York City	0-2		5226	1		3	4		6	7	8	9	10	11				5		2	
27		16	SOUTHPORT	1-1	Brownsword (p)	6870	1	2	3	4		6		8	9	10	11				5	7		
28		23	Chester	0-0		5186	1	2	3	4		6		8	9	10	11				5	7		
29	Feb	6	CREWE ALEXANDRA	2-2	Mosby, Haigh	7914	1	2	3	4		6		8	9	10	11				5	7		
30		13	Port Vale	1-7		17240	1	2	3			6		8	9	10	11			4	5	7		
31		20	BRADFORD PARK AVE.	4-1	Brown 2, Mosby, Wright (og)	8097	1	2	3			6	9	8	4	10	11				5	7		
32		27	ROCHDALE	1-1	Brown	7264	1	2	3			6	9	8	4	10	11				5	7		
33	Mar	6	Wrexham	1-3	Gregory	6522	1	2	3			6	9	8	4	10	11				5	7		
34		10	Stockport County	1-1	Brownsword (p)	2939	1	2	3	4	5	6	7	8	9	10							11	
35		13	MANSFIELD TOWN	2-2	Gregory, Haigh	6516	1	2	3	4		6	9	8		10	11				5	7		
36		18	ACCRINGTON STANLEY	1-2	McGill	5187	1	2	3	4	5	6		8	9	10	11					7		
37		20	Barrow	2-1	Gregory 2	4486	1	2	3	4				8	9	10	11				5	7		6
38		27	BRADFORD CITY	2-1	Haigh, Mosby	7035	1	2	3	4		6		8	9	10	11				5	7		
39	Apr	1	STOCKPORT COUNTY	2-0	Mosby, Jones	5849	1	2	3	4	5	6		8	9	10	11				5	7		
40		3	Chesterfield	0-1		5769	1	2	3	4		6	9	8		10	11				5	7		
41		10	TRANMERE ROVERS	3-1	Gregory 3	6180	1	4	3			6	9	8		10	11				5	7	2	
42		16	BARNSLEY	6-0	Gregory 2, Haigh, Brown, Jones, Thomas (og)	9975	1	6	3	4			9	8		10	7	11			5		2	
43		17	Halifax Town	3-0	Brown 2, Haigh	4674	1	6	3	4			9	8		10	11	7			5		2	
44		19	Barnsley	1-0	Haigh	10685	1	6	3	4			9	8		10	7	11			5		2	
45		24	CARLISLE UNITED	2-1	Hubbard, Gregory	7722	1	6	3	4			9	8		10	7	11			5		2	
46		27	Tranmere Rovers	1-1	Jones	4826	1	6	3	4	5		9	8		10	7	11					2	
			Apps				41	44	46	28	16	40	30	43	38	39	44	13	5	14	30	26	8	1
			Goals					1	8	2	1	2	10	10	9	16	9	1		1		5		

Two own goals

F.A. Cup

#	Date		Opponent	Score	Scorers	Att	Malan	Hubbard	Brownsword	McGill	Taylor	Bushby	Brown	Haigh	Whitfield	Gregory	Jones	Roberts	Barley	Sharpe	White	Mosby
R1	Nov	21	BOSTON UNITED	9-0	Haigh 3, Whitfield 2, Jones 2, Mosby, Gregory	8894	1	2	3			6		8	9	10	11			4	5	7
R2	Dec	12	BOURNEMOUTH	1-0	Brown	12005	1	2	3			6	7	8	9	10	11			4	5	
R3	Jan	9	Wrexham	3-3	Bushby 2, Mosby	17287	1	2	3	4		6		8	9	10	11				5	7
rep		14	WREXHAM	3-1	Whitfield, Gregory, Brownsword (p)	12862	1	2	3	4		6		8	9	10	11				5	7
R4		30	PORTSMOUTH	1-1	Jones	23735	1	2	3	4		6		8	9	10	11				5	7
rep	Feb	3	Portsmouth	2-2	Jones 2	30247	1	2	3	4		6		8	9	10	11				5	7
rep2		8	Portsmouth	0-4		24556	1	2	3	4		6		8	9	10	11				5	7

R4 replay a.e.t. R4 replay 2 at Highbury.

		P	W	D	L	F	A	W	D	L	F	A	Pts
1	Port Vale	46	16	7	0	48	5	10	10	3	26	16	69
2	Barnsley	46	16	3	4	54	24	8	7	8	23	33	58
3	SCUNTHORPE UNITED	46	14	7	2	49	24	7	8	8	28	32	57
4	Gateshead	46	15	4	4	49	22	6	9	8	25	33	55
5	Bradford City	46	15	6	2	40	14	7	3	13	20	41	53
6	Chesterfield	46	13	6	4	41	19	6	8	9	35	45	52
7	Mansfield Town	46	13	5	5	59	22	5	6	12	29	45	51
8	Wrexham	46	16	4	3	59	19	5	5	13	22	49	51
9	Bradford Park Ave.	46	13	6	4	57	31	5	8	10	20	37	50
10	Stockport County	46	14	6	3	57	20	4	5	14	20	47	47
11	Southport	46	12	5	6	41	26	5	7	11	22	34	46
12	Barrow	46	12	7	4	46	26	4	5	14	26	45	44
13	Carlisle United	46	10	8	5	53	27	4	7	12	30	44	43
14	Tranmere Rovers	46	11	4	8	40	34	7	3	13	19	36	43
15	Accrington Stanley	46	12	4	7	41	22	4	3	16	25	52	42
16	Crewe Alexandra	46	9	8	6	30	26	5	5	13	19	41	41
17	Grimsby Town	46	14	5	4	31	15	2	4	17	20	62	41
18	Hartlepools United	46	10	8	5	40	21	3	6	14	19	44	40
19	Rochdale	46	12	5	6	40	20	3	5	15	19	57	40
20	Workington	46	10	9	4	36	22	3	5	15	23	58	40
21	Darlington	46	11	3	9	31	27	1	11	11	19	44	38
22	York City	46	8	7	8	39	32	4	6	13	25	54	37
23	Halifax Town	46	9	8	6	26	21	3	4	16	18	52	34
24	Chester	46	10	7	6	39	22	1	3	19	9	45	32

1954/55   3rd in Division 3(N)

#	Date	Opponent	Score	Scorers	Att	Malan NF	Hubbard J	Brownsword NJ	McGill A	White R	Bushby A	Mosby H	Haigh J	Brown GA	Gregory JE	Jones JM	Lamb HT	Roberts H	Turner PS	Whitfield J	Lloyd WS	Sharpe LT	Barrett J	Marshall PW	Fawcett B
1	Aug 21	HALIFAX TOWN	2-2	Haigh 2	10388	1	2	3	4	5	6		7	8	9	10	11								
2	24	Grimsby Town	4-1	Brown 2, McGill, Gregory	19736	1	6	3	4	5			7	8	9	10	11	2							
3	28	York City	3-2	Gregory 3	12911	1	6	3	4	5			7	8	9	10	11	2							
4	Sep 2	GRIMSBY TOWN	1-0	Jones	15547	1	6	3	4	5			7	8	9	10	11	2							
5	4	Southport	2-0	Brown 2	9406	1	6	3	4	5			7	8	9	10	11	2							
6	9	BARNSLEY	1-0	Gregory	12158	1	6	3	4	5			7	8	9	10	11	2							
7	11	Barrow	3-1	Gregory, Brown, Haigh	6307	1	6	3	4	5			7	8	9	10	11	2							
8	15	Barnsley	0-1		16431	1	6	3	4	5			7	8	9	10	11	2							
9	18	WORKINGTON	1-1	Haigh	9403	1	6	3	4	5			7	8	9	10	11	2							
10	22	Wrexham	1-0	Gregory	8139	1	6	3	4	5				8	9	10	7	2	11						
11	25	Mansfield Town	1-2	McGill (p)	11809	1	6	3	4	5				8	9	10	7	2	11						
12	30	WREXHAM	1-0	Gregory	8810	1		3	4	5	6		7	8	9	10	11	2							
13	Oct 2	ACCRINGTON STANLEY	4-0	Brown 2, Turner, Haigh	11370	1	2		4	5	6			8	9	10	11	3		7					
14	9	Bradford Park Avenue	0-0		14402	1	2	3	4	5	6			8	9	10	11				7					
15	16	ROCHDALE	2-2	Brown 2	10331	1	2	3	4	5	6			8	9	10	11				7					
16	23	Tranmere Rovers	2-1	Brown, Haigh	5493	1	2	3	4	5	6		7	8	9	10	11								
17	30	STOCKPORT COUNTY	3-0	Brown, Bushby, Brownsword (p)	9956	1	2	3	4	5	6		7	8	9	10	11								
18	Nov 6	Hartlepools United	2-4	Gregory 2	7621	1	2	3	4	5	6		7	8	9	10	11								
19	13	Gateshead	0-2		9159	1	2	3	4	5	6			8	9	10	11					7			
20	27	CHESTERFIELD	2-1	Brown, Brownsword (p)	8739	1	2	3	4	5	6		7	8	9	10	11								
21	Dec 4	Crewe Alexandra	1-1	Gregory	3651	1	2	3	4	5	6		7	8	9	10	11								
22	18	Halifax Town	1-3	McGill	10981	1	2	3	4	5	6		7	8	9	10	11								
23	25	Bradford City	4-2	Brown 2, Gregory, Mosby	12587	1	2	3		5	6	4	7	8	9	10	11								
24	27	BRADFORD CITY	1-0	Brown	11016	1	2	3		5	6	4	7	8	9	10	11								
25	Jan 1	YORK CITY	1-2	Brownsword (p)	10593	1	2	3		5	6	4	7	8	9	10	11								
26	8	Chester	4-2	Whitfield 3, Brown	4083	1	2	3	4	5	6	7	8	9		11				10					
27	22	BARROW	3-0	Whitfield 2, Mosby	7348		2	3	4	5	6	7		9	10			11		8			1		
28	29	CHESTER	1-1	Brown	8328		2	3	4	5	6	7	8	9				11		10			1		
29	Feb 5	Workington	1-1	Gregory	8601		2	3	4	5	6	7		9	10	11				8			1		
30	12	MANSFIELD TOWN	2-0	Jones, Gregory	7132		2	3	4	5	6	7		9	10	11		8					1		
31	19	Accrington Stanley	1-2	Turner	10763		2	3	4	5	6			9	10	11		8	7				1		
32	Mar 5	Rochdale	0-2		6078		2	3	4	5	6			9	10	11		8					1		7
33	12	TRANMERE ROVERS	1-2	Gregory	7817	1	2	3	4	5	6		7	9	10	11		8							
34	19	Stockport County	2-4	Gregory, Brown	7005	1	6	3	4	5	8	7		9	10	11	2								
35	26	HARTLEPOOLS UNITED	5-1	Hubbard 4, Gregory	4155	1	8	3	4	5	6	7		9	10	11	2								
36	Apr 2	Gateshead	1-0	Brown	4217	1	8	3	4	5	6	7		9	10	11	2								
37	8	Oldham Athletic	1-1	Hubbard	9396	1	8	3	4	5	6	7		9	10	11	2								
38	9	DARLINGTON	1-0	McGill	8268	1	8	3	4	5	6	7		9	10	11	2								
39	11	OLDHAM ATHLETIC	6-1	Brown 2, Hubbard 2, Gregory 2	8471	1	8	3	4	5	6	7		9	10	11	2								
40	16	Chesterfield	0-2		7314	1	8	3	4	5	6	7		9	10	11	2								
41	18	CARLISLE UNITED	1-0	Gregory	7263	1	8	3	4	5	6	7		9	10	11	2								
42	23	CREWE ALEXANDRA	3-1	Gregory, Brown, McGill	5316	1	8	3	4	5	6			9	10	11	2			7					
43	27	Darlington	1-1	Whitfield	3395	1	8	3	4	5	6			9	10	11	2			7					
44	30	Carlisle United	2-1	Brown, Brownsword (p)	4636	1	8	3	4	5	6	7		9	10	11				8					
45	May 5	BRADFORD PARK AVE.	1-1	Gregory	5136	1	2	3	4	5	6	7		9	10	11				8					
46	7	Southport	1-1	Mosby	2407	1	2	3	4	5	6	7		9	10	11				8					
				Apps		40	45	45	43	46	36	35	28	46	44	44	22	4	5	12	1	2	1	6	1
				Goals			7	4	5			1	3	6	23	22	2			2	6				

F.A. Cup

	Date	Opponent	Score	Scorers	Att																				
R1	Nov 20	Horden Colliery	1-0	McGill	5949	1	2	3	4	5		7	8	10	9	11					6				
R2	Dec 11	Coventry City	0-4		21360	1	2	3	4	5	6	7	8	9	10	11									

		P	W	D	L	F	A	W	D	L	F	A	Pts
1	Barnsley	46	18	3	2	51	17	12	2	9	35	29	65
2	Accrington Stanley	46	18	2	3	65	32	7	9	7	31	35	61
3	SCUNTHORPE UNITED	46	14	6	3	45	18	9	6	8	36	35	58
4	York City	46	13	5	5	43	27	11	5	7	49	36	58
5	Hartlepools United	46	16	3	4	39	20	9	2	12	25	29	55
6	Chesterfield	46	17	1	5	54	33	7	5	11	27	37	54
7	Gateshead	46	15	3	5	38	26	9	5	9	27	43	52
8	Workington	46	11	7	5	39	23	7	7	9	29	32	50
9	Stockport County	46	13	4	6	50	27	5	8	10	34	43	48
10	Oldham Athletic	46	14	5	4	47	22	5	5	13	27	46	48
11	Southport	46	10	9	4	28	18	6	7	10	19	26	48
12	Rochdale	46	13	7	3	39	20	4	7	12	30	46	48
13	Mansfield Town	46	14	4	5	40	28	4	5	14	25	43	45
14	Halifax Town	46	9	9	5	41	27	6	4	13	22	40	43
15	Darlington	46	10	7	6	41	28	4	7	12	21	45	42
16	Bradford Park Ave.	46	11	7	5	29	21	4	4	15	27	49	41
17	Barrow	46	12	6	5	39	34	5	2	16	31	55	40
18	Wrexham	46	9	6	8	40	35	4	6	13	25	42	38
19	Tranmere Rovers	46	9	6	8	37	30	4	5	14	18	40	37
20	Carlisle United	46	12	1	10	53	39	3	5	15	25	50	36
21	Bradford City	46	9	5	9	30	26	4	5	14	17	29	36
22	Crewe Alexandra	46	8	10	5	45	35	2	4	17	23	56	34
23	Grimsby Town	46	10	4	9	28	32	3	4	16	19	46	34
24	Chester	46	10	3	10	23	25	2	6	15	21	52	33

1955/56 9th in Division 3(N)

#	Date		Opponent	Score	Scorers	Att	Malan NF	Hubbard J	Brownsword N	McGill A	White R	Bushby A	Davies JR	Haigh J	Brown GA	Gregory JE	Jones JM	Barrett J	Callaghan R	Marshall PW	Thompson D	Sharpe LT	Benson JR	Lamb HT	Heward B	Parrott JF	Mullen A	Wainwright L
1	Aug	20	Bradford Park Avenue	0-2		12604	1	2	3	4	5	6	7	8	9	10	11											
2		22	Mansfield Town	2-3	Haigh, Gregory	9730	1	2	3	4	5	6	7	8	9	10	11											
3		27	OLDHAM ATHLETIC	2-1	Haigh, Callaghan	8839	1	2	3		5	6		8	9	10	11	4	7									
4		31	MANSFIELD TOWN	3-0	Gregory 2, Plummer (og)	8923	1	2	3		5	6		8	9	10	11	4	7									
5	Sep	3	Workington	2-1	Callaghan, Gregory	7087		2	3		5	6		8		9	11	4	7	1	10							
6		7	WREXHAM	1-1	Brown	9566		2	3		5	6		8	9	10	11	4	7	1								
7		10	YORK CITY	1-1	Callaghan	9720		2	3		5	6		8	9	10	11	4	7	1								
8		14	Wrexham	1-0	Brownsword (p)	8902		2	3		5	6		8	9	10	11	4	7	1								
9		17	Derby County	2-2	Callaghan 2	18237		2	3		5	6	11		9	10		4	7	1	8							
10		21	HALIFAX TOWN	1-0	Davies	8434		2	3		5	6	11	8	9	10		4	7	1								
11		24	CREWE ALEXANDRA	1-1	Brown	8271		2	3		5			7	8	9	10	4		1		6						
12		26	Stockport County	2-3	Brown, Jones	4146		2	3	4	5			7	8	9	10	11		1		6						
13	Oct	1	Hartlepools United	2-0	Gregory, Jones	8170		2	3	4	5			7	8	9	10	11		1		6						
14		8	CARLISLE UNITED	4-0	Gregory 2, Davies, Haigh	8623		2	3	4	5	6	7		8	9	10	11		1								
15		15	Rochdale	2-3	Brown, Gregory	6110		2	3	4	5	6	7		8	9	10	11		1								
16		22	BARROW	2-0	Gregory, Brownsword (p)	7030	1	2	3	4	5		7		8		10	11	6		9							
17		29	Accrington Stanley	0-2		7443	1	2	3	4	5		7		8		10	11	6	9								
18	Nov	5	DARLINGTON	0-1		7642	1	2		4	5			8	7		10	11	6	9				3				
19		12	Gateshead	0-1		3765	1	10	3	4				7	8		9	11	6					2	5			
20		26	Tranmere Rovers	1-2	Brown	4748	1	6	3	4				7	8	9	10	11						2	5			
21	Dec	3	CHESTERFIELD	2-0	Jones, Brownsword (p)	7114	1	6	3	4					8	9			7					2	5	10		
22		17	BRADFORD PARK AVE.	4-2	Brown 3, Gregory	5942	1	6	3	4				7	8	10	9	11						2	5			
23		24	Oldham Athletic	1-2	Jones	5852	1	6	3	4				7	8	10	9	11						2	5			
24		26	Bradford City	3-4	Gregory 2, Brown	7896	1	6	3	4				7	8	10	9	11						2	5			
25		27	BRADFORD CITY	2-0	Haigh, McGill	7978		6	3	4				7	8	10	9	11		1				2	5			
26		31	WORKINGTON	3-1	Brown 2, Davies	7446		6	3	4				7	8	10	9	11		1				2	5			
27	Jan	21	DERBY COUNTY	0-2		10361		6	3	4				7	8	10	9	11		1				2	5			
28	Feb	4	Crewe Alexandra	2-1	Gregory, Jones	2432		2	3	4		6	7	8	10	9	11			1					5			
29		11	HARTLEPOOLS UNITED	5-1	Jones 2, Brown, Bushby, McGill(p)	5614		2	3	4		6	7	8	10	9	11			1					5			
30		18	Carlisle United	2-1	Haigh, Gregory	4928		2	3	4		6	7	8	10	9	11			1					5			
31	Mar	3	Barrow	2-2	Callaghan, Haigh	4001		2	3	4		6		8	10	9	11		7	1					5			
32		10	ACCRINGTON STANLEY	2-3	Brown 2	10049		2	3	4		6		8	10	9	11			1					5			
33		17	Southport	2-2	Brown, Mullen	5610		2	3	4		6	7	8	10					1					5		11	
34		22	ROCHDALE	1-2	Gregory	4865		2	3	4		6	7	8	10	9				1					5		11	
35		24	GATESHEAD	1-1	Brown	4702		2	3	4		6		8	10	9			7	1					5		11	
36		30	Grimsby Town	1-0	Brown	23399		2	3	4		6		8	10	9			7	1					5		11	
37		31	Darlington	0-1		4797			3	4		6	7	8	10	9				1				2	5		11	
38	Apr	2	GRIMSBY TOWN	0-1		19067			3	4		6		8	10	9	11		7	1				2	5			
39		7	TRANMERE ROVERS	2-1	Brown, Gregory	4443		2	3			6		8	10	9		4	7	1					5		11	
40		9	York City	0-0		9045		2	3			6		8	10	9		4	7	1					5		11	
41		14	Chesterfield	0-2		5592		2	3			6		8	10	9		4	7	1					5		11	
42		18	SOUTHPORT	0-1		4452		2	3			6	7	8	10	9	11			1			4		5			
43		21	CHESTER	2-1	Gregory, Haigh	4333		6	3				7	8		10	11	9	1			4		5				2
44		26	Stockport County	1-5	Gregory	3780		6	3				7	8		9	10			1			4		5		11	2
45		28	Halifax Town	3-0	Haigh, Gregory, Brown	2839			3	4			7	8	10	9	11			1			6	2	5			
46	May	2	Chester	5-3	Brown 2, Gregory, McGill(p), Bushby	3253			3	8		6	7		10	9	11			1			4	2	5			
					Apps		13	42	45	31	18	28	31	44	40	45	36	16	19	33	3	6	2	14	28	1	9	2
					Goals				3	3		2	3	8	21	20	7		6								1	

One own goal

F.A. Cup

#	Date		Opponent	Score	Scorers	Att	Malan	Hubbard	Brownsword	McGill	White	Bushby	Davies	Haigh	Brown	Gregory	Jones	Barrett	Callaghan	Marshall	Thompson	Sharpe	Benson	Lamb	Heward	Parrott	Mullen	Wainwright
R1	Nov	19	SHILDON COLLIERY	3-0	Davies, Brown, Gregory	8868	1	8	3	4			7		9	10	11	6						2	5			
R2	Dec	10	Bishop Auckland	0-0		13500	1	6	3	4				8	10		11		7					2	5	9		
rep		15	BISHOP AUCKLAND	2-0	Davies, Hubbard	9923	1	6	3	4			7	8	10	9	11							2	5			
R3	Jan	7	Rotherham United	1-1	Brown	16144		6	3	4			7	8	10	9	11			1				2	5			
rep		12	ROTHERHAM UNITED	4-2	Brown 3, Davies	13262		6	3	4			7	8	10	9	11			1				2	5			
R4		28	Liverpool	3-3	Davies 2, Gregory	53393		2	3	4		6	7	8	10	9	11			1					5			
rep	Feb	6	LIVERPOOL	1-2	Davies	19612		2	3	4		6	7	8	10	9	11			1					5			

R4 replay a.e.t.

		P	W	D	L	F	A	W	D	L	F	A	Pts
1	Grimsby Town	46	20	1	2	54	10	11	5	7	22	19	68
2	Derby County	46	18	4	1	67	23	10	3	10	43	32	63
3	Accrington Stanley	46	17	4	2	61	19	8	5	10	31	38	59
4	Hartlepools United	46	18	2	3	47	15	8	3	12	34	45	57
5	Southport	46	12	9	2	39	18	11	2	10	27	35	57
6	Chesterfield	46	18	1	4	61	21	7	3	13	33	45	54
7	Stockport County	46	16	4	3	65	22	5	5	13	25	39	51
8	Bradford City	46	16	5	2	57	25	2	8	13	21	39	49
9	SCUNTHORPE UNITED	46	12	4	7	40	26	8	4	11	35	37	48
10	Workington	46	13	4	6	47	20	6	5	12	28	43	47
11	York City	46	12	4	7	44	24	7	5	11	41	48	47
12	Rochdale	46	13	5	5	46	39	4	8	11	20	45	47
13	Gateshead	46	15	4	4	56	32	2	7	14	21	52	45
14	Wrexham	46	11	5	7	37	28	5	5	13	29	45	42
15	Darlington	46	11	6	6	41	28	5	3	15	19	45	41
16	Tranmere Rovers	46	11	4	8	33	25	5	5	13	26	59	41
17	Chester	46	10	8	5	35	33	3	6	14	17	49	40
18	Mansfield Town	46	13	6	4	59	21	1	5	17	25	60	39
19	Halifax Town	46	10	6	7	40	27	4	5	14	26	49	39
20	Oldham Athletic	46	7	12	4	48	36	3	6	14	28	50	38
21	Carlisle United	46	11	7	5	39	25	4	5	14	26	59	38
22	Barrow	46	11	6	6	44	25	1	3	19	17	58	33
23	Bradford Park Ave.	46	13	4	6	47	38	0	3	20	14	84	33
24	Crewe Alexandra	46	9	4	10	32	35	0	6	17	18	70	28

~ 226 ~

1956/57 14th in Division 3(N)

		Date	Opponent	Score	Scorers	Att	Marshall PW	Hubbard J	Brownsword NJ	McGill A	Hussey FM	Bushby A	Whiteside WR	Haigh J	Brown GA	Fletcher D	Jones JM	Gregory JE	Sharpe LT	Luke GB	Heward B	Lewis K	Charlesworth T	Davies JR	Horstead JB	Waldock R	Mullen A	Gleadall E	Hardwick K	Whitnall B
1	Aug	18	DARLINGTON	1-2	Brown	7923		2	3	4	5	6	7	8	9	10	11													
2		21	Southport	2-2	Brown 2	6625		2	3	4	5	6	7	8	9	10	11													
3		25	Barrow	2-1	Brown, Fletcher	8455		2	3	4	5	6		8	9	10	11	7												
4		30	SOUTHPORT	1-0	Brown	7768		2	3	4	5	6		8	9	10	11	7												
5	Sep	1	HULL CITY	1-1	Brown	11004		2	3		5	6		8	9	10	11	7	4											
6		3	Bradford Park Avenue	2-1	Haigh, Gregory	8564		2	3		5	6		8	9	10	11	7	4											
7		8	Workington	2-2	Haigh, Jones	11073		2	3		5	6		8	7	10	11		4	9											
8		13	BRADFORD PARK AVE.	2-2	Brown, Luke	7855		2	3		5	6		8	7	10	11		4	9											
9		15	HALIFAX TOWN	6-1	Luke 2, Jones 2, Fletcher, Brown	7143		2	3		5	6		8	7	10	11		4	9											
10		19	Crewe Alexandra	1-2	Luke	5425		2	3		5	6		8	7	10	11		4	9											
11		22	Rochdale	0-3		6320		2	3		5	6		8	7	10	11		4	9											
12		27	CREWE ALEXANDRA	5-1	Gregory 2, Haigh, Fletcher, Brown	5776		2	3	4	5	6		8	7		11	10		9											
13		29	MANSFIELD TOWN	0-1		7774		2	3	4	5	6		8	7	11		10		9											
14	Oct	6	Chesterfield	0-1		9017		2	3	4		6		8		11	7	10		9	5										
15		13	CHESTER	3-0	Brown, McGill, Gill (og)	6377		2	3	4		6		8	7	11		10		9	5										
16		20	York City	2-0	Gregory, Hubbard	8881		2	3	4		6		8	7	11		10		9	5										
17		27	BRADFORD CITY	1-1	Brown	6837		2	3	4		6		8		7	11	10		9	5										
18	Nov	3	Stockport County	3-1	Brown, Bushby, Jones	12313		2	3	4		6		8		7	11	10		9	5										
19		10	CARLISLE UNITED	1-2	Luke	5564		2	3	4		6		8		11		10		9	5	7									
20		24	TRANMERE ROVERS	1-4	Gregory	5228		2	3	4		6		8		7	11	10		9	5										
21	Dec	1	Hartlepools United	0-0		7881		2	3	4		6		8		10	11			9	5		1	7							
22		15	Darlington	2-1	Fletcher 2	3421		2	3			6		8	9		10	4			5		1	7							
23		22	BARROW	1-1	Haigh	3324		2	3			6		8	9	11		10	4		5		1	7							
24		25	Derby County	0-4		11266		2	3	4		6		8	9	7	11				5		1		10						
25		26	DERBY COUNTY	1-4	McGill (p)	4103		2	3	4		6		8	9	7	11				5		1		10						
26		29	Hull City	2-2	Fletcher 2	12873			3	4		6		8	9	7	11	10			5		1			2					
27	Jan	1	Accrington Stanley	1-0	Brown	8880	3			4		6		8	9	7	11	10			5		1			2					
28		12	WORKINGTON	2-1	Brown, R Brown (og)	5707			3	4		6		8	9	7	11	10			5		1			2					
29		19	Halifax Town	0-1		4496			3	4		6		8	9		11	10			5		1	7		2					
30	Feb	2	ROCHDALE	1-0	Haigh	6080			3	4		6		10	9						5			7		2	8	11			
31		9	Mansfield Town	1-1	Davies	8823			3	4		6		10	9		11				5			7	2	8					
32		16	CHESTERFIELD	5-1	Waldock 3, Fletcher, McGill	6854			3	4		6		10	9		11				5			7	2	8					
33		23	Chester	2-2	Waldock, Haigh	2691			3	4		6		10	9		11				5			7	2	8					
34	Mar	2	YORK CITY	2-1	Davies, Jones	7848			3	4	5	6		10	9		11							7	2	8					
35		9	Bradford City	1-3	Waldock	13475			3	4		6		10	9		11			5					2	8		7			
36		16	STOCKPORT COUNTY	2-3	Waldock, Bushby (p)	6829			3	4	5	6		10	9		11						1		2	8		7			
37		23	Carlisle United	0-0		8165		3		4	5	6			9		11						1	7	2	10		8			
38		30	ACCRINGTON STANLEY	2-3	Fletcher, Haigh	6602			3	4	5	6		10	9		11						1	7	2	8					
39	Apr	4	WREXHAM	4-3	Haigh, Waldock, Fletcher, Davies	4196	3		3	4	5	6		10	9		11						1	7	2	8					
40		6	Tranmere Rovers	2-4	Waldock, Haigh	5491	9		3	4	5	6		10			11						1	7	2	8					
41		10	Wrexham	1-1	Luke	4340		2	3	4	5	6		10			11			9			1	7		8					
42		13	HARTLEPOOLS UNITED	1-2	Fletcher	4599			3	4	5	6		10	9		11							7	2	8					
43		19	GATESHEAD	1-2	Waldock	4044			3	4	5	6		10	9		11							7	2	8			1		
44		20	Oldham Athletic	1-1	Fletcher	5897		2	3	4		6		10	9		11				5			7		8			1		
45		22	Gateshead	0-0		3324		2	3			6		10	9		11	4			5			7		8			1		
46		27	OLDHAM ATHLETIC	0-0		3903	3		2			6		10	9		11	4			5			7		8			1	3
			Apps				1	32	43	35	22	46	2	45	38	28	38	19	11	18	24	1	17	19	17	17	1	3	4	1
			Goals					1			3		2		9	14	12	5	5		6			3		9				

Two own goals

F.A. Cup

		Date	Opponent	Score	Scorers	Att	Marshall PW	Hubbard J	Brownsword NJ	McGill A	Hussey FM	Bushby A	Whiteside WR	Haigh J	Brown GA	Fletcher D	Jones JM	Gregory JE	Sharpe LT	Luke GB	Heward B	Lewis K	Charlesworth T	Davies JR
R1	Nov	17	ROCHDALE	1-0	Brown	8655	1	2	3	4		6		8		7	11	10		9	5			
R2	Dec	8	WREXHAM	0-0		9153		2	3	4		6		8		10	11	9			5		1	7
rep		11	Wrexham	2-6	Gregory 2	11549		2	3	4		6		8	9		11	10			5		1	7

R2 replay a.e.t.

		P	W	D	L	F	A	W	D	L	F	A	Pts
1	Derby County	46	18	3	2	69	18	8	8	7	42	35	63
2	Hartlepools United	46	18	4	1	56	21	7	5	11	34	42	59
3	Accrington Stanley	46	15	4	4	54	22	10	4	9	41	42	58
4	Workington	46	16	4	3	60	25	8	6	9	33	38	58
5	Stockport County	46	16	3	4	51	26	7	5	11	40	49	54
6	Chesterfield	46	17	5	1	60	22	5	4	14	36	57	53
7	York City	46	14	4	5	43	21	7	6	10	32	40	52
8	Hull City	46	14	6	3	45	24	7	4	12	39	45	52
9	Bradford City	46	14	3	6	47	31	8	5	10	31	37	52
10	Barrow	46	16	2	5	51	22	5	7	11	25	40	51
11	Halifax Town	46	16	2	5	40	24	5	5	13	25	46	49
12	Wrexham	46	12	7	4	63	33	7	3	13	34	41	48
13	Rochdale	46	14	6	3	38	19	4	6	13	27	46	48
14	SCUNTHORPE UNITED	46	9	5	9	44	36	6	10	7	27	33	45
15	Carlisle United	46	9	9	5	44	36	7	4	12	32	49	45
16	Mansfield Town	46	13	3	7	58	38	4	7	12	33	52	44
17	Gateshead	46	9	6	8	42	40	8	4	11	30	50	44
18	Darlington	46	11	5	7	47	36	6	3	14	35	59	42
19	Oldham Athletic	46	9	7	7	35	31	3	8	12	31	43	39
20	Bradford Park Ave.	46	11	2	10	41	40	5	1	17	25	53	35
21	Chester	46	8	7	8	40	35	2	6	15	15	49	33
22	Southport	46	7	8	8	31	34	4	16	21	60	32	
23	Tranmere Rovers	46	5	9	9	33	38	2	4	17	18	53	27
24	Crewe Alexandra	46	5	7	11	31	46	1	2	20	12	64	21

~ 227 ~

1957/58 Champions Division 3(N)

#	Date		Opponent	Score	Scorers	Att	Hardwick K	Horstead JB	Brownsword NJ	Marshall F	Heward B	Bushby A	Marriott JL	Waldock R	Fletcher D	Haigh J	Jones JM	Hussey FM	Hubbard J	Stokes AW	Whitnall B	Sharpe LT	Davies JR	Gleadall E	Davis EWC	Maw J	Minton AE
1	Aug	24	Chesterfield	1-1	Marriott	10768	1	2	3	4	5	6	7	8	9	10	11										
2		26	Tranmere Rovers	4-1	Waldock 3, Fletcher	13197	1	2	3	4	5	6	7	8	9	10	11										
3		31	DARLINGTON	5-0	Marriott 2, Waldock 2, Fletcher	8506	1	2	3	4	5	6	7	8	9	10	11										
4	Sep	5	TRANMERE ROVERS	1-0	Fletcher	10480	1	2	3	4	5	6	7	8	9	10	11										
5		7	Gateshead	2-1	Waldock, Fletcher	5666	1	2	3	4	5	6	7	8	9	10	11										
6		12	CREWE ALEXANDRA	3-2	Marriott, Haigh, Brownsword (p)	9679	1	2	3	4	5	6	7	8	9	10	11										
7		14	MANSFIELD TOWN	3-3	Haigh, Brownsword(p), Chamberlain(og)	9533	1	2	3	4		6	7	8	9	10	11	5									
8		18	Crewe Alexandra	2-0	Haigh, Williams (og)	4159	1	5	3	4		6	7	8	9	10	11		2								
9		21	Workington	2-3	Haigh, Fletcher	8839	1	5	3	4		6	7	8	9	10	11		2								
10		25	Rochdale	4-1	Haigh, Waldock, Marriott, Fletcher	5278	1	5	3	4		6	7	8	9	10	11		2								
11		28	BRADFORD CITY	0-2		9576	1	5	3	4		6	7	8	9	10	11		2								
12	Oct	3	ROCHDALE	2-0	Haigh, Stokes	11636	1	5	3	4		6	7		8	10	11		2	9							
13		5	Hull City	0-2		12009	1	5	3	4		6			8	10	11				2						
14		12	Accrington Stanley	1-2	Fletcher	7388	1	5		4		6	7		8	10	11		3	9	2						
15		19	BRADFORD PARK AVE.	6-2	Davies 2, Fletcher 2, Brownsword 2(2p)	7591	1	5	3	4		6	11	8	9	10			2				7				
16		26	Carlisle United	4-3	Gleadall, Fletcher, Marriott	10579	1	5	3	4		6	11		9	10			2				7	8			
17		31	HALIFAX TOWN	1-1	Davies	9373	1	5	3	4		6	11		9	10			2				7	8			
18	Nov	2	SOUTHPORT	1-0	Fletcher	8305	1	5	3	4		6	11	8	9	10			2				7				
19		9	York City	0-0		8276	1	5	3	4		6	11	8	9	10			2				7				
20		23	Oldham Athletic	1-2	Davis	8150	1	5	3	4		6		8		10	11		2				7		9		
21		30	BURY	1-0	Waldock	10926	1	5	3	4		6	7	8	9	10	11		2								
22	Dec	14	Chester	2-1	Fletcher 2	4604	1	5	3	4		6	7	8	9	10	11		2								
23		21	CHESTERFIELD	1-1	Fletcher	7741	1	5	3	4		6		8	9	10	11		2				7				
24		26	Halifax Town	1-0	Waldock	9942	1	5	3	4		6		8	9	10	11				2	7					
25		28	Darlington	1-1	Waldock	7833	1	5	3	4		6		8		10	11				2	7		9			
26	Jan	11	GATESHEAD	2-1	Waldock 2	7750	1	5	3	4		6	7	8		10	11				2				9		
27		18	Mansfield Town	5-3	Davis 2, Waldock, Haigh, Marriott	8415	1	5	3	4		6	7	8		10	11				2				9		
28	Feb	1	WORKINGTON	2-2	Waldock 2	9060	1	5	3	4		6		8		10	11				2				9	3	
29		20	HULL CITY	2-0	Davis, Feasey (og)	11408	1	5	3	4		6	7	8		10	11		2						9		
30		22	OLDHAM ATHLETIC	1-1	Waldock	10036	1	5	3	4		6		8	10		11		2				7		9		
31	Mar	1	Bradford Park Avenue	2-1	Waldock 2	13467	1	5	3	4		6		8		10	11		2				7		9		
32		13	STOCKPORT COUNTY	4-0	Waldock 2, Davis 2	8446	1	5	3	4	6			8		10	11		2				7		9		
33		15	Southport	2-1	Waldock, Davis	3366	1	5	3	4		6		8		10	11		2				7		9		
34		22	ACCRINGTON STANLEY	1-0	Davis	11304	1	5	3	4	6			8		10	11		2				7		9		
35		29	Barrow	1-0	Davies	5261	1	5	3	4	6			8		10	11		2				7		9		
36	Apr	4	Wrexham	0-1		14280	1	5	3	4	6			8		10	11		2				7		9		
37		5	HARTLEPOOLS UNITED	2-0	Davis 2	8684	1	5	3	4				8		10	11		2				6	7	9		
38		7	WREXHAM	1-0	Brownsword (p)	9879	1	5	3	4			7		8	10	11		2				6		9		
39		12	Bury	1-2	Haigh	12508	1	5	3	4			7			8	11		2				6		9	10	
40		17	BARROW	1-0	Stokes	9609	1	5	3	4			7		8		11		2	10			6		9		
41		19	YORK CITY	1-2	Davis	10083	1	5	3	4			7		8		11		2	10			6		9		
42		21	Stockport County	1-2	Davis	14005	1	5	3	4			7	8		10	11		2				6		9		
43		24	Bradford City	3-2	Minton 2, Davis	18240	1	5	3	4			7			10	11		2				6		9		8
44		26	CHESTER	2-1	Haigh, Davis	10403	1	5	3	4			7			10	11		2				6		9		8
45		28	Hartlepools United	2-1	Davis 2	8159	1	5	3	4			7			10	11		2				6		9		8
46	May	1	CARLISLE UNITED	3-1	Davis, Haigh, Brownsword (p)	12555	1	5	3	4			7	8		10	11		2						9		
					Apps		46	46	44	46	11	31	34	33	26	45	41	1	33	5	1	16	17	3	23	1	3
					Goals			6					7	21	14	10				2			4	2	17		2

Three own goals

F.A. Cup

#	Date		Opponent	Score	Scorers	Att	Hardwick K	Horstead JB	Brownsword NJ	Marshall F	Heward B	Bushby A	Marriott JL	Waldock R	Fletcher D	Haigh J	Jones JM	Hussey FM	Hubbard J	Stokes AW	Whitnall B	Sharpe LT	Davies JR	Gleadall E	Davis EWC	Maw J	Minton AE
R1	Nov	16	GOOLE TOWN	2-1	Fletcher, Davies	8931	1	5	3	4		6	11	8	9	10			2				7				
R2	Dec	7	BURY	2-0	Waldock, Jones	12106	1	5	3	4		6	7	8	9	10	11		2								
R3	Jan	4	BRADFORD CITY	1-0	Haigh	11645	1	5	3	4		6	7	8	9	10	11				2						
R4		25	Newcastle United	3-1	Davis 2, Haigh	33407	1	5	3	4		6	7	8		10	11				2				9		
R5	Feb	15	LIVERPOOL	0-1		23000	1	5	3	4		6	7	8		10	11				2				9		

		P	W	D	L	F	A	W	D	L	F	A	Pts
1	SCUNTHORPE UNITED	46	16	5	2	46	19	13	3	7	42	31	66
2	Accrington Stanley	46	16	4	3	53	28	9	5	9	30	33	59
3	Bradford City	46	13	7	3	42	19	8	8	7	31	30	57
4	Bury	46	17	4	2	61	18	6	6	11	33	44	56
5	Hull City	46	15	6	2	49	20	4	9	10	29	47	53
6	Mansfield Town	46	16	3	4	68	42	6	5	12	32	50	52
7	Halifax Town	46	15	5	3	52	20	5	6	12	31	49	51
8	Chesterfield	46	12	8	3	39	28	6	7	10	32	41	51
9	Stockport County	46	15	4	4	54	28	3	7	13	20	39	47
10	Rochdale	46	14	4	5	50	25	5	4	14	29	42	46
11	Tranmere Rovers	46	12	6	5	51	32	6	4	13	31	44	46
12	Wrexham	46	13	8	2	39	18	4	4	15	22	45	46
13	York City	46	11	8	4	40	26	6	4	13	28	50	46
14	Gateshead	46	12	5	6	41	27	3	10	10	27	49	45
15	Oldham Athletic	46	11	7	5	44	32	3	10	10	28	52	45
16	Carlisle United	46	13	3	7	56	35	6	3	14	24	43	44
17	Hartlepools United	46	11	6	6	45	26	5	6	12	28	50	44
18	Barrow	46	9	7	7	36	32	4	8	11	30	42	41
19	Workington	46	11	6	6	46	33	3	7	13	26	48	41
20	Darlington	46	15	3	5	53	25	2	4	17	25	64	41
21	Chester	46	7	10	6	38	26	6	3	14	35	55	39
22	Bradford Park Ave.	46	8	6	9	41	41	5	5	13	27	54	37
23	Southport	46	8	3	12	29	40	3	3	17	23	48	28
24	Crewe Alexandra	46	6	5	12	29	41	2	2	19	18	52	23

1958/59 18th in Division 2

#	Date	Opponent	Score	Scorers	Att	Hardwick K	Hubbard J	Brownsword NJ	Marshall F	Horstead JB	Sharpe LT	Marriott JL	Waldock R	Davis EWC	Haigh J	Ormond W	Jones JM	Heward B	Wood BW	Minton AE	Neale P	Jones K	Harburn PAP	Ward JR	Bushby A	Pearce DG	Donnelly P	Grant J
1	Aug 23	IPSWICH TOWN	1-1	Davis	13317	1	2	3	4	5	6	7	8	9	10	11												
2	28	Swansea Town	0-3		21056	1	2	3	4	5	6	7	8	9	10	11												
3	30	Bristol Rovers	0-4		24221	1	2	3	4	5	6	7	8	9	10	11												
4	Sep 4	SWANSEA TOWN	3-1	Davis 2, Waldock	13592	1	2	3	4	5	6	7	8	9	10		11											
5	6	DERBY COUNTY	2-2	Marriott, Haigh	13318	1	2	3	4	5	6	7	8	9	10		11											
6	10	Stoke City	3-4	Waldock, Sharpe, M Jones	17824	1	2	3	4	5	6	7	8	9	10		11											
7	13	Leyton Orient	1-2	Waldock	15955	1	2	3	4	5	6	7	8	9	10		11											
8	18	STOKE CITY	1-1	M Jones	14159	1	2	3	4	10	6	7	8	9			11	5										
9	20	ROTHERHAM UNITED	2-0	Wood, Brownsword (p)	13959	1	2	3	4		6	7		9	8		11	5	10									
10	27	SHEFFIELD WEDNESDAY	1-4	Brownsword (p)	17488	1	2	3	4		6	7		9	8		11	5	10									
11	Oct 4	Fulham	1-1	Bentley (og)	24569	1	2	3	4		6	7			10	8	11	5		9								
12	11	Sheffield United	1-4	M Jones	22084	1	2	3	4		6	7	10	9	8		11	5										
13	18	BRIGHTON & HOVE ALB	2-3	Waldock, Haigh	11921	1		3			2	7	8	9	4		11	5		10	6							
14	25	Grimsby Town	1-1	Waldock	16753	1	2	3		5	6	7	9		8		11	4		10								
15	Nov 1	BARNSLEY	1-0	Waldock	12956	1	2	3			6	7	8	9	4		11	5		10								
16	8	Middlesbrough	1-6	Neale	23020	1	2	3			6	7	8	9	4		11	5		10								
17	15	CHARLTON ATHLETIC	3-3	Waldock, Hewie(og),Brownsword(p)	11023	1	2	3	4	5	6	7	9		8		11			10								
18	22	Bristol City	1-0	Marriott	20306	1	2	3	4	5	6	7	9		8		11			10								
19	Dec 6	Huddersfield Town	1-0	Marriott	13888	1	2	3	4	5	6	7	9		8		11			10								
20	13	LIVERPOOL	1-2	Waldock	11194	1	2	3	4	5	6	7	9		8		11			10								
21	18	CARDIFF CITY	1-0	Marriott	10365	1	2	3	4	5	6	7	9		8		11			10								
22	20	Ipswich Town	1-3	Waldock	13204	1	2	3		5	4	7	10	9	8		11			6								
23	26	SUNDERLAND	3-2	Ashurst (og), Neale, Sharpe	14509	1	2	3	4	5	6	7	9		8		11			10								
24	27	Sunderland	1-3	Neale	27550	1	2	3	4		6	7	9		8		11	5		10								
25	Jan 3	BRISTOL ROVERS	0-0		11130		2	3	4	5		7	9		8		11	6		10	1							
26	17	Derby County	1-3	Harburn	13941	1	2	3	4	5	6	7		10	8		11						9					
27	31	LEYTON ORIENT	2-0	Harburn, Waldock	10259	1	2	3	4	5	6	7	10		8		11						9					
28	Feb 7	Rotherham United	0-1		9843	1	2	3	4	5	6	7	10		8		11						9					
29	14	Sheffield Wednesday	0-2		21801	1	2	3	4	5	6	7	10		8		11						9					
30	21	FULHAM	1-2	Waldock	10080		2	3	4	5	6	7	11							8	1	9	10					
31	28	MIDDLESBROUGH	0-3		11171		2	3	4	5	6	7	10		8					11	1	9						
32	Mar 7	Brighton & Hove Albion	1-2	Haigh	17795		2	3	4	5		7	9		8		11			10	1			6				
33	14	GRIMSBY TOWN	1-3	Marriott	13539		2	3		5		7	9		8		11	6		10	1				4			
34	21	Barnsley	1-0	Harburn	6032	1	2	3	4	5		7	8		10		11			6			9					
35	27	Lincoln City	3-3	Harburn, Waldock, Jones M	14679	1	2	3	4	5		7	8		10		11			6			9					
36	28	SHEFFIELD UNITED	1-3	Harburn	12353		2	3	4			7	8		10		11	5		6			9					
37	30	LINCOLN CITY	3-1	Donnelly 2, Harburn	13742		2	3				7	8		4		11	5		6	1		9				10	
38	Apr 4	Charlton Athletic	3-2	Harburn 2, Waldock	15285	1	2	3	4			7	8		10		11	5		6			9					
39	11	BRISTOL CITY	3-3	Donnelly 2 (1 p), McCall (og)	11101	1	2	3				7	8		4		11	5		6			9				10	
40	18	Cardiff City	2-0	Haigh, Waldock	13003	1	2	3	4				8		10		7	5		6			9				11	
41	22	Liverpool	0-3		13976	1	2	3	4				8		10		7	5	11	6			9					
42	25	HUDDERSFIELD T	0-3		9035	1		3	4				8		10		11	5		6			9			2		7
				Apps		35	40	42	34	27	30	39	38	17	40	3	37	19	3	26	7	1	15	1	1	2	3	1
				Goals				3			2	5	14	3	4		4		1	3			8				4	

Four own goals

F.A. Cup

| R3 | Jan 10 | BOLTON WANDERERS | 0-2 | | 23706 | 1 | 2 | 3 | 4 | 5 | 6 | 7 | | 9 | | 8 | | 11 | | | 10 | | | | | | | |

		P	W	D	L	F	A	W	D	L	F	A	Pts
1	Sheffield Wed.	42	18	2	1	68	13	10	4	7	38	35	62
2	Fulham	42	18	1	2	65	26	9	5	7	31	35	60
3	Sheffield United	42	16	2	3	54	15	7	5	9	28	33	53
4	Liverpool	42	15	3	3	57	25	9	2	10	30	37	53
5	Stoke City	42	16	2	3	48	19	5	5	11	24	39	49
6	Bristol Rovers	42	13	5	3	46	23	5	7	9	34	41	48
7	Derby County	42	15	1	5	46	29	5	7	9	28	42	48
8	Charlton Athletic	42	13	3	5	53	33	5	4	12	39	57	43
9	Cardiff City	42	12	2	7	37	26	6	5	10	28	39	43
10	Bristol City	42	11	3	7	43	27	6	4	11	31	43	41
11	Swansea Town	42	12	5	4	52	30	4	4	13	27	51	41
12	Brighton & Hove A.	42	10	9	2	46	29	5	2	14	28	61	41
13	Middlesbrough	42	9	7	5	51	26	6	3	12	36	45	40
14	Huddersfield Town	42	12	3	6	39	20	4	5	12	23	35	40
15	Sunderland	42	13	4	4	42	23	3	4	14	22	52	40
16	Ipswich Town	42	12	4	5	37	27	5	2	14	25	50	40
17	Leyton Orient	42	9	4	8	43	30	5	4	12	28	48	36
18	SCUNTHORPE UNITED	42	7	6	8	32	37	5	3	13	23	47	33
19	Lincoln City	42	10	5	6	45	37	1	2	18	18	56	29
20	Rotherham United	42	9	5	7	32	28	1	4	16	10	54	29
21	Grimsby Town	42	7	7	7	41	36	2	3	16	21	54	28
22	Barnsley	42	8	4	9	34	34	2	3	16	21	57	27

~ 229 ~

1959/60   15th in Division 2

#		Date	Opponent	Score	Scorers	Att	Hardwick K	John DCJ	Brownsword NJ	Sharpe LT	Horstead JB	Neale P	Marriott JL	Waldock R	Harburn PAP	Haigh J	Donnelly P	Heward B	Bakes MS	Thomas BEB	Williams I	Middleton H	Jones K	Pashley R	Passmoor T	Hubbard J	Needham A
1	Aug	22	BRISTOL CITY	1-1	Brownsword (p)	10863	1	2	3	4	5	6	7	8	9	10	11										
2		24	Plymouth Argyle	0-4		25888	1	2	3	4	5	6	7	8	9	10	11										
3		29	Huddersfield Town	0-2		14730	1	2	3	6	5	10	7	11	9	8		4									
4	Sep	3	PLYMOUTH ARGYLE	2-0	Sharpe, Haigh	12165	1	2	3	6	5		7	8	9	10		4	11								
5		5	Rotherham United	1-1	Haigh	10764	1	2	3	6	5		7	8	9	10		4	11								
6		9	Liverpool	0-2		31713	1	2	3	6	5	9	7	8		10		4	11								
7		12	CARDIFF CITY	1-2	Haigh	10933	1	2	3	6	5	9	7	8		10		4	11								
8		17	LIVERPOOL	1-1	Donnelly	11822	1	2	3	4		6	7	8		10	9	5	11								
9		19	Hull City	2-0	Waldock, Donnelly	18459	1	2	3	4		6	7	8		10	9	5	11								
10		26	SHEFFIELD UNITED	1-1	Marriott	15384	1	2	3	4		6	7			10	9	5	11	8							
11	Oct	3	Middlesbrough	1-3	Thomas	27979	1	2	3	4		6	7			10	9	5	11	8							
12		10	IPSWICH TOWN	2-2	Middleton, Thomas	11408		2	3	4		6	7			10	11	5		8	1	9					
13		17	Bristol Rovers	1-1	Donnelly	15225		2	3	4		6	7			8	10	5	11		1	9					
14		24	SWANSEA TOWN	3-1	Marriott, Donnelly, Middleton	9675		2	3	4		6	7			8	10	5	11		1	9					
15		31	Brighton & Hove Albion	1-0	Middleton	18927		2	3	4		6	7			8	10	5	11		1	9					
16	Nov	7	STOKE CITY	1-1	Haigh	10827		2	3	4		6	7			8	10	5	11		1	9					
17		14	Portsmouth	0-4		14949		2	3	4		6	7			8	10	5	11		1	9					
18		21	SUNDERLAND	3-1	Donnelly 2, Thomas	11682		2	3	6			7			4	10	5	11	8	1	9					
19		28	Aston Villa	0-5		37367		2	3	6			7			4	10	5	11	8	1	9					
20	Dec	5	LINCOLN CITY	5-0	Middleton 2, Thomas, Bakes, Brownsword (p)	13945		2	3	6			7			4	10	5	11	8		9	1				
21		12	Leyton Orient	1-1	Haigh	9588		2	3	6			7			4	10	5	11	8		9	1				
22		19	Bristol City	2-0	Marriott, Middleton	9099		2	3	6			7			4	10	5	11	8		9	1				
23		26	DERBY COUNTY	3-2	Middleton 2, Donnelly	13342		2	3	6			7			4	10	5	11	8		9	1				
24		28	Derby County	0-3		17677		2	3	6			7			4	10	5	11	8		9	1				
25	Jan	2	HUDDERSFIELD T	0-2		12228		2	3	6			7			4	10	5	11	8		9	1				
26		16	ROTHERHAM UNITED	2-1	Donnelly, Middleton	12745		2	3	6			7			4	10	5	11	8		9	1				
27		23	Cardiff City	2-4	Thomas, Middleton	16759		2	3	6			7			4	10	5	11	8		9	1				
28	Feb	6	HULL CITY	3-0	Middleton, Thomas, Donnelly	10885		2	3	6			7			4	10	5	11	8		9	1				
29		13	Sheffield United	1-2	Thomas	16460		2	3	6			7			4	10	5	11	8		9	1				
30		20	MIDDLESBROUGH	1-1	Thomas	10817		2	3	6			7			4	10	5	11	8		9	1				
31		27	Ipswich Town	0-1		12829		2	3	6			7			4	10	5	11	8		9	1				
32	Mar	5	BRISTOL ROVERS	3-4	Thomas 2, Donnelly	9277		2	3	6			7			4	10	5	11	8		9	1				
33		12	Swansea Town	1-3	Donnelly	11646		2	3	6			7			4	10	5	11	8		9	1				
34		19	ASTON VILLA	1-2	Marriott	13084		2	3	4			6	7			10	5	11	8		9	1				
35		26	Stoke City	3-1	Marriott, Pashley, Bakes	6234		2	3	4			6	7				9	5	11	10			1	8			
36	Apr	2	PORTSMOUTH	1-0	Donnelly	8675		2	3	4			6	7				9	5	11	10			1	8			
37		9	Sunderland	0-1		16952		2	3	4			6	7				9		11	10			1	8	5		
38		15	CHARLTON ATHLETIC	1-1	Haigh	8741		2	3	4			6	7		8				11	9		10	1		5		
39		16	LEYTON ORIENT	2-1	Bakes, Brownsword (p)	8192		2	3	4			6			8	10			11	7		9	1		5		
40		18	Charlton Athletic	2-5	Bakes, Donnelly	10787		2	3	4			6	7		8	10			11			9	1		5		
41		23	Lincoln City	1-2	Donnelly	12691		2	3				7			8	10	5	11				9	1			4	6
42		30	BRIGHTON & HOVE ALB	1-2	Donnelly	6537			3	8	2	10				4	11	5	7				9	1				6
					Apps		11	41	42	41	8	23	40	9	5	38	36	36	38	25	8	28	23	3	4	1	2
					Goals				3	1			5	1		6	15		4	10		11		1				

F.A. Cup

		Date	Opponent	Score	Scorers	Att		John DCJ	Brownsword NJ	Sharpe LT		Neale P	Marriott JL			Haigh J	Donnelly P	Heward B	Bakes MS	Thomas BEB		Middleton H	Jones K	Pashley R			
R3	Jan	9	CRYSTAL PALACE	1-0	Middleton	12651		2	3	6			7			4	10	5	11	8		9	1				
R4		30	PORT VALE	0-1		14043		2	3	4			6	7		10	9	5		8			1	11			

		P	W	D	L	F	A	W	D	L	F	A	Pts
1	Aston Villa	42	17	3	1	62	19	8	6	7	27	24	59
2	Cardiff City	42	15	2	4	55	36	8	10	3	35	26	58
3	Liverpool	42	15	3	3	59	28	5	7	9	31	38	50
4	Sheffield United	42	12	5	4	43	22	7	7	7	25	29	50
5	Middlesbrough	42	14	5	2	56	21	5	5	11	34	43	48
6	Huddersfield Town	42	13	3	5	44	20	6	6	9	29	32	47
7	Charlton Athletic	42	12	7	2	55	28	5	6	10	35	59	47
8	Rotherham United	42	9	9	3	31	23	8	4	9	30	37	47
9	Bristol Rovers	42	12	6	3	42	28	6	5	10	30	50	47
10	Leyton Orient	42	12	4	5	47	25	3	10	8	29	36	44
11	Ipswich Town	42	12	5	4	48	24	7	1	13	30	44	44
12	Swansea Town	42	12	6	3	54	32	3	4	14	28	52	40
13	Lincoln City	42	11	3	7	41	25	5	4	12	34	53	39
14	Brighton & Hove A.	42	7	8	6	35	32	6	4	11	32	44	38
15	SCUNTHORPE UNITED	42	9	7	5	38	26	4	3	14	19	45	36
16	Sunderland	42	8	6	7	35	29	4	6	11	17	36	36
17	Stoke City	42	8	3	10	40	38	6	4	11	26	45	35
18	Derby County	42	9	4	8	31	28	5	3	13	30	49	35
19	Plymouth Argyle	42	10	6	5	42	36	3	3	15	19	53	35
20	Portsmouth	42	6	6	9	36	36	4	6	11	23	41	32
21	Hull City	42	7	6	8	27	30	3	4	14	21	46	30
22	Bristol City	42	8	3	10	27	31	3	2	16	33	66	27

1960/61 9th in Division 2

#	Date		Opponent	Score	Scorers	Att	Jones K	John DCI	Brownsword NJ	Gibson A	Heward B	Neale P	Marriott JL	Godfrey BC	Thomas BEB	Bonson J	Bakes MS	Horstead JB	Sharpe LT	Middleton H	Kaye J	Turner J	Thorpe AW	Passmoor T	Needham A	Hemstead DW
1	Aug	20	Charlton Athletic	1-1	Thomas	12590	1	2	3	4	5	6	7	8	9	10	11									
2		25	IPSWICH TOWN	4-0	Marriott, Neale, Thomas, Godfrey	11130	1	2	3	4	5	6	7	8	9	10	11									
3		27	LEYTON ORIENT	2-2	Thomas 2	10107	1	2	3	4	5	6	7	8	9	10	11									
4		30	Ipswich Town	0-2		12426	1	2	3	4	5	6	7	8	9	10	11									
5	Sep	3	Derby County	5-2	Bonson 2, Thomas, Godfrey, Brownsword (p)	16944	1	2	3	4	5	6	7	8	9	10	11									
6		10	BRISTOL ROVERS	2-1	Thomas 2	10262	1	2	3	4	5	6	7	8	9	10	11									
7		15	MIDDLESBROUGH	1-1	Thomas	13852	1	2	3	4	5	6	7	8	9	10	11									
8		17	Liverpool	2-3	Thomas, Marriott	23797	1	2	3	4	5	6	7	8	9	10	11									
9		21	Middlesbrough	3-1	Thomas 2, Bonson	19744	1	2	3	4	5	6	7	8	9	10	11									
10		24	ROTHERHAM UNITED	1-1	Marriott	12724	1	2	3	4	5	6	7	8	9	10	11									
11	Oct	1	Southampton	2-4	Thomas 2	17464	1	2	3	4	5	6	7	8	9	10	11									
12		8	Sheffield United	0-2		14160	1	2	3	4	5	6	7	8	9	10	11									
13		15	STOKE CITY	1-1	Godfrey	8777	1	2	3	4	5	6	7	8	9	10	11									
14		24	Swansea Town	2-2	Bonson 2	9599	1	2	3	4			7	8	9	10	11	5	6							
15		29	LUTON TOWN	1-0	Thomas	8643	1	2	3	4			7	8	9	10	11	5	6							
16	Nov	5	Lincoln City	2-0	Godfrey, Thomas	10262	1	2	3	4			7	8	9	10	11	5	6							
17		12	PORTSMOUTH	5-1	Thomas 2, Godfrey 2, Sharpe	8335	1	2	3	4			7	8	9	10	11	5	6							
18		19	Huddersfield Town	2-1	Thomas, McGarry (og)	8617	1	2	3			4	7	8	9	10	11	5	6							
19		26	SUNDERLAND	3-3	Thomas, Bonson, Brownsword (p)	9156	1	2	3			4	7	8	9	10	11	5	6							
20	Dec	3	Plymouth Argyle	1-3	Sharpe	11925	1	2	3	4			7	8	9	10	11	5	6							
21		10	NORWICH CITY	2-1	Thomas, Godfrey	8444	1	2	3	4			7	8	9	10	11	5	6							
22		23	BRIGHTON & HOVE ALB	2-2	Brownsword 2 (2p)	9277	1	2	3	4			7	8	9	10	11	5	6							
23		27	Brighton & Hove Albion	1-1	Godfrey	20602	1	2	3	4			7	8	9	10	11	5	6							
24		31	Leyton Orient	1-2	Bonson	8450	1	2	3	4			7	8	9	10	11	5	6							
25	Jan	14	DERBY COUNTY	1-2	Godfrey	10067	1	2	3	4				8	9	10	11	5	6	7						
26		21	Bristol Rovers	3-3	Thomas 2, Marriott	11276	1	2	3			4	7	8	9	10	11	5	6							
27	Feb	4	LIVERPOOL	2-3	Thomas, Bonson	7970	1	2	3	4	6		7		9	10	11	5		8						
28		11	Rotherham United	0-4		8225	1	2	3	4	6		7		9	10	11	5		8						
29		18	SOUTHAMPTON	2-0	Thomas, Godfrey	8268			3	4	5		7	8	9	10	11	2	6		1					
30		25	SHEFFIELD UNITED	1-1	Godfrey	10873			3	4	5		7	8	9	10	11	2	6		1					
31	Mar	4	Stoke City	0-2		12667			3	4	5		7	8	9	10		2	6		1	11				
32		11	SWANSEA TOWN	1-2	Brownsword (p)	7926			3	4			7	8	9			2			10	1	11	5	6	
33		18	Norwich City	1-0	Godfrey	20598		2	3	4			7	8	9	10	11	5	6		1					
34		25	LINCOLN CITY	3-1	Bonson 2, Marriott	6981		2	3	4			7	8	9	10		5	6		1	11				
35	Apr	1	Sunderland	0-2		18242		2	3	4			7	8	9	10		5	6		1	11				
36		3	LEEDS UNITED	3-2	Godfrey, Thomas, Bakes	8725		2	3	4			7	8	9	10	11	5	6		1					
37		8	HUDDERSFIELD T	0-1		8352		2	3	4			7	8	9	10	11	5	6		1					
38		11	CHARLTON ATHLETIC	0-0		7303		2	3	4			7	8	9		11	5	6	10	1					
39		15	Portsmouth	2-2	Kaye, Godfrey	15223		2	3	4		5	7	9	8		11		6	10	1					
40		22	PLYMOUTH ARGYLE	2-0	Thomas, Bonson	5762		2	3	4		5	7	8	9	10	11		6		1					
41		25	Leeds United	2-2	Godfrey, Thorpe	6975		2	3	4		6	7	8	9	10		5			1	11				
42		29	Luton Town	0-0		8373		2				6	7		9	10		5	4	8	1	11				3
						Apps	28	38	41	38	18	20	40	39	42	40	36	27	25	1	6	14	6	1	1	1
						Goals			5				1	5	15	26	11	1		2		1		1		

One own goal

F.A. Cup

							Jones K	John DCI	Brownsword NJ	Gibson A	Heward B	Neale P	Marriott JL	Godfrey BC	Thomas BEB	Bonson J	Bakes MS	Horstead JB	Sharpe LT	Middleton H
R3	Jan	7	BLACKPOOL	6-2	Thomas 3, Bonson 3	19303	1	2	3	4				8	9	10	11	5	6	7
R4		28	Norwich City	1-4	Bakes	15485	1	2	3	4			7	8	9	10	11	5	6	

F.L. Cup

R1	Oct	10	Rochdale	1-1	Bonson	4274	1	2	3	4	5	6	7	11	9	10			8	
rep		20	ROCHDALE	0-1		5727	1	2	3	4	5		7	8	9		11	6	10	

		P	W	D	L	F	A	W	D	L	F	A	Pts
1	Ipswich Town	42	15	3	3	55	24	11	4	6	45	31	59
2	Sheffield United	42	16	2	3	49	22	10	4	7	32	29	58
3	Liverpool	42	14	5	2	49	21	7	5	9	38	37	52
4	Norwich City	42	15	3	3	46	20	5	6	10	24	33	49
5	Middlesbrough	42	13	6	2	44	20	5	6	10	39	54	48
6	Sunderland	42	12	5	4	47	24	5	8	8	28	36	47
7	Swansea Town	42	14	4	3	49	26	4	7	10	28	47	47
8	Southampton	42	12	4	5	57	35	6	4	11	27	46	44
9	SCUNTHORPE UNITED	42	9	8	4	39	25	5	7	9	30	39	43
10	Charlton Athletic	42	12	3	6	60	42	4	8	9	37	49	43
11	Plymouth Argyle	42	13	4	4	52	32	4	4	13	29	50	42
12	Derby County	42	9	6	6	46	35	6	4	11	34	45	40
13	Luton Town	42	13	5	3	48	27	2	4	15	23	52	39
14	Leeds United	42	7	7	7	41	38	7	3	11	34	45	38
15	Rotherham United	42	7	5	9	37	24	5	3	6	12	28	40	37
16	Brighton & Hove A.	42	9	6	6	33	26	5	3	13	28	49	37
17	Bristol Rovers	42	13	4	4	52	35	2	3	16	21	57	37
18	Stoke City	42	9	6	6	39	26	3	6	12	12	33	36
19	Leyton Orient	42	10	5	6	31	29	4	3	14	24	49	36
20	Huddersfield Town	42	7	5	9	33	33	6	4	11	29	38	35
21	Portsmouth	42	10	6	5	38	27	1	5	15	26	64	33
22	Lincoln City	42	5	4	12	30	43	3	4	14	18	52	24

1961/62 4th in Division 2

						Jones K	John DCJ	Agnew DY	Gibson A	Horstead JB	Howells R	Marriott JL	Godfrey BC	Thomas BEB	Bonson J	Thorpe AW	Brownsword NJ	Turner J	Hemstead DW	Kaye J	Neale P	Lindsey B	Bakes MS	Wilson A	Sharpe LT	Hodgson K	McGuigan JJ	McDowall JC
1	Aug	19	BRIGHTON & HOVE ALB	3-3	Marriott (p), Godfrey, Thomas	7965	1	2	3	4	5	6	7	8	9	10	11											
2		23	Norwich City	2-2	Thomas 2	27407	1	2		4	5	6	7	8	9	10	11	3											
3		26	Bury	1-4	Gibson	11236		2		4	5	6	7	8	9	10	11	3	1										
4		29	NORWICH CITY	2-0	Thomas 2	8803				4	5	6	7	8	9	10	11	3	1	2									
5	Sep	1	CHARLTON ATHLETIC	6-1	Godfrey 2,Thomas,Marriott,Thorpe,Brownsword(p)	9639				4	5	6	7	8	9	10	11	3	1	2									
6		5	BRISTOL ROVERS	2-1	Godfrey, Thomas	9558				4	5	6	7	8	9	10	11	3	1	2									
7		9	Liverpool	1-2	Godfrey	46837				4	5	6	7	8	9	10	11	3	1	2									
8		15	ROTHERHAM UNITED	5-2	Thomas 2, Godfrey 2, Thorpe	11823	1			4		6	7	10	9		11	3		2	8	5								
9		18	Bristol Rovers	1-2	Thomas	14107	1			4		6	7		9	10	11	3		2	8	5								
10		23	Sunderland	0-4		35112				4		6	7		9			3	1	2	8	5	10	11						
11		29	STOKE CITY	2-2	Thomas, Kaye	10347				4	5	6	7		9	10	11	3	1	2	8									
12	Oct	7	Swansea Town	1-2	Thomas	12479				4	2	6	7		9	10		3	1		8	5			11					
13		13	SOUTHAMPTON	5-1	Thomas 2,Wilson,Kaye,Davies(og)	10638	1			4	2	6	7	10	9			3			8	5			11					
14		21	Luton Town	2-1	Thomas, Kaye	9766	1			4	2	6	7	10	9			3			8	5			11					
15		27	NEWCASTLE UNITED	3-2	Thomas 2, Brownsword (p)	13988	1			4	2	6	7	10	9			3			8	5			11					
16	Nov	4	Middlesbrough	2-1	Thomas 2	12142	1			4	2	6	7	10	9			3			8	5			11					
17		11	PLYMOUTH ARGYLE	5-1	Thomas 4, Thorpe	8780	1			4	2	6	7	10	9		11	3			8	5								
18		18	Derby County	2-2	Brownsword (p), Wilson	21134	1			4	2		7	10	9			3			8	5			11	6				
19		24	LEYTON ORIENT	0-2		11812	1			4	2	6	7	10	9			3			8	5			11					
20	Dec	2	Preston North End	1-4	Thomas	8326	1			4	2	6		7	9			3			10	5	8		11					
21		16	Brighton & Hove Albion	3-0	Thomas, Kaye, Sitford(og)	9377	1			4	5	6	11		9	10		3		2	8						7			
22		22	BURY	1-2	Thomas	8287	1			4	5	6	11	8	9	10		3		2							7			
23		26	Leeds United	4-1	Thomas 4	19481	1			4	5	6	11	10	9			3			8						7			
24	Jan	13	Charlton Athletic	3-3	Thomas, Hodgson, Hinton(og)	13672	1			4	2	6	11	10	9			3			8	5					7			
25		20	LIVERPOOL	1-1	Howells	11162	1			4	2	6	7	8				3			9	5			11		10			
26	Feb	2	Rotherham United	1-0	Kaye	12528	1			4	2	6	7	8				3			9	5							11	10
27		10	SUNDERLAND	3-1	McGuigan, Kaye, Godfrey	11436	1			4	2	6	7	8				3			9	5							11	10
28		17	Stoke City	0-1		16578	1			4	2	6	7					3			9	5			11			8		10
29		20	LEEDS UNITED	2-1	Hodgson, McGuigan	9011	1			4	2	6	11	8				3			9	5						7		10
30		23	SWANSEA TOWN	2-0	Hodgson, McGuigan	8246	1			4	2	6	11	8				3			9	5						7		10
31	Mar	3	Southampton	4-6	McGuigan,Marriott,Brownsword (p),Kaye	10455				4	2	6	7					3			9	5			11			8	10	1
32		6	WALSALL	2-1	McGuigan, Hodgson	7028	1			4	2	6	7					3			9	5			11			8	10	
33		10	LUTON TOWN	2-0	McGuigan, Kaye	7709	1		2			6	7				11	3			9	5						8	10	
34		17	Newcastle United	1-2	McGuigan	37931	1		2	4		6	11					3			9	5			7			8	10	
35		23	MIDDLESBROUGH	1-1	McGuigan	7978	1			4	2	6	7	8				3			9	5			11				10	
36		31	Plymouth Argyle	1-3	Kaye	15913	1		2			4		8				3			9	5			11	6	7		10	
37	Apr	6	DERBY COUNTY	2-0	Kaye, McGuigan	6981	1		2	4		6	7	8						3	9	5			11				10	
38		14	Leyton Orient	1-0	Kaye	16867	1		2	4		6	7	8				3			9	5			11				10	
39		20	PRESTON NORTH END	2-1	Hodgson 2	11147	1			4		6	7					3		2	9	5			11		8		10	
40		23	Huddersfield Town	2-1	Wilson, Gibson	12397	1			4		6	7					3		2	9	5			11		8		10	
41		24	HUDDERSFIELD T	1-3	Hodgson	10573	1		2	4		6	7	8				3				5			11		9		10	
42		28	Walsall	1-4	McGuigan	7173	1			4	2	6	7					3				5	8		11		9		10	
						Apps	33	9	1	41	31	41	40	29	24	12	12	39	8	15	32	31	3	1	21	2	19	17	1	
						Goals				2		1	3	8	31		3	4			11				3			7	10	

Three own goals

F.A. Cup

| R3 | Jan | 6 | Charlton Athletic | 0-1 | | 20694 | 1 | | | 4 | 5 | 6 | 11 | 10 | 9 | | | 3 | | 2 | 8 | | | | | | 7 | | | |

F.L. Cup

| R1 | Sep | 13 | Newcastle United | 0-2 | | 14340 | | | | 4 | 5 | 6 | 7 | 8 | 9 | 10 | 11 | 3 | 1 | 2 | | | | | | | | | | |

		P	W	D	L	F	A	W	D	L	F	A	Pts
1	Liverpool	42	18	3	0	68	19	9	5	7	31	24	62
2	Leyton Orient	42	11	5	5	34	17	11	5	5	35	23	54
3	Sunderland	42	17	3	1	60	16	5	6	10	25	34	53
4	SCUNTHORPE UNITED	42	14	4	3	52	26	7	3	11	34	45	49
5	Plymouth Argyle	42	12	4	5	45	30	7	4	10	30	45	46
6	Southampton	42	13	3	5	53	28	5	6	10	24	34	45
7	Huddersfield Town	42	11	5	5	39	22	5	7	9	28	37	44
8	Stoke City	42	13	4	4	34	17	4	4	13	21	40	42
9	Rotherham United	42	9	6	6	36	30	7	3	11	34	46	41
10	Preston North End	42	11	4	6	34	23	4	6	11	21	34	40
11	Newcastle United	42	10	5	6	40	27	5	4	12	24	31	39
12	Middlesbrough	42	11	3	7	45	29	5	4	12	31	43	39
13	Luton Town	42	12	1	8	44	37	5	4	12	25	34	39
14	Walsall	42	11	7	3	42	23	3	4	14	28	52	39
15	Charlton Athletic	42	10	5	6	38	30	5	4	12	31	45	39
16	Derby County	42	10	7	4	42	27	4	4	13	26	48	39
17	Norwich City	42	10	6	5	36	28	4	5	12	25	42	39
18	Bury	42	9	4	8	32	36	8	1	12	20	40	39
19	Leeds United	42	9	6	6	24	19	3	6	12	26	42	36
20	Swansea Town	42	10	5	6	38	30	2	7	12	23	53	36
21	Bristol Rovers	42	11	3	7	36	31	2	4	15	17	50	33
22	Brighton & Hove A.	42	7	7	7	24	32	3	4	14	18	54	31

1962/63 9th in Division 2

#		Date	Opponent	Score	Scorers	Att	Jones K	Gannon MJ	Brownsword NJ	Gibson A	Neale P	Howells R	Marriott JL	Godfrey BC	Kaye J	McGuigan JJ	Hodgson K	Hemstead DW	Wilson A	Lindsey B	Horstead JB	Anderson AA	Bakes MS	Thorpe AW	Crawford I	Passmoor T	Reeves TB
1	Aug	18	SOUTHAMPTON	2-1	Hodgson, Knapp(og)	9583	1	2	3	4	5	6	7	8	9	10	11										
2		22	Chelsea	0-3		18190	1	2	3	4	5	6	7	8	9	10	11										
3		25	Grimsby Town	0-3	Kaye 3	16303	1		3	4	5	6	7	8	9	10	11	2									
4		28	CHELSEA	3-0	Kaye 3	10976	1		3	4	5				9	10	11	2	7	8							
5	Sep	1	Bury	2-0	Kaye, Lindsey	8418	1		3	4	5	6			9	10	11		7	8	2						
6		4	NEWCASTLE UNITED	2-1	Wilson, McGuigan	14053	1		3	4	5	6			9	10	11		7	8	2						
7		8	ROTHERHAM UNITED	1-0	Kaye	12911	1		3	4	5	6			9	10	11		7	8	2						
8		11	SWANSEA TOWN	1-0	Hodgson	10468	1		3	4	5	6			9	10	11		7	8	2						
9		15	Charlton Athletic	0-1		13259	1		3	4	5	6			9	10	7			11	8	2					
10		18	Swansea Town	0-1		10793	1		3	4	5	6			9	10	11		7		2						
11		22	STOKE CITY	0-0		11683	1		3	4	5	6		8	9	11			7	10	2						
12		29	Sunderland	0-0		42980	1		3	4	5			7		10	9		11	8	2	6					
13	Oct	6	PLYMOUTH ARGYLE	2-2	Godfrey, Hodgson	8497	1				5	4		7	9	10	11	3		8	2	6					
14		13	Preston North End	1-3	Kaye	9919	1		3	4	5			7	9					8	2	6	11				
15		19	PORTSMOUTH	1-2	Brownsword (p)	8375	1		3	4	5			7	9	10				8	2	6	11				
16		27	Cardiff City	0-4		11883	1		3	4	5			8	9	10	9			7	2	6		11			
17	Nov	2	HUDDERSFIELD T	2-2	Hodgson 2	8695	1		3	4	5	6		8	9	10	7				2			11			
18		10	Middlesbrough	3-4	Thorpe, McGuigan, Brownsword (p)	10536	1		3	4	5	6	7		9	10	8				2			11			
19		16	DERBY COUNTY	2-1	Howells, Hodgson	6094	1		3	4	5	6	7		9	10	8				2			11			
20		24	Newcastle United	1-1	Marriott	26221	1		3	4	5	6	7		9	10	8				2			11			
21		30	WALSALL	2-0	Brownsword (p), McPherson(og)	7074	1		3	4	5	6	7		9	10	8				2			11			
22	Dec	8	Norwich City	3-3	Kaye 2, Howells	13387	1		3	4	5	6	7		9	10	8				2			11			
23		15	Southampton	1-1	Hodgson	11159	1		3	4	5	6	7		9	10	8				2			11			
24		21	GRIMSBY TOWN	1-1	Gibson	12542	1		3	4	5	6	7		9	10	8				2			11			
25	Feb	23	Plymouth Argyle	3-2	McGuigan, Howells, Brownsword (p)	11696	1		3	4	5	6		8	9	10	11		7		2						
26	Mar	9	Portsmouth	2-1	Hodgson, Wilson	8464	1		3	4	5	6	11	8			9		7	10	2						
27		15	CARDIFF CITY	2-2	Kaye, Brownsword (p)	7844	1		3	4	5	6		8	9				7	10	2						
28		23	Huddersfield Town	0-2		10929	1				4	5	6		8	9	10	7	3		2			11			
29		26	PRESTON NORTH END	4-1	McGuigan 2, Wilson, Hodgson	7002	1		3	4		6			9	10	8		7		2			11	5		
30		29	MIDDLESBROUGH	1-1	Gibson	7249	1		3	4					9	10	8		7		2			11	5		
31	Apr	3	Leeds United	0-1		15783	1		3	4					9	10	8		7		2	6		11	5		
32		6	Derby County	2-6	Hodgson 2	8933	1		3	4		6			9	10	8		7		2			11	5		
33		12	LUTON TOWN	2-0	McGuigan, Gibson	7528	1		3	4		6			9	10	8		7		2			11	5		
34		15	Luton Town	0-1		9043	1	6		4					9	10		3	7	8	2			11	5		
35		20	Walsall	1-1	Wilson	6839	1	6		4	5				9	10		3	7	8	2			11			
36		23	LEEDS UNITED	0-2		7794	1	6	3	4	5			8	9	10			7		2			11			
37		26	NORWICH CITY	3-1	Kaye 2, Wilson	5797		6	3	4					9	10	11		7		2				8	5	1
38		30	SUNDERLAND	1-1	Ashurst (og)	8853		6	3	4					9	10	11		7		2				8	5	1
39	May	4	Stoke City	3-2	McGuigan, Kaye, Hodgson	25509		6	3	4					9	10	11		7		2				8	5	1
40		7	CHARLTON ATHLETIC	2-0	Crawford, Tocknell(og)	6572		6	3	4					9	10	11		7		2				8	5	1
41		10	BURY	1-0	Kaye	6427		6	3						9	10	11		7	4	2				8	5	1
42		17	Rotherham United	0-1		7367		6	3	4				8		10	9		7		2				11	5	1
					Apps		36	11	38	40	30	28	11	17	39	40	36	6	26	16	38	6	2	9	15	12	6
					Goals				5	3		3	1	1	13	7	12		5	1				1	1		

Four own goals

F.A. Cup

		Date	Opponent	Score	Scorers	Att																					
R3	Jan	26	Portsmouth	1-1	Godfrey	15500	1		3	4		6	11	8	9	10			7		2				5		
rep	Mar	7	PORTSMOUTH	1-2	McGuigan	9765	1		3	4	5	6			8	9	10	11	7		2						

F.L. Cup

		Date	Opponent	Score	Scorers	Att																					
R2	Sep	24	Southampton	1-1	McGuigan	5905	1		3	4	5			7		10	9			11	8	2	6				
rep	Oct	2	SOUTHAMPTON	2-2	Gibson, Godfrey	6506	1		3	4	5			7		10	9			11	8	2	6				
rep2		9	Southampton	3-0	Godfrey, McGuigan, Wimhurst (og)	4984	1		3	4	5			7	9	10					8	2	6	11			
R3		17	Sunderland	0-2		18154	1		3	4	5			7	9	10					8	2	6	11			

R2 replay a.e.t. R2 replay 2 at Peterborough.

		P	W	D	L	F	A	W	D	L	F	A	Pts
1	Stoke City	42	15	3	3	49	20	5	10	6	24	30	53
2	Chelsea	42	15	3	3	54	16	9	1	11	27	26	52
3	Sunderland	42	14	5	2	46	13	6	7	8	38	42	52
4	Middlesbrough	42	12	4	5	48	35	8	5	8	38	50	49
5	Leeds United	42	15	2	4	55	19	4	8	9	24	34	48
6	Huddersfield Town	42	11	6	4	34	21	6	8	7	29	29	48
7	Newcastle United	42	11	8	2	48	23	7	3	11	31	36	47
8	Bury	42	11	6	4	28	20	7	5	9	23	27	47
9	SCUNTHORPE UNITED	42	12	7	2	35	18	4	5	12	22	41	44
10	Cardiff City	42	12	5	4	50	29	6	2	13	33	44	43
11	Southampton	42	15	3	3	52	23	2	5	14	20	44	42
12	Plymouth Argyle	42	13	4	4	48	24	2	8	11	28	49	42
13	Norwich City	42	11	6	4	53	33	6	2	13	27	46	42
14	Rotherham United	42	11	3	7	34	30	6	3	12	33	44	40
15	Swansea Town	42	13	5	3	33	17	2	4	15	18	55	39
16	Portsmouth	42	9	5	7	33	27	4	6	11	30	52	37
17	Preston North End	42	11	6	4	43	30	2	5	14	16	44	37
18	Derby County	42	10	5	6	40	29	2	7	12	21	43	36
19	Grimsby Town	42	8	6	7	34	26	3	7	11	21	40	35
20	Charlton Athletic	42	8	4	9	33	38	5	1	15	29	56	31
21	Walsall	42	7	7	7	33	37	4	2	15	20	52	31
22	Luton Town	42	10	4	7	45	40	1	3	17	16	44	29

~ 233 ~

1963/64 — 22nd in Division 2: Relegated

#	Date	Opponent	Score	Scorers	Att	Reeves TB	Horstead JB	Brownsword NJ	Lindsey B	Neale P	Gannon MJ	Wilson A	Hodgson K	Lawther WI	Smillie AT	Crawford I	Jones K	Hutton J	Gibson A	Passmoor T	Hemstead DW	Harper IT	Mahy B	Godfrey BC	Marriott JL	Conde JP	Needham A	Kirkman AJ	Sloan D	Mason CE	Ellis KD
1	Aug 24	Swindon Town	0-3		18447	1	2	3	4	5	6	7	8	9	10	11															
2	27	NORTHAMPTON T	1-2	Lawther	8496		2	3	4	5	6		8	9	10	11	1	7													
3	30	CARDIFF CITY	1-2	Lawther	8123		2	3		6		7	8	9	10	11	1		4	5											
4	Sep 3	Northampton Town	0-2		15899		2	3		6		7	8	9	10	11	1		4	5											
5	7	Norwich City	1-2	Lawther	16099		2	3		6		7	8	9	10	11	1		4	5											
6	9	SUNDERLAND	1-1	Smillie	10261			3		5		7	9		10	11	1		4		2	6	8								
7	12	SWANSEA TOWN	2-2	Evans (og), Brownsword (p)	8297			3		5		7	8	9	10	11	1		4		2	6									
8	18	Sunderland	0-1		36128		6	3		5		7	8	9		11	1		4		2			10							
9	21	PORTSMOUTH	1-1	Hodgson	6673		6	3		5		7	8	9		11	1		4		2			10							
10	28	Rotherham United	1-2	Crawford	8655		3		8	5	6	7		9	10	11	1		4		2										
11	Oct 1	LEYTON ORIENT	0-0		6293			3	6	5		11	9		10	8	1		4		2			7							
12	5	LEEDS UNITED	0-1		10793		4	3	6	5		11	9		10	8	1				2			7							
13	19	MIDDLESBROUGH	1-0	Wilson	7126		6	3	8	9		7		10		11	1		4	5	2										
14	26	Preston North End	0-1		15622		6	3	8	9		7		10		11	1		4	5	2										
15	Nov 2	HUDDERSFIELD T	1-0	Neale	5840		6	3	8	9		10	11				1		4	5	2			7							
16	16	PLYMOUTH ARGYLE	1-0	Neale	5513		6	3	8	9		11		10			1		4	5	2			7							
17	23	Charlton Athletic	1-0	Hodgson	19648		6	3				11	8	10			1		4	5	2			7	9						
18	30	GRIMSBY TOWN	2-2	Conde, Lawther	8156		6	3				11	8	10			1		4	5				7	9	2					
19	Dec 7	Newcastle United	1-3	Hodgson	24717		6	3				11	8	10			1		4	5				7	9	2					
20	14	SWINDON TOWN	3-0	Hodgson, Lawther, Woodruff (og)	4986		6	3				11	8	10			1		4		2		9	7							
21	26	Manchester City	1-8	Lawther	26134		5	3			6	11	8	10			7	1	4		2							9			
22	28	MANCHESTER CITY	2-4	Brownsword (p), Kirkman	9088		5	3	6			11	8	10			7	1	4		2							9			
23	Jan 11	NORWICH CITY	2-2	Kirkman, Hodgson	5021			3	4	5		11	8	10			7	1			2						6	9			
24	16	Swansea Town	1-4	Sloan	7187		6	3	4	5		11		10			7	1											2	9	
25	25	Derby County	2-2	Hodgson, Sloan	8964		6	3	4	5		7	11	9				1			2								10	8	
26	29	Southampton	2-7	Sloan, Hodgson	13999		6	3	4	5		7	11	9				1			2								10	8	
27	Feb 1	Portsmouth	4-3	Hodgson 3, Smillie	11724		2	3	4	5		7	11	6	10			1							9					8	
28	8	ROTHERHAM UNITED	4-3	Lindsey, Wilson, Sloan, Madden (og)	7415			3	4	5		11	9	6	10			1									3	7		8	
29	15	Leeds United	0-1		28868		2			4	5	11	9	6			1	7				10					3			8	
30	22	SOUTHAMPTON	1-2	Brownsword	5591		2	3	4	5		11	9	6			1	7				10								8	
31	Plymouth Argyle		1-3	Hodgson	10162		6	3	4	5		11	9	10			1												8	2	
32	Mar 7	PRESTON NORTH END	1-0	Lindsey	6271		6	3	8	5		11	7	10			1				2									4	9
33	14	Leyton Orient	2-2	Wilson, Mason	4376		6	3	8	5		11	7	10			1				2									4	9
34	20	DERBY COUNTY	3-2	Wilson, Ellis, Brownsword (p)	6846		6	3		5		11	7	10			1				2								8	4	9
35	26	BURY	0-0		7406		6	3		5		11	7	10			1				2								8	4	9
36	28	Middlesbrough	0-2		8630		6	3	8	5			11	10			1				2								7	4	9
37	31	Bury	2-3	Lindsey, Wilson	6369		6	3	10	5		11		9			1	7			2								8	4	
38	Apr 4	CHARLTON ATHLETIC	1-1	Ellis	5138			3	6	5		11		10			1	7			2								8	4	9
39	8	Cardiff City	1-3	Lawther	9409			3	6	5		7	11	10			1				2							8		4	9
40	11	Grimsby Town	0-2		10406			3	6	5		7	11	10			1										2	8		4	9
41	18	NEWCASTLE UNITED	2-0	Lawther, Ellis	6434			3	6	5		7		10			1	11									2	8		4	9
42	25	Huddersfield Town	2-3	Ellis 2	5024			3	6	5		7		10			1	11									2	8		4	9
		Apps				1	33	39	28	37	4	40	33	38	12	20	41	6	19	10	25	2	4	2	8	4	10	12	12	12	10
		Goals						4	2	2		5	11	9	2	1									1			2	4	1	5

3 own goals

F.A. Cup

| R3 | Jan 4 | BARNSLEY | 2-2 | Wilson, Lawther | 11160 | | 6 | 3 | 8 | 5 | | 11 | 7 | 10 | | | 1 | | 4 | | 2 | | | 9 | | | | | | | |
| rep | 7 | Barnsley | 2-3 | Brownsword 2 (2p) | 21337 | | 6 | 3 | 4 | 5 | | 11 | 8 | 10 | | | 7 | 1 | | | 2 | | | | | | | 9 | | | |

Replay a.e.t.

F.L. Cup

R2	Sep 25	STOKE CITY	2-2	Smillie, Wilson	6945			3	8	5	6	7		9	10	11	1		4		2										
rep	Oct 16	Stoke City	3-3	Horstead, Crawford, Neale	11062		6	3	8	9		7		10		11	1		4	5	2										
rep2	22	Stoke City	0-1		4297		6	3	8	9		7		10		11	1		4	5	2										

Replay a.e.t. Replay 2 at Hillsborough.

		P	W	D	L	F	A	W	D	L	F	A	Pts
1	Leeds United	42	12	9	0	35	16	12	6	3	36	18	63
2	Sunderland	42	16	3	2	47	13	9	8	4	34	24	61
3	Preston North End	42	13	7	1	37	14	10	3	8	42	40	56
4	Charlton Athletic	42	11	4	6	44	30	8	6	7	32	40	48
5	Southampton	42	13	3	5	69	32	6	6	9	31	41	47
6	Manchester City	42	12	4	5	50	27	6	6	9	34	39	46
7	Rotherham United	42	14	3	4	52	26	5	4	12	38	52	45
8	Newcastle United	42	14	2	5	49	26	6	3	12	25	43	45
9	Portsmouth	42	9	7	5	46	34	7	4	10	33	36	43
10	Middlesbrough	42	14	4	3	47	16	1	7	13	20	36	41
11	Northampton Town	42	10	2	9	35	31	6	7	8	23	29	41
12	Huddersfield Town	42	11	4	6	31	25	4	6	11	26	39	40
13	Derby County	42	10	6	5	34	27	4	5	12	22	40	39
14	Swindon Town	42	11	5	5	39	24	3	5	13	18	45	38
15	Cardiff City	42	10	7	4	31	27	4	3	14	25	54	38
16	Leyton Orient	42	8	6	7	32	32	5	4	12	22	40	36
17	Norwich City	42	9	7	5	43	30	2	6	13	21	50	35
18	Bury	42	8	5	8	35	36	5	4	12	22	37	35
19	Swansea Town	42	11	6	4	43	28	1	5	15	19	48	33
20	Plymouth Argyle	42	6	8	7	26	32	2	8	11	19	35	32
21	Grimsby Town	42	6	7	8	28	34	3	7	11	19	41	32
22	SCUNTHORPE UNITED	42	8	8	5	30	25	2	2	17	22	57	30

1964/65 — 18th in Division 3

#	Date	Opponent	Score	Scorers	Att	Reeves TB	Betts JB	Horstead JB	Lindsey B	Neale P	Bannister J	Hutton J	Kirkman AJ	Lawther WI	Sloan D	Ratcliffe JB	Brownsword NJ	Needham A	Wilson A	Smillie AT	Hemstead DW	Mahy B	Brown MR	Scott RSA	Bramley JS	Thomas BEB	Harper IT	Sidebottom G	Barton F	Smith RW
1	Aug 22	BRISTOL CITY	5-2	Lawther 2, Sloan 2, Kirkman	5562	1	2	3	4	5	6	7	8	9	10	11														
2	26	Gillingham	0-0		14067	1		2	4	5	6	7	8	9	10	11	3													
3	28	Queen's Park Rangers	1-2	Kirkman	6550	1		2	4	5	6	7	8	9	10	11	3													
4	Sep 4	SHREWSBURY TOWN	3-2	Lawther, Sloan, Ratcliffe	6694	1		2	4	5	6	7	8	9	10	11		3												
5	9	Hull City	2-1	Lawther 2	8012	1		2	4	5	6		8	9	10	11		3	7											
6	12	Reading	0-2		6726	1		2		5	6		8	9	10	11		3	7	4										
7	15	HULL CITY	1-1	Ratcliffe	7297	1		4		5	6		8	9	10	11		3	7		2									
8	18	SOUTHEND UNITED	2-1	Sloan, Lawther	5953	1	2	4	4	5	6		8	9	10	11			7											
9	25	Barnsley	0-2		6061	1	2	5			6		8	9	10			3	11			4	7							
10	29	WORKINGTON	1-1	Scott	4993	1	2			5			8	9	10		3	6	11				7	4						
11	Oct 3	Mansfield Town	2-3	Lawther 2	7803	1	2	6		5		7	8	9	10			3	11					4						
12	6	Workington	0-2		3842	1	2	6		5		7		9	10			3	11		8			4						
13	10	PETERBOROUGH UTD.	2-3	Scott, Sloan	5133	1	2	6	4	5		7		9	10			3	11					8						
14	13	WALSALL	4-0	Lawther 2 (1p), Scott, Hutton	4007	1		6	4	5		7		9	8			3	11		2			10						
15	17	Bournemouth	1-2	Horstead	8264	1		6	4	5		7		9	8			3	11		2			10						
16	20	Walsall	2-1	Scott, Lawther	5391	1		6	4	5		7		9				3	11		2			10	8					
17	24	EXETER CITY	0-0		4086	1		6	4	5		7		9				3	11		2			10	8					
18	28	Luton Town	1-1	Scott	3876	1		6	4	5				9	7			3	11		2			10	8					
19	31	Oldham Athletic	1-2	Lawther	9258	1		6	4	5				9	7			3	11		2			10	8					
20	Nov 3	GILLINGHAM	2-3	Scott (p), Lawther	4290	1		5	4					9	10	11		3	7		2			6	8					
21	7	BRISTOL ROVERS	1-1	Lindsey	4213	1		5	4					9	10	11		3	7		2			6	8					
22	20	COLCHESTER UNITED	0-0		7610	1		4	8	5					10	11		3			2			6	7	9				
23	28	Port Vale	1-0	Ratcliffe	4620	1		4	8	5					10	11	3				2			6	7	9				
24	Dec 12	Bristol City	2-2	Thomas 2	8387	1		6	4	5		7	10			11					3			8	9	2				
25	18	QUEEN'S PARK RANGERS	2-1	Ratcliffe, Neale	5344	1				5		7	10			11	3				2			6	8	9	4			
26	26	GRIMSBY TOWN	2-1	Ratcliffe, Kirkman	10867	1			4	5		7	10			11					3			6	8	9	2			
27	Jan 2	Shrewsbury Town	2-3	Hutton, Scott	4707	1			4	5		7	10								3	11		6	8	9	2			
28	8	Exeter City	3-1	Thomas 2, Hutton	6092	1			4	5		7	10			11					3			6	8	9	2			
29	15	READING	1-1	Thomas	5992	1			4	5		7	10			11					3			6	8	9	2			
30	23	Southend United	1-0	Thomas	7630			3	4	5		7	10			11								6	8	9	2	1		
31	29	CARLISLE UNITED	0-1		6710			3	4	5		7	10			11								6	8	9	2	1		
32	Feb 5	BARNSLEY	2-3	Hutton, Thomas	6516				6	4	5	7				11		3						8	10	2	1	9		
33	12	MANSFIELD TOWN	0-1		6115				6	4	5	7				11		3						8	10	2	1	9		
34	26	BOURNEMOUTH	3-1	Ratcliffe, Bramley, Brown	5110					6	5	7				11					3		9	4	8	10	2	1		
35	Mar 6	Carlisle United	1-3	Thomas	9418					6	5	7			8	11					3		9			10	2	1		4
36	8	Peterborough United	2-2	Brown 2	9661	1			3	8	5	7				11							9	6		10	2	1		4
37	12	OLDHAM ATHLETIC	1-1	Brown	5795				3	8	5	7				11							9	6		10	2	1		4
38	20	Bristol Rovers	0-2		6650				3	6	5	7											9	11	8	10	2	1		4
39	26	BRENTFORD	2-0	Ratcliffe, Scott	5081				3	8	5	7				11							9	6		10	2	1		4
40	Apr 3	Colchester United	1-2	Lindsey	3212				3	8	5	7				11							9	6			2	1	10	4
41	6	Grimsby Town	0-3		6756				3	8	5	7	10			11							9	6			2	1		4
42	9	PORT VALE	0-0		3894	1			3	8	5	7											9	6		10	2			4
43	16	Watford	0-5		7140					2	10	5	7			11					3			6	8	9		1		4
44	20	WATFORD	0-2		3597					2	6	5				11			7		3	10			8	9		1		4
45	24	LUTON TOWN	8-1	Thomas 5, Wilson, Mahy, Bramley	2755					2	6	5				11			3	10		8	7	9		1		4
46	27	Brentford	0-4		6167					2	6	5				11			3	10				8	7	9		1		4
				Apps		31	7	38	39	43	9	31	20	22	21	26	3	20	25	1	25	6	11	32	24	23	19	15	3	12
				Goals				1	2	1		4	3	13	5	7			1			1	4	8	2	13				

F.A. Cup

| R1 | Nov 14 | DARLINGTON | 1-2 | Greener (og) | 5121 | 1 | | 6 | 4 | 5 | | 7 | | 9 | 8 | | | 3 | 11 | | 2 | | | 10 | | | | | | |

F.L. Cup

| R1 | Sep 23 | WORKINGTON | 0-1 | | 3910 | 1 | | 2 | 5 | | 6 | | 8 | 9 | 10 | 11 | | 3 | 7 | | | 4 | | | | | | | | |

Division 3 Final Table

		P	W	D	L	F	A	W	D	L	F	A	Pts
1	Carlisle United	46	14	5	4	46	24	11	5	7	30	29	60
2	Bristol City	46	14	6	3	53	18	10	5	8	39	37	59
3	Mansfield Town	46	17	4	2	61	23	7	7	9	34	38	59
4	Hull City	46	14	6	3	51	25	9	6	8	40	32	58
5	Brentford	46	18	4	1	55	18	6	5	12	28	37	57
6	Bristol Rovers	46	14	7	2	52	21	6	8	9	30	37	55
7	Gillingham	46	16	5	2	45	13	7	4	12	25	37	55
8	Peterborough Utd.	46	16	3	4	61	33	6	4	13	24	41	51
9	Watford	46	13	8	2	45	21	4	8	11	26	43	50
10	Grimsby Town	46	11	10	2	37	21	5	7	11	31	46	49
11	Bournemouth	46	12	4	7	40	24	6	7	10	32	39	47
12	Southend United	46	14	4	5	48	24	5	4	14	30	47	46
13	Reading	46	12	8	3	45	26	4	6	13	25	44	46
14	Queen's Park Rgs.	46	15	5	3	48	23	2	7	14	24	57	46
15	Workington	46	11	7	5	30	22	6	5	12	28	47	46
16	Shrewsbury Town	46	10	6	7	42	38	5	6	12	34	46	42
17	Exeter City	46	8	7	8	33	27	4	10	9	18	25	41
18	SCUNTHORPE UNITED	46	9	8	6	42	27	5	4	14	23	45	40
19	Walsall	46	9	4	10	34	36	6	3	14	21	44	37
20	Oldham Athletic	46	10	3	10	40	39	3	7	13	21	44	36
21	Luton Town	46	6	8	9	32	36	5	3	15	19	58	33
22	Port Vale	46	7	6	10	27	33	2	8	13	14	43	32
23	Colchester United	46	7	6	10	30	34	3	4	16	20	55	30
24	Barnsley	46	8	5	10	33	31	1	6	16	21	59	29

1965/66 4th in Division 3

#		Date	Opponent	Score	Scorers	Att	Sidebottom G	Lindsey K	Hemstead DW	Scott RSA	Horstead JB	Burkinshaw KH	Hutton J	Barton F	Brown MR	Lindsey B	Colquhoun J	Smith RW	Sloan D	Mahy B	Bedford NB	Goodwin F	Thomas BEB	Bramley JS	Neale P	Ash M	Burrows F	Clemence RN	Taylor SR	Barker J	Coatsworth FW
1	Aug	21	Hull City	2-3	Brown, Hutton	18829	1	2	3	4	5	6	7	8	9	10	11														
2		25	MANSFIELD TOWN	0-1		6894	1	2	3	4	5	6	7		9	10	11	8													
3		28	READING	2-0	Brown, Smith	4335	1	2	3	4	5	6			9	10	11	8	7	12											
4	Sep	4	Exeter City	0-4		5818	1		3	4	5	6	7		9	8	11	2			10										
5		11	PETERBOROUGH UTD.	1-1	Bedford	4828	1				3	6			9	4		2	11		10	5	7	8							
6		14	QUEEN'S PARK RANGERS	1-2	Bedford	5362	1				3	6			9	4		2	11		10	5	7	8							
7		18	Millwall	2-2	Snowdon(og), Hutton	11525	1	2			3	6	7		9	4	11	8			10				5						
8		25	GILLINGHAM	0-1		4325	1	2	3			6	7		9	4	11	8			10				5						
9	Oct	2	Oldham Athletic	3-1	Barton, Bedford, Colquhoun	6363	1	2	3			6	12	9		4	11	8			10				5	7					
10		4	Queen's Park Rangers	0-1		6726	1	2	3			6	7	9		4	11	8	12		10				5						
11		9	Brentford	1-0	Smith	7729	1		3	4		6	7	9		2	11				10	12			5						
12		16	BRISTOL ROVERS	3-0	Goodwin, Barton, Bedford	4219	1	2	3	4		6	7	9			11	8	12		10	5									
13		30	OXFORD UNITED	1-2	Smith (p)	4030	1	2	3	4		6	7	9			11	8			10	5									
14	Nov	6	Swansea Town	4-3	Ash, Thomas, Bedford, B.Lindsey	8853	1	2	3						6	11	4	7			10	5	9			8					
15		19	Workington	2-1	Thomas, Bedford	2934	1		3	6	5					2	11	4	7		10		9			8					
16		27	BOURNEMOUTH	3-0	Bedford 2, Smith	2766	1		3	6	5					2	11	4	7		10		9			8					
17	Dec	4	York City	3-1	Sloan, Bedford, Ash	4175	1		3	6	5		9			2	11	4	7		10					8					
18		11	SWINDON TOWN	2-1	Bedford 2	4483	1		3	6	5		9			2	11	4	7		10					8					
19		27	Shrewsbury Town	4-1	Bedford 3, Hutton	7520	1		3	6	5		9			2	11	4	7		10					8					
20		28	SHREWSBURY TOWN	1-4	Bedford	6249	1		3	6	5		9			2	11	4	7		10					8					
21	Jan	1	BRENTFORD	3-2	Sloan, Ash, Thomas	5738	1		3	6	5					2	11	4	7		10	9				8					
22		8	Walsall	0-3		7059	1		3	6	5	12				2	11	4	7		10	9				8					
23		15	YORK CITY	4-1	Burkinshaw, Sloan 2, Bedford	3680	1		3		5	6	9			2	11	4	7		10						12	8			
24		29	HULL CITY	2-4	Colquhoun, Ash	15570	1		3			6	9			2	11	4	7		10					8		5			
25	Feb	5	Reading	0-2		7102	1		3			6	9			2	11	4	7		10					8		5			
26		12	Brighton & Hove Albion	1-0	Bedford	12659	1		3		5	6		8		2	11	4	9		10				12	7					
27		19	EXETER CITY	2-1	Barton, Smith (p)	4576	1		3		5	6		8			11	4	9		10				2	7					
28		26	Peterborough United	1-3	Sloan	6696	1		3		5	6		8			11	4	9		10				12	7					
29	Mar	5	BRIGHTON & HOVE ALB	2-2	Sloan, Barton	4657	1		3		2			8		12	11	4	7		10			9	5		6				
30		7	Mansfield Town	2-2	Bedford, Smith (p)	6678	1	3	2					8		10	11	4	7		9				5		6				
31		12	MILLWALL	4-4	Snowdon(og),Smith,Colquhoun,Barton	5800	1	2	3			6		8		10	11	4	7		9				5						
32		19	Gillingham	1-0	Sloan	6110	1	2	3			6		8		10	11	4	7		9										
33		26	OLDHAM ATHLETIC	1-1	Bedford	5211	1	2	3			6		8		10	11	4	7		9				5						
34		29	Bristol Rovers	0-2		7376	1	2	3			6				10	11	4	7	8	9				5						
35	Apr	2	SWANSEA TOWN	1-1	Thomas	2914			2			6		8		10	11	4	7				9			12	5	1	3		
36		8	Grimsby Town	3-1	Sloan 3	10960	1		2			6		8			11	4	7		9					10	5		3		
37		12	GRIMSBY TOWN	2-2	Bedford, Colquhoun	7783	1		3		2	6				12	11	4	7		9		8			10	5		3		
38		16	WORKINGTON	4-1	Thomas 3, Sloan	4088	1		2			6		8			11	4	7		9					10	5		3		
39		23	Bournemouth	2-1	Burrows, Thomas	6161	1					6		8			11	4	7		9					10	5	2	3		
40		26	Watford	1-2	Barton	4072	1		2			6		8			11	4	7		9					10	5				
41		30	SOUTHEND UNITED	0-0		4399	1		2			6		8			11	4	7		9					10	5		3		
42	May	7	Swindon Town	0-0		9251	1		2			6					11	4	7		9					10	5		3		8
43		13	Southend United	1-0	Sloan	7326			3			6		8	2	11	4	7			9					10	5	1			
44		17	WATFORD	1-1	Colquhoun	3913			3			6				11	4	7	2	9		8				10	5	1			
45		21	WALSALL	4-2	Sloan 2, Thomas, Bedford	3429			3			6				11	4	7	2	9		8				10	5	1			
46		28	Oxford United	3-0	Thomas, Bedford, Mahy	4505	1					6				11	4	7	2	9		8				10	5				
					Apps		42	15	41	15	21	36	17	21	8	34	44	45	38	5	35	6	19	3	13	28	19	4	8	1	1
					Goals							1	3	6	2	1	5	7	14	1	22	1	10			4	1				

2 own goals

F.A. Cup

| R1 | Nov | 13 | Crewe Alexandra | 0-3 | | 5148 | 1 | 2 | 3 | | | | | | 6 | 11 | 4 | 7 | | | 10 | 5 | 9 | | | 8 | | | | | |

F.L. Cup

| R1 | Sep | 1 | DARLINGTON | 0-2 | | 2856 | 1 | 2 | 3 | 7 | 4 | 6 | | | 9 | | 11 | 8 | 10 | | | | | | 5 | | | | | | |

		P	W	D	L	F	A	W	D	L	F	A	Pts
1	Hull City	46	19	2	2	64	24	12	5	6	45	38	69
2	Millwall	46	19	4	0	47	13	8	7	8	29	30	65
3	Queen's Park Rgs.	46	16	3	4	62	29	8	6	9	33	36	57
4	SCUNTHORPE UNITED	46	9	8	6	44	34	12	3	8	36	33	53
5	Workington	46	13	6	4	38	18	6	8	9	29	39	52
6	Gillingham	46	14	5	4	33	19	8	4	11	29	35	52
7	Swindon Town	46	11	8	4	43	18	8	5	10	31	30	51
8	Reading	46	13	5	5	36	19	6	8	9	34	44	51
9	Walsall	46	13	7	3	48	21	7	3	13	29	43	50
10	Shrewsbury Town	46	13	7	3	48	22	6	4	13	25	42	49
11	Grimsby Town	46	15	6	2	47	25	2	7	14	21	37	47
12	Watford	46	12	4	7	33	19	5	9	9	22	32	47
13	Peterborough Utd.	46	13	6	4	50	26	4	6	13	30	40	46
14	Oxford United	46	11	3	9	38	33	8	5	10	32	41	46
15	Brighton & Hove A.	46	13	4	6	48	28	3	7	13	19	37	43
16	Bristol Rovers	46	11	10	2	38	15	3	4	16	26	49	42
17	Swansea Town	46	14	4	5	61	37	1	7	15	20	59	41
18	Bournemouth	46	9	8	6	24	19	4	4	15	14	37	38
19	Mansfield Town	46	10	5	8	31	36	5	3	15	28	53	38
20	Oldham Athletic	46	8	7	8	43	13	21	48	37			
21	Southend United	46	15	1	7	43	28	1	3	19	11	55	36
22	Exeter City	46	9	6	8	26	28	3	5	15	17	51	35
23	Brentford	46	9	4	10	34	30	1	8	14	14	39	32
24	York City	46	5	7	11	30	44	4	2	17	23	62	27

1966/67 — 18th in Division 3

League

#	Date		Opponent	Result	Scorers	Att.
1	Aug	20	GILLINGHAM	1-2	Thomas	5050
2		27	Orient	1-3	Ash	5475
3	Sep	3	BOURNEMOUTH	0-1		4173
4		7	Grimsby Town	1-7	Bedford	8044
5		10	Swansea Town	1-0	Lindsey	6165
6		17	MIDDLESBROUGH	3-2	Bramley, Barton, Lindsey	3948
7		24	Shrewsbury Town	3-4	Ash, Barton, Smith	4300
8		27	GRIMSBY TOWN	0-0		11105
9		30	COLCHESTER UNITED	3-1	Loughton (og), Thomas, Smith	5222
10	Oct	8	Walsall	0-2		9326
11		14	PETERBOROUGH UTD.	1-0	Smith (p)	5723
12		18	Oldham Athletic	0-2		13975
13		22	Torquay United	1-1	Colquhoun	5418
14		24	Bristol Rovers	1-1	Thomas	11015
15		28	BRIGHTON & HOVE ALB	0-1		5512
16	Nov	5	Darlington	1-2	Smith	6650
17		12	QUEEN'S PARK RANGERS	0-2		4912
18		15	OLDHAM ATHLETIC	1-1	Colquhoun	3580
19		19	Watford	1-0	Barton	7084
20	Dec	3	Reading	0-4		5080
21		9	DONCASTER ROVERS	2-1	Smith, Burkinshaw	6300
22		17	Gillingham	1-0	Ash	5468
23		23	MANSFIELD TOWN	2-1	Sloan, Barton	6263
24		27	Mansfield Town	1-3	Lindsey	10292
25		30	ORIENT	2-2	Sloan, Barton	5343
26	Jan	14	SWANSEA TOWN	4-3	Hemstead, Rusling, Lindsey, Sloan	4461
27		21	Middlesbrough	1-2	Burrows	19007
28		28	Bournemouth	0-0		3941
29	Feb	4	SHREWSBURY TOWN	2-0	Rusling 2	4447
30		11	Colchester United	1-0	Sloan	3965
31		18	Oxford United	1-2	Burkinshaw	7013
32		24	WALSALL	2-0	Colquhoun, Barton	4839
33	Mar	4	Peterborough United	0-1		5485
34		10	OXFORD UNITED	2-2	Barton (p), Sloan	4616
35		17	TORQUAY UNITED	3-1	Coatsworth, Smith (og), Sloan	4353
36		25	Brighton & Hove Albion	2-2	Colquhoun, Hemstead	11624
37		27	WORKINGTON	4-1	Colquhoun, Barton 2 (1 p), Sloan	5486
38		28	Workington	0-1		2079
39		31	DARLINGTON	2-0	Sloan, Rusling	4621
40	Apr	8	Queen's Park Rangers	1-5	Rusling	13113
41		14	WATFORD	1-0	Colquhoun	4927
42		22	Swindon Town	1-2	Sloan	12786
43		24	BRISTOL ROVERS	3-1	Barton 2, Coatsworth	4080
44		28	READING	0-2		4984
45	May	5	Doncaster Rovers	0-3		3948
46		12	SWINDON TOWN	1-2	Colquhoun	3544

F.A. Cup

	Date		Opponent	Result	Scorers	Att.
R1	Nov	26	Lincoln City	4-3	Smith, Burrows, Barton, Mahy	6223
R2	Jan	7	Mansfield Town	1-2	Foxon	9446

F.L. Cup

	Date		Opponent	Result	Scorers	Att.
R1	Aug	24	Chesterfield	1-2	Barton	5418

Division 3 Final Table

		P	W	D	L	F	A	W	D	L	F	A	Pts
1	Queen's Park Rgs.	46	18	4	1	66	15	8	11	4	37	23	67
2	Middlesbrough	46	16	3	4	51	20	7	6	10	36	44	55
3	Watford	46	15	5	3	39	17	5	9	9	22	29	54
4	Reading	46	13	7	3	45	20	9	2	12	31	37	53
5	Bristol Rovers	46	13	8	2	47	28	7	5	11	29	39	53
6	Shrewsbury Town	46	15	5	3	48	24	5	7	11	29	38	52
7	Torquay United	46	17	3	3	57	20	4	6	13	16	34	51
8	Swindon Town	46	14	5	4	53	21	6	5	12	28	38	50
9	Mansfield Town	46	12	4	7	48	37	8	5	10	36	42	49
10	Oldham Athletic	46	15	4	4	51	16	4	6	13	29	47	48
11	Gillingham	46	11	9	3	36	18	4	7	12	22	44	46
12	Walsall	46	12	8	3	37	16	6	2	15	28	56	46
13	Colchester United	46	14	3	6	52	30	3	7	13	24	43	44
14	Orient	46	10	9	4	36	27	3	9	11	22	41	44
15	Peterborough Utd.	46	12	4	7	40	31	2	11	10	26	40	43
16	Oxford United	46	10	8	5	41	29	5	5	13	20	37	43
17	Grimsby Town	46	13	5	5	46	23	4	4	15	15	45	43
18	SCUNTHORPE UNITED	46	13	4	6	39	26	4	4	15	19	47	42
19	Brighton & Hove A.	46	10	8	5	37	27	3	7	13	24	44	41
20	Bournemouth	46	8	10	5	24	24	4	7	12	15	33	41
21	Swansea Town	46	9	9	5	50	30	3	6	14	35	59	39
22	Darlington	46	8	7	8	26	28	5	4	14	21	53	37
23	Doncaster Rovers	46	11	6	6	40	40	1	2	20	18	77	32
24	Workington	46	9	3	11	35	35	3	4	16	20	54	31

1967/68   24th in Division 3: Relegated

#	Date		Opponent	Score	Scorers	Att	Arblaster BM	Hemstead DW	Barker J	Lindsey B	Burrows F	Burkinshaw KH	Sloan D	Barton F	Harney D	Colquhoun J	Foley P	Taylor SR	Foxon DN	Horstead JB	Webster AJ	Drake S	Verity DA	Naylor G	Deere SH	Rusling G	Blyth MR	Lavery J	Welbourne D	Foxton DG	Punton WH	Kerr GAM	Heath RT
1	Aug	19	Peterborough United	1-1	Barton	6984	1	2	3	4	5	6	7	8	9	10	11															
2		25	MANSFIELD TOWN	3-3	Sloan, Barton (p), Burrows	6372	1	2	3	4	5	6	7	8	9	10	11	12														
3	Sep	2	Watford	0-4		6675	1	2	3	4	5	6	7	8	9	10	11															
4		4	Bournemouth	0-1		6302	1	2	3	4	5	6	8	9		10	12	11														
5		9	SOUTHPORT	1-0	Sloan	4655	1	2	3	4	5	6	7	8	9	10		11														
6		16	Grimsby Town	1-2	Barton	7825	1	2		4	5	6	9	8	12	10	7	3	11													
7		23	Oldham Athletic	4-3	Barton, Sloan 2, Horstead	5263	1	2		4	5	6	7	8	9	10		3	11	12												
8		26	BOURNEMOUTH	1-1	Barton	4936	1	2		4	5	6	7	8	9	10		3	11	12												
9		30	BRISTOL ROVERS	1-1	Sloan	3848	1	2			5	6	7	8	9	10		3	11	4												
10	Oct	3	Bury	3-4	Harney, Colquhoun 2	5932	1	2			5	6	7	4	9	10	8	3	11	12												
11		7	WALSALL	2-5	Barton 2 (1 p)	4170		2			5	6	7	8	9	10		3	11		4	1	12									
12		14	Northampton Town	0-1		10099		2			5	6	7	8	9	10		3	11	4		1										
13		21	ORIENT	1-1	Foxon	3431		2			5	6	7	8	9	10		3	11	4		1										
14		24	BURY	3-1	Sloan, Horstead, Barton	3847		2			5	6	7	8	9	10		3	11	4		1										
15		27	Tranmere Rovers	0-2		6977		2			5	6	7	8	9	10		3	11		4	1		12								
16	Nov	3	STOCKPORT COUNTY	0-2		4338		2			5	6	7	8	9	10		3	11	4		1		12								
17		11	Brighton & Hove Albion	1-3	Deere	11251		2			5	6	7	8	11	10		3	12			1		4	9							
18		14	WATFORD	1-1	Rusling	3445		2			5		7	8		9		3	11			1		4	6	10						
19		17	SHREWSBURY TOWN	0-0		3104		2			5		7	8		9		3	11			1		4	10		6					
20		25	Swindon Town	0-2		11944		2			5		7	8		9		3	11			1		4	10		6					
21	Dec	1	READING	1-2	Colquhoun	3541		2			5		7	8		9		3	11			1		4	10	12	6					
22		15	PETERBOROUGH UTD.	2-1	Deere, Barton	3519		2			5	6	7	8		11		3				1		4	9		10					
23		23	Mansfield Town	0-3		4907		2	3		5	6	7	8		11						1		4	9		10					
24		26	OXFORD UNITED	1-1	Sloan	3839		2	3		5	6	7	8		11			12			1		4	9		10					
25		30	Oxford United	3-2	Deere 2, Sloan	6392		2	3		5	6	7	8					11			1		4	9			1	10			
26	Jan	20	GRIMSBY TOWN	0-3		6886		2	3		5	6	7		8				11						9		10	1	4	12		
27		26	GILLINGHAM	2-1	Blyth 2	3484		2	3	4	5	6	8		9	7									10		1				11	
28	Feb	3	OLDHAM ATHLETIC	2-0	Sloan, Foley	3697		2	3	4	5	6	8		9	7									10		1				11	
29		10	Bristol Rovers	0-4		5666		2	3	4	5	6	8		9	7									10		1				11	
30		17	BARROW	2-4	Lindsey, Sloan	3229		2		4	5	6	8		9	7	3								10		1				11	
31		24	Walsall	0-0		8987		2		8	5	6			11		3		4						9		10	1			7	
32		26	Colchester United	0-1		3979		2			5	6			11		3		4	8					9		10	1	12		7	
33	Mar	2	NORTHAMPTON T	1-1	Kerr	2475		2	3	4	5				8					7							6	1	10		11	9
34		9	COLCHESTER UNITED	5-1	Colquhoun 2, Punton, Heath, Deere	3098		2	3	4	5				7										9		6	1			11	8	10
35		16	Orient	1-2	Heath	5067		2	3	4	5				7										9		6	1			11	8	10
36		22	TRANMERE ROVERS	1-1	Colquhoun	3986		2	3	4	5				7										9		6	1			11	8	10
37		29	Stockport County	1-4	Heath	6779		2	3	4	5				7			12							9		6	1			11	8	10
38	Apr	6	BRIGHTON & HOVE ALB	1-3	Burrows (p)	2845		2	3	4	5				8			7							9		6	1			11		10
39		13	Shrewsbury Town	0-4		5578			3	4	5				7										9		6	1		2	11	8	10
40		15	Gillingham	1-3	Kerr	5031			3	4	5				7					12		1				9	6		2	11	8	10
41		19	SWINDON TOWN	3-1	Heath, Kerr 2	2725			3	4	5				7					1						9	6		2	11	8	10
42		25	Torquay United	1-2	Heath	10362			3	4	5				7					1						9	6		2	11	8	10
43		27	Reading	1-2	Colquhoun	3879			3	4	5				7					1	10					9	6		2	11	8	
44	May	3	TORQUAY UNITED	2-0	Rusling, Blyth	2700			3	4	5				7	12				1						9	6		2	11	8	10
45		6	Southport	1-1	Colquhoun	3238		2		4	5				11	7				1	12				9	6			3		8	10
46		11	Barrow	1-2	Kerr	3782			3	4	5			7	11	9				1						6		2		8	10
					Apps		10	46	18	27	46	28	30	25	18	45	13	24	20	9	5	21	4	10	19	8	27	15	4	9	16	15	12
					Goals					1	2		10	9	1	8	1			1	2				5	2	3				1	5	5

F.A. Cup

R	Date		Opponent	Score	Scorers	Att																										
R1	Dec	9	SKELMERSDALE UNITED	2-0	Colquhoun, Barton (p)	3847		2			5	6	7	8		11		3				1		4	10	9						
R2	Jan	6	Halifax Town	0-1		7804		2	3		5	6	7	8		11						1		4	9				1	10			

F.L. Cup

R	Date		Opponent	Score	Scorers	Att																										
R1	Aug	23	Doncaster Rovers	2-1	Barton, Foley	8666	1	2	3	4	5	6	7	8	9	10	11															
R2	Sep	13	NOTTM. FOREST	0-1		13523	1	2	3	4	5	6	9	8	11	10	7		12													

		P	W	D	L	F	A	W	D	L	F	A	Pts
1	Oxford United	46	18	3	2	49	20	4	10	9	20	27	57
2	Bury	46	19	3	1	64	24	5	5	13	27	42	56
3	Shrewsbury Town	46	14	6	3	42	17	6	9	8	19	32	55
4	Torquay United	46	15	6	2	40	17	6	5	12	20	39	53
5	Reading	46	15	5	3	43	17	6	4	13	27	43	51
6	Watford	46	15	6	5	59	20	6	5	12	15	30	50
7	Walsall	46	12	7	4	47	22	7	5	11	27	39	50
8	Barrow	46	14	6	3	43	13	7	2	14	22	41	50
9	Peterborough Utd.	46	14	4	5	46	23	6	6	11	33	44	50
10	Swindon Town	46	13	8	2	51	16	3	9	11	23	35	49
11	Brighton & Hove A.	46	11	8	4	31	14	5	8	10	26	41	48
12	Gillingham	46	13	6	4	35	19	5	6	12	24	44	48
13	Bournemouth	46	13	7	3	39	17	3	8	12	17	34	47
14	Stockport County	46	16	5	2	49	22	3	4	16	21	53	47
15	Southport	46	13	6	4	35	22	4	6	13	30	43	46
16	Bristol Rovers	46	14	3	6	42	25	3	6	14	30	53	43
17	Oldham Athletic	46	11	3	9	37	32	7	4	12	23	33	43
18	Northampton Town	46	10	8	5	40	25	4	5	14	18	47	41
19	Orient	46	10	6	7	27	24	2	11	10	19	38	41
20	Tranmere Rovers	46	10	7	6	39	28	4	5	14	23	46	40
21	Mansfield Town	46	8	7	8	32	31	4	6	13	19	36	37
22	Grimsby Town	46	10	7	6	33	21	4	2	17	19	48	37
23	Colchester United	46	6	8	9	29	40	3	7	13	21	47	33
24	SCUNTHORPE UNITED	46	8	9	6	36	34	2	3	18	20	53	32

~ 238 ~

1968/69 16th in Division 4

#	Date		Opponent	Score	Scorers	Att	Barnard G	FoxtonDG	Hemstead DW	Lindsey B	Holt R	Welbourne D	Colquhoun J	Kerr GAM	Harney D	Heath RT	Punton WH	Deere SH	Barker J	Foley P	Davidson I	Keegan JK	Wilson AP	Taylor SR	Cassidy N	Jackson NA	Rusling G	Currie JT
1	Aug	10	Rochdale	2-3	Kerr, Deere	3253	1	2	3	4	5	6	7	8	9	10	11	12										
2		17	BRENTFORD	1-1	Deere	3685	1	2	3	4	5	6	7	8		10	11	9										
3		23	Doncaster Rovers	3-4	Heath 2, Kerr	10474	1	2	3	4	5	6		8		10	11	9	12									
4		26	Colchester United	4-0	Kerr 2, Heath, Deere	3771	1		2	4	5	6	7	8		10	11	9	3									
5		30	CHESTER	2-2	Kerr, Colquhoun	4983	1		2	4	5	6	7	8		10	11	9	3									
6	Sep	6	BRADFORD CITY	1-0	Deere	5997	1	12	2	4	5	6	7	8		10	11	9	3									
7		14	York City	1-2	Colquhoun	5071	1		2	4	5	6	11	8		10		9	3	7	12							
8		16	Peterborough United	2-3	Foley, Heath	5401	1		2	4	5		11		12	10		9	3	8	6	7						
9		21	EXETER CITY	2-1	Deere, Foley (p)	3534	1		2	4	5	6	11			10		9	3	8	12	7						
10		28	Port Vale	1-4	Heath	3823	1		2		5	6	11			10		9	3	8	4	12	7					
11	Oct	4	HALIFAX TOWN	0-1		3942	1	2	3		5	6			8	10	11	9			4		7					
12		8	COLCHESTER UNITED	2-3	Kerr, Heath	2849	1	2	3		5	6		8		10	11	9			4		7					
13		12	Workington	1-1	Welbourne	2287	1	2	3		5	6		8		10	11	9			4		7					
14		18	NEWPORT COUNTY	1-0	Heath (p)	3360	1	2	3		5	6	11	8	12	10		9			4		7					
15		26	Aldershot	2-3	Heath, Rafferty (og)	4991	1		2	12	6		11	8		10		9	3		4		7					
16	Nov	1	SWANSEA TOWN	3-1	Kerr, Wilson 2	3451	1		2		5	6	11	8		10		9	3		4	12	7					
17		6	GRIMSBY TOWN	1-2	Colquhoun	5368	1		2		5	6	11	8		10		9	3		4	12	7					
18		9	Wrexham	1-0	Kerr	5848	1		2		5	6	4	8	11	10		9	3				7					
19		23	Darlington	1-0	Heath	4903	1		2		5	6		9		10	11		3		4	8	7					
20		30	LINCOLN CITY	0-0		5855	1		2		5			9			10	11	12	6	4	8	7	3				
21	Dec	6	BRADFORD PARK AVE.	1-0	Deere	3158	1		2		5	6		9			11	10	3		4	8	7					
22		26	Halifax Town	0-2		7092	1		2			5		8			11		6		4	10	7	3	9			
23	Jan	4	NOTTS COUNTY	2-1	Kerr, Cassidy	3410	1		2			5		8			11	10	6		4	12	7	3	9			
24		11	Swansea Town	0-2		4888	1				5	6		8	12		11	10	2		4	7		3	9			
25		25	Grimsby Town	1-0	Cassidy	5983	1		2	10	5	6		8			11		3		4	7			9			
26		28	WORKINGTON	0-1		4425	1		2	10	5			8			11	12	6		4	7			9	3		
27	Feb	1	Bradford Park Avenue	2-2	Kerr, Keegan	3050	1		2	10	5	6		8			11	12	3		4	7			9			
28		15	Lincoln City	2-1	Kerr, Cassidy	8186	1		2	10	5	6		8			11	12			4	7			9	3		
29		24	Newport County	1-1	Lindsey	1504	1		2	10	5			8			11		6		4	7			9	3		
30	Mar	1	ROCHDALE	0-0		3102	1		2	10	5			8			11		6		4	7		3	9			
31		5	Notts County	0-1		3311	1		2			6		8	12		11	5	3		4	10	7		9			
32		8	Brentford	1-2	Heath (p)	5456	1		2			6		8		10	11	5	3		4	7			9			
33		14	DONCASTER ROVERS	0-2		6650	1		2			6		8			10	5	3		4	11	7		9		12	
34		17	Southend United	3-0	Heath, Haydock(og), Cassidy	10131	1		2			6		8			10	5	3		4	7	11		9			
35		22	Chester	2-0	Wilson, Cassidy	5483	1		2			6		8			10	5	3		4	11	7		9			
36		25	WREXHAM	1-0	Wilson	2876	1		2			6		8			10	5			4	7	11	3	9			
37		29	Bradford City	0-3		6584	1		2			6		8			10	5			4	7	11	3	9			
38	Apr	5	PORT VALE	0-1		2966	1		2			6		8			10	11	5		4	7			9			
39		7	PETERBOROUGH UTD.	1-2	Punton	2822	1		2			6		8			10	11	5			7			9	3	4	
40		8	Chesterfield	2-1	Heath, Kerr	3793	1		2		5			8			4	11	6			10	7		9	3		
41		12	Exeter City	1-3	Heath (p)	4566	1		2		5			8			4	11	6			10	7		9	3		
42		15	CHESTERFIELD	0-1		2398	1		2		5			8			4	11	6		12	10	7		9	3		
43		18	YORK CITY	2-1	Kerr, Heath (p)	2300	1			3	5	6			7	12		10	11		4	8			9	2		
44		29	ALDERSHOT	4-1	Rusling, Cassidy, Keegan, Heath	2220	1		2		5			7			11		6	3	4	8			9		10	
45	May	2	Darlington	0-0		2500	1		2		5			7				11	6	3	4	8			9		10	
46		12	SOUTHEND UNITED	4-1	Cassidy 2, Rusling 2	1850	1		2		5	6		7				11	3			8			9		10	4

Players substituted in games 1 and 23 unknown.

	Barnard G	FoxtonDG	Hemstead DW	Lindsey B	Holt R	Welbourne D	Colquhoun J	Kerr GAM	Harney D	Heath RT	Punton WH	Deere SH	Barker J	Foley P	Davidson I	Keegan JK	Wilson AP	Taylor SR	Cassidy N	Jackson NA	Rusling G	Currie JT
Apps	46	8	45	16	35	36	15	42	7	33	29	43	30	4	35	33	23	8	25	8	5	1
Goals				1		1	3	13		15	1	6		2		2	4		8		3	

2 own goals

F.A. Cup

R1	Nov	16	Workington	0-2		3325	1		2		5	6		8				9	10		4	11	7	3				

F.L. Cup

R1	Aug	13	ROTHERHAM UNITED	2-1	Deere 2	4643	1	2	3	4	5	6	7	8		10	11	9										
R2	Sep	3	LINCOLN CITY	2-1	Kerr 2	11098	1		2	4	5	6	7	8		10	11	9	3									
R3		25	ARSENAL	1-6	Simpson (og)	17230	1		2		5	6	11			10		9	3	8	4	7			12			

		P	W	D	L	F	A	W	D	L	F	A	Pts
1	Doncaster Rovers	46	13	8	2	42	16	8	9	6	23	22	59
2	Halifax Town	46	15	5	3	36	18	5	12	6	17	19	57
3	Rochdale	46	14	7	2	47	11	4	13	6	21	24	56
4	Bradford City	46	11	10	2	36	18	7	10	6	29	28	56
5	Darlington	46	11	6	6	40	26	6	12	5	22	19	52
6	Colchester United	46	12	8	3	31	17	8	4	11	26	36	52
7	Southend United	46	15	3	5	51	21	4	10	9	27	40	51
8	Lincoln City	46	13	6	4	38	19	4	11	8	16	33	51
9	Wrexham	46	13	7	3	41	22	5	7	11	20	30	50
10	Swansea Town	46	11	8	4	35	20	8	3	12	23	34	49
11	Brentford	46	12	7	4	40	24	6	5	12	24	41	48
12	Workington	46	8	11	4	24	17	7	6	10	16	26	47
13	Port Vale	46	12	8	3	33	15	4	6	13	13	31	46
14	Chester	46	12	4	7	43	24	4	9	10	33	42	45
15	Aldershot	46	13	3	7	42	23	6	4	13	24	43	45
16	SCUNTHORPE UNITED	46	10	5	8	28	22	8	3	12	33	38	44
17	Exeter City	46	11	8	4	45	24	5	3	15	21	41	43
18	Peterborough Utd.	46	8	9	6	32	23	5	7	11	28	34	42
19	Notts County	46	10	8	5	33	22	2	10	11	15	35	42
20	Chesterfield	46	7	7	9	24	22	6	8	9	19	28	41
21	York City	46	12	8	3	36	25	2	3	18	17	50	39
22	Newport County	46	9	9	5	31	26	2	5	16	18	48	36
23	Grimsby Town	46	5	7	11	25	31	4	8	11	22	38	33
24	Bradford Park Ave.	46	5	8	10	19	34	0	2	21	13	72	20

1969/70 12th in Division 4

#		Date	Opponent	Score	Scorers	Att	Barnard G	Foxton DG	Barker J	Deere SH	Holt R	Welbourne D	Kerr GAM	Keegan JK	Cassidy N	Heath RT	Rusling G	Davidson AG	Jackson NA	Currie JT	Lindsey B	Atkin JM	Drake S
1	Aug	9	CHESTER	2-3	Rusling, Deere	3361	1	2	3	4	5	6	7	8	9	10	11						
2		15	Southend United	0-3		8808	1	2	3	4	5	6	7	8	9	10	11	12					
3		23	PETERBOROUGH UTD.	2-1	Heath, Deere	2582	1	2	3	4	5	6		8	9	10	11	7	12				
4		26	BRADFORD PARK AVE.	2-0	Rusling, Keegan	3191	1	2	3	4	5	6		8	9	10	11	7					
5		30	Oldham Athletic	3-1	Deere, Davidson, Cassidy	5426	1	2	3	4	5	6		8	9	10	11	7					
6	Sep	6	EXETER CITY	0-0		4073	1	2	3	4	5	6		8	9	10	11	7					
7		13	Grimsby Town	1-1	Heath (p)	7335	1	2	3	4	5	6		8	9	10	11	7					
8		15	Wrexham	1-2	Heath	9575	1	2	3	4	5	6	12	8	9	10	11	7					
9		20	ALDERSHOT	0-0		3596	1	2		4	5	6	3	8	9	10	11	7	12				
10		27	York City	2-3	Keegan 2	4610	1	2		4	5	6	11	8	9	10		7	3				
11		29	Colchester United	2-0	Deere, Heath	6328	1	2		4	5	6	11	8	9	10		7	3				
12	Oct	4	CHESTERFIELD	1-2	Cassidy	3889	1	2		4	5	6	11	8	9	10	12	7	3				
13		7	SOUTHEND UNITED	2-0	Rusling, Cassidy	2964	1	2		4	5	6		8	9	10	11	7	3	12			
14		11	Brentford	0-3		7490	1	2		4	5	6		8	9	10	11	7	3	12			
15		18	Lincoln City	2-1	Cassidy 2	8172	1	2		6				7	8	10	9	11	3		4	5	
16		25	HARTLEPOOL	3-1	Cassidy, Keegan, Rusling	3583	1	2		6				7	8	10	9	11	3		4	5	
17	Nov	1	Crewe Alexandra	2-0	Heath 2	3190	1	2		6				7	8	10	9	11	3		4	5	
18		8	DARLINGTON	2-0	Cassidy, Rusling	3488	1	2		6				7	8	10	9	11	3		4	5	
19		22	PORT VALE	2-1	Heath (p), Sproson(og)	5516	1	2	3	6				7	8	10	9	11			4	5	
20		25	WORKINGTON	1-0	Davidson	3256	1		3	6				7	8	10	9	11	2		4	5	
21		29	Notts County	1-3	Ball (og)	3497	1		3	6				7	8	10	9	11	2		4	5	
22	Dec	13	GRIMSBY TOWN	1-1	Cassidy	7154	1	2	3	6			9	7	8	10		11			4	5	
23		20	Exeter City	1-4	Cassidy	3534	1	2	3	6			9	7	8	10		11			4	5	
24		26	Peterborough United	2-2	Barker, Kerr	7796		2	3	5		6	8	7		10	9	11			4		1
25		27	OLDHAM ATHLETIC	2-1	Davidson, Cassidy	4949		2	3	5		6	9	7	8	10		11			4		1
26	Jan	10	Aldershot	1-3	Davidson	5520	1	2	3	4	5	6	9	7	8	10		11					
27		17	YORK CITY	1-1	Davidson	4740	1	2		4		6	9	7	8	10		11	3		5		
28		27	COLCHESTER UNITED	1-1	Cassidy	6276	1	2		4		6	9		8	10	12	11	3		5		
29		31	Chesterfield	1-2	Cassidy	11921	1	2	3	10		6	9	7	8		12	11			4	5	
30	Feb	10	BRENTFORD	1-1	Heath	5109	1	2	3	5		6	9	7	8	10		11			4		
31		14	Chester	1-1	Heath	3968	1	2	3	5		6	9	7	8	10		11			4		
32		18	Northampton Town	1-2	Heath (p)	3735	1	2	3	4		6	9	7		10	8	11		12	5		
33		20	Hartlepool	2-1	Heath, Kerr	1480	1	2	3	5		6	9	7	8	10		11			4		
34		28	LINCOLN CITY	2-1	Cassidy 2	6857	1	2	3	5		6	9	7	8	10		11			4		
35	Mar	3	SWANSEA TOWN	1-2	Keegan	4988	1	2	3	5		6	9	7	8	10		11			4		
36		9	Newport County	0-3		1917	1	2	3	5		6	9	7	8	10	12	11			4		
37		14	NOTTS COUNTY	2-3	Kerr, Cassidy	4166	1	2	3			6	9	7	8		10	11	12	4			
38		17	NORTHAMPTON T	1-0	Davidson	2984	1	2		5		6	9		8	10		11	3		4		
39		21	Swansea Town	1-2	Barker	10228	1	2	4	5		6	9	7		10		11	3				
40		23	Port Vale	2-1	Cassidy 2	6394	1	2	4	5			9	7	8	10		11	3			6	
41		28	NEWPORT COUNTY	4-0	Kerr, Cassidy 2, Davidson	3805	1	2		5		6	4	9	8	10		11	3			5	
42		30	Darlington	0-2		1717	1	2		5		6		9	8	10		11	3			5	
43		31	CREWE ALEXANDRA	0-1		3665	1	2		4		6		7	8	10	9	11			12	5	
44	Apr	4	Bradford Park Avenue	5-0	Kerr 2, Heath, Cassidy, Davidson	2563	1	2		5		6	9	7	8	10		11	3		4		
45		8	Workington	2-2	Heath, Cassidy	2475	1	2		5		6	9	7	8	10		11	3		4		
46		14	WREXHAM	1-3	Davidson	4107	1	2		5		6	9	7	8	10		11	3		4		
						Apps	44	44	27	46	15	36	31	46	44	44	26	45	25	5	22	17	2
						Goals			2	4			6	6	21	13	5	8					

2 own goals

F.A. Cup

		Date	Opponent	Score	Scorers	Att																	
R1	Nov	15	Macclesfield Town	1-1	Heath	5476	1	2	3	6				7	8	10	9	11			4	5	
rep		18	MACCLESFIELD TOWN	4-2	Keegan 2, Rusling, Cassidy	5131	1	2	3	6			12	7	8	10	9	11			4	5	
R2	Dec	6	Stockport County	0-0		4200	1	2	3	6				7	8	10	9	11			4	5	
rep		9	STOCKPORT COUNTY	4-0	Cassidy, Kerr 2, Keegan	5646	1	2	3	6			9	7	8	10		11			4	5	
R3	Jan	3	MILLWALL	2-1	Deere, Heath	7675	1	2	3	6	5	9		7	8	10		11			4	12	
R4		24	Sheffield Wednesday	2-1	Barker, Cassidy	38047	1	2	3	4		6	9	7	8	10	12	11				5	
R5	Feb	7	Swindon Town	1-3	Cassidy	24612	1	2	3	4		6	9	7	8	10		11				5	

F.L. Cup

		Date	Opponent	Score		Att																	
R1	Aug	12	HARTLEPOOL	0-2		2800	1	2	3	4	5	6	7	8	9	10	11	12					

		P	W	D	L	F	A	W	D	L	F	A	Pts
1	Chesterfield	46	19	1	3	55	12	8	9	6	22	20	64
2	Wrexham	46	17	6	0	56	16	9	3	11	28	33	61
3	Swansea Town	46	14	8	1	43	14	7	10	6	23	31	60
4	Port Vale	46	13	9	1	39	10	7	10	6	22	23	59
5	Brentford	46	14	8	1	36	11	6	8	9	22	28	56
6	Aldershot	46	16	5	2	52	22	4	8	11	26	43	53
7	Notts County	46	14	5	4	44	21	8	4	11	29	41	52
8	Lincoln City	46	11	8	4	38	20	6	8	9	28	32	50
9	Peterborough Utd.	46	13	8	2	51	21	4	6	13	26	48	48
10	Colchester United	46	14	5	4	38	22	3	9	11	26	41	48
11	Chester	46	14	3	6	39	23	7	3	13	19	43	48
12	SCUNTHORPE UNITED	46	11	8	4	34	23	7	4	12	33	42	46
13	York City	46	14	7	2	38	16	2	7	14	17	46	46
14	Northampton Town	46	11	7	5	41	19	5	5	13	23	36	44
15	Crewe Alexandra	46	12	6	5	37	18	4	6	13	14	33	44
16	Grimsby Town	46	9	9	5	33	24	5	6	12	21	34	43
17	Southend United	46	12	8	3	40	28	3	2	18	19	57	40
18	Exeter City	46	13	5	5	48	20	1	6	16	9	39	39
19	Oldham Athletic	46	11	4	8	45	28	2	9	12	15	37	39
20	Workington	46	9	9	5	31	21	3	5	15	15	43	38
21	Newport County	46	12	3	8	39	24	1	8	14	14	50	37
22	Darlington	46	8	7	8	31	27	5	3	15	22	46	36
23	Hartlepool	46	7	7	9	31	30	3	3	17	11	52	30
24	Bradford Park Ave.	46	6	5	12	23	32	0	6	17	18	64	23

1970/71   17th in Division 4

#	Month	Date	Opponent	Score	Scorers	Att	Barnard G	Foxton DG	Jackson NA	Barker J	Deere SH	Welbourne D	Keegan JK	Cassidy N	Kerr GAM	Heath RT	Davidson AG	Lindsey B	McDonald CB	Atkin JM	Rusling G	Muldoon T	Kisby CN	Woolmer AJ	Kirk HJ	O'Riley P	Williams MJ
1	Aug	15	Exeter City	1-1	Keegan	5456	1	2	3	4	5	6	7	8	9	10	11	12									
2		22	SOUTHEND UNITED	3-0	Kerr, Foxton, Heath	3930	1	2	3	4	5	6	7	8	9	10	12		11								
3		28	Stockport County	0-2		4164	1	2	3	4	5	6	7	8	9	10	11	12									
4	Sep	1	OLDHAM ATHLETIC	2-3	Lindsey, Heath	4217	1	2		3		6	7	8	9	10		4	11	5							
5		5	CAMBRIDGE UNITED	0-0		3995	1	2		3	6		7	8	9	10	12	4	11	5							
6		11	Aldershot	1-0	Rusling	5959	1	2		3	5		7		9	10	11	4			6	8					
7		19	YORK CITY	0-1		3723	1	2		3	6		7	8	9	10	11	4			5	12					
8		22	BARROW	1-1	Keegan (p)	3030	1	2		3	6	12	10	8	9		11	4	7	5							
9		26	Workington	0-0		2242	1	2		3	5	6	10	8	9		11	4			12		7				
10		30	Bournemouth	2-0	Deere, Davidson	8219	1	2		3	5	6	10	8	9	11	7	4						12			
11	Oct	3	GRIMSBY TOWN	1-2	Keegan (p)	6945	1	2		3	5	6	10	8	9	11	7							4			
12		6	Oldham Athletic	1-1	Davidson	8341	1	2		3	5	6	10	8	9	11	7							4			
13		10	Newport County	3-2	Cassidy 2, Davidson	3539	1	2		3	5	6	10	8	9	11	7							4			
14		17	EXETER CITY	3-0	Keegan, Cassidy 2	3684	1	2		3	5	6	10	8	9	11	7							4			
15		20	PETERBOROUGH UTD.	5-2	Keegan, Heath 2, Cassidy, Barker	3801	1	2	12	3	5	6	10	8	9	11	7							4			
16		24	Crewe Alexandra	1-3	Davidson	2385	1	2		3	5	6	10	8	9	11	7							4			
17		31	NOTTS COUNTY	0-1		5559	1	2	3		5	6	10	8		11	7			4	9						
18	Nov	7	Lincoln City	1-4	Cassidy	7469	1	2	3	12	5	6	10	8		11	7			4				9			
19		9	Darlington	0-3		3651	1	2	12	3	5	6	10	8		11	7			4				9			
20		14	CHESTER	0-2		3099	1	2		3	5	6	10	8		11	7			4				9			
21		28	NORTHAMPTON T	2-2	Barker, Woolmer	3265	1	2		3	5	6	10			7				4	9			8	11		
22	Dec	4	Southport	1-5	Keegan	2444	1	2	12	3	5	6	10			7				4	9			8	11		
23		18	Southend United	2-2	Davidson, Kirk	4606	1	2		3	5	6				4	7		10		9			8	11		
24		26	BRENTFORD	1-1	Heath	4736	1	2		3	5		10			4	7				6	9		8	11		
25	Jan	9	BOURNEMOUTH	1-1	Heath	4140	1	2		3	5	6	10			4	7			8	9				11		
26		16	Peterborough United	2-1	Davidson, Kirk	4500	1	2		3	5	6	10			4	7			8	9				11		
27		23	HARTLEPOOL	2-1	McDonald, Kirk	3657	1		3		5	6	10			4	2		8	12	9			7	11		
28		30	Northampton Town	0-1		4607	1		3		5	6	10			4	2		8		9			7	11		
29	Feb	6	SOUTHPORT	2-0	Deere, Keegan	3228	1		3		5	6	10			4	2		8		9			7	11		
30		13	Hartlepool	1-1	Rusling	1261	1		3		5	6	10			4	2		8		9			7	11		
31		20	DARLINGTON	0-0		3505	1		3		5	6	10			4	2		8		9			7	11		
32		27	Notts County	0-3		10750	1		3		5	6	10			4	2		8	12	9			7	11		
33	Mar	6	CREWE ALEXANDRA	1-1	Woolmer	2633	1		3		5	6	10			4	2		8	11	9			7			
34		8	Barrow	2-1	Davidson, Heath	1604	1		3		5	6	10			4	2		8	11	9			7			
35		13	Chester	0-2		3738	1		3		5	6	10			4	2		8	11	12			7		9	
36		16	COLCHESTER UNITED	2-0	Woolmer, O'Riley	3715	1		3		5	6	10			4	2		8					7	11	9	
37		20	LINCOLN CITY	3-1	O'Riley 2, McDonald	5607	1		3		5	6	10			4	2		8					7	11	9	
38		22	Colchester United	0-2		5592			3		5	6	10			4	2		8					7	11	9	1
39		27	Cambridge United	1-1	Keegan	3627	1		3		5	6	10			4	2		8		12			7	11	9	
40	Apr	3	STOCKPORT COUNTY	1-2	Keegan	2666	1	2	3				10			4	7			5			6	8	11	9	
41		9	Grimsby Town	0-1		7639	1	2	3	6			10			4	8			5				7	11	9	
42		10	Brentford	1-0	Heath	7560	1	2	6	3			10			4	7			5	12			8	11	9	
43		13	ALDERSHOT	2-1	O'Riley, Heath	3031	1	2	6	3			10			4	8			5	11			7		9	
44		17	NEWPORT COUNTY	0-1		2880	1	2	3				10			4	8		12	5	11		6	7		9	
45		24	York City	0-2		4823	1	2	6	3			10			4	7		8	5				9	11		
46	May	1	WORKINGTON	4-0	Jackson, Heath 2, Kirk	2568	1	2	4	3			6			8	7			5					11	9	
					Apps		45	33	28	30	38	36	45	19	16	43	44	9	22	25	22	1	9	26	21	11	1
					Goals			1	1	2	2		9	6	2	10	7	1	2		2			3	4	4	

F.A. Cup

#	Month	Date	Opponent	Score	Scorers	Att																					
R1	Nov	21	Tranmere Rovers	1-1	Woolmer	3757	1	2		3	5	6	10			11	7			4	9			8			
rep		24	TRANMERE ROVERS	0-0		5431	1	2	12	3	5	6	10			11	7			4	9			8			
rep2		30	Tranmere Rovers	1-0	Rusling	7235	1	2	12	3	5	6	10			11	7			4	9			8			
R2	Dec	12	MANSFIELD TOWN	3-0	Rusling 2, Kirk	7656	1	2		3	5	6	10			4	7				9			8	11		
R3	Jan	2	West Bromwich Alb.	0-0		21960	1	2		3	5	6	10			4	7				9			8	11		
rep		11	WEST BROM ALB.	1-3	Deere	15926	1	2		3	5	6	10			4	7		8		9				12	11	

R1 replay and replay 2 a.e.t. Replay 2 at Goodison Park. R3 replay a.e.t.

F.L. Cup

#	Month	Date	Opponent	Score	Scorers	Att																					
R1	Aug	18	NORTHAMPTON TOWN	2-3	Keegan (p), Jackson	4470	1	2	3	4	5	6	7	8	9	10	11	12									

		P	W	D	L	F	A	W	D	L	F	A	Pts
1	Notts County	46	19	4	0	59	12	11	5	7	30	24	69
2	Bournemouth	46	16	5	2	51	15	8	7	8	30	31	60
3	Oldham Athletic	46	14	6	3	57	29	10	5	8	31	34	59
4	York City	46	16	6	1	45	14	7	4	12	33	40	56
5	Chester	46	17	2	4	42	18	7	5	11	27	37	55
6	Colchester United	46	14	6	3	44	19	7	6	10	26	35	54
7	Northampton Town	46	15	4	4	39	24	4	9	10	24	35	51
8	Southport	46	15	2	6	42	24	6	4	13	21	33	48
9	Exeter City	46	12	7	4	40	23	5	7	11	27	45	48
10	Workington	46	13	7	3	28	13	5	5	13	20	36	48
11	Stockport County	46	12	8	3	28	17	4	6	13	21	48	46
12	Darlington	46	15	3	5	42	22	2	8	13	16	35	45
13	Aldershot	46	8	10	5	32	23	6	7	10	34	48	45
14	Brentford	46	13	3	7	45	27	5	5	13	21	35	44
15	Crewe Alexandra	46	13	1	9	49	35	5	7	11	26	41	44
16	Peterborough Utd.	46	14	3	6	46	23	4	4	15	24	48	43
17	SCUNTHORPE UNITED	46	9	7	7	36	23	6	6	11	20	38	43
18	Southend United	46	8	11	4	32	24	6	4	13	21	42	43
19	Grimsby Town	46	13	4	6	37	26	5	3	15	20	45	43
20	Cambridge United	46	9	9	5	31	27	6	4	13	20	39	43
21	Lincoln City	46	11	4	8	45	33	2	9	12	25	38	39
22	Newport County	46	8	3	12	32	36	2	5	16	23	49	28
23	Hartlepool	46	6	10	7	28	27	2	2	19	6	47	28
24	Barrow	46	5	5	13	25	38	2	3	18	26	52	22

~ 241 ~

1971/72 4th in Division 4: Promoted

#	Date		Opponent	Score	Scorers	Att	Barnard G	Foxton DG	Barker J	Jackson NA	Deere SH	Welbourne D	McDonald CB	Fletcher JR	Woolmer AJ	Heath RT	Kirk HJ	Davidson AG	Kisby CN	Hutchinson DN	Kerr GAM	Atkin JM	Markham P
1	Aug	14	Grimsby Town	1-4	Fletcher	7497	1	2	3	4	5	6	7	8	9	10	11	12					
2		21	LINCOLN CITY	2-1	Heath, Jackson	4868	1	2	3	4	5	6		7		8	11	9	10				
3		28	Crewe Alexandra	2-0	Jackson (p), Davidson	2800	1	2	3	6	4	5		9		8	11	10	7				
4		30	Southend United	3-2	Davidson 2, Fletcher	6704	1	2	3	4	5	6	7	9		10	11	8					
5	Sep	4	DONCASTER ROVERS	0-0		5047	1	2	3	8	4	5	6	9		7	11	10					
6		11	Peterborough United	1-0	Heath	6387	1	2	3	6	4	5		9		8	11	10	7				
7		17	NORTHAMPTON T	0-0		5253	1	2	3	4	5	6	12	8		10	11	9	7				
8		25	Aldershot	1-1	Heath	4675	1	2	3	4	5	6		9		8	11	10	7	12			
9		28	COLCHESTER UNITED	2-0	Fletcher, Davidson	5111	1	2		3	5	6	4	8		10	11	9	7				
10	Oct	2	DARLINGTON	3-1	Kisby, Davidson, Heath	5321	1	2	3	6	4	5		9		7	11	10	8				
11		9	Bury	1-3	Davidson	2733	1	2	3	6	5	4		9		8	11	10	7	12			
12		16	GRIMSBY TOWN	1-2	Deere	11510	1	2	3	6	4	5	12	9		7	11	10	8				
13		23	Barrow	1-0	3556	2190	1	2	3	8	5	6		9		7	11	4		10			
14		30	BRENTFORD	0-0		5859	1	2	3	8	5	6		9			11	4		10	7		
15	Nov	6	Exeter City	0-1		3556	1	2	3		5	6					11	7	4	9	10	12	
16		13	WORKINGTON	2-0	Kisby, McDonald	4535	1	2	3		5		7	9			11	10	4		8	6	
17		27	READING	1-1	Fletcher	4321	1	2	3		5	6		9		7	11	10	4		8		
18	Dec	4	Gillingham	1-0	Fletcher	6988	1		3	2	5	6	12	9		7	11	8			10	4	
19		11	CHESTER	2-0	McDonald, Fletcher	3776	1		3	2	5	6	6	9			11	7		12	10	4	
20		18	Doncaster Rovers	2-0	Fletcher, Kerr	5534	1		3	2	5		4	9		8	11	7			10	6	
21		27	HARTLEPOOL	2-2	McDonald, Kerr	6940	1	12	3	2	5		7	8		10	11	4			9	6	
22	Jan	1	Northampton Town	2-0	Jackson, Kerr	3929	1	2	3	8	4		7	9			11	6			10	5	
23		8	CREWE ALEXANDRA	2-0	Kerr 2	4323	1	2	3	4	5		7	9			11	8			10	6	
24		15	Southport	1-1	McDonald	3602	1	2	3	4	5		7	9			11	8			10	6	
25		21	Colchester United	1-1	Fletcher	4867	1	2	3	10	5		7	8			11	4			9	6	
26		29	NEWPORT COUNTY	1-0	Davidson	4580	1	2	3	6	5		8	9			11	7			10	4	
27	Feb	5	Stockport County	0-0		2452	1	2	3	8	5		7	9			11	4			10	6	
28		12	BARROW	2-1	Fletcher 2	5127	1	2	3	8	5		7	9	12		11	4			10	6	
29		19	Brentford	3-0	McDonald, Fletcher 2	11910	1	2	3	8	5		7	10			11	4			9	6	
30		26	EXETER CITY	3-0	Giles(og), Jackson, Fletcher	6250	1	2	3	7	5		6	10	9		11	8				4	
31	Mar	4	Workington	1-2	Fletcher	1977	1	2	3	10	5		4	9			11	7			8	6	
32		11	BURY	3-0	Saile(og), Fletcher 2	5082	1	2	3	8	5		4	9			11	7	12		10	6	
33		14	SOUTHPORT	1-0	Dunleavy (og)	6800	1	2	3	10	5		7	8			11	4			9	6	
34		18	Lincoln City	0-1		16498	1	2	3	10	6		7	8	12		11	4			9	5	
35		25	PETERBOROUGH UTD.	0-0		5555	1	2	3	10	4		6	7	8		11				9	5	
36		31	Darlington	1-0	Fletcher	2960	1	2	3	10	5		7	8	12		11	4			9	6	
37	Apr	1	Hartlepool	0-1		6192	1	2		3	10	5		7	8	9		11	4	12			
38		4	ALDERSHOT	1-0	Kirk	6929	1		3	10	5		7	8			11	4			9	6	2
39		8	STOCKPORT COUNTY	0-2		7183	1		3		5		10	8	12		11	7	4		9	6	2
40		11	CAMBRIDGE UNITED	2-1	Fletcher 2	5916	1			3	5		7	8	10		11	4			9	6	2
41		15	Reading	0-2		4163	1		3	2	5		7	8	10		11	4		12	9	6	
42		19	Chester	0-0		2347	1		3	10	5			8	7		11	4			9	6	2
43		22	GILLINGHAM	3-3	Kirk, Kerr, McDonald	5504	1	2	3	10	5		4	8	12		11	7			9	6	
44		25	SOUTHEND UNITED	1-1	Kirk	8540	1		3	10	5		7	8			11	4			9	6	2
45		29	Cambridge United	0-2		3927	1		3	10	5	12		8	9		11	4		7		6	2
46	May	1	Newport County	0-1		3686	1		3	10	5			8	7		11	4	12	9		6	2
					Apps		46	35	44	42	46	19	33	46	14	17	46	45	16	9	29	31	7
					Goals					4	1		6	19		4	4	7	2		6		

Player substituted in game 45 not known

3 own goals

F.A. Cup

	Date		Opponent	Score	Scorers	Att																	
R1	Nov	20	South Shields	3-3	Deere, Kerr 2	4000	1	2	3		5			9			7	11	8	4	10	6	
rep		29	SOUTH SHIELDS	2-3	Fletcher, Kirk	5272	1	2	3		5	6	12	8			7	11	9	4	10		

F.L. Cup

	Date		Opponent	Score		Att																	
R1	Aug	18	LINCOLN CITY	0-1		5864	1	2	3	4	5	6		8	9	10	11	7					

		P	W	D	L	F	A	W	D	L	F	A	Pts
1	Grimsby Town	46	18	3	2	61	26	10	4	9	27	30	63
2	Southend United	46	18	2	3	56	26	6	10	7	25	29	60
3	Brentford	46	16	2	5	52	21	8	9	6	24	23	59
4	SCUNTHORPE UNITED	46	13	8	2	34	15	9	5	9	22	22	57
5	Lincoln City	46	17	5	1	46	15	4	9	10	31	44	56
6	Workington	46	12	9	2	34	7	4	10	9	16	27	51
7	Southport	46	15	5	3	48	21	3	9	11	18	25	50
8	Peterborough Utd.	46	14	6	3	51	24	3	10	10	31	40	50
9	Bury	46	16	4	3	55	22	3	8	12	18	37	50
10	Cambridge United	46	11	8	4	38	22	6	6	11	24	38	48
11	Colchester United	46	13	6	4	38	23	6	4	13	32	46	48
12	Doncaster Rovers	46	11	8	4	35	24	5	6	12	21	39	46
13	Gillingham	46	11	5	7	33	24	5	8	10	28	43	45
14	Newport County	46	13	5	5	34	20	5	3	15	26	52	44
15	Exeter City	46	11	5	7	40	30	5	6	12	21	38	43
16	Reading	46	14	3	6	37	26	3	5	15	19	50	42
17	Aldershot	46	5	13	5	27	20	4	9	10	21	34	40
18	Hartlepool	46	14	2	7	39	25	3	4	16	19	44	40
19	Darlington	46	9	9	5	37	24	5	2	16	27	58	39
20	Chester	46	10	11	2	34	16	0	7	16	13	40	38
21	Northampton Town	46	8	9	6	43	27	4	4	15	23	52	37
22	Barrow	46	8	8	7	23	26	5	3	15	17	45	37
23	Stockport County	46	7	10	6	33	32	2	4	17	22	55	32
24	Crewe Alexandra	46	9	4	10	27	25	1	5	17	16	44	29

1972/73 24th in Division 3: Relegated

						Barnard G	Foxton DG	Barker J	Davidson AG	Deere SH	Welbourne D	Kerr GAM	Fletcher JR	Collier GR	Heath RT	Kirk HJ	Jackson NA	McDonald CB	Sargent GS	Atkin JM	Sowden M	Kisby CN	Williams MJ	Markham P	Warnock N	Charnley DL	Krzywicki RL	Keeley NB
1	Aug	12	SWANSEA CITY	1-0	Davidson	5655	1	2	3	4	5	6	7	8	9	10	11											
2		18	Tranmere Rovers	1-2	Kirk (p)	3537	1	2	3		5	6	7	8	9	10	11	4	12										
3		26	WREXHAM	1-1	Deere	4135	1	2	3	7	5	6	12	8	9	10	11	4											
4		29	WALSALL	2-1	Fletcher, Kirk	4159	1	2	3	7	5	6	9	8		10	11	4											
5	Sep	2	Bournemouth	1-1	Fletcher	10034	1	2	3	4	5	6	10	9		7	11	8											
6		8	HALIFAX TOWN	0-3		4848	1	2	3	7	5	6	9	8		10	11	4												
7		16	Charlton Athletic	0-2		4970	1	2	3	7	5	6	9	8		10	11	4		12										
8		19	ROCHDALE	1-2	McDonald	3530	1	2	3	8	5	6	12	9		10	11	4	7											
9		23	GRIMSBY TOWN	1-2	Deere	10540	1		3		5	6	10	9	8	7	11	2	4											
10		25	Southend United	0-1		6411	1	2	3		5	6		8		10	11	4	7	9										
11		30	Blackburn Rovers	0-3		5764	1	2	3		5	6	9			7	11	4	8	10										
12	Oct	7	BRENTFORD	1-0	Welbourne	3143	1	2			5	6		8			11	3	7	9	4	10								
13		10	PLYMOUTH ARGYLE	1-1	Kirk	3650	1	2			5	6		8	12		11	3	7	9	4	10								
14		14	Bolton Wanderers	0-0		7175	1	2		8	5	6	9				11	3	7	10	4									
15		21	YORK CITY	1-0	Sargent	3538	1	2		7	5	6		8		12	11	3	10	9	4									
16		24	Oldham Athletic	0-3		5269	1		3	10	5	6		8			11	2	7	9	4		12							
17		28	Rotherham United	1-2	McDonald	4317			3	10	5	6		8		9	11		7		4		12	1	2					
18	Nov	4	SOUTHEND UNITED	0-0		3157			3	7	5	6		8		9	11		10		4			1	2					
19		11	Rochdale	2-0	Heath, Kirk	2551			3		5	6		8		9	11		10		4			1	2	7				
20		25	SHREWSBURY TOWN	1-0	Fletcher	2596		2	3		5		8	9			11		6		4			1		7				
21	Dec	2	Bristol Rovers	1-5	Fletcher	5715		2			5		7	9	12	8	10		6		4			3	1		11			
22		16	Port Vale	0-2		3833	1	2	3		5	6		8		9	11		10		4					7				
23		23	NOTTS COUNTY	1-0	Davidson	3820	1	2	3	10	5	6		8		9	11				4					7				
24		26	Grimsby Town	0-1		16580	1	2	3	10	5	6		8		9	11				4		12			7				
25		30	TRANMERE ROVERS	1-5	Fletcher	3374	1	2	3	10	5	4		8	12	9			11				6			7				
26	Jan	6	Wrexham	2-1	Heath, Fletcher	2595	1		3		5	4	10	8		9	11				6				2	7				
27		20	BOURNEMOUTH	1-1	Kirk (p)	3458	1			7	5	4	10	8		9	11				6		3		2					
28		27	Halifax Town	0-1		1769	1		3	7	5	4	10	8		9	11				6				2					
29	Feb	3	Swansea City	1-2	McDonald	1607	1		3	7	5	6	10	8		9	11		12			4			2					
30		6	Plymouth Argyle	0-3		10008			3	4	5	6	10	8		9	11		7					2	1		12			
31		10	CHARLTON ATHLETIC	0-2		2818			3	7	5	4	10	8			11		12		6		2	1			9			
32		24	PORT VALE	0-1		2580			3	2	5	4		9		8	11				6		12	1		7		10		
33	Mar	3	Brentford	0-1		7760			3	2	5			9	4		11				6		8	1		7		10		
34		6	Watford	1-5	Fletcher	4578			3	2	5	6		8	10		11			9	12			1		7	4			
35		10	BOLTON WANDERERS	1-1	Fletcher	4424			3	2	2	6		8	9		11		12	10	4			1		7				
36		13	OLDHAM ATHLETIC	0-0		2779			3		5	6		8	10		11		4	9	2			1		7				
37		17	York City	1-3	Kirk	2848			3		5	6	12	8	10		11		4	9	2			1		7				
38		20	CHESTERFIELD	0-1		2048			3		5	6	12	8	10		11		4	9	2			1		7				
39		24	ROTHERHAM UNITED	2-1	Kirk (p), Fletcher	2199		12	3		5	4		8	10		11		6	9	2			1		7				
40		30	Shrewsbury Town	2-4	Kirk (p), Collier	2277		2	3		5	6		8	10		11		4	9	12			1		7				
41	Apr	7	BRISTOL ROVERS	0-2		1784		2	3	10	5	4		8	9		11		6		12			1		7				
42		14	Chesterfield	1-2	Warnock	3678			3	4	5	6	9		10		11		8					1		2	7			
43		21	WATFORD	1-0	Fletcher	1544			3	4	5	6	12	9	10		11		8					1		2	7			
44		23	Notts County	0-2		15697		12	3	2	5	6	4	9	10		11		8					1			7			
45		24	BLACKBURN ROVERS	1-1	Garbett (og)	2546		12	3	2	5		4	9	10		11		8							6	1	7		
46		28	Walsall	1-1	Collier	3402			3	2	4		6	10	8		11		7							5	1			9
					Apps	24	25	40	30	46	41	24	45	21	27	45	15	31	15	27	3	14	22	9	23	1	2	1				
					Goals				2	2	1		10	2	2	8		3	1						1						

One own goal

F.A. Cup

R1	Nov	18	Hartlepool United	0-0		4568			3	7	5	6		9		10	11		8		4			1	2					
rep		21	HARTLEPOOL UNITED	0-0		4478			3		5	6		8	12	9	11		10		4	7		1	2					
rep2		27	Hartlepool United	2-1	Dawes (og), Deere	7917		2			5		7	8		9	11		10		4		6	1	3					
R2	Dec	9	HALIFAX TOWN	3-2	Heath, Fletcher, Barker	4037	1	2	3		5	6		9		10	11		8		4					7				
R3	Jan	13	CARDIFF CITY	2-3	Welbourne, Kirk	6379	1		3	12	5	6	10	8		9	11				4				2	7				

R1 replay 2 at Roker Park. R1 replay and replay 2 a.e.t.

F.L. Cup

R1	Aug	15	CHESTERFIELD	0-0		5619	1	2	3		5	6	7	8	9	10	11	4	
rep		23	Chesterfield	0-5		8288	1	2	3		5	6	7	8	9	10	11	4	

		P	W	D	L	F	A	W	D	L	F	A	Pts
1	Bolton Wanderers	46	18	4	1	44	9	7	7	9	29	30	61
2	Notts County	46	17	4	2	40	12	6	7	10	27	35	57
3	Blackburn Rovers	46	12	8	3	34	16	8	7	8	23	31	55
4	Oldham Athletic	46	12	7	4	40	18	7	9	7	32	36	54
5	Bristol Rovers	46	17	4	2	55	20	3	9	11	22	36	53
6	Port Vale	46	15	6	2	41	21	6	5	12	15	48	53
7	Bournemouth	46	14	6	3	44	16	3	10	10	22	28	50
8	Plymouth Argyle	46	14	3	6	43	26	6	7	10	31	40	50
9	Grimsby Town	46	16	2	5	45	18	4	6	13	22	43	48
10	Tranmere Rovers	46	12	8	3	38	17	3	8	12	18	35	46
11	Charlton Athletic	46	12	7	4	46	24	5	4	14	23	43	45
12	Wrexham	46	11	9	3	39	23	3	8	12	16	31	45
13	Rochdale	46	8	8	7	22	26	6	9	8	26	28	45
14	Southend United	46	13	6	4	40	14	4	4	15	21	40	44
15	Shrewsbury Town	46	10	10	3	31	21	5	4	14	15	33	44
16	Chesterfield	46	13	4	6	37	22	4	5	14	20	39	43
17	Walsall	46	14	3	6	37	26	4	4	15	19	40	43
18	York City	46	8	10	5	24	14	5	5	13	18	32	41
19	Watford	46	11	8	4	32	23	1	9	13	11	25	41
20	Halifax Town	46	9	8	6	29	23	4	7	12	14	30	41
21	Rotherham United	46	12	4	7	34	27	5	3	15	17	38	41
22	Brentford	46	12	5	6	33	18	3	2	18	18	51	37
23	Swansea City	46	11	5	7	37	29	3	4	16	14	44	37
24	SCUNTHORPE UNITED	46	8	7	8	18	25	2	3	18	15	47	30

~ 243 ~

1973/74 18th in Division 4

#	Date		Opponent	Score	Scorers	Att
1	Aug	25	Lincoln City	0-1		6327
2	Sep	1	BARNSLEY	3-0	Houghton, Barker, Keeley	3441
3		8	Peterborough United	0-1		6399
4		12	Gillingham	2-7	Houghton, Welbourne	4610
5		14	CREWE ALEXANDRA	0-0		3476
6		18	BRADFORD CITY	2-1	Pilling, Fletcher	3155
7		21	Northampton Town	0-2		5049
8		29	HARTLEPOOL	1-1	Houghton	2466
9	Oct	3	Bradford City	1-2	Podd(og)	2445
10		6	Swansea City	2-1	Collier, Money	1743
11		13	NEWPORT COUNTY	0-0		2607
12		19	Colchester United	0-2		4862
13		23	GILLINGHAM	1-1	Simpkin	2402
14		27	BRENTFORD	4-1	Woods 2, Simpkin, Keeley	2376
15	Nov	2	Stockport County	1-3	Welbourne	2419
16		10	CHESTER	2-1	Keeley, Collier	2164
17		13	READING	1-0	Davidson	2526
18		17	Torquay United	1-1	Davidson	3064
19	Dec	8	MANSFIELD TOWN	5-3	Houghton 2(1 p), Horsfall 2, Davidson	2420
20		22	Hartlepool	0-3		832
21		26	DONCASTER ROVERS	2-1	Pilling, Barker	5582
22		29	PETERBOROUGH UTD.	2-1	Collier, Keeley	5004
23	Jan	1	Barnsley	0-5		5940
24		12	Crewe Alexandra	0-1		1591
25		19	LINCOLN CITY	1-1	Keeley	5379
26	Feb	3	Darlington	0-3		3006
27		10	NORTHAMPTON T	1-2	Collier	3421
28		17	Newport County	1-2	Warnock	3051
29		23	SWANSEA CITY	0-0		2238
30	Mar	2	Doncaster Rovers	0-1		1587
31		9	Brentford	1-2	Roberts	4050
32		16	COLCHESTER UNITED	1-0	Keeley	2134
33		19	DARLINGTON	1-0	Roberts	1715
34		23	Chester	0-2		2038
35		26	Bury	0-0		5190
36		30	STOCKPORT COUNTY	2-1	Davidson, Collier	1739
37	Apr	6	Reading	0-0		3562
38		10	Workington	2-1	Davidson, Keeley	1326
39		13	TORQUAY UNITED	0-0		2370
40		15	Rotherham United	1-1	Keeley	2341
41		16	ROTHERHAM UNITED	3-0	Warnock 2, Roberts	2610
42		20	Mansfield Town	2-2	Roberts, Andrews	2342
43		22	Exeter City	0-4		2226
44		27	WORKINGTON	0-1		1890
45		30	BURY	1-2	Keeley	2014

Home game with Exeter City not played.
Scunthorpe awarded two points.

F.A. Cup

	Date		Opponent	Score	Scorers	Att
R1	Nov	24	DARLINGTON	1-0	Houghton	3191
R2	Dec	15	Mansfield Town	1-1	Houghton	4511
rep		18	MANSFIELD TOWN	1-0	Warnock	2679
R3	Jan	5	MILLWALL	1-1	Collier	7275
rep		8	MILLWALL	1-0	Pilling	4789
R4		26	Newcastle United	1-1	Keeley	37870
rep		30	NEWCASTLE UNITED	0-3		19028

F.L. Cup

	Date		Opponent	Score	Scorers	Att
R1	Aug	29	Peterborough United	2-2	Pilling, Keeley	6339
rep	Sep	4	PETERBOROUGH UNITED	2-1	Keeley 2	4472
R2	Oct	9	BRISTOL CITY	0-0		4418
rep		16	Bristol City	1-2	Welbourne	7837

Division 4 Final Table

		P	W	D	L	F	A	W	D	L	F	A	Pts
1	Peterborough Utd.	46	19	4	0	49	10	8	7	8	26	28	65
2	Gillingham	46	16	5	2	51	16	9	7	7	39	33	62
3	Colchester United	46	16	5	2	46	14	8	7	8	27	22	60
4	Bury	46	18	3	2	51	14	6	8	9	30	35	59
5	Northampton Town	46	14	7	2	39	14	6	6	11	24	34	53
6	Reading	46	11	9	3	37	13	5	10	8	21	24	51
7	Chester	46	13	6	4	31	19	4	9	10	23	36	49
8	Bradford City	46	14	7	2	45	20	3	7	13	13	32	48
9	Newport County	46	13	6	4	39	23	3	8	12	17	42	45
10	Exeter City	45	12	5	6	37	20	6	3	13	21	35	44
11	Hartlepool	46	11	4	8	29	16	5	8	10	19	31	44
12	Lincoln City	46	10	8	5	40	30	6	4	13	23	37	44
13	Barnsley	46	15	5	3	42	16	2	5	16	16	48	44
14	Swansea City	46	11	6	6	28	15	5	13	17	31	43	
15	Rotherham United	46	10	9	4	33	22	5	4	14	23	36	43
16	Torquay United	46	11	7	5	37	23	2	10	11	15	34	43
17	Mansfield Town	46	13	8	2	47	24	0	9	14	15	45	43
18	SCUNTHORPE UNITED	45	12	7	3	37	17	2	5	16	14	47	42
19	Brentford	46	9	7	7	31	20	3	9	11	17	30	40
20	Darlington	46	9	8	6	29	24	4	5	14	11	38	39
21	Crewe Alexandra	46	11	5	7	28	30	3	5	15	15	41	38
22	Doncaster Rovers	46	10	7	6	32	22	2	4	17	15	58	35
23	Workington	46	10	8	5	33	26	1	5	17	10	48	35
24	Stockport County	46	4	12	7	22	25	3	8	12	22	44	34

1974/75 Bottom of Division 4

		Date	Opponent	Score	Scorers	Att	Barnard G	Markham P	Atkin JM	Simpkin CJ	Peacock JC	Keeley NB	Money R	Collier GR	Sproates A	Roberts DE	Davidson AG	Warnock N	Lavery J	Taylor EK	Welbourne D	Earl S	Barker J	Charnley DL	Anderson TK	Lynch BJ	Marshall B	Mountfotd RW	Pilling S	Oates RA	Norris M
1	Aug	17	Workington	1-1	Davidson	1656	1	2	3	4	5	6	7	8	9	10	11														
2		24	MANSFIELD TOWN	0-1		2794	1	2	3	4	5	6	7	8		10	11	9													
3		31	Bradford City	0-3		3255	1	2	3	4	5	6	7	8	9	10	11														
4	Sep	3	Barnsley	2-2	Collier, Roberts	5428		2	4	3	5	8	7	6		10	9		1	11											
5		7	READING	0-1		1693		2		5	3	9	4	7		10	6	8	1	11											
6		14	Darlington	1-3	Davidson	1863	1	2		3	5	11	7	8			9				10	4	6								
7		17	Doncaster Rovers	1-1	Roberts	3116		2		4	5	11	12	7		9	6		1	8	3	10									
8		21	HARTLEPOOL	1-1	Roberts	1663		2		5	12	11		7		9	6		1	8	4	10	3								
9		24	TORQUAY UNITED	0-2		1654		2	4				12	7		9	6		1	8	3	10	5	11							
10		28	Shrewsbury Town	0-5		3381		2	5		12		4	7		9	6		1	8		10	3		11						
11	Oct	1	BARNSLEY	1-0	Warnock	2157		2				11	4	7		10	6	9	1			3		5		8	12				
12		5	Chester	0-1		2857		2				11	4	7	10	9		12	1			6		5		3	8				
13		12	CAMBRIDGE UNITED	2-0	Warnock, Keeley	1774		2		5	3	11	6		12	9		7	1			4				10		8			
14		15	SOUTHPORT	3-3	Markham, Roberts, Keeley	1869		2		4	5	11	6			10		9	1			3				8		7	12		
15		19	Stockport County	2-3	Welbourne, Keeley	1500				10	5	11	4			9	7		1			3				6	2	8	12		
16		26	ROTHERHAM UNITED	0-3		2838	1			5	3		6	4		10	7	9								8	2		11	12	
17	Nov	2	CREWE ALEXANDRA	1-1	Roberts	1501	1	2				11	4			9		7			5		3		10					8	
18		9	Exeter City	0-0		3058	1	2		4		11	7			10	12	9				3		5		6				8	
19		16	ROCHDALE	2-2	Pilling 2	1621	1	2		6		11	7			10	12	9				3		5		4				8	
20		30	SWANSEA CITY	1-2	Roberts	1037	1	2	6	4			8	7	12	11		10				3		5						9	
21	Dec	7	Newport County	0-2		3139	1	2				11	4	6	7		10	9				3		5						8	
22		21	Brentford	0-2		4360	1	2				11	6	4	7		10	9				5		3						8	
23		26	DARLINGTON	1-1	Davidson (p), Collier	2122	1	2				10	4	7	6		11	9				5				3				8	
24		28	Lincoln City	0-1		7883	1	2				10	4	7	6	12	11	9				5				3				8	
25	Jan	4	DONCASTER ROVERS	0-0		2326	1	2				10	6	7	4	9	11					5				3				8	
26		11	NEWPORT COUNTY	4-1	Roberts 3, Collier	1529	1	2				12	6	7	4	10	11	9				5				3				8	
27		18	Swansea City	0-1		1428	1	2				9	4	7	6	10	11					5				3				8	
28	Feb	1	EXETER CITY	2-1	Collier, Roberts	1846	1	2					4	7	6	10	11	9				5				3				8	
29		8	Crewe Alexandra	1-1	Davidson	1986	1	2				12	4	7	6	10	11	9				5				3				8	
30		11	Northampton Town	0-3		3079	1	2					4	7	6	10	11	9				5				3				8	
31		15	NORTHAMPTON T	2-1	Roberts, Pilling	1833	1	2				9	6	7	4	10	11					5				3				8	
32		22	Rochdale	2-4	Collier, Roberts	1430	1	2				9	4	7	6	10						5			11	3				8	6
33	Mar	1	BRADFORD CITY	1-2	Charnley	1959	1	2				9	4	7	6	10						5			11	3				8	
34		8	Torquay United	1-1	Warnock	1822		2			6	9	4	7				11				5				3				8	10	1
35		15	SHREWSBURY TOWN	1-0	Davidson	1663		2			5	10	7	9			11					6				3				8	4	1
36		18	WORKINGTON	2-1	Davidson (p), Collier	1913		2			4	9	7	10		12	11					5				3				8	6	1
37		22	Reading	1-1	Davidson	4475		2			6	10	11	7			9					5				3				8	4	1
38		28	Hartlepool	0-1		2471		2			4	9	7	10		12	11					5				3				8	6	1
39	Apr	1	LINCOLN CITY	1-1	Davidson	5463		2			4	9		7	12	10	11					5	3							8	6	1
40		5	Rotherham United	2-3	Keeley, Roberts	6469		2			5	6	9		7	12	10	11					3							8	4	1
41		8	Southport	0-1		924		2			4			5	7	12	10	11					3		9					8	6	1
42		12	CHESTER	1-3	Earl	1877		12			5	3		6	7		9	10							11			2		8	4	1
43		15	BRENTFORD	1-2	Pilling	1439		2				3		4	7	6	10								9		11			8	5	1
44		19	Cambridge United	0-2		3278		2	5		3		6	7	4	11									9					8	10	1
45		21	Mansfield Town	0-7		11020					5	4	3	6	7		10								9		2			11	8	1
46		26	STOCKPORT COUNTY	0-0		1438	1			6	5	2		8	7	11	10								9					3	4	
			Apps				14	42	10	27	19	34	43	40	24	39	34	20	11	7	33	7	13	8	10	22	3	3	31	14	12
			Goals					1				4		5		13	8	3			1	1		1					4		

F.A. Cup

		Date	Opponent	Score	Scorers	Att																									
R1	Nov	23	ALTRINCHAM	1-1	Keeley	2627	1	2		4		11	7	6		10	9	12				3		5						8	
rep		25	Altrincham	1-3	Collier	3500	1	2				11	7	6		10	9	12				3		5						8	

F.L. Cup

		Date	Opponent	Score	Scorers	Att																									
R1	Aug	20	SHEFFIELD WEDNESDAY	1-0	Davidson (p)	5214	1	2	3	4	5	9	6	7	8	10	11	12													
R2	Sep	10	Manchester City	0-6		14790		2	4	3	5	10	7	8		11	6		1	9						12					

	P	W	D	L	F	A	W	D	L	F	A	Pts
1 Mansfield Town	46	17	6	0	55	15	11	6	6	35	25	68
2 Shrewsbury Town	46	16	3	4	46	18	10	7	6	34	25	62
3 Rotherham United	46	13	7	3	40	19	9	8	6	31	22	59
4 Chester	46	17	5	1	48	9	6	6	11	16	29	57
5 Lincoln City	46	14	8	1	47	14	7	7	9	32	34	57
6 Cambridge United	46	15	5	3	43	16	5	9	9	19	28	54
7 Reading	46	13	6	4	38	20	8	4	11	25	27	52
8 Brentford	46	15	6	2	38	14	3	7	13	15	31	49
9 Exeter City	46	14	3	6	33	24	5	8	10	27	39	49
10 Bradford City	46	10	5	8	32	21	7	8	8	24	30	47
11 Southport	46	13	7	3	36	19	2	10	11	20	37	47
12 Newport County	46	13	5	5	43	30	6	4	13	25	45	47
13 Hartlepool	46	13	6	4	40	24	3	5	15	12	38	43
14 Torquay United	46	10	7	6	30	25	4	7	12	16	36	42
15 Barnsley	46	10	7	6	34	24	5	4	14	28	41	41
16 Northampton Town	46	12	6	5	43	22	3	5	15	24	51	41
17 Doncaster Rovers	46	10	9	4	41	29	4	3	16	24	50	40
18 Crewe Alexandra	46	9	9	5	22	16	2	9	12	12	31	40
19 Rochdale	46	9	9	5	35	22	4	4	15	24	53	39
20 Stockport County	46	10	8	5	26	27	2	6	15	17	43	38
21 Darlington	46	11	4	8	38	27	2	6	15	16	40	36
22 Swansea City	46	9	4	10	25	31	6	2	15	21	42	36
23 Workington	46	7	5	11	23	29	3	6	14	13	37	31
24 SCUNTHORPE UNITED	46	7	8	8	27	29	0	7	16	14	49	29

1975/76 — 19th in Division 4

#	Date		Opponent	Score	Scorers	Att
1	Aug	16	Darlington	0-2		1920
2		23	EXETER CITY	0-1		1660
3		30	Newport County	0-0		2735
4	Sep	6	HUDDERSFIELD T	0-1		1992
5		13	Hartlepool	2-1	Hemmerman, Collier	1970
6		20	TORQUAY UNITED	3-1	Collier, Woodward 2	1989
7		22	Tranmere Rovers	1-2	Money	2308
8		27	Swansea City	0-2		3098
9	Oct	4	READING	2-1	Keeley, Collier	2177
10		11	ROCHDALE	1-3	Green	2508
11		18	Crewe Alexandra	0-1		1939
12		21	Watford	0-1		3581
13		25	NORTHAMPTON T	0-2		1965
14	Nov	1	Brentford	2-5	Charnley, Green	4220
15		4	CAMBRIDGE UNITED	0-1		1526
16		8	WORKINGTON	3-0	Keeley, Green 2	1503
17		15	Bournemouth	0-1		4333
18		28	Lincoln City	0-3		8494
19	Dec	6	SOUTHPORT	1-2	Collier	1817
20		13	Reading	0-1		5575
21		20	STOCKPORT COUNTY	0-0		1570
22		26	Bradford City	0-0		3465
23		27	DONCASTER ROVERS	2-1	Davidson, Woodward	5801
24	Jan	3	Barnsley	0-1		2823
25		10	NEWPORT COUNTY	1-2	Money	1739
26		17	Torquay United	0-1		2776
27	Feb	7	Cambridge United	2-2	Keeley, Davidson	1777
28		10	WATFORD	0-1		2200
29		14	Workington	3-2	Green 2, Davidson	1273
30		21	BOURNEMOUTH	2-0	Money, Charnley	2068
31		24	TRANMERE ROVERS	2-2	Wiggington (p), O'Connor	3049
32		27	Northampton Town	1-2	O'Connor	6804
33	Mar	2	HARTLEPOOL	5-1	Collier 2, Green 2, Oates	2966
34		6	BRENTFORD	2-1	Green, O'Connor	3225
35		12	Rochdale	1-1	Green	1430
36		16	CREWE ALEXANDRA	1-0	Green	3126
37		20	LINCOLN CITY	0-2		10329
38		26	Southport	1-1	Collier	1805
39		29	Stockport County	0-0		2078
40	Apr	3	DARLINGTON	2-1	Irvine, Davidson	2492
41		6	SWANSEA CITY	1-1	Green	3015
42		10	Huddersfield Town	1-1	Davidson	6502
43		17	BRADFORD CITY	2-0	Green, O'Connor	3254
44		19	Doncaster Rovers	1-0	Green	4097
45		20	BARNSLEY	1-0	O'Connor	4770
46		23	Exeter City	4-5	Green, Woodward 2, Wiggington	1863

F.A. Cup

R1	Nov	22	Preston North End	1-2	Green	8119

F.L. Cup

R1/1	Aug	20	Mansfield Town	0-4		4810
R1/2		26	MANSFIELD TOWN	0-2		1412

Division 4 Final Table

		P	W	D	L	F	A	W	D	L	F	A	Pts
1	Lincoln City	46	21	2	0	71	15	11	8	4	40	24	74
2	Northampton Town	46	18	5	0	62	20	11	5	7	25	20	68
3	Reading	46	19	3	1	42	9	5	9	9	28	42	60
4	Tranmere Rovers	46	18	3	2	61	16	6	7	10	28	39	58
5	Huddersfield Town	46	11	6	6	28	17	10	8	5	28	24	56
6	Bournemouth	46	15	5	3	39	16	5	7	11	18	32	52
7	Exeter City	46	13	7	3	37	17	5	7	11	19	30	50
8	Watford	46	16	4	3	38	18	6	2	15	24	44	50
9	Torquay United	46	12	6	5	31	24	6	8	9	24	39	50
10	Doncaster Rovers	46	10	6	7	42	31	9	5	9	33	38	49
11	Swansea City	46	14	8	1	51	21	2	7	14	15	36	47
12	Barnsley	46	12	8	3	34	16	2	8	13	18	32	44
13	Cambridge United	46	7	10	6	36	28	7	5	11	22	34	43
14	Hartlepool	46	10	6	7	37	29	6	4	13	25	49	42
15	Rochdale	46	7	11	5	27	23	5	7	11	13	31	42
16	Crewe Alexandra	46	10	7	6	36	21	3	8	12	22	36	41
17	Bradford City	46	9	7	7	35	26	3	10	10	28	39	41
18	Brentford	46	12	7	4	37	18	2	6	15	19	42	41
19	SCUNTHORPE UNITED	46	11	3	9	31	24	3	7	13	19	35	38
20	Darlington	46	11	7	5	30	14	3	3	17	18	43	38
21	Stockport County	46	8	7	8	23	23	5	5	13	20	53	38
22	Newport County	46	8	7	8	35	33	5	2	16	22	57	35
23	Southport	46	6	6	11	27	31	2	4	17	14	46	26
24	Workington	46	5	4	14	19	43	2	3	18	11	44	21

1976/77 20th in Division 4

#	Date		Opponent	Score	Scorers	Att	Letheran G	Czuczman M	Peacock JC	Oates RA	Wiggington CA	Money R	Wadsworth M	Collier GR	Keeley NB	Green R	Pilling S	Davidson AG	O'Connor D	Markham P	O'Meara AM	Bridges B	Dale AG	Lee R	Kilmore K	Lumby JA	Walton IJ	Barnard G
1	Aug	21	ROCHDALE	0-1		3391	1	2	3	4	5	6		7	8	9	10	11	12									
2		28	Watford	1-2	Wadsworth	5950	1	4	3	6	5		8	7	10	9		2	11									
3	Sep	3	CREWE ALEXANDRA	4-0	Wiggington 2(1p), Keeley, O'Connor	3286	1	6	3	4	5		7		9	10		8	11	2								
4		11	Bournemouth	2-2	Green 2	4297	1	2	3	4	5	6	7		8	10	9		12	11								
5		18	WORKINGTON	3-1	Wiggington (p), Keeley, Peacock	3466	1		3	4	5	6		7	8	10		9	11	2								
6		24	Southend United	1-1	Keeley	5288	1		3	6	4	5		7	8	10		9	11	2								
7		29	Exeter City	0-2		2934	1		3	4	5	6		8	9	10	12	7	11	2								
8	Oct	2	HARTLEPOOL	2-0	Keeley, Davidson	3287	1		3	4	5	6		7	10	11	8	9		2								
9		9	Halifax Town	1-0	Wiggington	1854	1		3	4	5	6	12	7	10	11	8	9		2								
10		15	Cambridge United	0-1		3412	1		3	4	5	6	12	8	9	10	11	7		2								
11		23	COLCHESTER UNITED	2-0	Keeley, Pilling	3157	1		3	4	5	6	12	7	11	10	8	9		2								
12		30	DARLINGTON	3-0	Davidson, Green, Wadsworth	3905	1		3	4	5	6	12	7	10	11		8	9	2								
13	Nov	2	SOUTHPORT	1-1	Davidson	4768	1		3	4	5	6	12	8	9	10	11	7		2								
14		6	Barnsley	1-5	Pilling	4440	1		3		5	6	7	4	10	11	8	9		2								
15		13	ALDERSHOT	1-3	Keeley	3586	1		3	4	5	6	7	8	10	11		9		2								
16		27	Torquay United	3-1	O'Connor 3	2098	1		3	4	5	6		7	10	9		8	11	2								
17	Dec	11	Swansea City	0-2		2392	1	12	3	4	5	6		7	10	9		8	11	2								
18		17	Stockport County	0-1		2827	1	7	3	4	5	6		8	9	10		12	11	2								
19		27	DONCASTER ROVERS	1-1	Green	7003	1	7	3	4	5	6	12	8	9	10			11	2								
20		28	Huddersfield Town	0-1		7028	1	7	3	4	5	6	11	8	9	10		12		2								
21	Jan	8	BRADFORD CITY	2-1	Wiggington, Keeley	4218	1	4	3	12	5	6	11	7	8	9		10		2								
22		22	Rochdale	0-5		1640	1	6	3	12	5	4	11	7	10	9		8		2								
23		25	BRENTFORD	2-1	Wadsworth, Keeley	2726			2	4	5		11	8	9	10	3	7			1	6	12					
24		28	Newport County	0-0		1601		6	2	4	5		11	8	9	10	3	7			1							
25	Feb	5	WATFORD	0-0		3201	1	6	2	4	5		11	7	10	9	3	8						12				
26		8	BARNSLEY	1-2	Pilling	4557	1	6	2	4	5		11	8	9	10	3	7			1			12				
27		12	Crewe Alexandra	1-2	Keeley	2189	1	6	2	4	5		11	12	9	10	3	7						8				
28		19	BOURNEMOUTH	0-0		2715	1	6	2	4	5		11	7	10		3	9						8	12			
29		26	Workington	0-1		1200	1	6	2	4	5	7	12		10		3	9						8	11			
30	Mar	5	SOUTHEND UNITED	1-0	Lumby	2752	1	7	2	4	5	6			11		3							8	9	10		
31		7	Darlington	2-5	Kilmore, Keeley	2134		6	2	4	5	7			9		3				1			12	11	8	10	
32		12	Hartlepool	0-3		1673		7	2	4	5	6		8	9		3		11		1				10			
33		15	EXETER CITY	4-1	Lumby 2, Czuczman, Hore(og)	2147		7	2	4	5	6			9		3				1				11	8	10	
34		19	HALIFAX TOWN	2-1	Lumby. Keeley	2902		7	2	4	5	6			9		3				1				11	8	10	
35		26	CAMBRIDGE UNITED	0-2		3611		7	2	4	5	6			9		3	12			1				11	8	10	
36	Apr	2	Colchester United	1-1	Lumby	3799		7	2	4	5	6			9		3	12			1				11	8	10	
37		9	HUDDERSFIELD T	0-4		4207		4	2		5	6	12		9		3	7			1				11	8	10	
38		11	Doncaster Rovers	0-3		4676			2	4	5	6			9		3	7			1				11	8	10	
39		12	Southport	1-2	Lumby	941		7	2	4	5	6			9		3	8			1				12	10		11
40		16	SWANSEA CITY	0-3		2079			2	4	5	6	8	7	9		3	11			1				12	10		
41		19	NEWPORT COUNTY	1-0	Keeley	1883		2		4	5	6	7		9		3	11							8	10		1
42		23	Aldershot	1-1	Kilmore	2392		2	12	4	5	6	9		8		3	7							11	10		1
43		30	TORQUAY UNITED	0-0		2105		2		4	5	6	9		11		3	7							8	10		1
44	May	4	Bradford City	0-4		5982		2		4	5	6			12		3	7							11	8	10	1
45		7	Brentford	2-4	Kilmore, Lumby	5300		2		4	5	6			12	9	3	7							11	8	10	1
46		14	STOCKPORT COUNTY	2-2	Lumby, Oates	2135		2		4	5	6			9		3	7							11	8	10	1
					Apps		27	31	41	44	46	38	28	31	46	27	33	41	10	19	13	1	2	16	19	16	1	6
					Goals			1	1	1	5		3		12	4	3	3	4						3	8		

One own goal

F.A. Cup

	Date		Opponent	Score	Scorers	Att			Peacock	Oates	Wiggington	Money		Wadsworth	Keeley	Green		Davidson	O'Connor	Markham								
R1	Nov	20	CHESTERFIELD	1-2	Keeley	5404			3	4	5	6		7	10	9		8	11	2	1							

F.L. Cup

	Date		Opponent	Score	Scorers	Att	Letheran	Czuczman	Peacock	Oates	Wiggington	Money	Wadsworth	Collier	Keeley	Green	Pilling	Davidson	O'Connor	Markham								
R1/1	Aug	14	Mansfield Town	0-2		5224	1	2	3	4	5	6		8	9	10	11	7										
R1/2		17	MANSFIELD TOWN	2-0	Keeley, Wiggington	3164	1	2	3	4	5	6	7	8	9	10	11											
rep		24	MANSFIELD TOWN	2-1	O'Connor, Wadsworth	4319	1	2	3	4	5	6	7	8	9	10		12	11									
R2		31	Notts County	0-2		6208	1	6	3	4	5		7	8	9	10		2	11									

		P	W	D	L	F	A	W	D	L	F	A	Pts
1	Cambridge United	46	16	5	2	57	18	10	8	5	30	22	65
2	Exeter City	46	17	5	1	40	13	8	7	8	30	33	62
3	Colchester United	46	19	2	2	51	14	6	7	10	26	29	59
4	Bradford City	46	16	7	0	51	18	7	6	10	27	33	59
5	Swansea City	46	18	3	2	60	30	7	5	11	32	38	58
6	Barnsley	46	16	5	2	45	18	7	4	12	17	21	55
7	Watford	46	15	7	1	46	13	8	12	21	37	51	
8	Doncaster Rovers	46	16	2	5	47	25	5	7	11	24	40	51
9	Huddersfield Town	46	15	5	3	36	15	4	7	12	24	34	50
10	Southend United	46	11	9	3	35	19	4	10	9	17	26	49
11	Darlington	46	13	5	5	37	25	5	8	10	22	39	49
12	Crewe Alexandra	46	16	6	1	36	15	3	5	15	11	45	49
13	Bournemouth	46	13	8	2	39	13	2	10	11	15	31	48
14	Stockport County	46	10	10	3	29	19	3	9	11	24	38	45
15	Brentford	46	14	3	6	48	27	4	4	15	29	49	43
16	Torquay United	46	12	5	6	33	22	5	4	14	26	45	43
17	Aldershot	46	10	8	5	29	19	6	3	14	20	40	43
18	Rochdale	46	8	7	8	32	25	5	5	13	18	34	38
19	Newport County	46	11	6	6	33	21	3	4	16	9	37	38
20	SCUNTHORPE UNITED	46	11	6	6	32	24	2	5	16	17	49	37
21	Halifax Town	46	11	6	6	36	18	0	8	15	11	40	36
22	Hartlepool	46	8	9	6	30	20	2	3	18	17	53	32
23	Southport	46	12	8	17	28	0	7	16	16	49	25	
24	Workington	46	3	7	13	23	42	1	4	18	18	60	19

1977/78 — 14th in Division 4

#	Date	Opponent	Score	Scorers	Att	Crawford PG	Czuczman M	Peacock JC	Pilling S	Money R	Bridges B	Oates RA	Kilmore K	Keeley NB	Lumby JA	Heron B	Kavanagh EA	Farrell KM	Wigg RG	Cooper T	Davy SJ	Lee R	O'Donnell JD	Grimes V	Holyoak P	Deere SH	Couch GR
1	Aug 20	Southport	1-1	Lumby (p)	2068	1	2	3	4	5	6	7	8	9	10	11											
2	23	CREWE ALEXANDRA	3-0	Keeley, Kilmore, Lumby	3283	1	2	3	4	5	6	7	8	9	10	11											
3	26	BOURNEMOUTH	0-0		4110	1	2	3	4	5	6	7	8	9	10	11											
4	Sep 3	Hartlepool United	0-1		1946	1	2	3	4	5	6	7	8	9	10	11	12										
5	10	SOUTHEND UNITED	1-2	Lumby	2768	1	2	3	4	5	6	7	8	9	10	11											
6	13	Barnsley	0-3		5725	1	2	3	4	5	6	7	8		10	11	12										
7	17	WIMBLEDON	3-0	Lumby, Oates 2	2618	1	2	3	12	5	6	7	10	9	8	11	4										
8	24	Brentford	0-2		6120	1	2	3	12	5	6	7	8	9	10	11	4										
9	27	SWANSEA CITY	1-0	Kilmore	2654	1	2	3		5	6	7	8	9	10	11	4										
10	Oct 1	NORTHAMPTON T	2-2	Heron, Lumby (p)	2580	1	2	3	12	5	6	7	8	9	10	11	4										
11	4	Newport County	1-3	Farrell	3191	1	2	3	8	5	6	7		9	10	11	4	12									
12	8	Grimsby Town	0-0		5249	1	2	3	8	5		6		9	10	11	4	7									
13	15	READING	0-1		2569	1	2	3	7	5		6	12	9	10	11	4	8									
14	22	Torquay United	2-4	Lumby (p), Green (og)	2529	1	2			3	5	6	7	8	9	10			11								
15	29	HALIFAX TOWN	2-0	Lumby (p), Keeley	2420	1	2	3		5	6	7	8	9	10		4		11								
16	Nov 5	HUDDERSFIELD T	1-1	Lumby	3068	1	2	3		5	6	7	8	9	10	11	4										
17	12	Watford	1-4	Lumby	10565	1	2	3	12	5		7	8	9	10		4		11	6							
18	19	ROCHDALE	1-0	Kilmore	2078	1	2	3	12	5		7	8	9			11	4	10	6							
19	Dec 3	Aldershot	0-4		3070	1	6	3	8			5		9	10	12			11	4	2	7					
20	10	DARLINGTON	3-0	Lumby, Keeley, Oates	1803	1	5	3				4	8	9	10	12			11	6	2	7					
21	26	Doncaster Rovers	1-1	Wigg	5097	1	5	3		12	6	8		9	10				11		2	7	4				
22	27	YORK CITY	2-1	Lumby 2	3242	1	5	3			6	4		9	10	7			11		2		8				
23	31	Huddersfield Town	1-4	Lumby (p)	4000	1	5	3			6	4	12	9	10	7			11		2		8				
24	Jan 2	STOCKPORT COUNTY	3-0	Oates, Lumby 2	3237	1	5	3			6	4		9	10				7	11	2		8				
25	7	Crewe Alexandra	1-1	Lumby	1926	1	5	3			6	4	12	9	10				7	11	2		8				
26	14	SOUTHPORT	0-2		2574	1	5	3	12		6	4		9	10				7	11	2		8				
27	21	Bournemouth	1-1	Keeley	2869	1	5	3			6	4	8	9	10	7			12	11	2						
28	Feb 3	Southend United	0-2		6879	1	5	3			6	4		9	10	7				11	12		2	8			
29	11	Wimbledon	0-0		1603	1	5		3			4		9	10		11		12		2		8	7	6		
30	25	Northampton Town	2-1	Lumby, Deere	2972	1	5		3			4		9	10				11		2		8	7		6	
31	Mar 3	GRIMSBY TOWN	2-1	Lumby 2 (1p)	7612	1	6	3				4		9	10				11		2		8	7		5	
32	7	BARNSLEY	1-0	Keeley	4828	1	6	3				4		9	10				11		2		8	7		5	
33	11	Reading	0-1		3410	1	6	3	12			4		9	10				11		2		8	7		5	
34	14	BRENTFORD	1-1	Wigg	2925	1	6	3				4	12	9	10				11		2		8	7		5	
35	18	TORQUAY UNITED	0-1		2169	1	6		3			4		9	10	12			11		2		8	7		5	
36	24	York City	2-0	Grimes, Kilmore	2408	1	6		3			4	8	9	10				11		2			7		5	
37	27	DONCASTER ROVERS	0-0		3592	1	6		3			4	8	9	10				11		2			7		5	
38	28	Halifax Town	2-2	Lumby (p), Grimes	2215	1	6		3			4	8	9	10				11				2	7		5	
39	31	Stockport County	1-1	Keeley	2774	1	5					4	8	9	10				11		2		3	7		6	
40	Apr 4	NEWPORT COUNTY	2-0	Kilmore 2	2457	1	6					4	8	9	10				11		2		3	7		5	
41	8	WATFORD	0-1		5202	1	6		3			4	8	9		12			11		2			7		5	10
42	15	Rochdale	1-1	Oates	1005	1	6		3			4		9		8			11	12	2			7		5	10
43	18	HARTLEPOOL UNITED	2-0	Kilmore 2	2181	1	6		3			4	8	9					11		2			7		5	10
44	22	ALDERSHOT	1-1	Oates	2555	1	6		3			4	8	9					11		2			7		5	10
45	25	Swansea City	1-3	Oates	13228	1	6		3			4	8	9					11	12	2			7		5	10
46	29	Darlington	1-1	Wigg	1302	1	6		3			4	8	9		12			11		2			7		5	10
			Apps			46	46	31	30	18	22	46	32	46	39	25	15	7	32	4	24	3	23	18	1	17	6
			Goals									7	8	6	20	1		1	3					2		1	

One own goal

F.A. Cup

	Date	Opponent	Score	Att																						
R1	Nov 26	Stockport County	0-3	4512	1	6	3			5	8	9	10		4	12	11		2	7							

F.L. Cup

	Date	Opponent	Score	Scorers	Att																						
R1/1	Aug 13	Darlington	0-0		2800	1	2	3		5	6	7	8	9	10	11			4								
R1/2	16	DARLINGTON	3-1	Lumby, Kilmore, Oates	2971	1	2	3	12	5	6	7	8	9	10	11			4								
R2	30	Peterborough United	1-1	Pilling	3697	1	2	3	4	5	6	7	8	9	10	11	12										
rep	Sep 6	PETERBOROUGH UTD.	0-1		4564	1	2	3	4		6	7	8	9	10	11	5										

		P	W	D	L	F	A	W	D	L	F	A	Pts
1	Watford	46	18	4	1	44	14	12	7	4	41	24	71
2	Southend United	46	15	5	3	46	18	10	5	8	20	21	60
3	Swansea City	46	16	5	2	54	17	7	5	11	33	30	56
4	Brentford	46	15	6	2	50	17	6	8	9	36	37	56
5	Aldershot	46	15	8	0	45	16	4	8	11	22	31	54
6	Grimsby Town	46	14	6	3	30	15	7	5	11	27	36	53
7	Barnsley	46	15	4	4	44	20	3	10	10	17	29	50
8	Reading	46	12	7	4	33	23	6	7	10	22	29	50
9	Torquay United	46	12	6	5	43	25	4	9	10	14	31	47
10	Northampton Town	46	9	8	6	32	30	8	5	10	31	38	47
11	Huddersfield Town	46	13	5	5	41	21	2	10	11	22	34	45
12	Doncaster Rovers	46	11	8	4	37	26	3	9	11	15	39	45
13	Wimbledon	46	8	11	4	39	26	6	5	12	27	41	44
14	SCUNTHORPE U	46	12	6	5	31	14	2	10	11	19	41	44
15	Crewe Alexandra	46	11	8	4	34	25	4	6	13	16	44	44
16	Newport County	46	14	6	3	43	22	2	5	16	22	51	43
17	Bournemouth	46	12	6	5	28	20	2	9	12	13	31	43
18	Stockport County	46	14	4	5	41	19	2	6	15	15	37	42
19	Darlington	46	10	8	5	31	22	4	5	14	21	37	41
20	Halifax Town	46	7	10	6	28	23	3	11	9	24	39	41
21	Hartlepool United	46	12	4	7	34	29	3	3	17	17	55	37
22	York City	46	8	7	8	27	31	4	5	14	23	38	36
23	Southport	46	5	13	5	30	32	1	6	16	22	44	31
24	Rochdale	46	8	6	9	29	28	0	2	21	14	57	24

1978/79   12th in Division 4

							Crawford PG	Davy SJ	Peacock JC	Oates RA	Deere SH	Czuczman M	Grimes V	Wigg RG	Keeley NB	Pilling S	Kilmore K	Bloomer BMc	O'Donnell JD	Gibson D	Kavanagh EA	Couch GR	Armstrong KT	Earl S	Hall DA
1	Aug	19	Port Vale	2-2	Wigg, Pilling	3025	1	2	3	4	5	6	7	8	9	10	11	12							
2		22	BOURNEMOUTH	1-0	Pilling	2433	1		3	4	5	6	7	9	10	11	8	12	2						
3		25	HUDDERSFIELD T	3-1	Pilling, Grimes, Kilmore	3029	1		3		5	6	7	9	10	11	8		2	4					
4	Sep	1	Doncaster Rovers	0-0		4667	1		3	4	5	6	7	9	10	11	8	12	2						
5		9	BARNSLEY	0-1		7612	1		3	4	5	6	7	9		11	8	12	2	10					
6		12	Portsmouth	0-0		10965	1		3	4	5	6	7	9		11	8		2	10	12				
7		15	Northampton Town	0-1		3858	1		3	4	5	6	7	9		11	8		2	10	12				
8		23	STOCKPORT COUNTY	1-0	Wigg	2691	1		3	4	5	6	7	9		12	8		2	10	11				
9		26	ALDERSHOT	2-0	Kilmore 2	2566	1		3	4	5	6	7	9		11	8		2	10					
10		30	Wigan Athletic	0-1		4459	1		3	4	5	6	7	9		11	8		2	12	10				
11	Oct	7	NEWPORT COUNTY	2-3	Deere, Oates	2453	1		3	4	5	6		9			8	10	2	7	11				
12		14	Wimbledon	1-3	Wigg	3808	1		3	4	5	6	7	9		10	8		2		11				
13		17	Hartlepool United	1-1	Kilmore	2981	1	2		4	5	6	7	9		3	8			10	11	12			
14		21	BRADFORD CITY	3-2	Couch, Kilmore 2 (1 p)	2778	1	2		4	5	6	7		9	3	8			10	11				
15		28	York City	0-1		1970	1	2		4	5		7	6	9	3	8			10	11				
16	Nov	4	READING	0-3		2424	1	2		4	5	6	7	11	9	3	8			10	12				
17		11	DONCASTER ROVERS	0-0		3250	1	2		4		6	7	9	11	3	8		5		10				
18		18	Huddersfield Town	2-3	Oates, Keeley	3375	1	2		4	5	6	7	9		11	3	8		10	12				
19	Dec	9	Torquay United	1-0	Kilmore (p)	2794	1			4	5	6	7			10	3	8	2		11			9	
20		16	HEREFORD UNITED	4-2	Kilmore 2, Pilling, Earl	1683	1			4	5	6	7			10	3	8	2		11			9	
21		23	Darlington	2-2	Kilmore 2	1512	1			4	5	6	7			10	3	8	2		11			9	
22		26	GRIMSBY TOWN	2-1	Kilmore (p), Grimes	8008	1			4	5	6	7			11	3	8	2		10			9	
23		30	ROCHDALE	0-4		2620	1			4	5	6	7	12	10	3	8		2		11			9	
24	Feb	3	Aldershot	0-2		3669	1			4	5	6	7			11	3	8	2	12	10			9	
25		26	Stockport County	2-0	Kavanagh, Earl	2676	1			4	5	6	7			11	3	8	2	12	10			9	
26	Mar	3	Bradford City	1-1	Pilling	4988	1		12	4	5	6	7			11	3	8	2		10			9	
27		10	YORK CITY	2-3	Kilmore 2 (2p)	2261	1			4	5	6	7			11	3	8	2		10			9	
28		13	Barnsley	1-4	Grimes	9308	1			4	5	6	7			11	3	8	2	9	10				
29		16	Reading	1-0	Keeley	5144	1			4	5	6	7			11	3	8	2	12	10			9	
30		20	NORTHAMPTON T	0-3		1763	1			4	5	6	7			11	3	12	2	8	10			9	
31		24	Bournemouth	0-0		3028	1			4	5	6	7			11		8	2		10			9	
32		27	PORT VALE	2-0	Grimes, Earl	1472	1		3	4	5	6	7			11		8	2		10			9	
33		31	CREWE ALEXANDRA	0-1		1868	1		3	4	5		7					8			10	11		9	6
34	Apr	3	PORTSMOUTH	2-2	Couch, Bloomer	1535	1	12	3	4	5		7					8	9	2		10	11		6
35		7	Hereford United	1-3	Kilmore (p)	2859	1	12	3	4	5	6	7					8	9	2		10		11	
36		10	DARLINGTON	1-0	Craig (og)	1372	1		12	4	5	2	7				9	8		3		10	11		6
37		14	Grimsby Town	1-1	Kavanagh	10197	1		3	4	5	6	7					8	2		12	10	11		9
38		16	HALIFAX TOWN	1-0	Earl	1624	1		3	4	5	2	7					8			11	10	12	9	6
39		18	Newport County	0-2		2572	1		3	4	5	2	7					8			11	10		9	6
40		21	Rochdale	0-1		1224	1	2	3	4	5		7					8		11		10	12	9	6
41		24	HARTLEPOOL UNITED	3-1	Oates, Earl 2	1226	1	2		4	5	3	7					8			10	9		11	6
42		28	TORQUAY UNITED	2-2	Kilmore (p), Earl	1426	1		2	4	5	3	7					8			10	9		11	6
43	May	1	WIGAN ATHLETIC	0-1		1582	1		3	4	5	2	7					8		11	10	9		6	12
44		5	Crewe Alexandra	2-0	Couch 2	1121	1	2	3	4	5		7			11		8			10	9		6	
45		8	WIMBLEDON	2-0	Kilmore (p), Earl	1777	1	2	3	4	5		7		6			8			10	9		11	
46		18	Halifax Town	3-2	Couch, Grimes, Gibson	1037	1	2	3	4	5		7					8		11	10	9			6

	Apps	46	14	28	45	45	39	45	18	25	30	46	7	32	18	39	18	1	23	11
	Goals				3	1		5	3	2	5	17	1		1	2	5		8	

One own goal

F.A. Cup

| R1 | Nov | 25 | SHEFFIELD WEDNESDAY | 1-1 | Pilling | 8697 | 1 | | | 4 | 5 | 6 | 7 | 9 | | 11 | 3 | 8 | 2 | | 10 | | | | |
| rep | | 28 | Sheffield Wednesday | 0-1 | | 9760 | 1 | | | 4 | 5 | 6 | 7 | 9 | | 11 | 3 | 8 | 2 | | 10 | | | | |

F.L. Cup

| R1/1 | Aug | 12 | NOTTS COUNTY | 0-1 | | 2389 | 1 | | 3 | 4 | 5 | 6 | 7 | 9 | | 10 | 11 | 12 | 2 | 8 | | | | | |
| R1/2 | | 15 | Notts County | 0-3 | | 5064 | 1 | | 3 | 4 | 5 | 6 | 7 | 9 | | 10 | 11 | 12 | 2 | 8 | | | | | |

		P	W	D	L	F	A	W	D	L	F	A	Pts
1	Reading	46	19	3	1	49	8	7	10	6	27	27	65
2	Grimsby Town	46	15	5	3	51	23	11	4	8	31	26	61
3	Wimbledon	46	18	3	2	50	20	7	8	8	28	26	61
4	Barnsley	46	15	5	3	47	23	9	8	6	26	19	61
5	Aldershot	46	16	5	2	38	14	4	12	7	25	33	57
6	Wigan Athletic	46	14	5	4	40	24	7	8	8	23	24	55
7	Portsmouth	46	13	7	3	35	12	7	5	11	27	36	52
8	Newport County	46	12	5	6	39	28	9	5	9	27	27	52
9	Huddersfield Town	46	13	8	2	32	15	5	3	15	25	38	47
10	York City	46	11	6	6	33	24	7	5	11	18	31	47
11	Torquay United	46	14	4	5	38	24	5	4	14	20	41	46
12	SCUNTHORPE UI	46	12	3	8	33	30	5	8	10	21	30	45
13	Hartlepool United	46	7	12	4	35	28	6	6	11	22	38	44
14	Hereford United	46	12	8	3	35	18	3	5	15	18	35	43
15	Bradford City	46	11	5	7	38	26	6	4	13	24	42	43
16	Port Vale	46	8	10	5	29	28	6	4	13	28	42	42
17	Stockport County	46	11	5	7	33	21	3	7	13	25	39	40
18	Bournemouth	46	11	6	6	34	19	5	5	13	29	39
19	Northampton Town	46	12	4	7	40	30	3	5	15	24	46	39
20	Rochdale	46	11	4	8	25	26	4	5	14	22	38	39
21	Darlington	46	8	8	7	25	21	3	7	13	24	45	37
22	Doncaster Rovers	46	8	8	7	25	22	5	3	15	25	51	37
23	Halifax Town	46	7	5	11	24	32	2	3	18	15	40	26
24	Crewe Alexandra	46	3	7	13	24	41	3	7	13	19	49	26

~ 249 ~

1979/80 — 14th in Division 4

#		Date	Opponent	Score	Scorers	Att
1	Aug	18	Torquay United	0-3		3063
2		21	HARTLEPOOL UNITED	1-3	Kavanagh	1710
3		25	Portsmouth	1-6	Pilling	12234
4	Sep	1	BOURNEMOUTH	2-1	Green, Earl	1471
5		8	Aldershot	0-2		2709
6		14	HUDDERSFIELD T	1-1	Green	2546
7		18	YORK CITY	6-1	Green 2, Partridge 3(1p), Cammack	2365
8		22	Bradford City	0-2		6248
9		28	DONCASTER ROVERS	0-0		4465
10	Oct	2	York City	0-2		2397
11		6	WALSALL	2-2	Green, O'Berg	2492
12		9	Hartlepool United	2-3	Partridge (p), Green	2810
13		13	Lincoln City	0-4		4933
14		20	NEWPORT COUNTY	1-3	Keeley	1875
15		23	DARLINGTON	3-0	O'Berg, Cammack, Green	1559
16		26	Tranmere Rovers	2-1	Green, Pilling	1876
17	Nov	3	TORQUAY UNITED	1-1	Cammack	1868
18		6	Darlington	1-3	Cammack	1306
19		10	STOCKPORT COUNTY	1-1	Cammack	1853
20		17	Wigan Athletic	1-4	Partridge	4618
21		30	ROCHDALE	2-0	Oates 2	1771
22	Dec	8	Northampton Town	0-0		2120
23		15	Newport County	1-2	Stewart	4158
24		21	HALIFAX TOWN	1-0	Cammack	1473
25		26	Port Vale	0-1		3432
26		29	HEREFORD UNITED	1-0	Green	1764
27	Jan	5	Peterborough United	1-3	Davy	3014
28		26	PORTSMOUTH	1-0	Partridge	2609
29	Feb	9	BRADFORD CITY	3-3	Pilling, Partridge 2	2819
30		16	Doncaster Rovers	0-5		3304
31		23	LINCOLN CITY	1-0	Pilling	3672
32	Mar	4	CREWE ALEXANDRA	1-1	O'Berg	1903
33		8	TRANMERE ROVERS	2-2	Pilling, Cammack	1779
34		15	Walsall	1-1	Partridge	5078
35		21	Stockport County	2-1	Stewart, Partridge	2215
36		25	Bournemouth	3-3	Pilling 2, Stewart	2675
37		29	WIGAN ATHLETIC	1-3	Cammack	2140
38	Apr	5	PORT VALE	1-0	Pilling	1855
39		7	Crewe Alexandra	1-1	Cammack	2596
40		8	Halifax Town	2-2	Oates, Cammack	1660
41		12	PETERBOROUGH UTD.	1-0	Stewart	1908
42		15	Huddersfield Town	1-2	Partridge	10900
43		18	Rochdale	1-0	Partridge	1018
44		22	ALDERSHOT	1-1	Partridge	1562
45		25	NORTHAMPTON T	3-0	Stewart, Cammack 2	1676
46	May	3	Hereford United	1-1	Pilling	2099

F.A. Cup

Round	Date	Opponent	Score	Scorers	Att
R1	Nov 24	Rochdale	1-2	Pilling	1985

F.L. Cup

Round	Date	Opponent	Score	Att
R1/1	Aug 11	Grimsby Town	0-2	5083
R1/2	Aug 14	GRIMSBY TOWN	0-0	3908

Division 4 Final Table

		P	W	D	L	F	A	W	D	L	F	A	Pts
1	Huddersfield Town	46	16	5	2	61	18	11	7	5	40	30	66
2	Walsall	46	12	9	2	43	23	11	9	3	32	24	64
3	Newport County	46	16	5	2	47	22	11	2	10	36	28	61
4	Portsmouth	46	15	5	3	62	23	9	7	7	29	26	60
5	Bradford City	46	14	6	3	44	14	10	6	7	33	36	60
6	Wigan Athletic	46	13	5	5	42	26	8	8	7	34	35	55
7	Lincoln City	46	14	8	1	43	12	4	9	10	21	30	53
8	Peterborough Utd.	46	14	3	6	39	22	7	7	9	19	25	52
9	Torquay United	46	13	7	3	47	25	2	10	11	23	44	47
10	Aldershot	46	10	7	6	35	23	6	6	11	27	30	45
11	Bournemouth	46	8	9	6	32	25	5	9	9	20	26	44
12	Doncaster Rovers	46	11	6	6	37	27	4	8	11	25	36	44
13	Northampton Town	46	14	5	4	33	16	2	7	14	18	50	44
14	SCUNTHORPE UNITED	46	11	9	3	37	23	6	6	14	21	52	43
15	Tranmere Rovers	46	10	4	9	32	24	4	9	10	18	32	41
16	Stockport County	46	9	7	7	30	31	5	5	13	18	41	40
17	York City	46	9	6	8	35	34	5	5	13	30	48	39
18	Halifax Town	46	11	9	3	29	20	2	4	17	17	52	39
19	Hartlepool United	46	10	7	6	36	28	4	3	16	23	36	38
20	Port Vale	46	8	6	9	34	24	4	6	13	22	46	36
21	Hereford United	46	8	7	8	22	21	3	7	13	16	31	36
22	Darlington	46	7	11	5	33	26	2	6	15	17	48	35
23	Crewe Alexandra	46	10	6	7	25	27	1	7	15	10	41	35
24	Rochdale	46	6	7	10	20	28	1	6	16	13	51	27

1980/81 16th in Division 4

#	Date		Opponent	Score	Scorers	Att	Neenan JP	Davy SJ	Jarvis NC	Grimes V	Dall DG	Oates RA	Pugh JG	Cammack SR	Lambert AJ	Partridge M	O'Berg PJ	Ashworth PA	Pilling S	Boxall AR	Stewart CD	Gordon JS	Cowling C	Wood HS	Green R	Duffy VG
1	Aug	16	ALDERSHOT	2-2	Grimes, Cammack	1325	1	2	3	4	5	6	7	8	9	10	11									
2		19	Rochdale	0-4		2427	1	2	3	4	5	6	7	8	9	10	11	12								
3		23	Bradford City	0-0		3177	1	2				6	7	8	9	10			3	5	11					
4		30	WIMBLEDON	1-2	O'Berg	1624				4	2	6	7	8	9	10	12		3	5	11	1				
5	Sep	6	CREWE ALEXANDRA	1-1	Partridge	1516				4	5	6	2	8	9	10	12		3		11	1	7			
6		13	Halifax Town	0-1		1226	1			4	5	6	2	8	9	10	12	7	3		11					
7		16	Darlington	1-0	Cammack	2633	1	2		4	5	6	7	8	9	12	11	10	3							
8		19	STOCKPORT COUNTY	2-0	Cammack, O'Berg	1985	1	2		4	5	6	7	8	9		11	10	3							
9		27	Lincoln City	2-2	Ashworth, Thompson (og)	4209	1	2		4	5	6	7	8	9	12	11	10	3							
10		30	DARLINGTON	3-0	Cammack 2, Partridge (p)	2106	1			4	5	6	7	8		2	11	10	3		12					
11	Oct	4	Bournemouth	2-2	Lambert, O'Berg	3079	1			4	5	6	7	8	9	2	11	10	3		12					
12		7	HARTLEPOOL UNITED	3-3	Cammack, Ashworth 2	2900	1			4	5	6	7	8	9	2	11	10	3							
13		11	NORTHAMPTON T	0-2		2650	1			4	5	6	7	8	9	2	11	10	3		12					
14		17	Southend United	0-2		5271	1		3	4	5	6	7	8		2	11	10			9			12		
15		22	Peterborough United	2-0	Lambert, Partridge	4262	1		3	4	5	6	7	8	9	2	11								10	
16		25	TORQUAY UNITED	0-2		2254	1		3	4	5	6	7	8	9	2	11	12							10	
17		28	DONCASTER ROVERS	1-1	Cammack	4053	1		3	4	5	6	7	8	9	2	11	12							10	
18	Nov	1	York City	0-1		1959	1		3	4	5	6	7	8	9	2	11	12							10	
19		4	Hartlepool United	0-2		4357	1		3	4	5	6	7	8	9	2	11	10							12	
20		8	HEREFORD UNITED	3-1	Stewart 2, Cammack	1539	1					6		8	12	7	11			5	9				10	
21		11	ROCHDALE	1-1	Stewart	2019	1	2	3	4		6		8		7	11			5	9				10	
22		15	Aldershot	0-0		2512	1	2	3	4		6		8		7	11			5	9				10	
23	Dec	6	Wigan Athletic	1-1	Partridge (p)	3672	1	2	3	4		6	12	8		7	11			5	9				10	
24		20	TRANMERE ROVERS	2-0	Lambert, Stewart	1664	1	2	3	4		6	10	8	7	9				5	12				11	
25		26	Mansfield Town	0-1		4261	1	2	3	4		6	10	8	7	9		12		5	11					
26		27	BURY	2-2	Boxall, Cammack	2960	1	2	3	4		6	10	8	7	9	12			5	11					
27	Jan	10	PETERBOROUGH UTD.	1-1	Green	2064	1	2	3	4		6	10	8			7			5	11				9	
28		19	Wimbledon	2-2	Green, O'Berg	2112	1	2	3	4	5	6	10	8		12	7				11				9	
29		31	BRADFORD CITY	1-0	Cammack	2558	1	2	3			6	10	8	4		7			5	11				9	
30	Feb	4	Torquay United	1-2	Green	1760	1	2	3	4	5	6	10	8		11	7				12				9	
31		7	HALIFAX TOWN	2-2	Stewart, Grimes	2073	1	2	3	4		6	10	8			7			5	11				9	
32		14	Crewe Alexandra	0-1		2231	1	2		4		6	10	8			7		3	5	11				9	
33		21	LINCOLN CITY	2-2	O'Berg, Pilling	4848	1			4		6	10	8		2	7	12	3	5	11				9	
34		24	PORT VALE	1-1	Cammack (p)	1946	1			4		6	10	8		2			3	5	11				9	12
35		27	Stockport County	0-2		1675	1	2		4		6	10	8		9	7	12	3	5	11					
36	Mar	3	Port Vale	2-2	Partridge (p), Cammack	2277	1	2		4		6	10	8		9	7	12	3	5	11					
37		6	BOURNEMOUTH	1-1	Partridge (p)	2392	1	2		4		6		8		9	7	10	3	5	11				12	
38		13	Northampton Town	3-3	Grimes, O'Berg, Green	2046	1	2		4		6		8		10	7		3	5	11				9	
39		22	SOUTHEND UNITED	2-1	Pilling, Green	3605	1	2		4		6		8		9	7		3	5	11				10	
40		27	Doncaster Rovers	0-1		8001	1	2		4		6		8		9	7		3	5	11				10	
41	Apr	4	YORK CITY	3-2	Green 2, Stewart	1694	1	2		4		6		8		9	7		3	5	11				10	
42		11	Hereford United	1-2	Price (og)	2009	1	2		4	6			9	8		7		3	5	11				10	
43		18	Bury	1-6	Stewart	2357	1	2		4	6			9	8		7	12	3	5	11					
44		20	MANSFIELD TOWN	2-0	O'Berg, Cammack	1850	1	2	3	4			10	8	12	5	7	6		11					9	
45		24	Tranmere Rovers	2-1	Pilling, Stewart	1063	1	2		4			10	8		5	7	6	3		11				9	
46	May	2	WIGAN ATHLETIC	4-4	O'Berg 2, Cammack 2	1704	1	2		4				8	10	5	7	6	3		11	9				
			Apps				44	31	21	45	22	40	38	46	24	40	43	23	26	24	34	2	2	1	27	1
			Goals							3				15	3	6	9	3	3	1	8				7	

Two own goals

F.A. Cup

	Date		Opponent	Score	Scorers	Att																				
R1	Nov	22	HARTLEPOOL UNITED	3-1	Grimes, Green, Partridge (p)	5165	1	2	3	4		6		8		7	11			5	9				10	
R2	Dec	13	ALTRINCHAM	0-0		3672	1	2	3	4		6	12	8		7	11			5	9				10	
rep		15	Altrincham	0-1		5176	1	2	3	4		6	7	8	11			12		5	9				10	

F.L. Cup

	Date		Opponent	Score	Scorers	Att																				
R1/1	Aug	9	BARNSLEY	0-1		4550	1	2	3	4	5	6	7	8	9	10	12				11					
R1/2		12	Barnsley	1-2	Cammack	8430	1	2	3	4	5	6	7	8	9	10	12				11					

		P	W	D	L	F	A	W	D	L	F	A	F	A	Pts
1	Southend United	46	19	4	0	47	6	11	3	9	32	25	79	31	67
2	Lincoln City	46	15	7	1	44	11	10	8	5	22	14	66	25	65
3	Doncaster Rovers	46	15	4	4	36	20	7	8	8	23	29	59	49	56
4	Wimbledon	46	15	4	4	42	17	8	5	10	22	29	64	46	55
5	Peterborough Utd.	46	11	8	4	37	21	6	10	7	31	33	68	54	52
6	Aldershot	46	12	9	2	28	11	6	5	12	15	30	43	41	50
7	Mansfield Town	46	13	5	5	36	15	7	4	12	22	29	58	44	49
8	Darlington	46	13	6	4	43	23	6	5	12	22	36	65	59	49
9	Hartlepool United	46	14	3	6	42	22	6	6	11	22	39	64	61	49
10	Northampton Town	46	11	7	5	42	26	7	6	10	23	41	65	67	49
11	Wigan Athletic	46	13	4	6	29	16	5	7	11	22	39	51	55	47
12	Bury	46	10	8	5	38	21	7	3	13	32	41	70	62	45
13	Bournemouth	46	9	8	6	30	21	7	5	11	17	27	47	48	45
14	Bradford City	46	9	9	5	30	24	5	7	11	23	36	53	60	44
15	Rochdale	46	11	6	6	33	25	3	9	11	27	45	60	70	43
16	SCUNTHORPE UNITED	46	8	12	3	40	31	3	8	12	20	38	60	69	42
17	Torquay United	46	12	2	8	38	26	5	3	15	17	37	55	63	41
18	Crewe Alexandra	46	10	7	6	28	20	3	7	13	20	41	48	61	40
19	Port Vale	46	10	8	5	40	23	2	7	14	17	47	57	70	39
20	Stockport County	46	10	5	8	29	25	6	2	15	15	32	44	57	39
21	Tranmere Rovers	46	12	5	6	41	24	1	5	17	18	49	59	73	36
22	Hereford United	46	8	8	7	29	20	5	5	15	9	42	38	62	35
23	Halifax Town	46	9	3	11	28	32	2	9	12	16	39	44	71	34
24	York City	46	10	2	11	31	23	2	7	14	16	43	47	66	33

1981/82   23rd in Division 4

F.A. Cup

	Date	Opponent	Result	Scorers	Att
R1	Nov 21	BRADFORD CITY	1-0	Cowling	3339
R2	Jan 2	Crewe Alexandra	3-1	Cowling, Telfer, Dall	2729
R3	6	HEREFORD UNITED	1-1	Stewart	3781
rep	20	Hereford United	1-4	Grimes	4025

Milk Cup (F.L. Cup)

	Date	Opponent	Result	Att
R1/1	Sep 1	MANSFIELD TOWN	0-0	2249
R1/2	14	Mansfield Town	0-2	2258

Final Division 4 Table

	Team	P	W	D	L	F	A	W	D	L	F	A	F	A	Pts
1	Sheffield United	46	15	8	0	53	15	12	7	4	41	26	94	41	96
2	Bradford City	46	14	7	2	52	23	12	6	5	36	22	88	45	91
3	Wigan Athletic	46	17	5	1	47	18	9	8	6	33	28	80	46	91
4	Bournemouth	46	12	10	1	37	15	11	9	3	25	15	62	30	88
5	Peterborough Utd.	46	16	3	4	46	22	8	7	8	25	35	71	57	82
6	Colchester United	46	12	6	5	47	23	8	6	9	35	34	82	57	72
7	Port Vale	46	9	12	2	26	17	9	4	10	30	32	56	49	70
8	Hull City	46	14	3	6	36	23	5	9	9	34	38	70	61	69
9	Bury	46	13	7	3	53	26	4	10	9	27	33	80	59	68
10	Hereford United	46	10	9	4	36	25	6	10	7	28	33	64	58	67
11	Tranmere Rovers	46	7	9	7	27	25	7	9	7	24	31	51	56	60
12	Blackpool	46	11	5	7	40	26	4	8	11	26	34	66	60	58
13	Darlington	46	10	5	8	36	28	5	8	10	25	34	61	62	58
14	Hartlepool United	46	9	6	8	23	34	4	8	11	34	50	73	84	55
15	Torquay United	46	9	8	6	30	25	5	5	13	17	34	47	59	55
16	Aldershot	46	8	7	8	34	29	5	8	10	23	39	57	68	54
17	York City	46	9	5	9	45	37	5	3	15	24	54	69	91	50
18	Stockport County	46	10	5	8	34	28	2	8	13	14	39	48	67	49
19	Halifax Town	46	6	11	6	28	30	3	11	9	23	42	51	72	49
20	Mansfield Town	46	8	6	9	39	39	5	4	14	24	42	63	81	47
21	Rochdale	46	7	9	7	26	22	3	7	13	24	40	50	62	46
22	Northampton Town	46	9	5	9	32	27	2	6	15	25	57	57	84	42
23	SCUNTHORPE UNITED	46	7	9	7	26	35	2	6	15	17	44	43	79	42
24	Crewe Alexandra	46	3	6	14	19	32	3	3	17	10	52	29	84	27

~ 252 ~

1982/83 4th in Division 4: Promoted

#	Date		Opponent	Score	Scorers	Att
1	Aug	28	Hartlepool United	0-0		1009
2	Sep	4	ALDERSHOT	1-1	Hunter	1309
3		7	STOCKPORT COUNTY	3-0	Telfer 2, Cowling	1335
4		11	Wimbledon	2-2	O'Berg 2	1611
5		19	YORK CITY	0-0		2436
6		25	Bristol City	2-0	O'Berg, Parkinson	3890
7		28	Darlington	1-0	Hunter	1574
8	Oct	2	COLCHESTER UNITED	2-1	O'Berg, Angus	2616
9		9	Peterborough United	1-0	Angus	3075
10		15	HULL CITY	0-1		7483
11		18	Mansfield Town	2-0	Hunter, Cowling	2647
12		23	TRANMERE ROVERS	2-1	Baines, Cowling	3052
13		30	Torquay United	1-1	Cammack	3005
14	Nov	2	PORT VALE	1-0	Cammack	3766
15		6	NORTHAMPTON T	5-1	O'Berg 2, Cammack 3	3412
16		12	Crewe Alexandra	1-0	O'Berg	2195
17		27	BURY	0-1		6335
18	Dec	4	Hereford United	2-0	Cammack, Cartwright	2103
19		18	Blackpool	1-3	Cammack	2860
20		27	ROCHDALE	1-1	Cammack	4845
21		28	Halifax Town	1-3	Parkinson (p)	2270
22	Jan	1	CHESTER	2-0	Cammack 2	3639
23		3	Swindon Town	2-2	Parkinson, Cammack	6728
24		16	HARTLEPOOL UNITED	3-0	Hunter, Cowling, Parkinson	4261
25		23	York City	1-2	Cowling	7097
26		29	WIMBLEDON	0-0		3846
27	Feb	5	BRISTOL CITY	1-1	Parkinson	3624
28		12	Stockport County	1-1	Cammack	2328
29		26	Hull City	1-1	Leman	###
30	Mar	1	MANSFIELD TOWN	2-2	Cammack 2	3562
31		5	Tranmere Rovers	4-0	Leman, Cammack 2, Parkinson	1652
32		12	TORQUAY UNITED	2-0	Hunter 2	3342
33		15	Aldershot	1-1	O'Berg	1422
34		20	Northampton Town	1-2	Cowling	2634
35		25	CREWE ALEXANDRA	2-0	Hunter 2	2938
36	Apr	1	HALIFAX TOWN	2-0	Lester, Cammack	3775
37		4	Rochdale	1-0	Graham	2056
38		8	HEREFORD UNITED	1-2	Cammack (p)	3785
39		15	Colchester United	1-5	Cammack	3155
40		23	BLACKPOOL	4-3	Cowling 2, Cammack 2 (1p)	2791
41		26	PETERBOROUGH UTD.	3-0	Lester, Cammack, Pointon	3211
42		30	Bury	0-1		4739
43	May	2	SWINDON TOWN	2-0	Cammack, Lester	3546
44		7	DARLINGTON	2-2	Cammack 2	3305
45		9	Port Vale	1-0	Cowling	6212
46		14	Chester	2-1	Graham 2	2560

F.A. Cup

	Date		Opponent	Score	Scorers	Att
R1	Nov	20	Darlington	1-0	Cammack	2540
R2	Dec	11	NORTHWICH VICTORIA	2-1	Cowling, O'Berg	5457
R3	Jan	8	GRIMSBY TOWN	0-0		###
rep		11	Grimsby Town	0-2		9509

Milk Cup (F.L. Cup)

	Date		Opponent	Score	Scorers	Att
R1/1	Aug	31	GRIMSBY TOWN	1-2	Cowling	2620
R1/2	Sep	14	Grimsby Town	0-0		3347

F.L. Trophy

	Date		Opponent	Score	Scorers	Att
Gp	Aug	14	LINCOLN CITY	1-1	Hunter	1022
Gp		17	SHEFFIELD UNITED	0-0		1874
Gp		21	Grimsby Town	0-2		2334

Division 4 Final Table

		P	W	D	L	F	A	W	D	L	F	A	F	A	Pts
1	Wimbledon	46	17	4	2	57	23	12	7	4	39	22	96	45	98
2	Hull City	46	14	8	1	48	14	11	7	5	27	20	75	34	90
3	Port Vale	46	15	4	4	37	16	11	6	6	30	18	67	34	88
4	SCUNTHORPE UNITED	46	13	7	3	41	17	10	7	6	30	25	71	42	83
5	Bury	46	15	4	4	43	20	8	8	7	31	26	74	46	81
6	Colchester United	46	17	5	1	51	19	7	4	12	24	36	75	55	81
7	York City	46	18	4	1	59	19	4	9	10	29	39	88	58	79
8	Swindon Town	46	14	3	6	45	27	5	8	10	16	27	61	54	68
9	Peterborough Utd.	46	13	6	4	38	23	4	7	12	20	29	58	52	64
10	Mansfield Town	46	11	6	6	32	26	5	7	11	29	44	61	70	61
11	Halifax Town	46	9	8	6	31	23	7	4	12	28	43	59	66	60
12	Torquay United	46	12	3	8	38	30	5	4	14	18	35	56	65	58
13	Chester	46	8	6	9	28	24	7	5	11	27	36	55	60	56
14	Bristol City	46	10	8	5	32	25	3	9	11	27	45	59	70	56
15	Northampton Town	46	10	8	5	43	29	4	4	15	22	46	65	75	54
16	Stockport County	46	11	8	4	41	31	3	4	16	19	48	60	79	54
17	Darlington	46	8	5	10	27	30	5	8	10	34	41	61	71	52
18	Aldershot	46	11	5	7	40	35	1	10	12	21	47	61	82	51
19	Tranmere Rovers	46	8	8	7	30	29	5	3	15	19	42	49	71	50
20	Rochdale	46	11	8	4	38	25	0	8	15	17	48	55	73	49
21	Blackpool	46	10	8	5	32	23	3	4	16	23	51	55	74	49
22	Hartlepool United	46	11	5	7	30	24	2	4	17	16	52	46	76	48
23	Crewe Alexandra	46	9	5	9	35	32	2	3	18	18	39	53	71	41
24	Hereford United	46	8	6	9	19	23	3	2	18	23	56	42	79	41

1983/84   23rd in Division 3: Relegated

#	Date		Opponent	Score	Scorers	Att	Neenan JP	Longden DP	Pointon NG	Brolly MJ	Boxall AR	Hunter L	Graham T	Cammack SR	Cowling C	Dey G	Broddle JR	Webster IA	Green JR	Lester MJ	Holden R	O'Berg PJ	Richardson R	Snow SG	Hill DM	Wilson DJ	Leman D	Botham IT	Matthews M	Whitehead A	Bell DM	Pratley RG	Parkinson ND	Steele SP
1	Aug	27	Port Vale	0-0		4565	1	2	3	4	5	6	7	8	9	10	11	12															
2	Sep	3	EXETER CITY	3-1	Lester, Cammack, Graham	2768	1	2	3	4		6	7	8	9	11			5	10													
3		7	OXFORD UNITED	0-0		3516	1	2	3	4		6	7	8	9	11			5	10													
4		9	Orient	0-1		2702	1	2	3	4			7	8	9	11	12		5	10													
5		16	BOLTON WANDERERS	1-0	Cowling	4406	1	2	3	4	7	6		8	9	11			5	10	12												
6		24	Newport County	1-1	Green	2679	1	2	3	4	7	6			9	11			5	10	8	12												
7		27	Plymouth Argyle	0-4		3821	1	2	3	4	7	6			9	11			5	10	8	12												
8		30	SOUTHEND UNITED	1-6	Holden (p)	3335	1			3	4		6						5	10	8	7	2	9	11									
9	Oct	8	Bradford City	2-2	Leman, Lester	2476	1	2	3	7		6			9				5	10	8	12				4	11							
10		15	ROTHERHAM UNITED	1-2	Lester	3139	1	2	3	7		6	12		9				5	10	8					4	11							
11		18	WIGAN ATHLETIC	0-0		2345	1	2	3	7		6			9				5	10	8	11				4								
12		22	Bristol Rovers	1-4	Pointon	5324	1	2	3	7		6			9			12	5	10	8	11				4								
13		29	WIMBLEDON	5-1	Peters(og),Wilson 2(1p),Cammack 2	2347	1	2	3	7				8	6		9		5	10		11				4								
14	Nov	1	Sheffield United	3-5	Dey, Broddle, Wilson	10502	1	2	3					8	6	7	9		5	10		11				4								
15		5	WALSALL	0-0		2932	1	2	3	7				8	6	4	9		5	10		11												
16		12	Lincoln City	1-2	O'Berg	4657	1	2	3	7				8	6	4	9		5	10		11												
17		26	Millwall	1-2	Cammack	3776	1	2	3	7			4	8			9	6	5	10		11												
18	Dec	3	BOURNEMOUTH	1-2	Cammack	2344	1	2	3	7			4	8			9	6	5	10		11		12										
19		17	GILLINGHAM	2-0	Cammack (p), Cowling	2127	1	2	3	4				8	7			6	5	10		11												
20		26	Hull City	0-1		18461	1	2	3	4				8	7				5	10		11					9							
21		27	PRESTON NORTH END	1-5	Cammack	3986	1	2	3	12		4		8	7				5	10		11					9	6						
22		31	Burnley	0-5		7632	1	2	3	7		6	9	8					5	10		11				4								
23	Jan	2	BRENTFORD	4-4	Graham, Cammack 2, O'Berg	2239	1		3	7		6	9	8					5	10		11	2			4								
24		21	Bolton Wanderers	0-0		5379	1	2	3	7			9	8					5	10		11				4		6						
25	Feb	3	Southend United	0-0		1976	1	2	3	7			9	8		10	12	6	5							4			11					
26		10	NEWPORT COUNTY	3-3	Brolly 2, Cammack	2879	1	2	3	7				8			11	6	5	10						4			9					
27		18	Wimbledon	1-1	Cammack (p)	3117	1	2	3	7				8				11	6	5	10					4			9					
28		25	BRISTOL ROVERS	2-2	Cammack (p), O'Berg	2737	1	2	3	7				8					6	5	10		11			4			9					
29	Mar	3	Wigan Athletic	0-2		3092	1	2	3	7			11	8					5	10						4			9	6				
30		6	Walsall	1-1	Bell	4735	1	2	3	7			11	8					5	10						4			9	6				
31		10	LINCOLN CITY	0-0		3889	1	2	3	7			11	8					5	10						4			9	6				
32		17	BRADFORD CITY	2-1	Cammack, Matthews	3274	1	2	3	7			11	8					5	10						4			9	6				
33		27	SHEFFIELD UNITED	1-1	Bell	6750	1	2	3	7				8					5							4			10	9	6	11		
34		31	Oxford United	0-1		6747	1	2	3	7			12	8					5							4			10	9	6	11		
35	Apr	7	PLYMOUTH ARGYLE	3-0	Bell. Brolly, Cammack	2780	1	2	3	7			11	8					5							4			10	9	6			
36		11	Exeter City	1-1	Brolly	2003	1	2	3	7			11	8					5							4			10	9	6			
37		14	Bournemouth	1-1	Cammack	3501	1			7			11	8			3	2	5										10	9	6	12		
38		17	PORT VALE	1-1	Bell	2952	1	2	3	7			11	8					5	4									10	9	6			
39		21	HULL CITY	2-0	Bell (p), Cammack	8286	1	2	3	7			11	8					5							4			10	9		6		
40		24	Preston North End	0-1		3403	1	2	3	7			11	8					5							4			10	9		6		
41		27	MILLWALL	0-1		2867	1	2	3	7			11	8					5							4			10	9		6		
42	May	1	ORIENT	3-1	Graham 2, Parkinson	2284		2	3				11	8					5			7				4			10	9		6	1	
43		5	Brentford	0-3		4561		2	3				11	8	12				5			7				4			10	9		6	1	
44		7	BURNLEY	4-0	Cammack 2(1p),Cowling,Green	2620		2	3				11	8	9				5			7				4			10			6	1	
45		12	Gillingham	1-1	Cowling	3513		2	3						8	9			5	11		7				4			10			6	1	
46		15	Rotherham United	0-3		4298		2	3	6			11	8			9	12	5			7				4			10				1	

	Apps	41	43	45	41	4	15	27	39	22	12	13	9	45	33	7	25	2	1	2	6	2	3	25	15	19	10	10	5
	Goals			1	4			4	18	4	1	1		2	3	1	3				3	1		1		5		1	

One own goal

F.A. Cup

Rd	Date		Opponent	Score	Scorers	Att																										
R1	Nov	19	PRESTON NORTH END	1-0	Cammack (p)	3484	1	2	3	7			12	8	6	4	9		5	10		11												
R2	Dec	10	BURY	2-0	Pashley(og), Cammack	3246	1	2	3	4				8			7	6	5	10		11			9									
R3	Jan	7	Leeds United	1-1	Cammack	17130	1		3	7			9	8		4		6	5	10		11	2											
rep		10	LEEDS UNITED	1-1	Dey	13129	1	2	3	7			9	8		4		6	5	10		11												
rep2		16	LEEDS UNITED	4-2	Brolly, Cammack, Lester, Graha	13312	1	2	3	7			9	8		4		6	5	10		11												
R4	Feb	1	West Bromwich Albion	0-1		18235	1	2	3	7			9	8		10		6	5			11				4								

R3 replay a.e.t.

Milk Cup (F.L. Cup)

Rd	Date		Opponent	Score	Scorers	Att																										
R1/1	Aug	30	DONCASTER ROVERS	1-1	Cammack	4295	1	2	3	4	5	6	7	8	9	11				10														
R1/2	Sep	13	Doncaster Rovers	0-3		4377	1	2	3	4		6	7	8	9	11	5			10	12														

Associate Members Cup

Rd	Date		Opponent	Score	Scorers	Att																										
R1	Feb	21	CHESTERFIELD	2-1	Cammack, Brolly	2507	1	2	3	7				8		11		6	5	10						4			9					
R2	Mar	13	CREWE ALEXANDRA	4-4	Bell 3 (1 pen), Matthews	1524	1	2	3	7			11	8					5			10				4			9		6	12		
R3		20	SHEFFIELD UNITED	2-3	Matthews, Cammack	2720	1	2		7			11	8	12				5	10		3				4			9	6				

R2 won on penalties, a.e.t. R3 a.e.t.

FINAL LEAGUE TABLES: 1983/84 - 1990/91

Final League Table 1983/84 Division 3

		Pl.	Home					Away					F.	A.	Pts
			W	D	L	F	A	W	D	L	F	A			
1	Oxford United	46	17	5	1	58	22	11	6	6	33	28	91	50	95
2	Wimbledon	46	15	5	3	58	35	11	4	8	39	41	97	76	87
3	Sheffield United	46	14	7	2	56	18	10	4	9	30	35	86	53	83
4	Hull City	46	16	5	2	42	11	7	9	7	29	27	71	38	83
5	Bristol Rovers	46	16	5	2	47	21	6	8	9	21	33	68	54	79
6	Walsall	46	14	4	5	44	22	8	5	10	24	39	68	61	75
7	Bradford City	46	11	9	3	46	30	9	2	12	27	35	73	65	71
8	Gillingham	46	13	4	6	50	29	7	6	10	24	40	74	69	70
9	Millwall	46	16	4	3	42	18	2	9	12	29	47	71	65	67
10	Bolton Wanderers	46	13	4	6	36	17	5	6	12	20	43	56	60	64
11	Orient	46	13	5	5	40	27	5	4	14	31	54	71	81	63
12	Burnley	46	12	5	6	52	25	4	9	10	24	36	76	61	62
13	Newport County	46	11	9	3	35	27	5	5	13	23	48	58	75	62
14	Lincoln City	46	11	4	8	42	29	6	6	11	17	33	59	62	61
15	Wigan Athletic	46	11	5	7	26	18	5	8	10	20	38	46	56	61
16	Preston North End	46	12	5	6	42	27	3	6	14	24	39	66	66	56
17	Bournemouth	46	11	5	7	38	27	5	2	16	25	46	63	73	55
18	Rotherham United	46	10	5	8	29	17	5	4	14	28	47	57	64	54
19	Plymouth Argyle	46	11	8	4	38	17	2	4	17	18	45	56	62	51
20	Brentford	46	8	9	6	41	30	3	7	13	28	49	69	79	49
21	SCUNTHORPE U	46	9	9	5	40	31	0	10	13	14	42	54	73	46
22	Southend United	46	8	9	6	34	24	2	5	16	21	52	55	76	44
23	Port Vale	46	10	4	9	33	29	1	6	16	18	54	51	83	43
24	Exeter City	46	4	8	11	27	39	2	7	14	23	45	50	84	33

Final League Table 1984/85 Division 4

		Pl.	Home					Away					F.	A.	Pts
			W	D	L	F	A	W	D	L	F	A			
1	Chesterfield	46	16	6	1	40	13	10	7	6	24	22	64	35	91
2	Blackpool	46	15	7	1	42	15	9	7	7	31	24	73	39	86
3	Darlington	46	16	4	3	41	22	8	9	6	25	27	66	49	85
4	Bury	46	15	6	2	46	20	9	6	8	30	30	76	50	84
5	Hereford United	46	16	2	5	38	21	6	9	8	27	26	65	47	77
6	Tranmere Rovers	46	17	1	5	50	21	7	2	14	33	45	83	66	75
7	Colchester United	46	13	7	3	49	29	7	7	9	38	36	87	65	74
8	Swindon Town	46	16	4	3	42	21	5	5	13	20	37	62	58	72
9	SCUNTHORPE U	46	14	6	3	61	33	5	8	10	22	29	83	62	71
10	Crewe Alexandra	46	10	7	6	32	28	8	5	10	33	41	65	69	66
11	Peterborough Utd.	46	11	7	5	29	21	5	7	11	25	32	54	53	62
12	Port Vale	46	11	8	4	39	24	3	10	10	22	35	61	59	60
13	Aldershot	46	11	6	6	33	20	6	2	15	23	43	56	63	59
14	Mansfield Town	46	10	8	5	25	15	3	10	10	16	23	41	38	57
15	Wrexham	46	10	6	7	39	27	5	3	15	28	43	67	70	54
16	Chester City	46	11	3	9	35	30	4	6	13	25	42	60	72	54
17	Rochdale	46	8	7	8	33	30	5	7	11	22	39	55	69	53
18	Exeter City	46	9	7	7	30	27	4	7	12	27	52	57	79	53
19	Hartlepool United	46	10	6	7	34	29	4	4	15	20	38	54	67	52
20	Southend United	46	8	8	7	30	34	5	3	15	28	49	58	83	50
21	Halifax Town	46	9	3	11	26	32	6	2	15	16	37	42	69	50
22	Stockport County	46	11	5	7	40	26	2	3	18	18	53	58	79	47
23	Northampton Town	46	10	1	12	32	32	4	4	15	21	42	53	74	47
24	Torquay United	46	5	11	7	18	24	4	3	16	20	39	38	63	41

Final League Table 1985/86 Division 4

		Pl.	Home					Away					F.	A.	Pts
			W	D	L	F	A	W	D	L	F	A			
1	Swindon Town	46	20	2	1	52	19	12	4	7	30	24	82	43	102
2	Chester City	46	15	5	3	44	16	8	10	5	39	34	83	50	84
3	Mansfield Town	46	13	8	2	43	17	10	4	9	31	30	74	47	81
4	Port Vale	46	13	9	1	42	11	8	7	8	25	26	67	37	79
5	Orient	46	11	6	6	39	21	9	6	8	40	43	79	64	72
6	Colchester United	46	12	6	5	51	22	7	7	9	37	41	88	63	70
7	Hartlepool United	46	15	6	2	41	20	5	4	14	27	47	68	67	70
8	Northampton Town	46	9	7	7	44	29	9	3	11	35	29	79	58	64
9	Southend United	46	13	4	6	43	27	5	6	12	26	40	69	67	64
10	Hereford United	46	15	6	2	55	30	3	4	16	19	43	74	73	64
11	Stockport County	46	9	9	5	35	28	8	4	11	28	43	63	71	64
12	Crewe Alexandra	46	10	6	7	35	26	8	3	12	19	35	54	61	63
13	Wrexham	46	11	5	7	34	24	6	4	13	34	56	68	80	60
14	Burnley	46	11	3	9	35	30	5	8	10	25	35	60	65	59
15	SCUNTHORPE U	46	11	7	5	33	23	4	7	12	17	32	50	55	59
16	Aldershot	46	12	5	6	45	25	5	2	16	21	49	66	74	58
17	Peterborough Utd.	46	9	11	3	31	19	4	6	13	21	45	52	64	56
18	Rochdale	46	12	7	4	41	29	2	6	15	16	48	57	77	55
19	Tranmere Rovers	46	9	1	13	46	41	6	8	9	28	32	74	73	54
20	Halifax Town	46	10	8	5	35	27	4	4	15	25	44	60	71	54
21	Exeter City	46	10	4	9	26	25	3	11	9	21	34	47	59	54
22	Cambridge United	46	12	2	9	45	38	3	7	13	20	42	65	80	54
23	Preston North End	46	7	4	12	32	41	4	6	13	22	48	54	89	43
24	Torquay United	46	8	5	10	29	32	1	5	17	14	56	43	88	37

Final League Table 1986/87 Division 4

		Pl.	Home					Away					F.	A.	Pts
			W	D	L	F	A	W	D	L	F	A			
1	Northampton Town	46	20	2	1	56	20	10	7	6	47	33	103	53	99
2	Preston North End	46	16	4	3	36	18	10	8	5	36	29	72	47	90
3	Southend United	46	14	4	5	43	27	11	1	11	25	28	68	55	80
4	Wolverhampton W.	46	12	3	8	36	24	12	4	7	33	26	69	50	79
5	Colchester United	46	15	3	5	41	20	6	4	13	23	36	64	56	70
6	Aldershot	46	13	5	5	40	22	7	5	11	24	35	64	57	70
7	Orient	46	15	2	6	40	25	5	7	11	24	36	64	61	69
8	SCUNTHORPE U	46	15	3	5	52	27	3	9	11	21	30	73	57	66
9	Wrexham	46	8	13	2	38	24	7	7	9	32	27	70	51	65
10	Peterborough Utd.	46	10	7	6	29	21	7	7	9	28	29	57	50	65
11	Cambridge United	46	12	6	5	37	23	5	5	13	23	39	60	62	62
12	Swansea City	46	13	3	7	31	21	4	8	11	25	40	56	61	62
13	Cardiff City	46	6	12	5	24	18	9	4	10	24	32	48	50	61
14	Exeter City	46	11	10	2	37	17	0	13	10	16	32	53	49	56
15	Halifax Town	46	10	5	8	32	32	5	5	13	27	42	59	74	55
16	Hereford United	46	10	6	7	33	23	4	5	14	27	38	60	61	53
17	Crewe Alexandra	46	8	9	6	38	35	5	5	13	32	37	70	72	53
18	Hartlepool United	46	6	11	6	24	30	5	7	11	20	35	44	65	51
19	Stockport County	46	9	6	8	25	27	4	6	13	15	42	40	69	51
20	Tranmere Rovers	46	6	10	7	32	37	5	7	11	22	35	54	72	50
21	Rochdale	46	8	8	7	31	30	3	9	11	23	43	54	73	50
22	Burnley	46	9	7	7	31	35	3	6	14	22	39	53	74	49
23	Torquay United	46	8	8	7	28	29	2	10	11	28	43	56	72	48
24	Lincoln City	46	8	7	8	30	27	4	5	14	15	38	45	65	48

Final League Table 1987/88 Division 4

		Pl.	Home					Away					F.	A.	Pts
			W	D	L	F	A	W	D	L	F	A			
1	Wolverhampton W.	46	15	3	5	47	19	12	6	5	35	24	82	43	90
2	Cardiff City	46	15	6	2	39	14	9	7	7	27	27	66	41	85
3	Bolton Wanderers	46	15	6	2	42	12	7	6	10	24	30	66	42	78
4	SCUNTHORPE U	46	14	5	4	42	20	6	12	5	34	31	76	51	77
5	Torquay United	46	10	7	6	34	16	11	7	5	32	25	66	41	77
6	Swansea City	46	9	7	7	35	28	11	3	9	27	28	62	56	70
7	Peterborough Utd.	46	10	5	8	28	26	10	5	8	24	27	52	53	70
8	Leyton Orient	46	13	4	6	55	27	6	8	9	30	36	85	63	69
9	Colchester United	46	10	5	8	23	22	9	5	9	24	29	47	51	67
10	Burnley	46	12	5	6	31	22	8	2	13	26	40	57	62	67
11	Wrexham	46	13	3	7	46	26	7	3	13	23	32	69	58	66
12	Scarborough	46	12	8	3	38	19	5	6	12	18	29	56	48	65
13	Darlington	46	13	6	4	39	25	5	5	13	32	44	71	69	65
14	Tranmere Rovers	46	14	2	7	43	20	5	7	11	18	33	61	53	64
15	Cambridge United	46	10	6	7	32	24	6	7	10	18	28	50	52	61
16	Hartlepool United	46	9	7	7	25	25	6	7	10	25	32	50	57	59
17	Crewe Alexandra	46	7	11	5	25	19	6	8	9	32	34	57	53	58
18	Halifax Town	46	11	7	5	37	25	3	7	13	17	34	54	59	55
19	Hereford United	46	8	7	8	25	27	6	5	12	16	32	41	59	54
20	Stockport County	46	7	7	9	26	26	5	8	10	18	32	44	58	51
21	Rochdale	46	5	9	9	28	34	6	6	11	19	42	47	76	48
22	Exeter City	46	8	6	9	33	29	3	7	13	20	39	53	68	46
23	Carlisle United	46	9	5	9	38	33	3	3	17	19	53	57	86	44
24	Newport County	46	4	5	14	19	36	2	2	19	16	69	35	105	25

Final League Table 1988/89 Division 4

		Pl.	Home					Away					F.	A.	Pts
			W	D	L	F	A	W	D	L	F	A			
1	Rotherham United	46	13	6	4	44	18	9	10	4	32	17	76	35	82
2	Tranmere Rovers	46	15	6	2	34	13	6	11	6	28	30	62	43	80
3	Crewe Alexandra	46	13	7	3	42	24	8	8	7	25	24	67	48	78
4	SCUNTHORPE U	46	11	9	3	40	22	10	5	8	37	35	77	57	77
5	Scarborough	46	12	7	4	33	23	9	7	7	34	29	67	52	77
6	Leyton Orient	46	16	2	5	61	19	5	10	8	25	31	86	50	75
7	Wrexham	46	12	7	4	44	28	7	7	9	33	35	77	63	71
8	Cambridge United	46	13	7	3	45	25	5	7	11	26	37	71	62	68
9	Grimsby Town	46	11	9	3	33	18	6	6	11	32	41	65	59	66
10	Lincoln City	46	12	6	5	39	26	6	4	13	25	34	64	60	64
11	York City	46	10	8	5	43	27	7	5	11	19	36	62	63	64
12	Carlisle United	46	9	6	8	26	25	6	9	8	27	27	53	52	60
13	Exeter City	46	14	4	5	46	23	4	2	17	19	45	65	68	60
14	Torquay United	46	15	2	6	32	23	2	6	15	13	37	45	60	59
15	Hereford United	46	11	8	4	40	27	3	8	12	26	45	66	72	58
16	Burnley	46	12	6	5	35	20	2	7	14	17	41	52	61	55
17	Peterborough Utd.	46	10	3	10	29	32	4	9	10	23	42	52	74	54
18	Rochdale	46	10	10	3	32	26	3	4	16	24	56	56	82	53
19	Hartlepool United	46	10	6	7	33	33	4	4	15	17	45	50	78	52
20	Stockport County	46	8	10	5	31	20	2	11	10	23	32	54	52	51
21	Halifax Town	46	10	7	6	42	27	3	4	16	27	48	69	75	50
22	Colchester United	46	8	7	8	35	30	4	7	12	25	48	60	78	50
23	Doncaster Rovers	46	9	6	8	32	32	4	4	15	17	46	49	78	49
24	Darlington	46	3	12	8	28	38	5	6	12	25	38	53	76	42

Final League Table 1989/90 Division 4

		Pl.	Home					Away					F.	A.	Pts
			W	D	L	F	A	W	D	L	F	A			
1	Exeter City	46	20	3	0	50	14	8	2	13	33	34	83	48	89
2	Grimsby Town	46	14	4	5	41	20	8	9	6	29	27	70	47	79
3	Southend United	46	15	3	5	35	14	7	6	10	26	34	61	48	75
4	Stockport County	46	13	6	4	45	27	8	5	10	23	35	68	62	74
5	Maidstone United	46	14	4	5	49	21	8	3	12	28	40	77	61	73
6	Cambridge United	46	14	3	6	45	30	7	7	9	31	36	76	66	73
7	Chesterfield	46	12	9	2	41	19	7	5	11	22	31	63	50	71
8	Carlisle United	46	15	4	4	38	20	6	4	13	23	40	61	60	71
9	Peterborough Utd.	46	10	8	5	35	23	7	9	7	24	23	59	46	68
10	Lincoln City	46	11	6	6	30	27	7	8	8	18	21	48	48	68
11	SCUNTHORPE U	46	9	9	5	42	25	8	6	9	27	29	69	54	66
12	Rochdale	46	11	4	8	28	23	9	2	12	24	32	52	55	66
13	York City	46	10	5	8	29	24	6	11	6	26	29	55	53	64
14	Gillingham	46	9	8	6	28	21	8	3	12	18	27	46	48	62
15	Torquay United	46	12	2	9	33	29	3	10	10	20	37	53	66	57
16	Burnley	46	6	10	7	19	18	8	4	11	26	37	45	55	56
17	Hereford United	46	7	4	12	31	32	8	6	9	25	30	56	62	55
18	Scarborough	46	10	5	8	35	28	5	5	13	25	45	60	73	55
19	Hartlepool United	46	12	4	7	45	33	3	6	14	21	55	66	88	55
20	Doncaster Rovers	46	7	7	9	29	29	7	2	14	24	31	53	60	51
21	Wrexham	46	8	8	7	28	28	5	4	14	23	39	51	67	51
22	Aldershot	46	8	7	8	28	26	4	7	12	21	43	49	69	50
23	Halifax Town	46	5	9	9	31	29	7	4	12	26	36	57	65	49
24	Colchester United	46	9	3	11	26	25	2	7	14	22	50	48	75	43

Final League Table 1990/91 Division 4

		Pl.	Home					Away					F.	A.	Pts
			W	D	L	F	A	W	D	L	F	A			
1	Darlington	46	13	8	2	36	14	9	9	5	32	24	68	38	83
2	Stockport County	46	16	6	1	54	19	7	7	9	30	28	84	47	82
3	Hartlepool United	46	15	5	3	35	15	9	5	9	32	33	67	48	82
4	Peterborough Utd.	46	13	9	1	38	15	8	8	7	29	30	67	45	80
5	Blackpool	46	17	3	3	55	17	6	7	10	23	30	78	47	79
6	Burnley	46	17	5	1	46	16	6	5	12	24	35	70	51	79
7	Torquay United	46	14	7	2	37	13	4	11	8	27	34	64	47	72
8	SCUNTHORPE U	46	17	4	2	51	20	3	7	13	20	42	71	62	71
9	Scarborough	46	13	5	5	36	21	6	7	10	23	35	59	56	69
10	Northampton Town	46	14	5	4	34	21	4	8	11	23	37	57	58	67
11	Doncaster Rovers	46	12	5	6	36	22	5	9	9	20	24	56	46	65
12	Rochdale	46	10	9	4	29	22	5	8	10	21	31	50	53	62
13	Cardiff City	46	10	6	7	26	23	5	9	9	17	31	43	54	60
14	Lincoln City	46	10	7	6	32	27	4	10	9	18	34	50	61	59
15	Gillingham	46	9	9	5	35	27	3	9	11	22	33	57	60	54
16	Walsall	46	7	12	4	25	17	5	5	13	23	34	48	51	53
17	Hereford United	46	9	10	4	32	19	4	4	15	21	39	53	58	53
18	Chesterfield	46	8	12	3	33	26	5	2	16	14	36	47	62	53
19	Maidstone United	46	9	5	9	42	34	4	7	12	24	37	66	71	51
20	Carlisle United	46	12	3	8	30	30	1	6	16	17	59	47	89	48
21	York City	46	8	6	9	21	23	3	7	13	24	34	45	57	46
22	Halifax Town	46	9	6	8	34	29	3	4	16	25	50	59	79	46
23	Aldershot	46	8	7	8	38	43	2	4	17	23	58	61	101	41
24	Wrexham	46	8	7	8	33	34	2	3	18	15	40	48	74	40

1984/85 9th in Division 4

#	Date		Opponent	Score	Scorers	Att.	Neenan JP	Longden DP	Pointon NG	Matthews M	Green JR	Whitehead A	Brolly MJ	Dey G	Bell DM	Lester MJ	Cowling C	Webster IA	Cammack SR	Broddle JR	Hill DM	Graham T	Lees T	Gregory PG	Botham IT	Shutt SJ	O'Berg PJ	Finney SB	Ferry W	Atkins MN	Stobart SA	Stanley P
1	Aug	25	Chester City	1-1	Whitehead	2050	1	2	3	4	5	6	7	8	9	10	11	12													
2		31	COLCHESTER UNITED	2-2	Cammack, Cowling	1818	1	2	3	4	5	6		7		10	11		8	9											
3	Sep	8	Exeter City	1-2	Lester	2658	1	2	3	4	5	6	7	8		10	11			9											
4		15	CHESTERFIELD	2-4	Broddle, Cowling	2853	1	2	3	4	6	5	7	8		10	11			9											
5		18	CREWE ALEXANDRA	2-3	Scott(og), Cowling	1619	1	2	3	4	6	5	7	8		10	11			9											
6		22	Darlington	1-2	Bell	1762	1		3	4	2	5			8	10	11	6		9	7										
7		28	HALIFAX TOWN	4-0	Broddle, Cowling, Brolly, Matthews	1929	1	2	3	4	6		7			10	11	5		9		8	12								
8	Oct	3	Peterborough United	1-3	Brolly	3620	1	2	3	4	6	5	7			10	11			9		8									
9		6	Northampton Town	2-0	Matthews, Cowling	1873			3	4	6	5	7			10	11			9		8	2								
10		13	BLACKPOOL	1-1	Bell (pen)	2366	1		3	4	6	5	7		9	10	11			12		8	2								
11		19	Southend United	1-1	Cowling	2204			3	4	6	5	7			10	11		9	12		8	2	1							
12		23	TORQUAY UNITED	2-0	Broddle 2	2046			3	4	6	5				10	11		9	7		8	2	1							
13		27	Bury	1-0	Lester	3324			3	4	6	5				10	11		8	7		9	2	1							
14	Nov	3	ALDERSHOT	2-1	Cowling, Cammack	2253			3	4	6	5				10	11		8	7		9	2	1							
15		6	Swindon Town	0-0		2867			3	4	6	5				10	11		8	7		9	2	1							
16		9	HEREFORD UNITED	1-1	Graham	2902			3	4	6	5				10	11		8	7		9	2	1							
17		24	Hartlepool United	2-3	Cowling 2	1903			3	4	6	5				10	11		8	7		9	2								
18		30	WREXHAM	5-2	Cammack 3(1 p), Matthews, Whitehead	2180	1		3	4	6	5				10	11		8	7		9	2								
19	Dec	22	Port Vale	1-1	Graham	2521			3	4	6	5	12				11		8	7	10	9	2	1							
20		26	STOCKPORT COUNTY	1-0	Cammack	2881		2	3	4	6	5					11		8	7	9	10		1							
21	Jan	1	Tranmere Rovers	0-2		1943	1		3	4	6	5				10			8	7	11	9	2		12						
22		26	Chesterfield	0-1		3698			3		6	5	7			10	11		8	12	4	9	2	1							
23	Feb	1	Halifax Town	2-1	Whitehead, Broddle	1317			3	4	6	5				10	11			7	8	9	2	1							
24		8	DARLINGTON	0-1		1762			3		6	5	4			10	11			7	8	9	2	1							
25		12	PETERBOROUGH UTD.	2-1	Broddle, Brolly	1212			3		6	5	7				10		8	11	4	9	2	1	12						
26		16	Crewe Alexandra	1-1	Shutt	1782			3		6	5	11			10				7	4	9	2	1		8					
27		23	Aldershot	2-1	Graham, Broddle	1926			3		6	5	11			10			8	7	4	9	2	1							
28		26	ROCHDALE	4-2	Cammack 2, Brolly 2	1694			3		6	5	11			10			8	7	4	9	2	1							
29	Mar	2	BURY	2-2	Graham, Cammack	2710			3		6	5	7			10			8	11	4	9	2	1							
30		5	Torquay United	0-0		1158			3		6	5	7			10			8	11	4	9	2	1							
31		8	SOUTHEND UNITED	2-1	Cammack, Graham	1912		2	3		6	5	7			10			8	11	4	9	2	1							
32		12	CHESTER CITY	2-1	Cammack 2 (1 p)	1875		2	3		6	5	7			10			8	11	4	9	2	1							
33		16	Blackpool	0-1		3937			3		6	5	7			10	12		8	11	4	9	2	1							
34		19	EXETER CITY	7-1	*See below	1566			3		6	5	7			10	12		8	11	4	9	2	1							
35		22	NORTHAMPTON T	2-1	Hill, Broddle	2024			3		6	5	7			10			8	11	4	9	2	1			12				
36		29	SWINDON TOWN	6-2	Cammack, Broddle, Brolly, Hill, Graham, Greer	2042			3		6	5	7			10			8	11	4	9	2	1							
37	Apr	2	Colchester United	1-1	Broddle	2409			3		6	5	7			10	12		8	11	4	9	2	1							
38		6	Stockport County	0-2		1285			3		6	5	7			10	12		8	11	4	9	2	1							
39		9	TRANMERE ROVERS	5-2	Brolly 2, Cammack 2, Broddle	2260			3		6	5	7			10			8	11	4	9	2	1			12				
40		13	Hereford United	0-1		3412			3		6	5	7			10			8	11	4	9	2	1							
41		19	HARTLEPOOL UNITED	2-0	Broddle, Lester	2037		2	3		6	5	7			10			8	11	4			1		9		12			
42		24	Mansfield Town	1-0	Cammack	1963		2	3		6	5	7			10			8	11	4			1				9	12		
43		27	Wrexham	1-2	Cammack	1352		2	3		6	5	7			10			8	11	4	9		1						12	
44	May	4	MANSFIELD TOWN	2-2	Cammack 2	1705			3		6	5	7			10			8	11	4	9		1					2		
45		6	Rochdale	3-3	Cammack 2 (2p), Stobart	1482		2	3		6	5	7			10			8	11	4	9		1						12	
46		10	PORT VALE	3-3	Graham, Broddle, Cammack	1867	1		3		6	5	7			10			8	11	4	9	2							12	

Scorers in game 34: Broddle, Whitehead,
Cammack 2 (1p), Graham 2, Brolly

Apps	14	14	46	22	46	45	34	5	3	44	27	3	34	45	29	38	31	32	2	2	2	1	2	2	0
Goals				3	1	4	9		2	3	9		24	14	2	9				1				1	

One own goal

F.A. Cup

R1	Nov	17	Nuneaton Borough	1-1	Dixey (og)	4287	1		3	4	6	5				10	11		8	7				2						9
rep		20	NUNEATON BOROUGH	2-1	Lester, Cammack	3334	1		3	4	6	5	12			10	11		8	7				2							9
R2	Dec	7	Port Vale	1-4	Ridley (og)	4268	1	12	3	4	6	5	10				11		8	7	9			2							

R1 replay a.e.t. (90 mins. 1-1)

Milk Cup (F.L. Cup)

R1/1	Aug	28	MANSFIELD TOWN	0-1		2106	1	2	3	4	5	6	7	9		10	11		8	12											
R1/2	Sep	5	Mansfield Town	2-1	Brolly, Cowling	3107	1	2	3	4	5	6	7	8		10	11	12		9											
R2/1		24	ASTON VILLA	2-3	Lester, Whitehead	6212	1	2	3	4	5	6	7		12	10	11			9		8									
R2/2	Oct	10	Aston Villa	1-3	Pointon	11421	1		3	4	6	5	7			10	11			9		8	2								

R1 won on away goals rule

Freight Rover Trophy (Associate Members Cup)

R1/1	Jan	22	BRADFORD CITY	1-4	Graham	1380			3	4	6	5	7			10	11		8		12	9	2	1	14						
R1/2	Feb	6	Bradford City	1-2	Brolly	2388		2	3	4	6	5	7					12		11	8	9		1	10		14				

1985/86 15th in Division 4

#		Date	Opponent	Result	Scorers	Att	Gregory PG	Russell WM	Pointon NG	Lister SH	Whitehead A	Green JR	Brolly MJ	Cammack SR	Broddle JR	Graham T	Hill DM	Lester MJ	Hawley JE	Matthews M	Smith MC	Longden DP	Money R	Ferry W	Matthews N	Barnes DO	Dixon KL	Webster IA	Stevenson AJ	Travis DA	Johnson P	Hunter L	Houchen KM
1	Aug	17	TORQUAY UNITED	4-0	Graham, Broddle, Cammack, Green	1929	1	2	3	4	5	6	7	8	9	10	11															
2		23	Halifax Town	1-2	Cammack (p)	1094	1	2	3	4	5	6	7	8	9	10	11															
3		26	WREXHAM	1-1	Broddle	2097	1	2	3	4	5	6	7	8	9	10	11															
4		31	Peterborough United	0-1		2928	1	2	3	4	5	6		8	9	10	11	7	12													
5	Sep	6	TRANMERE ROVERS	0-1		2058	1	2	3	4	5		7	8	9	11		10	12													
6		14	Southend United	1-2	Cammack (p)	2974	1	2	3	4	5	6	7	8	9			10	12														
7		18	Exeter City	0-2		1723	1	2	3	4	5	6		8	12	7	11	10	9													
8		21	MANSFIELD TOWN	0-3		1780	1	2	3	4	5	6	7		8		11	10	9	12												
9		28	Aldershot	1-2	Graham	1056	1	2	3	4	5			8	9	7	11	10		6	12											
10	Oct	1	CREWE ALEXANDRA	3-1	Graham, Holland(og), Hill	1443	1		3		5	6	7	8	9	4	11	10				2										
11		5	Orient	0-3		2847	1	12	3	6	5		7	8	9	4	11	10				2										
12		11	CAMBRIDGE UNITED	0-0		1496	1		3	6	5		7	8		4	11	10	9			2										
13		18	Colchester United	1-1	Broddle	3462	1	2	3	4	5		7	8	9		11	10				6										
14		22	PORT VALE	0-0		1888	1	2	3	4	5		7	8	9		11	10				6										
15		25	HEREFORD UNITED	2-1	Whitehead, Cammack	1564	1	2	3	4	5		7	8	9	12	11	10				6										
16	Nov	2	Northampton Town	2-2	Brolly, Lister	2343	1	2	3	4	5		7	8	9		11	10				6										
17		5	Preston North End	1-0	Cammack	2007	1	2	3	4	5		7	8	9							6	11									
18		9	SWINDON TOWN	0-2		1920	1	2		4	5		7	8		12	3	10				6	11	9								
19		23	Rochdale	0-1		1430	1	2		4	5		7	8	9	12	11	10				3	6									
20		30	BURNLEY	1-1	Hawley	2001	1	2		4	5				9	10	11		8			3	6		7							
21	Dec	14	Chester City	1-1	Hawley	2657	1	2			5				9		11	10	8	4		3	6		7							
22		22	HALIFAX TOWN	3-3	Hawley 3 (1 p)	2285	1	2		12	5				9		11	10	8	4		3	6		7							
23		26	HARTLEPOOL UNITED	1-0	Matthews M	2495	1	2		11	5				9	10			8	4		3	6		7							
24	Jan	1	Stockport County	0-0		3504	1	2		10	5				9	11			8	4		3	6		7							
25		11	PETERBOROUGH UTD.	2-0	Broddle, Whitehead	1832	1	2		4	5				9	10	11		8	12		3	6		7							
26		18	Torquay United	0-1		1064	1	2			5				9	10	11		8	4		3	6			7						
27		24	SOUTHEND UNITED	2-0	Hill, Broddle	1463	1	2		5					9	10	11		8	4		3	6			7	12					
28		31	Tranmere Rovers	1-2	Hawley	1417	1	2		4	5				9	10	11		8			3	6			7						
29	Feb	3	Port Vale	1-3	Graham	2977	1	2		4	5				9	10	11		8			3	6			7	12					
30	Mar	1	ALDERSHOT	1-0	Hawley	1270	1	2		4	5				9	10	11		8	7		3				6						
31		4	Crewe Alexandra	0-4		1072	1	2		4	5				9	10	11		8	7		3				6						
32		8	ORIENT	2-2	Whitehead, Cammack	1478	1	2		4	5			12	9		11		8			3			7	6		10				
33		15	Cambridge United	1-0	Cammack	1785	1	2		4	5			10	12		11		8			3	6		7			9				
34		18	NORTHAMPTON T	1-0	Broddle	1355	1	2			5				9	12	4		8			3			7	6		10				
35		22	Hereford United	1-1	Graham	2367		2			5				8	9	4		11			3			7			10	1	6		
36		25	Mansfield Town	1-1	Travis	3919		2			5				9	8	4		11			3			7			10	1	6		
37		28	STOCKPORT COUNTY	2-3	Dixon, Cammack	2025		2		4	5				9	8	12		11			3			7			10	1	6		
38	Apr	1	Hartlepool United	1-0	Cammack	2781					5				8		4		11			2	3		7			10	1	6		9
39		4	PRESTON NORTH END	1-3	Cammack	2261				12	5				8		4		11			2	3		7			10	1	6		9
40		12	Swindon Town	1-1	Hunter	6783		2		4	5				8				11			3			7			10	1	6		9
41		15	COLCHESTER UNITED	1-0	Dixon	1238		2		4	5				8	12			11			3			7			10	1	6		9
42		18	ROCHDALE	3-1	Broddle, Houchen, Lister	1406		2		4				7	8	12			11			3	5					10	1	6		9
43		22	EXETER CITY	1-0	Cammack	1343		2						7	8	4	10		11			3	5						1	6		9
44		26	Burnley	2-1	Houchen, Overson (og)	2542		2						12	8	4	7		11			3	5					10	1	6		9
45		29	Wrexham	0-1		1042		2		4	5				8	7			11			3	10						1	6		9
46	May	3	CHESTER CITY	2-0	Brolly, Cammack	2256		2		4				7	8	10			11			3	5				12		1	6		9

	Apps	34	42	17	37	41	9	20	33	41	31	42	18	21	11	1	31	25	2	1	6	14	5	2	12	12	12	9
	Goals				2	3	1	2	12	7	5	2		7	1						2					1		1	2

Two own goals

F.A. Cup

		Date	Opponent	Result	Scorers	Att																										
R1	Nov	16	Halifax Town	3-1	Hill, Broddle, Lister	1501	1	2		4	5		7	8	9	12	11	10				3	6									
R2	Dec	7	ROCHDALE	2-2	Graham, Hill	2868	1	2		7	5				9	10	11		8	4		3	6									
rep		10	Rochdale	1-2	Broddle	5066	1	2		4	5				9	7	11	10	8			3	6									

Milk Cup (F.L. Cup)

		Date	Opponent	Result	Scorers	Att																										
R1/1	Aug	20	Darlington	2-3	Lister, Cammack	2159	1	2	3	4	5	6	7	8	9	10	11		12													
R1/2	Sep	10	DARLINGTON	0-0		1504	1	2	3	4	5	6	7	8	9			11	10	12												

Freight Rover Trophy (Associate Members Cup)

		Date	Opponent	Result	Scorers	Att																										
R1	Jan	15	Lincoln City	3-1	Money, Hawley (p), Whitehead	1235	1	2			5				9	10	11		8	4		3	6		7							
R1		21	HALIFAX TOWN	3-2	Matthews M, Hawley 2	1244	1	2		4	5				9	10	11		8	7		3	6				12	14				
QF	Mar	10	PORT VALE	1-1	Hawley	1415	1	2		4	5			9		12	11		8	7		3	6					10				

QF lost on penalties (4-3) a.e.t.

1986/87 8th in Division 4

#	Date	Opponent	Score	Scorers	Att
1	Aug 23	NORTHAMPTON T	2-2	Cammack, Hunter	2302
2	30	Burnley	0-1		2958
3	Sep 7	CREWE ALEXANDRA	2-1	Johnson, Hunter	2098
4	13	Orient	1-3	Birch	1857
5	16	Aldershot	1-2	McLean	1696
6	19	PRESTON NORTH END	4-0	Lister 2, Broddle, Russell	2689
7	30	CAMBRIDGE UNITED	1-1	Broddle	1694
8	Oct 5	WOLVERHAMPTON W.	0-2		3296
9	11	Swansea City	2-1	Whitehead, Broddle	5412
10	17	TORQUAY UNITED	2-0	McLean, Johnson	1703
11	21	Tranmere Rovers	0-1		1469
12	25	Cardiff City	1-1	Johnson	2145
13	Nov 1	WREXHAM	3-3	Richardson, Johnson, Broddle	1948
14	4	Southend United	1-3	Johnson	2789
15	9	HALIFAX TOWN	2-1	Johnson, Lister	2059
16	21	COLCHESTER UNITED	5-2	Lister, Broddle, Johnson 2, McLean(p)	1725
17	29	Hereford United	2-2	Rodgerson (og), Hill	2003
18	Dec 13	Rochdale	1-1	Lister	1244
19	19	EXETER CITY	3-1	Reeves 2, Hill	1545
20	26	Peterborough United	1-1	Russell	4267
21	27	LINCOLN CITY	2-1	Harle, Lister	4299
22	Jan 1	HARTLEPOOL UNITED	1-2	Richardson	2726
23	3	Colchester United	0-1		2100
24	24	Crewe Alexandra	2-2	De Mange, Broddle	1430
25	31	TRANMERE ROVERS	6-0	*See below	1611
26	Feb 7	ALDERSHOT	2-0	North 2	1991
27	10	ORIENT	0-2		2087
28	14	Preston North End	1-2	Birch	7968
29	21	STOCKPORT COUNTY	1-2	Hunter	1752
30	28	Cambridge United	0-1		2136
31	Mar 3	Wrexham	1-1	Lister	1360
32	7	CARDIFF CITY	1-3	Smith	1936
33	11	Northampton Town	0-1		5352
34	14	Torquay United	2-2	Johnson, Flounders	1393
35	21	SWANSEA CITY	3-2	Johnson, Flounders, Lister	1590
36	28	Wolverhampton Wan.	0-1		7348
37	Apr 3	Halifax Town	1-1	Lister (p)	1232
38	11	SOUTHEND UNITED	3-0	Broddle, Johnson 2	1602
39	13	Stockport County	0-1		1773
40	17	Hartlepool United	2-0	Harle, Flounders	1713
41	20	PETERBOROUGH UTD.	2-0	Hill, Gage (og)	2470
42	25	Exeter City	0-0		1525
43	28	BURNLEY	2-1	Johnson 2	1770
44	May 1	HEREFORD UNITED	3-1	Johnson, Broddle, Russell	1660
45	4	Lincoln City	2-1	Flounders 2	2567
46	9	ROCHDALE	2-0	Lister, Flounders	2347

Scorers in game 25: Hunter, Lister, De Mange, Johnson, Broddle 2

Two own goals

F.A. Cup

Rd	Date	Opponent	Score	Scorers	Att
R1	Nov 15	SOUTHPORT	2-0	Hill, Broddle	2601
R2	Dec 6	RUNCORN	1-0	Broddle	3006
R3	Jan 10	Tottenham Hotspur	2-3	Johnson S, De Mange	19339

Littlewoods Challenge Cup (F.L. Cup)

Rd	Date	Opponent	Score	Scorers	Att
R1/1	Aug 26	DARLINGTON	2-0	Lister, Hill	1350
R1/2	Sep 2	Darlington	2-1	Lister 2	1469
R2/1	23	IPSWICH TOWN	1-2	Broddle	3919
R2/2	Oct 7	Ipswich Town	0-2		6587

Freight Rover Trophy (Associate Members Cup)

Rd	Date	Opponent	Score	Scorers	Att
PR	Nov 25	Lincoln City	0-1		1003
PR	Dec 2	HARTLEPOOL UNITED	1-0	Broddle	952
R1	Jan 27	WREXHAM	1-2	Hunter	1227

1987/88 4th in Division 4

					Green RR	Russell WM	Longden DP	McLean DJ	Brown AJ	Nicol PJ	Dixon KL	Harle D	Daws A	Flounders AJ	Hill DM	Atkins MN	Johnson SA	Broddle JR	Stevenson AJ	Lister SH	Heyes D	Money R	Birch A	Taylor K	Reeves D	Cowling DR	Taylor MJ	Shearer DJ	Richardson IP	Johnson P
1	Aug	15	TRANMERE ROVERS	3-0 Russell, Flounders 2	2277	1	2	3	4	5	6	7	8	9	10	11														
2		22	Carlisle United	1-3 Johnson	2074	1	2	3	4		6	7	8		10	11	5	9	12											
3		29	COLCHESTER UNITED	2-2 Johnson, Flounders	2003	1	2	3	4	5	6	7	8		10	11		9	12											
4		31	Wolverhampton Wan.	1-4 Flounders	6672	1	2	3	4	5	6	7	8		10			9	11	12										
5	Sep	5	ROCHDALE	1-0 Dixon	1969	1	2	3		5		7	8		10	11	6	9	4										
6		12	Cambridge United	3-3 Flounders 2, Harle	1830	1	2	3		5		7	8		10		6	9	11	4										
7		15	BOLTON WANDERERS	1-1 Russell (p)	2501		2	3		5		7	8		10		6	9	11	4	1									
8		19	NEWPORT COUNTY	3-1 Flounders 2, Atkins	2004		2	3		5		7	8		10		6	9	11	4	1									
9		26	Darlington	4-1 Russell, Dixon, Lister, Flounders	1638	1	2	3			5	7	8		10		6	9		4		11								
10		29	STOCKPORT COUNTY	0-0	2181	1	2	3			5	7	8		10		6	9		4		11	12							
11	Oct	3	Peterborough United	1-1 Dixon	3594	1	2	3		5		7	8		10		6	9		4		11	12							
12		10	HALIFAX TOWN	1-0 Johnson	2105	1	2					7	8		10	11	3	9		5		6		4						
13		17	Hereford United	3-2 Reeves 3	2092	1	2	11				7	8		10		3			5		6		4	9					
14		20	Burnley	1-1 Flounders	6323	1	2	11				7	8		10		3		12	5		6		4	9					
15		24	CARDIFF CITY	2-1 Ford(og), Taylor	2872	1	2	11				7	8		10		3		12	5		6		4	9					
16		31	Hartlepool United	0-1	2763	1	2	11			6	7	8		10		3		12	5				4	9					
17	Nov	7	WREXHAM	3-1 Reeves, Flounders 2	2348	1	2	3			5	7	8		10					5		6		4	9					
18		7	SCARBOROUGH	0-1	4506	1	2	3				7	8		10		14	12		5		6		4	9	11				
19		21	Crewe Alexandra	2-2 Atkins, Flounders	2045	1	2	3				7	8		10		11	9		5		6		4						
20		28	SWANSEA CITY	1-2 Flounders	2309	1	2	3				7	8	12	10		11	9		5		6		4						
21	Dec	12	Exeter City	1-1 Johnson	1831		2	3				7	8	12	10		11		14	5	1	6		4						
22		18	TORQUAY UNITED	2-3 Impey(og), Russell	2261		7	3					8	11	10		2	9		14		5		4		1				
23		26	DARLINGTON	1-0 Flounders	3140		2	3			6		7	8	11	10		9		5				4		1				
24		28	Leyton Orient	1-1 Harle	5542		2	3				9	7	8	11	10				5		6		4		1				
25	Jan	1	Colchester United	3-0 Daws 2, Lister	2287		2	3				9	7	8	11	10				5				4		1				
26		2	CAMBRIDGE UNITED	3-2 Hill, Taylor K, Daws	3252		2	3		12	6		7	8	9	10	11			5				4		1				
27		16	Newport County	1-1 Taylor K	1760			3		6			7		9	10	11		12	8		5	2	4		1				
28		30	WOLVERHAMPTON W.	0-1	5476		2	3		6			7	8		10	11	9		5				4		1				
29	Feb	6	Rochdale	1-2 Flounders	1455		2	3		6			7	8		10	11	12		5		9		4		1				
30		13	LEYTON ORIENT	3-2 Harle 2, Shearer	2951	1	2	3		6				8		10	11	12		5		7		4				9		
31		20	Tranmere Rovers	3-1 Flounders 2, Lister	2803	1	2	3		6				8		10	11	12		5		7		4				9		
32		27	PETERBOROUGH UTD.	5-0 Shearer, Flounders 3, Gunn(og)	3378	1	2	3		6				8		10	11			5		7		4				9		
33	Mar	1	Stockport County	1-1 Shearer	1834	1	2	3				6	14	8		10	11	12		5		7		4				9		
34		5	HEREFORD UNITED	3-0 Hill, Taylor, Lister	3413	1		3				6	12	8		10	11			5		7		4				9		
35		12	Halifax Town	2-2 Harle (p), Lister	1807	1		3		12		6	7	8		10	11	9		5		2		4						
36		19	HARTLEPOOL UNITED	3-0 Flounders, Dixon, Hill	3783	1		3				6	7	8		10	11	12		5		2		4				9		
37		26	Cardiff City	1-0 Shearer	4527	1		3		12		6	7		8	10	11	2	14	5		2		4				9		
38	Apr	2	Scarborough	0-0	4677	1		3				6	7	8		10	11			5		2		4				9		
39		4	CREWE ALEXANDRA	2-1 Flounders, Taylor K	4091	1		3				6	7	8		10	11	12		5		2		4				9		
40		9	Wrexham	1-2 Shearer	2589	1		3		12		6	7	8			11	10	14	5		2		4				9		
41		12	CARLISLE UNITED	1-0 Shearer	3514	1		3				6	7	8		10	11			5		2		4				9		
42		19	Bolton Wanderers	0-0	6669	1						6	7	8		10	11	3		5		2		4				9		
43		23	BURNLEY	1-1 Harle (p)	5347	1		3		5	6	7	8			10	11	2	12					4				9		
44		30	Swansea City	1-1 Lister	3482	1	7	3		12	6	14	8			10	11			5		2		4				9		
45	May	2	EXETER CITY	1-1 Shearer	6736	1		3		7	6		8			10	11		12	5		2		4				9		
46		7	Torquay United	2-1 Flounders, Richardson	4989	1		3			6		8	9		10	11		14	12	5	2		4					7	

| | Apps | 35 | 34 | 44 | 4 | 22 | 25 | 41 | 45 | 10 | 45 | 26 | 22 | 32 | 7 | 8 | 39 | 3 | 32 | 2 | 35 | 6 | 1 | 8 | 15 | 1 | 0 |
| | Goals | | 4 | | | | | 4 | 6 | 3 | 24 | 3 | 2 | 4 | | | 6 | | | | 5 | 4 | | | 7 | 1 | |

Three own goals

Play Offs

SF1	May	15	Torquay United	1-2 Flounders	4602	1		3	8		6				9	10	11			2	5				4				12	7	
SF2		18	TORQUAY UNITED	1-1 Lister (p)	6482	1		3	6					12		9	10	11	14		2	5				4				8	7	

F.A. Cup

R1	Nov	14	BURY	3-1 Russell 3 (1 p)	3151	1	2	3				7	8		10		11	9		5		6		4							
R2	Dec	5	SUNDERLAND	2-1 Taylor, Harle	7178	1	2	3				7	8		10		11	9		5		6		4							
R3	Jan	9	BLACKPOOL	0-0	6217		2	3		6			7	8	9	10	11			5				4							1
rep		12	Blackpool	0-1	6127		2	3		6			7	8	9	10	11		14	5		12		4							1

Littlewoods Challenge Cup (F.L. Cup)

R1/1	Aug	18	HARTLEPOOL UNITED	3-1 Hill, Nicol, Russell (p)	1613	1	2	3	4	5	6	7	8		10	11		9													
R1/2		26	Hartlepool United	1-0 Johnson	872	1	2	3	4	5	6	7	8		10	11		9													
R2/1	Sep	23	Leicester City	1-2 Flounders	7718		2	3			5	7	8		10		6	9				4	1	11	12						
R2/2	Oct	6	LEICESTER CITY	1-2 Johnson	4031	1	2	12		5		7	8		10		6	9				4		3	11						

Freight Rover Trophy (Associate Members Cup)

PR	Oct	13	GRIMSBY TOWN	2-0 Dixon, Stevenson	1710		2	11				7	8		10		3	9	12	5	1	6		4							
PR	Nov	24	Halifax Town	0-3	686		2			6	4	7	8	9	10		11	12		5	1										
Po	Dec	15	Grimsby Town	2-1 Harle, Flounders	970			3			5	7	8	11	10			9	2		1	6		4							
R2	Jan	19	Mansfield Town	0-1	3637			3				7	8	9	10	12	6	14		11	5		2	4							

1988/89 4th in Division 4

#	Date		Opponent	Score	Scorers	Att	Musselwhite PS	Longden DP	Rumble P	Taylor K	Lister SH	Brown AJ	Hodkinson AJ	Winter J	Shearer DJ	Flounders AJ	Cowling DR	Daws A	Stevenson AJ	Richardson IP	Money R	Smalley PT	Harle D	Hamilton IR	Brown DJ	Nicol PJ	Cork D	Cotton P	Alexander G
1	Aug	27	HEREFORD UNITED	3-1	Cowling, Daws, Taylor	3663	1	2	3	4	5	6	7	8	9	10	11	12											
2	Sep	3	Crewe Alexandra	2-3	Flounders, Lister (p)	1514	1	2		4	5	6	7	8		10	11	9	3	12									
3		10	GRIMSBY TOWN	1-1	Lister	6037	1	2	3	4	5	6	7	8		10	11	9											
4		17	York City	2-1	Daws 2	2735	1	2	3	4	5		7	8		10	11	9	6										
5		20	CARLISLE UNITED	1-1	Flounders	3113	1	2	3	4	5	6	7			10	11	9	8	12	14								
6		24	Exeter City	2-2	Daws, Rumble	1876	1	2	3	4	5	6	7			10	11	9	8	12									
7	Oct	1	SCARBOROUGH	0-3		4167	1			3	4	5	7			10		9				11	2	8					
8		5	Lincoln City	0-1		5443	1			3	4	5	12	7		10		9	6		11		2	8					
9		8	Colchester United	2-1	Flounders, Richardson	1299	1	12	3	4	5	11	7			10		9	6	14			2	8					
10		15	CAMBRIDGE UNITED	1-0	Taylor	3514	1		3	4	5	11	7			10		9	6				2	8					
11		22	Rochdale	0-1		2250	1		3	4	5	6	7			10	11	9					2	8					
12		25	WREXHAM	3-1	Daws, Hodkinson, Flounders	2999	1		3	4	5		7			10	11	9	6				2	8					
13		29	Peterborough United	2-1	Hodkinson, Harle (p)	3532	1		3		5		7			10	11	9	6		4		2	8					
14	Nov	5	BURNLEY	2-1	Flounders, Lister	6358	1		3		5		7			10	11	9	6		4		2	8					
15		8	Rotherham United	3-3	Flounders, Lister, Hodkinson	5923	1		3		5		7			10	11	9	6		4		2	8					
16		12	LEYTON ORIENT	2-2	Daws 2	4239	1		3		12	5	7			10	11	9	6	14	4		2	8					
17		26	TORQUAY UNITED	1-0	Daws	3359	1		3	4	5	12	7			10	11	9	6				2	8					
18	Dec	3	Darlington	3-3	Smalley, Daws, Lister	1745	1		3	4	5	11	7			10		9	6				2	8					
19		17	Doncaster Rovers	2-2	Hodkinson, Flounders	3381	1		3	4	5	6	7			10	11	9	2	12				8					
20		26	HARTLEPOOL UNITED	1-1	Harle (p)	4595	1		3	4	5	6	7			10	11	9	12				2	8	14				
21		31	TRANMERE ROVERS	0-1		4154	1		3	4	5	6	7			10	11	9	14				2	8	12				
22	Jan	2	Halifax Town	1-5	Hamilton	2650	1		3	4	5	6	7			12		9	11				2	8	10				
23		7	Stockport County	2-1	Flounders, Daws	2656	1		3	4	5		7			10	14	9	6				2	8	11	1	12		
24		14	CREWE ALEXANDRA	2-2	Daws 2	4032	1	12		4	5	14	7			10	3	9	6				2	8	11	1			
25		21	Hereford United	2-1	Hodkinson, Daws	2024			3	4		6	7			10	8	9					2		11	1	5		
26		28	YORK CITY	4-2	Smith(og), Brown A, Daws 2	4196			3	4		6	7			10	8	9					2		11	1	5		
27	Feb	4	Carlisle United	3-0	Lister, Taylor (p), Flounders	2627			3	4	7	6				10	8	9					2		11	1	5		
28		11	EXETER CITY	2-0	Lister, Cowling	4102	1			4	7	6				10	8	9	3				2		11				
29		18	COLCHESTER UNITED	2-3	Lister, Nicol	4286	1			4	7	6	12			10	8	9	3				2		11		5	14	
30		25	Cambridge United	3-0	Taylor, Flounders, Daws	2563	1			4	7	6	3			10	8	9					2		11		5		
31		28	Wrexham	0-2		2609	1		3	4	7	6	5			10	8	9					2		11		12		
32	Mar	4	ROCHDALE	4-0	Daws 2, Brown A, Hodkinson	4098	1		3	4	7	6	5			10	8	9					2		11		14	12	
33		11	Burnley	1-0	Lister	6813	1		3		7	6				10	8	9					2		11		5	4	
34		14	PETERBOROUGH UTD.	3-0	Flounders 3	3983	1		3		7	6				10	8	9					2		11		5	4	
35		18	Grimsby Town	1-1	Flounders	9796	1		3	12	7	6				10	8	9					2		11		5	4	
36		25	HALIFAX TOWN	0-0		4591	1		3	4	7	6	12			10	8	9							11		5		
37		27	Hartlepool United	2-0	Flounders, Daws	1923	1		3	4		6	7			10	8	9					2		11		5	12	
38	Apr	1	DONCASTER ROVERS	2-1	Taylor (p), Hodkinson	5334	1		3	4		6	7			10	8	9					2		11		5	12	
39		4	STOCKPORT COUNTY	1-1	Taylor (p)	3958	1		3	4			7			10	8	9	6				2		11		5	12	14
40		8	Tranmere Rovers	1-2	Daws	10465	1		3	4			12			10	8	9	6		7		2		11		5	14	
41		15	Scarborough	0-1		4456	1		3	4		6	7			10	8	9					2		11		5	12	
42		22	LINCOLN CITY	0-0		5729	1		3	4			7			10	8	9					2		11		5	6	
43		28	Torquay United	2-0	Daws, Hodkinson	2544	1		3	4			7			10	8	9	12				2		11		5	6	
44	May	1	ROTHERHAM UNITED	0-0		8775	1		3	4			7			10		9	8	12			2		11		5	6	
45		6	DARLINGTON	5-1	Daws 3, Taylor, Flounders	5296	1		3	4			7			10	8	9					2		11		5	6	
46		13	Leyton Orient	1-4	Taylor	6366	1		3	4			7			10	8	9					2		11		5	6	
			Apps				41	41	8	41	34	32	41	4	1	46	39	46	26	9	6	39	18	27	5	23	15	1	0
			Goals						1	8	9	2	8			16	2	24		1		1	2	1		1			

One own goal

Play Offs

	Date		Opponent	Score	Scorers	Att																							
SF1	May	21	Wrexham	1-3	Cowling	5449	1		3	4			7			10	8	9					2		11		5	6	12
SF2		24	WREXHAM	0-2		5516	1		3	4			7			10	8	9		14	12		2		11		5	6	

F.A. Cup

	Date		Opponent	Score	Scorers	Att																							
R1	Nov	19	Blackpool	1-2	Harle (p)	3976	1		3	4	5	14	7			10	11	9	6	12			2	8					

Littlewoods Challenge Cup (F.L. Cup)

	Date		Opponent	Score	Scorers	Att																							
R1/1	Aug	30	HUDDERSFIELD TOWN	3-2	Flounders, Lister, Hodkinson	3820	1	2		4	5	6	7			10	11	9	3	12	8								
R1/2	Sep	6	Huddersfield Town	2-2	Flounders 2	4237	1	2		4	5	6	7			10	11	9	3		8								
R2/1		27	CHELSEA	4-1	Daws 2, Stevenson, Taylor	5061	1		3	4	5	6	7			10		9	2	11				8					
R2/2	Oct	12	Chelsea	2-2	Harle (p), Flounders	5814	1		3	4	5	11	7			10		9	6	12			2	8					
R3	Nov	2	Bradford City	1-1	Daws	8011	1		3		5		7			10	11	9	6		4		2	8					
rep		22	BRADFORD CITY	0-1		5793	1		3	4	5	12	7			10	11	9	6				2	8					

R1/2 a.e.t.

Sherpa Van Trophy (Associate Members Cup)

	Date		Opponent	Score	Scorers	Att																							
PR	Dec	6	HALIFAX TOWN	1-2	Harle (p)	1547	1		3		4	5	11	7		10		9	6				2	8					12
PR		13	Huddersfield Town	0-1		2216	1		3			5	4	7		12	10	9	6	11			2	8					

1989/90 11th in Division 4

#	Date		Opponent	Score	Scorers	Att	Litchfield P	Smalley PT	Longden DP	Taylor K	Knight IJ	Tucker G	Hodkinson AJ	Cowling DR	Cotton P	Flounders AJ	Marshall G	Nicol PJ	Money R	Butler MC	Daws A	Hamilton IR	Musselwhite PS	Stevenson AJ	Lillis MA	Lister SH	Ward PT	Hall RA	Bramhall J	Alexander G	Cox NJ
1	Aug	19	Lincoln City	0-1		4504	1	2	3	4	5	6	7	8	9	10	11	12													
2		26	ROCHDALE	0-1		2808	1	2	12	4	3	6		8		10	11	5	7	9											
3	Sep	2	Gillingham	3-0	Taylor (p), Flounders 2	3467		2	3	4		6	7	8		10	11	5			9	12	1								
4		9	SCARBOROUGH	0-1		3330		2	3	4		6	7			10	11	5			9	8	1								
5		16	Peterborough United	1-1	Taylor	4350		2	3	4		6	7			10	11	5		9		8	1	12							
6		23	EXETER CITY	5-4	Lillis 2, Hamilton 2, Taylor	2935		2	3	4		6	7	12		10	11	5				8	1		9						
7		26	TORQUAY UNITED	2-0	Flounders, Lillis (p)	3242		2	3	4		6	7			10	11	5				8	1		9						
8		30	Aldershot	2-4	Lillis, Tucker	1892		2	3	4		6	7	14		10	11	5			12	8	1		9						
9	Oct	7	Hartlepool United	2-3	Lillis, Daws	1823		2	3	4		6	7	12		14	11	5			10	8			9						
10		14	MAIDSTONE UNITED	1-0	Lister (p)	3165	1	2	3	4			7			12	11				10	8			6	9	5				
11		17	Carlisle United	1-0	Lillis	4793	1	2	3	4		12	7			14	11				10	8			6	9	5				
12		21	COLCHESTER UNITED	4-0	Stevenson, Daws, Hamilton, Taylor	3254	1	2	3	4			7				11				10	8			6	9	5				
13		28	Cambridge United	3-5	Marshall, Daws, Hamilton	2395	1	2	3	4						14	11				10	8			6	9	5	12			
14		31	YORK CITY	1-1	Flounders	3800	1	2	3				5	7		10	11				9	8			6			4			
15	Nov	4	Doncaster Rovers	2-1	Daws, Flounders	3374	1		3					2		10	11	5			9	8			6	7		4			
16		11	BURNLEY	3-0	Marshall, Ward (p), Hamilton	4745	1		3					9	2	10	11	5				8			6	7		4			
17		25	Stockport County	2-4	Ward, Flounders	3259	1		3					9	2	10	11	5				8			6	7		4			
18	Dec	2	SOUTHEND UNITED	1-1	Ward	3714	1	2	3	8			9		14	10	11	5							6	7	12	4			
19		16	Hereford United	2-1	Nicol, Lillis	1924	1	2	3	8				4	14	12	11	6			9	10				7	5				
20		26	GRIMSBY TOWN	2-2	Daws, Marshall	8384	1	2	3	8				4		12	11	6			9	10				7			5		
21		30	CHESTERFIELD	0-1		5006		2	3	8				4		9	11	5			12	10	1		6	7					
22	Jan	1	Wrexham	0-0		1887		2	3	4			7	11		10		6			9	8	1	5							
23		6	HALIFAX TOWN	1-1	Taylor	3051		2	3	4				11	6	10	7				12	8	1	5	9						
24		13	Rochdale	0-3		1781		2	3	4				8	6	10	7				9	11	1	5							
25		20	LINCOLN CITY	1-1	Lillis	3830		2	3	14				8	6	10	7				9	11	1		12		4		5		
26		27	Scarborough	0-0		2329		2	3	6				8			7				9	11	1		10		4		5		
27	Feb	10	PETERBOROUGH UTD.	0-0		3188		2	3	6				8		12	7				9	11	1		10		4		5		
28		13	GILLINGHAM	0-0		2226		2	3	6				8		9	7				12	11	1		10		4		5		
29		16	Southend United	0-0		3154		2	3	6				8		10					9	11	1	12	7		4		5		
30		24	STOCKPORT COUNTY	5-0	Lillis 2, Daws 2, Ward	3280		2	3	6				8		10					9	11	1	12	7		4		5		
31	Mar	3	Halifax Town	1-0	Daws	1793		2	3				7	8		10					9	11	1	6			4		5		
32		6	ALDERSHOT	3-2	Lillis, Hamilton, Flounders	3202		2	3				8			10	12				9	11	1	6	7		4		5		
33		10	Torquay United	3-0	Daws, Flounders, Lillis	1935		2	3				6	8		10					9	11	1	12	7		4		5		
34		17	HARTLEPOOL UNITED	0-1		3868		2	3	14			6	8		10	12	5			9	11	1		7		4				
35		21	Maidstone United	1-1	Flounders	1299		2	3	6				8		10	7				9	11					4		5		
36		24	CARLISLE UNITED	2-3	Flounders, Lillis (p)	3406		2	3	6				8	9	10	7					11	1		12		4		5		
37		28	Exeter City	0-1		5805		2	3	6				8	9	10						11	1		7		4		5		
38		31	Colchester United	0-1		2920		2	3	6				8	9	10	14				12	11	1		7		4		5		
39	Apr	7	CAMBRIDGE UNITED	1-1	Taylor	2486		2	3	6					12	10					9	11	1	8	7		4		5		
40		10	York City	1-0	Taylor	2232		2	3	6				7		9	10					11	1	8			4		5		
41		14	WREXHAM	3-1	Flounders 2 (1 p), Taylor	2820		2	3	6				7		9	10	4				11	1	8					5		
42		17	Grimsby Town	1-2	Flounders	11894		2	3	6				7		9	10	4				11	1	8					5		
43		21	HEREFORD UNITED	3-3	Flounders 2 (1 p), Pejic (og)	2247		2	3	6				7	4	9	10				8	11	1	12					5		
44		28	Burnley	1-0	Cotton	3902	1	2	3	6					7	9	10				8	11					4		5		
45	May	1	Chesterfield	1-1	Daws	3469	1	2	3	6		7				9	10				8	11					4		5		
46		5	DONCASTER ROVERS	4-1	Flounders 3, Daws	3020	1	2	3	6		7				9	10				8	11					4		5		
						Apps	17	44	46	39	2	15	21	32	17	44	34	18	1	2	33	43	29	24	29	6	25	1	21	0	0
						Goals				8		1			1	18	3	1			11	6		1	13	1	4				

One own goal

F.A. Cup

	Date		Opponent	Score	Scorers	Att																									
R1	Nov	18	MATLOCK TOWN	4-1	Lillis 3, Hodkinson	4307	1	12	3					9	2	10	11	5				8			6	7		4			
R2	Dec	9	BURNLEY	2-2	Taylor 2	5698	1	12	3	8				9	2	10	11								6	7	5	4			
rep		12	Burnley	1-1	Daws	7682	1	2	3	10				12		14	11				9	8			6	7	5	4			
rep2		18	Burnley	0-5		7429	1	2	3	8				4		12	14	11	6		9	10				7	5				

R2 replay a.e.t.

Littlewoods Challenge Cup (F.L. Cup)

	Date		Opponent	Score	Scorers	Att																									
R1/1	Aug	23	Scarborough	0-2		2259	1	2	3	4		6		8	9	10	11	5	7						12						
R1/2		29	SCARBOROUGH	1-1	Flounders	1853		2	3	4		6	7	8		10	11	5		9			1								

Leyland DAF Trophy (Associate Members Cup)

	Date		Opponent	Score	Scorers	Att																									
PR	Nov	7	SCARBOROUGH	1-0	Flounders	1496	1		3					9	2	10	11	5				8			6	7		4			
PR	Dec	22	Carlisle United	1-1	Taylor	1942		2	3	8					7	10					9	11	1	6					5	4	12
R1	Jan	9	Tranmere Rovers	1-2	Cotton	2766		2	3	4			14	11	6	10	7	12			9	8	1	5							

1990/91 8th in Division 4

#		Date	Opponent	Score	Scorers	Att	Litchfield P	Longden DP	Cowling DR	Ward PT	Hicks SJ	Hall RA	Taylor K	Hamilton IR	Lillis MA	Flounders AJ	Marshall G	Miller I	Daws A	Smalley PT	Cotton P	Musselwhite PS	Cox NJ	Bramhall J	Powell G	Stevenson AJ	Joyce JP	Humphries G	Hill DM	Hine M	Lister SH	Alexander G	Tucker G
1	Aug	25	BLACKPOOL	2-0	Flounders, Hamilton	3024	1	2	3	4	5	6	7	8	9	10	11																
2	Sep	1	Aldershot	2-3	Flounders (p), Daws	2001	1	2	3	4	5	6	7	12		10	11	8	9	14													
3		8	PETERBOROUGH UTD.	1-1	Flounders	3028	1	2	3	4	5			8	9	10	11	7			6												
4		15	Maidstone United	1-6	Lillis	1778	1	2	3	4	5		11	8	9	10		7			6												
5		18	Torquay United	1-1	Lillis	2811	1	2	3	4	5	6	12	8	9	10	11	7		14													
6		22	LINCOLN CITY	2-1	Hicks, Hall	2844	1	2	3	4	5	6	12	8	9	10	11	7															
7		29	CARDIFF CITY	0-2		2573	1	2	3	4	5	6	12	8	9	10	11	7	14														
8	Oct	2	Walsall	0-3		3676	1	2	3	4	5	6		8		10	11	7	9														
9		6	Halifax Town	0-0		1468		2	3	4	5	6	8			12			9		10	1	7	11									
10		13	GILLINGHAM	1-0	Hall	2357		2		4	5	6	8			10		3	9			1	7	11									
11		20	SCARBOROUGH	3-0	Daws 2, Taylor	2786		2		4	5	6	8			10		3	9			1	7	11									
12		23	Chesterfield	0-1		3371		2		4	5	6	8			10		3		14	9		12	1	7	11							
13		27	Darlington	0-0		3852		2		4	5	6	8			10		3	9			1	7	11									
14	Nov	3	STOCKPORT COUNTY	3-0	Lillis, Flounders (p), Daws	2826		2		4	5	6	8			10		3	9			1	7	11									
15		10	ROCHDALE	2-1	Flounders, Cotton	3070		2			5	6	8			10		3	9		12	1	7	11									
16		24	Wrexham	0-1		1333		2			5	6	8			10		3			4	1	7	11	9	12							
17	Dec	1	York City	2-2	Hall, Powell	2495		2		10	5	6	8			3	12		14		4	1	7	11	9								
18		15	DONCASTER ROVERS	1-1	Flounders	3963		2	11	4	5	6	14			3	10		9			8	1	7		12							
19		22	Hereford United	0-2		2218		2	11		5	6	4	12	3	10						8	1	7		9							
20		29	CARLISLE UNITED	2-0	Flounders (p), Lillis	2971		2	11		5			4	9	3	10					8	1	7	6								
21	Jan	1	Burnley	1-1	Lillis	8557		2	11	12	5			4	9	3	10		14			8	1	7	6								
22		12	ALDERSHOT	6-2	Cowling,Flounders 3(1p),Hamilton,Lillis	2727		2	11	8	5	6	4	9	3							12	1	7									
23		19	Blackpool	1-3	Cowling	2494		2	11	8	5	6				10					12	3	1	7									
24		26	MAIDSTONE UNITED	2-2	Ward, Daws	2703		2	11	3	5	6	4	9		10			8				1	7									
25	Feb	2	TORQUAY UNITED	3-0	Cowling, Cox, Flounders	2502		2	11		5	6		8		3			9			4	1	7		12							
26		23	Rochdale	1-2	Daws	1832		2	11	4	5			8	3	10			9				1			6	7						
27		26	HARTLEPOOL UNITED	2-1	Taylor, Lillis	2220		2		4	5		11	8	3	10			9				1			6	7						
28	Mar	2	YORK CITY	2-1	Ward, Daws	2860		2		4	5		11	8	3	10			9				1			6	7						
29		5	NORTHAMPTON T	3-0	Daws, Chard(og), Lillis	2852		2		4	5		11	8	3	10			9				1			6	7						
30		8	Doncaster Rovers	3-2	Flounders 2, Daws	4015		2		4	5		11	8	3	10			9				1				7	6					
31		12	WALSALL	1-0	Daws	3352		2		4	5		11	8	3	10			9				1				7	6					
32		16	Cardiff City	0-1		2873		2		4	5		11	8	3	10			9				1				7	6					
33		19	Gillingham	1-1	Flounders	2324		2		4	5		11	8	3	10			9				1				7	6					
34		23	HALIFAX TOWN	4-4	Flounders (p),Taylor,Humphries,Lillis	3134		2		4	5		11	8	3	10			9			12	1				7	6					
35		30	Northampton Town	1-2	Taylor	3728		2			5		11	8	12	10			9				1				7	6	3	4			
36	Apr	1	HEREFORD UNITED	3-0	Flounders 2, Daws	3001		2			5		11	8	12	10			9				1				7	6	3	4			
37		6	Carlisle United	3-0	Hill, Hine, Dalziel(og)	1909		2			5		11	8		10			9				1				7	6	3	4			
38		9	Hartlepool United	0-2		2840		2			5			11	8	12	10		9				1				7	6	3	4			
39		13	BURNLEY	1-3	Hine	4449		2			5			11	8	12	10		9			14	1				7	6	3	4			
40		17	Lincoln City	2-1	Flounders 2 (1p)	3212		2			5			11		8	10		9				1			12	7		3	4	6		
41		20	Scarborough	1-2	Flounders (p)	2026		2			5			11	12	8	10		9				1			14	7		3	4	6		
42		23	Peterborough United	0-0		5774		2			5			11		8	10		9				1				7		3	4	6		
43		27	CHESTERFIELD	3-0	Daws, Flounders 2	3046		2			5			11	8	3	10		9				1				7			4	6	12	
44	May	4	DARLINGTON	2-1	Flounders, Daws	5769		2			5			11	8	3	10		9				1				7			4	6		
45		7	WREXHAM	2-0	Daws, Lillis	3572		2			5			11	8	3	10		9				1				7			4	6		
46		11	Stockport County	0-5		6212		2			5			11	8	3	10		9				1			12	7		14	4	6		
					Apps		8	46	18	30	46	21	42	34	39	46	7	12	34	3	15	38	17	11	4	9	21	10	9	12	7	1	0
					Goals				3	2	1	3	4	2	10	23			14		1			1		1		1	1	2			

Two own goals

Play Offs

		Date	Opponent	Score	Scorers	Att		Longden			Hicks			Hamilton	Lillis	Flounders			Daws			Musselwhite	Cox			Stevenson	Joyce		Hill	Hine	Lister	Alexander	
SF1	May	19	BLACKPOOL	1-1	Lillis	6536		2			5			11	12	3	10		9				1				7		8	4	6		
SF2		22	Blackpool	1-2	Hill	7596		2			5			11	4	3	10		9				1			6	7		8	12			

F.A. Cup

		Date	Opponent	Score	Scorers	Att		Longden	Cowling	Ward	Hicks	Hall	Taylor	Hamilton	Lillis	Flounders	Marshall	Miller	Daws		Cotton	Musselwhite	Cox	Bramhall	Powell	Stevenson							
R1	Nov	17	Rochdale	1-1	Hicks	3259		2			5	6	8			3	10		9				1		4	1	7	11					12
rep		20	ROCHDALE	2-1	Flounders, Lillis	3761		2			5	6	8			3	10		9				4	1	7	11	12						
R2	Dec	8	TRANMERE ROVERS	3-2	Ward, Lillis, Flounders	3576		2	11	4	5	6		12	3	10			9			8	1	7									
R3	Jan	5	Brighton & Hove Albion	2-3	Flounders (p), Bramhall	7785		2	11	12	5			4	9	3	10					8	1	7	6								

R1 replay a.e.t.

Rumbelows Cup (F.L. Cup)

		Date	Opponent	Score	Scorers	Att	Litchfield	Longden	Cowling	Ward	Hicks	Hall	Taylor	Hamilton	Lillis	Flounders	Marshall	Miller															
R1/1	Aug	28	Carlisle United	0-1		2531	1	2	3	4	5	6	7	8		10	11		9														
R1/2	Sep	4	CARLISLE UNITED	1-1	Lillis	2130	1	2	3	4	5	6			8	9	10	11	7	12													

Leyland DAF Trophy (Associate Members Cup)

		Date	Opponent	Score	Scorers	Att		Longden			Hicks	Hall		Hamilton	Lillis	Flounders	Marshall	Miller	Daws	Smalley	Cotton	Musselwhite	Cox	Bramhall	Powell	Stevenson	Joyce						Tucker
PR	Nov	27	Doncaster Rovers	0-1		1394		2		12	5	6	8			3	10					4	1	7		9	11						
PR	Dec	18	CHESTERFIELD	3-1	Lillis 2, Taylor	859		2	11		5	6	4			3	10		9			8	1	7		12							
R1	Jan	15	Doncaster Rovers	0-0		1635		2	11	8	5	6	4	9			10				12	3	1	7									
R2		29	PRESTON NORTH END	1-4	Flounders	2155		2	11	3	5		4	9			10				8	12	1	7									6

R1 won on penalties (4-3) a.e.t.

1991/92 5th in Division 4

#	Date	Opponent	Score	Scorers	Att	Musselwhite PS	Batch N	Joyce JP	Longden DP	Hine M	Hicks SJ	Humphries G	Alexander G	Hamilton IR	Daws A	Buckley JW	Helliwell I	Martin DS	Lister SH	Hyde GS	Hill DM	White JG	Stevenson AJ	Whitehead PM	Marples C	Samways M	Elliott MS
1	Aug 17	Gillingham	0-4		3480		1	2	3	4	5	6	7	8	9	10	11	12									
2	24	DONCASTER ROVERS	3-2	Helliwell, Alexander, Daws	3505	1		2	3	4	5	6	7	8	9	10	11										
3	31	Blackpool	1-2	Buckley	3273	1		2	3		5	6	7	8	9	10	11	4	12	14							
4	Sep 3	SCARBOROUGH	1-1	Joyce	3185	1		2	3	4	5	6	7	8	9	10	11										
5	7	MAIDSTONE UNITED	2-0	Hill, Daws	2738	1		2	3	4	5	6	7	8	9		11		12	14	10						
6	14	Chesterfield	1-0	Humphries	3338	1		2	3			5	7	8	9		11	4	12		10						
7	17	Barnet	2-3	Humphries, White	3094	1		2	3			6	7	8	9		11	4	5		10	12					
8	21	CREWE ALEXANDRA	1-0	Hamilton	3021	1		2	3			6	7	8	9			4	5	12	10	11					
9	28	Wrexham	0-4		1635	1		2	3	14		6	7	8	9	12	11	4	5		10						
10	Oct 5	HEREFORD UNITED	1-1	Daws (p)	2384	1		2	3	8		6	14		9	7	11	4	5		10		12				
11	12	Carlisle United	0-0		1988	1		2	3			6	12	8	9	7	11	4	5		10						
12	19	Northampton Town	1-0	Helliwell	2575	1		2	3			6		8	9	7	11	4	5		10						
13	26	MANSFIELD TOWN	1-4	Daws	3610	1		2	3		5			8	9	7	11	4			10		6				
14	Nov 2	Cardiff City	2-2	Hill, Own goal (Pike)	2356	1		2	3		5		7	8	9	12	11	4	6		10						
15	5	ROCHDALE	6-2	*see below	2331	1		2	3		5		7	8	9		11	4	6		10						
16	9	ROTHERHAM UNITED	1-0	Daws	4175	1		2	3			5	7	8	9		11	4	6		10						
17	23	Lincoln City	2-4	Martin, Alexander	3078	1			3			5	2	8	9	7	11	4	6		10						
18	30	YORK CITY	1-0	Hamilton	2887			2	3			5	7	8	9		11	4	6		10		1				
19	Dec 14	Burnley	1-1	Own goal (Pender)	8419			2	3		5		7	8	9		11	4		6	10	12	1				
20	20	Doncaster Rovers	2-1	Humphries, Alexander	1825			2	3		5	6	7	8	9		11	4		12	10	14	1				
21	26	GILLINGHAM	2-0	White, Martin	3883			2	3		5	6	7	8	9			4			10	11	1				
22	28	BLACKPOOL	2-1	White 2	4271			2	3		5	6	7	8	9			4		12	10	11	1				
23	Jan 1	Scarborough	1-4	White	2237			2	3		5	6	7	8	9		12	4		14	10	11	1				
24	18	Halifax Town	4-1	White 3, Hamilton	1232			2				5	6	7	8	9		11	4		3	10	1				
25	25	WALSALL	1-1	White	3165			2	3			5	6	7	8			11	4		10	9	1				
26	Feb 8	Mansfield Town	3-1	Alexander, Hamilton (p), White	3496	1		2	3			6	7	8		5	11				10	9					
27	11	York City	0-3		2255	1		2	3	14	5		7	8		6	11	4		12	10	9					
28	15	BURNLEY	2-2	Helliwell, White	5303			2	3	12	5		7	8	14	6	11	4			10	9		1			
29	Mar 3	HALIFAX TOWN	1-0	Buckley	2448	1		2	3		5		7	8	12	10	11	4	6			9					
30	7	Walsall	1-2	Buckley	2722	1		2	3			5	7	8	12	10	11	4	6		14	9					
31	10	Rochdale	0-2		2036	1		2	3	7				8	9	10	11	4	6		5	12					
32	14	CARDIFF CITY	1-0	Buckley	2766	1		2	3	7			12	8	9	10	11	4	6		5	14					
33	21	Rotherham United	0-5		4528	1		2	3			5	14	8	9	10	11	4	6		7	12					
34	28	LINCOLN CITY	0-2		3297	1		2	14		5	6	7	8	9	10	11	4			3	12					
35	31	CHESTERFIELD	2-0	Helliwell, Hamilton (p)	2224				2			6	7	8			10	11	4		3	9				1	5
36	Apr 4	Maidstone United	1-0	Hamilton	1237			2	3			6	7	8			10	11			4	9				1	5
37	11	BARNET	1-1	Hamilton (p)	3361			2	3			6	7	8	12	10	11				4	9				1	5
38	14	NORTHAMPTON T	3-0	Hill, Buckley, Daws	2286			2	3			6	12	8	9	10	11	7			4					1	5
39	18	Crewe Alexandra	1-1	Helliwell	3313			2	3			6		8	9	10	11	7			4					1	5
40	20	WREXHAM	3-1	Joyce, Hamilton (p), Buckley	2900			2	3			6		8		10	11	7			4	9				1	5
41	25	Hereford United	2-1	Helliwell 2	1587			2	3			6	12	8	9	10	11	7			4					1	5
42	May 2	CARLISLE UNITED	4-0	Elliott, Daws, Hill, Helliwell	3851			2	3			6		8	9	10	11	7			4					1	5

Scorers in game 15: Hamilton, A Brown (og), Lister, Helliwell, Alexander, Hill

	Apps	24	1	40	41	10	21	32	36	41	36	28	39	37	19	8	37	22	2	8	1	8	8
	Goals			2				3	5	9	7	6	9	2	1		5	11					1

Three own goals

Play Offs

	Date	Opponent	Score	Scorers	Att			Joyce	Longden			Humphries	Alexander	Hamilton	Daws	Buckley	Helliwell	Martin			Hill	White				Samways	Elliott
SF1	May 10	Crewe Alexandra	2-2	Helliwell 2	6083			2	3			6	12	8	9	10	11	7			4					1	5
SF2	13	CREWE ALEXANDRA	2-0	Martin, Hamilton	7938			2	3			6		8	9	10	11	7			4					1	5
F	23	Blackpool	1-1	Daws	22741			2	3			6	14	8	9	10	11	7		12	4					1	5

Final Played at Wembley. Lost on penalties (4-3) a.e.t.

F.A. Cup

	Date	Opponent	Score	Scorers	Att				Longden		Hicks	Humphries	Alexander	Hamilton	Daws	Buckley	Helliwell	Martin	Lister	Hyde	Hill	White					
R1	Nov 16	ROTHERHAM UNITED	1-1	Helliwell	4511	1			3		5	2	8	9	7	11	4	6	12	10	14						
rep	26	Rotherham United	3-3	Helliwell, Daws, White	4829	1			3	12	5	2	8	9	7	11	4	6		10	14						

Lost on penalties (7-6) a.e.t.

Rumbelows Cup (F.L. Cup)

	Date	Opponent	Score	Scorers	Att																						
R1/1	Aug 20	Wrexham	0-1		1621	1		2	3	4	5	6	7	8	9	10	11		12								
R1/2	27	WREXHAM	3-0	Humphries, Alexander, Helliwell	2125	1		2	3	4	5	6	7	8	9	10	11		12								
R2/1	Sep 24	LEEDS UNITED	0-0		8392	1		2	3			6	7	8	9		11	4	5		10						
R2/2	Oct 8	Leeds United	0-3		14558	1		2	3	14			12	8	9	7	11	4	5		10	6					

Autoglass Trophy (Associate Members Cup)

	Date	Opponent	Score	Scorers	Att																						
PR	Oct 22	BURY	1-3	Hamilton	1122	1		2	3			6	14	8	9	7	11	4	5	12	10						
PR	Jan 7	Halifax Town	2-0	White, Alexander	646			2	3		5		7	8	9			4	6	10		11	1				
R1	21	Hartlepool United	1-2	Hamilton	1351			2			5	6	7	8		12	11	4		9	3	10	1				

FINAL LEAGUE TABLES: 1991/92 - 1998/99

Final League Table 1991/92 Division 4

		Pl.	Home					Away					F.	A.	Pts
			W	D	L	F	A	W	D	L	F	A			
1	Burnley	42	14	4	3	42	16	11	4	6	37	27	79	43	83
2	Rotherham United	42	12	6	3	38	16	10	5	6	32	21	70	37	77
3	Mansfield Town	42	13	4	4	43	26	10	4	7	32	27	75	53	77
4	Blackpool	42	17	3	1	48	13	5	7	9	23	32	71	45	76
5	SCUNTHORPE U	42	14	5	2	39	18	7	4	10	25	41	64	59	72
6	Crewe Alexandra	42	12	6	3	33	20	8	4	9	33	31	66	51	70
7	Barnet	42	16	1	4	48	23	5	5	11	33	38	81	61	69
8	Rochdale	42	12	6	3	34	22	6	7	8	23	31	57	53	67
9	Cardiff City	42	13	3	5	42	26	4	12	5	24	27	66	53	66
10	Lincoln City	42	9	5	7	21	24	8	6	7	29	20	50	44	62
11	Gillingham	42	12	5	4	41	19	3	7	11	22	34	63	53	57
12	Scarborough	42	12	5	4	39	28	3	7	11	25	40	64	68	57
13	Chesterfield	42	6	7	8	26	28	8	4	9	23	33	49	61	53
14	Wrexham	42	11	4	6	31	26	3	5	13	21	47	52	73	51
15	Walsall	42	5	10	6	28	26	7	3	11	20	32	48	58	49
16	Northampton Town	42	5	9	7	25	23	6	4	11	21	34	46	57	46
17	Hereford United	42	9	4	8	31	24	3	4	14	13	33	44	57	44
18	Maidstone United	42	6	9	6	24	22	2	9	10	21	34	45	56	42
19	York City	42	6	9	6	26	23	2	7	12	16	35	42	58	40
20	Halifax Town	42	7	5	9	23	35	3	3	15	11	40	34	75	38
21	Doncaster Rovers	42	6	2	13	21	35	3	6	12	19	30	40	65	35
22	Carlisle United	42	5	9	7	24	27	2	4	15	17	40	41	67	34

Final League Table 1992/93 Division 3 (Formerly Division 4)

		Pl.	Home					Away					F.	A.	Pts
			W	D	L	F	A	W	D	L	F	A			
1	Cardiff City	42	13	7	1	42	20	12	1	8	35	27	77	47	83
2	Wrexham	42	14	3	4	48	26	9	8	4	27	26	75	52	80
3	Barnet	42	16	4	1	45	19	7	6	8	21	29	66	48	79
4	York City	42	13	6	2	41	15	8	6	7	31	30	72	45	75
5	Walsall	42	11	6	4	42	31	11	1	9	34	30	76	61	73
6	Crewe Alexandra	42	13	3	5	47	23	8	4	9	28	33	75	56	70
7	Bury	42	10	7	4	36	19	8	2	11	27	36	63	55	63
8	Lincoln City	42	10	6	5	31	20	8	3	10	26	33	57	53	63
9	Shrewsbury Town	42	11	3	7	36	30	6	8	7	21	22	57	52	62
10	Colchester United	42	13	3	5	38	26	5	2	14	29	50	67	76	59
11	Rochdale	42	10	3	8	38	29	6	7	8	32	41	70	70	58
12	Chesterfield	42	11	3	7	32	28	4	8	9	27	35	59	63	56
13	Scarborough	42	7	7	7	32	30	8	2	11	34	41	66	71	54
14	SCUNTHORPE U	42	8	7	6	38	25	6	5	10	19	29	57	54	54
15	Darlington	42	5	6	10	23	31	7	8	6	25	22	48	53	50
16	Doncaster Rovers	42	6	5	10	22	28	5	9	7	20	29	42	57	47
17	Hereford United	42	7	9	5	31	27	3	6	12	16	33	47	60	45
18	Carlisle United	42	7	5	9	29	27	4	6	11	22	38	51	65	44
19	Torquay United	42	6	4	11	18	26	6	3	12	27	41	45	67	43
20	Northampton Town	42	6	5	10	19	28	5	3	13	29	46	48	74	41
21	Gillingham	42	9	4	8	32	28	0	9	12	16	36	48	64	40
22	Halifax Town	42	3	5	13	20	35	6	4	11	25	33	45	68	36

Final League Table 1993/94 Division 3

		Pl.	Home					Away					F.	A.	Pts
			W	D	L	F	A	W	D	L	F	A			
1	Shrewsbury Town	42	10	8	3	28	17	12	5	4	35	22	63	39	79
2	Chester City	42	13	5	3	35	18	8	6	7	34	28	69	46	74
3	Crewe Alexandra	42	12	4	5	45	30	9	6	6	35	31	80	61	73
4	Wycombe Wands.	42	11	6	4	34	21	8	7	6	33	32	67	53	70
5	Preston North End	42	13	5	3	46	23	5	8	8	33	37	79	60	67
6	Torquay United	42	8	10	3	30	24	9	6	6	34	32	64	56	67
7	Carlisle United	42	10	4	7	35	23	8	6	7	22	19	57	42	64
8	Chesterfield	42	8	8	5	32	22	8	6	7	23	26	55	48	62
9	Rochdale	42	10	5	6	38	22	6	7	8	25	29	63	51	60
10	Walsall	42	7	5	9	28	26	10	4	7	20	27	48	53	60
11	SCUNTHORPE U	42	9	7	5	40	26	6	7	8	24	30	64	56	59
12	Mansfield Town	42	9	3	9	28	30	6	7	8	25	32	53	62	55
13	Bury	42	9	6	6	33	22	5	5	11	22	34	55	56	53
14	Scarborough	42	8	4	9	29	28	7	4	10	26	33	55	61	53
15	Doncaster Rovers	42	8	6	7	24	26	6	4	11	20	31	44	57	52
16	Gillingham	42	8	8	5	27	23	4	7	10	17	28	44	51	51
17	Colchester United	42	8	4	9	31	33	5	6	10	25	38	56	71	49
18	Lincoln City	42	7	4	10	26	29	5	7	9	26	34	52	63	47
19	Wigan Athletic	42	6	7	8	33	33	5	5	11	18	37	51	70	45
20	Hereford United	42	6	4	11	34	33	6	2	13	26	46	60	79	42
21	Darlington	42	7	5	9	24	28	3	6	12	18	36	42	64	41
22	Northampton Town	42	6	7	8	25	23	3	4	14	19	43	44	66	38

Final League Table 1994/95 Division 3

		Pl.	Home					Away					F.	A.	Pts
			W	D	L	F	A	W	D	L	F	A			
1	Carlisle United	42	14	5	2	34	14	13	5	3	33	17	67	31	91
2	Walsall	42	15	3	3	42	18	9	8	4	33	22	75	40	83
3	Chesterfield	42	11	7	3	26	10	12	5	4	36	27	62	37	81
4	Bury	42	13	7	1	39	13	10	4	7	34	23	73	36	80
5	Preston North End	42	13	3	5	37	17	6	7	8	21	24	58	41	67
6	Mansfield Town	42	10	5	6	45	27	8	6	7	39	32	84	59	65
7	SCUNTHORPE U	42	12	2	7	40	30	6	6	9	28	33	68	63	62
8	Fulham	42	11	5	5	39	22	5	9	7	21	32	60	54	62
9	Doncaster Rovers	42	9	5	7	28	20	8	5	8	30	23	58	43	61
10	Colchester United	42	8	5	8	29	30	8	5	8	27	34	56	64	58
11	Barnet	42	8	7	6	37	27	7	4	10	19	36	56	63	56
12	Lincoln City	42	10	7	4	34	22	5	4	12	20	33	54	55	56
13	Torquay United	42	10	8	3	35	25	4	5	12	19	32	54	57	55
14	Wigan Athletic	42	7	6	8	28	30	7	4	10	25	30	53	60	52
15	Rochdale	42	8	6	7	25	23	4	8	9	19	44	44	67	50
16	Hereford United	42	9	6	6	22	19	3	7	11	23	43	45	62	49
17	Northampton Town	42	8	5	8	25	29	2	9	10	20	38	45	67	44
18	Hartlepool United	42	9	5	7	33	32	2	5	14	10	37	43	69	43
19	Gillingham	42	8	7	6	31	25	2	4	15	15	39	46	64	41
20	Darlington	42	7	5	9	25	24	4	3	14	18	33	43	57	41
21	Scarborough	42	4	7	10	26	31	4	3	14	23	39	49	70	34
22	Exeter City	42	5	5	11	25	36	3	5	13	11	34	36	70	34

Final League Table 1995/96 Division 3

		Pl.	Home					Away					F.	A.	Pts
			W	D	L	F	A	W	D	L	F	A			
1	Preston North End	46	11	8	4	44	22	12	9	2	34	16	78	38	86
2	Gillingham	46	16	6	1	33	6	6	11	6	16	14	49	20	83
3	Bury	46	11	6	6	33	21	11	7	5	33	27	66	48	79
4	Plymouth Argyle	46	14	5	4	41	20	8	7	8	27	29	68	49	78
5	Darlington	46	10	6	7	30	21	10	12	1	30	21	60	42	78
6	Hereford United	46	13	5	5	40	22	7	9	7	25	25	65	47	74
7	Colchester United	46	13	7	3	37	22	5	11	7	24	29	61	51	72
8	Chester City	46	11	9	3	45	22	7	7	9	27	31	72	53	70
9	Barnet	46	13	6	4	40	19	5	10	8	25	26	65	45	70
10	Wigan Athletic	46	15	3	5	36	21	5	7	11	26	35	62	56	70
11	Northampton T.	46	9	10	4	32	22	9	3	11	19	22	51	44	67
12	SCUNTHORPE U	46	8	8	7	36	30	7	7	9	31	31	67	61	60
13	Doncaster Rovers	46	11	6	6	25	19	5	5	13	24	41	49	60	59
14	Exeter City	46	9	9	5	25	22	4	9	10	21	31	46	53	57
15	Rochdale	46	7	8	8	32	33	7	5	11	25	28	57	61	55
16	Cambridge United	46	8	8	7	34	30	6	4	13	27	41	61	71	54
17	Fulham	46	10	9	4	39	26	2	8	13	18	37	57	63	53
18	Lincoln City	46	8	7	8	32	26	5	7	11	25	47	57	73	53
19	Mansfield Town	46	6	10	7	25	29	5	10	8	29	35	54	64	53
20	Hartlepool United	46	8	9	6	30	24	4	4	15	17	43	47	67	49
21	Leyton Orient	46	11	4	8	29	22	1	7	15	15	41	44	63	47
22	Cardiff City	46	8	6	9	24	22	3	6	14	17	42	41	64	45
23	Scarborough	46	5	11	7	22	28	3	5	15	17	41	39	69	40
24	Torquay United	46	4	9	10	17	36	1	5	17	13	48	30	84	29

Final League Table 1996/97 Division 3

		Pl.	Home					Away					F.	A.	Pts
			W	D	L	F	A	W	D	L	F	A			
1	Wigan Athletic	46	17	3	3	53	21	9	6	8	31	30	84	51	87
2	Fulham	46	13	5	5	41	20	12	7	4	31	18	72	38	87
3	Carlisle United	46	16	3	4	41	21	8	9	6	26	23	67	44	84
4	Northampton T.	46	14	4	5	43	17	6	8	9	24	27	67	44	72
5	Swansea City	46	13	5	5	37	20	8	3	12	25	38	62	58	71
6	Chester City	46	11	8	4	30	16	7	8	8	25	27	55	43	70
7	Cardiff City	46	11	4	8	30	23	9	5	9	26	31	56	54	69
8	Colchester United	46	11	9	3	36	23	6	8	9	26	28	62	51	68
9	Lincoln City	46	10	8	5	35	25	8	4	11	35	44	70	69	66
10	Cambridge United	46	11	5	7	30	27	7	6	10	23	32	53	59	65
11	Mansfield Town	46	9	8	6	21	17	7	8	8	26	28	47	45	64
12	Scarborough	46	9	9	5	36	31	7	6	10	29	37	65	68	63
13	SCUNTHORPE U	46	11	3	9	36	33	7	6	10	23	29	59	62	63
14	Rochdale	46	10	6	7	34	24	4	10	9	24	34	58	58	58
15	Barnet	46	9	9	5	32	23	5	7	11	14	28	46	51	58
16	Leyton Orient	46	11	6	6	28	20	4	6	13	22	38	50	58	57
17	Hull City	46	9	8	6	29	26	4	10	9	15	24	44	50	57
18	Darlington	46	11	5	7	37	28	3	5	15	27	50	64	78	52
19	Doncaster Rovers	46	9	7	7	29	23	5	3	15	23	43	52	66	52
20	Hartlepool United	46	8	6	9	33	32	6	3	14	20	34	53	66	51
21	Torquay United	46	9	4	10	24	24	4	7	12	22	38	46	62	50
22	Exeter City	46	6	9	8	25	30	6	3	14	23	43	48	73	48
23	Brighton & Hove A.	46	12	6	5	41	27	1	4	18	12	43	53	70	47
24	Hereford United	46	6	8	9	26	25	5	6	12	24	40	50	65	47

Final League Table 1997/98 Division 3

		Pl.	Home					Away					F.	A.	Pts
			W	D	L	F	A	W	D	L	F	A			
1	Notts County	46	14	7	2	41	20	15	5	3	41	23	82	43	99
2	Macclesfield Town	46	19	4	0	40	11	4	9	10	23	33	63	44	82
3	Lincoln City	46	11	7	5	32	24	9	8	6	28	27	60	51	75
4	Colchester United	46	14	5	4	41	24	7	6	10	31	36	72	60	74
5	Torquay United	46	14	4	5	39	22	7	7	9	29	37	68	59	74
6	Scarborough	46	14	6	3	44	23	5	9	9	23	35	67	58	72
7	Barnet	46	10	8	5	35	22	9	5	9	26	29	61	51	70
8	SCUNTHORPE U	46	11	7	5	30	24	8	5	10	26	28	56	52	69
9	Rotherham United	46	10	9	4	41	30	6	10	7	26	31	67	61	67
10	Peterborough Utd.	46	13	6	4	37	16	5	7	11	26	35	63	51	67
11	Leyton Orient	46	14	5	4	40	20	5	7	11	22	27	62	47	66*
12	Mansfield Town	46	11	9	3	42	26	5	8	10	22	29	64	55	65
13	Shrewsbury Town	46	12	3	8	35	28	4	10	9	26	34	61	62	61
14	Chester City	46	12	7	4	34	15	5	3	15	26	46	60	61	61
15	Exeter City	46	10	8	5	39	25	5	7	11	29	38	68	63	60
16	Cambridge United	46	11	8	4	39	27	3	10	10	24	30	63	57	60
17	Hartlepool United	46	10	12	1	40	22	2	11	10	21	31	61	53	59
18	Rochdale	46	15	3	5	43	15	2	4	17	13	40	56	55	58
19	Darlington	46	13	6	4	43	28	1	6	16	13	44	56	72	54
20	Swansea City	46	8	8	7	24	16	5	3	15	25	46	49	62	50
21	Cardiff City	46	5	13	5	27	22	4	10	9	21	30	48	52	50
22	Hull City	46	10	6	7	36	32	1	2	20	20	51	56	83	41
23	Brighton & Hove A.	46	3	10	10	21	34	3	7	13	17	32	38	66	35
24	Doncaster Rovers	46	3	3	17	14	48	1	5	17	16	65	30	113	20

* 3 points deducted

Final League Table 1997/98 Division 3

		Pl.	Home					Away					F.	A.	Pts
			W	D	L	F	A	W	D	L	F	A			
1	Brentford	46	16	5	2	45	18	10	2	11	34	38	79	56	85
2	Cambridge United	46	13	6	4	41	21	10	6	7	37	27	78	48	81
3	Cardiff City	46	13	7	3	35	17	9	7	7	25	22	60	57	80
4	SCUNTHORPE U	46	14	3	6	42	28	8	5	10	27	30	69	58	74
5	Rotherham U.	46	11	8	4	41	26	9	5	9	38	35	79	61	73
6	Leyton Orient	46	12	6	5	40	30	7	9	7	28	29	68	59	72
7	Swansea City	46	11	9	3	33	19	8	5	10	23	29	56	48	71
8	Mansfield Town	46	15	2	6	38	18	4	8	11	22	40	60	58	67
9	Peterborough U.	46	11	4	8	41	29	7	8	8	31	27	72	60	66
10	Halifax Town	46	10	8	5	33	25	7	7	9	25	31	58	56	66
11	Dalington	46	10	6	7	41	24	8	5	10	28	34	69	58	65
12	Exeter City	46	13	5	5	32	18	4	7	12	15	32	47	50	63
13	Plymough Argyle	46	11	6	6	32	19	6	4	13	26	35	58	54	61
14	Chester City	46	6	12	5	28	30	7	6	10	29	36	57	66	57
15	Shrewsbury Town	46	11	6	6	36	29	3	8	12	16	34	52	63	56
16	Barnet	46	10	5	8	30	31	4	8	11	24	40	54	71	55
17	Brighton & H.A.	46	8	3	12	25	35	8	4	11	24	31	49	66	55
18	Southend United	46	8	6	9	24	21	6	6	11	28	37	52	58	54
19	Rochdale	46	9	8	6	22	21	4	7	12	20	34	42	55	54
20	Torquay United	46	9	9	5	29	20	3	8	12	18	38	47	58	53
21	Hull City	46	8	5	10	25	28	6	6	11	19	34	44	62	53
22	Hartlepool United	46	8	7	8	33	27	5	5	13	19	38	52	65	51
23	Carlisle United	46	8	8	7	25	21	3	8	12	18	32	43	53	49
24	Scarborough	46	8	3	12	30	39	6	3	14	20	38	50	77	48

1992/93 — 14th in Division 3

Re-classification of Divisions; Division 4 became Division 3.

#	Date	Opponent	Result	Scorers	Att
1	Aug 22	Halifax Town	0-0		1793
2	29	SHREWSBURY TOWN	1-1	Alexander	3438
3	Sep 1	WALSALL	2-0	Elliott, Helliwell	2828
4	5	Lincoln City	0-1		3764
5	12	Northampton Town	0-1		1835
6	19	CREWE ALEXANDRA	3-3	Goodacre, Humphries, Daws (p)	2995
7	26	Carlisle United	2-0	Helliwell 2	4772
8	Oct 3	Chesterfield	2-1	Goodacre, White	3552
9	10	YORK CITY	1-2	White	4114
10	17	Barnet	0-3		2924
11	24	COLCHESTER UNITED	3-1	Daws, Martin, Helliwell	2473
12	31	Cardiff City	0-3		6027
13	Nov 3	Wrexham	2-0	Stevenson, Buckley	2930
14	7	DONCASTER ROVERS	0-1		4451
15	21	Torquay United	1-0	Helliwell	1860
16	28	SCARBOROUGH	1-2	McCullagh	2807
17	Dec 12	HEREFORD UNITED	3-1	Alexander, Elliott 2	1970
18	19	Darlington	2-2	White 2	1801
19	26	Rochdale	0-2		3043
20	28	GILLINGHAM	2-2	Daws 2 (1 p)	2835
21	Jan 16	CARLISLE UNITED	0-0		2570
22	26	Shrewsbury Town	1-2	Helliwell	2190
23	30	HALIFAX TOWN	4-1	Helliwell 2, Martin, Buckley	2460
24	Feb 13	LINCOLN CITY	1-1	Stevenson	3748
25	20	Walsall	2-3	Stevenson, Helliwell	2935
26	27	York City	1-5	Farrell	2990
27	Mar 6	CHESTERFIELD	0-1		2725
28	9	BURY	2-0	Alexander, Platnauer	2589
29	13	Doncaster Rovers	1-0	Elliott	2760
30	20	WREXHAM	0-0		3282
31	23	Scarborough	2-1	White, Alexander	2007
32	27	TORQUAY UNITED	2-2	Alexander, Elliott	2568
33	30	NORTHAMPTON T	5-0	Elliott, Goodacre 2, Helliwell, Thompstone	2307
34	Apr 3	Bury	0-0		2509
35	6	Hereford United	2-2	Helliwell, Goodacre	1740
36	10	ROCHDALE	5-1	Helliwell, Goodacre 2, Platnauer, Martin	2926
37	12	Gillingham	1-1	Thompstone	3859
38	17	DARLINGTON	1-3	Goodacre	2774
39	20	Crewe Alexandra	0-1		3006
40	24	BARNET	2-0	Goodacre, Helliwell	2810
41	May 1	Colchester United	0-1		3421
42	8	CARDIFF CITY	0-3		7407

Played in game 10: TJ Ryan (at 6).

F.A. Cup

Round	Date	Opponent	Result	Scorers	Att
R1	Nov 14	HUDDERSFIELD TOWN	0-0		4312
rep	25	Huddersfield Town	1-2	Buckley	4841

Replay a.e.t.

Coca Cola Cup (F.L. Cup)

Round	Date	Opponent	Result	Scorers	Att
R1/1	Aug 18	Darlington	1-1	Helliwell	1489
R1/2	25	DARLINGTON	2-0	Daws, Alexander	2299
R2/1	Sep 22	Leeds United	1-4	Helliwell	10113
R2/2	Oct 27	LEEDS UNITED	2-2	Helliwell 2	7419

Autoglass Trophy (Associate Members Cup)

Round	Date	Opponent	Result	Scorers	Att
R1	Dec 8	Rotherham United	1-3	Goodacre	1634
R1	14	LINCOLN CITY	2-2	Clarke (og), Alexander	1263
R2	Feb 2	Rochdale	2-1	Daws 2	1312
QF	9	Wigan Athletic	1-2	Humphries (p)	1512

1993/94 11th in Division 3

#	Date		Opponent	Score	Scorers	Att	Samways M	Thompstone IP	Mudd PA	Carmichael M	Elliott MS	Bradley R	Alexander G	Martin DS	Trebble ND	Thornber SJ	Smith MC	Hope CJ	Goodacre SD	Juryeff IM	Toman JA	Watson JI	White JG	Knill AR	Henderson DR	Sansam C	Bullimore WA	Danzey MJ	Ryan TJ	Heath M	Jobling KA
1	Aug	14	Wigan Athletic	2-0	Mudd, Smith	2353	1	2	3	4	5	6	7	8	9	10	11	12	14												
2		21	BURY	1-1	Thompstone	3375	1	7	3	2	5		14	4	12		11	6	8	9	10										
3		28	Mansfield Town	1-0	Toman	2751	1	7	3	8	5		2	4			11	6	12	9	10										
4		31	Walsall	0-0		2519	1	7	3	4	5		2	8	12	11		6		9	10										
5	Sep	4	HEREFORD UNITED	1-2	Thompstone	3091	1	7	3	8	5		2	4	14	12	11	6		9	10										
6		11	Chester City	2-0	Toman, Juryeff	2195	1	7	3	11	5	6	2	4	8	12		4		9	10										
7		18	CARLISLE UNITED	2-1	Carmichael 2	3361	1	7	3	11	5	6	2	8			12	4		9	10	14									
8		25	Gillingham	0-1		2872	1	2	3	11	5	6	7	8	14	10	12	4					9								
9	Oct	2	SCARBOROUGH	1-1	Thompstone	2910	1	7	3	11	5	6	2	8	11			12			10		9								
10		9	Colchester United	1-2	Carmichael	3405	1	7	3	4	5	6	2	8	14		9	10		11			12								
11		16	NORTHAMPTON T	7-0	Carmichael 3, Thompstone, Smith, Elliott, Toman	2814	1	7	3	9	5	6	2	8			11	4		14	10		12								
12		23	Torquay United	1-1	Toman	3241	1	7	3	9	5	6	2	8	11			4			10	12	14								
13		30	DARLINGTON	3-0	Carmichael (p), Alexander, Trebble	3025	1	7	3	9	5	6	2		11	8		4			10	12	14								
14	Nov	1	Doncaster Rovers	1-3	Trebble	4439	1	7	3	9	5	6	2		11	8		4			10	14	12								
15		6	WYCOMBE WANDERERS	0-0		3604	1	7	3	9		6	2			8	14	4			10	11	12	5							
16		20	Shrewsbury Town	0-0		2436	1	7	3	9		6	2	8			11	4	12		10			5							
17		27	ROCHDALE	2-1	Toman, Thompstone	3106	1	7	3	9		6	2	8			11	4	12		10		14	5							
18	Dec	11	Bury	0-1		2389	1	7	3	9		6	2	8			11	4						5	10						
19		18	WIGAN ATHLETIC	1-0	Carmichael	2873	1		3	9		6	2	8		11		4	12	14				5	10	7					
20		27	Lincoln City	0-2		6030	1		3	9		6	2	8		10	7	4		11				5	12						
21		28	CHESTERFIELD	2-2	Carmichael (p), Mudd	3266	1		3	9		6	2	8				4		12				5	11	7	10				
22	Jan	1	Preston North End	2-2	Knill, Carmichael	7669	1		12	9		6	2	8	3			4		11				5	10	7	14				
23		3	WALSALL	5-0	Martin, Smith, Bullimore, Carmichael, Henderson	3417	1		12	9		6		8	7		11	4		3				5	10	14	2				
24		22	COLCHESTER UNITED	1-1	Carmichael	2854	1	7	3	9		6	2				11	4						5	8	12	10				
25		29	Darlington	1-2	Carmichael	2142	1	7	3	9		6	2	8				4						5	11		10				
26	Feb	5	TORQUAY UNITED	1-3	Carmichael	2755	1		3	9		6	2	8				4						5	7	12	10	11			
27		12	Crewe Alexandra	3-3	Martin, Carmichael, Danzey	3507	1		3	9			2				12	11	4					5	7			10			
28		19	MANSFIELD TOWN	2-3	Carmichael 2	3089	1	12	3	9		6	2	8			14	11	4					5	7			10			
29	Mar	5	CHESTER CITY	1-1	Mudd	2669	1	7	3	9		6	2	8	11		10	12	4	14				5							
30		8	Northampton Town	0-4		3192	1	2	10	6			7	8				3	4					5	9	11					
31		12	Carlisle United	1-3	Goodacre	4076	1		3	6			2				10	11	4	7	9			5	14	12	8				
32		15	CREWE ALEXANDRA	2-1	Alexander, Thornber	2122	1		3	6			2				8	11	4	7	9			5	14	12	10				
33		19	GILLINGHAM	1-1	Juryeff	2386	1			3		6	2				8	11	4	7	9			5	14	12	10				
34		26	Scarborough	1-0	Smith	1571	1	3		6	5	2					10	11	4	7	9				8						
35		29	Hereford United	2-1	Carmichael, Juryeff	1767	1	3		6	5	2					10	11	4	7	9				8				12		
36	Apr	2	LINCOLN CITY	2-0	Alexander, Goodacre	3571	1	3		6	5	2					10	11	4	7	9				8						
37		4	Chesterfield	1-1	Alexander	3629	1	3		6	5	2					10		4	7				11	14	8			12		
38		9	PRESTON NORTH END	3-1	Smith, Bradley, Bullimore	3790	1	3		6	5	2					8	11		9				4	7		10				
39		16	DONCASTER ROVERS	1-3	Goodacre	4151	1	3		6	5	2					10	11	12	9				4	7		8				
40		23	Wycombe Wanderers	2-2	Smith, Bullimore (p)	5755				6	5	2					10	11	3	12	9			4	7		8		1		
41		30	SHREWSBURY TOWN	1-4	Juryeff	4587	1			6	5	2					10	11	3	12	9			4	7		8				
42	May	7	Rochdale	3-2	Thornber, Juryeff, Lancaster (og)	3118	1	3		6	5	2					10	11	12	7	9			4			8				
			Apps				41	30	33	42	14	34	41	26	14	24	30	41	18	23	15	5	9	25	20	10	18	3	1	2	0
			Goals					5	3	18	1	1	4	2	2	2	6		3	5	5			1	1		3	1			

One own goal

F.A. Cup

Rd	Date		Opponent	Score	Scorers	Att																								
R1	Nov	14	Accrington Stanley	3-2	Toman, Goodacre 2	5816	1	7	3	6			2	8			11	4	12		10			9	5						
R2	Dec	4	Walsall	1-1	Carmichael	4962	1	7	3	9		6	2	8			11	4			10			12	5						
rep		14	WALSALL	0-0		3300	1	7	3	9		6	2	8		14	12	4	10	11					5						
R3	Jan	8	Wimbledon	0-3		4944	1		3	9		6	2	8	7		11	4			12				5		10				

R2 replay won on penalties (7-6) a.e.t.

Coca Cola Cup (F.L. Cup)

Rd	Date		Opponent	Score	Scorers	Att																								
1/1	Aug	17	Shrewsbury Town	0-1		1939	1	2	3	4	5		7	8		10	11	6	12				14	9							
1/2		24	SHREWSBURY TOWN	1-1	Martin	2320	1	7	3		5		2	4	12		11	6	8		10	9									

Autoglass Trophy (Associate Members Cup)

Rd	Date		Opponent	Score	Scorers	Att																								
R1	Sep	27	Scarborough	2-2	Carmichael 2 (1 p)	412	1		3	7	5	6	2	8	10		11	4		9					12						
R1	Oct	19	HULL CITY	1-1	Carmichael	2366	1		3	9	5	6	2	8			11	4		7	10	12	14								
R2	Dec	1	Scarborough	2-0	Carmichael 2	679	1	7	3	9		6	2	8		10		4						12	5						
QF	Jan	11	Stockport County	0-2		4404	1		3	9		6	2		12		11	4	7						5		10				8

1994/95 7th in Division 3

#	Date		Opponent	Result	Scorers	Att.	Samways M	Ford T	Mudd PA	Thornber SJ	Knill AR	Bradley R	Alexander G	Bullimore WA	Juryeff JM	Henderson DR	Smith MC	Carmichael M	Goodacre SD	Hope CJ	Martin DS	Thompstone IP	Sansam C	Nicholson M	Eyre JR	Young SR	Eli R	Turnbull LM	Gregory NR	Kiwomya AD	Housham SJ	Walsh MS
1	Aug	13	Barnet	2-1	Henderson, Juryeff	2208	1	2	3	4	5	6	7	8	9	10	11															
2		20	FULHAM	1-2	Juryeff	3165	1	2	3	4	5	6	7	8	9	10	11	12	14													
3		27	NORTHAMPTON T	1-1	Bradley	2499	1	2	3	4		6	7	8	9	10	11	12		5	14											
4		30	GILLINGHAM	3-0	Thornber, Henderson, Smith	2098	1	2	3	4	5	6	7	8		10	11			9		12										
5	Sep	3	CARLISLE UNITED	2-3	Juryeff, Thornber	3217	1	2	3	4	5	6	7	8	9	10	11		12		14											
6		10	Bury	0-2		2540	1	4	3		5	6	7	8	9	10	11	2														
7		13	Darlington	3-1	Bullimore, Ford, Alexander	2181	1	4	3		5	6	7	8	9	10	11	2				12										
8		17	BARNET	1-0	Juryeff	2481	1	2	3	4	5	6	7	8	9	10	11															
9		24	WIGAN ATHLETIC	3-1	Thornber, Alexander, Bullimore (p)	2602	1	2	3	4	5	6	7	8	9	10	11															
10	Oct	1	Hereford United	1-2	Bradley	2267	1	2	3	4	5	6	7	8	9	10	11			14	12											
11		8	Preston North End	1-0	Alexander	6895	1	2	3	4	5	6	7	8	9	10				11												
12		15	WALSALL	0-1		3609	1	2	3	4	5	6	7	8	9	10	12			11		14										
13		22	Exeter City	2-2	Henderson, Juryeff	2511	1	2	3	4	5		7		9	10	11		14	8		12										
14		29	HARTLEPOOL UNITED	0-0		2624	1	2	3	4	5	6	7		9	10	11	12	14	8												
15	Nov	5	Torquay United	1-1	Juryeff	3036	1	2	3	4	5	6	7		9	10	11	12		8												
16		19	MANSFIELD TOWN	3-4	Bullimore, Nicholson, Juryeff	2975	1	4	3		5	6	7	8	9					2				10	11							
17		26	Colchester United	2-4	Thornber, Knill	2904	1				5		7	8	9			6		12				14	10	11						
18	Dec	10	Fulham	0-1		3358	1	2	3	4	5		7	8	9	10	11	12		14												
19		16	Northampton Town	1-0	Knill	3845	1	2	3	4	5	6	7	8	9			11	14					12		10							
20		26	LINCOLN CITY	2-0	Juryeff, Eyre	4785	1	2	3	4	5	6	7	8	9			11	14					12		10							
21		27	Doncaster Rovers	1-1	Carmichael	3852	1	2	3	4	5	6	7	8	9			11	14					12		10							
22		31	ROCHDALE	4-1	Mudd, Bullimore (p), Eyre, Thompstone	2653	1	2	3	4		6	7	8				11	5			12				10	9						
23	Jan	7	EXETER CITY	3-0	Eyre 2, Alexander	2463	1	2	3	4		6	7	8				11	5							10	9						
24		14	Chesterfield	1-3	Bullimore (p)	3245	1	2	3	4	5	6	7	8				11	14					12		9	10						
25		21	TORQUAY UNITED	3-2	Smith, Eyre, Carmichael	2229	1	2		4	5	6	7	8				11	12														
26		28	Hartlepool United	4-1	Knill, Young, Thornber, Eyre	1660	1	2	3	4	5		7	8				11	6					12		14	10	9					
27	Feb	4	COLCHESTER UNITED	3-4	Bullimore, Eyre 2	2748	1	2	3	4	5		7	8					12	6				14		11	10	9					
28		18	CHESTERFIELD	0-1		3566	1	2		4	5		7		10					6		3		8		11		9	12				
29		21	Mansfield Town	0-1		3079	1	2		4	5		7					12	6			3		8	10	11		9	14				
30		25	HEREFORD UNITED	1-0	Nicholson	2193	1	2		4	5		7	8					12	6				10		11		9					
31		28	Scarborough	0-3		1179	1	2	3	4	5		7	11		14	12			6		9			10			8					
32	Mar	11	BURY	3-2	Gregory 2, Hughes(og)	2767	1	2	3	4	5							12		6					7	11			9	8	10		
33		18	Gillingham	2-2	Young, Turnbull	2459	1	2	3	4	5		7	14				12		6						11			8	10			
34		25	Carlisle United	1-2	Kiwomya	6704	1	2	3	4	5		7	9						6									8	10	11		
35	Apr	1	DARLINGTON	2-1	Gregory 2	2449	1	2	3	4	5		7	9						6		12							8	10	11		
36		4	Wigan Athletic	0-0		1307	1		3	4	5		7	9						6		2							8	10	11		
37		8	Rochdale	2-1	Turnbull, Kiwomya	1720	1			3	4		5					7	12	6					9			14	8	10	11		
38		15	DONCASTER ROVERS	0-5		4366	1				4	5	12	7	9				3	6		2						14	8	10	11		
39		17	Lincoln City	3-3	Turnbull, Gregory, Nicholson	3330	1				5		7	4					3	6				9				8	10	11	2		
40		22	SCARBOROUGH	3-1	Gregory, Kiwomya, Nicholson	2079	1	7		4	5			8						6				9				10	11	2	3		
41		29	Walsall	1-2	Gregory	4539	1	7			5	12	8							6				14	9			4	10	11	2	3		
42	May	6	PRESTON NORTH END	2-1	Ford, Knill	3691	1	7			5		17	12	8					6				10	9			4		11	2	3		
			Apps				42	38	35	37	39	25	40	35	21	17	32	20	5	24	5	19	6	15	9	14	2	10	10	9	4	3
			Goals					2	1	5	4	2	4	6	8	3	2	2		1		4		8	2			3	7	3		

One own goal

F.A. Cup

	Date		Opponent	Result	Scorers	Att.																									
R1	Nov	12	Bradford City	1-1	Hope	5481	1	8	3		5	6	7	4	9		11			2				10								
rep		22	BRADFORD CITY	3-2	Carmichael, Alexander, Thompstone	4514	1	4	3	11	5	6	7	8	9			12		2		14	10									
R2	Dec	2	Birmingham City	0-0		13832	1	2	3	4	5	6	7	8	9	10	11	12				14										
rep		14	BIRMINGHAM CITY	1-2	Bullimore	6280	1	2	3	4	5	6	7	8	9		11	12				10	14									

R1 replay a.e.t.

Coca Cola Cup (F.L. Cup)

	Date		Opponent	Result	Scorers	Att.																									
R1/1	Aug	16	HUDDERSFIELD TOWN	2-1	Henderson, Bullimore	2841	1	2	3	4	5	6	7	8	9	10	11															
R1/2		23	Huddersfield Town	0-3		6455	1	2	3		5	6	7	8	9	10	11	12	14		4											

Auto Windscreen Trophy (Associate Members Cup)

	Date		Opponent	Result	Scorers	Att.																									
R1	Sep	27	ROTHERHAM UNITED	1-3	Alexander	1404	1	2	3	4	5	6	7	8		10	11			9		12		14								
R1	Nov	8	Chesterfield	1-1	Bullimore (pen)	1424	1			6	5	3	7	8			11	9	10	2		4	14								12	

1995/96 12th in Division 3

#		Date	Opponent	Score	Scorers	Att	Samways M	Walsh MS	Wilson PA	Thornber SJ	Knill AR	Bradley R	Ford T	Turnbull LM	McFarlane AA	Eyre JR	Nicholson M	Hope CJ	Bullimore WA	Young SR	Housham SJ	Graham DWT	Sansam C	Murfin AJ	Varadi I	Paterson JR	Clarkson PI	D'Auria DA	Jones RA	Butler LS	Germaine GP	O'Halloran KJ
1	Aug	12	CAMBRIDGE UNITED	1-2	Eyre	2561	1	2	3	4	5	6	7	8	9	10	11															
2		19	Wigan Athletic	1-2	Turnbull	3153	1	2	3	4		6	7	8	9	10	11	5	12	14	13											
3		26	BARNET	2-0	Thomas (og), McFarlane	1970	1		3	4	7	6			9	10	11	5	8		2											
4		28	Lincoln City	2-2	Graham, Eyre	2674	1		3	4	7	6			9	10	11	5	8		2	12										
5	Sep	2	Exeter City	0-1		2893	1	3		4	5				9	10		6	8	12	2	7		11								
6		9	Gillingham	1-1	Hope	2423	1		3	4	5	6	12		9	10	11	7	8	13	2											
7		12	CHESTER CITY	0-2		1875	1		3	4	5	6	12		9	10	11	7	8	14	2	13										
8		16	Preston North End	2-2	Bullimore (p), Sansam	7391	1	2	3		5	14	4		12	10	11	6	8	9	7		13									
9		23	Mansfield Town	1-1	McFarlane	2478	1	2	3		5	14	4		12	10	11	6	8	9	7		13									
10		30	COLCHESTER UNITED	1-0	Eyre	2051	1		3	8	5	6	4		14	10	13	2		9	7				11	12						
11	Oct	7	NORTHAMPTON T	0-0		2455	1		3	8	5	6	4		13	10	12	2		9	7				11	14						
12		14	Hartlepool United	0-2		2608	1		3	8	5	6	4		13	10		2	12	9	7		14		11							
13		21	LEYTON ORIENT	2-0	Paterson, Hope	2315	1		3	6	5		4		9	10	13	2	8	12	7				11							
14		28	Torquay United	8-1	McFarlane 4, Eyre 2, Knill, Ford	2137	1	12	3	7	5		4		9	10	14	6	8	13	2				11							
15		31	Cardiff City	1-0	McFarlane	2024	1	12	3	7	5	6	4		9	10	13				2				11	8						
16	Nov	4	ROCHDALE	1-3	Ford	3003	1		3	7	5	6	4		9	10			12		2				11	8						
17		18	Darlington	0-0		2078	1	2	3	12	5	6	4		9	10			8						11	7						
18		25	SCARBOROUGH	3-3	Ford, Clarkson, Bullimore (p)	2231	1	2	3		5	6	4		9	10	13	12	8						11	7						
19	Dec	9	MANSFIELD TOWN	1-1	McFarlane	2552	1	2	3			6	4	12	9	10		7	5		13				11		8					
20		16	Colchester United	1-2	Young	2138	1	2	3			6	4	7	9			12	5	10					11		8					
21		19	Hereford United	0-3		2516	1	2	3	13		6	4	7	9			12	5	10					11		8					
22	Jan	13	WIGAN ATHLETIC	3-1	Jones, D'Auria, McFarlane	2288	1	2	3			6	4	13	9	10		12	5						11		8	7				
23		20	Cambridge United	2-1	McFarlane, Wilson (p)	2413	1	2	3			6	4	13	9	10	12	5							11		8	7				
24		23	Plymouth Argyle	3-1	Hope, Turnbull, McFarlane	4712	1	2	3			6	4	10	9		11	5		12							8	7				
25		30	Fulham	3-1	D'Auria, Jones, Paterson	2176	1	2	3			6			4	10	9	12	6		13				11		8	7				
26	Feb	3	Barnet	0-1		1674	1	2	3		6		4	10	9	12	8	5		13					11			7				
27		10	PLYMOUTH ARGYLE	1-1	McFarlane	2789		2	3		5	6	12		9	10									11	4	8	7	1			
28		17	Chester City	0-3		2401		2	3			6	4		9		12	5							11	10	8	7	1			
29		24	PRESTON NORTH END	1-2	Jones	3638	1	2			5	6	4		9	13	14	3		12					11	10	8	7				
30		27	Gillingham	0-0		5557	1				5	6	4		9	10		2		3					11	7	8					
31	Mar	2	Bury	0-3		3035	1	13			5	6	4	14	9	10	12	2							11	8	7				
32		5	LINCOLN CITY	2-3	Eyre, Clarkson	2411	1	2	3		5	6	4	13	9	10	12								11	8	7					
33		9	HEREFORD UNITED	0-1		1903		2	3		5	6	4	13	9	10	12	14							11	8	7		1			
34		16	Doncaster Rovers	0-2		1920		2	3		5	6	4	12	9	10	11	7							13	8			1			
35		23	FULHAM	3-1	Knill, Ford, D'Auria	1919			3		5	6	4	7	9	10		2			12				11	8			1			
36		26	EXETER CITY	4-0	Eyre 2, Ford, McFarlane	1615	1		3		5	6	4	7	9	10		2							12	8						11
37		30	Northampton Town	2-1	Clarkson, McFarlane	4290			3		5	6	4	7	9	10		2							11	8			1			
38	Apr	2	HARTLEPOOL UNITED	2-1	Ford, Bradley	2100			3		5	6	4		9	10		2							11	8			1	7		
39		6	TORQUAY UNITED	1-0	Ford	2247			3		5		4		9	10	13	2		6					12	11	8		1	7		
40		8	Leyton Orient	0-0		2814			3		5			7	9	10	12	2		6					4	11	8		1			
41		13	CARDIFF CITY	1-1	Knill	2044			3		5		4	7	9	10	13	2							12	11	8		1	6		
42		16	BURY	1-2	Nicholson	2132			3		5	6	4	7	9		13	2							11	12	8		1			10
43		20	Rochdale	1-1	Clarkson	1654			3		5	6		7	9		12	2		13					10	11	8		1			4
44		23	DONCASTER ROVERS	2-2	Turnbull, Clarkson	2614	1				5	6		7	9	10	12	2		3					4	11	8					13
45		27	Scarborough	4-1	McFarlane, Clarkson, D'Auria 2(1p)	1738	1		3		5	6		7	9	12	10	2		4					13	11	8					
46	May	4	DARLINGTON	3-3	Eyre 2, McFarlane	4847			3		5	6		9	10	12	2			4				7	11	8			1			

	Apps	Goals
Samways M	33	
Walsh MS	25	1
Wilson PA	40	
Thornber SJ	16	3
Knill AR	38	1
Bradley R	38	7
Ford T	38	3
Turnbull LM	23	16
McFarlane AA	46	10
Eyre JR	39	1
Nicholson M	36	3
Hope CJ	40	2
Bullimore WA	14	1
Young SR	14	
Housham SJ	28	
Graham DWT	3	1
Sansam C	5	1
Murfin AJ	1	
Varadi I	2	
Paterson JR	26	2
Clarkson PI	24	6
D'Auria DA	27	5
Jones RA	11	3
Butler LS	2	
Germaine GP	11	
O'Halloran KJ	7	

One own goal

F.A. Cup

		Date	Opponent	Score	Scorers	Att	Samways M	Walsh MS	Wilson PA	Thornber SJ	Knill AR	Bradley R	Ford T	Turnbull LM	McFarlane AA	Eyre JR	Nicholson M	Hope CJ	Bullimore WA	Young SR	Housham SJ				Paterson JR
R1	Nov	11	Northwich Victoria	3-1	Ford, McFarlane 2	2685	1		3	7	5	6	4		9	10	12		8		2				11
R2	Dec	2	SHREWSBURY TOWN	1-1	Eyre	2718	1	2	3		6	4	7	9	10	8	5								11
rep		12	Shrewsbury Town	1-2	Paterson	3313	1	2	3			6	4	7		10	12	5	8	9					11

Coca Cola Cup (F.L. Cup)

		Date	Opponent	Score	Scorers	Att															
R1/1	Aug	15	ROTHERHAM UNITED	4-1	Eyre 2, McFarlane, Ford	2110	1	2	3	4	5	6	7	8	9	10	11	12	13	14	
R1/2		22	Rotherham United	0-5		2206	1	2	3	4		6	7	8	9	10	11	5	13	12	

R1/2 a.e.t.

Auto Windscreens Shield (Associate Members Cup)

		Date	Opponent	Score	Scorers	Att																
R1	Sep	26	Wigan Athletic	1-1	Housham	1064	1		3	8	5	6	4		9		12	2		10	7	11
R1	Oct	17	BURY	4-0	McFarlane 2, Matthewson (og), Eyre	877	1			3	5	6	4		9	10	12	2	8	13	7	14	11
R2	Nov	28	YORK CITY	0-3		1734	1	2	3			6	4	7	9	10	12	5	8	13		11

1996/97 13th in Division 3

					Samways M	Hope C	Wilson P A	Sertori M	Knill A	Bradley R	O'Auria D	Moss D	McFarlane A	Eyre J	Clarkson P	Francis J	Walsh M	Paterson J	Gavin M	Housham S	Borland J	Dunn I	Jackson K	Baker P	Calvo-Garcia A	Turnbull L	Lucas D	Laws B	Clarke T	Jones G	Forrester J	McAuley S	Walker J	Wilson P D
1	Aug 17	Leyton Orient	1-0	Clarkson	4430	1	2	3	4	5	6	7	8	9	10	11	12																	
2	24	TORQUAY U.	1-0	Clarkson	2236	1	2	3	4	5	6	7	8	9	10	11	12	13																
3	27	SCARBOROUGH	0-2		2512	1	2	3	4	5	6	7	8	9	10	11	12		13																
4	31	Brighton & H.A.	1-1	Eyre	4365	1	2	3	4	5	6	7	8	9	10	11	12																	
5	Sep 7	Wigan Ath.	0-3		3321	1	2	3	4	5	6	7			10	11	9			8	12													
6	10	CAMBRIDGE U.	3-2	McFarlane, Clarkson, Wilson	1643	1	2	3	4		6			9	10	11		5		8	7													
7	14	CARDIFF C.	0-1		2121	1	2	3	4		6			9	10	11		5	12	8	7	13												
8	21	Chester C.	0-1		1901	1	2	3	4	5	6				10	11			12	8	7		9	13										
9	28	BARNET	1-2	Clarkson	1942	1	2	3	4		6	5			10	11			12	8	7		9											
10	Oct 1	Hereford U.	2-3	Bradley, Jackson	1785	1	2	3	4		6	10		12		11		5	13	8	7		9	14										
11	5	Hull C.	2-0	Clarkson, Baker	5414	1	2	3	4		6	10				11		5	12	8	7			14	9	13								
12	12	LINCOLN C.	2-0	Housham, D'Auria	3274	1	2	3	4		6	8		12	10	11		5		7					9									
13	15	NORTHAMPTON T.	2-1	D'Auria, Hope	2079	1	2	3	4			6		8	12	10	11	5	13	7					9									
14	19	Swansea C.	1-1	Eyre	2373	1	2	3	4			6	8			10	11	5	12	7					9									
15	26	ROCHDALE	2-2	Baker, Eyre(p)	2628	1	2	3	4			6	8		12	10	11	5	13	7					9	14								
16	29	Fulham	1-2	Hope	4566	1	2	3	4	5	6		8			10	11		13	12	7				9									
17	Nov 2	Mansfield T.	0-2		2210	1	2	3	4	5		6	8		12	10	11		13	7					9									
18	9	DONCASTER R.	1-2	Clarkson	3270	1	2	3	4	5			8			10	11	12	6	7					9	13								
19	19	Colchester U.	1-1	Clarkson	1842	1		5	3	4			8		12	10	11	2	6	7					9									
20	23	DARLINGTON	3-2	Clarkson, Baker(2)	2366	1		5	3	4			8				11	2	6		7	12			9	10									
21	30	Rochdale	2-1	Baker, Eyre	1969	1		5	3	4		6	8		10	11		2							9	7	12								
22	Dec 3	HARTLEPOOL U.	2-1	Baker, Clarkson	1778	1		5	3	4		6	8			10	11	2							9	7									
23	14	Exeter C.	4-1	Calvo-Garcia, Sertori, Clarkson(2)	2000	1		5	3	4		6	8			10	11	2		12					9	7									
24	21	Carlisle U.	2-3	Clarkson, McFarlane	5646	1		5	3	4	6		8		12	10	11	2	13		7				9		14								
25	28	WIGAN ATH.	2-3	Eyre(p), McFarlane	2833	1		5	3				8	9	10		11	6	7		2					12	4	1							
26	Jan 18	HEREFORD U.	5-1	Housham,Clarkson,Eyre(p),Baker(2)	1986		6	3		5	8				10	11		2			7				9		4	1							
27	25	FULHAM	1-4	Turnbull	3259		6	3		5	8					10	11	2	13	12	7				9		4	1							
28	Feb 1	Doncaster R.	1-1	Baker	3022		6	3					8			10	11	2	7						9			1	4						
29	8	MANSFIELD T.	0-2		2600		6	3	4	5						10		2	12	11	7				9			1	8						
30	15	Darlington	0-2		2245		6	3	4	5			8			10		2		11	7				9	12		1							
31	18	CHESTER C.	0-2		1524	1	6	3	4	5			8					2	12	11	7				9	10									
32	22	COLCHESTER U.	2-1	D'Auria, Jones	2738		6	3	4	5			8			12		2			7				9		11			1	10				
33	25	Cambridge U.	2-0	Eyre, Housham	2033		6	3	4	5			8			9		2			7						11			1	10				
34	Mar 1	Hartlepool U.	1-0	Eyre	1300		6	3	4	5			8			9		2			7					12	11			1	10				
35	8	CARLISLE U.	0-0		3470		6	3	4	5			8			9		2			7						11			1	10				
36	15	Exeter C.	1-0	Jones	3378		6	3	4	5			8			9		2	7							12	11			1	10				
37	22	Torquay U.	2-1	Forrester, Jones	1761		6	3	4	5			8			9			7								11			1	10	2			
38	29	LEYTON ORIENT	1-2	Forrester	3365		6		4	5			8			9			7								11			1	10	2	3	12	
39	31	Scarborough	2-3	Jones, Forrester	3212		6		4	5			8			9				12							11			1	10	7	3	2	
40	Apr 5	BRIGHTON & H.A.	1-0	Hope	2925		6		4	5			8			9		12		11										1	10	7	3	2	
41	8	Barnet	1-1	Jones	1393		6		4	5			8			9		2	12	11							-			1	13	10	3	7	
42	12	HULL C.	2-2	Forrester(2)	4257		5		4	6			8			9		2	11											1	12	10	3	7	
43	15	Cardiff C.	0-0		4490		5		4	6			8			9		2	11										12	1		10	3	7	12
44	19	Lincoln C.	0-2		4755		5		4	6			8			9		2	11											1		10	3	7	
45	26	SWANSEA C.	1-0	Forrester	3130		5		4				8			9		2	12		6					11				1		10	3	7	
46	May 3	Northampton T.	0-1		6828		5		4				8			9		2	12		6					11	13		14	1		10	3	7	
				Apps.		25	46	37	42	29	22	39	4	14	42	28	5	36	29	11	34	2	3	4	21	13	14	6	4	15	11	10	9	9	1
				Goals			3	1	1		1	3			3	8	13				3				1	9	1	1				5	6			

F.A. Cup

R1	Nov 16	Rotherham U.	4-1	Baker(2), D'Auria, Clarkson	3896	1		3	4	5		8			10	11		2	6		7				9										
R2	Dec 7	Wrexham	2-2	Baker(2)	3780	1		5	3	4		6	8		12	10	11	2							9	7									
rep	17	WREXHAM	2-3	Baker, Clarkson	3976	1		5	3	4			8		12	10	11	2	14	6					9	7									

Coca-Cola Cup (F.L. Cup)

R1/1	Aug 30	BLACKPOOL	2-1	Moss, Clarkson	1880	1	2	3	4	5	6	7	8	9	10	11																			
R1/2	Sep 3	Blackpool	0-2		2560	1	2	3	4	5	6	7		9	10	11	12			8	14														

Auto Windscreens Shield (Ass. Members Cup)

R1	Jan 28	NOTTS COUNTY	1-1	Hope	1076		6	3	12	5			8				11		7	15	2			14	9	10		1	4						
R2	Feb 11	Shrewsbury T.	1-2	Hope	1728		6	3	4	5			12			10		2		11	7				9			1	8						

Rd 1 won 4-2 on penalties
Rd 2 lost on 'sudden death' (first goal in extra time)

1997/98 8th in Division 3

		Date	Opponent	Score	Scorers	Att.
1		Aug 9	Peterborough U.	1-0	Forrester	5761
2		16	LEYTON ORIENT	1-0	Forrester	3068
3		23	Swansea	0-2		4865
4		30	MANSFIELD T.	1-0	Calvo-Garcia	3414
5	Sep 2		CHESTER C.	2-1	Eyre(2,1p)	2633
6		7	Notts Co.	1-2	Strodder (og)	5009
7		13	DONCASTER R.	1-1	Eyre	3378
8		20	Barnet	1-0	Eyre (p)	1951
9		27	HULL C.	2-0	Forrester, Calvo-Garcia	4905
10	Oct 4		Rochdale	0-2		2087
11		18	LINCOLN C.	0-1		4152
12		21	SHREWSBURY T.	1-1	Forrester	2362
13		25	Exeter C.	3-2	Walsh, Hope, D'Auria	4552
14		31	Colchester U.	3-3	Hope, D'Auria(2)	3134
15	Nov 4		CAMBRIDGE U.	3-3	Forrester, Eyre, D'Auria	2417
16		8	HARTLEPOOL U.	1-1	Hope	3272
17		11	Cardiff C.	0-0		2340
18		18	Rotherham U.	3-1	Eyre(2), Forrester	3355
19		22	Torquay U.	4-2	Calvo-Garcia(2), D'Auria, Wilcox	2152
20		29	BRIGHTON & H.A.	0-2		3187
21	Dec 13		SCARBOROUGH	1-3	D'Auria	2535
22		20	Darlington	0-1		2267
23		26	NOTTS CO.	1-2	Hendon (og)	4781
24		28	Chester C.	0-1		2263
25	Jan 10		PETERBOROUGH U.	1-3	Forrester	3584
26		17	Mansfield T.	0-1		2375
27		20	Macclesfield T.	0-2		1450
28		24	SWANSEA C.	1-0	D'Auria	2123
29		30	Doncaster R.	2-1	D'Auria, Housham	2086
30	Feb 7		BARNET	1-1	Walker	2313
31		14	ROCHDALE	2-0	Regis, Eyre	2284
32		21	Hull C.	1-2	Regis	4904
33		24	Lincoln C.	1-1	Forrester	3407
34		28	CARDIFF C.	3-3	Eyre(p), Forrester, Calvo-Garcia	2135
35	Mar 3		Hartlepool U.	1-0	Wilcox	1588
36		7	COLCHESTER U.	1-0	McAuley	2143
37		14	Cambridge U.	2-2	Forrester, Stamp	2423
38		21	ROTHERHAM U.	1-1	Eyre	4011
39		28	TORQUAY U.	2-0	Hope, Calvo-Garcia	3264
40	Apr 4		Brighton & H.A.	1-2	Hope	2141
41		11	MACCLESFIELD T.	1-0	D'Auria	2949
42		13	Scarborough	0-0		3427
43		18	DARLINGTON	1-0	Sertori	2267
44		21	Leyton Orient	0-1		2735
45		25	EXETER C.	2-1	D'Auria, Harsley	2024
46	May 2		Shrewsbury T.	2-0	Marshall, Forrester	2704

Two own goals

F.A. Cup

	Date	Opponent	Score	Scorers	Att.
R1	Nov 15	SCARBOROUGH	2-1	Wilcox, Calvo-Garcia	3039
R2	Dec 6	ILKESTON	1-1	Forrester	4187
rep	17	Ilkeston	2-1		2109
R3	Jan 3	Crystal Palace	0-2		11624

Coco-Cola Cup (F.L. Cup)

	Date	Opponent	Score	Scorers	Att.
R1/1	Aug 12	Scarborough	2-0	Calvo-Garcia(2)	1907
R1/2	26	SCARBOROUGH	2-1	Calvo-Garcia(2)	2149
R2/1	Sep 16	EVERTON	0-1		7145
R2/2	Oct 1	Everton	0-5		11562

Auto Windscreens (Associate Members Cup)

	Date	Opponent	Score	Scorers	Att.
R1	Dec 9	CHESTER C.	2-1	Eyre(2p)	813
R2	Jan 6	Hartlepool U.	2-1	Calvo-Garcia, Housham	1491
QF	27	GRIMSBY T.	0-2		4596

1998/99 4th in Division 3

#	Date	Opponent	Result	Scorers	Att	Clarke T	Marshall L	McAuley S	Harsley P	Hope C	Fickling A	Walker J	Calvo-Garcia A	Eyre J	Gayle J	Forrester J	Stamp D	Bull G	Wilcox R	Logan R	Housham S	Stanton N	Atkinson G	Dawson A	Evans T	Sheldon G	Witter A
1	Aug 8	Shrewsbury	1-2	Forrester	3600	1	2	3	4	5	2	7	8	9	10	11											
2	15	CARLISLE U.	3-1	Hope, Eyre, Gayle	2810	1		3	4	6	2	7	11	9	10	8	12	13	5	14							
3	22	Hartlepool U.	2-1	Calvo-Garcia, Logan	2697	1		3	4	6	2	7	11	9	10	8	12	13	5	14							
4	29	PLYMOUTH A.	0-2		2868	1		3	4	6	2	7	11	9	10	8	12	13	5	14							
5	31	Swansea C.	2-1	Eyre(p), Forrester	4024	1	13	3		6	2	7	11	9	10	8	12		5								
6	Sep 5	TORQUAY U.	2-0	Hope, Gayle	2421	1	13	3		6	2	7	11	9	10	8		14	5	4							
7	8	CAMBRIDGE U.	3-2	Forrester(2), Logan	2431	1	13	3		6	2	7	11	9	10	8			5	4							
8	12	Rochdale	2-2	Forrester, Stamp	1929	1	13	3		6	2	7	11	9	10	8	12	14	5	4							
9	19	MANSFIELD T.	3-2	Forrester, Eyre(2)	3554	1		3		6	2	7	11	9	10	8	12		5	4							
10	26	Brighton & H.A.	3-1	Stamp(2), Eyre	2623	1		3		6	2	7	11	9		8	10	14	5	4							
11	Oct 3	HALIFAX T.	0-4		4989	1	13	3		6	2	7	11	9	10	8	12	14	5	4							
12	10	SOUTHEND U.	1-1	Calvo-Garcia	3747	1				6	2	7	11	9	10	8	12		5	4	3						
13	17	Exeter C.	2-2	Forrester, Hope	2885	1	13			6	2	7	11	9	10	8	12		5	4	3						
14	20	Brentford	1-2	Forrester	4700	1		13		6	2	7	11	9	10	8			5	4	3						
15	24	ROTHERHAM U.	4-3	Wilcox, Eyre(p), Knill (og), Logan	4783	1			13	6	2	7	11	9	10	8	12	14	5	4	3						
16	31	Leyton Orient	0-1		3919	1	13			6	2	7	11		10	8	12	9	5	4	3						
17	Nov 7	CHESTER C.	2-1	Forrester, Logan	3160	1		3		6	2	7	11	9		8	10		5	4							
18	10	Barnet	0-1		1314	1	13	3	14	6		7	11		10	8	12	9	5	4	2						
19	21	HULL C.	3-2	Gayle, Forrester, Marshall	5633	1	13	3	7	6			11	9	10	8	12		5	4	2						
20	28	Peterborough U.	1-2	Calvo-Garcia	5160	1	13	3	7	6		14	11	9	10	8			5	4	2						
21	Dec 12	CARDIFF C.	0-2		3200	1	4	3	10	6	2	7		9		8		12	5		11	14	13				
22	19	Darlington	1-3	Brumwell (og)	2456	1	13		3	6	2	7	14	9	10	8			5	4		11					
23	26	HARTLEPOOL U.	1-0	Forrester	3621		13		5	6	2	7	11	9	10	8			4					3	1		
24	28	Scarborough	4-1	Hope, Calvo-Garcia, Forrester(2)	2300				5	6	2	7	11	9	10	8		12	4					3	1		
25	Jan 9	SHREWSBURY	3-0	Forrester, Eyre, Gayle	2860				5	6	2	7	11	9	10	8			4					3	1		
26	16	Carlisle U.	1-0	Eyre	3044		13		5	6	2	7	11	9	10	8			4					3	1		
27	30	SCARBOROUGH	5-1	Logan, Calvo-Garcia(2), Eyre, Hope	3779				5	6		7	11	9		8		10	4			2		3	1	12	
28	Feb 6	Torquay United	0-1		2071				5	6	4	7	11	9		8	12	10				14	2	3	1		
29	13	Cambridge United	0-0		5596				5	6	2	7		9		8						11		3	1		4
30	20	ROCHDALE	0-1		3749		11		5	6	2	7		9		8	10	12	14			13		3	1		4
31	27	Mansfield Town	1-2	Forrester	3208				10	6	2	7	11	9		8						5	14	3	1		
32	Mar 6	BRIGHTON & H.A.	3-1	Eyre(3)	4148				5	6		7	11	9	10	8	14	12	4					3	1		2
33	13	Chester City	2-0	Calvo-Garcia, Forrester	2215				5	6		7	11		10	8	14		4					3	1	9	2
34	20	LEYTON ORIENT	2-0	Calvo-Garcia, Forrester	4163				5	6		7	11	9	10	8		2	4	13				3	1		
35	23	SWANSEA CITY	1-2	Walker	3631				5	6		7	11	9	10	8	14	12	2	4	13			3	1		
36	27	Rotherham U.	0-0		4939				5	6		7	11	9	10	8			4					3	1	14	2
37	30	Plymouth A.	0-5		3589		13		5	6		7	11	9	10	8	12	14	4					3	1		2
38	Apr 3	EXETER CITY	2-0	Eyre, Logan	3419		7		5	6			11	9	10	8		12	4					3	1		2
39	5	Southend U.	1-0	Sheldon	4814		7		5	6			11		10				12	4				3	1	9	2
40	10	BRENTFORD	0-0		5604				5	6			11		10	8	13	14	4	7				3	1	9	2
41	13	PETERBOROUGH U.	1-1	Forrester	3296				5	6			11	9	10	8	13		4					3	1	7	2
42	17	Hull City	3-2	Forrester, Stamp, Eyre	9835				5	6		7		9		8	10	12	4					3	1	13	2
43	24	BARNET	3-1	Calvo-Garcia, Eyre, Forrester	3930				5	6	3	7	11	9	10	8			4						1	13	2
44	May 27	Halifax Town	0-1		3486				5	6		7	11	9	10	8			14	4				3	1	13	2
45	1	Cardiff City	0-0		12455				5	6		7	11	9	12	8		13	14	4				3	1	10	2
46	8	DARLINGTON	0-1		4238				5	6	13	7		9	10	8		12	2	4				3	1	14	

	Apps	22	19	17	34	46	29	41	43	41	37	46	25	22	27	41	16	4	1	24	24	11	14
	Goals		1			5		1	9	15	4	20	4		1	6						1	

Two own goals

Play-offs

#	Date	Opponent	Result	Scorers	Att	Clarke	Marshall	McAuley	Harsley	Hope	Fickling	Walker	Calvo-Garcia	Eyre	Gayle	Forrester	Stamp	Bull	Wilcox	Logan	Housham	Stanton	Atkinson	Dawson	Evans	Sheldon	Witter
SF1	May 15	Swansea City	0-1		7822	1				6	4	7	11	9	10	8			5	2				3			
SF2	18	SWANSEA CITY	3-1	Dawson, Sheldon(2)	7089	1			2	6		7	11	9	10	8			5	4	12			3		13	
F	29	Leyton Orient	1-0	Calvo-Garcia	36985				2	6		7	11		10	8	13	14	5	4	12			3	1	9	

* a.e.t. Full time 1-0

F.A.Cup

#	Date	Opponent	Result	Scorers	Att																						
R1	Nov 14	Woking	1-0	Forrester	3399	1	9	3	14	6		7	11			8	10		5	4	2						
R2	Dec 5	BEDLINGTON	2-0	Eyre(p), Forrester	4719	1	15	3	7	6	2		11	9		8	10	12	5	4							
R3	Jan 2	Wrexham	3-4	Housham, Eyre, Harsley	4429		14	3	5	6	2	7	11	9	10	8			4	15			1				

Worthington Cup (F.L.Cup)

#	Date	Opponent	Result	Scorers	Att																						
R1/1	Aug 11	Blackpool	0-1		1813	1		3	4	5	6	7	8	9	10	11	14	12	2								
R1/2	18	BLACKPOOL	1-1	Forrester	2211	1	16	3	4	6	2	7	11	9	10	8			5								

Auto Windscreen Shield (Ass. Members Cup)

#	Date	Opponent	Result	Scorers	Att																						
R2	Jan 19	Carlisle U.	1-1	Walker	1507				5	6	2	7	11	9	10	8		12		4	14			3	1	13	

Lost 4-3 on penalties a.e.t.

FINAL LEAGUE TABLES 1999/2000 - 2004/05

Final League Table 1999/2000 Division 3

		Pl	Home					Away					F	A	Pts
			W	D	L	F	A	W	D	L	F	A			
1	Preston North End	46	15	4	4	37	23	13	7	3	37	14	74	37	95
2	Burnley	46	16	3	4	42	23	9	10	4	27	24	69	47	88
3	Gillingham	46	16	3	4	46	21	9	7	7	33	27	79	48	85
4	Wigan Athletic	46	15	3	5	37	14	7	14	2	35	24	72	38	83
5	Millwall	46	14	7	2	41	18	9	6	8	35	32	76	50	82
6	Stoke City	46	13	7	3	37	18	10	6	7	31	24	68	42	82
7	Bristol Rovers	46	13	7	3	34	19	10	4	9	35	26	69	45	80
8	Notts County	46	9	6	8	32	27	9	5	9	29	28	61	55	65
9	Bristol City	46	7	14	2	31	18	8	5	10	28	39	59	57	64
10	Reading	46	10	9	4	28	18	6	5	12	29	45	57	63	62
11	Wrexham	46	9	6	8	23	24	8	5	10	29	37	52	61	62
12	Wycombe Wands.	46	11	4	8	32	24	5	9	9	24	29	56	53	61
13	Luton Town	46	10	7	6	41	35	7	3	13	20	30	61	65	61
14	Oldham Athletic	46	8	5	10	27	28	8	7	8	23	27	50	55	60
15	Bury	46	8	10	5	38	33	5	8	10	23	31	61	64	57
16	Bournemouth	46	11	6	6	37	19	5	3	15	22	43	59	62	57
17	Brentford	46	8	6	9	27	31	5	7	11	20	30	47	61	52
18	Colchester United	46	9	4	10	36	40	5	6	12	23	42	59	82	52
19	Cambridge United	46	8	6	9	38	33	4	6	13	26	32	64	65	48
20	Oxford United	46	6	5	12	24	38	6	4	13	19	35	43	73	45
21	Cardiff City	46	5	10	8	23	34	4	7	12	22	33	45	67	44
22	Blackpool	46	4	10	9	26	37	4	7	12	23	40	49	77	41
23	SCUNTHORPE U.	46	4	6	13	16	34	5	6	12	24	40	40	74	39
24	Chesterfield	46	5	7	11	17	25	2	8	13	17	38	34	63	36

Final league Table 2000/01 Division 3

		Pl	Home					Away					F	A	Pts
			W	D	L	F	A	W	D	L	F	A			
1	Brighton & Hove A.	46	19	2	2	52	14	9	6	8	21	21	73	35	92
2	Cardiff City	46	16	7	0	56	20	7	6	10	39	38	95	58	82
3	Chesterfield	46	16	5	2	46	14	9	9	5	33	28	79	42	80
4	Hartlepool United	46	12	8	3	40	23	9	6	8	31	31	71	54	77
5	Leyton Orient	46	13	7	3	31	18	7	8	8	28	33	59	51	75
6	Hull City	46	12	7	4	27	18	7	10	6	20	21	47	39	74
7	Blackpool	46	14	4	5	50	26	8	2	13	24	32	74	58	72
8	Rochdale	46	11	8	4	36	25	7	9	7	23	23	59	48	71
9	Cheltenham Town	46	12	5	6	37	27	6	9	8	22	25	59	52	68
10	SCUNTHORPE U.	46	13	7	3	42	16	5	4	14	20	36	62	52	65
11	Southend United	46	10	8	5	29	23	5	10	8	26	30	55	53	63
12	Plymouth Argyle	46	13	5	5	33	17	2	8	13	21	44	54	61	58
13	Mansfield Town	46	12	7	4	40	26	3	6	14	24	46	64	72	58
14	Macclesfield Town	46	10	5	8	23	21	4	9	10	28	41	51	62	56
15	Shrewsbury Town	46	12	5	6	30	26	3	5	15	19	39	49	65	55
16	Kidderminster H.	46	10	6	7	29	27	3	8	12	18	34	47	61	53
17	York City	46	9	6	8	23	26	4	7	12	19	37	42	63	52
18	Lincoln City	46	9	9	5	36	28	3	6	14	22	38	58	66	51
19	Exeter City	46	8	9	6	22	20	4	5	14	18	38	40	58	50
20	Darlington	46	10	6	7	28	23	2	7	14	16	33	44	56	49
21	Torquay United	46	8	9	6	30	29	4	4	15	22	48	52	77	49
22	Carlisle United	46	8	8	7	26	26	3	7	13	16	39	42	65	48
23	Halifax Town	46	7	6	10	33	32	5	5	13	21	36	54	68	47
24	Barnet	46	9	8	6	44	29	3	1	19	23	52	67	81	45

Final league Table 2001/02 Division 3

		Pl	Home					Away					F	A	Pts
			W	D	L	F	A	W	D	L	F	A			
1	Plymouth Argyle	46	19	2	2	41	11	12	7	4	30	17	71	28	102
2	Luton Town	46	15	5	3	50	18	15	2	6	46	30	96	48	97
3	Mansfield Town	46	17	3	3	49	24	7	4	12	23	36	72	60	79
4	Cheltenham Town	46	11	11	1	40	20	10	4	9	26	29	66	49	78
5	Rochdale	46	13	8	2	41	22	8	7	8	24	30	65	52	78
6	Rushden & Diamonds	46	14	5	4	40	20	6	8	9	29	33	69	53	73
7	Hartlepool United	46	12	6	5	53	23	8	5	10	21	25	74	48	71
8	SCUNTHORPE U.	46	14	5	4	43	22	5	9	9	31	34	74	56	71
9	Shrewsbury Town	46	13	4	6	36	19	7	6	10	28	34	64	53	70
10	Kidderminster H.	46	13	6	4	35	17	6	3	14	21	30	56	47	66
11	Hull City	46	12	6	5	38	18	4	7	12	19	33	57	51	61
12	Southend United	46	12	5	6	36	22	3	8	12	15	32	51	54	58
13	Macclesfield Town	46	7	7	9	23	25	8	6	9	18	27	41	52	58
14	York City	46	11	5	7	26	20	5	4	14	28	47	54	67	57
15	Darlington	46	11	6	6	37	25	4	5	14	23	46	60	71	56
16	Exeter City	46	7	9	7	25	32	7	4	12	23	41	48	73	55
17	Carlisle United	46	11	5	7	31	21	1	11	11	18	35	49	56	52
18	Leyton Orient	46	10	7	6	37	25	3	6	14	18	46	55	71	52
19	Torquay United	46	8	6	9	27	31	4	9	10	19	32	46	63	51
20	Swansea City	46	7	8	8	26	26	6	4	13	27	51	53	77	51
21	Oxford United	46	8	7	8	34	28	3	7	13	19	34	53	62	47
22	Lincoln City	46	8	4	11	25	27	2	12	9	19	35	44	62	46
23	Bristol Rovers	46	8	7	8	28	28	3	5	15	12	32	40	60	45
24	Halifax Town	46	5	9	9	24	28	3	3	17	15	56	39	84	36

Final league Table 2002/03 Division 3

		Pl	Home					Away					F	A	Pts
			W	D	L	F	A	W	D	L	F	A			
1	Rushden & Diam.	46	16	5	2	48	19	8	10	5	25	28	73	47	87
2	Hartlepool United	46	16	5	2	49	21	8	8	7	22	30	71	51	85
3	Wrexham	46	12	7	4	48	26	11	8	4	36	24	84	50	84
4	Bournemouth	46	14	7	2	38	18	6	7	10	22	30	60	48	74
5	SCUNTHORPE U.	46	11	8	4	40	20	8	7	8	28	29	68	49	72
6	Lincoln City	46	10	9	4	29	18	8	7	8	17	19	46	37	70
7	Bury	46	8	8	7	25	26	10	8	5	32	30	57	56	70
8	Oxford United	46	9	7	7	26	20	10	5	8	31	27	57	47	69
9	Torquay United	46	9	11	3	41	31	7	7	9	30	40	71	71	66
10	York City	46	11	9	3	34	24	6	6	11	18	29	52	53	66
11	Kidderminster H.	46	8	8	7	30	33	8	7	8	32	30	62	63	63
12	Cambridge United	46	10	7	6	38	25	6	6	11	29	45	67	70	61
13	Hull City	46	9	10	4	34	19	5	7	11	24	34	58	53	59
14	Darlington	46	8	10	5	36	27	4	8	11	22	32	58	59	54
15	Boston United	46	11	6	6	34	22	4	7	12	21	34	55	56	54
16	Macclesfield Town	46	8	6	9	29	28	6	6	11	28	35	57	63	54
17	Southend United	46	12	1	10	29	23	5	2	16	18	36	47	59	54
18	Leyton Orient	46	9	6	8	28	24	5	5	13	23	37	51	61	53
19	Rochdale	46	7	6	10	30	30	5	10	8	33	40	63	70	52
20	Bristol Rovers	46	7	7	9	25	27	5	8	10	25	30	50	57	51
21	Swansea City	46	9	6	8	28	25	3	7	13	20	40	48	65	49
22	Carlisle United	46	5	5	13	26	40	8	5	10	26	38	52	78	49
23	Exeter City	46	7	7	9	24	31	4	8	11	26	33	50	64	48
24	Shrewsbury Town	46	5	6	12	34	39	4	8	11	28	53	62	92	41

Final league Table 2003/04 Division 3

		Pl	Home					Away					F	A	Pts
			W	D	L	F	A	W	D	L	F	A			
1	Doncaster Rovers	46	17	4	2	47	13	10	7	6	32	24	79	37	92
2	Hull City	46	16	4	3	50	21	9	9	5	32	23	82	44	88
3	Torquay United	46	15	6	2	44	18	8	6	9	24	26	68	44	81
4	Huddersfield Town	46	16	4	3	42	18	7	8	8	26	34	68	52	81
5	Mansfield Town	46	13	5	5	44	25	9	4	10	32	37	76	62	75
6	Northampton Town	46	13	4	6	30	23	9	5	9	28	28	58	51	75
7	Lincoln City	46	9	11	3	36	23	10	6	7	32	24	68	47	74
8	Yeovil Town	46	14	3	6	40	19	9	2	12	30	38	70	57	74
9	Oxford United	46	14	8	1	34	13	4	9	10	21	31	55	44	71
10	Swansea City	46	10	7	6	37	26	6	6	11	22	35	59	62	61
11	Boston United	46	11	7	5	35	21	5	4	14	15	33	50	54	59
12	Cambridge United	46	6	7	10	26	32	8	7	8	31	35	57	67	56
13	Bury	46	10	7	6	29	26	5	4	14	25	38	54	64	56
14	Bristol Rovers	46	9	7	7	29	28	5	6	12	21	35	60	63	55
15	Kidderminster Harr	46	9	5	9	28	29	5	8	10	17	30	45	59	55
16	Cheltenham Town	46	11	4	8	37	38	3	9	11	20	34	57	72	55
17	Southend United	46	8	4	11	27	29	6	8	9	24	34	51	63	54
18	Darlington	46	10	4	9	30	28	4	7	12	23	33	53	61	53
19	Leyton Orient	46	8	9	6	28	27	5	5	13	20	38	41	65	53
20	Macclesfield Town	46	8	9	6	28	25	5	4	14	26	44	42	67	52
21	Rochdale	46	7	8	8	28	26	5	6	12	21	32	49	58	50
22	SCUNTHORPE U.	46	7	10	6	36	27	4	6	13	33	45	69	83	49
23	Carlisle United	46	8	5	10	23	27	4	4	15	23	42	46	69	45
24	York City	46	7	6	10	22	29	3	8	12	13	37	35	64	44

Final league Table 2004/05 Division 2 (Formerly 3)

		Pl	Home					Away					F	A	Pts
			W	D	L	F	A	W	D	L	F	A			
1	Yeovil Town	46	16	4	3	57	28	9	4	10	33	37	90	65	83
2	SCUNTHORPE U.	46	16	5	2	43	16	6	9	8	26	26	69	42	80
3	Swansea City	46	15	5	3	36	16	9	3	11	26	27	62	43	80
4	Southend United	46	13	5	5	31	14	9	7	7	34	32	65	46	78
5	Macclesfield Town	46	15	3	5	39	24	7	6	10	21	25	60	49	75
6	Lincoln City	46	11	8	4	37	22	9	4	10	27	25	64	47	72
7	Northampton Town	46	11	9	3	35	20	9	3	11	27	31	62	51	72
8	Darlington	46	13	4	6	33	21	7	8	8	24	28	57	49	72
9	Rochdale	46	11	8	4	34	21	5	10	8	20	27	54	48	66
10	Wycombe Wands.	46	8	7	8	28	26	9	7	7	30	26	58	52	65
11	Leyton Orient	46	10	8	5	40	30	6	7	10	25	37	65	67	63
12	Bristol Rovers	46	10	12	1	39	22	3	9	11	21	35	60	57	60
13	Mansfield Town	46	9	8	6	29	24	6	7	10	27	32	56	56	60
14	Cheltenham Town	46	10	5	8	27	23	6	7	10	24	31	51	54	60
15	Oxford United	46	11	4	8	29	24	5	7	11	21	39	50	63	59
16	Boston United	46	11	8	4	39	24	3	8	12	23	34	62	58	58
17	Bury	46	8	9	6	26	18	6	7	10	28	36	54	54	58
18	Grimsby Town	46	8	10	5	28	19	6	6	11	23	33	51	52	58
19	Notts County	46	6	7	10	21	27	7	6	10	25	35	46	62	52
20	Chester City	46	7	8	8	25	33	5	8	10	18	36	43	69	52
21	Shrewsbury Town	46	9	7	7	34	18	2	9	12	14	35	48	53	49
22	Rushden & Diam.	46	8	6	9	29	29	2	8	13	13	34	42	63	44
23	Kidderminster H.	46	6	6	11	21	39	4	2	17	18	46	39	85	38
24	Cambridge United	46	7	6	10	22	27	1	10	12	17	35	39	62	30

1999/2000 23rd in Division 2

						Att	Evans	Harsley	Dawson	Logan	Wilcox	Hope	Walker	Hodges	Graves	Gayle	Calvo-Garcia	Housham	Stamp	Marshall	Humphreys	Stanton	Fickling	Sheldon	Sparrow	Ipoua	Guinan	Perez	Marcelle	Bull	Cornforth	McAuley	Omoyinmi	Hyldgaard	Torpey	Quailey	Jackson	Hodgson	Clarke	Turner	Barwick
1	Aug 17	a	Wigan Athletic	0 3		7481	1	2	3	4	5	6	7	8	9	10	11	12	13	14																				
2	14	h	Wycombe Wanderers	0 1		4092	1	2	3	4	5	6	7	8	12		11		10		9																				
3	21	a	Notts County	0 3		5506	1	2	3		5	6	7	8		10	11		14			9	4	12	13																	
4	28	h	AFC Bournemouth	3 1	Humphreys(2,1p), Ipoua	3376	1	2	3	4		6	7	8			11			12	9			5	10		13															
5	30	a	Cardiff City	1 1	Ipoua	8006	1	2	3	4		6	7	8			11			13	9	12		5	14		10															
6	Sep 4	h	Bristol Rovers	0 2		4496	1	2	3	4		6	7	8			11	12			9	13		5	14		10															
7	11	a	Colchester United	1 0	Hodges	3280	1	2	3		5	6		8			11				9		4	7	12	10	13															
8	18	h	Bristol City	1 2	Guinan	4542	1	2	3		5	6		8		12	11						4			7	9	10														
9	25	h	Chesterfield	0 0		4321	1	2	3	4	5	6	7	8		13	11								12		9	10														
10	Oct 2	a	Stoke City	0 1		13068	1	2	3	4	5	6	7	8		12			10					13	11	9																
11	10	a	Burnley	2 1	Ipoua	10752		2	3	4	5	6	7	8		14	11							12		13	9		1	10												
12	16	h	Preston North End	1 1	Ipoua(P)	5326		2	3	4	5	6	7	8			11							12			9		1	10												
13	19	a	Oxford United	1 0	Ipoua	3829		2	3	4		6	7	8		12	11							5			9		1	10												
14	23	a	Chesterfield	1 1	Fickling	3464		2	3	4		6	7	8		13	11							5		12	9		1	10												
15	Nov 2	a	Cambridge United	3 1	Hope, Hardisley., Hodges	3285		2	3		5	6	7	8			13	11					12	4			9		1	10	14												
16	6	h	Millwall	1 4	Cornforth	4550		2	3		5	6	7	8			13	11					12	4			9		1	10		14											
17	12	a	Brentford	3 4	Ipoua (p), Hardley, Calvo-Garcia	4657	12	2	3		5	6	7	8		13	14	11						4			9		1	10													
18	23	h	Gillingham	1 4	Ipoua	3444		2		4		6	7	8			14	11					12	5			9		1	10			13	3									
19	27	a	Reading	1 1	Hodges	6142		2				6	13	8	14		11						7	5			9		1	12		10	3										
20	Dec 4	h	Wigan Athletic	1 2	Hodges	3463		2		4		6	7	8	11								8	5			9		1	12			3										
21	18	h	Bury	0 2		3137		2	3	4		6	7	8					10	13			11	5	12			1		9													
22	26	a	Oldham Athletic	1 1	Hope	5998		2	3	4		6	7	8	10								5		12		9		1				11										
23	28	h	Blackpool	1 0	Omoyimni	4476		2	3	4		6	7	8	10								5	12			9		1				11										
24	Jan 3	a	Luton Town	1 4	Hodges	5574	1	2	3	4	12		7	8	10			13					6	5		14	9						11											
25	15	a	Wycombe Wanderers	1 2	Sheldon	4850		2	12		5		7	8					11				6	4	10		9					3		1									
26	22	h	Notts County	1 0	Ipoua	4035		2	12	4		6	7	8					10					5	13		9					3	11	1									
27	29	a	AFC Bournemouth	1 1	Dawson	4802		2	8	4		6	7						10				14	5	13	12	9					3	11	1									
28	Feb 1	h	Wrexham	0 2		2851		2	11	4		6	7			8	12						13	5	14		9				10	3	7	1									
29	5	h	Cardiff City	0 0		3614		2	11	4		6	7	8									5			12						3		1	9	10							
30	12	a	Bristol Rovers	1 1	Hope	8236	1	2	3	4		6	7	8	12								11	5		13									9	10							
31	19	h	Reading	2 2	Torpey, Quailey	4082	1	2	3	4		6		8	12			7					11	5	13										9	10							
32	26	a	Bristol City	1 2	Quailey	9897	1	2	3	4		6	12	8				7					11	5	13		9									10							
33	Mar 4	h	Colchester United	0 0		4253	1	2	3	4		6	7					8					11	5	14	13	9				12						10							
34	7	a	Millwall	2 1	Logan, Quailey	8772	1	2	3	4		6	7		9			8					11	5	12	13											10							
35	11	h	Cambridge United	0 3		2964	1	2	3	4		6	7		13								5			12										9	10	8	11				
36	18	a	Gillingham	1 3	Harsley	6822	1	12	3	4		6	7			11							8	5		13	14										9	10	2				
37	21	h	Brentford	0 0		2686	1	2	3	4		6	7			11							8		13		12										9	10	5				
38	25	h	Oldham Athletic	1 2	Quailey	3807	1	2	3	4		6	7	12	11								8			13											9	10	5				
39	Apr 28	a	Wrexham	1 3	Quailey	2139	1	2	12	4		6	7	8			5						3	14		13											9	10		11			
40	1	a	Bury	0 3		3546	1	2	3	4		12	7	8				5	13				6		11	10												9						
41	8	h	Luton Town	1 2	Dawson	3811	1	2	3	4		6	7	8	12								5		11	10												9						
42	15	a	Blackpool	2 0	Bull, Sheldon	5542	1	2	3	4		6	7	8	14								5	12	11	10					13							9						
43	22	a	Preston North End	0 1		15518	1	2	3	4		6	7	8	14				12				5		11	13					10							9						
44	24	h	Stoke City	0 2		5435	1	2	3	4		6	7	8									5		11	12					10							9	13					
45	29	a	Oxford United	0 2		6753	1	2	3	4		6	7	8			13						11		12												9	10	5				
46	May 6	h	Burnley	1 2	Hodges	5862		2	3	4		6	7	8									11		13												9	10	5		1	12	
					Apps		28	46	43	39	14	44	42	40	19	12	18	9	10	5	6	34	30	22	11	40	3	13	10	6	4	8	6	5	15	14	6	1	1	1	1
					Goals			3	2	1		3		7			1			2			1	3		9	1				1	1				1	5						

F A Cup

| R1 | Oct 29 | A | Rushden & Diamonds | 0 2 | | 4112 | 1 | 2 | 3 | 4 | | 6 | 7 | 8 | | | 11 | | | | | | 12 | 5 | 14 | | 9 | | | | 10 | 13 | | | | | | | | | | |

Worthington Cup (F.L.Cup)

| R1/1 | Aug 10 | H | Huddersfield Town | 0 2 | | 3398 | 1 | 2 | 3 | 4 | 5 | 6 | 7 | 8 | 9 | 10 | 11 | | 12 | 13 | | | | | | | | | | | | | | | | | | | | | | | |
| R1/2 | 24 | A | Huddersfield Town | 0 0 | | 4345 | 1 | 2 | 3 | | | 6 | 7 | 8 | 12 | | 11 | 13 | 10 | | | | 4 | 5 | 9 | 14 | | | | | | | | | | | | | | | | | | | |

Auto Windscreen Shield (Associate Members Cup)

| R2 | Jan 8 | A | Lincoln City | 2 1 | Hodges, Sheldon | 3617 | | 2 | | | 5 | | 7 | 8 | | | | | 10 | | | 6 | 4 | 9 | 12 | | | | | | | 3 | 11 | 1 | | | | | | | | | | |
| QF | 25 | H | Chesterfield | 1 2 | Stamp | 2532 | | 2 | 3 | | 5 | 6 | | | | 11 | | | 10 | | | 7 | | 12 | 9 | | | | | 8 | | | | 1 | | | | | | | | | | |

Pounewatchy was no.4 in QF

2000/01   10th in Division 3

League results and appearance/goal tables omitted due to complexity of the scorecard grid.

F A Cup

	Date		Opponent	Score	Scorers	Att
R1	Nov 18	h	Hartlepool United	3 1	Ipoua (3)	3552
R2	Dec 9	h	Brighton & Hove Albion	2 1	Toprey, Sheldon	3879
R3	Jan 6	a	Burnley	2 2	Hosges, Ipoua	8054
rep	23	h	Burnley (5-4 on pens.)	1 1	Dawson	4709
R4	28	a	Bolton Wanderers	1 5	Calvo-Garcia	11737

Worthington Cup (F.L.Cup)

	Date		Opponent	Score	Scorers	Att
R1/1	Aug 25	a	Wigan Athletic	0 1		2725
R1/2	Sep 5	h	Wigan Athletic	1 4	Torpey	2062

LDV Vans Trophy (Associate Members Cup)

	Date		Opponent	Score	Scorers	Att
R1	Dec	a	Hartlepool United	2 3	Sheldon, Quailey	1538

2001/02 8th in Division 3

						Evans	Bradshaw	Dawson	Jackson	Thom	Stanton	Sheldon	Graves	Carruthers	Grant	Beagrie	Quailey	Croudson	Wilcox	Brough	Barwick	Ridley	Torpey	Kell	Hodges	Cotterill	Calvo-Garcia	McCoombe	Sparrow	Dudley	Anderson	McGibbon	Parton	Pepper	Jeffrey	Vaughan
1	Aug 11	a	Kidderminster Harriers	0 1		3173	1	2	3	4	5	6	7	8	9	10	11	12																			
2	18	h	Bristol Rovers	1 2	Quailey	3593		6	3	4			7	8	9		11	10	1	2	12																	
3	25	a	Exeter City	4 0	Carruthers(2), Grant, Bradshaw	2798		2	3	4	5	6	14	8	9	10	11		1	12		7	13															
4	27	h	Lincoln City	1 1	Beagrie	4349		2	3	4	5	6	12	8	9	10	11		1			7	13															
5	Sep 1	a	Macclesfield Town	3 4	Jackson, Carruthers, Sheldon	1740		2	3	4	5	6	7	8	10		11		1		12			9														
6	8	h	Hartlepool United	1 0	Torpey	3206	1	6	3	4	5			8	10		11			2	12	7		9														
7	15	a	Rochdale	2 2	Brough, Beagrie (p)	3468	1	2	3	4	5	6					11			12	10	7		9	8	13												
8	18	h	Swansea City	2 2	Carruthers, Torpey	2574	1	2	3	4		6			10	14	11			5	7	13		9	8	12													
9	22	h	Mansfield Town	0 0		3857	1	2	3	4	5	6			10		11	13			7			9	8	12													
10	25	a	Torquay United	0 0		1982	1	2	3	4	5	6			10		11	12			13			9	8	7													
11	Oct 29	a	Shrewsbury Town	3 1	Thom, Carruthers, Quailey	3047	1	2	3	4	5	6			9		11	10			14	12			8	7	13												
12	5	a	Halifax Town	0 0		2603	1	2	3	4	5	12			9		11	10			13			14	8	7		6											
13	13	h	Luton Town	0 2		3939	1	2	3	4		6	12		9		11	10						14	8	7		5	13										
14	20	a	Oxford United	1 0	Torpey	5006	1		3	4	5	13	12		14		11				7	2		9	8			6	10										
15	23	h	Southend United	2 0	Carruthers, Beagrie	2956	1	2	3	4	5	12			10		11	14			13			9	8	7		6											
16	Nov 27	a	Cheltenham Town	3 3	Carruthers, Beagrie, Quailey	3295	1		3	4	5	2			10		11	14		12	13			9	8	7		6											
17	3	h	Leyton Orient	4 1	Torpey (2), Hodges, Beagrie	3356	1		3	4		5			10		11	13			14			9	8	7		6	2	12									
18	9	a	York City	2 0	Carruthers, Calvo-Garcia	3192	1		3	4		5			10		11	13			12			9	8	7		6	2	14									
19	20	a	Rushden & Diamonds	0 0		3533	1		3	4		5			10		11	12						9	8	7		6	2										
20	24	h	Darlington	7 1	Carruthers(2),Torpey(2),Beagrie(p),Sheldon,Kell	3662	1	12	3	4		5	14		10		11				13			9	8	7		6	2										
21	Dec 1	a	Carlisle United	0 3		2702	1	12	3	4		5			10		11	13						9	8	7		6	2										
22	15	h	Hull City	2 1	Hodges, Torpey	6479	1	14	3	4		5			10		11				12	13		9	8	7		6	2										
23	22	h	Plymouth Argyle	2 1	Hodges (2)	3602	1	6	3	4		5			10						8			9		7		11	2	12									
24	29	a	Lincoln City	2 3	Calvo-Garcia, Beagrie	5235	1	6	3	4		5					11	10						9		7		8	2										
25	Jan 12	a	Bristol Rovers	1 1	Calvo-Garcia	6691	1		3	4	12	5		7	10		11							9				8	2	6									
26	15	h	Exeter City	3 4	Torpey, Beagrie(p), Quailey	2877	1		3	4	12	5		8	10		11	14						9		7		6	2	13									
27	19	h	Kidderminster Harriers	1 0	Torpey	3360	1		3	4	5	6			11			10				2		9		7		8											
28	22	a	Plymouth Argyle	1 2	Carruthers	5804	1		3	4	5	6			11		14							9		13		8	12	2									
29	26	h	Halifax Town	4 0	Thom,Torpey(2), Calvo-Garcia	3465	1		3	4	5	6			10		11	13			14			9		7		8	12	2									
30	29	a	Hartlepool United	2 3	Beagrie (2, 1p)	3294	1		3	4	13	5		7	10		11	12						9				8	2	6									
31	Feb 2	a	Shrewsbury Town	2 2	Jackson, Quailey	3345	1		3	4		6		7			11	10						9			5	8	12	2	13								
32	9	h	Oxford United	1 0	Hodges	3504	1		3	4					11			10	2					9		7	5	8		6	9	12							
33	12	h	Macclesfield Town	1 1	Torpey	2870	1		3	4		6			11			10						9		7	5	8		2	12								
34	16	a	Luton Town	3 2	Beagrie, Graves, Sparrow	6371	1		3	4		6		7			11	10						9		12		8		2		5							
35	23	h	Rochdale	2 1	Graves (2)	4521	1		3	4		6		7			11	10						9		12		8		2	13	5							
36	26	a	Swansea City	2 2	Calvo-Garcia,Quailey	3085	1	6	3	4								10	2			7		9		13	12	11		8		5							
37	Mar 2	h	Mansfield Town	1 2	Quailey	6292	1		3	4		6	12					10						9		7	5	11		2				8					
38	5	h	Torquay United	1 0	Quailey	2838	1		3	4		6	8					10						9		7		11		2		5	12						
39	9	a	Hull City	1 0	Jackson	12529	1		3	4		6	8					10				12		9		7		11		2		5							
40	16	h	Carlisle United	2 1	Jeffrey, Hodges	4109	1		3	4			6	8										9		7	4	11	12	2		5					10		
41	23	a	Southend United	0 2		3818	1	2		4			6		14			13		5			3	9			7	11	12	8							10		
42	30	h	Cheltenham Town	1 2	Calvo-Garcia	5086	1			4			6		12	13		11					3	9		7		8		2							10		5
43	Apr 1	a	Leyton Orient	0 0		4221	1		3	4			6		7	10		11	13					9		12		8		2									5
44	6	h	Rushden & Diamonds	1 1	Underwood (o.g)	4794	1		3	4			6	12	7	10		11						9				8		2							13		5
45	13	a	Darlington	1 2	Carruthers	4218	1		3	4			6	12	7	10		11						9		14		8		2							13		5
46	20	h	York City	1 0	Carruthers	5159	1		3	4			6					10			11	13				7		8	12	2								9		5
			Apps				42	21	44	45	20	42	14	17	33	4	40	30	4	9	19	10	4	39	16	35	10	34	17	24	4	1	6	1	1	6	5
			Goals							1	3	2		2	3	13	1	11	7					13	1	6		6		1						1	

1 own goal

F A Cup

R1	Nov 1	a	Doncaster Rovers	3 2	Hodges, Carruthers, Calvo-Garcia	6222	1		3	4		5			10		11	12						9	8	7		6	2									
R2	Dec 8	h	Brentford	3 2	Carruthers (2), Calvo-Garcia	3457	1		3	4		5			10		11							9	8	7		6	2									
R3	Jan 5	a	Millwall	1 2	McCoombe	9244	1			4	12	5			10		11	13			3	9			7		8	2	6									

Worthington Cup (F.L.Cup)

R1 Aug 20	a	Rotherham United	0 2		2589		2	3	4	5	6	7	12	9	10	11		1	14	13		8														

LDV Vans Trophy(Associate Members Cup)

R1 Oct 16	h	Lincoln City	3 1	Torpey, Beagrie(2)	1662	1		3	4	2				10		11				13		12	9	8	7		5	6									
R2 30	h	Darlington	3 0	Hodges, Carruthers, McCoombe	1626	1		3	4	2				10			11	14		12	13		9	8	7		6	5									
Q/F Dec 4	a	Huddersfield Town	1 4	Torpey, Beagrie(2)	3587	1	2	3	4			13	12	10			14			8			9	11	7		6	5									

2002/03 5th in Division 3

#	Date		Opponent	Score	Scorers	Att	Evans	Sparrow	Dawson	Stanton	Jackson	Cotterill	Graves	Calvo-Garcia	Carruthers	Wheatcroft	Beagrie	Brough	McCoombe	Torpey	Barwick	Ryan	Wright	Parton	Ridley	Balmer	Featherstone	Kilford	Byrne	Hayes	O'Connor	Taylor	Dalglish	Strong
1	Aug 10	h	Wrexham	1 1	Calvo-Garcia	3879	1	2	3	4	5	6	7	8	9	10	11	12	13														
2	13	a	Exeter City	1 1	Carruthers	3722	1	2	3	4	5	6	7	8	9	10	11	12															
3	17	a	Leyton Orient	0 2		4028	1	2	3	4	5		7	8	10	14	11	12			9	13											
4	24	h	York City	2 1	Smith (o.g.), Carruthers	3540	1	2	3	4	5	6	7	8	10		11	12			9	13											
5	26	a	Rushden & Diamonds	0 2		3849	1	2	3	4	5	6	7	8	10	12	11	14	13	9													
6	31	h	Bristol Rovers	2 2	Dawson, Carruthers	3178	1	2	3	4	5	6	7	8	10		11	14	13	9	12												
7	Sep 7	a	Lincoln City	0 1		4204	1	2	3	4	5	6	7	8	10		11	13	12	9		14											
8	14	h	Kidderminster Harriers	1 1	Brough	2676	1		3		5		7	8	10		11	6	4	9			2	13	12								
9	17	h	Carlisle United	3 1	Torpey (2), Carruthers	2342	1	6	3		5		7	11	10			8	4	9			12	2									
10	21	a	Macclesfield Town	3 2	Carruthers, Torpey (2)	1929	1	2	3	4	5		7	11	10			8	6	9	13			12									
11	28	a	Shrewsbury Town	1 1	Sparrow	2988	1	2	3	4	5		7	11	10		12	8	6	9													
12	Oct 5	a	Oxford United	1 0	Beagrie (p)	5658	1	2	3	4	5		7	8	10		11		6	9													
13	12	h	Cambridge United	1 2	Sparrow,	3140	1	2	3	4			7	8	10		11		6	9							5	12					
14	19	a	Rochdale	2 1	Carruthers (2)	3442	1	2	3	4			7	8	10		11	12	6	9							5	13					
15	26	h	Torquay United	5 1	Carruthers, Torpey (3), McCoombe	2911	1	2	3	4			7	8	10		11	12	6	9							5	13					
16	29	h	Darlington	1 1	Carruthers	3059	1	2	3	4			7	8	10		11		6	9							5	12					
17	Nov 2	a	Hull City	0 2		11885	1		3	2			7	8	10		11	13	4	9	6						5	12					
18	9	h	Boston United	2 0	Beagrie (p), Torpey	3730	1		3	2			7	8	10		11		4	9							5	6	12				
19	23	h	Swansea City	2 0	Carruthers (p), Sparrow	2886	1	8	3	2			7		10				4	9								6	11	5				
20	30	a	AFC Bournemouth	1 2	Sparrow,	6527	1	8	3	2				12	10			7	4	9					13			6	11	5				
21	Dec 14	h	Bury	0 1		3011	1	8		2			7		10			11	4	9					3			6		5	12	13		
22	21	a	Hartlepool United	2 2	Brough, Carruthers	4089	1	8	3	2	12		7		10			11	4	9								14	6	5		13		
23	26	h	Rushden & Diamonds	0 0		4096	1	8	3	2	4			13	11	10		7		9					12			6		5				
24	29	a	Southend United	2 1	Carruthers, Torpey	4248	1	8	3	2	4		7		10			13		9					12			6	11	5				
25	Jan 1	a	York City	3 1	Torpey (p), Carruthers, Graves	4554	1	8	3	2	4		7	14	10				12	13	9							6	11	5				
26	11	h	Leyton Orient	2 1	Sparrow, Kilford	3242	1	8	3	2	4		7	13	10					9					12			6	11	5				
27	18	a	Bristol Rovers	1 2	Carruthers	6617	1	8	3	2	4		7	12	10					9						11		6		5		13		
28	21	h	Exeter City	1 1	Carruthers	2461	1	8	3	2	4		7		10		13		12	9								6	11	5				
29	25	h	Southend United	4 1	Carruthers, Kilford, Calvo-Garcia, Hayes	3096	1		3	2	5		7	11	10		13	8	4									9	6		12			
30	Feb 1	a	Wrexham	1 2	Sparrow	3129	1	8	3		2			11	10		12	7	4									9	6	5	13			
31	8	a	Boston United	0 1		3358	1	7	3	2	4			8	10			11	12									6	5	9				
32	15	h	Hull City	3 1	Hayes, Sparrow (2)	6284	1	7		2	4			12	8	10		11	14	13					3			6	5	9				
33	22	h	Lincoln City	0 0		5141	1	7	3	2	5			12	8	10		11	4									6		9				
34	Mar 1	a	Kidderminster Harriers	3 1	Beagrie (2, 1p), Carruthers	2834	1	8	3	4	5	13	7		10		11						12	2				6		9				
35	8	h	Macclesfield Town	1 1	Hayes	3398	1	8	3	4	5		7	12	10		11							2				6		9	13			
36	11	h	Carlisle United	2 1	Beagrie, Dawson	3124	1	8	3	4	5		7	12	10		11							2			13	6		9	14			
37	15	a	Torquay United	1 1	Sparrow	2486	1	8	3	4	5		7	12	10		11							2			14	6		9	13			
38	18	h	Rochdale	3 1	Hayes (2), Kilford	3616	1	8	3	2	5		7		12		11		4								13	6		9		10		
39	22	h	Darlington	0 1		3904	1	8	3	5		12	7		10		11		4					2				6		9		14	13	
40	29	a	Cambridge United	1 1	Hayes	3951	1	8	3	2			12				11		4									6		9		10	7	5
41	Apr 5	h	AFC Bournemouth	0 2		4488	1	8	3	2			12		13		11		4									6		9		10	7	5
42	12	a	Swansea City	1 1	Carruthers	6014	1	8	3	2			7		13		11		4									6		9		10	12	5
43	19	a	Hartlepool United	4 0	Hayes, Carruthers(2), Calvo-Garcia	5280	1	8	3	2	4		12	11	10											13		6		9			7	5
44	21	a	Bury	0 0		3898	1	2			4		7	11	10		12								13	3		6		9			8	5
45	26	h	Oxford United	2 0	Hayes, Dalglish	5629	1	7	3	2	4			8	10		11		12									6		9			13	5
46	May 3	a	Shrewsbury Town	2 1	Daglish (2)	4127	1	7	3	2	4			8	10		11		12									13	6				9	5
					Apps		46	42	43	42	33	9	41	35	45	4	34	23	31	28	5	2	2	8	11	6	20	28	13	18	3	8	8	7
					Goals			9	2				1	3	20		5	2	1	10									3	8			3	

1 own goal

Play-offs

#	Date		Opponent	Score	Scorers	Att																											
S/F1	May 10	a	Lincoln City	3 5	Calvo-Garcia(2), Stanton	8902	1	7	3	2	4			8	10		11			13								6		9			12	5
S/F2	14	h	Lincoln City	0 1		8295	1	8	3	2	4		13	11	14				12	9								6		10			7	5

FA Cup

#	Date		Opponent	Score	Scorers	Att																											
R1	Nov 16	a	Northwich Victoria	3 0	Torpey (3)	1724	1		3	5			7	11	10			8	4	9			2					6	12					
R2	Dec 7	h	Carlisle United	0 0		3590	1	8	3	2			12		10			7	4	9								6	11	5				
rep	23	a	Carlisle United	1 0	Carruthers	6809	1	8	3	2	4		7	12	10		11		9						13			6	5					
R3	Jan 4	h	Leeds United	0 2		8329	1	8	3	2	4		7	14	10				12						13			6	11	5				

Worthington Cup (F.L.Cup)

#	Date		Opponent	Score	Scorers	Att																											
R1	Sep 11	a	Preston North End	1 2	Torpey	5594	1	6	3	4	5		7	11	10			8		9	13		2	12										

LDV Vans Trophy (Associate Members Cup)

#	Date		Opponent	Score	Scorers	Att																											
R1	Oct 22	h	Blackpool	2 3	Torpey, Dawson	1475	1	8	3	2			7		10		11	6	4	9					13		5	12						

2003/04   22nd in Division 3

#		Date		Opponent	Score	Scorers	Att	Evans	Stanton	Sharp	Jackson	Byrne	Kilford	Sparrow	Kell	Torpey	Hayes	Beagrie	MacLean	Graves	Calvo-Garcia	McCoombe	Ridley	Featherstone	Russell	Barwick	Butler	Keegan	Hunt	Gulliver	Taylor	Smith	Parton	Holloway	Groves	Williams
1	Aug	9	h	Bristol Rovers	1 2	Beagrie (p)	4186	1	2	3	4	5	6	7	8	9	10	11	12																	
2		16	a	Bury	3 2	Torpey (2), Beagrie	2761	1	2	3	4	5	6	7	8	9	10	11	12																	
3		23	h	Oxford United	1 1	Beagrie (p)	3617	1	2	3	4	5		7	8	9	10	11	12		6															
4		26	a	Mansfield Town	0 5		5142	1		3	4	5	6		8	9	10	11	7	13	12	2														
5		30	h	Torquay United	2 1	McaLean, Calvo-Garcia	3080	1		3	4	5	6		8	9	10	11	13	7	12	2														
6	Sep	6	a	Boston United	1 1	Sharp (p)	3154	1		3	4	5			8	9			10	7	11		2	6												
7		13	h	Swansea City	2 2	Calvo-Garcia (2)	3510	1	2	6	4	5	13	7	8	9	12		10		11		3													
8		16	a	Kidderminster Harriers	2 0	Byrne, MacLean	2162			3	12	5	6	7	8	9			10			11	4	2	14	1	13									
9		20	a	Leyton Orient	1 1	Kell	3663		2	3	4	5		7	8	9	14		10			11	6		12	1		13								
10		27	h	Southend United	1 1	MacClean	3390		2	6		5		7	8	9		11	10				4			1		3								
11		30	h	Cheltenham Town	5 2	MacClean (3, 1p), Beagrie, Torpey	2857		2	3		5		7	8	9	13	11	10		6					1	12	4								
12	Oct	4	a	Rochdale	0 2		2838		2	3		5		7	8	9	12	11	10		6			13	1		4									
13		11	h	Lincoln City	1 3	Hayes	5045		2	3		5		7	8	9	12	11	10		6				1		4									
14		17	a	Northampton Town	1 1	Kell	4827			13	4	5		2	8	9	14	11	10	12				6	1	7	3									
15		21	a	Carlisle United	4 1	Torpey, MacLean, Sharp,Beagrie (p)	3437			3	4	5	6			9	14	11	10	7			12			1	8	2	13								
16		25	h	York City	6 2	Beagrie, Sparrow, Barwick, MacLean(3)	3807		13	3	4	5		8		9	12	11	10	7						1	8	2									
17	Nov	1	h	Huddersfield Town	2 2	Beagrie, MacLean	4715			3	4	5		6	7	9		11	10	14			12			1	8	2	13								
18		15	a	Macclesfield Town	4 0	Hayes, MacLean (3)	2205	1			4	5		7	8		9	11	10				3				6	2									
19		22	h	Cambridge United	2 2	Torpey, Beagrie (p)	3397	1		3	4	5	12	7	8		9	11	10								6	2									
20		29	a	Darlington	1 1	Beagrie (p)	3606	1		3	4	5	6	7			13	9	11	10	12						8	2									
21	Dec	13	h	Hull City	1 1	Beagrie (p)	6426	1		3				7	8	9	12	11	10	2		4					6	5									
22		20	a	Yeovil Town	1 2	Beagrie (p)	5714	1	2	3	12	5		7	8		9	11	10					14			6	4		13							
23		26	a	Doncaster Rovers	0 1		8961	1	2	3		5		7	8	9	13		10	12				11			6	4									
24		28	h	Boston United	0 1		4346	1	2	3		5	13	7	8	9	14		10	12				11			6	4									
25	Jan	10	a	Bristol Rovers	0 1		5789	1				5	13	7	8	9	14		10	2		12	3	11			6	4									
26		17	h	Bury	0 0		3869	1	2	3		5	6	7	12	9	13					14					8			4	10	11					
27		27	h	Mansfield Town	0 0		3113	1	4	3		5		7		9	10	11		2							6				8		12				
28	Feb	7	h	Doncaster Rovers	2 2	Torpey, Butler	5681	1	2	3		5		7	12	9	10	11									6	4			8		13				
29		11	a	Oxford United	2 3	Torpey (2)	5118	1	2	3		5		7		9	12	11			13						8	4			6	10					
30		14	a	Lincoln City	1 1	Taylor C.	5324	1	2	3		5			7	9	10	11	13		12						6	4			8						
31		21	h	Northampton Town	1 0	Ridley	3566	1	2	3		5	6	7		9		11	10	12		13	14					4			8						
32		24	h	Torquay United	0 1		2561	1	2	12	11	5		7		9			10	2		13	3				6	4			8	14					
33	Mar	6	h	Yeovil Town	3 0	MacLean (2), Holloway	3355	1	4	11						9			10	2		5	3								8			6	7	12	
34		9	a	York City	3 1	Groves (2), MacLean (p)	2676	1	4	11						9			10	2		12	3				13	5			8				6	7		
35		13	h	Hull City	1 2	MacLean	19076	1	2	11		5				9		12	10				3					4			8				6	7		
36		16	h	Kidderminster Harriers	0 2		2512	1	2	11			5		12	9	13	11	10									4			8				6	7		
37		20	a	Swansea City	2 4	Taylor C. (2)	4400	1	4					7		9	13	12	10				3				6	5			8			2	11		
38		23	h	Carlisle United	2 3	MacLean (2, 1p)	2326	1	4	13				7		9	12		10	2			3				6	5			8				11		
39		27	h	Leyton Orient	1 1	Sparrow	2822	1	4	12			13	7		9	14		10	2			3				6	5			8				11		
40	Apr	2	a	Southend United	2 4	Sparrow, Torpey	4976	1					5			7	9	12		10				3	11		6	4			8			2			
41		10	h	Rochdale	2 2	MacLean, Butler	3564	1	4							7			9	12	13	10			3	11	6	5			8			2			
42		12	h	Cheltenham Town	1 2	Groves	3409	1	2					5	13	7			9	12	14	10			3		6	4			8				11		
43		17	a	Huddersfield Town	2 3	Sodge o.g., MacLean	12108	1	2	3			5	12	7			9		11	10						6	4							8		
44		20	a	Macclesfield Town	1 0	Torpey	4334	1	2	3			5		7			9	13		10		12				6	4							8		
45	May	1	a	Cambridge United	2 3	Beagrie, Torpey	4498	1	2	3			5		7			11	10	12	14						6	4			13				8		
46		8	h	Darlington	0 1		4801	1	2	3			5		7	12	9	14	11	10	13	6						4			8						
						Apps		36	33	40	17	39	18	38	24	43	35	32	42	21	12	15	18	11	10	30	35	2	1	2	20	1	3	5	13	1
						Goals				2				1		3	2	11	2	11	23		2		1			1	2			3			1	3	

1 own goal

F A Cup

R1	Nov	8	h	Shrewsbury Town	2 1	Hayes(2)	3232	1		3		5		7	8		9	11	10			2					6	4		12							
R2	Dec	6	h	Sheffield Wednesday	2 2	Torpey(2)	7418	1		3	4	5		7	8	9		11	10							12	6	2									
rep		17	a	Sheffield Wednesday	0 0	(a.e.t. 3-1 on pens.)	11722	1	12	3		5		7	8	9	13	11	10	2							6	4									
R3	Jan	3	a	Barnsley	0 0		10839	1	2	3		5	13	7	8	9	14	11	10							12	6	4									
rep		13	h	Barnsley	2 0	Torpey, McCoombe	6293	1	4			5	6	7	13	9	11		10	2		14	3	12			8										
R4		24	a	Portsmouth	1 2	Parton	17508	1	4	3		5	6	7		9	10	11		2				12			8						13				

Carling Cup (F.L.Cup)

| R1 | Aug | 8 | h | Oldham Athletic | 2 1 | Hayes(2) | 2366 | 1 | 2 | 3 | 4 | 5 | 6 | 7 | 8 | 9 | 10 | 11 | 14 | 12 | 13 | | | | | | | | | | | | | | | | |
| R2 | Sep | 23 | h | Burnley | 2 3 | MacLean, Beagrie | 2915 | | | 3 | | 5 | | 7 | 8 | 9 | 13 | 12 | 10 | | 4 | | 11 | 1 | 6 | 2 | | | | | | | | | | | |

LDV Vans Trophy (Associate Members Cup)

R1	Oct	14	h	Shrewsbury Town	2 1	Jackson, Kell	1265		2	3	12	5		7	8	14	9	11	10		6				1	13	4										
R2	Nov	4	a	Hull City	3 1	Torpey, Sparrow, MacLean	6656	1		3	4	5	6	7	12	9		11	10			13				8	2										
Q/F	Dec	9	a	Bury (a.e.t.)	1 0	Hayes	1246	1		3		5		7	8	9	13	11	10	12		4		14		6	2										
S/F	Jan	20	a	Sheffield Wednesday	0 4		10236	1	2	3		5	6	7	13	9	14		11				12			8				4	10						

2004/05   2nd in Division 2

Re-classification of the Divisions: Division 3 became Division 2

#	Date	H/A	Opponent	Score	Scorers	Att	Musselwhite	Stanton	Ridley	Butler	Crosby	Baraclough	Taylor	Kell	Bailey	Hayes	Beagrie	Sparrow	Keogh	Parton	Brighton	Featherstone	Rankine	Evans	Jackson	Byrne	Barwick	Torpey	Graves	Williams	Sharp	Teggart	Walters	Angus	Corden	Hinds
1	Aug 7	h	Rochdale	3-1	Taylor, Hayes, Sparrow	4409	1	2	3	4	5	6	7	8	9	10	11	12	13																	
2	10	a	Cheltenham Town	2-0	Kell, Keogh	3647	1	2	3	4	5	6	7	8	9	10	11	13	12																	
3	14	a	Oxford United	1-1	Hayes	4920	1	2	3	4	5	6	7	8	13	10	11	12	9																	
4	21	h	Lincoln City	3-2	Kell, Butler (2)	5215	1	2	3	4	5	6	7	8	13	10	11	12	9																	
5	28	h	Macclesfield Town	2-2	Sparrow, Hayes	2321	1	2	3	4	5	6	12	8		10	11	7	9																	
6	30	h	Northampton Town	2-0	Keogh, Crosby (p)	4201	1	2	3	4	5	6	7	8		10		11	9																	
7	Sep 4	a	Darlington	0-0		3983	1	2	3	4	5	6	7	8		10		11	9	12																
8	11	h	Chester City	1-2	Butler	4203	1	2	3	4	5	6	7	8		10		11	9	13	12															
9	18	a	Bury	1-0	Rankine	2846	1	2	3	4	5	6	12	8		10	11	7	9			13														
10	25	h	Mansfield Town	1-1	Baraclough	5463	1	2	3	4	5	6	14	8		10	11	7	9	12		13														
11	Oct 2	a	Boston United	1-1	Hayes	3640	1	2	3	4	5	6	7	8		10	11	12	9			14					13									
12	8	h	Wycombe Wanderers	2-0	Hayes, Crosby (p)	3373	1	2	3	4	5	6	7	8		10		14	13		11				12		9									
13	16	a	Kidderminster Harriers	2-3	Torpey, Hayes	2167	1	2	3	4	5	6	7	8		10		14			11				13		12	9								
14	19	h	Southend United	3-2	Torpey, Hayes (2)	3402	1	2	3	4	5	6	7	8		10	11	12							13			9								
15	23	h	Yeovil Town	1-0	Butler	4470	1	2	3	4	5	6	7	8		10	11	12							13			9								
16	30	a	Leyton Orient	1-1	Torpey	4359	1	2	3	4	5	6	12	8		10	11	7							13	14		9								
17	Nov 6	h	Grimsby Town	2-0	Hayes (2)	8054	1		3	4	5	6	12	8		10	11	7							13		2	9								
18	20	a	Bristol Rovers	3-0	Hayes (2), Torpey	7039	1		3	4	5	6	12	8		10	11	7									2	9								
19	27	h	Shrewsbury Town	3-1	Beagrie (p), Hayes, Taylor	4418	1		3	4	5	6	12	8		10	11	7							13		2	9								
20	Dec 7	a	Cambridge United	2-1	Torpey, Tayloe	2666	1	12	3	4	5	6	14	8		10	11	7							13		2	9								
21	11	h	Swansea City	1-0	Torpey	5075	1		3	4	5	6	12	8		10	11	7							13		2	9								
22	18	a	Rushden & Diamonds	3-1	Butler (2), Torpey	3198	1	12	3	4	5	6	13	8		10	11	7									2	9								
23	26	a	Chester City	1-1	Torpey	3216	1	12	3	4	5	6	8			10	11	7									2	9								
24	28	h	Notts County	0-0		6399	1	2	3	4	5	6	12	8		10	11	7							13			9								
25	Jan 1	h	Darlington	0-1		5131	1	2	3	4	5	6	12	8		10	11	7							14	13										
26	3	a	Mansfield Town	0-1		5315	1		2			6	12	8		10	11	7		13		9		4	5				3		9						
27	15	h	Bury	3-2	Butler, Torpey (2)	5365	1		3	4	5	6	12	8		10	11	7							13		2	9								
28	22	a	Notts County	0-2		6429	1		3	4	5	6	13	8		10	11	7							14		2	9		12						
29	29	h	Boston United	1-1	Butler	5056	1		3	4	5	6	13	8		10	11	7							14		2	9		12						
30	Feb 5	h	Kidderminster Harriers	2-1	Baraclough, Hayes	5023	1			4	5	6	12	8		13	11	7									2	9			3	10				
31	11	a	Southend United	0-0		8224	1				5	6	11	8		12		7									4	9			3	10	2			
32	15	a	Wycombe Wanderers	1-2	Sparrow	4089	1		12		5		6	8		14	11	7	13								4	9			3	10	2			
33	19	h	Leyton Orient	1-0	Keogh	5162	1		3		5	6	12	8		10	11	7	13									9					2	14		
34	22	h	Yeovil Town	3-4	Hayes (2), Butler	7598	1		3	4	5		6	8		10		7	14						12			9	13				2	11		
35	26	a	Swansea City	1-2	Butler	7249	1		3	4		6	12	8		10		7	13						5			9	14				2	11		
36	Mar 5	h	Rushden & Diamonds	4-1	Beagrie	4932	1		3	4	5	6	8			10	11		7				14		12			9					2	13		
37	12	h	Cheltenham Town	4-1	Sparrow (2), Kell, Byrne	4659	1		3		5	6	13	8		10	11	7	14						4			9	12				2			
38	19	a	Rochdale	0-0		3605	1		3			12	6	8		10	11	7	13						5			9					2	14	4	
39	25	h	Oxford United	1-1	Baraclough	5977	1		3		5	6	13	8		14	11	7	10						12			9					2		4	
40	28	a	Lincoln City	0-2		6729	1		3			5	6	14	8		13	11	7	10						4		9	12							2
41	Apr 2	h	Macclesfield Town	0-0		5536	1		3			5	6	12	8		10		7	11				13		4		9								2
42	9	a	Northampton Town	2-1	Hayes, Kell	6523	1		3			5	6	13	8		10		7					12		4		9						11		2
43	16	a	Cambridge United	4-0	Kell, Crosby, Tayloe (2)	5642	1		3	12	5	6	13	8		10	11	7	14						4			9								2
44	23	a	Grimsby Town	0-0		7941	1		3	4	5	6	12	8		10	11	7					13				2	9					14			
45	30	h	Bristol Rovers	4-0	Torpey (2), Hayes, Taylor	6925	1		3	4	5	6	7	8		10	11		12								2	9							14	13
46	May 7	a	Shrewsbury Town	0-0		6285	1		3	4	5	6	8			10	11	7	12								2	9								
Apps							46	21	44	37	44	45	44	43	4	46	36	44	25	1	5	1	21		3	29		29	4	6	1	3	9	8	7
Goals										#	3	3	6	5		#	2	5	3				1			1		#							

F A Cup

R	Date	H/A	Opponent	Score	Scorers	Att	Musselwhite	Stanton	Ridley	Butler	Crosby	Baraclough	Taylor	Kell	Bailey	Hayes	Beagrie	Sparrow	Keogh	Parton	Brighton	Featherstone	Rankine	Evans	Jackson	Byrne	Barwick	Torpey	Graves	Williams	Sharp	Teggart	Walters	Angus	Corden	Hinds
R1	Nov 13	h	Chesterfield	2-0	Hayes, Baraclough	4869	1		3	4	5	6	12	8		10	11	7							14		2	9		13						
R2	Dec 3	h	Wrexham	2-0	Ridley, Sparrow	5698	1		3	4	5	6	12	8		10	11	7									2	9								
R3	Jan 8	a	Chelsea	1-3	Hayes	40019	1		3	4	5	6	12	8		10	11	7							9		2			13						

Carling Cup (F.L.Cup)

R	Date	H/A	Opponent	Score	Att	Musselwhite	Stanton	Ridley	Butler	Crosby	Baraclough	Taylor	Kell	Bailey	Hayes	Beagrie	Sparrow	Keogh
R1	Aug 25	a	Nottingham Forest	0-2	7344	1	2	3	4	5	6	7	8	9	10	11	12	13

LD Vans Trophy (Associate Members Cup)

R	Date	H/A	Opponent	Score	Scorers	Att	Musselwhite	Stanton	Ridley	Butler	Crosby	Baraclough	Taylor	Kell	Bailey	Hayes	Beagrie	Sparrow	Keogh	Parton	Brighton	Featherstone	Rankine	Evans	Jackson	Byrne	Barwick	Torpey	Graves	Williams	Sharp
R1	Sep 28	a	Hereford United	1-1	Torpey (a.e.t. 3-4 on pens.)	1414		4					7			14		2		11	6	10	1	3	5	8		9	12	13	

2005/06 — 12th in Division 1

#	Date		Opponent	Score	Scorers	Att.
1	Aug 6	a	Brentford	0 2		5952
2	9	h	Barnsley	2 1	Crosby (p), Taylor	7152
3	13	h	Gillingham	1 1	Hinds	5007
4	20	a	Nottingham Forest	1 0	Sharp	19091
5	26	h	Southend United	1 0	Barocliffe	5569
6	29	a	Hartlepool United	3 3	Sharpe(2), Keough	5044
7	Sep 2	a	Huddersfield Town	4 1	Beagrie(p), Keough (2), Sparrow	14112
8	10	h	Port Vale	2 0	Hinds, Keough	5694
9	17	a	Doncaster Rovers	1 3	Sharp	6699
10	24	h	Walsall	1 3	Sharp	4973
11	27	a	Milton Keynes Dons	0 1		4682
12	Oct 1	h	Yeovil Town	3 4	Keough, Sharp (2)	4311
13	7	a	Tranmere Rovers	2 0	Kough, Sharp	7522
14	15	h	Rotherham United	2 2	Sharp (2)	6649
15	22	a	Swindon Town	1 1	Sparrow	4972
16	29	a	Oldham Athletic	4 2	Butler, Sharp(2), Crosby	5055
17	Nov 13	h	Blackpool	2 5	Sharp (2,1p)	6016
18	19	h	Tranmere Rovers	1 2	Sharp (p)	4602
19	26	h	Brentford	1 3	Goodwin	4322
20	Dec 6	a	Swansea City	0 2		13207
21	10	a	Barnsley	2 5	Beagrie (p), MacKenzie	8197
22	16	h	Nottingham Forest	3 1	Ridley, Taylor, Byrne	5857
23	26	h	Chesterfield	2 2	Baraclough, Johnsonj	5866
24	31	h	Bradford City	0 0		5269
25	Jan 2	a	AFC Bournemouth	1 1	Sharp	6259
26	10	h	Huddersfield Town	2 2	Beagrie, Keough	4450
27	14	a	Bristol City	1 1	Keough	11692
28	21	h	Doncaster Rovers	1 1	Goodwin	6978
29	Feb 4	h	Milton Keynes Dons	2 0	Sharp (2, 1 p)	4631
30	7	a	Colchester United	0 1		4416
31	11	a	Walsall	2 2	Keough, MacKenzie	4911
32	14	h	Bristol City	0 2		3786
33	18	h	Swansea City	2 2	Sharp, Torpey	4352
34	25	a	Gillingham	3 1	Sparrow, Hinds, Keough	6029
35	28	a	Port Vale	2 1	Sparrow, Taylor	3984
36	Mar 10	a	Southend United	0 3		8717
37	14	h	Hartlepool United	2 0	Baraclough, Sparrow	4550
38	18	a	Chesterfield	2 1	Hinds, Crosby	4406
39	25	h	Colchester United	0 0		4608
40	Apr 1	a	Bradford City	2 4	Beagrie (p), Hinds	8409
41	8	h	AFC Bournemouth	2 2	Beagrie (p), Hinds	4136
42	14	a	Yeovil Town	1 0	Sharp	6759
43	17	h	Swindon Town	1 2	Sharp	5207
44	22	a	Rotherham United	1 1	Keough	5778
45	29	h	Blackpool	1 0	Sharp	5917
46	May 6	a	Oldham Athletic	1 1	Sharp	5544

F A Cup

Rd	Date		Opponent	Score	Scorers	Att.
R1	Nov 5	a	Bury	2 2	Keough, Baraclough	2940
rep	15	h	Bury	1 0	Johnson (a.e.t. 0-0 at 90 mins.)	4006
R2	Dec 3	a	Aldershot Town	1 0	Keough	3548
R3	7	a	Manchester City	1 3	Keough	27779

Carling Cup (F.L.Cup)

Rd	Date		Opponent	Score	Scorers	Att.
R1	Aug 23	h	Tranmere Rovers	2 1	Ryan, Hinds	2738
R2	Sep 20	h	Birmingham City	0 2		6109

LDV Vans Trophy (Associate Members Cup)

Rd	Date		Opponent	Score	Scorers	Att.
R1	Oct 18	h	Hartlepool United	1 0	Crosby (p)	2028
R2	Dec 13	a	Halifax Town	3 1	Sharp, Keough, Johnson	1124
Q/F	20	a	Hereford United	0 2		1452

Final League Table 2005/06 Division 1

		Pl	Home					Away					F	A	Pts
			W	D	L	F	A	W	D	L	F	A			
1	Southend United	46	13	6	4	37	16	10	7	6	35	27	72	43	82
2	Colchester United	46	15	4	4	39	21	7	9	7	19	19	58	40	79
3	Brentford	46	10	8	5	35	23	10	8	5	37	29	72	52	76
4	Huddersfield Town	46	13	6	4	40	25	6	10	7	32	34	72	59	73
5	Barnsley	46	11	11	1	37	19	7	7	9	25	25	62	44	72
6	Swansea City	46	11	9	3	42	23	7	8	8	36	32	78	55	71
7	Nottingham Forest	46	14	5	4	40	15	5	7	11	27	37	67	52	69
8	Doncaster Rovers	46	11	6	6	30	19	9	3	11	25	32	55	51	69
9	Bristol City	46	11	7	5	38	22	7	4	12	28	40	66	62	65
10	Oldham Athletic	46	12	4	7	32	24	6	7	10	26	36	58	60	65
11	Bradford City	46	8	9	6	28	25	6	10	7	23	24	51	49	61
12	SCUNTHORPE U.	46	8	8	7	36	33	7	7	9	32	40	68	73	60
13	Port Vale	46	10	5	8	30	26	6	7	10	19	28	49	54	60
14	Gillingham	46	13	4	6	31	21	3	8	12	19	43	50	64	60
15	Yeovil Town	46	8	8	7	27	24	7	3	13	27	38	54	62	56
16	Chesterfield	46	6	7	10	31	37	8	7	8	32	36	63	73	56
17	Bournemouth	46	7	11	5	25	20	5	8	10	24	33	49	53	55
18	Tranmere Rovers	46	7	8	8	32	30	6	7	10	18	22	50	52	54
19	Blackpool	46	9	8	6	33	27	3	9	11	23	37	56	64	53
20	Rotherham United	46	7	9	7	31	26	5	7	11	21	36	52	62	52
21	Hartlepool United	46	6	10	7	28	30	5	7	11	16	29	44	59	50
22	M. K. Dons	46	8	8	7	28	25	4	6	13	17	41	45	66	50
23	Swindon Town	46	9	5	9	31	31	2	10	11	15	34	46	65	48
24	Walsall	46	7	7	9	27	34	4	7	12	20	36	47	60	47

Final League Table 2006/07 Division 1

		Pl	Home					Away					F	A	Pts
			W	D	L	F	A	W	D	L	F	A			
1	SCUNTHORPE U.	46	15	6	2	40	17	11	7	5	33	18	73	35	91
2	Bristol City	46	15	5	3	35	20	10	5	8	28	19	63	39	85
3	Blackpool	46	12	6	5	40	25	12	5	6	36	24	76	49	83
4	Nottingham Forest	46	14	5	4	37	17	9	8	6	28	24	65	41	82
5	Yeovil Town	46	14	3	6	22	12	9	7	7	33	27	55	39	79
6	Oldham Athletic	46	13	4	6	36	18	8	8	7	33	29	69	47	75
7	Swansea City	46	12	6	5	36	20	8	6	9	33	33	69	53	72
8	Carlisle United	46	12	5	6	35	24	7	6	10	19	31	54	55	68
9	Tranmere Rovers	46	13	5	5	33	22	5	8	10	25	31	58	53	67
10	Millwall	46	11	8	4	33	19	8	1	14	26	43	59	62	66
11	Doncaster Rovers	46	8	10	5	30	23	8	5	10	22	24	52	47	63
12	Port Vale	46	12	3	8	35	26	6	3	14	29	39	64	65	60
13	Crewe Alexandra	46	11	4	8	39	38	6	5	12	27	34	66	72	60
14	Northampton Town	46	8	5	10	27	28	7	9	7	21	23	48	51	59
15	Huddersfield Town	46	9	8	6	37	33	5	9	9	23	36	60	69	59
16	Gillingham	46	14	2	7	29	24	3	6	14	27	53	56	77	59
17	Cheltenham Town	46	8	6	9	25	27	7	3	13	24	34	49	61	54
18	Brighton & H.A.	46	5	7	11	23	34	9	4	10	26	24	49	58	53
19	Bournemouth	46	10	5	8	28	27	3	8	12	22	37	50	64	52
20	Leyton Orient	46	6	10	7	30	32	6	5	12	31	45	61	77	51
21	Chesterfield	46	9	5	9	29	22	3	6	14	16	31	45	53	47
22	Bradford City	46	5	9	9	27	31	6	5	12	20	34	47	65	47
23	Rotherham United	46	8	4	11	37	39	5	5	13	21	36	58	75	38
24	Brentford	46	5	8	10	24	41	3	5	15	16	38	40	79	37

Final League Table 2007/08 Championship

		Pl	Home					Away					F	A	Pts
			W	D	L	F	A	W	D	L	F	A			
1	West Bromwich A.	46	12	8	3	51	27	11	4	8	37	28	88	55	81
2	Stoke City	46	12	7	4	36	27	9	9	5	33	28	69	55	79
3	Hull City	46	13	7	3	43	19	8	5	10	22	28	65	47	75
4	Bristol City	46	13	7	3	33	20	7	7	9	21	33	54	53	74
5	Crystal Palace	46	9	9	5	31	23	9	8	6	27	19	58	42	71
6	Watford	46	8	7	8	26	29	10	9	4	36	27	62	56	70
7	Wolverhampton W.	46	11	6	6	31	25	7	10	6	22	23	53	48	70
8	Ipswich Town	46	15	7	1	44	14	3	8	12	21	42	65	56	69
9	Sheffield United	46	10	8	5	32	24	7	7	9	24	27	56	51	66
10	Plymouth Argyle	46	9	9	5	37	22	8	4	11	23	28	60	50	64
11	Charlton Athletic	46	9	7	7	38	29	8	6	9	25	29	63	58	64
12	Cardiff City	46	12	4	7	31	21	4	12	7	28	34	59	55	64
13	Burnley	46	7	9	7	31	31	9	5	9	29	36	60	67	62
14	Q.P. Rangers	46	10	6	7	32	27	4	10	9	28	39	60	66	58
15	Preston North End	46	11	5	7	29	20	4	6	13	21	36	50	56	56
16	Sheffield Wed.	46	9	5	9	29	25	5	8	10	25	30	54	55	55
17	Norwich City	46	10	6	7	30	22	5	4	14	19	37	49	59	55
18	Barnsley	46	11	7	5	35	26	3	6	14	17	39	52	65	55
19	Blackpool	46	8	11	4	35	27	4	7	12	24	37	59	64	54
20	Southampton	46	9	5	9	26	27	4	10	9	30	45	56	72	54
21	Coventry City	46	8	8	7	25	26	6	3	14	27	38	52	64	53
22	Leicester City	46	7	7	9	23	19	5	9	9	19	26	42	45	52
23	SCUNTHORPE U.	46	7	8	8	31	33	4	5	14	15	36	46	69	46
24	Colchester United	46	4	8	11	31	41	3	9	11	31	45	62	86	38

Final League Table 2008/09 Division 1

		Pl	Home					Away					F	A	Pts
			W	D	L	F	A	W	D	L	F	A			
1	Leicester City	46	13	9	1	41	16	14	6	3	43	23	84	39	96
2	Peterborough U.	46	14	6	3	41	22	12	5	6	37	32	78	54	89
3	M.K. Dons	46	12	4	7	42	25	14	5	4	41	22	83	47	87
4	Leeds United	46	17	2	4	49	20	9	4	10	28	29	77	49	84
5	Millwall	46	13	4	6	30	21	12	3	8	33	32	63	53	82
6	SCUNTHORPE U.	46	13	5	5	44	24	9	5	9	38	39	82	63	76
7	Tranmere Rovers	46	15	5	3	41	20	6	6	11	21	29	62	49	74
8	Southend United	46	13	2	8	29	20	8	6	9	29	41	58	61	71
9	Huddersfield Town	46	9	8	6	32	28	9	6	8	30	37	62	65	68
10	Oldham Athletic	46	9	9	5	35	24	7	8	8	31	41	66	65	65
11	Bristol Rovers	46	11	4	8	44	29	6	8	9	35	32	79	61	63
12	Colchester United	46	7	4	12	21	24	11	5	7	37	34	58	58	63
13	Walsall	46	10	3	10	34	36	7	7	9	27	30	61	66	61
14	Leyton Orient	46	6	6	11	24	33	9	5	9	21	24	45	57	56
15	Swindon Town	46	8	7	8	37	34	4	10	9	31	37	68	71	53
16	Brighton & H. A.	46	6	6	11	32	40	7	7	9	23	30	55	70	52
17	Yeovil Town	46	6	10	7	26	29	6	5	12	15	37	41	66	51
18	Stockport County	46	9	7	7	34	28	7	5	11	25	29	59	57	50
19	Hartlepool United	46	8	7	8	45	40	5	4	14	21	39	66	79	50
20	Carlisle United	46	8	7	8	36	32	4	7	12	20	37	56	69	50
21	Northampton Town	46	8	8	7	38	29	4	5	14	23	36	61	65	49
22	Crewe Alexandra	46	8	4	11	30	38	4	6	13	29	44	59	82	46
23	Cheltenham Town	46	7	6	10	30	38	2	6	15	21	53	51	91	39
24	Hereford United	46	6	4	13	23	28	3	3	17	19	51	42	79	34

Final League Table 2009/10 Championship

		Pl	Home					Away					F	A	Pts
			W	D	L	F	A	W	D	L	F	A			
1	Newcastle United	46	18	5	0	56	13	12	7	4	34	22	90	35	102
2	West Bromwich Alb.	46	16	3	4	48	21	10	10	3	41	27	89	48	91
3	Nottingham Forest	46	18	2	3	45	13	4	11	8	20	27	65	40	79
4	Cardiff City	46	12	6	5	37	20	10	4	9	36	34	73	54	76
5	Leicester City	46	13	6	4	40	18	8	7	8	21	27	61	45	76
6	Blackpool	46	13	6	4	46	22	6	7	10	28	36	74	58	70
7	Swansea City	46	10	10	3	21	12	7	8	8	19	25	40	37	69
8	Sheffield United	46	12	8	3	37	20	5	6	12	25	35	62	55	65
9	Reading	46	10	7	6	39	22	7	5	11	29	41	68	63	63
10	Bristol City	46	10	10	3	38	34	5	8	10	18	31	56	65	63
11	Middlesbrough	46	9	8	6	25	21	7	6	10	33	29	58	50	62
12	Doncaster Rovers	46	9	7	7	32	29	6	8	9	27	29	59	58	60
13	Q. P. Rangers	46	8	9	6	36	28	6	6	11	22	37	58	65	57
14	Derby County	46	12	3	8	37	32	3	8	12	16	31	53	63	56
15	Ipswich Town	46	8	11	4	24	23	4	9	10	26	38	50	61	56
16	Watford	46	10	6	7	36	26	4	6	13	25	42	61	68	54
17	Preston North End	46	9	10	4	35	26	4	5	14	23	47	58	73	54
18	Barnsley	46	8	7	8	25	29	6	5	12	28	40	53	69	54
19	Coventry City	46	8	9	6	27	29	5	6	12	20	35	47	64	54
20	SCUNTHORPE U.	46	10	7	6	40	32	4	3	16	22	52	62	84	52
21	Crystal Palace	46	8	5	10	24	27	6	12	5	26	26	50	53	49
22	Sheffield Wed.	46	8	6	9	30	31	3	8	12	19	38	49	69	47
23	Plymouth Argyle	46	5	6	12	20	30	6	2	15	23	38	43	68	41
24	Peterborough U.	46	6	5	12	32	37	2	5	16	14	43	46	80	34

Final League Table 2010/11 Championship

		Pl	Home					Away					F	A	Pts
			W	D	L	F	A	W	D	L					
1	Q.P.Rangers	46	14	7	2	43	15	10	9	4	28	17	71	32	88
2	Norwich City	46	13	6	4	47	30	10	9	4	36	28	83	58	84
3	Swansea City	46	15	5	3	41	11	9	3	11	28	31	69	42	80
4	Cardiff City	46	12	7	4	41	25	11	4	8	35	29	76	54	80
5	Reading	46	12	7	4	43	25	8	10	5	34	26	77	51	77
6	Nottingham Forest	46	13	8	2	43	22	7	7	9	26	28	69	50	75
7	Leeds United	46	11	8	4	47	34	8	7	8	34	36	81	70	72
8	Burnley	46	12	6	5	40	30	6	8	9	25	31	65	61	68
9	Millwall	46	12	6	5	39	22	6	7	10	23	26	62	48	67
10	Leicester City	46	13	6	4	48	27	6	4	13	28	44	76	71	67
11	Hull City	46	7	8	8	21	19	9	9	5	31	32	52	51	65
12	Middlesbrough	46	10	7	6	37	32	7	4	12	31	36	68	68	62
13	Ipswich Town	46	10	3	10	33	37	8	5	10	29	31	62	68	62
14	Watford	46	9	7	7	39	32	7	6	10	38	39	77	71	61
15	Bristol City	46	10	4	9	30	29	7	5	11	32	36	62	65	60
16	Portsmouth	46	8	9	6	31	26	7	4	12	22	34	53	60	58
17	Barnsley	46	11	6	6	32	23	3	8	12	23	43	55	66	56
18	Coventry City	46	9	5	9	27	26	5	8	10	27	32	54	58	55
19	Derby County	46	8	4	11	35	32	5	6	12	23	39	58	71	49
20	Crystal Palace	46	11	6	6	28	24	1	6	16	16	45	44	69	48
21	Doncaster Rovers	46	7	9	7	26	31	4	6	13	29	50	55	81	48
22	Preston North End	46	7	4	12	27	36	3	8	12	27	43	54	79	42
23	Sheffield United	46	7	5	11	27	36	4	4	15	17	43	44	79	42
24	SCUNTHORPE U	46	5	5	13	21	40	7	1	15	22	47	43	87	42

2006/07 — 1st in Division 1

#	Date		Opponent	Score	Scorers	Att	Murphy	Mulligan	Ridley	Foster	Crosby	Goodwin	Sparrow	Hinds	Keogh	Sharp	Baraclough	Torpey	Taylor	MacKenzie	Ferretti	Byrne	Williams	Foy	Paul	McBreen	Morris	Winn	Allanson	Lillis	Talbot	Butler	Beckford	Hurst
1	Aug 5	a	Bristol City	0 1		13268	1	2	3	4	5	6	7	8	9	10	11	12	13	14														
2	8	h	Swansea City	2 2	Crosby (p), Sharp	4187	1	2	3	4	5		8	6	9	10	11		7			12												
3	12	h	Crewe Alexandra	2 2	Sharp, Crosby (p)	4329	1	2	3	4	5		8	6	9	10	11		7			12												
4	19	a	Rotherham United	1 2	Sharp	4708	1	2	3	4	5		8	6	9	10	11		7	12	13	14												
5	26	h	Brentford	1 1	Mousinho o.g.	3942	1	7		4	5		8	6	9	10	12			13			14	2	3	11									
6	Sep 1	a	Gillingham	2 0	Hinds, Sparrow	5749	1	2		4			8	5		10	6	12	7						3		9	11							
7	9	a	Oldham Athletic	0 1		4812	1	2		4			8	5	9	10	6	13	7						3		12	11							
8	12	h	Port Vale	3 0	Sharp (2), Morris	3473	1	2		4	12		8	5	14	10	6	9	7						3		13	11							
9	16	h	Cheltenham Town	1 0	Keyho	4288	1	2		4	12		8	5	13	10	6	9	7						3			11							
10	23	a	AFC Bournemouth	1 1	MacKenzie	5256	1			4	5		8	6	9	10	12		7	11			2	3			14	11							
11	27	a	Chesterfield	1 0	Sharp	4849	1			4	5		8	2	9	10	6		7	13			12	3			14	11							
12	30	h	Doncaster Rovers	2 0	Sharp, Keyho	6441	1	2		4	12		8	5	9	10	6		7						3		13	11							
13	Oct 7	a	Nottingham Forest	4 0	Taylor, Keyho, Morris, Sharp	22640	1			4	5		8	2	9	10			6				7	13	3		12	11							
14	14	h	Brighton & Hove Albion	1 2	Sharp	5607	1	12		4	5		8	2	9	10	6	14	7	13					3			11							
15	21	a	Bradford City	1 0	Sharp	8723	1	2			5		8	4	13	10	6	9	7						3		12	11							
16	28	h	Leyton Orient	3 1	Sharp (2), Sparrow	4795	1	2			5	13	8	4	9	10	6	14	7				12		3			11							
17	Nov 4	a	Huddersfield Town	1 1	Sparrow	10456	1			4	5		8	2	9	10	6		7						3			11							
18	18	h	Northampton Town	1 0	Crosby (p)	4758	1			4	5	13	8	2	9	10	6		7				12		3	14		11							
19	25	a	Yeovil Town	2 0	Sharp 2)	5921	1	12		4	5	6	8	3	9	10	11	13	7				2												
20	Dec 5	h	Tranmere Rovers	1 1	Keyho	4572	1			4	5	12	8	2	9	10	6		7				13	3				11							
21	9	a	Carlisle United	2 0	Sharp, Keyho	6956	1			4	5	6	8	11	9	10	12	14	7				2	3				13							
22	15	h	Blackpool	1 3	Baraclough	4527	1			4	5	6		8	9	10	12	14	7				2	3	13			11							
23	22	a	Millwall	1 0	Torpey	7192			13	4		6		5	9	10	8	14	7	12			2	3				11		1					
24	26	h	Chesterfield	1 0	Sharp	6123	1			4	5	6		8	9	10	14	11	7	13			2	3				12							
25	30	h	AFC Bournemouth	3 2	Crosby, Keyho, Sharp	4794	1		12	4	5	6		13	9	10	8		7				2	3				11							
26	Jan 1	a	Port Vale	0 0		4869	1			4	5	12		8	9	10	6		7	11			2	3	13			14							
27	13	h	Oldham Athletic	1 1	Cregan o.g.	7685	1			4	5	6		2	9	10			7				12	3				11			13	14			
28	16	a	Cheltenham Town	1 1	Sharp	3036	1		12	4	5	6		2	9	10	8			7				3	13			11							
29	20	a	Doncaster Rovers	2 2	Keyho, Talbot	12414	1	12	2	4	5	6		8	9				7	13				3							11	14	10		
30	27	h	Millwall	3 0	Goodwin, Crosby (p), Beckford	5001	1	2	3	4	5	6				10			7	8				11										9	
31	Feb 5	h	Bristol City	1 0	Sharp	5108	1		3	4	5	6		8		10			7				2					13					12	9	11
32	17	h	Rotherham United	1 0	Beckford	5978	1	12	3	4	5	6		8		10			7	14			2					13						9	11
33	20	a	Swansea City	2 0	Sharp, Beckford	10746	1	2	3	4	5	6		8		10			7	14								13					12	9	11
34	24	h	Gillingham	3 1	Hinds, Mulligan, Morris	5312	1	2	3	4	5	6	13	8		10			7	12								14						9	11
35	27	a	Crewe Alexandra	3 1	Sharp (2), Beckford	4842	1	2	3	4	5	6	8	11		10			7	12			13											9	
36	Mar 3	a	Brentford	2 0	Beckford, taylor	5645	1	2	3	4		6		8		10			7	13			12										5	9	11
37	10	h	Nottingham Forest	1 1	Sharp	8906	1	2	3	4	5	6	8	11		10			7															9	
38	17	a	Brighton & Hove Albion	1 1	Beckford	6276	1	2	3	4	5	6	8	11		10			7	13								12					14	9	
39	24	a	Leyton Orient	2 2	MacKenzie, Sharp	5869	1	2	3	4	5	6		13		10			7	8			12					11						9	14
40	31	h	Bradford City	2 0	Sharp, Beckford	6437	1			4	5	6		13		10	14		7	8			2	3									12	9	11
41	Apr 6	h	Yeovil Town	1 0	Jones o.g.	7883	1			4	5	6		12		10	13		7	8			2	3										9	11
42	9	a	Northampton Town	1 2	Sharp	6381	1			4	5	6		8		10			12	7			2	3									13	9	11
43	14	h	Huddersfield Town	2 0	Sharp (2, 1p)	7518	1			4			6	13	14		10	12	7	8			2	3									5	9	11
44	21	a	Tranmere Rovers	2 0	Butler, Sharp	6721	1			4		12	6	13		10			7	8			2	3				14					5	9	11
45	28	a	Blackpool	1 3	Sharp	9482	1			4		12	8			10	6		7				2	3				13					5	9	11
46	May 5	h	Carlisle United	3 0	Taylor, Sparrow, Beckford	8720	1			4	5	6	8	12		10	11	9	7				2	3										13	14
					Apps		45	24	18	44	39	31	29	44	28	45	33	14	45	24		4	24	35	5		7	28		1	3	11	18	13
					Goals				1		5	1	4	2	7	30	1	1	3	2					3			1			1	8		

3 own goals

F A Cup

	Date		Opponent	Score	Scorers	Att																													
R1	Nov 10	a	Cheltenham Town	0 0		2721	1			4	5	13	8	2	9	10	6		7				12	3			14	11							
rep	21	h	Cheltenham Town	2 0	Barraclough, Sharp	3074	1	14		4	5	13	8	2	9	10	6		7				12	3	11										
R2	Dec 2	h	Wrexham	0 2		5054	1			4	5		8	3	9	10	6	13	7				2	12				11							

Carling (F.L.Cup)

	Date		Opponent	Score	Scorers	Att																													
R1	Aug 28	h	Lincoln City *	4 3	Torpey, Mulligan, Paul, Barroclough	3445	1	7		4	5		8	6		10	14	9	12			2	3	11	13										
R2	Sep 20	h	Aston Villa	1 2	Sharp	6502	1	2		4			8	5	9	10	6		7						3			11							

* a.e.t. 2-2 at 90 mins.

Johnstone's Paint Trophy (Associate Members Cup)

	Date		Opponent	Score	Scorers	Att																													
R1	Oct 17	a	Bradford City	2 1	Foy, Goodwin (p)	1936	1	2		4		13	6		12				9			11	5	3	7		10		8	14					
R2	30	h	Port Vale	0 0	(a.e.t. lost 5-3 on pens.)	3421	1	7	3	4	5	6		8					9				2	11	13		10		14		12					

2007/08 — 23rd in Championship

#	Date	H/A	Opponent	Score	Scorers	Att	Murphy	Byrne	Williams	Iriekpen	Crosby	Goodwin	Taylor	Baraclough	Hayes	Forte	Hurst	Sparrow	Paterson	Lillis	Youga	Butler	Cork	May	Logan	Morris	Ameobi	Winn	Martis	Seck	McCann	Hobbs	Horsfield	Weston	Wright
1	Aug 11	a	Charlton Athletic	1-1	Iriekpen	23151	1	2	3	4	5	6	7	8	9	10	11	12	13															
2	18	h	Burnley	2-0	Paterson, Goodwin	6975	1	2	3	4	5	6	13	8	9	11	7	14	10			12													
3	25	a	Bristol City	1-2	Peterson	12474	1	2	3		5	6	7		9	12	11	8	10		13	4	14												
4	Sep 1	h	Sheffield United	3-2	Crosby, Paterson, Sparrow	8801	1	2			5	6	13	8	9	12	11	7	10		3	4													
5	15	a	Barnsley	0-2		11230	1			3	12	5	6		8	9	13	11	7	10	2	4													
6	19	h	Preston North End	2-1	Crosby, Hayes	5754	1	2			14	5	6	12	8	9	13	11	7	10	3	4													
7	22	h	West Bromwich Albion	2-3	Crosby (p), Paterson	8307	1	2			12	5	6	13	8	9	14	11	7	10	3	4													
8	29	a	Colchester United	1-0	Hayes	5218	1	5	12			6	7		9	10	11	8			3	4	2	13											
9	Oct 2	a	Norwich City	0-0		23176	1	2			12	5	6	7		9	10	11	8	14	3	4		13											
10	6	h	Watford	1-3	Forte	7515	1	2				5	6	7	13	10	11	8	9		3	4	12	14											
11	20	h	Leicester City	0-0		6006	1	2				5	6			9	7	11	8	10	3	4		12											
12	23	a	Sheffield Wednesday	2-1	Paterson (2)	21557	1	2	12			5	6	7		9	13	11	8	10	3	4		14											
13	27	a	Cardiff City	1-1	Goodwin	11850	1	2				5	6	7		9	13	11		10	12	3	4	8											
14	Nov 3	h	Crystal Palace	0-0		6778	1		12			5	6	7		9	13	11	8	10	3	4	2												
15	6	h	Stoke City	2-3	Hayes, Goodwin	5521	1	2	12			5	6	7	8	9		11		10	3	4	8												
16	10	a	Blackpool	0-1		8051	1		14			5	6	7		9	13	11		10	3	4	2		8	12									
17	24	h	Hull City	1-2	Forte	8633	1		6			5				9	10	11	8	12	3	4	2		7	13									
18	27	a	Coventry City	1-1	Cork	14036	1		3			5	6	13		9	10	11		12	14	2	4	8	7										
19	Dec 1	a	Plymouth Argyle	0-3		10520			3			5	6		7	11	14	10	13	8	9		4	6		2	12								
20	3	h	Blackpool	1-1	Butler	4407	1		3			5	6			9	12	11	7	10		4	8												
21	8	h	Queen's Park Rangers	2-2	Paterson, Forte	5612	1		3			5	6			9	7	11	8	10		4	2			12	13								
22	15	a	Ipswich Town	2-3	Paterson (2)	19306	1		3			5	6	12	8	9	14	11		10		4	2			7	13								
23	22	h	Norwich City	0-1		6648	1		3			5	6	13	4	9	8	11	14	10			2			7	12								
24	26	a	Preston North End	1-0	Paterson	12920	1	2	3			5	6		4	9	14	11	13	10			8			7	12								
25	29	a	West Bromwich Albion	0-5		25238	1		3			5	6	7	4	12	10		9		2		8			11	13	14							
26	Jan 1	h	Barnsley	2-2	Morris, Youga	6897	1		3			5	6	12	4	9	14	11		10	2		8			7	13								
27	12	a	Southampton	1-8		18146	1	2	3			5				9	14	11	8	10			6			7	13		4	12					
28	19	h	Wolverhampton Wanderers	0-2		7465	1	2	3			5				9	14	11	8	10			6	13		7		4		12					
29	26	a	Burnley	0-2		14516	1		3				12			13	14		8	10		4	6	9		7		2		11	5				
30	Feb 2	h	Charlton Athletic	1-0	Paterson	6084	1	2	3			5	6			9		11		14		4	7			13				8	12	10			
31	9	a	Sheffield United	0-0		25668	1	2	3			5	6			9	10		12			4	8	13		7				11	4				
32	12	h	Bristol City	0-1		5423	1	2	3			5	6			7	14	11	13	10		12	8									4	9		
33	15	a	Stoke City	2-3	Paterson, Hobbs	20979	1		3			5	6			13	14		7	10		4	8	12		11					2	9			
34	23	h	Southampton	1-1	Crosby	6035	1		3	12	5	6					13		7	10		4	8	14		11					2	9			
35	Mar 1	a	Coventry City	2-1	Paterson, Cork	5866	1		3	4	5	6							10			8	9			7				11	2				
36	8	a	Hull City	0-2		20906	1		3	4	5	6				13			10			8	9			7				11	2	12	14		
37	11	h	Plymouth Argyle	1-0	Morris	4920	1			4	5	6	3						10			2	8	13		7				11	12	9	14		
38	15	a	Queen's Park Rangers	1-3	McCann	14499	1			4	5	6	3		9		12	7				2	8	13						11		10			
39	18	a	Wolverhampton Wanderers	1-2	Butler	21628	1				5	6	3					8	10			4	2	13		7				11		9	12		
40	22	h	Ipswich Town	1-2	May	6636	1				5	6	3					8	10			4	2	12	7					11		9	14	13	
41	29	a	Leicester City	0-1		22165	1	2		4		6			3	12		11	13			5		10	14					8		9	7		
42	Apr 5	a	Sheffield Wednesday	1-1	Morris	7425	1	2	3	4		6				13	10		12			5		14		11				8		9	7		
43	12	a	Crystal Palace	0-2		15975	1	2	3	4		6				12	7		10			5			11					8		9	13		
44	19	h	Cardiff City	3-2	Hayes (2, 1p), Hurst	4727	1	2	3	4		6			9	7	11		10			5	8	13	12	14									
45	26	a	Watford	1-0	Hayes	16454	1	2	3	4					9	8	11	14				5	6	10	7	12									13
46	May 4	h	Colchester United	3-3	Forte, Hayes (2)	5554	1	2	3	4					9	7		8				5	6	10	11	13				12					
			Apps				45	25	34	17	38	40	20	17	40	38	33	32	40	3	19	36	34	21	4	25	9	4	3	14	9	12	7	2
			Goals							1	4	3			8	4	1	1	13		1	2	2	1		3					1	1			

F A Cup

| R3 | Jan 5 | a | Preston North End | 0-1 | | 4616 | 1 | 2 | 3 | | 5 | | | | 9 | 13 | 11 | 8 | 10 | 12 | | 6 | | | 7 | 14 | | 4 | | | | | | |

Carling (F.L.Cup)

| R1 | Aug 14 | h | Hartlepool United | 1-2 | Paterson | 2965 | | 2 | 3 | 4 | 5 | 14 | 7 | | 9 | 13 | 11 | 8 | 10 | 1 | | 6 | 12 | | | | | | | | | | | | |

2008/09   6th in Division 1

#	Date		Opponent	Score	Scorers	Att	Lillis	Byrne	Williams	Iriekpen	Milne	McCann	Morris	Thompson	Hayes	Hooper	Hurst	May	Forte	Sparrow	Wright	Mirfin	Togwell	Murphy	Pearce	Woolford	Lea	Crosby	Lansbury	Mills	Trotter	Odejayi
1	Aug 9	h	Leeds United	1-2	Hooper	8315	1	2	3	4	5	6	7	8	9	10	11	12	13	14												
2	16	a	Walsall	1-2	Thompson	4162	1	2	3	4		6	14	8	9	10	11	12			13	5	7									
3	23	h	Peterborough United	1-0	Hayes (p)	4217		2	3	4		6	12	8	9	10	11				14		7	1	5	13						
4	30	a	Stockport County	3-0	Hooper, McCann	6348		2	3			6		8	9	10	11	13			12	5	7	1	4	14						
5	Sep 6	a	Brighton & Hove Albion	4-1	Woolford, Hooper (3)	5529		2	3			6	14	7	9	10		13			12		5	8	1	4	11					
6	13	h	Carlisle United	2-1	Sparrow, Hayes	5188		2	3	12		6		7	9	10	11				13		5	8	1	4	14					
7	20	a	Hereford United	2-1	Togwell, Hooper	3004		2	3	4		6	12	13	9	10					7			8	1	5	11					
8	27	h	Yeovil Town	2-0	Iriekpen, Forbes o.g.	4829		2	3	4		6			9	10		12			7			8	1	5	11					
9	Oct 4	a	Leyton Orient	2-2	Iriekpen, Hayes	4244	13	2	3	4		6			9	10			12		7			8	1	5	11					
10	11	h	Crewe Alexandra	3-0	Woolford, Hayes, Iriekpen	4790		2	3	4			7		9	10		14	13		8	12	5	6	1		11					
11	18	a	Cheltenham Town	2-1	Hooper, Sparrow	3682		2	3			6			9	10		12	14		7	13	5	8	1	4	11					
12	21	h	Southend United	1-1	Hayes (p)	4324		2	3	12		6			9	10					7		5	8	1	4	11					
13	25	h	Millwall	3-2	Hooper, Hayes (p), Sparrow	5670		2	3	4		6			9	10		12	13		7			8	1	5	11					
14	28	a	Oldham Athletic	0-3		6057		2	3	4		6			9	10		14	13		7		12	8	1	5	11					
15	Nov 1	h	Swindon Town	3-3	McCann, Woolford, Hayes	4744		2	3	4		6	13		9			12	10		7			8	1	5	11					
16	14	a	Bristol Rovers	2-1	McCann, iriekpen	7173		2				6	14	13	9	10		12			7		5	8	1	4	11					
17	22	h	Leicester City	1-2	Hayes	4957		2	3	4		6	7		9	10		12			8		5		1	13	11					
18	25	h	Tranmere Rovers	0-2		4564		2	3	4		6	12	14	9	10		13			7		5	8	1		11					
19	Dec 6	a	Milton Keynes Dons	2-0	Morris, Thompson	11550		2	3			6	13	14		10		9			7	12	5	8	1	4	11					
20	13	h	Northampton Town	4-4	May(2), Hooper (2)	3976		2	3	4			7			10		9			8			6	1	5	11					
21	23	a	Colchester United	0-0		4606		4	3			6	12	7	13	10		9				2		8	1	5	11					
22	26	h	Hartlepool United	3-0	McCann, Hooper, Hayes (p)	5347		4	3			6	13	7	14	10		9			12	2		8	1		11					
23	28	a	Huddersfield Town	0-2		15228		4	3			6	13	12	14	10		9			7	2		8	1	5	11					
24	Jan 13	a	Yeovil Town	2-1	Togwell, Hooper	3275			3			6		7	9	10	14	12			13	2	5	8	1	4						
25	17	a	Crewe Alexandra	2-3	Hayes, O'Donnell	3811		4	3			6		7	9	10	13				12	2	5	8	1	14	11					
26	24	h	Leyton Orient	2-1	Hayes, Thompson	4230		2				6	12	7	9	10	14				8	3	5	13	1	4	11					
27	27	h	Oldham Athletic	2-0	McCann, Hooper	4447		2				6	13	7	9	10	14				8	3	5	12	1	4	11					
28	31	a	Millwall	2-1	Hooper (2)	8868		2				6	14	7	9	10	12				8	3	5	13	1	4	11					
29	Feb 14	h	Bristol Rovers	0-2		4156		2				6	12	7	9	10					8	3	5	13	1	4	11		14			
30	21	a	Swindon Town	2-4	Hooper, Lansbury	6852		2				6		14	13	10	9				7	3	5	8	1	4	12		11			
31	24	a	Southend United	0-2		6028						6	14	7	9	10						2		8	1	4		5	12	3	13	
32	28	a	Leeds United	2-3	Hooper (2)	24921		2				6		12	14	10					7			8	1	4	11		5	13	3		9
33	Mar 3	h	Walsall	1-1	Odejayi	3423		2				6			9	10	11						12	5	1	8			7	3		13
34	7	h	Stockport County	2-1	Hurst, Hooper	4890		2				6			9	10	11					14	5	8	1	4			7	3	12	13
35	10	a	Peterborough United	1-2	Lansbury	5637		2				6			9	10	11				13	12	5	8	1	4			7	3		14
36	14	a	Carlisle United	1-1	Hayes	4867		2				6			9	10	11						5	8	1		12	4	7	3	13	14
37	17	h	Hereford United	3-0	Hooper, Hurst, Hayes	3672		2				6			9	10					8	12	5		1	4	14		7	3	13	
38	21	h	Brighton & Hove Albion	2-0	Hooper, McCann (p)	4404		2				6			9	10					8	12	5		1	4			7	3	13	14
39	28	h	Colchester United	3-0	Hooper (2), Lansbury	4304			3			6			9	10	11	13			8	2	5	14	1	4	12		7		6	
40	Apr 10	h	Huddersfield Town	1-2	Woolford	5543		4				6			9	10	14	13				2	5	8	1		11		7	3	12	
41	13	a	Hartlepool United	2-2	McCann, Hayes (2)	3998		4				6			9	10		13			12	2	5	8	1		11		7	3	14	
42	18	a	Milton Keynes Dons	0-1		4873		4				6			9	10		14			13	2	5		1	12	11		7	3	8	
43	21	a	Northampton Town	3-3	Trotter, McCann, Sparrow	4416		2				6			9	10					7	3	5		1	4	11				8	
44	24	a	Leicester City	2-2	Hayes, McCann (p)	30542		2				6			9	10					7	3	5	14	1	4	11		13	12	8	
45	28	h	Cheltenham Town	3-0	Hayes, Byrne, Lansbury	3635	1	2	3			6		14	9	10	12							5	8	4		13	7	11		
46	May 2	h	Tranmere Rovers	1-1	Byrne	8029	1	2				6		14	9	10					7	12	5	8		4	11			3	13	
					Apps		5	43	26	16	1	43	20	24	44	45	20	23		8	36	28	33	40	42	39	39		4	16	14	12	6
					Goals			2		4		9	1	3	17	24	2	2		4			2			4			4		1	1

1 own goal

Play-Offs

S/F1	May 8	h	Milton Keynes Dons	1-1	Woolford	6599	12	2				6	3	14	9	10					7		5	8	1	13	11		4			
S/F2	15	a	Milton Keynes Dons	0-0	(a.e.t won 7-6 on pens.)	14479		2				6	3	10	9					13	7		5	12	1		11		4		8	
F	24	n	Millwall	3-2	Sparrow (2), Woolford	59661		2				6	3		9	10				13	7		5	8	1		11		4		12	

Final Played at Wembley

F A Cup

R1	Nov 8	a	Walsall	3-1	Hooper (2), Hurst	2318		2		4		6	12	13	9	10	14				7		5	8	1		11	3				
R2	29	h	Alfreton Town	4-0	May, Hooper (2), Togwell	4249		2	3			6	12		9	10	14	13			7		5	8	1	4	11					
R3	Jan 3	a	Watford	0-1		8690		4	3			6			7	9	10	14			13	12	2		8	1	5	11				

Carling Cup (F.L.Cup)

R1	Aug 12	a	Hartlepool United	0-3		2076	1	2	3	4	5	6	7	8		10	11	14	9	13	12											

Johnstone's Paint Tropy (Associate Members Cup)

R1	Sep 2	h	Notts County	2-1	Hayes (2)	1755		2	3			6	7		9	13		10	14	8		5				4	11	12				
R2	Oct 7	h	Grimsby Town	2-1	Togwell, Morris	4844	1	2	3				7		9	10		12	13	8		5	6				11		4			
Q/F	Nov 7	h	Rochdale	1-0	Mirfin	2474		2		4		6	12		9			14	13	10	7		5	8	1		11	3				
S/F	Dec 16	h	Tranmere Rovers	2-1	May, Hayes	2669		4	3					7	10	13		9			8	2		6	1	12	11		5			
l/F1	Jan 20	h	Rotherham United	2-0	Woolford, Pearce	6038		2	3						12	7	9	10			13	8	6	5		4	11					
l/F2	Feb 17	a	Rotherham United	1-0	Hooper	6555		2				6	13	7	9	10					12	3	5	8	1	4	11		14			
F	Apr 5	n	Luton Town	2-3	Hooper, McCann	55378		2	3			6			9	10	11				8	12	5	14	1	4	13		7			

Final played at Wembley. a.e.t. 2-2 at 90 mins.

2009/10   20th in Championship

#	Date		Opponent	Score	Scorers	Att.	Murphy	Byrne	Togwell	Jones	Mirfin	McCann	Sparrow	Morris	Hayes	Hooper	Woolford	O'Connor	Forte	Wright I	Lillis	Wright A	Williams	Thompson	Spence	Canavan	Slocombe	Friend	Ngala	May	Milne	Moloney	McDermott	Raynes	McNulty
1	Aug 8	a	Cardiff City	0 4		22264	1	2	3	4	5	6	7	8	9	10	11	12	13	14															
2	15	h	Derby County	3 2	Hooper (2), Woolford	7352	1	5	12	4		8	7		9	10	11	6	14	13		2	3													
3	18	h	Middlesbrough	0 2		8274	1	2			4	8	7		9	10	11	6		12			3	13	5											
4	22	a	Sheffield Wednesday	0 4		20215	1	2	14	4		8	7		9	10	11	6		13			3		5	12										
5	29	h	Queen's Park Rangers	0 1		5866	1	2	6		5	12	7		9	10	11	8		14			3	13	4											
6	Sep 12	a	Crystal Palace	4 0	Forte, Hayes, Togwell, O'Connor	12912	1		6	4	5			12	9	13	11	8	10	7			3	14	2											
7	15	h	Preston North End	3 1	McCann, Hooper (2)	5383	1	13	6	4	5	11	12		9	10		8	7				3		2											
8	19	a	Bristol City	1 1	McCann	14203	1		6	4	5	14	12		9	13	11	8	10	7			3		2											
9	26	h	Doncaster Rovers	2 2	Byrne, McCann (p)	7945	1	12	6	4	5	11			9		14	8	10	7			3	13	2											
10	30	a	Nottingham Forest	0 2		18332	1	2	6	4		11			9		14	8	10	7	12		3	13	5											
11	Oct 3	a	Plymouth Argyle	1 2	Hooper (p)	9780		5	3	4		6	7	11	9	10	13	12		8	1	2		14												
12		h	Sheffield United	3 1	McCann (2), Hayes	7599	1	2	6	4	5	11			9	10	14	8	13	7			3	12												
13	17	h	Newcastle United	2 1	Woolford (2)	8921	1	2	6	4	5	8			9	10	11		13	7		12	3	14												
14	24	a	Peterborough United	0 3		8051	1	2	6	4		11			9		13	8	10	7		12	3	14	5											
15	31	h	Swansea City	0 2		5201	1	4	6		5	11	14		9	10	12	8		7			3	13												
16	Nov 7	a	Blackpool	1 4	Hayes	7727	1	2	6	4	5	11	10		9			8	13			7					12	3	14							
17	21	a	Watford	0 3		13241		2	6	4	5		7		9	10	11	13		8	1							3	12							
18	28	h	Leicester City	1 1	Woolford	6884	1	2	6	4	5	11			9	10	12	8		7			3	13												
19	Dec 6	h	Coventry City	1 0	Hooper	5013	1			4	5	6			9	10	11	8		7	12		3	14												
20	9	a	Barnsley	1 1	Hayes	11657	1	2	6	4	5	11			9	10			13	7		14	3	8			12									
21	12	a	Reading	1 1	Hooper	15274		2	6	4	5	11			9	10		13	14	7	1	12	3	8												
22	26	h	Middlesbrough	0 3		20647	1	2			4	5	6	12	9		11	8	14	7		13	3	10												
23	28	h	West Bromwich Albion	1 3	Jones	7221	1		6	4	5	11			9		12	8	13	7		2	3	10					14							
24	Jan 9	a	Derby County	4 1	Hooper, Thompson(2), Forte	28106		4	14		5			12	9	10	11	6	13	7	1	2	3	8												
25	16	a	Cardiff City	1 1	O'Connor	5032		4	6		5	14	12		9	10	11	8	13			1	2	3	7											
26	27	h	Sheffield Wednesday	2 0	Hooper, McCann	7038	1	2	6	4	5	8			9	10	11		13	14			3	7					12							
27	30	a	Queen's Park Rangers	1 0	Thompson	13105	1	2	6	4	5	8			9	10	11		13	12			3	7						14						
28	Feb 6	h	Crystal Palace	1 2	Mirfin	7543	1	2	6	4	5	8			9	10			12	13			3	7						14	11					
29		6	a	West Bromwich Albion	0 2		23146	1	2	6		4	5	13	7	12		10	14	8			11										3	9			
30	13	a	Leicester City	1 5	Hayes	21626	1		6	4	5	11			9	10		8		7			3											2		
31	16	h	Barnsley	2 1	Hooper, Hayes	5648	1		6	4	5	13	7		9	10	11	14		8		12	3											2		
32	20	h	Watford	2 2	Hooper (2,1p)	5411	1	2	12		5	6	7		9	10		8	13				3	14										4		
33	23	h	Ipswich Town	1 1	Byrne	5828	1	2	6		5		7		9	10	11		12				3	8										4		
34	27	a	Coventry City	1 2	Mcann	16197	1	2	6		5	13	7		9	10	11			8			3	14									12	4		
35	Mar 13	a	Ipswich Town	0 1		19378	1	2	6		5	8	7		9		11	13	12				3	10										4		
36	17	a	Newcastle United	0 3		39301	1		12	4		11			9		13	6	10	7		2	3	8										14	5	
37	20	h	Plymouth Argyle	2 1	Thompson, Woolford	5153	1		6		5	8	7		9		11		12			2	3	10										4		
38	23	h	Peterborough United	4 0	hayes, Thompson (2), Togwell	4995	1		6		5	8	7		9		11	13				2	3	10	12					4				14		
39	28	a	Sheffield United	1 0	Hayes	23005	1		6		5	8			9		11	13	14			2	3	7	12									10	4	
40	Apr 2	h	Blackpool	2 4	McCann (p), Hooper	7508	1		6			8	7		9	13	11		12			2	3	10						5		14		4		
41	5	a	Swansea City	0 3		14830	1	4				6	7		9	13	14		8			3	11		2									10	5	12
42	10	a	Preston North End	2 3	Thompson (2)	12441	1	2			5	6	7		9	10	11	12		13			8											4	3	
43	17	h	Bristol City	3 0	Hooper (3)	5430	1	2	12		5	6	7		9	10	11						3	8					4							
44	20	h	Reading	2 2	Hooper, Sparrow	5299	1	4	13		5	6	7		9	10	11		12			3		8	2												
45	24	a	Doncaster Rovers	3 4	Hooper (2), Hayes	12124	1	2	12		5	6	7		9	10	11		13	14		3		8					4							
46	May 2	h	Nottingham Forest	2 2	Canavan, Thompson	8119		4	6		5	8	12		9	10	11		13		1		7	2												3
			Apps				40	36	41	28	37	42	30	3	45	35	40	32	28	35	8	19	37	36	9	7	1	4	2	1	4	3	9	12	3
			Goals					2	2	1	1	8	1		9	19	5	2	2					9		1										

F A Cup

							Murphy	Byrne	Togwell	Jones	Mirfin	McCann	Sparrow	Morris	Hayes	Hooper	Woolford	O'Connor	Forte	Wright I	Lillis	Wright A	Williams	Thompson	Spence	Canavan
R3	Jan 2	h	Barnsley	1 0	Hayes	5457		2	6	4	5		13		9		11		10	7	1		3	8			12
R4	24	h	Manchester City	2 4	Hayes, Boyatta o.g.	8861	1	2	6	4	5	8			9	10	11		14	13			3	7			12

Carling Cup (F.L.Cup)

							Murphy	Byrne	Togwell	Jones	Mirfin	McCann	Sparrow	Morris	Hayes	Hooper	Woolford	O'Connor	Forte	Wright I	Lillis	Wright A	Williams	Thompson	Spence	Canavan	Slocombe
R1	Aug 11	h	Chesterfield	2 1	Sparrow, Hayes	2501		5	12	4			7		9	10	11	6	13	14	1	2	3	8			
R2	25	a	Swansea City *	2 1	Canavan, Hooper	7321	1		6		5		7		9	12	11	13	10	8			3	14	4	2	
R3	Sep 29	h	Port Vale	2 0	Hayes, Mccann	3383	1		13		5	8	7		9		14	6	10	11			3		4	2	12
R4	Oct 28	a	Manchester City	1 5	Forte	36358	1	2	13	4	5	6			9	14	11	8	10	7			3			12	

* a.e.t. 1-1 at 90 mins.

2010/11 24th in Championship

								Murphy	Nolan	McNulty	Jones	Mirfin	Togwell	Wright J	O'Connor	Dagnall	Forte	Thompson	Raynes	Wright A	Woolford	Slocombe	Byrne	Collins	Grant	Canavan	Boyes	Godden	Sears	Warner	McDonald	N'Guessan	McClenahan	Cowan-Hall	Reid	Ibrahim	Lillis	Hughes	Duffy	Garner	Nelson	Miller	Gordon	Nunez	Williams
1 Aug	7	a	Reading	2	1	Thompson, Jones	15914	1	2	3	4	5	6	7	8	9	10	11	12	13	14																								
2	14	h	Norwich City	0	1		6042	1	2	3	4	5		7	6	9	10	8		13	11			12																					
3	21	a	Queen's Park Rangers	0	2		12046	1	2	3			6	7	8	9	10		5		11		12		13	4																			
4	28	h	Crystal Palace	3	0	Forte (2), O'Conner (p)	5292	1	3		4	5	6	7	8	9	10				12		2	11	13																				
5 Sep	11	h	Bristol City	0	2		5185	1	3		4	5	6	7	8	9	10				14		2	11	12	13																			
6	14	a	Sheffield United	4	0	Dagnall (2), Mirfin, Woolford	19390	1	3			5	6	7	8	9	10		12		13		2	11	14	4																			
7	18	a	Swansea City	0	2		13537	1	3		13	5	6	7	8	9	10				14		2	11	12	4																			
8	25	h	Ipswich Town	1	1	Mirfin	5931	1	3		4	5	6	7	12	9	10				11		2	8	13																				
9	28	h	Barnsley	0	0		5421	1	3		4	5	6	7	12	9	10				11		2	8	13																				
10 Oct	2	a	Leicester City	1	3	O'Connor	20652	1	3			5	6	7	13	9	10				11		2	12	8	4																			
11	16	h	Doncaster Rovers	1	3	Woolford	7005	1	3		4	5	6	7	12	9	10	14			11		2	8	13																				
12	19	a	Preston North End	3	2	Dagnall, O'Connor, Woolford	11179	1	3		4	5		7	6	9		14	13		11	12	2	8					10																
13	23	a	Watford	2	0	Byrne, Woolford	12366		3			5	6	7	8	9	13	12	4		11		2						10	1															
14	30	h	Leeds United	1	4	Byrne	8122		3			5	6	7	8	9	13	14	4		11		2			12			10	1															
15 Nov	6	a	Hull City	1	0	O'Connor	21873	1	3				6	7	8	9	12		5		11		2	13	14	4			10																
16	9	h	Middlesbrough	0	2		5475	1	3					7	6	9	14		5		11		2	8	12	4			10		13														
17	13	h	Cardiff City	2	4	MacDonald, N'Guessan	5333	1	3	12	4				6	14	9		5		11		2		13				10		8	7													
18	20	a	Derby County	2	3	Forte, O'Connor (p)	25189	1		3	4			7	6		9	13	5		14		2						10		8	11	12												
19	27	h	Coventry City	0	2		4397	1	2	3	4			7	6	13	9	12					5						10		8	11													
20 Dec	4	a	Millwall	0	3		8937	1	3		4		6	7	8	9	13	14		2	11		5						10		12														
21	28	a	Burnley	2	0	Woolford, Dagnall	15043	1	3		4		6	13	8	9	10	7		2	11		5	12				14																	
22 Jan	1	a	Doncaster Rovers	0	3		9447	1	3			5	6	12	8	9	10	13		2	11		4	7				14																	
23	3	h	Watford	1	2	Woolford	4498	1	3			5	12	7	6	9	10	8		2	11		4					14						13											
24	15	a	Leeds United	0	4		25446	1	3				6			9	12		4	2	11			8	7			13							5	10									
25	22	h	Burnley	0	0		4334		12				6			9	10		4	2	11				13			14							5	8	1	3	7						
26 Feb	1	a	Middlesbrough	0	2		14364		3				6	12		9				2				13	11										5	8	1	4	7	10					
27	5	h	Hull City	1	5	Garner	6835		3				6							2				12	11										4		1	8	7	10	5	9			
28	12	a	Cardiff City	0	1		21604		2				6	7										14	12										4	13	1	8	11	10	5	9	3		
29	16	h	Nottingham Forest	1	0	Dagnall	5578		2				6	7		9			14	12					13										4		1	8	11		5	10	3		
30	19	h	Derby County	0	0		5696						6	7						2				12	13										4	14	1	8	11	10	5	9	3		
31	22	h	Sheffield United	3	2	Garner (2,1p), Miller	6281						6	7					14	2				13											4	12	1	8	11	10	5	9	3		
32	26	a	Bristol City	0	2		14423						6	7					12	2					13										4	14	1	8	11	10	5	9	3		
33 Mar	1	a	Portsmouth	0	2		14252		2			6		7					4					8											11	1	12	10	13	5	9	3		
34	5	h	Swansea City	1	0	Garner (p)	4608						6	7					4	2				8	13											14	1	11	12	10	5	9	3		
35	8	a	Barnsley	1	2	Collins	10250						6	7		14			4	2				8													13	1	11	12	10	5	9	3		
36	12	h	Leicester City	0	3		6528		12					7		9			4	2				13													14	1	6	11	10	5	8	3		
37	15	h	Preston North End	0	3		4190		3					7	12	14			2	13				8										4		1	6	11	10	5	9			
38	19	a	Ipswich Town	0	2		17787		2			4		7	8	13								14	12												1	6	11	10	5	9	3		
39 Apr	2	a	Norwich City	0	6		2652	1	2				12		8	13			6					10										4			11	14	9	5		3	7	
40	9	h	Queen's Park Rangers	4	1	Garner(2), O'Connor, Duffy	6061	1				4	6	13	8	9			12																		2	11	10	5	14	3	7	
41	12	h	Reading	0	2		4458	1				4	6	12	8	9																					2	11	10	5	13	3	7	
42	16	a	Crystal Palace	2	1	Mirfin, Nunez	17810	1				4	6			9								8	13													2	11	10	5	12		7	3
43	22	a	Coventry City	1	1	Nunez	16705	1				4	6		12	9								8	10													2	11		5	13	14	7	3
44	25	h	Millwall	1	2	O'Connor (p)	5190	1	2			4	6		12	9								8	13														11	10	5			7	3
45	30	a	Nottingham Forest	1	5	O'Connor (p)	27949	1	12			4	6		8	9				2				14	10														11		5	13		7	3
46 May	7	h	Portsmouth	1	1	Nunez	5142						6		8					2		12		13	10										4		1		11	9	5	14		7	3
							Apps	29	35	6	14	23	36	36	32	37	24	12	22	20	24	2	21	32	27	8		5	9	2	5	3	1	1	12	11	15	19	22	18	20	18	14	8	5
							Goals				1	3		1	9	7	4	1			8		2	3							1	1							1	6		1		3	

F.A.Cup

								Murphy	Nolan	McNulty	Jones	Mirfin	Togwell	Wright J	O'Connor	Dagnall	Forte	Thompson	Raynes	Wright A	Woolford	Slocombe	Byrne	Collins	Grant	Canavan	Boyes	Godden	Sears	Warner	McDonald	N'Guessan	McClenahan	Cowan-Hall	Reid	Ibrahim	Lillis	Hughes	Duffy	Garner	Nelson	Miller	Gordon	Nunez	Williams
R3 Jan	8	h	Everton	1	5	Collins	7028	1	3		4	5	13	7	6	9	10		12	2	11			8				14																	

Carling Cup (F.L. Cup)

								Murphy	Nolan	McNulty	Jones	Mirfin	Togwell	Wright J	O'Connor	Dagnall	Forte	Thompson	Raynes	Wright A	Woolford	Slocombe	Byrne	Collins	Grant	Canavan	Boyes	Godden	Sears	Warner	McDonald	N'Guessan	McClenahan	Cowan-Hall	Reid	Ibrahim	Lillis	Hughes	Duffy	Garner	Nelson	Miller	Gordon	Nunez	Williams
R1 Aug	10	h	Oldham Athletic	2	1	Forte, Woolford	2602			3	4		13	7	6	9	10	8	5		11	1	2	12	14																				
R2	24	h	Sheffield Wednesday	4	2	Collins, Dagnell(2), O'Connor	4680	1	3				6	7	8	9	10		5	12			2	11	14	4	13																		
R3 Sep	22	h	Manchester United	2	5	Wright J., Woolford	9077	1	3			5	6	7	8	9	10				11		2	12	13	4		14																	

2011/12   18th in Division 1

F A Cup

Carling Cup (F.L.Cup)

Johnstone's Paint Trophy (Associate Members Cup)

~ 286 ~

League Record Summaries: 1912-13 to 2011-12

		P	W	D	L	F	A	Pts.	Pos.
Midland League	1912-13	38	13	08	17	55	78	34	15th
Midland League	1913-14	34	16	04	14	55	55	36	7th
Midland League	1914-15	38	13	09	14	70	79	35	13th

First World War (No competitive football)

		P	W	D	L	F	A	Pts.	Pos.
Midland League	1919-20	34	18	07	09	71	39	43	3rd
Midland League	1920-21	38	18	09	11	64	43	45	4th
Midland League	1921-22	42	22	08	12	87	60	52	4th
Midland League	1922-23	42	18	13	11	85	58	49	6th
Midland League	1923-24	42	21	07	14	55	49	49	6th
Midland League	1924-25	28	12	05	11	45	41	29	7th
Subsidiary League	1924-25	12	2	01	09	11	21	05	7th
Midland League	1925-26	40	19	09	12	86	78	47	7th
Midland League	1926-27	38	28	04	06	121	44	60	1st
Midland League	1927-28	44	23	04	17	118	85	50	9th
Midland League	1928-29	50	20	14	16	98	96	54	11th
Midland League	1929-30	50	26	06	18	124	98	58	7th
Midland League	1930-31	46	19	11	16	98	101	45	11th
Midland League	1931-32	46	18	09	19	83	99	45	9th
Midland League	1932-33	44	23	05	16	104	100	51	8th
Midland League	1933-34	32	14	05	13	76	73	33	6th
Midland League	1934-35	38	17	03	18	67	82	37	11th
Midland League	1935-36	40	16	08	16	73	77	40	11th
Midland League	1936-37	42	19	03	20	75	86	41	14th
Midland League	1937-38	42	22	05	15	109	78	49	6th
Midland League	1938-39	42	28	08	06	133	57	64	1st
Midland League	1939-40	14	09	03	02	55	27	21	1st
Midland League	1939-40	13	10	01	02	49	18	21	2nd

Second World War (No competitive football)

		P	W	D	L	F	A	Pts.	Pos.
Scunthorpe (Wartime) Lge.	1944-45	22	16	02	04	100	52	34	1st
Midland League	1945-46	36	17	06	13	82	66	40	6th
Midland League	1946-47	42	24	09	09	121	61	57	4th
Midland League	1947-48	42	23	09	10	89	59	55	2nd
Midland League	1948-49	42	24	06	12	104	56	54	4th
Midland League	1949-50	46	29	06	11	99	44	64	3rd
Division Three North	1950-51	46	13	18	15	58	57	46	12th
Division Three North	1951-52	46	14	16	16	65	74	44	14th
Division Three North	1952-53	46	16	14	16	62	56	46	15th
Division Three North	1953-54	46	21	15	10	77	56	57	3rd
Division Three North	1954-55	46	23	12	11	81	53	58	3rd
Division Three North	1955-56	46	20	08	18	75	63	48	9th
Division Three North	1956-57	46	15	15	16	71	69	45	14th
Division Three North	1957-58	46	29	08	09	88	50	66	1st
Division Two	1958-59	42	12	09	21	55	84	33	18th
Division Two	1959-60	42	13	10	19	57	71	36	15th
Division Two	1960-61	42	14	15	13	69	64	43	9th
Division Two	1961-62	42	21	07	14	86	71	49	4th

		P	W	D	L	F	A	Pts.	Pos.
Division Two	1962-63	42	16	12	14	57	59	44	9th
Division Two	1963-64	42	10	10	22	52	82	30	22nd
Division Three	1964-65	46	14	12	20	65	72	40	18th
Division Three	1965-66	46	21	11	14	80	67	53	4th
Division Three	1966-67	46	17	08	21	58	73	42	18th
Division Three	1967-68	46	10	12	24	56	87	32	24th
Division Four	1968-69	46	18	08	20	61	60	44	16th
Division Four	1969-70	46	18	10	18	67	65	46	12th
Division Four	1970-71	46	15	13	18	56	61	43	17th
Division Four	1971-72	46	22	13	11	56	37	57	4th
Division Three	1972-73	46	10	10	26	36	72	30	24th
Division Four	1973-74	46	14	12	19	47	64	42	18th
Division Four	1974-75	46	07	15	24	41	78	29	24th
Division Four	1975-75	46	14	10	22	50	59	38	19th
Division Four	1976-77	46	13	11	22	49	73	37	20th
Division Four	1977-78	46	14	16	16	50	55	44	14th
Division Four	1978-79	46	17	11	18	54	60	45	12th
Division Four	1979-80	46	14	15	17	58	75	43	14th
Division Four	1980-81	46	11	20	15	60	69	42	16th
Division Four	1981-82	46	09	15	22	43	79	42	23rd
Division Four	1982-83	46	23	14	09	71	42	83	4th
Division Three	1983-84	46	09	19	18	54	73	46	21st
Division Four	1984-85	46	19	14	13	83	62	71	9th
Division Four	1985-86	46	15	14	17	50	55	59	15th
Division Four	1986-87	46	18	12	16	73	57	66	8th
Division Four	1987-88	46	20	17	09	76	51	77	4th
Division Four	1988-89	46	16	14	11	77	57	77	4th
Division Four	1989-90	46	17	15	14	69	54	66	11th
Division Four	1990-91	46	20	11	15	71	62	71	8th
Division Four	1991-92	42	21	09	12	64	59	72	5th
Division Three *	1992-93	42	14	12	16	57	54	54	14th
Division Three	1993-94	42	15	14	13	64	56	59	11th
Division Three	1994-95	42	18	08	16	68	63	62	7th
Division Three	1995-96	46	15	15	16	67	61	60	12th
Division Three	1996-97	46	18	09	19	59	62	63	13th
Division Three	1997-98	46	19	12	15	56	52	69	8th
Division Three	1998-99	46	22	08	16	69	58	74	4th
Division Two	1999-00	46	09	12	25	40	74	39	23rd
Division Three	2000-01	46	18	11	17	62	52	65	10th
Division Three	2001-02	46	19	14	13	74	56	71	8th
Division Three	2002-03	46	19	15	12	68	49	72	5th
Division Three	2003-04	46	11	16	19	69	72	49	22nd
Division Two **	2004-05	46	22	14	10	69	42	80	2nd
Division One	2005-06	46	15	15	16	68	73	60	12th
Division One	2006-07	46	26	13	07	73	35	91	1st
Championship	2007-08	46	11	13	22	46	69	46	23rd
Division One	2008-09	46	22	10	14	82	63	76	6th
Championship	2009-10	46	14	10	22	62	84	52	20th
Championship	2010-11	46	12	06	28	43	87	42	24th
Division One	2011-12	46	10	22	14	55	59	52	18th

Structure of Football League changes: * Division 4 became Division 3.   ** Division 3 Became Division 2

MEMORABLE SEASONS

SEASON 1901-02
Scunthorpe United Junior Section
Known as 'The Centrals', this is the oldest known team group of any Scunthorpe club.

Back: Lawson, Symes, E.Hollingsworth, Bones, Floyd, Kennington, Jacques
Middle: Northall (Captain), Lings, Todd
Front: Laird, Walker, Dustin, J.Honningsworth, Bray

SEASON 1911-12
Winners of the North Lindsey League, the Frodingham Charity Cup, the (Scunthorpe Nursing) Charlesworth Cup, the Ironstone Cup and the Grimsby Charity Cup

(Players only) Back: Wogin. Second row: Parrot, Long. Third row: Cox, Holland, Brown,
Front: Hollin, Rusling, Hill, Blanchard, Ibbotson, Harrison

SEASON 1919-20
3rd in Midland League

Back: Moran (Trainer), Hill, Robson, Pattison, Hannah, Bullivant, Wield, Dixon (Asst. Trainer)
Front: Butler, Spavin, Brown, Lemon, Booth, Allcock (Secretary)

SEASON 1926-27 (Players only)
Midland League Champions

Standing: Smith, Skull, Reynolds, Hunter, Moore
Seated: Thompson, Johnson, Simms, Allen, Alford, Kneeling: McKenzie, Holland

**SEASON 1938-39
Midland League Champions**

Standing: Allcock (Secretary), Stocks, Millington, Thorpe, Poxton, T.Jones, Allen, Cliff (Chairman)
Seated: Norris, Fleetwood, Johnson, Nightingale, Wilkinson, Lloyd (Trainer)

**SEASON 1947-48
Midland League Runners-up**

Standing: Johnson (Masseur), Lloyd (Trainer), Leeman, Watford, Rymer, Harper, Brownsword, Millington, Douglas (Groundsman), Allcock (Secretary)
Seated: Smith, Rowney, Bowers, Wallace, Robertshaw, Norris

**SEASON 1950-51
First season in Football league**

Standing: Barker, Brownsword, Allen, Thompson, Taylor, McCormick
Seated: Mosby, Payne, Gorin, Rees, Boyes

**SEASON 1957-58
Champions Football League Div. 3 North**

Standing: Hubbard, Marshall, Horstead, Hardwick, Sharpe, Brownsword
Seated: Marriott, Minton, Davis, Haigh, Jones

SEASON 1961-62
4th in Division 2 (Highest League position to date)

Back: Bonson, Neale, Gibson, Hemstead,
Bakes, Godfrey, Brownsword
Middle: Strong (Masseur), Passmoor, Horstead,
Turner, unknown, unknown, Barker (Trainer)
Seated: Marriott, John, Duckworth (Manager),
Wharton (Chairman), Sharpe, Middleton, Thomas

SEASON 1971-72
4th in Division 4 (Promoted)

Back: Kisby, Barry, Hutchinson, William,
Barnard, Foxton, Jackson, Davidson
2nd row: Strong (Masseur), Cowling (Secretary),
Woolmer, Deere, John Barker, Atkin, Brownsword
(Coach), Jeff Barker (Scout), Ashman (Manager)
3rd row: Fletcher, McDonald, Kerr,
Archer (Director), Johnson (Director)
Kirk, Heath, Welbourne
Seated: Sargent, Markham, Bawden,
Mullen, Crellin, Sowden

SEASON 1974-75
The Worst Season! (Bottom Division 4)

Back: Davidson, Oates, Unknown,
Barnard, Norris, Money, Roberts
Middle: Collier, Sproates, Keeley, Pilling,
Simpson, Warnock Front: Atkin, Unkonwn,
Peacock, Markham, Charnley

SEASON 1982-83
4th in Division 4 (Promoted)

Back: Boxall, Fowler, Johnson,
Neenan, Hunter, Cowling
Middle: Keeley, Snow, Pointon,
Telfer, Grimes, Cammack
Front: Leman, Baines (Player Coach),
Duncan (Player Manager),
McLoughlin (Y.T. Coach), Parkinson, O'Berg

SEASON 1987-88
4th in Division 4 (Lost in play-off Final)

Back: Birch, Richardson, Harle, Russell, Flounders, McLean, Broddle, Longden, Daws
Middle: Green (Asst. Manager), Talbot, Mountain, Huxford, Stevenson, Nicol, Atkins, Shaw, Dunnill, Young, McLoughlin (Physio)
Front: Money, Hayes, Johnson, Brown, Lister, Green, Hill

SEASON 1988-89
4th in Division 4 (Lost in play-off Final)

Back: Money (Youth Dev. Off.), Buxton (Manager), Mountain, Stevenson, Thompson, Musselwhite, Nicol, Lister, Brown, Shearer, Green (Asst. Man), McLouchlin (Physio)
Front: Flounders, Cowling, Longden, Daws, Harle, Richardson, Taylor

SEASON 1991-92
5th in Division 4
(Lost in play-off Final)

Back: McLoughlin (Physio), Martin, Alexander, Stevenson, Hyde, Lillis, Musselwhite, Lister, Hick, Humphries, Hamilton, Joyce, Cowling (Youth Team Coach)
Front: Daws, Hine, Goodacre, Moore (Asst. Man), Green (Manager), Buckley, Godfrey, Longden

SEASON 1998-99
4th in Division 3 (Promoted after play-off win)

Front: Marshall, Hope, Clarke, Logan, Evans, Fickling, McAuley
Middle: Adkins (Physio), Eyre, Wilcox, Neil, Gayle, Featherstone, Stamp, Bull, Wilson (Youth Dev. Off.)
Front: Page, Housham, Calvo-Garcia, Lillis (Asst. Manager), Laws (Manager), Forrester, Harsley, Nottingham

THE SQUADS - 1999-2000 TO 2011-2012

Season 1999-2000
Back: Dawson, Bell, Hope, Evans, Adkins (Pysion) Clarke, Fickling, McAuley
Middle: Wilson (Youth Dev. Off.c) Housham, Stamp, Gayle, Logan, Walker, Stanton, Daly (Physio)
Front: Sheldon, Graves, Calo-Garcia, Wilcox (Caoch) Laws (Manager), Marshall, Hodges, Harsley

Season 2000-01
Back: Pepper, Sheldon, Wilson (Youth Dev.Off.), Dawson, Harsley
(Middles: Adkins (Physio), Stamp, Dewhurst, Evans, Torpey, Herrick, Quailey, Kackson, Daly (Assist.Physio)
Front: Fickling, Calvo-Garcia, Morrison, Laws (Manager), Wilcox (Assist.Man.), Graves, Hodges, Stanton

Season 2001-02
Back: Pepper, Stanton, Thom, Torpey, Anderson, Sheldan,
Middle: Adkins (Physio), Jackson, Sparrow, Carruthers, Evans, Quailey, Doherty, Cotterill, Ridley, Morrison, Wilson (Youth Dev.Off.)
Front: Graves, Calvo-Garcia, Bough, Laws (Manager) Beagriw, Dawson, Bradshaw

Season 2002-03
Back: S.Ridley, L.Ridley, Stanton, Torpey, Jackson, Cotterill
Middle: Sparrow, Barwick, Carruthes, Bennion, MvCoombe, Evans, Wheatcroft, Kell, Graves, Adkins(Physio)
Front: Brough, Calvo-Garcia, Wilcox (Assist.Man.), Laws (Manager) Beagrie, Dawson, Parton

Season 2003-04
Back: Sparrow, Evans, Barwick, Capp, Kilford,
Middles: Graves, Stanton, Byrne, McCoombe, Torpey, Hayes, Featherstone, Butler, Kell, Jackson, Rowing (Chief Exec.), Collen (Director)
Front: Beagrie (P/Coach), Calvo-Garcia, Parton, Willcox (P/Assist.Man.), Holland (Chairman), Laws (Manager), Ridley, Sharp, Adkin (Physio)

Season 2004-05
Back: (Coach), Sparrow, Hayes, Kell, Torpey, Butler, Crosby, Featherstone, Barraclough, Wilson, (Youth Dev.Off.)
Middle: Hammond (Chief Exec.), Sharp, Partin, Byrne, Evans, Capp, Musselwhite, (?) , Ridley, Stanton, Mouatt (Youth Physio), Oxenforth
Front: Grave, Taylor, Barwick, Wilcox, (Assist.Man.), Cartin (Assist.Chairman), Wharton (Chairman), Elliott (Director), Laws (Manager), Beagrie, Jackson, Williams

Season 2005-06
Back: Mouatt, Sparrow, Rankine, Torpey, Evas, Musselwhite, Hinds, Crosby, Butler, Parkin
Middle: Adkins, Ridley, Stanton, Corden, Parton, Capp, Keogh, Johnson, Ryan, Williams, Daws, Beeby
Front: Blackburn (Assist.Director), Barraclough, Taylor, Wilcox, Elliott, Laws (Manager), Wharton (Chairman), Carton, Beagrie, Byrne, Goodwin, Oxenforth

Season 2006-07
Back: Taylor, Goodwin, Hinds, Foster, Keogh
Middle: Adkins (Physio), Abramson, Callister, McKenzie, Lillis, Murphy, Torpey, Butler, Allanson, Dalton (Physio), Mouatt (Physio), Daws
Front: Mullican, Sharp, Ridley, Byrne, Wilcox (Assist.Man.), Wharton (Chairman), Laws (Manager), Crosby, Barraclough, Williams, Twibey

Season 2007-08
(Inset- Morris) Back: Mouatt, Finn, Youga, Morfaw, Taylor, Goodwin, Butler, Sparrow, Forte, Wilcox, Pressman, Noonan
Middle: Beeby, Turnbull, Dalton, Paterson, Iriekpen, McBreen, Murphy, Lillis, Hurst, Hayes, Winn, Parkin, Daws, Wagstaff, Hammond
Front: Milligan, Byrne, Barraclough, Wharton, Adkins, Garton, Crosby, Williams, Cork

Season 2008-09
Back: Forte, Hurst, Sparrow, Williams, Winn, McCann, Hooper
Middle: Byrne, Morris, Hayes, May, Murphy, Iriekpen, Lillis, Milne, Thompson, Wilcox, Picton, Wright
Front: Turnbull (Chief Scout), Parkin, (Coach), Barraclough (P/Coach), Adkins (Manager), Crosby (P/Assist Man.),
Daws (Reserve Team Man.), Pressman ('Keeper Coach)

Season 2009-10
Back: Thompson, Woolford, Mirfin, Morris, Jones, Milne, Canavan, May, Boyes, Hayes, Hooper
Middle: Mouatt (Youth Physio), Dalton (Physio), Hurst, J.Wright, Forte, A.Wright, Slocombe, Murphy, Lilles, Pickton,
Coleman, McCann, Winn, Turnbull (Chief Scout), Pressman ('Keeper Coach)
Front: Godden, Sparrow, Byrne, Barraclough (Coach), Adkins (Manager), Crosby (Assis.Man.), O'Connor, Togwell, Williams.

Season 2010-11
Back: Forte, Collins, Mirfin, Woolford, Raynes, Jones, McNulty, Canavan, Boyes
Middle: Crawford (Kit Man), Coleman, McClelland, Wright, Lillis, Murphy, Slocombe, Williams, J.Wright, Turnbull (Chief Scout), Milne (Coach)
Front: Godden, Dagnall, Togwell, Byrne, Pressman (Assist.Man./'Keeper Coach), Barraclough (Manager), Parkin (Coach), Grant, Cowan-Hall, Nolan, O'Connor

Season 2011-12
Back: Godden, Collins, Wright, Canavan, Raynes, Robertson, Reid, Thompson, Collins
Middle: Dalton (Physio), Cutler ('Keeper Coach), Grant, Wint, Slocombe, Lillis, Turner, Barcham, Hughes, Crawford (Kit Man), Rands (Statistician)
Front; Duffy, Dagnall, Toowell, Byrne, Brass (Assist.Man.), Knill (manager), Nelson, Ryan, Nolan, Thewws

Yore Publications

Was formed by Dave Twydell in 1991, and during these twenty-one years,
a large number and variety of football books have been published.

We specialise in Football League club histories (arguably the leading publisher in this field), currently around 40 titles, plus several updated reprints and Scottish clubs (we published the original Scunthorpe United book in 1999). Recent tiles have included: The complete histories of Barnsley (2012), Chester City (2011), Doncaster Rover (2010) and 'Well Again (The Official History of Motherwell (2004). These are all large, quality, hardback books, 300 plus pages with well illustrated written histories and detailed statistics.

We have also produced around twenty players' Who's Who books, covering both English and some Scottish clubs, notably, 'Timeless Bees' (Brentford), Dundee Legends, Royals Remembered (Reading), etc.

With a keen interest in non-League football, the 'Gone But Not Forgotten' series of books, two per year, is now in its twentieth year. Each addition covers, in reasonable detail,
around six clubs that have folded or grounds that are no more.

For a full and detailed list of all our publications, see our website:
www.yore.demon.co.uk or write to:
Yore Publications, 12 The Furrows, Harefield, Middx. UB9 6AT